ALAI

Association Littéraire et Artistique Internationale

ALAI Study Days

Copyright in cyberspace

Copyright and the Global Information Infrastructure

Amsterdam, 4-8 June 1996

Journées d'Étude de l'ALAI

Le droit d'auteur en cyberspace

Le droit d'auteur et l'infrastructure mondiale de l'information

Amsterdam, 4-8 juin 1996

Editor / *Rédacteur* - Marcel Dellebeke

Otto Cramwinckel 1997

Editor / *Rédacteur*

Marcel Dellebeke

Editorial preparation / *Préparation rédactionnelle*

Marcel Dellebeke Institute for Information Law (University of Amsterdam) /
Institut du droit de l'information (Université d'Amsterdam)
Esmée Faûth Buma/Stemra
Juliette Jonkers Buma/Stemra

French double-check / *Contrôle supplémentaire du français*

Nicole van der Kroft-de Taeye

Cover design / *Styliste de couverture*

Airline

Publisher / *Éditeur*

Otto Cramwinckel (otto.cram@cram.nl)

Cataloguing Data / *Données de catalogage*

Copyright in cyberspace, Copyright and the Global Information Infrastructure / *Le droit d'auteur en cyberspace, Le droit d'auteur et l'infrastructure mondiale de l'information*
Dellebeke, M. (ed./*réd.*)
ISBN 90 75727 917
Cramwinckel / Amsterdam

Table of contents
Table des matières

II

Authenticity of authorship and work
L'authenticité de la qualité d'auteur et de l'oeuvre

III

Private international law aspects
Les aspects de droit international privé

IV

Provisions on circumvention of technical protection devices
Les dispositions tendant à interdire les appareils à contourner les mesures techniques anti-copie

V

Protection of and vis-à-vis databases
La protection en faveur des et vis-à-vis des banques de données

Preface
Préface

V. NABHAN

I have the pleasure to present to you the proceedings of the 63rd Congress of the ALAI, which has taken place in Amsterdam from 4 to 8 June 1996.

The Congress will no doubt be remembered in the history of the ALAI and this even more so as well by the importance of the theme as by the number and quality of the contributions. The theme which concentrates on the coming electronic highway in conjunction with digital technique is decidedly novel. At the onset of the twenty first century, copyright is finding itself once more at a turning point, so to speak. Having said that, one could have expected a certain resistance to tackle a subject which could result in 'cutting one's throat'. But the contrary has been the case. Far from taking a defensive attitude or waiting comfortably at a distance, the challenge has stimulated the minds. The evidence thereof is this voluminous work which contains the fruits of our labours and which testifies the vitality of our association.

Thanks should be extended to all participants who in one form or other have enriched this volume with their contributions. The result is impressive and constitutes a work of reference which shall be frequently consulted. The Dutch organisers also deserve our praise, not only for having magnificently acquitted themselves of their duty as organisers, but also for having undertaken and having succeeded to publish this volume without undue delay. Taking into account the totality of the information which it contains and the speed of technical evolution, the choice to go ahead speedily with the publication of the proceedings is a wise decision which will be well received by countless readers of this work.

J'ai le plaisir de vous présenter les actes du 63ième Congrès de l'ALAI qui s'est tenu à Amsterdam du 4 au 8 juin 1996.

Ce Congrès fera sans doute date dans l'histoire de l'ALAI et ceci tant en raison de l'importance de la thématique abordée que par le foisonnement et la qualité des contributions. La thématique, qui met en vedette l'avènement des autoroutes de l'information conjugué à la technique numérique, est assurément nouvelle. À l'aube du vingt et unième siècle, le droit d'auteur se trouve encore une fois, comme on se plaît à le dire, "à un tournant". Devant ce constat, on aurait pu ainsi craindre une certaine résistance à se lancer à l'assaut d'un sujet somme toute "casse-cou". Mais bien au contraire. Loin de nous acculer à une attitude défensive ou de nous figer dans un attentisme confortable et de bon aloi, le défi a plutôt stimulé les esprits. À preuve cet ouvrage volumineux qui constate le fruit de nos travaux et qui témoigne de la vitalité de notre association.

Il faut donc savoir gré à tous les participants qui à un titre ou un autre ont enrichi ce volume de leur contribution. Le résultat est impressionnant et constituera un ouvrage de référence qui sera fréquemment consulté. Les organisateurs néerlandais méritent aussi nos éloges, non seulement pour s'être magnifiquement acquittés de leur tâche d'organisateurs, mais aussi pour s'être employés et avoir réussi à publier ce volume dans des délais courts. Compte tenu de la somme de renseignements qu'il contient, et de la rapidité d'évolution des techniques, il s'agit là d'une décision judicieuse qui sera fort bien accueillie par les nombreux lecteurs de cet ouvrage.

Editorial note
Note du rédacteur

The editorial policy regarding the contents of this book has been the following. Included are the general reports, the questionnaires, the national reports, the texts of speeches of the panelists and the interventions which have been presented during the Study Days, only as far as we have received or have succeeded in retrieving the text thereof. The reports, speeches and interventions are included in the language as presented, which is either English or French. The other texts in this book are in both languages.

Le rédacteur a procédé, en ce qui concerne le contenu du présent livre, de la manière suivante. Il a inclu les rapports généraux, les questionnaires, les rapports nationaux, les conférences, les interventions des membres des panels et celles d'autres participants qui ont été présentés au cours des Journées d'Étude, dans la mesure toutefois où ces textes lui ont été transmis ou ont pu être transcrit. Les rapports, allocutions et interventions sont édités dans la langue dans laquelle ils ont été prononcées, c'est-à-dire en anglais ou en français. Les autres textes compris dans ce livre sont dans les deux langues.

Amsterdam, December/*décembre* 1996

Study Days organizing committee
Comité organisateur des Journées d'Étude

E.A. Mout-Bouwman (Chairwoman/*Présidente*)
J. Jonkers
R.L. du Bois
J.A. Schaap
P.R.C. Solleveld
M. Gielen
Lidy Groot Congress Events

ALAI 1996 Steering Committee
Commission d'experts de l'ALAI 1996

A.A. Quaedvlieg (Chairman/*Président*)
H. Cohen Jehoram
J. Jonkers
N. van Lingen
E.A. Mout-Bouwman
D.H.M. Peeperkorn
J.H. Spoor

Study Days programme

Tuesday 4 June 1996

17.30   Welcome reception

Wednesday 5 June 1996

10.00   **Welcome**
               V. Nabhan, President of ALAI
               J.H. Spoor, Vice-President of the Dutch Copyright Association
               (Vereniging voor Auteursrecht, VVA)

               Opening
               W. Sorgdrager, Minister of Justice of the Netherlands

               **Latest developments regarding the Protocol to the Berne
               Convention and the New Instrument**
               M. Ficsor, WIPO

               **The European Union's approach to copyright regarding the
               Global Information Infrastructure**
               J. Reinbothe, European Commission DG-XV

14.00   **The economic rights involved**

               General reporter   *J.H. Spoor*

               Moderator   *J. Corbet*

               Panel members   *P.H. Dumont*
                                         J.M. Gutton
                                         C. Clark

20.15   Ballet performance by the *Nederlands Dans Theater*
               in the *Muziek Theater*

Thursday 6 June 1996

9.30   **Authenticity of authorship and work**

            General reporter   *A. Dietz*

            Moderator   *Y. Gendreau*

            Panel members   *E. Franchi*
                                    G.W.G. Karnell
                                    F. Pollaud-Dulian
                                    A.A. Quaedvlieg

14.00   **Private international law aspects**

            General reporter   *G. Koumantos*

            Moderator   *J.C. Ginsburg*

            Panel members   *Th. Dreier*
                                    P.Y. Gautier
                                    J.M.B. Seignette

17.00   General Assembly ALAI

18.30   Cocktails and private viewing of the Amsterdam
            Historical Museum, offered by the City of Amsterdam
            and the Ministry of Justice

Friday 7 June 1996

9.30   **Provisions on circumvention of technical protection devices**

            General reporter   *A. Lucas*

            Moderator   *G. Roussel*

            Panel members   *E. Franchi*
                                    M. Lehman
                                    N.A. Smith
                                    J.P. Triaille

14.00   **Protection of and vis-à-vis databases**

            General reporter   *W.R. Cornish*

Moderator   *J. Rosén*

Panel members   *M.A. Leaffer*
                            P.B. Hugenholtz

19.00   Boat trip and closing dinner at the Renaissance Hotel

Saturday 8 June 1996

9.15   Excursion to Haarlem

Visits of Frans Hals Museum and Teylers Museum
Private concert in Haarlem Cathedral
Visit of secret gardens

Programme des Journées d'Étude

Mardi 4 juin 1996

17.30   Réception de bienvenue

Mercredi 5 juin 1996

10.00   **Allocutions de bienvenue**
V. Nabhan, Président de l'ALAI
J.H. Spoor, Vice-Président de l'Association néerlandaise du droit
d'auteur *(Vereniging voor Auteursrecht, VVA)*

Ouverture des sessions
W. Sorgdrager, Ministre néerlandais de la Justice

**Derniers développements concernant le Protocole de la Convention
de Berne et le Nouvel Instrument**
M. Ficsor, OMPI

**Le droit d'auteur et l'infrastructure globale de l'information; approche
de l'Union européenne**
J. Reinbothe, Commission européenne DG-XV

14.00   **Les droits économiques concernés**

Rapporteur général   *J.H. Spoor*

Modérateur   *J. Corbet*

Membres du panel   *P.H. Dumont*
                              J.M. Gutton
                              C. Clark

20.15   Représentation de ballet par le *Nederlands Dans Theater*
au *Muziek Theater*

Jeudi 6 juin 1996

9.30 **L'authenticité de la qualité d'auteur et de l'oeuvre**

Rapporteur général   *A. Dietz*

Modérateur   *Y. Gendreau*

Membres du panel   *E. Franchi*
G.W.G. Karnell
F. Pollaud-Dulian
A.A. Quaedvlieg

14.00 **Les aspects de droit international privé**

Rapporteur général   *G. Koumantos*

Modérateur   *J.C. Ginsburg*

Membres du panel   *Th. Dreier*
P.Y. Gautier
J.M.B. Seignette

17.00 Assemblée générale ALAI

18.30 Réception et visite privée du Musée d'histoire d'Amsterdam,
offertes par la Ville d'Amsterdam et par le Ministère de la Justice

Vendredi 7 juin 1996

9.30 **Les dispositions tendant à interdire les appareils à contourner
les mesures techniques anti-copie**

Rapporteur général   *A. Lucas*

Modérateur   *G. Roussel*

Membres du panel   *E. Franchi*
M. Lehman
N.A. Smith
J.P. Triaille

14.00 **La protection en faveur des et vis-à-vis des banques de données**

Rapporteur général   *W.R. Cornish*

Modérateur	*J. Rosén*
Membres du panel	*M.A. Leaffer* *P.B. Hugenholtz*

19.00   Promenade en bateau et dîner de clôture à l'Hôtel Renaissance

Samedi 8 juin 1996

9.15   Excursion à Haarlem

Visites des musées Frans Hals et Teyler'
Concert privé dans l'ancienne Cathédrale
Promenade dans les jardins secrets de Haarlem

Allocution de bienvenue

V. Nabhan

Madame le Ministre de la Justice,
Monsieur le Représentant de la Commission européenne,
Monsieur le Représentant de l'OMPI,
Monsieur le Vice-Président de l'Association néerlandaise du droit d'auteur,
Mesdames, Messieurs,
Chers amis,

Il y a quelques décennies, un compatriote canadien illustre, Marshall McLuhan, dont le nom est familier à plusieurs, prédisait qu'avec le développement des moyens de communication, le monde allait se réduire un jour, comme une peau de chagrin, aux dimensions d'un grand village. Ces propos, sans doute révolutionnaires pour l'époque où ils furent tenus, ont été accueillis par les uns avec sarcasme et scepticisme, et par les autres avec foi et enthousiasme. Mais nul ne réalisait encore à quel point ces prévisions tenaient en réalité de la prophétie. On peut même se demander si l'auteur de ces prévisions, Marshall McLuhan, en mesurait pleinement la portée. Si celui-ci revenait miraculeusement un jour sur terre, parmi nous, il n'est pas interdit de croire qu'il serait pour le moins étonné de constater la justesse de sa prédiction et, qui sait, l'ampleur de son génie. Nul doute qu'il embrasserait avec célérité la religion Internet, se livrant avec régularité, dévotion et ferveur à ses pratiques quotidiennes d'"internaute surfeur".

Le phénomène décrit par McLuhan, des distances qui se réduisent à la faveur des techniques de communication qui se perfectionnent, ne nous est pas totalement inconnu à l'ALAI. Déjà en 1982, ici même, en cette magnifique ville d'Amsterdam, qui représente non seulement la quintessence de la tolérance mais aussi du raffinement - car comment qualifier autrement ce lieu qui comporte une si forte concentration de musées et de cafés terrasses, bordant des plans d'eau attrayants et inspirant la douceur de vivre - l'ALAI tenait un important congrès, organisé de main de maître par nos amis néerlandais, qui portait sur les problèmes juridiques découlant de la retransmission des oeuvres par câble. A l'époque, ce nouveau mode de diffusion nous semblait susciter des problèmes graves, très graves même.

Depuis lors, beaucoup d'eau a coulé sous les ponts d'Amsterdam. Et ce n'est pas sans un curieux hasard, et un juste retour des choses, que nous nous retrouvons de nouveau en cette même ville, à notre grand bonheur d'ailleurs, afin de débattre encore une fois de l'impact des nouveaux modes de communication sur le droit d'auteur. Mais cette fois-ci, le phénomène n'a plus aucune commune mesure avec le passé. Les techniques de communication ont fait un bond prodigieux, vertigineux.

Les distances ne se sont plus simplement rapprochées ou réduites. Elles sont maintenant pratiquement abolies, elles ont disparu. Grâce aux autoroutes de l'information, tout un chacun est diffuseur, et la planète est son champ d'action. Plus de limites. Plus de frontières.

Devant ces développements, certains crient au miracle et multiplient les génuflexions. D'autres nous mettent en garde et se perdent en lamentations. Car il va sans dire que ces nouvelles techniques provoquent des bouleversements qui ne laissent personne indifférent. Bouleversements d'abord dans nos habitudes de vie, nos façons de travailler. Dorénavant, l'accès à l'information, ce bien précieux entre tous, est facilité. Mais face à ce flot constant et irrépressible de données qui nous submerge, disposera-t-on encore du temps et du recul nécessaires pour assimiler, discerner, réfléchir? Assistera-t-on, comme certains se plaisent à l'évoquer, à la disparition du livre, du support matériel? Verra-t-on le clivage s'accentuer entre les *"haves"* et les *"have-nots"*, les privilégiés, possesseurs de l'information et ceux qui en sont dépourvus?

Mais il n'y a pas que nos modes de vie et nos façons de faire qui peuvent être affectés. Le droit se ressent inévitablement du choc des nouvelles techniques et en subit les contrecoups. La protection de la vie privée est en danger, la répression de la littérature haineuse ou pornographique pose problème, pour ne mentionner que certaines des questions qui sont vivement discutées à l'heure actuelle. Et bien sûr, plus près de nos préoccupations, tout l'univers du droit d'auteur est interpellé par le nouvel environnement numérique.

Ces journées vont nous permettre de mener en profondeur une réflexion concentrée sur les défis auxquels nous sommes confrontés face à l'avènement de cette société d'information globale. Il s'agit là d'un sujet d'actualité que nous ne pouvions ignorer et il faut savoir gré au groupe néerlandais, et particulièrement au professeur Cohen Jehoram, d'avoir relevé le défi en l'inscrivant comme thème de ces Journées d'Étude.

Il m'appartient maintenant, fort de mes fonctions redoutables de président, de déclarer officiellement l'ouverture de ces Journées d'Étude, et de nous souhaiter à tous des échanges qui, je n'en doute pas, seront intéressants et féconds.

Welcoming speech

J.H. Spoor

Your Excellency,
Mr Chairman,
Ladies and Gentlemen,

One century ago, the eminent French scholar Pouillet already stressed the importance of meetings like these Study Days. In the foreword to his major copyright law treatise, he wrote: *'Dans tous les pays, il y a des hommes de bonne volonté qui travaillent, sans bruit, et qui échangent leurs idées; des congrès se réunissent, en vue de l'unification des lois qui protègent le droit des auteurs'*, *'Everywhere, people of good will are working quietly and exchanging ideas. Congresses are organized in view of harmonizing copyright laws'*. No doubt, this will sound familiar to you. Although a hundred years have passed, this is precisely why we have met for these Amsterdam Study Days.

Pouillet then went on to say that *'Un jour viendra où les législateurs trouveront la législation toute faite, et ils s'étonneront de la trouver uniforme dans tous les pays'*, *'One day, governments will find the laws have all been made, and will be surprised to notice them to be uniform anywhere'*. This was rather an optimistic statement. It is true that, thanks to international cooperation, national copyright laws of different countries are quite similar. Our discussions are made much easier by the fact that our laws are mostly based on the same principles and the same concepts. But, as any lawyer knows, we never find laws to have been all made. Times change and we change with them; the laws have to follow suit. Since the days of Pouillet, technology changed the world, and copyright was adapted time and again, in order to cope with developments such as broadcasting, tape recording, reprography, satellites and computer software.

The present challenge is called cyberspace, or Internet, or Global Information Highway, or whatever. In many respects it is new and unprecedented; certainly its potential is immense. Distance no longer forms an obstacle to the diffusion of works, which can take place at virtually no cost. From now on, worldwide demand for a work may be satisfied by one single server. Some Internet gurus are already predicting the end of copyright, while right owners are preparing to make the best of it.

But what this new technology first of all requires, is study and discussion. Once more, like in Pouillet's days, that is what has brought us together on these Study Days. The Dutch group of ALAI is honoured by your presence, and wishes you all a very heartily welcome. Our only regret is the absence of our chairman Herman Cohen

Jehoram. He chaired the decision to invite ALAI for this event; he announced it; and he should have been here to welcome you. Unfortunately, a temporary but prolonged illness has prevented him from being present. We all send him our very best wishes.

I wish you a fruitful meeting and a pleasant stay in Amsterdam.

Opening speech

W. SORGDRAGER

Ladies and gentlemen,

You have made an excellent choice of subject for your Study Days, as this is a theme that is currently enjoying a flood of interest. At the end of the year a Diplomatic Conference will take place in the framework of the World Intellectual Property Organisation. On this occasion decisions must be made about amendments and additions to the Berne Convention. If these amendments are indeed effectuated - in the form of one or more conventions - they will be the first in 25 years, making the Conference a historic event. This historic event will have been triggered in the first place by the technological developments of recent years and the growing awareness that rules are needed at international level to govern copyright and neighbouring rights.

With respect to the exercise of copyright on the electronic highway, we have seen the appearance of several important government reports over the past twelve months: in the United States, Canada, Japan and the European Community. This has already led in several cases to proposals for amendments to existing legislation: in a very small number of cases, amendments have already been made. It is essential for the scholarly community to make its voice heard in good time, and to exert its influence on the decision-making process, now that international rules are under discussion.

Besides bearing responsibility for copyright, there are other ways in which the Ministry of Justice is confronted with the impact of new technologies. The new media are also used to disseminate less exalted products of the human mind, such as racist texts and child pornography. If standards of decency are violated and criminal offences committed, action should be taken.

One should be aware that criminal law is fully applicable to electronic networks. Anyone who commits a criminal offence by disseminating certain information runs the risk of criminal prosecution. Persons who give anonymous authors or authors outside the bounds of national jurisdiction the opportunity to disseminate information relevant to the criminal law, are likewise criminally liable.

In the case of traditional information channels, freedom of expression is safeguarded by provisions designed to limit any self-censorship on the part of the printer and the publisher. They are not themselves liable, and may exculpate themselves if they do not hide themselves in anonimity and if they reveal the offender's name. But with the advent of new technologies, new positions have come into being, such as that of service providers and bulletin board servers. Persons occupying such positions will have to realise that the opposite side of the coin of freedom of expression, is that they bear a certain responsibility in relation to the dissemination of information. This leads to the need for rules of conduct in cyberspace.

The new electronic media share certain specific features: an attenuated relationship between information and location, the scope for anonimity, and the international forum. But these characteristics do not justify a 'free-for-all' mentalitity. Technological anarchy on the Internet is not a very appealing prospect. Cyberspace participants will have to be made aware of their own responsibilities. In the network world this point has sunk in. In some cases, service providers decide voluntarily to be less cooperative in the dissemination of unlawful information. It is in the first place a task of the interested parties themselves to devise rules about access to networks.

Where the precise limits will lie, will have to emerge from practice. Court decisions can serve as a useful guideline. A case that has attracted a lot of publicity in the Netherlands is the dispute between the Scientology Church and 22 service providers operating in the Netherlands, about the dissemination on the Internet of information that is protected by copyright. At the beginning of this year, the court ruled that service providers could only be said to have violated copyright under certain specified circumstances. The court reasoned that service providers merely provide the opportunity to publicise information; they do not influence the content of the message disseminated, and may even be ignorant of it. Only once it is crystal clear that a publication is in violation of copyright and that it is reasonable to assume that the service provider concerned was aware of this (for example, after receiving a demand letter), then there are grounds for liability. As an appeal is pending, these rules may be adjusted.

In the wave of new technologies, we must endeavour to strike a balance between all the interests that are at stake, from the makers of creative products and those involved in marketing them, to libraries, the press and ordinary users - in short, the general public. We have to devise the appropriate instrument to achieve this balance. In the debate thus far, the emphasis has been on the risks that the new technologies may pose to persons with rights to protect. Little or no attention is paid to the risks they may pose to the public at large. When the new technologies enter into the private sphere, rules of privacy are at stake. And the accessibility of public domain information may be obstructed by technical devices.

The instrument I am referring to should not necessarily be legislation, whether at national or international level. We might alternatively wish to consider codes of conduct, or agreements concluded between interested parties. A promising approach used in the United States are the conferences on fair use. At such a conference, interested parties sit down together and endeavour to reach agreement on where the use of protected material is free, and where it must be paid for. This avoids a situation in which the business of finding a solution to the problems is left solely to those who have rights to protect.

The responsibility of the legislature is in the first place to ensure that all the interests at stake receive due consideration. The legislature also has to guard against unnecessarily detailed pieces of legislation being enacted in response to specific incidents. I will give an example. The Dutch Copyright Act is based on two general concepts of a high level of abstraction: communication to the public and reproduction. These concepts arose in the analogue age, and appear highly usable in a digital environment. Technologically speaking, they are neutral concepts.

In interpreting these concepts, the courts have a significant role to play. No-one will deny that copyright has taken on greater significance for the commercial sector. This was recently observed by the *Hoge Raad*, the highest court in the Netherlands. It observed that the Dutch legislature could not have predicted, over 80 years ago, all the cases that would one day be submitted to the courts. The *Hoge Raad* then ruled that the Copyright Act did not have a completely closed system of restrictions to the rights concerned. According to the Dutch Supreme Court, when balancing the interests of copyright holders against the social or economic rights of others, or against the public interest, the limits of copyright have to be more sharply defined in cases for which the legislature has not provided. With this ruling, the *Hoge Raad* created a framework that will allow lower courts to resolve frictions that arise in the exercise of copyright in cyberspace. In this way, the social and economic interests of others help to determine the limits of copyright.

I believe that this approach is equally useful when we are speaking of international regulations. In my opinion, in setting out to amend the Berne Convention to accommodate the new technologies, what we should be doing is to clarify and redefine existing concepts in the light of new technologies, rather than introduce new rights or new restrictions on rights.

Much has been written about the likely shipwreck of traditional copyright in the tidal wave of new technologies. It cannot be denied that more and more questions relating to copyright are being raised as a result of these new applications. It is equally undeniable, however, that a certain consensus is emerging about how we should approach these issues. I think the question that scholarship and politics must seek to answer is how rights can be exercised in cyberspace. New technologies create a fresh scope for the dissemination of information and lead to the opening up of new markets. They also create new ways of ensuring the protection and exercise of rights, and hence of controlling use.

In many cases, fees have to be paid to a collecting body when a work is used. New technologies hold out the prospect of a more individualised exercise of rights, with their collective exercise being dictated not by the nature of the right, but by the freely elected decision of the person concerned. In cyberspace too, right holders remain free to exercise their rights collectively. However, the new technologies will create fresh opportunities for the conclusion of contracts on an individual basis.

In conclusion, I should like to recall briefly the main points I have made, the three themes which I believe should receive attention in the coming debate. First, the cyberspace participant's own responsibility for his or her actions, second, the positive role to be played by the legislature, and third, the scope for a more individualised exercise of rights.

The relationship between copyright and the electronic highway prompts a host of questions. I should like to wish the ALAI every success in tackling them during these Study Days. The tangible results of your work will help us to exercise our own responsibilities - as legislators, as the makers of creative products, and as the consumers of information.

Thank you.

Latest developments regarding the Protocol to the Berne Convention and the New Instrument

M. Ficsor

Your Excellency,
Mr President,
Ladies and gentlemen,
Dear colleagues and friends,

It is a great pleasure and honour for me to be here with you today.

For WIPO, ALAI is not just one of the numerous non-governmental organizations which participate in our meetings, but it has a specific and eminent status with our organization. It not only played a decisive role in the creation of the Berne Convention, which is administered by WIPO, but its congresses, study days and the participation of representatives of ALAI in our meetings have always contributed to the development of the international system of copyright and neighbouring rights.

This system is faced with a challenge now to which we have to give an urgent answer. Nothing shows better that ALAI is ready and capable to play the role of catalyst in producing certain changes that are needed, and at the same time play the role of the guardian of the basic copyright and neighbouring rights values, than that this subject matter – 'copyright in cyberspace' – has been chosen for these Study Days. I think that this is the best moment possible.

'Copyright in cyberspace' is one of the many possible synonymous expressions, the others being copyright on the digital superhighway, copyright in the information society, copyright in the Global Information Infrastructure, copyright in the era of multimedia and so on. We have spoken a lot about this subject recently. We have just calculated in WIPO that, if we accepted all invitations during these months to all the meetings where these questions are discussed, then every staff member of WIPO dealing with copyright would have to be at 1.8 meetings a day at various points in the world. Also here, I see a great many people who yesterday were still in Florence to attend the meeting of the European Commission on the same subject matter, where I was one of the speakers in the first panel, after having just arrived from Cannes from a conference of the Business Software Alliance dealing with the same issues.

The discussions on the impact of digital technology on copyright have gone through three stages. First, there was a stage of euphoria at one side and a kind of panic on

29

the other side. It was said that copyright should be fundamentally changed, that copyright was out of date, that copyright only had one duty now, namely that it should die and be buried as deep as possible. The second stage was a kind of antithesis to this very strong thesis. It was responded that nothing should be changed, copyright may continue to exist without any revision, digital technology was not so important that we have to address its impact at the international level, and at the level of national laws, the existing rules should continue being applied. We are now in the third stage; the happy stage of synthesis. We know that changes are needed, but basically they should consist only of an adaptation of the system to the new requirements and that there is no need for a basic transformation of the copyright system.

I have said that ALAI has chosen the best moment to deal with this issue. One of the reasons why I have said this is that just about two weeks ago the competent governing bodies of WIPO decided that we should convene a Diplomatic Conference in December of this year on what the title of the Conference indicates: 'Certain copyright and neighbouring rights questions'. The Diplomatic Conference is to address the matters which have been discussed by the WIPO Committees dealing with the Berne Protocol and the New Instrument on certain neighbouring rights. It will take place in Geneva in the Conference Center, and not at the headquarters of WIPO, because even the biggest room at WIPO would be too small for this and we don't want the representatives of non-governmental organizations such as ALAI to sit in a separate room and not to be able to participate appropriately. The diplomatic conference, of course, will not cover all questions which were on the agenda of the Committees, but it is absolutely clear that, if we wanted to adopt a meaningful, important treaty, then it should deal with the questions raised by digital technology and it should give an answer to the most important questions raised by that technology.

You know that the projects under the titles of the Berne Protocol and the New Instrument started at the beginning of the nineties. At that time, another important process was also on the way: the negotiations in the Uruguay Round. The effect of that was that the preparatory work in WIPO was slowed down. Nobody wanted any interference with that series of negotiations. But when the TRIPs Agreement was adopted in April 1994, the situation suddenly changed and a political will emerged that we should accelerate the preparatory work in the two WIPO Committees. By that time, it became absolutely clear that the TRIPs Agreement was unable to give answers to certain important questions raised by the new technologies and particularly by the digital technology. This wasn't a surprise, because the spectacular acceleration of Internet took place just after practically everything had been agreed upon in the draft text of the TRIPs Agreement and, of course, nobody wanted to reopen the negotiations just because of some brand new developments. So, the preparatory work became much more serious in WIPO and we started discussing all the aspects of digital technology.

It is clear that, in the new treaty or treaties to be adopted in December, we should give responses to the most important items on the agenda of the two Committees, but we don't have to deal with all issues which have been discussed at the various meetings. First of all, in the treaty or treaties (the number of treaties is as yet uncertain) we don't have to address the question of digitization because there is agreement that this is just a form of reproduction. Furthermore, we don't have to deal with the copyright status of multimedia productions. It is understood and agreed upon by practically everybody that multimedia productions are protected by copyright under article 2(1) and/or (5) of the Berne Convention. We may have to revisit this issue later, but for the time being any international regulation would seem premature.

The real issue is not the copyright status of multimedia productions, the real issue is the Net, that is, the storage and transmission of works in the Internet-type systems. In their last sessions, the two WIPO Committees discussed the proposals submitted by the European Commission about a clarification to be included in the records of the future diplomatic conference concerning the storage of works in computer memories. It was proposed that somewhere in the records an agreed statement should be included according to which the storage of works in computer memories, even temporary storage, should be considered as reproduction. This was supported very strongly, and the support went so far as that it was suggested that this be included not in the records but rather in the text of the treaty or treaties. But there was also some hesitation. The hesitation related to the question of how far the temporary nature of storage could go so that what is taking place still might be qualified as reproduction. It was said that the adjective 'temporary' is very much subjective, and it is really subjective if one tries to define this by identifying the duration by minutes or seconds or nanoseconds. At the same time, there is a possible test that may and should be applied, namely, whether or not a new fixation takes place which is sufficient and appropriate so that the signs, the images and/or the sounds, in which the work is expressed, may be perceived and so that a further fixation may be made on the basis of it. If the response is positive to this question, such a fixation should be considered as a reproduction.

The other issue emerging with the Internet, which is an even more difficult issue, is the digital transmission of works, that is the very complex process of uploading, transmitting, downloading and so on. Actually, the way it will take place, as it is predicted, may be in the form of encrypted signals included in some 'software envelopes', where you may be able to see what kind of work is made available in encrypted form and you may find the menu of the various uses, for example, indicating that you don't have to pay for some limited browsing, you have to pay a certain amount if you want to study something more thoroughly, or listen to a sound recording, or watch a film without making a more or less permanent copy, and, of course, you have to pay more if you would like to have such a copy. For the users, all this will be one single phenomenon. They don't care whether their obligations emerge on the basis of the right of reproduction, the right of communication to the public or the right of distribution, they only care how much they have to pay for this or that. Therefore, at the beginning, the idea emerged that we should address this phenomenon as it exists, that we should call it 'making available of works in electronic systems' and that we should provide for a new right to cover this kind of use. However, we cannot forget about the basic truth so eloquently expressed by

Wolfgang Goethe in his *Faust*: '*Es erben sich Gesetze und Rechte, wie eine ewige Krankheit fort*', 'We inherit laws and rights as an eternal disease'. We cannot get rid of the past. We cannot neglect that there are certain rights included in the Berne Convention and in national laws. We cannot forget about the *a contrario* implications. We cannot forget about contracts to be applied. So we should first - and probably also last - try to address the existing rights.

Now, if we review the existing rights, it is clear that there is an absolute candidate for taking care of storage and transmission of works in the Internet and in similar future systems, namely the right of reproduction. As I have said, there is some hesitation about the extent of its application in respect of 'temporary' reproduction, but I hope that an appropriate solution will be found during the coming months (for example, by not denying that reproduction is reproduction just because it is temporary, but at the same time allowing certain exceptions where a transient reproduction is technically indispensable to carry out an act authorized by the author or by the law).

But the right of reproduction is not sufficient for various reasons. One of the most important reasons is that frequently reproduction will be carried out by consumers. Of course, there is also reproduction at the uploading point, but if we only concentrate on such acts we may neglect a commercially more relevant aspect of the activity of service and content providers, namely making works available to the public. Therefore, a right which takes care of that truly commercial aspect is also needed.

I have used the expression 'making available to the public'. This is a very broad notion. Actually, there are two basic forms of making available of works to the public. The first basic form is making available in the form of copies for use, which is a kind of deferred possibility to see, to read, to watch and so on. The second basic form is making available directly through broadcasting and other communication to the public, by public performance, and so on. These two forms are related to the right of distribution and the right of communication to the public, which have been considered from the beginning as candidates to be partners for the right of reproduction. In this respect, we have to see that the Internet-type networks create some hybrid forms, such as making available copies only for the time of seeing, watching, listening to the work which then after that disappears, or making available copies – even permanently – through electronic signals. The first form is similar to communication to the public and the other, in a way, is similar to distribution of copies.

You can argue either way and in both cases there are some doubts, of course. Because distribution is related traditionally to the distribution of tangible copies. Under many laws, it is very difficult to think of 'immaterial distribution' as a subject matter of the right of distribution. As far as communication to the public is concerned, there are also problems; such as the notion of 'public' and also the structure of the act. Traditionally, a communication or a transmission means that the communicator, the transmitter acts, and you may or may not receive what is transmitted, you are passive. But in the case of 'digital transmission', the act is composed of two steps: a work is made available for access only and the members of the public should cause the system to actually transmit or communicate. Therefore, it should be clarified that all these acts are now covered by the concept of distribution or the concept of communication to the public. Furthermore, the Berne Convention doesn't have general rights of distribution and communication to the public, and the gaps in the Convention should be filled in.

The European Commission presented a very important draft text for the last sessions of the Committees, held just two weeks ago. I quote this text, because of its importance. It is proposed that the following should be included in the text of the Berne Protocol and the New Instrument: *'Without prejudice to the rights provided in Articles 11, 11*bis*, 11*ter*, 14 and 14*bis *of the Berne Convention, authors of literary and artistic works shall enjoy the exclusive right of authorizing any communication to the public of their works'*. It goes on, and here is the essence: *'... including the making available to the public of their works by wire or wireless means in such a way that members of the public may access these works from a place and at a time individually chosen by them'*. I think this is an excellent text and it may be a basis for a compromise between the various systems; it may be the basis for a 'interoperable' solution at the international level.

Of course, those who have read my testimony presented at the Congress of the United States in November last year may ask how it is possible that I have said about the US draft legislation, which is based on the right of distribution, that it is excellent, simple and elegant, and now I say that the proposal coming from the European Commission, which is based on the opposite idea: communication to the public, is also excellent. You may say that I behave like the 'hero' of the following anecdote. At a meeting, a participant says about something that it is white and the chairman says: 'You are right'. Another participant says the opposite, that it is black and the chairman says: 'You are right'. A third person asks for the floor and tells the chairman that it cannot be true that the same thing is both black and white, and the chairman says: 'You are also right'. This situation, however, is not the same, because the dimension is not the same. I think that the proposed legislation embodied in the National Information Infrastructure Bills is very good for the United States, for the US legal system, but it is not necessarily good – and I said so at the hearing in the Congress – at the international level, because national laws differ very much in this respect. The proposal of the European Community is actually a combination of the communication to the public approach with the famous 'umbrella solution'. It is sufficiently broad so that it might be applied at the national level in a flexible way. In my view, that is the essence, that is the solution for the communication to the public, right of distribution, making available to the public phenomenon.

The 'digital agenda' still contains some other items. Namely, that the existence of rights in the Internet is not sufficient; they may not be exercized appropriately without technological measures of protection and without appropriate rights management information, like identification numbers and the like. Proposals have been discussed at the meetings of the Committees and will be discussed during the remaining part of the preparatory work. The treaty or treaties should include provisions obliging contracting parties to introduce sanctions against those who manufacture, import and distribute devices for defeating or circumventing technological measures of protection and who falsify or delete, without authority, rights management information. There is broad agreement on that, but still much should be done as far as the wording of the provisions is concerned. The most important players agree that we need this and I hope that there will be appropriate provisions in the treaty or treaties on this subject.

Finally, I should like to also mention that at the last session of the two Committees, the United States presented a draft treaty about *sui generis* protection of databases. It follows the idea of the system included in the recently adopted directive of the European Community, but it differs in many aspects. I mention the duration of protection which in the directive is 15 years, while the Americans propose 25 years. This may create some problems. We already have the experience of the Integrated Circuits Treaty, where there was a similar problem; at the end, we agreed on a compromise term of protection, which then was no good for anybody, for some countries because it was too long and for other countries because it was too short.

Until the diplomatic conference, there will be a frantic program of preparatory work. The chairman of the two Committees is supposed to produce a basic proposal with the assistance of the International Bureau of WIPO by 1 August, which will then be translated into the various languages, and made available by 1 September. Then there will be some negotiations, consultations during the months of September, October and November, and we hope that on 20 December, when the diplomatic conference is scheduled to be completed, those who care for an appropriate protection of copyright and neighbouring rights will receive a nice Christmas present.

We are in a decisive period. You know the saying: people can be divided into three groups; those who make things happen, those who watch things happen and those who wonder what has happened. I think that the international copyright community is in the second group now; it is watching what is happening and is ready to react. If in December we succeed, we may say that we belong to the first group of people who make things happen, that we are in the big league, and we should, because it is important for everybody. Not only for WIPO or for ALAI, or for the European Community or for the United States, not only for authors or owners of neighbouring rights, but I think it is important for society in general, and, in this borderless world, it is important for the entire mankind.

Thank you.

The European Union's approach to copyright regarding the Global Information Infrastructure

J. REINBOTHE

Ladies and gentlemen,

In the limited time I have at hand, I will try to debrief you on what has happened in the conference organized by the European Commission in Florence, yesterday and the day before yesterday, and what should happen in Brussels over the next few months. In Florence we had very good discussions, excellent speakers and even consensus on many items.

Let me first make some general points about the way the European Commission looks at intellectual property in the information society, and also about what the mandate of the European Commission in this area is. Firstly, I would say that 'copyright in cyberspace' is not a revolution but an evolution, which has taken place in part or is taking place. The history of copyright has always been a history of adaptation towards new technologies - look for example at photos, films, phonograms, television, and now the information society. The difference of course is that this time it is not a new category of works or a new way of marketing of works or subject matter that we are faced with, but a new environment. Therefore, the Information Society is certainly a new challenge of technology, probably even the biggest so far in copyright. It is no revolution, though the dimension of this challenge is certainly beyond what we have seen so far. So I would draw the conclusion not to panic. However, this time we need action rather than reaction.

The question is, of course, *who* should act. It is clear that the national legislator has had to react to challenges of technology in the area of copyright and it always did. For more than 100 years now, reactions have also come from international fora, notably the WIPO. Conventions and their revisions had to deal with challenges of technology for quite some time now. There is yet another entity that has emerged since the mid-eighties; the European Community. Also the European Community has to react or - rather - act. What does the European Community/Commission have to do with it? They are involved mainly for three reasons. First, the single market for goods and services had to be established also for copyright goods and services. This mandate the European Community has according to the EC-treaty. Copyright goods and services do form part of the single market. Another reason is that the competitivity of the European cultural industry and of creators has to be safeguarded on a Community level. This second reason is in my opinion as important as the first. The common market has to be, of course, also the economic reality for copyright; it gives us the economic framework for copyright protection in the European Community. The third reason is that we have to ensure that the rules on competition are also respected in the area of copyright, be it by collecting societies or others.

I would like to remind you of how the European Community has already reacted to the previous challenges of technology. The EC has reacted in two sectors: domestic and international. With respect to the domestic sector, legislative action in the copyright area was initiated by the Green Paper of 1988, which was already called *Copyright and the challenge of technology*. That Green Paper dealt with the protection of computer programs and databases, with problems of piracy and with distribution and rental rights. Since then the Council has adopted five directives in a little more than five years; the software directive, the rental directive, the cable and satellite directive, the directive on the harmonization of duration of protection and, most recently in March of this year, the directive on databases. Therefore, the domestic record is not bad at all.

Internationally, the European Community has been involved in the TRIPs negotiations, which were concluded in substance in 1991. These also dealt with new technologies with respect to copyright; in the TRIPs text (article 10) there is a provision on the protection of computer programs. The provision on databases is also related to new technologies, although less than the software provision. The TRIPs Agreement covers, of course, many different subjects, only to a rather small extent new technologies with regard to copyright. The other international area where the European Commission, on behalf of the Community, has been very active, relates to WIPO: the future Berne Protocol will deal with the protection of authors, and the Possible New Instrument will deal with the protection of phonogram producers and performers. The Commission has been and still is very active in these negotiations which will culminate in the Diplomatic Conference in December 1996. When explaining the international activities of the European Commission, it should be remembered that the Commission proposed some five years ago two decisions for adoption by the Council. These draft decisions suggested that all Member States should adhere to the Rome Convention and the Berne Convention. Though these decisions were never adopted by the Council, mainly for political reasons, they indicate clearly the direction taken by the Commission for quite some time now.

With respect to the initiatives of the European Commission on copyright in the information society, again, two sectors are worth mentioning: the domestic sector inside the Community and the international sector. In the domestic sector, in 1995 the Green Paper on copyright in the information society was issued, which initiated a consultation process. Part of this consultation process was the hearing that was organized in January of this year on some selected issues of the Green Paper. About 350 written comments from interested circles and Member States were received. The conference in Florence last week was in fact DG-XV's conference to sum up, and to conclude the consultation process. I will briefly describe the results of this conference.

There are four 'horizontal' conclusions, which also form a sort of mandate for the

Commission. The first conclusion is that most agree that the existing copyright concepts are still valid also in the framework of the information society. Secondly, adaptations and further harmonization on community level are needed in the area of the reproduction right, including private copying, the 'communication to the public' (or: 'making available to the public') and the physical distribution right for authors. The third 'horizontal' conclusion of the conference was that both the management of rights and enforcement issues are very important. The generic term 'enforcement' covers provisions against the abuse of anti-copy devices and the like. The fourth 'horizontal' conclusion concerns the international dimension, which has to be looked at in parallel to the harmonization exercise. The European Commission finds itself in a rather unique situation to draft proposals for the harmonization of copyright and neighbouring rights in parallel to negotiating in a diplomatic conference in the framework of WIPO. However, there is not much of a choice. We have to act now and cannot limit ourselves to only international negotiations or only domestic harmonization; we have to do both at the same time. There is no time to lose.

What will happen in the future on the domestic front is probably roughly the following. The European Commission services are preparing a Communication from the Commission to the Council. This document will describe the results of the consultation process in the Community. It will take positions and announce initiatives on all sectors, which I just described, including some others. In parallel or immediately after the publication of this paper, there will be one or several draft directive(s). On top of these measures, we envisage an explanatory document on applicable law and on enforcement questions in the context of the information society.

Last but not least, the subject of management of rights, including collective management should be tackled. Particularly collective management is worth looking at in the interest not only of users but also in the interest of those who are doing the collective management (collecting societies), and in the interest of those they represent. An initiative may be expected probably more in the medium term, not in the immediate future.

I would like to mention briefly the international negotiations. Since Mr Ficsor has already talked about this subject, I can limit myself to my personal assessments. The proposal that the Community has submitted in Geneva some ten days ago was welcomed by most participants, and I believe that we, the European Community, are on the right track. The direction that the European Community have chosen seems to be the right one, both for the reproduction right and the 'communication to the public' right, or the 'make available' right.

There are also some other points in the international negotiations worthwhile mentioning. One of these is the issue of publication; the question whether we need a provision in the new treaties on publication related to article 3 of the Berne Convention. Another big potential problem lies in the area of limitations to the rights. In the international area it is very difficult to come up with limitations which are more than some vague notions or indications of a direction. In the context of domestic harmonization I think we have to be much more precise on this point.

On another very important issue, the *sui generis* protection of databases, both the European Community and the USA have submitted proposals in Geneva. This topic is also essential in the framework of the information society and in the international context. While having recent legislation on this already in the European Community, we should also have, on an international level, an instrument in the WIPO-framework.

Some concluding remarks. Cyberspace is, of course, the issue of the day. It is fascinating and it clearly requires action. The Commission is determined to maintain the speed and quality of its action and will also try to take or maintain the lead in some areas. But I believe that we should not lose sight of the other areas of copyright. Today we have cyberspace, the information society, highways, etcetera - 'the digital agenda' as it was called by our American colleagues - but there is much more in copyright. The information society issue is only one of many in the context of copyright. We must not lose sight of the other areas of intellectual property and of the potential need for clarification or even harmonization there. I think management of rights is one key word in this context.

I thank you for your attention.

I

The economic rights involved

Les droits économiques concernés

The economic rights involved

J.H. SPOOR

I. Introduction

What is so special about the electronic highway?

The electronic highway brings together two technological developments. The first development is digitization. The electronic format allows, *inter alia*, unlimited copying at almost no cost. Moreover, it is extremely easy to make adaptations of electronic documents. The second development is networking. Networks, especially global networks such as the Internet, do away with traditional barriers for distribution and diffusion. From a user's viewpoint it is virtually irrelevant where a document is located. Whether it is stored next door or somewhere on another continent, its transmission to whoever requests it is a matter of seconds only. Even substantial files may be transmitted to the other side of the world; once more, at virtually no cost.

Electronic highway potential

The electronic highway brings an immense variety of applications. Some of these are quite new, others may seem more traditional but nevertheless turn out to offer new and tremendous potentialities. To mention just a few:
- E-mail permits transmission of all kinds of documents to any number of individual addressees.
- Newsgroups unite users from all over the world on an incidental or regular basis.
- Programs such as Gopher or WWW offer access to innumerable sites, where all kinds of materials may be found, ranging from Shakespeare's plays to the TRIPs Treaty and from Beethoven to beat music. Users may move around freely, access gigabytes of documents and download them at will.
- Hyperlinks permit users to move from one document to another by means of a mere mouse-click.

Copyright consequences

Together, these technological developments put existing copyright systems to the test, on the national as well as on the international level. From now on, any protected work may be transmitted through electronic networks, on a wide or a small scale, while the receiving person can store it and re-transmit it at will. Such transmissions may take place with or without the copyright holder's permission. Certain forms of control are possible, or even actually being practiced. Sites may be protected; users only get access by using a password which they can obtain by entering into a contract.

Documents will soon be provided with codes for identification, control and remuneration purposes. But such systems cannot offer protection if somebody uploads and transmits protected works without first asking the right holder's permission. To the extent that third party protection is required, copyright therefore remains mandatory.

This is not a new phenomenon. From the day when the printing process was invented, and perhaps even before, third party protection of art and literary works has required some form of copyright. Nor is new the fact that copyright needs to be re-adjusted to the demands of cyberspace, which are as such unprecedented. Copyright has been confronted with implementation problems before, resulting from technological changes. Earlier this century, copyright had to cope with new technologies such as gramophone records, broadcasting and reprography. Thus, it was a matter for debate whether gramophone records were 'frozen performances', and as such covered by the right of public performance, or tangible copies that were subject to the reproduction right (or perhaps both). It took some time before that matter was settled, but settled it was. Seen from this perspective, cyberspace is just the most recent challenge. Admittedly it is a rather dazzling challenge; all the more so if we take into account that the copyright system goes back to the days when printing was the core technology. Although it was adapted time and again, by now the system has grown rather old, to put it mildly. Some critics go further and state bluntly that copyright is simply out of date (and a pain in the neck as well). Certainly it was never intended to provide solutions for the electronic age. Hadn't we better forget all about it and start all over again?

The answer is quite easy - but then of course the question was a rhetorical one. Even if it would be better to forget about copyright and to invent something new - mind you, I don't say it would be better, but even supposing for a moment that it would be - it simply can't be done. Copyright is on the statute book, and likely to stay there, on the national as well as on the international level. It also is certain to be applied to electronic networks, and in fact has already been repeatedly applied to them by national courts. So for the moment let us forget about whether it is the best of all possible solutions, and simply see how it is currently being applied, or how the National Reports say it is likely to be interpreted in their respective jurisdictions.

Focus of this Report

In order to assess the copyright consequences of electronic networks, we first of all have to study how existing copyright rules apply to various kinds of network use of protected works, such as uploading and transmission by content providers, but also browsing and storage by the end-users. Once that comparison has been made we can review the results and discuss possible solutions, if needed. Of course, much work has already been done in this field, for example in the EC and US Green and White Papers respectively. The ALAI, however, has its own responsabilities. Moreover, the ALAI, by uniting copyright specialists from several continents, should be able to offer a unique contribution to the ongoing discussion on how copyright may deal with electronic network exploitation.

42

The National Reports

This General Report exists by virtue of ten very enlightening National Reports. Some Reports were accompanied by statutory texts or scholarly articles which were very useful in updating not only my knowledge but also my documentation. I am most grateful to the reporters. Together, they have highlighted the situation as regards the economic rights in cyberspace in the following countries: Austria (Dr Michel Walter)[*not included; not retrievable - ed.*], Belgium (Mr David Szafran), Canada (Mr Michel Racicot and Ms Lucie Guibault), Finland (Mr Jyrki Ojala), France (Prof. Pierre Sirinelli), Germany (Mr Oliver Schwenzer), Italy (Mr Alberto Pojaghi), the Netherlands (Mr Dirk Visser), Switzerland (Mr Jean Cavalli and Mr Vincent Salvadé), and the USA (Profs. Jane C. Ginsburg and Adria G. Kaplan).

Set-up of this Report

Below, I will first discuss the existing economic rights as well as the exceptions or defenses to those rights. Next, I will briefly focus on suggestions that have been made for changes in the law. Then we will turn to licensing. Finally, I will discuss some liability issues.

II. Applying current economic rights to electronic network use

Let us first analyze the current copyright implications of uploading, transmission, browsing and downloading. Suppose a work, say, an article by an eminent copyright scholar, is uploaded to a site, from where it may then be transmitted to others - the general public, or certain specific people, or just a couple of friends of the uploader. Or it may simply be accessible for anyone who cares to have a glance at that particular site, without the uploader actually sending it to anybody. Does the uploader need the author's permission? And what about the persons who care to consult the article? How do the various jurisdictions analyze and answer these questions?

a. *Mere uploading*

Not surprisingly, all Reports agree that uploading amounts to reproduction, since the article is fixed on a tangible medium: the web server's hard disk. Still, several Reports add comments that must be mentioned. The definition of 'reproduction' in Canadian law requires that at least an important part of the work must be copied. The Canadian Report doubts whether this requirement will always be satisfied as regards component parts of multimedia works, and in consequence expects this to be a likely defense in conflicts over multimedia network use. More as to principle, the Dutch Report, while accepting that uploading falls under the definition of reproduction, expresses concern over such a wide application of the notion of reproduction. The Report quotes from the Dutch National Group of ALAI's reaction to the EC Green Paper, where a reticent application of the notion of reproduction is advocated. According to this reaction, '*[e]xtending the Computer Programs Directive definition of reproduction to the reproduction of copyrighted works other than programs in a digital environment would obliterate the traditional right of private copying and should therefore be considered very carefully'.* In this respect, the Dutch seem to have a somewhat isolated position. Most Reports merely stress that although uploading amounts to reproduction, it may nevertheless be permissible under exceptions such as the private use exemption, or defenses such as the fair use defense.

b. *Making accessible*

Let us now assume the uploaded work is made accessible to others, without (as yet) also being actually transmitted. It is like a not so popular museum early in the morning. Although the doors are open, no visitors have as yet arrived, but anybody may at any time decide to enter the building and view the collection. All Reports agree that this situation is probably covered by some existing right, but there is less uniformity as to which right. It may be the right of public performance or the display right (Finland), or a form of broadcasting or cable television (Belgium), *'télédiffusion'* (France), or *'droit de diffusion à distance'* (Italy). The legal classification may also depend on the kind of work that is made accessible. Thus, in German law the right of public exhibition is only involved if unpublished works of visual arts are being shown.

Most Reports require that the uploaded work must at least be accessible for a public, but the definition of what constitutes a 'public', or rather of groups that are not considered as being a public, will vary, the most common limit being the group which consists of no more than family and close friends. The Belgian Report stresses that for the purpose of defining this limit, the mere membership of a cyberspace discussion group cannot be seen as 'friendship'. In Italian law, if there is 'diffusion at distance', there is no minimum size to the group that can be seen as a public. Certainly, as the Canadian and other Reports point out, the fact that prospective users may consult the work one by one (or even not at all, although they would be able to) does not prevent them from forming a public, as is for example pointed out in the Canadian Report. But according to that Report, e-mail, because of its one-to-one character, is not a communication to the public. Clearly this merely refers to individual e-mail, not to e-mail which is sent to a number of individual recipients. One might say mail is not public but mailings probably are.

c. *Transmission*

As a rule, works are not uploaded and made accessible simply to stay where they are; they will be transmitted to one or more users, either at the user's request or through the uploader's initiative. If such transmission reaches a public, as discussed in the last paragraph above, the rights of communication to the public mentioned in that paragraph will apply. What about the transmission as such, *i.e.* the activity of the networking organizations who provide the communication facilities, such as routers, nodes, satellite links and what else, may be involved? The Dutch Report stresses that this is merely a component part of the whole consultation process and cannot as such be considered an act of 'communication to the public', while such automatic temporary storage *en route* as results from electronic traffic jams or the intricate organization of cyberspace, should not be seen as 'reproduction'.

d. *Distribution?*

The question arises whether transmission may also be considered to be a form of 'distribution', thus bringing into play the distribution right in those countries where this right is recognized; the reasoning being that the transmission results in a copy being made available to the user. After all, the effect of the transmission will be that a copy of the work is made in the user's mailbox (usually a partition of a hard disk which is at his disposal on his access provider's server), or at least the work will be temporarily stored in the user's computer's internal (RAM) memory. I will come back later to the question whether storage in the RAM can be seen as such a copy.

Here, the answers are far from uniform. The US Report hints that even the mere use of the word 'distribution' in connection with electronic network transmission should be avoided. Indeed, from the classic copyright point of view, no distribution takes place on networks. On networks copies stay where they are, while additional copies are made at will whenever and wherever a document is requested. In a way, the Internet is essentially a global copying system. In consequence, if one right comes into play above all others, it is the reproduction right rather than the distribution right, which traditionally concerns the transfer of reproductions, *i.e.* physical objects once they have been made. But at the same time, seen from a functional perspective, one can very well say that, since copies are put at the user's disposal, the effect of cyberspace transmission is much the same as in the case of traditional distribution.

The question is not purely academic, as is for example stressed in the German and Austrian Reports. In German law performers and phonogram producers do not have absolute rights with respect to the public performance of their works, while they *do* have an exclusive distribution right. Nevertheless, the German Report takes a firm stand: although it is stressed that neighbouring right holders should have an exclusive right with respect to digital transmission, like in the US Report it is concluded that network transmission cannot be seen as distribution. The Italian Report on the other hand takes the opposite view, while the Austrian Report, if perhaps less outspoken, stresses the connexity of network transmission and distribution. It is pointed out that '*in qualifying digital diffusion as an act of reproduction and distribution the whole activity is covered*', a result that cannot be obtained through concepts such as broadcasting. This Report also mentions a precedent and an important precedent at that: in a judgment of 4 October 1994, the Austrian Supreme Court held the transmission of a photograph through an online-service of images (*'Bildfunk'*) to be distribution.

e. *On-line consultation*

Moving further down the line, the focus is on the user. As mentioned above, when a user accesses a work by means of gopher or on a web site, at least an act of temporary storage in the user's computer's RAM will take place. Although several Reports discuss the question whether on-line access may also be covered by public performance, display or broadcasting rights, the crucial question of course is, whether such copying - ephemeral though it will in all likelihood be - may nevertheless amount to 'reproduction'.

Answers to this question cover the whole range from an unequivocal 'yes' through 'subject to debate' to a modest 'probably not'. The 'probably not' is expressed in the Belgian Report, while a clear 'yes' comes from Italy as well as from the USA; but then of course that answer has a solid base in the US Copyright Act definition of 'reproduction'. The Swiss and French Reports are equally affirmative; the French Report points out that French law makes no distinction between *'durable, provisoire, éphémère ou intermédiaire'*. The Canadian Report, although reaching the same result with respect to Canadian law as it stands, nevertheless mentions that only as recently as 1988 a parliamentary committee advised to interpret 'reproduction' in such a way as *not* to cover RAM storage. Doubts as to whether reproduction should cover such storage are also expressed in the German, Finnish and Dutch Reports. According to this last Report, the Software Directive's broad interpretation of reproduction is 'arguably overstretched', and should not be adopted outside the software domain without further study.

f. *Downloading or printing*

If the user downloads the retrieved documents to disk or if he prints them, he reproduces them; there is no doubt about that. For the rest, the main question will be whether downloading or printing may nevertheless be permissible under existing statutory exceptions. The French Report points out that printed copies will in principle be subject to the reprography remuneration regime, as does the Belgian Report. Contrariwise, the prevaling opinion in the Netherlands is that the statutory license which lies at the basis of the reprography remuneration system should *not* apply to electronic copies, which should unequivocally remain subject to the author's exclusive right; except, perhaps, to the extent to which copies are made for mere personal study or use. The Finnish Report mentions Nordic discussions concerning an even more restrictive proposal to altogether abolish the freedom of copying for private use with respect to digital copies.

g. *Back-up copies*

Computers are utterly reliable until something goes wrong, which according to Murphy is bound to happen at the worst possible moment, so sensible people make back-ups all the time (except perhaps at just that one moment), and so do sensible access providers. But everywhere, back-up copies also qualify as reproductions, and therefore as a rule will require the copyright owner's permission. In some countries, however, they may be permissible under existing provisions which allow the making of copies in special situations, such as article 55 of the German Copyright Act which provides for the making of temporary copies by broadcasting organizations, or article 24 of the Swiss Copyright Act which allows the making of archival copies. According to the US Report, on the other hand, to the extent that a services provider makes back-up copies which serve an archival function (and which, so it is understood, may be accessed by third parties), such archival copies might, in the case of a law suit, strenghten the argument that the services provider is liable for direct copyright infringement.

h. *Exceptions and defenses*

General

Exceptions to copyright show too many national differences to deal with them in any detail here. Instead, we will focus on a few aspects of a more general nature. Exceptions and defenses do not simply vary from one country to another: the way in which they are applied is also subject to considerable differences. Perhaps the main common ground is found in article 9, paragraph 2 of the Berne Convention, where it is expressly stated that *'[i]t shall be a matter for legislation in the countries of the Union to permit the reproduction of such works in certain special cases, provided that such reproduction does not conflict with a normal exploitation of the work and does not unreasonably prejudice the legitimate interests of the author'*, although national interpretations of this provision show considerable variation, to say the least. Then, most civil law countries have a closed system of exceptions, while the common law countries use the often more flexible defenses of fair use (USA) or fair dealing (Canada). In the civil law group, the Netherlands are perhaps the only country to have an open system; at least, that is the conclusion which may be drawn from the Dutch Supreme Court's *Dior* judgment of 20 October 1995, where it was held that courts may also find exceptions to copyright in situations which the legislative bodies could not possibly have anticipated, provided such exceptions are in line with the existing ones. The potential of this doctrine in creating exceptions with respect to cyberspace use of protected works, however, requires further study and testing in court; all the more so because the *Dior* case did not itself have anything to do with electronic exploitation, let alone networking.

Application of existing exceptions

Most Reports consider that the existing provisions can, and indeed must be applied in the electronic environment. This is for example the case in Belgium, Finland, Switzerland and Canada. To a certain extent this is also the view in Germany, however with the proviso that such application of the exceptions must be in the public interest. The French Report, on the other hand, expresses doubt whether existing exceptions may be applied at all in the electronic domain. Thus, the French Report points out that the notion of *'cercle de famille'* was developed in view of traditional forms of exploitation, and may not simply be transferred to the electronic environment. Likewise, the Italian Report stresses that copying for private use is only permissible if it is done manually. Clearly, digital copying, in spite of its etymology, does not satisfy that condition.

Special exceptions?

None of the Reports mentions the existence as yet of special exceptions with respect to electronic networking (nor, indeed, of special rights). Neither, so the Swiss Report states, should the introduction of such exceptions be considered. Elsewhere, however, the subject of special exceptions is already under discussion - as is the restriction of certain existing exceptions to non-digital exploitations or uses only. The US

Report mentions attempts to develop guidelines for fair use in the area of on-line education. The Canadian Industry Department's Consultative Commission has discussed the status of browsing and, after some lobbying it appears, put forward proposals, the effect of which would be to subject browsing to copyright. The Canadian Report, however, is in favour of US case law (in the *Netcom* case) which tends to leave browsing free under the US fair use doctrine. Likewise, the Dutch Report suggests that to make a work *available* for *(inter alia)* browsing should be covered by copyright, rather than the act of browsing as such. The Finnish Report, finally, is in favour of special rules for the electronic environment as regards private use, while exceptions in the interest of the freedom of information and pressing social needs should receive universal treatment without a distinction being made between digital and non-digital situations.

i. *Do we need new rights?*

No, says the Canadian Report, as does the Italian; we can manage with the existing rights. *Yes*, says the Austrian Report; the introduction of a special *diffusion right* to complement the reproduction right should be considered. The Swiss, as usual, are well off, as their author's right is a general prerogative which may be extended as needed, while the statutorily defined faculties merely serve as examples. Meanwhile, the Dutch Report stresses that user freedom merits attention as well as authors' rights, and that in particular the reproduction right should not be enforced in the private user's sphere, for instance in case of e-mail. Taken all together, consensus is clearly lacking. Nor do we always need it, as implementation on the national level must accomodate for national differences and need not necessarily be uniform, the Austrian Report says.

j. *A few conclusions*

(1) Traditionally, the economic rights are often divided in two categories, dealing with exploitation by means of tangible and intangible media respectively. The first category concerns the making of copies and their distribution, while the second category deals with public performance or display, broadcasting and similar activities. On electronic networks this division is clearly under stress, to say the least. In cyberspace, any intangible communication will at the same time involve some form of (at least) temporary storage, which many consider to be a form of reproduction under existing copyright rules. They will point out that an extensive interpretation of 'reproduction' is mandatory, since the 'public' character of certain network operations may be hard to establish or even totally absent, while the act of uploading may be out of the right holder's reach because servers may be located in some country far away. Under those circumstances the reproduction right may well offer the last resort to right holders. At the same time, and even without extensive interpretation, the application of the reproduction right, jointly with other copyright prerogatives, may already lead to some form of 'overkill'.

(2) Incidentally, the desire to close any potential loophole even before it has really become manifest may well also explain the extensive interpretation of the 'distribu-

tion' concept. However, this general reporter is not convinced that such extensive interpretation is really needed. Moreover, there is a serious risk that such an interpretation may lead to serious confusion, especially as regards the related notion of 'exhaustion', a doctrine that is far too complex already.

(3) Finally, the single fact that digital technology makes copying and distribution much easier is not a sufficient argument to ban all freedom from the networking environment. It should at least be demonstrated that traditional copyright notions and exceptions lead to unacceptable results in actual practice before existing fences are made higher and additional fences are installed in cyberspace.

III. **Licensing**

a. *User licensing*

Whether users need permission to browse, download or print documents will first of all depend on the qualification of these activities under national law. No specific questions as to such licensing were asked in the questionnaire; reference is made to the relevant paragraphs in the preceding chapter. In practice, sites containing materials which are to be exploited commercially can *e.g.* be password-protected, and passwords will be granted on conditions which no doubt will fix, *inter alia*, permissible uses and pricing.

b. *Ownership of networking rights*

More complex licensing problems arise where it is the *content provider* who wishes to upload and make available certain protected works, especially where the rights in those works were acquired before electronic network transmission became fashionable or could even be anticipated at all. In several countries there is no doubt that transfers of copyright will never cover rights which did not exist at the time the contract was signed. This is *e.g.* the situation in Switzerland and Italy. In Italy, however, the transfer may cover technical methods which are not yet known, provided that the relevant rights exist already. This, on the other hand, is excluded in Belgium, where the transfer will not cover new exploitation methods. The French and German Reports stress that the transfer must be construed narrowly, with the result that the network rights will mostly belong to the author. Dutch and US law are mostly interpreted to permit full transfer of copyright, but the Dutch Report adds that in practice full transfers are rather rare. In the US, the question whether a grant of 'first publication rights' includes network rights is very controversial, and the object of the currently pending lawsuit *Tasini v. New York Times*. The US Report adds that *'as a result of the work-made-for-hire doctrine in the United States all rights in certain works are often consolidated in large entities, such as major periodicals or motion picture producers'*; including network rights. The same will often apply in the Netherlands, where employment contracts generally give the employer full title to employee's works, while (as mentioned above) full transfer of copyright is also considered possible. But taking all together, in most countries the network rights in existing works may offer serious problems, at least where exploitation is being envisaged by publishers or other entities to whom merely the traditional rights in those works were transferred. It will often be necessary to go back to the author or his/her heirs.

Satisfactory as this solution may perhaps seem from a traditional dogmatic copyright point of view, it may well form a serious practical impediment for electronic exploitation of existing works. Also, except for situations where a full transfer of copyright amounts to an abuse by the acquiring party of its bargaining power against individual authors, the dogmatic view that a full transfer of the copyright in a work should not be possible is not shared by this general reporter. Contract law must be equitable, and should not hinder effective exploitation and use of protected works; nor should it deprive authors of the authority to transfer their rights if they choose to do so themselves.

Be that as it may, it will certainly be necessary to develop effective licensing systems. It cannot be excluded that the advanced computing power of future computer and software generations will permit individual licensing and fully automatic remuneration, once electronic labels will not only have made it possible and cost effective to identify any single work, but to locate and contact its author (or other right owner) as well. For the time being, however, solutions will often have to be found in collective licensing.

c. *Compulsory licensing in cyberspace?*

It is sometimes argued that compulsory licences might be necessary to prevent individual right owners from hindering or altogether barring electronic network exploitation of their works. Leaving for the moment aside the question whether such a solution would be effective or at least feasible, the National Reports hardly give it any support, except perhaps as regards the extended application of existing compulsory licences, as the Swiss Report points out. In Canada the subject has come under discussion, but compulsory licensing was rejected as being incompatible with NAFTA obligations. For the rest, most Reports stress that practicable solutions should be found in collective licensing.

d. *Collective administration*

While further compulsory licensing is clearly not welcome, collective licensing is receiving considerable approval, and much work is under progress to give it some form of implementation on Internet and other electronic networks. The USA has several working systems already, in the field of photographs and database text reprints respectively, while the formation of an Author's Registry has been announced, which is *'to provide a simple accounting system for paying royalties to registered authors'*. In the field of music, ASCAP and BMI offer blanket licences for computerized on-line services. So, indeed, will SOCAN in Canada, provided its tariff proposals will receive the required official approval. Similar initiatives are being prepared elsewhere, *e.g.* in the Netherlands. Moreover, work is being done in the USA with respect to automatic clearance systems, while proposals have been put forward in Canada to come to a voluntary identification centre, and a 'virtual market'. More in general, the Austrian Report expects collecting societies will play an increasing role on electronic highways. The French Report mentions initiatives for collecting societies to cooperate in this field, which will prevent users from being confronted with a multitude of organizations. Similar initiatives are being taken in the Netherlands.

IV. **Liability issues**

In spite of these and other initiatives, until right owner identification and ease of concluding contracts will have become utterly sophisticated, while user readiness to apply for licences and right owner willingness to grant them will have reached equally unprecedented heights, copyright infringement on electronic networks will remain a topic that deserves to be discussed as well. This General Report will just address the question who will be liable in cases of unauthorized uploading, making available and transmission:

- the *contents* (or *information*) *provider*, *i.e.* the person or entity who makes certain information available to others, *e.g.* by exploiting a 'site' on a server or by uploading information to a bulletin board;
- the *services provider*, *i.e.* the person or entity who offers facilities to information providers, *e.g.* by exploiting a server on which sites may be exploited; or
- the *access provider*, *i.e.* the person or entity who enables its subscribers to access the network, in order to 'visit' site and consult or download information.[1]

a. *Liability of information (contents) providers*

It is evident that information providers who infringe copyright by uploading protected materials or making them accessible, etc., will be liable. The questionnaire does not further address this issue, except as regards the question whether a contents provider will even be liable for contents which he did not after all provide himself, but which some unknown person uploaded on his site. Several Reports answer that contents providers may well be liable for anything which is to be found on their sites, even if it was uploaded by persons unknown, although Swiss law in principle does not hold a provider liable in this situation. Anyway, in view of the ease with which many computers may be accessed by unauthorized persons who are sufficiently skilled in the art, providers are well advised to take what precautionary measures they can. The extent of this liability may vary; thus, in Finnish and Italian law, damages are only due in case of fault, while there is a no-fault liability for payment of a fair compensation.

b. *Liability of services providers*

Liability of the services provider is much more of an issue. The US cases *Playboy v. Frena* and *Religious Technology Center v. Netcom On-Line Communications Services* have attracted wide attention and are not only quoted in the US Report, but are even discussed in considerable detail in its Canadian counterpart. (For further details of both cases, reference is made to those Reports.) Cases have equally been reported from the Netherlands, which also has the dubious prerogative of being able to report a Scientology Internet case, as well as an earlier bulletin board liability judgment in *Bridgesoft v. Lenior*. As yet, no uniform conclusions can be drawn, perhaps not even per country. Generally speaking, the most common denominator probably is that a service provider must exercise reasonable care to avoid diffusing infringements, and almost certainly may not be aware of the infringement without taking action to prevent it from continuing. For providers who wish to stay clear from any liability this clearly is an Achilles' heel, for how are they to assess whether the warning is founded, so they can act upon it without risking a counterclaim from the contents provider?

In this respect, so the Dutch Report argues, the *Scientology* judgment is more satisfactory than *Bridgesoft*. In that latter case, an operator on whose bulletin board software had been infringingly uploaded, was found liable because in updating the Title Allocation Table he was considered to have actively made accessible to others, while by checking the accompanying information (but how realistic a demand was that?) he could have noticed its infringing nature. In *Scientology*, the court, on the other hand, required that infringements must be reasonably certain before service providers may be required to take action to stop them.

Precautionary measures

Whether a service provider must take precautionary measures is equally debated. The French and Italian Reports are affirmative. In the USA the issue is debated, the NII being in favour of such measures, a view that is shared by the German Report; provided, however, they do not lead to censorship, as this would be contrary to civil rights. Incidentally, the US Report mentions a similar remark from the *Netcom* judgment. Neither Belgian nor Swiss law requires measures to be taken, while the Dutch Report pleads against an obligation to require precautions.

c. *Liability of access provider*

Contrary to content or service providers, access providers generally have no power to stop infringements. All they can do is to prevent access, and thereby transmission. The key point in nevertheless discussing their liability, of course, is the fact that both content and service providers may be based in some far away country, while access providers operate nearby. Yet, several Reports consider that similar measures may be required from this group. The Finnish Report, however, states they certainly should be under no obligation to monitor transmissions. The Italian Report feels that access providers must prevent access when warned of infringements taking place through its connections, while the Dutch Report argues that access providers should not even be liable after they have been warned of infringements taking place, unless action should be both feasible and realistic.

V. Final remarks

Altogether, the National Reports, although agreeing on a number of points, show that views differ in many other respects. In fact, the divergencies were larger than I

had anticipated. Points that should be discussed include *inter alia*:
- Should the concept of 'distribution' be applied to networking?
- Should 'browsing' be considered to fall under the concept of reproduction?
- Should traditional notions as to when a communication may be considered to be 'public' apply to networking as well, or must even one-to-one communications such as e-mail be considered 'public'?
- Does networking require collective licensing and enforcement?
- What standards of liability should apply?

As a general reporter, I do not wish to anticipate on those discussions. I would, however, like to stress a more general aspect which I feel must be taken into account. One thing is certain: networking will change the way in which copyright works are exploited and communicated. Copyright should not form an obstruction to such changes; it must leave room for them to develop in a constructive way, which is profitable for both the authors and for their public. To make a comparison: as reprography was invented and matured, it did not just lead to more copies being made, it also led to a different way of using copyright works. A few decades ago, we used to study books in a library and make excerpts. Now we make copies instead, which we take home in order to read them at leisure (which, incidentally, rarely happens in practice, so they just pile up). We simply want to be able to consult them whenever we may need them, so we may even make additional copies to be stored in certain files or elsewhere. Authors certainly should be justly remunerated for such use of their works, but it is hardly wise and certainly unrealistic to charge royalties for such photocopies in the same way as for books. Network databases in turn may be used as libraries, where documents can be found time and again, whenever one needs them. Why download a document at all if your subscription allows you to consult it, without an additional per-page fee, whenever you want to look at it? Such an approach may lead to new and efficient ways to handle protected information.

If, however, any consultation of a document is considered to be a reproduction which should be taxed at a fixed price, users will be forced to download every document they consult, with the burden of having to store it in such a way that it can easily be retrieved, and regardless of whether they wish to consult it again or not, simply in order to prevent having to pay over and again every time renewed consultation turns out to be necessary. They also will be more tempted to 'share' such downloaded copies, *e.g.* by e-mailing them to friends and colleagues. In the end, a narrow way of licensing, based on a static application of traditional concepts therefore risks to lead to more copying and thereby to less control. I therefore think that copyright can continue to serve as a basis for protection and licensing, even in cyberspace. It should not, however, be considered a blueprint for accounting.

Footnote

1. These distinctions and definitions are somewhat different from those in the questionnaire, as some of the National Reports justly pointed out that these were not quite in line with what may now be considered to have developed as standard practice.

Questionnaire

1. **Rights which are involved**

Under your national law, are the following acts subject to certain economic rights (such as *e.g.* the reproduction right, distribution right, public performance right, display right, broadcasting right, cable transmission right, etc.)?

1.1. The storage of a work on a network computer, *e.g.* in a site on a server ('uploading').

1.2. Making that work available to others. If so, please specify whether it is relevant if it is made available at large or to a restricted group only.

1.3. Distribution of the work, *e.g.* to a newsgroup or a forum.

1.4. On-line consultation of the work, *i.e.* having it displayed on the consulting person's monitor (this will probably also require temporary fixation of that work in the consulting person's computer's internal memory).

1.5. Copying the consulted work on a hard disc or other media ('downloading').

1.6. Printing the consulted work.

1.7. Transmission of the work through the network in the course of it being consulted.

1.8. Making back-ups, perhaps fully automatic, by the services provider.

2. **Exceptions**

2.1. Will any of the acts, mentioned under 1.1-1.8, although in principle covered by certain economic rights, nevertheless be permissible in some situations under existing restrictions to copyright (*e.g.* restrictions for educational purposes, or for private use)? If so, please give details.

2.2. Does your national law provide for special exceptions regarding such acts in respect to network use of copyright works? Has there been any discussion about the need to implement such special exceptions? In your opinion, should such special exceptions be developed for certain specific situations?

3. **Licensing**

3.1. Are there special problems for information providers who want to acquire permission to upload and distribute existing works? For example, if the copyright has been transferred to a publisher before networking became possible or feasible, will it be clear whether the networking rights are owned by that publisher or still by the author?

3.2. Are there special facilities for information providers who want to acquire permission to upload and distribute existing works? *E.g.* is there any system of statutory or compulsory licensing that will cover these acts?

3.3. Are there any systems for collective administration of copyright which deal with these rights? If so, do those systems function in practice and do they have sufficient coverage (that is, will they be applicable for all or most of the works in a certain category of works)?

4. **Liability**

It is evident that persons who infringe copyright by up- or downloading will be liable. However, can action for copyright infringement also be taken against the mentioned persons in the following situations?

4.1. The information provider on whose site a work has been uploaded by an unknown person.

4.2. The services provider who owns the server on which a work has been infringingly uploaded by an information provider.

4.3. Does it make any difference if that services provider makes automatic back-ups which include the infringingly uploaded work?

4.4. Is a service provider required to take certain precautionary measures (such as reminding information providers of their obligations under copyright law, scanning uploaded subject matter for possible infringements, keeping a log on all uploading and consultations, etc.)?

4.5. The networking services provider, for transmitting the work through the network in the course of it being consulted.

4.6. Does it make any difference if that networking services provider has been informed that certain infringements may take place; assuming, moreover, that it would be technically feasible to monitor transmissions in order to detect potentially infringing transmissions?

General remarks

This topic deals with the question, whether and to which extent the economic rights (also called the exploitation rights) that form part of copyright are involved when works are made available, transmitted, consulted and copied through a network system such as the

Global Information Infrastructure (GII) is intended to be. It also deals with the way in which such rights can be exercised, through licensing or collective administration.

The topic only concerns copyright in works that may be transmitted through the GII, such as books and articles, photographs and drawings, musical compositions and computer programs. In consequence, some aspects fall outside its scope and should not be discussed, such as:
- the question when and whether certain objects are indeed copyrightable subject matter;
- rights in the GII itself or in its component parts, such as protocols, interfaces, accessing and routing software, etc.

Other forms of protection than copyright, which may be available to works or to non-copyrightable subject matter, may briefly be mentioned if this is considered useful to outline the copyright position, but should not be discussed in detail.

In this questionnaire, *information provider* means the person or entity who makes certain information available to others, for example by exploiting a 'site' on a server or by uploading information to a bulletin board. *Services provider* means the person or entity who offers facilities to information providers, for example by exploiting a bulletin board or a server on which sites may be exploited. *Network provider* means the person or entity who offers facilities for the transmission of data through the network, such as hubs, routers etc. Of course, one entity may be engaged in several or all of these activities.

Questionnaire

1. **Les droits concernés**

En vertu de votre droit national, les opérations suivantes sont-elles soumises à certains droits patrimoniaux (comme par exemple le droit de reproduction, le droit de distribution, le droit de communication au public, le droit d'exposer, le droit d'émettre, le droit de transmission par câble, etc.)?

1.1. La numérisation d'une oeuvre sur un réseau informatique, par exemple dans un site sur un serveur *("uploading")*.

1.2. Le fait de rendre cette oeuvre accessible à d'autres personnes. Dans l'affirmative, préciser si le caractère étendu ou restreint du groupe a une incidence éventuelle.

1.3. La distribution de l'oeuvre, par exemple à destination d'un groupe d'information ou d'un forum.

1.4. La consultation d'une oeuvre *on-line*, par exemple le fait de la diffuser sur l'écran de la personne qui la consulte (ce qui nécessitera aussi vraisemblablement la fixation de cette oeuvre dans la mémoire interne de l'ordinateur de la personne qui consulte).

1.5. Copier l'oeuvre consultée sur un disque dur ou sur une autre forme de support *("downloading")*.

1.6. L'impression de l'oeuvre consultée.

1.7. La transmission de l'oeuvre à travers le réseau suite à sa consultation.

1.8. La réalisation de *"back-ups"*, éventuellement entièrement automatiques, par le fournisseur d'accès.

2. **Exceptions**

2.1. Les opérations visées aux points 1.1 à 1.8 sont-elles autorisées dans certaines situations, en vertu de dérogations au droit d'auteur, malgré le fait que ces opérations soient soumises en principe à la protection de certains droits économiques (par exemple, les restrictions liées à des fins d'enseignement, ou à l'usage privé)? Dans l'affirmative, prière de bien vouloir détailler.

2.2. Votre droit national prévoit-il des exceptions spécifiques concernant ces opérations à propos d'oeuvres protégées par le droit d'auteur qui sont utilisées sur réseaux? Y a-t-il eu des discussions sur la nécessité d'introduire de pareilles exceptions spécifiques? A votre avis, pareilles exceptions particulières devraient-elles être appliquées à certaines situations spécifiques?

3. Licences

3.1. Existe-t-il des problèmes spécifiques pour les diffuseurs d'informations qui souhaitent obtenir l'autorisation de reproduire et de diffuser des oeuvres existantes? Par exemple, dans l'hypothèse où le droit d'auteur a été cédé à un éditeur avant que la numérisation sur réseau ne devienne possible ou réalisable, pourra-t-on déterminer clairement si les droits liés à l'utilisation du réseau sont détenus par cet éditeur ou s'ils appartiennent encore à l'auteur?

3.2. Existe-t-il des dispositions spécifiques permettant aux diffuseurs d'informations d'obtenir facilement l'autorisation de reproduire et de diffuser des oeuvres existantes? Par exemple, existe-t-il un système de licence légal ou contractuel qui couvre ces opérations?

3.3. Existe-t-il des systèmes de gestion collective des droits d'auteur qui concernent ces droits? Dans l'affirmative, ces systèmes fonctionnent-ils en pratique et ont-ils une couverture suffisante (cela étant, s'appliquent-ils à toutes les oeuvres ou à la plupart des oeuvres répertoriées dans une certaine catégorie d'oeuvres)?

4. Responsabilité

Il est évident que les personnes qui contreviennent aux dispositions sur le droit d'auteur en transmettant ou en reproduisant des oeuvres sur réseau seront responsables. Cependant, une action pour violation du droit d'auteur peut-elle être intentée à l'encontre des personnes mentionnées dans les situations suivantes?

4.1. Le diffuseur d'informations sur le site duquel une oeuvre a été diffusée par une personne inconnue.

4.2. Le fournisseur d'accès qui détient le serveur sur lequel une oeuvre a été illégalement diffusée par un diffuseur d'informations.

4.3. Quelle est l'incidence de *"back ups"* qui incluent une oeuvre illégalement diffusée, et qui sont réalisés automatiquement par le fournisseur d'accès?

4.4. Un fournisseur d'accès a-t-il l'obligation de prendre certaines mesures de précaution (comme par exemple, rappeler au diffuseurs d'informations leurs obligations résultant de la législation sur le droit d'auteur, examiner les transmissions susceptibles de constituer une infraction aux dispositions sur le droit d'auteur, conserver un relevé de tout enregistrement et consultation, etc.)?

4.5. Le fournisseur d'accès au réseau, pour avoir transmis sur réseau une oeuvre en cours de consultation.

4.6. Quelle est l'incidence du fait que le fournisseur d'accès au réseau a eu connaissance du fait que certaines irrégularilés peuvent survenir: considérant, de surcroît, qu'il est techniquement possible de contrôler les transmissions en vue de détecter les éventuelles transmissions illégales?

Belgique

D. SZAFRAN

1. **Les droits concernés**

En vertu de votre droit national, les opérations suivantes sont-elles soumises à certains droits patrimoniaux (comme par exemple le droit de reproduction, le droit de distribution, le droit de communication au public, le droit d'exposer, le droit d'émettre, le droit de transmission par câble, etc.)?

1.1. *La numérisation d'une oeuvre sur un réseau informatique, par exemple dans un site sur un serveur* ("uploading").

Le droit belge opère la distinction entre les droits moraux (droit de divulgation, droit de paternité, droit à l'intégrité de l'oeuvre) et les droits patrimoniaux ou économiques. Parmi ces derniers, on distingue le droit de reproduction et le droit de communication au public. Il convient de préciser d'emblée que les logiciels sont également protégés par le droit d'auteur: ils sont en principe assimilés aux oeuvres littéraires, protégées par la loi du 30 juin 1994 sur le droit d'auteur et les droits voisins, sous réserve des dispositions particulières comme la présomption de cession des droits patrimoniaux à l'employeur - consacrées par la loi du 30 juin 1994 transposant en droit belge la directive européenne du 14 mai 1991 concernant la protection juridique des programmes d'ordinateur.

Concernant le droit de reproduction, la loi belge du 30 juin 1994 sur le droit d'auteur et les droits voisins prévoit que "*l'auteur d'une oeuvre littéraire ou artistique a seul le droit de la reproduire ou d'en autoriser la reproduction*, de quelque manière et sous quelque forme que ce soit" (article 1er, § 1er, al. 1er). Par conséquent, la numérisation d'une oeuvre, fixée sur un support (disque dur, disquette, CD-ROM, etc.) en vue de la diffusion sur un réseau informatique, constitue un mode de reproduction qui nécessite l'autorisation de l'auteur, compte tenu du champ d'application de la disposition précitée - à l'exception notamment de la reproduction d'"oeuvres sonores et audiovisuelles effectuées dans le cercle de famille et réservées à celui-ci" (article 22, 1er, 5°; voy. également en ce sens la doctrine citée par B. Dauwe et M. Buydens dans leur réponse déposée à l'ABDA au questionnaire du Livre vert de la Commission Européenne sur le droit d'auteur et les droits voisins dans la Société de l'information: Gotzen, "L'ordinateur et la propriété intellectuelle", *Journal des Tribunaux* 1976, p. 89; Spoor, "Banques de données et droit d'auteur", *Droit de l'informatique* 1984, n° 2, p. 14; Travaux Capitant, "Nouveaux moyens de reproduction", T 37, Economica, 1988; Lamy, *Droit de l'informatique* 1995, p. 542).

1.2. *Le fait de rendre cette oeuvre accessible à d'autres personnes. Dans l'affirmative, préciser si le caractère étendu ou restreint du groupe a une incidence éventuelle.*

La loi belge précitée précise que *"l'auteur d'une oeuvre littéraire ou artistique a seul le droit de la communiquer au public* par un procédé quelconque" (article 1er, § 1er, al. 4). La jurisprudence a considéré que la transmission par un télédistributeur *"à une généralité indéterminée d'abonnés sans lien entre eux et dont il était loisible à quiconque d'en faire partie"* constitue une communication au public sanctionnée par le droit d'auteur (Bruxelles, 30 mars 1979, *JT*, p. 502; Cour de cassation belge, 3 septembre 1981, affaire *Coditel, Pasicrisie* 1982, I, p. 8; *Hoge Raad* des Pays-Bas, 30 octobre 1981, *RIDA* avril 1982, p. 168; Trib. Féd. suisse, 20 janvier 1981, *RIDA* janvier 1982, p. 196). La Cour de cassation belge a décidé que *"le caractère public ou non de l'exécution de la représentation d'une oeuvre musicale ne dépend pas du caractère du local où elle a lieu, mais des conditions de l'accès à ce local: en principe, devient publique l'assemblée d'un cercle privé dans laquelle, outre les membres adhérents, de soutien et d'honneur, leurs conjoints et leurs enfants mineurs, sont admises des personnes étrangères, quelles que soient les formalités présidant à leur admission"* (Cour de cassation, 25 mai 1972, *Pasicrisie* 1972, I, p. 885).

Concernant la loi du 30 juin 1994 relative au droit d'auteur et aux droits voisins, il a été souligné que *"comme auparavant, il reste aux tribunaux à apprécier suivant les cas de façon raisonnable (P. Wauwermans, Le droit des auteurs en Belgique, Bruxelles 1894, n°273). Ce qui doit être retenu, c'est la destination de l'exécution, combinée avec l'intimité réelle (Grenoble, 28 février 1966, RIDA n° LVII, p. 167; P.Y. Gautier, Propriété littéraire et artistique, PUF 1991, n° 139) qui unit ceux qui y assistent. S'il existe un lien familial, affectif ou professionnel particulier, des relations habituelles entre ceux qui assistent à la communication, elle reste privée"* (A. Berenboom, *Le nouveau droit d'auteur et les droits voisins*, Larcier 1995, p. 122, n° 88). La même solution peut être appliquée à la diffusion de textes, sons, images ou logiciels sur les réseaux informatiques, compte tenu des dispositions de la loi précitée, exprimée en termes généraux.

Le fait de rendre une oeuvre accessible à d'autres personnes est par conséquent susceptible de constituer une communication au public soumise à la protection du droit d'auteur, lorsqu'elle est destinée à une généralité indéterminée d'abonnés sans lien entre eux et dont il est loisible à quiconque d'en faire partie. A cet égard, le nombre de personnes appartenant à ce groupe peut constituer un des éléments pris en compte par un juge éventuellement saisi, pour déterminer le caractère public de la communication. En effet, l'augmentation du nombre de destinataires de la communication réduit les liens d'intimité pouvant exister entre les différents abonnés. Ainsi, dans l'hypothèse ou une communication par le réseau a lieu entre plusieurs personnes privées, le lien d'intimité sera souvent plus difficile à établir. Ce lien est d'autant plus ténu lorsque les personnes se sont rencontrées à l'occasion de l'utilisation d'un service sur le réseau et que l'accès à l'utilisation de ce service est ouvert à une généralité de personnes sans lien entre elles, au sens de la jurisprudence précitée. En l'absence de pareil lien, la communication par le réseau entre plusieurs personnes privées (*"bulletin board service"* par exemple) constitue par conséquent une communication au public.

De même, il a été précisé que *"[l]es nouvelles technologies qui permettent à chaque consommateur de choisir et de recevoir individuellement la transmission de programmes spécifiques ne doivent pas être interprétées ni sur le plan juridique, ni sur le plan pratique, comme une forme de communication privée qui échapperait dès lors à la protection des conventions actuellement en vigueur"* (traduction libre: *"New technologies allowing for selection by and transmission to individual consumers of specific programmes on a one-to-one basis, must not be misunderstood in legal or practical terms as a form of private communication which might then not be protected by existing Conventions"* (The American Film Marketing Association, *The Electronic Information Superhighway, AFMA's response to the European Union questionnaire and hearing on Copyright and Related Rights in the Information Society'*, 31 juillet 1994, in: Commission européenne, *Réponse des milieux intéressés sur "le droit d'auteur et les droits voisins dans la société de l'information"*, 1995, p. 26). Dans la mesure où elle est destinée à une généralité indéterminée d'abonnés sans lien entre eux et dont il est loisible à quiconque d'en faire partie, pareille communication semble en effet constituer une communication au public, eu égard à la jurisprudence précitée. Les mêmes critères semblent pouvoir être transposés, par analogie, à toute oeuvre communiquée au moyen de réseaux informatiques.

> *1.3. La distribution de l'oeuvre, par exemple à destination d'un groupe d'information ou d'un forum.*

Les critères évoqués au point 1.2 sont applicables à la distribution d'une oeuvre à un groupe d'information ou à un forum. En effet, pareille distribution est susceptible de constituer une communication au public soumise à la protection du droit d'auteur, lorsqu'elle est destinée à une généralité indéterminée d'abonnés sans lien entre eux et dont il est loisible à quiconque d'en faire partie. Dans l'hypothèse où une communication par le réseau intervient entre un grand nombre de personnes, le lien d'intimité sera souvent plus difficile à établir. Ce lien est d'autant plus ténu lorsque les personnes se sont rencontrées à l'occasion de l'utilisation d'un service sur le réseau et que l'accès à l'utilisation de ce service est ouvert à une généralité de personnes sans lien entre elles, au sens de la jurisprudence précitée. En l'absence de pareil lien, la communication par le réseau entre plusieurs personnes constitue par conséquent une communication au public.

> *1.4. La consultation d'une oeuvre* on-line, *par exemple le fait de la diffuser sur l'écran de la personne qui la consulte (ce qui nécessitera aussi vraisemblablement la fixation de cette oeuvre dans la mémoire interne de l'ordinateur de la personne qui consulte).*

La consultation d'une oeuvre par une personne, sans fixation sur un support permettant une consultation ultérieure de l'oeuvre, ne paraît pas devoir être considérée comme une reproduction de l'oeuvre. Une fixation temporaire de l'oeuvre dans la mémoire interne, destinée exclusivement à permettre la visualisation ponctuelle sur écran, ne paraît pas constituer une reproduction, en l'absence d'enregistrement sur un support fixe. Par contre, cette consultation est susceptible de constituer une communication au public dans l'hypothèse où le destinataire de la consultation fait partie d'une généralité indéterminée d'abonnés sans lien entre eux et dont il est loisible à quiconque d'en faire partie.

1.5. Copier l'oeuvre consultée sur un disque dur ou sur une autre forme de support ("downloading").

Contrairement à la fixation temporaire d'une oeuvre dans une mémoire interne destinée exclusivement à la visualisation de l'oeuvre sur écran, l'enregistrement de l'oeuvre sur un support fixe (disque dur, disquette d'ordinateur, etc.) constitue une reproduction soumise à la protection du droit d'auteur (cf. point 1.1).

1.6. L'impression de l'oeuvre consultée.

L'impression de l'oeuvre consultée constitue un procédé plus traditionnel de reproduction, soumis à la protection du droit d'auteur en application de la loi du 30 juin 1994 précitée (article 1er, § 1er, al. 1er).

1.7. La transmission de l'oeuvre à travers le réseau suite à sa consultation.

Pareille transmission est susceptible de constituer une communication au public dans l'hypothèse où le destinataire de la consultation fait partie d'une généralité indéterminée d'abonnés sans lien entre eux et dont il est loisible à quiconque d'en faire partie, au sens décrit ci-avant.

1.8. La réalisation de "back-ups", *éventuellement entièrement automatiques, par le fournisseur d'accès.*

La réalisation de *"back-ups"* implique l'enregistrement d'oeuvres sur un support fixe (disquette d'ordinateur, disque dur, etc.). Pareille opération constitue dès lors une reproduction au sens de la loi du 30 juin 1994 sur le droit d'auteur et les droits voisins.

2. Exceptions

2.1. Les opérations visées aux points 1.1 à 1.8 sont-elles autorisées dans certaines situations, en vertu de dérogations au droit d'auteur, malgré le fait que ces opérations soient soumises en principe à la protection de certains droits économiques (par exemple, les restrictions liées à des fins d'enseignement, ou à l'usage privé)? Dans l'affirmative, prière de bien vouloir détailler.

La loi du 30 juin 1994 relative au droit d'auteur et aux droits voisins prévoit notamment les exceptions suivantes aux droits patrimoniaux de l'auteur (articles 21 à 23). Lorsque l'oeuvre a été licitement publiée, l'auteur ne peut interdire, entre autres:

- *"la communication gratuite et privée effectuée dans le cercle de famille"* (article 22, § 1er, 3°);
- la reproduction d'oeuvres *"effectuée dans un but strictement privé ou didactique"* et ne portant pas *"préjudice à l'édition de l'oeuvre originale"* (article 22, § 1er, 4°);
- en ce qui concerne les oeuvres audiovisuelles et sonores, l'auteur ne peut interdire les reproductions *"effectuées dans le cercle de famille et réservées à celui-ci"* (article 22, § 1er, 5°); toutefois, ceux-ci ont droit à une rémunération, même *"pour la copie privée de leurs oeuvres"* (article 55, al. 1er); il s'agit donc d'un système de licence obligatoire;
- les citations (article 21);
- la reproduction et la communication au public de courts fragments d'oeuvres - voire l'intégralité en ce qui concerne les oeuvres plastiques - *"à l'occasion de comptes rendus d'évènements de l'actualité"* (article 22, § 1er, 1°); et
- les caricatures, parodies ou pastiches (article 22, § 1er, 6°).

Ces exceptions aux droits patrimoniaux des auteurs s'appliquent notamment aux reproductions et communications au public réalisées au travers de réseaux informatiques, dans la mesure où elles sont exprimées en termes généraux.

> **2.2.** *Votre droit national prévoit-il des exceptions spécifiques concernant ces opérations à propos d'oeuvres protégées par le droit d'auteur qui sont utilisées sur réseaux? Y a-t-il eu des discussions sur la nécessité d'introduire de pareilles exceptions spécifiques? A votre avis, pareilles exceptions particulières devraient-elles être appliquées à certaines situations spécifiques?*

Le droit national ne prévoit pas d'exceptions spécifiques à propos d'oeuvres protégées par le droit d'auteur qui sont utilisées sur réseaux. Des discussions ont eu lieu au niveau belge entre les différents intervenants, notamment en ce qui concerne la rémunération pour copie privée d'oeuvres sonores et audiovisuelles réalisées sur un support informatique. Certains ont émis l'idée qu'en pratique, les appareils et supports informatiques ne sont pas suffisamment utilisés pour la reproduction d'oeuvres sonores et audiovisuelles, malgré les possibilités techniques de réaliser pareilles reproductions; il en résulterait que celles-ci ne devraient pas donner lieu à une rémunération pour copie privée, au stade actuel. Cette solution paraît toutefois contraire à la loi du 30 juin 1994 précitée, qui prévoit une rémunération pour toute reproduction privée d'oeuvres sonores et audiovisuelles, quel que soit le mode de reproduction (article 55, § 1er). Cette rémunération représente 3% du prix de vente des appareils et supports permettant pareille reproduction, sauf disposition contraire fixant un taux différent (voy. l'article 56, § 2).

3. Licences

> **3.1.** *Existe-t-il des problèmes spécifiques pour les diffuseurs d'informations qui souhaitent obtenir l'autorisation de reproduire et de diffuser des oeuvres existantes? Par exemple, dans l'hypothèse où le droit d'auteur a été cédé à un éditeur avant que la numérisation sur réseau ne devienne possible ou réalisable, pourra-t-on déterminer clairement si les droits liés à l'utilisation du réseau sont détenus par cet éditeur ou s'ils appartiennent encore à l'auteur?*

La loi du 30 juin 1994 précise que *"[p]our chaque mode d'exploitation, la rémunéra-tion de l'auteur, l'étendue et la durée de la cession doivent être déterminés expressé-ment"* (article 3, § 1er, al. 4). Par ailleurs, *"[n]onobstant toute disposition contraire, la cession de droit concernant des formes d'exploitation encore inconnues est nulle"* (article 3, § 1er, al. 6). Par conséquent, dans l'hypothèse où le droit d'auteur a été cédé à un éditeur avant que la numérisation sur réseau ne devienne possible ou réalisable, les diffuseurs d'informations qui souhaitent obtenir l'autorisation de reproduire et de diffuser des oeuvres existantes doivent obtenir l'autorisation de l'auteur, et non celui de l'éditeur. Ce dernier ne pourra obtenir la cession des droits relatifs à ces nouvelles formes d'exploitation, qu'à partir du moment où celles-ci seront connues. Il résulte également de ce qui précède que l'autorisation accordée par l'auteur à un diffuseur d'informations, de reproduire et diffuser une oeuvre au moyen de nouvel-les formes d'exploitation encore inconnues serait entachée de nullité.

> *3.2. Existe-t-il des dispositions spécifiques permettant aux diffuseurs d'informations d'obtenir facilement l'autorisation de reproduire et de diffuser des oeuvres existantes? Par exemple, existe-t-il un système de licence légal ou contractuel qui couvre ces opérations?*

Il a été précisé qu'en ce qui concerne les oeuvres audiovisuelles et sonores, l'auteur ne peut interdire les reproductions *"effectuées dans le cercle de famille et réservées à celui-ci"* (article 22, § 1er, 5°; cf. point 2.1). Toutefois, ceux-ci ont droit à une rémunération, même *"pour la copie privée de leurs oeuvres"* (article 55, al. 1er). Il s'agit donc d'un système de licence obligatoire. Ce système permet aux diffuseurs d'information de réaliser pareilles reproductions, sans devoir obtenir l'autorisation de l'auteur. Par ailleurs, les exceptions aux droits patrimoniaux de l'auteur permet-tent de réaliser certaines reproductions ou communications au public, même en l'absence d'autorisation de l'auteur (cf. point 2.1: articles 21 à 23 de la loi du 30 juin 1994).

> *3.3. Existe-t-il des systèmes de gestion collective des droits d'auteur qui concernent ces droits? Dans l'affirmative, ces systèmes fonctionnent-ils en pratique et ont-ils une couverture suffisante (cela étant, s'appliquent-ils à toutes les oeuvres ou à la plupart des oeuvres répertoriées dans une certaine catégorie d'oeuvres)?*

La loi du 30 juin 1994 contient des dispositions relatives aux sociétés de gestion collective des droits (articles 65 à 78; voy. également l'arrêté royal du 6 avril 1995 relatif à l'autorisation des sociétés de gestion des droits visée à l'article 65 de la loi du 30 juin 1994 relative aux droits d'auteur et aux droits voisins). Ces systèmes fonctionnent en pratique, et semblent présenter une couverture suffisante. La plupart des sociétés de gestion collective sont spécialisées dans certaines catégories d'oeuvres.

4. **Responsabilité**

Il est évident que les personnes qui contreviennent aux dispositions sur le droit d'auteur en transmettant ou en reproduisant des oeuvres sur réseau seront responsables. Cependant, une action pour violation du droit d'auteur peut-elle être intentée à l'encontre des personnes mentionnées dans les situations suivantes?

4.1. *Le diffuseur d'informations sur le site duquel une oeuvre a été diffusée par une personne inconnue.*

La question de savoir si les réseaux informatiques ont le statut d'un transporteur de signal, d'un télédiffuseur ou d'un organe de presse, reste ouverte. En l'absence de dispositions légales ou réglementaires spécifiques, il ne semble pas qu'une solution uniforme en ce qui concerne la responsabilité du diffuseur d'informations sur le site duquel une oeuvre a été diffusée par une personne inconnue puisse être dégagée.

4.2. *Le fournisseur d'accès qui détient le serveur sur lequel une oeuvre a été illégalement diffusée par un diffuseur d'informations.*

Les considérations évoquées au point 4.1 sont également transposables aux fournisseurs d'accès.

4.3. *Quelle est l'incidence de "back-ups" qui incluent une oeuvre illégalement diffusée, et qui sont réalisés automatiquement par le fournisseur d'accès?*

Dans la mesure ou la réalisation de *back-ups* implique l'enregistrement d'oeuvres sur un support fixe (disquette d'ordinateur, disque dur, etc.), pareille opération constitue une reproduction au sens de la loi du 30 juin 1994 sur le droit d'auteur et les droits voisins, susceptible d'engager la responsabilité du fournisseur d'accès qui réalise ces *back-ups* (cf. points 1.1 et 1.8).

4.4. *Un fournisseur d'accès a-t-il l'obligation de prendre certaines mesures de précaution (comme par exemple, rappeler au diffuseurs d'informations leurs obligations résultant de la législation sur le droit d'auteur, examiner les transmissions susceptibles de constituer une infraction aux dispositions sur le droit d'auteur, conserver un relevé de tout enregistrement et consultation, etc.)?*

En l'absence de dispositions légales et réglementaires spécifiques, il n'existe pas d'obligation particulière dans le chef d'un fournisseur d'accès, telles que celles décrites ci-dessus. Toutefois, chaque personne est tenue d'une obligation générale de prudence, et est responsable des dommages causés du fait d'une simple négligence fautive (article 1382 du Code Civil). L'existence de la faute repose sur la notion de personne prudente et diligente placée dans les mêmes conditions; eu égard au caractère professionnel du fournisseur d'accès, l'absence d'information adéquate pourrait être qualifiée à tout le moins de négligence ou de faute légère, sous réserve d'appréciation de chaque cas d'espèce. Toutefois, le lien de causalité entre la faute (l'absence de contrôle ou d'information donnée par le fournisseur d'accès aux utilisateurs de réseaux) et le dommage (violation du droit d'auteur) semble être difficile à établir. La responsabilité des fournisseurs devra dès lors faire l'objet d'un examen au cas par cas.

4.5. *Le fournisseur d'accès au réseau, pour avoir transmis sur réseau une oeuvre en cours de consultation.*

Il a été constaté que la transmission sur réseau informatique d'une oeuvre protégée par le droit d'auteur constitue une communication au public sanctionnée par le droit d'auteur lorsqu'elle est destinée à une généralité indéterminée d'abonnés sans lien entre eux et dont il était loisible à quiconque d'en faire partie (cf. point 1.2). Par conséquent, les fournisseurs d'accès qui réalisent pareille opération engagent leur responsabilité.

4.6. *Quelle est l'incidence du fait que le fournisseur d'accès au réseau a eu connaissance du fait que certaines irrégularilés peuvent survenir: considérant, de surcroît, qu'il est techniquement possible de contrôler les transmissions en vue de détecter les éventuelles transmissions illégales?*

Il a été souligné qu'aucune disposition légale ou réglementaire spécifique n'impose au fournisseur d'accès un système de contrôle. Celui-ci a donc le droit en principe de refuser de réaliser un tel contrôle, qui peut en outre s'avérer coûteux. Néanmoins, dans l'hypothèse où le fournisseur d'accès au réseau a eu connaissance du fait que certaines irrégularités peuvent survenir, son refus de réaliser un contrôle est susceptible de constituer un abus de droit, dans la mesure où il est techniquement possible de contrôler les transmissions en vue de détecter les transmissions illégales. Par contre, le fournisseur d'accès peut être dégagé de sa responsabilité, notamment si les inconvénients résultant du contrôle (coût de ce contrôle) sont disproportionnés par rapport aux avantages en résultant (détection des violations du droit d'auteur). Outre la responsabilité des utilisateurs de réseaux qui contreviennent aux dispositions relatives au droit d'auteur, il est utile de préciser que leur responsabilité est également susceptible d'être engagée sur la base des dispositions suivantes (les présentes considérations sont en partie extraites d'un article paru au *Journal des Procès*, 26 janvier 1996, n° 297, p. 15 à 17).

Droit des marques

Le titulaire d'une marque déposée a le droit exclusif de reproduire et de diffuser, ou d'autoriser la reproduction et la diffusion de celle-ci sur un réseau informatique.

Protection de la vie privée

L'utilisation des réseaux informatiques permet de centraliser, traiter et stocker les images filmées par des caméras de vidéo-surveillance. D'autre part, le courrier électronique *(e-mail)* est protégé par le principe du secret de la correpondance, qui est inscrit dans la Constitution (article 29) et constitue un des aspects de la protection de la vie privée. Néanmoins, le législateur peut apporter des restrictions à ce principe, lorsque des mesures, prises par l'autorité publique, sont nécessaires notamment à la sécurité nationale, à la prévention des infractions, à la protection de la morale ou des droits et libertés d'autrui. Par ailleurs, l'utilisation des banques de données, notamment aux fins de publicité sur les réseaux informatiques, entre dans le champ d'application de la loi du 17 juin 1991 sur la protection des personnes à l'égard du traitement automatisé de données à caractère personnel.

Protection des consommateurs

Les commandes passées par des consommateurs sur les réseaux informatiques *(télé-shopping)* constituent une vente à distance réglementée par la loi du 14 juillet 1991 sur les pratiques du commerce et sur l'information et la protection du consommateur (article 77 *et seq.*).

Droits de l'homme et droit pénal

En matière pénale, certaines productions multimédias permettent de suivre au jour le jour l'évolution d'un procès, dans lequel sont mêlés reportages, déclarations des témoins, commentaires, pièces du dossier répressif et de procédure, etc. Ces procédés mettent en évidence le conflit de valeurs entre, d'une part, la liberté d'expression, en ce compris la liberté de la presse et le droit corrélatif du public à connaître des éléments ayant véritable "valeur d'information", et d'autre part, les droits d'autrui visés dans la Convention européenne des droits de l'homme, notamment le droit à l'honneur, à la réputation et la présomption d'innocence.

Responsabilité contractuelle

En matière contractuelle, un échange de consentement peut également intervenir sur les réseaux informatiques entre les utilisateurs, qui sont ainsi liés par un véritable contrat. Dès lors, certaines techniques ont été imaginées en vue d'apporter la preuve du consentement et de son contenu (intervention d'un tiers dépositaire du contrat conclu sur réseau, avec une clé d'accès empêchant toute modification ultérieure, formules mathématiques, etc.). Néanmoins, ces modes de preuve ne sont pas considérés comme des écrits en l'état actuel de la législation; tout au plus leur reconnaîtra-t-on une valeur de présomption ou de commencement de preuve.

Responsabilité civile et pénale

Les utilisateurs de réseaux qui commettent une faute ayant causé un préjudice sont susceptibles d'engager leur responsabilité (exemple: diffusion d'informations couvertes par le secret professionnel, divulgation d'un secret de fabrication, diffamation, diffusion d'un procédé de fabrication d'explosifs et incitation à commettre une infraction, etc.). En vertu du droit international privé belge, la loi applicable est la loi du lieu du fait dommageable, qui est soit le lieu de l'émission soit le lieu de la diffusion. La transmission d'images contraires aux bonnes moeurs sur réseau informatique est également susceptible d'engager la responsabilité pénale des émetteurs. En outre, la diffusion de messages incitant à la discrimination raciale est passible de sanctions prévues par la loi du 30 juillet 1981 tendant à réprimer certains actes inspirés par le racisme et la xénophobie.

Droit social

Le télétravail est une méthode d'organisation du travail qui permet notamment aux travailleurs de prester leurs services à domicile en étant relié à l'entreprise par un réseau informatique. Le projet de recommandation européenne et le projet de loi relatif au travail à domicile, déposé au Parlement, impliquent que le télétravailleur bénéficie de la protection sociale accordée aux travailleurs.

Droit fiscal

En droit fiscal, il convient de déterminer quel est l'état compétent pour soumettre à imposition les bénéfices réalisés au moyen de l'utilisation de réseaux informatiques. Cette localisation permet d'éviter que ces bénéfices échappent à toute imposition; elle permet également d'écarter le risque de double imposition des mêmes bénéfices par plusieurs états, en cas d'absence de convention internationale préventive de la double imposition. Les questions juridiques soulevées ont tendance à se multiplier au fur et à mesure de l'extension des réseaux informatiques. L'application des critères liés à la protection du droit d'auteur et des droits voisins est appelée à évoluer au fur et à mesure des innovations techniques et de la multiplicité de leurs applications. C'est pourquoi il semble opportun de conserver des critères d'appréciation suffisamment larges, tels que ceux évoqués ci-avant, afin de permettre leur application aux développements technologiques en constante évolution.

Canada

L. Guibault & M. Racicot

Introduction

La numérisation des oeuvres et leur distribution sur l'autoroute de l'information soulèvent de nombreuses questions en droit d'auteur. Afin d'éviter que le droit d'auteur soit encore une fois à la remorque des développements technologiques, le gouvernement canadien, à l'instar de nombreux gouvernements étrangers,[1] a constitué un groupe de travail destiné à étudier l'applicabilité des normes existantes de droit d'auteur aux oeuvres distribuées sur l'autoroute électronique. En effet, le ministère fédéral de l'Industrie mettait sur pied, au printemps 1994, le Comité consultatif sur l'autoroute de l'information. Ce Comité était composé des cinq groupes de travail suivants: compétitivité et création d'emplois; recherche-développement, applications et développement du marché; accès et incidences sociales; apprentissage et formation; culture et contenu canadiens.

Conscient de l'importance du droit d'auteur pour la protection et la circulation des oeuvres sur l'autoroute électronique, le Groupe de travail sur la culture et le contenu canadiens a jugé à-propos de former un Sous-comité spécial, chargé de faire des recommandations sur les façons d'utiliser le droit d'auteur pour optimaliser les avantages de l'autoroute de l'information pour tous les Canadiens.[2] Après avoir tenu des consultations publiques sur les conclusions de son rapport préliminaire, le Sous-comité sur le droit d'auteur a publié son rapport final au cours du mois de mars 1995.[3] Les recommandations du rapport final ont ensuite fait l'objet de discussions au sein du Comité consultatif sur l'autoroute de l'information, pour mener à l'adoption, à l'intérieur du rapport final du Comité consultatif, d'une série de recommandations spécifiques au droit d'auteur.[4] Les travaux du Sous-comité sur le droit d'auteur ont consisté essentiellement à examiner, à la lumière de la Loi sur le droit d'auteur,[5] l'ensemble des oeuvres protégées disponibles sous un format numérique, et leur utilisation sur l'autoroute électronique. À cette fin, l'étude du Sous-comité s'est limitée uniquement aux questions touchant le droit d'auteur, à l'exclusion des questions liées aux brevets et aux marques de commerce. De plus, en interprétant son mandat, le Sous-comité a précisé qu'il ne devait pas s'étendre à l'analyse des modifications proposées dans le cadre de la seconde phase de la réforme de la Loi sur le droit d'auteur, processus alors en cours au moment des travaux. De façon générale, le Sous-comité a donc revu les principes du droit d'auteur, en se souciant de préserver l'équilibre entre les besoins des créateurs et ceux des usagers.[6]

Au moment de rédiger le présent rapport, peu de commentaires ont été émis sur les conclusions tirées par ces comités. En raison de l'absence de commentaire doctrinal ou de jurisprudence canadienne directement pertinente, notre analyse doit donc puiser dans ces rapports comme source première d'information sur l'état du droit d'auteur et sur la politique législative que devrait adopter le gouvernement canadien, relativement à l'utilisation sur l'autoroute de l'information d'oeuvres protégées par le droit d'auteur. Ceci ne nous empêche pas cependant d'émettre nos propres commentaires sur la portée et la signification de certaines des recommandations formulées par les comités d'étude.

Les droits visés

Les droits exclusifs dont jouissent les titulaires de droits d'auteur sur leurs oeuvres sont prévus à l'article 3 de la Loi sur le droit d'auteur. Les principaux droits économiques reconnus aux titulaires sur leurs oeuvres sont la reproduction, la publication, la représentation publique, l'exposition publique, l'importation et la communication au public par télécommunication, de même que le droit de location pour les programmes d'ordinateurs et les enregistrements sonores. En examinant tour à tour chacun de ces droits, le Sous-comité s'est demandé s'ils pouvaient s'appliquer dans un environnement numérique ou s'ils devaient être modifiés pour tenir compte de l'utilisation d'oeuvres protégées sur l'autoroute de l'information.

Reproduction

En vertu du paragraphe 3(1) de la Loi sur le droit d'auteur, le titulaire d'un droit d'auteur a le droit exclusif de *"produire ou de reproduire une oeuvre, ou une partie importante de celle-ci, sous une forme matérielle quelconque".* Le Sous-comité souligne qu'une oeuvre continue d'être assujettie au droit d'auteur même si elle est reproduite électroniquement. Ainsi, une oeuvre fixée sous une forme matérielle quelconque sera réputée être reproduite si elle est téléchargée d'un babillard électronique et copiée sur une disquette, un disque dur ou un autre support de stockage. Le Sous-comité ajoute que l'accès à une oeuvre ou le téléchargement d'une oeuvre protégée transmise par courrier électronique sont assimilés à une reproduction.[7] Or, la notion de "partie importante" n'est pas définie dans la loi. L'évaluation de ce qui constitue la reproduction d'une partie importante d'une oeuvre est laissée à l'appréciation des tribunaux. En général, les tribunaux évaluent la partie utilisée d'une part en fonction de l'importance de l'extrait par rapport à la totalité de l'oeuvre originale, et d'autre part en fonction de l'importance de l'extrait par rapport à la totalité de l'oeuvre résultante. Si la portion utilisée n'est pas jugée importante, aucune redevance n'est alors due à l'auteur pour son utilisation.[8] Pourtant, dans le cas de la reproduction d'une oeuvre multimédia, dans lesquelles sont rassemblés notamment des textes, des extraits musicaux et des photographies, comment détermine-t-on l'importance d'une partie de l'oeuvre? Lorsque l'ensemble des composantes de l'oeuvre multimédia se résume à une série de nombres binaires, doit-on mesurer la taille d'une partie en fonction de l'espace de mémoire requis pour la sauvegarder? Sachant que les images et les sons exigent un espace de mémoire nettement supérieur à celui qui est nécessaire pour stocker un texte, doit-on considérer que la reproduction d'une seule photographie ou d'un extrait musical tiré d'une oeuvre multimédia, sans la reproduction du texte, est suffisamment importante pour justifier une condamnation pour violation de droit d'auteur?

Nulle part dans les rapports des comités ne discute-t-on de la notion de "partie importante" d'une oeuvre numérique. Dans la mesure où plusieurs actes fréquemment posés sur l'autoroute de l'information sont assimilés à une reproduction, l'importance relative d'une telle reproduction constituera dans bien des cas la seule défense disponible à une accusation de violation de droit d'auteur. Par surcroît, les médias numériques sont non linéaires, c'est-à-dire que les utilisateurs peuvent faire des recherches et établir une liaison avec un autre système sans passer par une voie donnant un résultat unique. En raison de la non-linéarité des systèmes, il devient toutefois difficile de savoir quelles oeuvres ou quelles parties d'une oeuvre sont reproduites par l'usager.[9] Compte tenu du silence de la loi et des rapports des comités, ces questions devront par conséquent être tranchées par les tribunaux.

De plus, il importe selon nous de distinguer l'acte qui consiste à télécharger une oeuvre sur le serveur d'un fournisseur de services,[10] de l'acte qui consiste à télécharger cette oeuvre du serveur vers l'ordinateur personnel d'un usager.[11] Ni le rapport du Sous-comité sur le droit d'auteur ni celui du Comité consultatif ne font une telle distinction et utilisent indistinctement les termes "accès" et "téléchargement". Or, ces deux actes n'entraînent pas nécessairement les mêmes conséquences en termes de reproduction d'une oeuvre sur l'autoroute de l'information. À titre d'analogie, prenons l'exemple d'un livre placé sur les rayons d'une bibliothèque: ce n'est pas le fait de mettre le livre sur les rayons qui viole le droit d'auteur mais de le copier.

Le fait de télécharger en amont un fichier sur le serveur d'un fournisseur de services n'implique pas nécessairement la reproduction du fichier, si le fichier est transmis au serveur plutôt que d'être reproduit. Toutefois on est en droit de penser qu'une telle reproduction sera effectuée dans la majorité des cas. La reproduction de fichiers placés sur le serveur constituera une violation des droits du titulaire si elle a été effectuée sans l'autorisation de ce dernier. Par contre, quand on télécharge en aval ce fichier du fournisseur à l'ordinateur de l'usager, on en fait nécessairement une reproduction. L'autorisation du titulaire est donc requise dans tous les cas où l'on télécharge un fichier dans un ordinateur personnel.

Communication au public par télécommunication

L'un des droits économiques ayant suscité le plus de discussions parmi les membres des différents comités est le droit exclusif du titulaire d'autoriser ou d'interdire la communication de son oeuvre au public par télécommunication.[12] Ce droit s'applique aux oeuvres littéraires, dramatiques, musicales ou artistiques et englobe *toute transmission de signes, signaux, écrits, images, sons ou renseignements de toute nature, par fil, radio, procédé visuel ou optique, ou autre système électromagnétique".*[13] En d'autres termes, le droit de communiquer une oeuvre au public par télécommunication couvre toute transmission par câble, par ondes radio, par satellite et par ligne téléphonique, lorsque cette transmission est destinée au public.[14]

La définition de ce qui constitue une transmission destinée au public n'apparaît pas dans la loi et a donc été développée par les tribunaux. De façon générale, on considère que l'expression "au public", applicable à la communication d'oeuvres par télécommunication, est plus large que l'expression "en public", invoquée en relation avec des représentations d'oeuvres.[15] Le paragraphe 3(1.2) de la Loi donne certaines indications sur ce qu'on entend par l'expression "public": *pour l'application de l'alinéa (1)f), font partie du public les personnes qui occupent les locaux d'un même immeuble d'habitation, tel un appartement ou une chambre d'hôtel, et la communica-tion qui leur est exclusivement destinée est une communication au public*". De plus, n'est pas considérée comme une communication au public, la communication effectuée entre les stations affiliées d'un même réseau de radiodiffusion.[16] À notre avis, le critère à prendre en considération dans l'évaluation de ce qui constitue une communication "au public" est la destination de la communication, non pas la situation dans laquelle se trouve la personne qui la reçoit.

Dans le contexte de l'autoroute de l'information, on s'est demandé si une commu-nication de point à point et une transmission sur demande à des abonnés individuels forment une transmission destinée au public par télécommunication, au sens normale-ment donné à cette expression. Le Sous-comité sur le droit d'auteur s'est notam-ment demandé si l'expression "au public" englobait les communications aux abon-nés de l'autoroute de l'information. De l'avis du Sous-comité, la communication point à point entre deux personnes au moyen du courrier électronique, même si elle porte sur une oeuvre protégée, ne constitue pas une communication de l'oeuvre au public, ni une exécution ou une représentation de cette oeuvre en public. Toutefois, de l'avis du Sous-comité, le téléchargement en aval par un usager d'une oeuvre protégée transmise par courrier électronique, est soumis au droit de reproduction.

Le Sous-comité a également ajouté que, lorsqu'une oeuvre est intégrée à un "babillard électronique" de façon à pouvoir être communiquée à tout membre du public ayant accès au réseau qui désire en prendre connaissance, il pourrait y avoir violation du droit exclusif du titulaire du droit d'auteur de communiquer son oeuvre au public si ce dernier n'a pas autorisé cette communication. Lors des travaux du Sous-comité, certaines parties ont avancé qu'il conviendrait de définir clairement le sens de l'expression "au public" dans la Loi. Le Sous-comité a estimé que l'expression "au public" doit être interprétée de façon à englober les transmissions du type décrit ci-dessus, même si chacun des membres du public peut recevoir cette transmission à sa guise et à son gré. On a fait remarquer que la jurisprudence ne traite pas expressément de cette question, et que toute précision apportée par interprétation judiciaire devrait donner lieu à des modifications appropriées dans la Loi sur le droit d'auteur, si cette interprétation judiciaire avait pour effet d'exclure de telles trans-missions.[17] À cet égard, la recommandation du Sous-comité s'énonce dans les termes suivants: *Le Sous-comité est d'avis que le droit d'auteur englobe la communication au public d'une oeuvre, peu importe si cette oeuvre est rendue accessible "sur demande". Si une étude plus approfondie établissait que la législation n'est pas claire à cet égard, la Loi sur le droit d'auteur devrait être modifiée pour indiquer clairement que la communication d'une oeuvre au public par télécommunication est soumise à l'autorisation préalable du titulaire du droit d'auteur, même si cette communication est faite sur demande et séparément à des usagers individuels.*"[18]

Influencés par les débats en cours aux États-Unis sur le droit d'auteur et l'autoroute de l'information, les membres du Sous-comité ont abordé la question du droit de "distribution", qui existe en droit américain. Dans l'état actuel du droit américain, aucune disposition ne prévoit la possibilité de transmettre des oeuvres au public par télécommunication ou par voie électronique. En effet, la loi américaine reconnaît au titulaire du droit d'auteur le droit exclusif *"to distribute copies or phonorecords of the copyrighted work to the public by sale or other transfer of ownership, or by rental, lease, or lending"*.[19] Le droit de distribution en vigueur aux États-Unis est épuisé une fois que la première distribution a eu lieu. Il s'agit de la doctrine de la première vente, qui empêche le titulaire du droit d'auteur d'interdire la redistribution de copies de son oeuvre dont il a précédemment autorisé la distribution initiale. Le Sous-comité a clos la discussion en déclarant que, comme la Loi canadienne comprend le droit de communiquer au public par télécommunication, qui s'applique aux transmissions électroniques, il ne convient ni de modifier la Loi pour y introduire un droit de distribution, ni d'adopter la doctrine de la première vente.[20]

Autres droits économiques

Les autres droits exclusifs contenus dans la Loi sur le droit d'auteur ont fait l'objet d'une étude moins poussée par le Sous-comité sur le droit d'auteur. Le droit de représentation publique et le droit de publication ont été interprétés comme pouvant englober la transmission d'une oeuvre par voie électronique. En relation avec le droit de représentation publique, le Sous-comité a rappelé que la Cour d'appel fédérale avait déjà indiqué que la transmission d'une oeuvre par des câblodistributeurs à leurs abonnés à la résidence privée de ces derniers pouvait être assimilée à une représentation de cette oeuvre "en public".[21] En ce qui a trait au droit de publication, le Sous-comité a conclu que les transmissions électroniques qui ont pour effet de mettre des copies à la disposition du public équivalent à une publication.[22]

En ce qui a trait au droit d'exposition publique,[23] le Sous-comité a déclaré que ce droit est beaucoup plus limité que le droit de présentation en public défini dans la loi américaine.[24] Le Sous-comité a ajouté que le droit d'exposition en public pourrait jouer un rôle important dans le contexte de l'autoroute de l'information et qu'il pourrait devenir nécessaire de revoir éventuellement la portée de ce droit, s'il devient aussi important que le droit de présentation en public américain.

Le Sous-comité a cependant porté une attention particulière sur le droit de location des programmes d'ordinateurs et des enregistrements sonores. Le droit de location a été introduit en droit canadien par la mise en oeuvre des obligations de l'Accord de libre-échange nord-américain,[25] à l'égard des programmes d'ordinateur et des enregistrements sonores. Ce droit ne s'applique pas aux oeuvres audiovisuelles ou cinématographiques, ni à aucune autre catégorie d'oeuvre. Bien que le Sous-comité ait convenu que la technologie actuelle ne permet pas de louer des oeuvres par la voie électronique (puisque la transmission d'une oeuvre équivaut davantage à une reproduction qu'à une location), il a quand même souligné le fait que la facilité avec laquelle on peut numériser une oeuvre et les méthodes de distribution de plus en plus diversifiées auront pour effet de mettre un plus grand nombre de copies entre les mains d'un plus grand nombre d'usagers, multipliant ainsi les possibilités d'activités de location commerciale non autorisée, en dehors de l'autoroute de l'information proprement dite. C'est pourquoi le Sous-comité n'a pas jugé à propos d'étendre le droit de location à d'autres oeuvres, dont les oeuvres multimédia, dans le contexte des oeuvres transmises sur l'autoroute de l'information.

Afin que les titulaires de droit d'auteur puissent faire respecter d'une manière plus efficace leur droit de location des programmes d'ordinateur ou des enregistrements sonores, le Sous-comité a recommandé que le libellé de la Loi sur le droit d'auteur soit précisé pour empêcher ou interdire la location commerciale non autorisée ou déguisée, comme l'imposition de "frais de réapprovisionnement". De plus, le Sous-comité a estimé qu'il conviendrait d'ajouter des dispositions prévoyant des dommages statutaires, inspirées du modèle américain, aux recours civils qui s'offrent aux titulaires de droit d'auteur en général, sans que ces dispositions soient limitées aux activités de location illicites.[26]

Malgré les demandes qui lui ont été faites par certains groupes, le Sous-comité sur le droit d'auteur a refusé de considérer la question de l'importation d'oeuvres par voie électronique, parce qu'à son avis, *"l'importation électronique est techniquement impossible, sur le plan pratique, puisque la transmission d'une oeuvre du point A au point B consiste à faire une copie supplémentaire de l'oeuvre originale ou de l'oeuvre copiée, qui, pour sa part, demeure au point A".*[27] Soulignons enfin que les droits moraux ont fait l'objet d'une étude approfondie de la part du Sous-comité, mais que cet aspect de la question n'entre pas dans le champs de notre analyse sur les droits économiques des titulaires de droits d'auteur.

En résumé, de l'avis du Sous-comité, les droits économiques actuellement prévus dans la Loi sur le droit d'auteur sont suffisamment souples pour inclure les transmissions d'oeuvres par voie électronique. De façon générale, seules de légères corrections devront être apportées, par souci de clarté, au libellé de quelques dispositions. Ces conclusions ont d'ailleurs été entérinées par le Comité consultatif qui n'a adressé au gouvernement que trois recommandations, la première portant sur une éventuelle clarification de la définition de l'expression "communication au public par télécommunication', la seconde portant sur la précision qu'on devrait apporter au libellé de la disposition relative au droit de location et la troisième sur l'adoption de dommages statutaires.

Les exceptions

Utilisation équitable

Les droits exclusifs conférés aux titulaires par la Loi sur le droit d'auteur peuvent toutefois être limités, dans les circonstances prévues par la Loi.[28] L'une des exceptions qui porte le plus à confusion en droit canadien est le concept d'utilisation équitable, défini aux alinéas 27(2)a et a.1) de la Loi.[29] La disposition sur l'utilisation équitable n'est pas une exception au droit d'auteur. Elle constitue plutôt une défense valide dans les cas où une violation a effectivement été constatée. Cette défense est possible, quelle que soit la forme que prend la violation des droits du titulaire. Elle est fondée sur le principe d'équité qui donne aux tribunaux la latitude nécessaire pour rendre un jugement équitable dans des situations où l'application de la Loi conduirait à des résultats excessivement sévères. Le Sous-comité a émis l'opinion que cette défense ne peut être vraiment utile que si elle demeure suffisamment vague pour être soulevée dans diverses circonstances imprévues, la clarté étant plutôt le domaine des exceptions.[30] Ainsi, alors même que la conduite d'une personne constituerait normalement une violation au droit d'auteur d'un titulaire, l'exception d'utilisation équitable permet à cette personne d'échapper à toute responsabilité.[31] Contrairement à ce que certains pensent, l'utilisation d'une oeuvre n'est pas nécessairement équitable si elle est faite pour l'une des cinq fins énumérées dans la Loi. L'utilisation doit d'abord être réputée équitable, et elle doit ensuite être faite pour l'une des fins énumérées dans la Loi.

Pourtant, la Loi ne contient aucune définition de ce que constitue l'utilisation équitable d'une oeuvre. L'évaluation de ce qui constitue une conduite équitable demeure donc à l'appréciation du tribunal. L'absence de définition est apparue pour certains comme une source d'imprécision, mais pour d'autres, comme une forme de souplesse qui permet aux tribunaux d'adapter la règle aux différentes situations factuelles. À ce titre, dans son livre blanc sur le droit d'auteur, paru lors de la première phase de la révision de la Loi,[32] le gouvernement canadien avait déploré le fait qu'il n'y ait pas eu de définition expresse de cette notion dans le texte de la Loi. De l'avis des auteurs de ce rapport, cette lacune avait contribué à la confusion dont souffrait cette notion.

Une source de confusion supplémentaire venait, selon le gouvernement, de la différence qui existait entre le concept américain d'usage équitable *("fair use")* et le concept canadien d'utilisation équitable *("fair dealing")*. Sans expliquer les raisons qui justifiaient le rejet du concept canadien en faveur de la notion américaine, le livre blanc proposait d'incorporer dans la Loi la définition suivante d'usage équitable: *"usage qui ne porte pas atteinte à l'exploitation normale de l'oeuvre ni ne cause un préjudice injustifié aux intérêts légitimes de l'auteur"*, inspirée de la loi américaine. Cette définition devait être accompagnée de critères exhaustifs d'évaluation et devait s'appliquer à toutes les oeuvres protégées rendues accessibles au public, qu'elles aient été publiées ou non.

Quelques mois après la publication du rapport *De Gutenberg à Télidon*, un sous-comité parlementaire s'était penché sur les recommandations formulées dans ce rapport.[33] Sur la question de l'utilisation équitable, le Comité parlementaire avait dit préférer conserver la notion d'utilisation équitable reconnue dans la Loi canadienne et dans les lois des autres pays du *Commonwealth* et qui n'avait donné lieu qu'à de rares litiges. Le Comité avait expliqué que le bon fonctionnement du système canadien tenait précisément au fait que, malgré l'absence de définition, les tribunaux avaient adopté une démarche claire pour l'application de cette exception: *"[i]l faut d'abord établir qu'il y a eu violation (...). Une fois la violation établie, on peut décider si une défense invoquant l'utilisation équitable permettra d'excuser la violation. La défense ne réussira que si l'utilisation était équitable et visait une des cinq fins énumérées".* En effet, la défense ne s'applique que si l'utilisation est équitable *et* si elle a été réalisée à des fins d'étude privée, de recherche, de critique, de compte rendu ou de préparation d'un résumé destiné aux journaux.[34]

Le Comité parlementaire avait donc refusé d'inclure dans la Loi une définition de la notion d'utilisation équitable, de même qu'il s'était opposé à énumérer les facteurs suivant lesquels une utilisation pouvait être jugée équitable. En outre, le Comité avait catégoriquement refusé que la défense d'utilisation équitable soit étendue de manière à s'appliquer à des oeuvres non publiées. Cependant, la recommandation voulant que la définition de "publication" soit élargie de manière à inclure les diverses méthodes, outre la distribution d'exemplaires, par lesquelles une oeuvre peut être rendue accessible au public, avait été approuvée sans réserve par le Comité parlementaire. De fait, l'ancienne définition de l'expression "publication", qui désignait auparavant l'édition d'exemplaires rendus accessibles au public,[35] avait été modifiée de la façon suivante: *"publication, par rapport à toute oeuvre, s'entend de la mise à disposition du public d'exemplaires de l'oeuvre".*[36]

Le Sous-comité sur le droit d'auteur s'est également penché sur le principe de l'utilisation équitable, cette fois dans le contexte de l'autoroute électronique. À nouveau, le système canadien a dû subir la comparaison avec le système américain d'usage équitable. Le système américain diffère du système canadien en ce qu'il s'applique à une gamme plus vaste d'activités, et notamment à l'enseignement et la préparation d'oeuvres savantes; il contient une énumération non exhaustive de facteurs en vertu desquels on détermine si une action constitue ou non un usage équitable; et il vise les oeuvres non publiées. Pour des raisons similaires à celles qu'avait invoquées le Comité parlementaire en 1985, la réponse du Sous-comité aux demandes des groupes de pressions a été de recommander le *status quo*: *"Compte tenu de l'état actuel de la technologie, le Sous-comité est d'avis que les dispositions relatives à l'utilisation équitable offrent une protection suffisante aux usagers d'oeuvres protégées par le droit d'auteur sur l'autoroute de l'information et qu'il ne convient donc pas de les modifier".*[37] Le Sous-comité recommandait pourtant du même souffle que, compte tenu de l'évolution de la technologie, la question de l'utilisation équitable soit examinée régulièrement par le gouvernement pour s'assurer que ces dispositions conservent leur pertinence sur l'autoroute de l'information.

De façon surprenante, le contenu des recommandations du Comité consultatif sur l'utilisation équitable ne reflète pas celui du rapport final du Sous-comité sur le droit d'auteur. Pour le Sous-comité, la diffusion de copies d'une oeuvre par voie électronique semblait clairement assimilable à une publication et, suivant ce principe, l'exception d'utilisation équitable pouvait donc s'appliquer à ces oeuvres car elles étaient publiées. Or, l'unique recommandation formulée à l'égard de l'utilisation équitable par le Comité consultatif porte sur cette question: *"La section de la Loi sur le droit d'auteur qui traite de l'utilisation équitable devrait être clarifiée. La Loi devrait comprendre des lignes directrices et des critères précis sur la portée de l'exception d'utilisation équitable, énonçant explicitement que l'utilisation équitable s'applique à la reproduction électronique d'une oeuvre ainsi qu'au stockage et à la transmission d'une copie de cette oeuvre par des moyens électroniques".*[38]

Survol

Parmi les exceptions dont on a envisagé la création dans le contexte de l'autoroute de l'information, se trouve celle portant sur la "consultation" d'oeuvres sur l'autoroute électronique, qu'on appelle également le "survol". La question de la "consultation" se rapporte essentiellement au droit de reproduction de l'oeuvre: lorsqu'un usager "consulte" une oeuvre d'un ordinateur à l'autre dans le but de déterminer s'il désire l'utiliser ou non, enfreint-il le droit d'auteur du titulaire? Dans son rapport final, le Sous-comité sur le droit d'auteur déclarait: *"La consultation d'une oeuvre sur l'autoroute électronique suppose la copie de cette oeuvre; pour la consulter, en effet, il faut d'abord y avoir accès. Le Sous-comité estime que le fait d'accéder à une oeuvre équivaut à la reproduire, même si c'est à titre temporaire ou passager. L'action de parcourir une oeuvre, ou une partie importante de celle-ci, devrait donc être assujettie au droit de reproduction".*[39] Autrement dit, suivant les termes du Sous-comité sur le droit d'auteur, la consultation d'une oeuvre, même si c'est à titre temporaire ou passager, est assujettie au droit de reproduction.

La notion de survol sur l'autoroute de l'information fait nécessairement appel à celle de fixation. En effet, la protection du droit d'auteur n'est accordée à une oeuvre que si elle est fixée sur un support matériel quelconque. Lors de la réforme de la Loi sur le droit d'auteur en 1988, le Sous-comité parlementaire avait analysé la question de la fixation des oeuvres. Il en était venu à la conclusion qu'une fixation devait avoir un certain degré de permanence, et avait recommandé l'adoption d'une définition suivant laquelle la fixation devait inclure tous les moyens capables de capter une oeuvre, y compris le captage par un support informatique, mais non le captage sur un support de nature volatile tel que la mémoire centrale ou l'écran d'affichage d'un ordinateur.[40] Dans sa réponse au rapport du Sous-comité parlementaire, le gouvernement avait déclaré que la recommandation du Sous-comité serait prise en compte dans la définition de la notion de fixation.

Pourtant, la notion de fixation n'a pas été définie dans la Loi et n'apparaît qu'indirectement dans la définition des programmes d'ordinateur: *"Ensemble d'instructions ou d'énoncés destiné, quelle que soit la façon dont ils sont exprimés, fixés, incorporés ou emmagasinés, à être utilisé directement ou indirectement dans un ordinateur en vue d'un résultat particulier".* De même, le législateur a ajouté, en 1993, une disposition qui prévoit que *"l'oeuvre est fixée même si sa fixation se fait au moment de sa communication".*[41] Cette disposition a été introduite lors de l'adoption de l'Accord de libre-échange Nord-américain,[42] principalement pour renverser le courant jurisprudentiel qui dominait jusque-là, voulant que les éléments d'une télédiffusion en direct n'étaient pas protégés par le droit d'auteur, puisqu'ils n'étaient pas fixés sur un support quelconque.[43] Là encore, le critère de fixation semble s'appliquer à l'oeuvre elle-même et non à sa transmission.

Aux fins de la violation du droit d'auteur, il convient ensuite de déterminer si, en vertu de la Loi, la copie doit également être fixée pour donner ouverture à un recours. En ce qui a trait à la reproduction d'une oeuvre, la question avait déjà été soulevée au moment de la réforme de la Loi sur le droit d'auteur, en matière de programmes d'ordinateur. Le Sous-comité sur la révision du droit d'auteur avait écrit dans son rapport: *"Toutefois, plusieurs témoins semblaient en déduire qu'il doit aussi y avoir fixation dans le cas d'une violation. C'est un malentendu. Il y a fixation quand on copie une oeuvre protégée, mais la reproduction d'une copie fixée d'une oeuvre protégée n'est qu'une des façons dont on peut porter atteinte à la protection s'appliquant à une oeuvre. Qu'on songe, par exemple, aux représentations publiques et à la transmission non autorisées. (...) Cette précision ayant été apportée, il demeure néanmoins une question au sujet des violations par reproduction. (...) En matière de technologie informatique, il y a lieu de définir ce qu'est une copie. Sur le plan juridique, la Loi sur le droit d'auteur reconnaît aux auteurs le droit exclusif de "reproduire une oeuvre... sous une forme matérielle quelconque'. Il faut alors se demander ce qu'est une "forme matérielle". Par exemple, est-ce qu'une copie d'une oeuvre contenue dans la mémoire centrale d'un ordinateur peut être considérée comme une reproduction sous une forme matérielle?".* [44]

Le Sous-comité sur la réforme en était venu à la conclusion que, en ce qui concernait le droit de reproduction, la forme matérielle devait avoir un certain degré de permanence. Pour cette raison, on n'avait pas cru opportun de créer, en faveur des titulaires, un nouveau droit d'affichage sur un écran d'ordinateur. Par surcroît, le Sous-comité avait conclu que la reproduction d'une oeuvre dans la mémoire centrale d'un ordinateur, *"alors que cette oeuvre serait perdue à jamais si le courant était coupé"*, n'avait pas ce caractère de permanence requis pour équivaloir à une violation du droit d'auteur. Aujourd'hui, le survol d'une oeuvre sur l'autoroute de l'information fait justement appel à la reproduction d'une oeuvre dans la mémoire vive des ordinateurs des usagers.

Rappelons que dans les cas de violation aux droits d'auteur, on doit d'abord prouver qu'il y a eu reproduction d'une oeuvre. On doit ensuite démontrer que cette reproduction porte sur la totalité de l'oeuvre ou sur une partie importante de celle-ci, puisque la reproduction a été effectuée sans le consentement du titulaire du droit. À cette étape, le défendeur peut invoquer la défense d'utilisation équitable, auquel cas le tribunal doit examiner premièrement si la reproduction est équitable et deuxièmement, si elle a été réalisée à l'une des fins prévues par la Loi.

Lors de la consultation publique qui s'est déroulée entre la publication du rapport préliminaire et celle du rapport final du Sous-comité sur le droit d'auteur, certaines parties ont fait valoir que si la consultation était assimilée à la reproduction, les usagers seraient indûment entravés dans leur capacité d'accéder à des oeuvres sur l'autoroute de l'information et de les utiliser. Le Sous-comité a estimé que les restrictions imposées aux usagers dans l'accès aux oeuvres n'est pas un problème majeur, du point de vue de la consultation électronique, dans la mesure où les titulaires de droit d'auteur sont déjà en mesure d'autoriser au préalable la reproduction de leurs oeuvres sous forme numérisée et de négocier les droits en conséquence. Le Sous-comité a fait remarquer qu'il appartient au titulaire du droit de décider si, et selon quelles modalités, la consultation doit être autorisée et, le cas échéant, de déterminer quelle valeur économique doit être rattachée à la consultation.

Certains participants aux consultations ont reconnu de plus que la consultation équivalait à une reproduction, mais ont soutenu qu'une telle utilisation pouvait être couverte par l'exception d'utilisation équitable. Après examen, le Sous-comité a conclu que la défense d'utilisation équitable n'aura pas à être invoquée dans la plupart des cas, puisque le titulaire du droit d'auteur aura généralement autorisé, implicitement ou explicitement, la reproduction d'une oeuvre transmise par voie électronique, notamment à des fins de consultation. Le Sous-comité a ajouté que dans les rares cas où une oeuvre serait placée sur l'autoroute de l'information sans que la consultation soit autorisée, l'usager pourrait vraisemblablement fonder sa défense sur l'utilisation équitable. Enfin, suivant l'opinion des membres du Sous-comité, ces cas limités ne justifiaient pas une modification aux dispositions actuelles portant sur l'utilisation équitable.

Divisé entre les intérêts des créateurs et ceux des usagers, le Comité consultatif s'est contenté d'approuver la recommandation du Sous-comité, voulant que l'auteur conserve la faculté de déterminer si et selon quelles modalités, la consultation doit être autorisée et, le cas échéant, de déterminer la valeur économique à rattacher à la consultation. Toutefois, en plus de suggérer qu'une étude plus approfondie de la question soit entreprise, le Comité consultatif a cru opportun de recommander que la Loi sur le droit d'auteur soit modifiée afin de préciser ce qui constitue un survol et ce qui constitue une oeuvre offerte au public. Conséquemment, le Comité consultatif a proposé que la définition suivante de "survol" soit ajoutée à la Loi: *"Le survol désigne la matérialisation temporaire d'une oeuvre sur un écran vidéo, un écran de télévision ou tout autre dispositif semblable, ou l'audition de la partie audio d'une telle oeuvre à l'aide d'un haut-parleur ou de tout autre dispositif semblable, sans toutefois inclure la reproduction permanente de l'oeuvre sous une forme matérielle quelconque"*.

L'application de cette recommandation aurait donc pour effet de consacrer le droit exclusif du titulaire d'autoriser ou d'interdire la reproduction de son oeuvre sur l'autoroute électronique, y compris la reproduction effectuée à des fins temporaires telle que le survol. La définition de survol n'aurait pour seule fonction que de clarifier les circonstances dans lesquelles le consentement du titulaire du droit d'auteur peut être exigé. La défense d'utilisation équitable ne serait donc pas recevable pour le survol sur l'autoroute de l'information, car même si la reproduction de l'oeuvre était jugée équitable, on n'a pas recommandé que le survol soit introduit dans l'énumération prévue aux paragraphes 27(2)a et a.1) de la Loi.

La question du "survol", ou *"browsing"* sur l'autoroute de l'information s'est posée également aux États-Unis, notamment dans l'arrêt *Religious Technology Center c. Netcom et al.*[45] *En obiter*, la Cour a examiné la question du survol en tant qu'élément d'une défense d'usage équitable. Techniquement le survol amène la reproduction de l'information numérique dans la mémoire de l'ordinateur. Les défendeurs ont reconnu que cette reproduction est fixée même lorsque l'information est placée temporairement dans la mémoire vive de l'ordinateur, mais que la reproduction temporaire effectuée lors du survol est nécessaire uniquement parce que l'information numérique n'est pas directement compréhensible par l'homme. Il s'agit donc de l'équivalent fonctionnel de la lecture, qui ne soulève pas l'application des lois sur le droit d'auteur et qui peut être faite par quiconque en bibliothèque sans l'autorisation du titulaire du droit d'auteur. On peut toutefois avancer que les effets du survol sont différents, puisque des millions de personnes peuvent consulter en même temps une seule copie d'une oeuvre sur l'autoroute de l'information, alors qu'une personne à la fois peut lire la copie de la bibliothèque.

La Cour a ajouté qu'en l'absence de but commercial ou d'incidences sur les revenus du titulaire de droit d'auteur, la consultation constitue probablement un usage équitable; un marché pourrait difficilement se développer pour l'octroi de licences de reproduction temporaire d'oeuvres numériques dans la mémoire vive d'ordinateurs pour permettre la consultation. À moins que cette utilisation soit de nature commerciale, dans le cas par exemple où une personne lit une oeuvre protégée à partir de l'autoroute de l'information et décide de ne pas en acheter de copie, la défense d'usage équitable est possible. La Cour a précisé de plus que, à moins que l'usager ait des raisons de croire que le message électronique contient du matériel protégé, il sera protégé par la doctrine de la violation involontaire qui permet aux tribunaux de ne pas accorder de dommages en cas de violation, dans des circonstances particulières. Enfin, la Cour a estimé que les usagers ne devraient pas s'inquiéter d'une accusation pour violation directe, en ce qu'il serait hautement improbable, d'un point de vue pratique, qu'un titulaire de droit d'auteur réussisse à prouver une telle violation ou intente une poursuite contre une telle personne.[46] Manifestement, cette conception rejoint celle qui a été adoptée par le Sous-comité sur le droit d'auteur.

Les licences

Application

Avant d'aborder la question de l'affranchissement des droits des titulaires de droits d'auteur, le Sous-comité sur le droit d'auteur a jugé important d'examiner les mécanismes législatifs, politiques ou techniques qui pourraient être implantés pour donner aux titulaires un moyen efficace de retirer une juste rémunération pour l'utilisation qui est faite de leurs oeuvres. Sur la base de l'étude réalisée par le Sous-comité, le Comité consultatif a ensuite formulé un certain nombre d'énoncés d'intention, adressés surtout au gouvernement mais aussi à l'industrie privée.

Ainsi, le Comité consultatif a exprimé le souhait que le gouvernement fédéral encourage la mise au point et la standardisation de techniques permettant de contrôler l'utilisation des oeuvres protégées, qui soient acceptables pour les usagers. Le gouvernement fédéral devrait également soutenir la mise au point et l'utilisation d'identificateurs pouvant être incorporés aux oeuvres protégées diffusées sous une forme numérique afin de faciliter l'identification des titulaires de droits d'auteur et le repérage des utilisations non autorisées d'oeuvres protégées. Le Comité consultatif a recommandé de plus que le gouvernement fédéral joue un rôle de chef de file dans une campagne d'éducation publique, menée en collaboration avec l'industrie et les groupes de créateurs et d'usagers, afin de mieux les informer sur l'utilisation du droit d'auteur. En outre, le Comité a estimé que le gouvernement fédéral devrait envisager d'avoir recours à tout l'éventail des instruments de politique mis à sa disposition pour assurer une protection efficace du droit d'auteur afin de favoriser la création de nouvelles oeuvres canadiennes. Enfin, le Comité a recommandé que l'altération ou le contournement des mesures de protection de toutes sortes, telles que le chiffrement ou les procédés anticopie, dans le but d'enfreindre le droit d'auteur, soient assimilés à un acte criminel en vertu de la Loi sur le droit d'auteur.

Affranchissement des droits

Dans le cadre de ses travaux, le Sous-comité sur le droit d'auteur s'est penché sur la nature des mesures administratives qui pourraient faciliter l'obtention des droits pour l'utilisation des oeuvres protégées sur l'autoroute de l'information et, en particulier, des oeuvres multimédias. L'affranchissement des droits d'auteur soulève deux problèmes majeurs: d'une part, les usagers et les créateurs d'oeuvres multimédias et d'autres oeuvres composites éprouvent de la difficulté à déterminer l'identité des titulaires des droits d'auteur sur des oeuvres ou des parties d'oeuvres, sans compter que le coût d'obtention des droits peut s'avérer prohibitif. D'autre part, de nombreux créateurs refusent d'accorder l'autorisation de reproduire leurs oeuvres sous une forme numérique par crainte que ces oeuvres soient utilisées d'une manière non autorisée ou qu'elles soient modifiées.

Le Sous-comité a proposé trois options, destinées à remédier aux difficultés posées par l'affranchissement des droits sur l'autoroute de l'information. La première consiste à créer un "centre d'identification volontaire des droits", où tous les titulaires de droits d'auteur pourraient enregistrer leurs oeuvres, décrire la nature des droits disponibles et fournir un contrat type pour l'octroi de licences. Tant les créateurs d'oeuvres multimédias que les usagers de l'autoroute de l'information, où circulent ces oeuvres, pourraient accéder à un système centralisé permettant d'identifier le titulaire des droits d'auteur et de négocier les conditions d'utilisation des oeuvres protégées. Le rapport du Sous-comité souligne que, pour être vraiment efficace, ce centre ne devrait pas être limité à l'obtention des droits pour l'utilisation d'oeuvres sur l'autoroute de l'information, mais devrait inclure *tous* les droits applicables à l'autoroute de l'information. L'idée d'instaurer un système d'identification volontaire des droits a été avancée sous une forme plus ou moins similaire par divers groupes consultatifs étrangers.[47] Ces centres d'identification couvriraient à la fois les oeuvres multimédias créées entièrement à partir de nouveau matériel et les oeuvres multimédias créées à partir d'oeuvres existantes.[48]

La seconde option serait d'adopter un mécanisme d'octroi obligatoire de licences, où la portée de certains droits pourrait être limitée. Même si le Sous-comité n'entrevoit son utilisation qu'à titre de "mécanisme d'exception" pour les cas particuliers où l'intérêt du public supplanterait les droits du créateur,[49] l'adoption d'une telle option affaiblirait sensiblement les droits des créateurs sur leurs oeuvres. À notre avis, cette solution pourrait difficilement être défendue au Canada, au regard de l'Accord de libre-échange nord-américain.[50] En effet, deux dispositions de l'Accord limitent grandement le pouvoir des États membres d'imposer des restrictions à l'exercice des droits économiques par leur titulaire. La première disposition se trouve au paragraphe 1705(3)a de l'Accord qui prévoit que: *"En ce qui concerne le droit d'auteur et les droits connexes, chacune des Parties fera en sorte que toute personne qui acquiert ou détient des droits patrimoniaux soit autorisée à les transférer librement et séparément, au moyen de contrats, en vue de leur exploitation et de leur utilisation par le bénéficiaire"*. La seconde disposition se trouve au paragraphe 1705(5) de l'Accord, qui s'énonce comme suit: *"Chacune des Parties restreindra les limitations ou les exceptions aux droits prévus dans le présent article à certains cas qui n'entrent pas en conflit avec l'exploitation normale de l'oeuvre et ne portent pas indûment préjudice aux intérêts légitimes du détenteur du droit"*.[51]

Le Sous-comité sur le droit d'auteur n'a pas retenu l'option du régime de licence obligatoire sur la base d'une analogie, pour le moins boîteuse, faite avec l'ancien mécanisme de licences obligatoires sur les médicaments brevetés. Contrairement à ce qu'avance le Sous-comité, l'abandon au Canada du régime de licence obligatoire sur les médicaments brevetés ne tient pas à un changement dans l'intérêt public, mais bien à la signature de l'Accord de libre-échange nord-américain, qui contient une disposition identique à celle du paragraphe 1705(3) en matière de brevets. Soulignons enfin qu'après examen de la question, le livre vert européen rejette également l'imposition d'un système de licences non volontaires comme solution aux problèmes de libération des droits d'auteur.[52]

La troisième option proposée par le Sous-comité consisterait à établir un marché électronique ou "virtuel" pour l'affranchissement des droits et, éventuellement, pour la négociation d'accords pour l'octroi de licences commerciales. Le Sous-comité entrevoit même que le marché pourrait être constitué d'un service Internet ou qu'il pourrait prendre la forme plus complexe d'une base de données commerciales. En d'autres termes, il revient à l'industrie de décider de la meilleure approche à utiliser pour l'affranchissement des droits sur les oeuvres utilisées sur l'autoroute de l'information.[53] À son tour, le Comité consultatif s'est contenté d'émettre deux énoncés d'intention relativement à l'affranchissement des droits d'auteur: d'une part, le gouvernement fédéral devrait encourager l'industrie, ainsi que les groupes de créateurs et d'usagers à créer des systèmes administratifs pour faciliter l'affranchissement des droits d'utilisation des oeuvres sur support numérique. Le Comité a souligné d'autre part, qu'il ne convient pas d'imposer sur le marché commercial un régime d'émission obligatoire de licences.[54]

Alors que dans son rapport final, le Sous-comité sur le droit d'auteur a déploré le peu d'intérêt manifesté par les sociétés de gestion collective de droits d'auteur face au problème de l'obtention des droits pour l'utilisation d'oeuvres numériques, la Société canadienne des auteurs, compositeurs et éditeurs de musique (SOCAN) a pris les devants en matière de perception des droits d'exécution sur des oeuvres protégées, utilisées sur l'autoroute de l'information. Elle a soumis à la Commission du droit d'auteur un projet de tarif pour l'année 1996.[55] S'il est approuvé par la Commission, le tarif numéro 22 permettra à la SOCAN de consentir des licences pour la communication au public par télécommunication, au Canada, des oeuvres faisant partie de son répertoire, *"à des abonnés par le biais d'un service de télécom-*

munications à l'aide d'un ordinateur ou d'un autre appareil raccordé à un réseau de télécommunications, lorsque chaque abonné peut avoir accès à la transmission de ces oeuvres de manière indépendante par rapport à toute autre personne ayant accès au service".[56] Aux fins de l'application du tarif, la SOCAN a proposé de plus une définition de l'expression "service de télécommunications", qui: *"s'entend notamment d'un service d'ordinateur interactif, d'un service de babillard électronique (BE), d'un serveur de réseau ou d'un fournisseur de service ou d'une installation comparable permettant ou sanctionnant l'encodage numérique, l'accès sélectif et/ou la mémorisation d'oeuvres musicales ou de portions d'oeuvres musicales numériquement codées en vue de leur transmission, sous une forme numérique, par le biais d'un réseau de télécommunications ou qui permet l'accès à un tel réseau de télécommunications à l'ordinateur d'un abonné ou à un autre appareil permettant à cet abonné d'avoir accès à la transmission de matériel de manière indépendante par rapport à toute autre personne ayant accès au service".*

À la suite de la publication de ce projet de tarif, au mois de septembre 1995, plusieurs organismes ont fait part de leurs objections auprès de la Commission du droit d'auteur. L'un des opposants souligne que le dépôt d'un tarif pour la perception des droits est prématuré, alors que le rapport final du Sous-comité sur le droit d'auteur vient tout juste d'être déposé et que plusieurs questions d'orientation de politique demeurent encore en suspens. Cet organisme considère en effet que les questions relatives à la responsabilité des opérateurs de babillards électroniques et des fournisseurs de services, à l'affranchissement des droits, à l'exception d'utilisation équitable et aux mesures destinées à assurer le respect des droits des créateurs doivent être débattues publiquement dans un forum politique approprié, et ne devraient pas être déterminées unilatéralement par la Commission du droit d'auteur à une étape si hâtive.

Dans leurs objections, des fournisseurs de services soutiennent que la SOCAN n'a aucune autorité pour exiger le versement de redevances, puisqu'à leur avis, l'accès sur demande des oeuvres musicales par des usagers individuels distincts constitue une communication privée qui n'est pas soumise à l'imposition d'une licence. Ils invoquent, à l'appui de leur argument, l'alinéa 3(1)f de la Loi sur le droit d'auteur, relatif à la transmission au public par télécommunication. Selon eux, les fournisseurs de services ne "communiquent" pas des oeuvres musicales, mais ne font que fournir le moyen par lequel une personne peut choisir d'accéder à cette oeuvre d'une tierce partie. Même si l'on considère qu'ils communiquent des oeuvres musicales, les fournisseurs de services prétendent qu'ils ne les communiquent pas "au public", dans le sens généralement entendu par cette expression dans la jurisprudence. Enfin, les fournisseurs de services estiment qu'ils devraient bénéficier de la restriction au droit d'auteur prévue à l'article 3(1.3) de la Loi, qui s'énonce comme suit: *"N'effectue pas une communication au public au titre de l'alinéa (1)f la personne qui ne fait que fournir à un tiers les moyens de télécommunication nécessaires pour que celui-ci l'effectue".*

De toute évidence, la portée de l'alinéa 3(1)f de la Loi n'est pas aussi claire que l'entrevoyait le Sous-comité sur le droit d'auteur. Or, l'essentiel des activités exercées sur l'autoroute de l'information le sont par "communication au public par télécommunication". À défaut de préciser la portée de ce concept, les fournisseurs de services se trouveront justifiés de remettre sans cesse en question le pouvoir de la Commission du droit d'auteur de fixer des tarifs pour l'utilisation d'oeuvres protégées sur l'autoroute de l'information. Si les fournisseurs refusent de verser des redevances pour l'utilisation qu'ils font des oeuvres protégées, les droits que peuvent faire valoir les créateurs sur leurs oeuvres demeureront purement théoriques. L'intervention législative suggérée par le Sous-comité sur le droit d'auteur, et reprise par le Comité consultatif, pourrait bien s'avérer nécessaire, de manière à indiquer clairement que toute communication d'une oeuvre par télécommunication même transmise sur demande et à des usagers individuels distincts constitue la "communication d'une oeuvre au public par télécommunication" et est soumise à l'autorisation préalable du titulaire du droit d'auteur.

La responsabilité

Prenant pour acquis que les activités des prestataires de services ne se limitent pas simplement à fournir les moyens de télécommunication nécessaires pour communiquer des oeuvres au public par télécommunication, ces prestataires ne sont alors pas couverts par l'exemption du paragraphe 3(1.3) de la Loi. Les fournisseurs de services et les opérateurs de babillards électroniques seraient donc susceptibles d'être tenus responsables de la communication non autorisée au public d'oeuvres protégées. Les différents groupes de travail ayant étudié la question ont tiré des conclusions bien sommaires et sans beaucoup de nuances sur la responsabilité qui devrait être imputée aux opérateurs de babillards électroniques.

De façon générale, le Comité consultatif s'est dit d'accord avec le principe, avancé dans les recommandations du Sous-comité sur le droit d'auteur, voulant que les propriétaires et les opérateurs de babillards électroniques ne soient pas tenus responsables des infractions au droit d'auteur, lorsqu'il peut être démontré que ces exploitants ignoraient réellement et ne pouvaient soupçonner que des abonnés portaient atteinte au droit d'auteur, alors qu'ils avaient pris des mesures raisonnables pour prévenir les abus.[57] Soulignons qu'aucun rapport ne va au-delà de l'étude de la responsabilité des opérateurs de babillards électroniques, et qu'aucun d'entre eux ne fait mention du degré de responsabilité imputable aux fournisseurs de services.

En vertu de la Loi sur le droit d'auteur, quiconque exécute, sans le consentement du titulaire du droit d'auteur, un acte que lui seul a la faculté d'exercer est considéré comme ayant porté atteinte au droit d'auteur sur une oeuvre.[58] L'exécution non autorisée d'actes que seul le titulaire du droit d'auteur a la faculté de poser donne ouverture pour le titulaire à des recours civils ou peut donner naissance à des recours pénaux, dans les circonstances prévues par la Loi. La responsabilité des opérateurs de babillards électroniques et de fournisseurs d'Internet varie selon les faits de chaque cas. Ainsi, tant en matière civile que pénale, la personne ayant causé l'acte de violation devra répondre des conséquences de cet acte.

Mais les activités en question mettent en jeu non seulement la responsabilité de leurs auteurs immédiats (usagers des babillards électroniques ou de l'Internet), mais également celle de l'opérateur ou du fournisseur, comme l'expliquent les auteurs Richard et Carrière: *"Although section 27 makes no such distinction, infringement of copyright may be categorized as direct or primary infringement, in which an owner's exclusive, legislated rights are violated, and indirect or secondary infringement, consisting of certain dealings with respect to infringing works. A distinguishing feature between the two is knowledge on the part of the infringer that copyright is being infringed. Such knowledge is required in the case of indirect infringement, whereas direct infringement may occur whether or not knowledge is present. A common feature of any infringement is the absence of consent on the part of the copyright owner."* [59]

Responsabilité civile

Les recours civils dont disposent les titulaires de droits d'auteur en réparation des actes de contrefaçon sont énoncés à l'article 34 de la Loi, où il est dit que le titulaire peut exercer tous les recours, par voie d'injonction, dommages-intérêts, reddition de compte ou autrement, que la loi accorde ou peut accorder pour la violation d'un droit. Les recours civils s'avèrent donc disponibles à l'égard de toute violation aux droits exclusifs du titulaire de droits d'auteur énoncés dans la Loi. Le titulaire jouit non seulement des droits exclusifs énoncés dans la Loi tels que le droit de produire, reproduire ou communiquer une oeuvre, mais aussi, en vertu de l'article 3(1) *in fine* de la Loi sur le droit d'auteur, du droit d'autoriser l'accomplissement de ces actes. Cette disposition permet d'atteindre les personnes qui, n'ayant pas elles-mêmes commis l'acte de violation, en ont pourtant autorisé l'accomplissement.[60]

Suivant la jurisprudence, l'autorisation résulte du fait d'avoir cautionné, encouragé, soutenu ou approuvé l'acte accompli. L'approbation peut elle-même consister en l'omission par une personne de prendre les mesures adéquates afin d'empêcher la perpétration de la violation alors qu'elle avait des raisons d'en soupçonner la commission et qu'elle était en position d'autorité pour la prévenir.[61] Même l'indifférence peut atteindre un degré dont on peut déduire une autorisation.[62] À notre avis, le fait pour un exploitant de babillard électronique ou un fournisseur d'Internet qui met son équipement et l'espace de mémoire à la disposition de ses abonnés, de n'avoir recouru à aucune mesure, sous forme d'avis, de politique etc. pour dissuader des activités illégales, pourrait être suffisant pour engager sa responsabilité à ce titre. L'autorisation serait encore plus flagrante si les actes de violation nc sont pas accomplis à l'insu de l'exploitant, mais plutôt avec sa tacite bénédiction. De plus, l'exploitant pourrait être tenu responsable des violations faites par ses employés dans le cadre de leurs fonctions même en l'absence d'autorisation.[63] La jurisprudence canadienne connaît des exemples où des personnes ont été tenues responsables des actes de leurs subordonnés ou de personnes sur les activités desquelles elles pouvaient exercer un contrôle.[64] En effet, les tribunaux canadiens ont reconnu qu'un employeur peut être tenu responsable de violations commises par son employé dans l'exercice de ses fonctions[65] et qu'un mandant est responsable des violations commises par son mandataire[66] et ce, même en l'absence d'autorisation de commettre cette violation.

Manifestement, les opérateurs de babillards électroniques et les fournisseurs de services sont responsables des actes de violation qu'ils accomplissent directement.

Mais rares sont les cas où un opérateur ou un fournisseur contrevient directement aux droits d'auteur d'un titulaire. Dans la plupart des cas de violation, les abonnés d'un babillard électronique ou d'un fournisseur de service téléchargent du matériel protégé sur le réseau, de manière à permettre à de nombreux autres abonnés de télécharger ce même matériel dans leur ordinateur personnel.

Les circonstances entourant la violation de droits d'auteur par un tel exploitant se rapprochent de celles dans lesquelles se trouve une institution d'enseignement qui met des appareils de photocopies à la disposition de son personnel et de ses étudiants. Mentionnons particulièrement l'arrêt *University of New South Wales c. Moorehouse*, dans lequel la Haute Cour australienne déclare: *"In the circumstances of the present case it is impossible to hold that the University itself did the act of photocopying (...). Mr Brennan was not the servant or agent of the University for the purpose of making the copies (...). It seems to me to follow these statements of principle that a person who has under his control the means by which an infringement of copyright may be committed - such as a photocopying machine - and who makes it available to other persons knowing, or having reason to suspect, that it is likely to be used for the purpose of committing an infringement, and omitting to take reasonable steps to limit the use to legitimate purposes, would authorize an infringement that resulted from its use."*[67]

Suivant la jurisprudence canadienne, la connaissance joue donc un rôle capital dans la détermination de la responsabilité d'une personne, lors de poursuites pour violation de droits d'auteur. Malgré les principes clairs qui se dégagent de la jurisprudence canadienne, le Sous-comité sur le droit d'auteur a préféré fonder son raisonnement sur les motifs de l'arrêt américain *Playboy Enterprises Inc. c. Frenaz*,[68] rendu par une Cour de District de la Floride. L'exploitant d'un babillard électronique faisait l'objet d'une poursuite pour avoir enfreint le droit exclusif du titulaire de distribuer et d'exposer au public des reproductions de photographies appartenant à *Playboy*. La Cour a tenu l'exploitant du babillard électronique responsable d'avoir distribué des photographies, sans l'autorisation du titulaire du droit d'auteur. La responsabilité de l'exploitant a été maintenue en dépit du fait que ce dernier ait affirmé son ignorance des actes commis par ses abonnés. Considérant probablement que la décision était trop sévère,[69] le Sous-comité a suggéré de prévoir un mécanisme de défense, lorsqu'il peut être démontré sans ambiguïté que le droit d'auteur a été enfreint à l'insu de l'exploitant.[70]

Depuis l'arrêt *Playboy Entreprises Inc.*, la Cour du District Nord de la Californie a rendu une autre décision reliée à l'autoroute de l'information, portant cette fois sur la violation des droits d'auteur de l'Église de Scientologie sur des écrits reproduits par les ordinateurs d'un opérateur de babillard électronique, Thomas Klemesrud, et d'un fournisseur de services, Netcom On-Line Communications Services Ltd.[71] Cette décision comporte un grand intérêt théorique, non seulement parce qu'elle représente la première décision qui aborde la responsabilité des fournisseurs de services, mais également parce que le juge Whyte analyse les trois cas où la responsabilité des exploitants de babillards électroniques et de services d'Internet peut être engagée: la responsabilité pour violation directe du droit d'auteur, la responsabilité pour acte contributoire à la violation du droit d'auteur et la responsabilité du commettant sur des employés dans l'exécution de leurs fonctions.

La Cour a distingué le cas de *Netcom* de celui de *Frena* d'une part, en ce que le droit atteint n'était pas le droit de distribuer ou d'exposer une oeuvre au public mais bien le droit de reproduction du titulaire et d'autre part, en ce que, contrairement à Frena, Netcom ne conservait pas dans son ordinateur des copies pour ses usagers, mais fournissait simplement un accès à l'Internet. De plus, Netcom n'exerçait aucun contrôle sur le contenu de l'information disponible pour ses abonnés. La Cour a conclu que la sauvegarde dans le système de Netcom de copies contrefaites et la retransmission à d'autres serveurs ne constituent pas une violation directe du droit de reproduire une oeuvre, lorsque de telles copies sont téléchargées par des usagers. Cette conclusion est renforcée par le fait que les systèmes du fournisseur et de l'opérateur de babillard électronique sauvegardent automatiquement et indistinctement tous les fichiers envoyés par leurs usagers. De plus, la Cour a mis en doute le bien fondé de l'arrêt *Frena*, relativement au lien ténu de causalité qui existe entre l'opérateur de babillard électronique et l'acte de distribution et d'exposition au public effectué par les usagers.

La Cour a déclaré que l'opérateur du babillard électronique et le fournisseur d'Internet ne sont pas libérés de toute responsabilité uniquement parce qu'il n'ont pas directement violé les droits d'auteur de la demanderesse sur ses oeuvres.[72] En effet suivant la jurisprudence américaine, une personne peut tout de même être tenue responsable pour avoir indirectement contribué à la violation des droits de la titulaire, lorsqu'il peut être prouvé que cette personne, connaissant l'existence des activités illicites, a incité, entraîné ou contribué matériellement à la conduite répréhensible d'une autre personne.[73] Dans son jugement sur l'injonction interlocutoire, la Cour a estimé que: *"However, the evidence reveals a question of fact as to whether Netcom knew or should have known that Erlich had infringed plaintiff's copyrights following receipt of plaintiff's letter. Because Netcom was arguably participating in Erlich's public distribution of plaintiff's works, there is a genuine issue as to whether Netcom knew of any infringement by Erlich before it was too late to do anything about it. If plaintiffs can prove the knowledge element, Netcom will be liable for contributory infringement since its failure to simply cancel Erlich's infringing message and thereby stop an infringing copy from being distributed worldwide constitutes substantial participation in Erlich's public distribution of the message."*
Sachant que Netcom et Klemesrud avaient la possibilité de prendre de simples mesures pour prévenir tout dommage supplémentaire aux oeuvres protégées appartenant à l'Église de Scientologie, la Cour a conclu à la responsabilité des deux défendeurs pour violation contributoire, alors qu'ils avaient connaissance de la présence de messages illicites et ont cependant continué d'aider l'usager dans l'accomplissement de ses fins.[74]

Aux États-Unis, la responsabilité des défendeurs pour les actes commis par leurs usagers peut être soulevée dans les circonstances suivantes: lorsqu'il est prouvé que le commettant a le droit et le pouvoir de contrôler les actes de la personne qui viole les droits d'auteur et qu'elle reçoit un avantage financier direct de la violation.[75] En ce qui concerne le premier élément, la Cour a noté que Netcom, dans sa prestation de services auprès de ses usagers, se réserve le droit de prendre des recours contre ses usagers et d'empêcher toute violation au droit d'auteur, de même qu'elle exige que ses abonnés l'indemnisent pour tout dommage à des tiers. De fait, la preuve a établi que Netcom avait déjà procédé à la suspension de milliers de comptes d'usagers et qu'elle pouvait retirer des messages spécifiques. Il était donc évident que Netcom exerçait un contrôle sur les activités de ses abonnés. Pourtant, aucune preuve n'a pu être faite sur l'intérêt financier que pouvait retirer Netcom de la transmission de messages illicites par ses usagers. Netcom reçoit une somme forfaitaire pour sa prestation de services et ses revenus n'augmentent pas grâce à la violation de droits d'auteur. Ce motif d'action a donc été rejeté par la Cour.

En résumé, le droit canadien comporte de grandes similarités avec le droit américain en ce qui a trait aux recours civils disponibles et aux critères d'évaluation de la responsabilité du défendeur. Dans le cas de violations directes, l'exploitant est tenu responsable, peu importe qu'il ait eu connaissance ou non de l'existence des droits du titulaire sur l'oeuvre contrefaite. Dans le cas de violations secondaires, plus particulièrement d'avoir apporté une contribution à l'acte commis par un tiers ou d'avoir entretenu un lien de subordination ou de contrôle par rapport à la personne qui accomplit cet acte, l'élément clé dans la détermination de la responsabilité des exploitants de babillards électroniques ou des fournisseurs d'Internet pour les actes demeure la connaissance. À la lumière de cette analyse, nous partageons la conclusion du Comité consultatif vis-à-vis de la responsabilité des opérateurs de babillards électroniques et des fournisseurs de services: ceux-ci ne devraient pas être tenus responsables des infractions au droit d'auteur, lorsqu'il peut être démontré que ces exploitants ignoraient réellement et ne pouvaient soupçonner que des abonnés portaient atteinte au droit d'auteur, alors qu'ils avaient pris des mesures raisonnables pour prévenir les abus.[76]

Responsabilité pénale

Outre les recours civils, la Loi sur le droit d'auteur contient une série de dispositions pénales sur les infractions et les peines, applicables à certains actes accomplis en violation de droits d'auteur. Les infractions, donnant lieu à des poursuites sur déclaration sommaire de culpabilité ou par voie de mise en accusation, sont énumérées de façon exhaustive au paragraphe 42(1) de la Loi.[77] Comme toute disposition pénale, celle-ci doit être interprétée de façon restrictive. Pour conclure à la responsabilité pénale de l'accusé, la poursuite doit prouver, hors de tout doute raisonnable, l'existence de deux éléments essentiels: l'accusé doit d'une part avoir commis ces actes sciemment et il doit d'autre part avoir commis ces actes dans un but commercial.[78] Suivant les termes de la disposition, les infractions à la Loi sur le droit d'auteur sont de responsabilité stricte, c'est-à-dire qu'un accusé peut se disculper de son accusation en prouvant qu'il ignorait réellement et ne pouvait soupçonner que des abonnés portaient atteinte au droit d'auteur, alors qu'il avait pris des mesures raisonnables pour prévenir les abus.[79]

À notre connaissance, aucun jugement motivé n'a encore été rendu au Canada concernant à la violation de droits d'auteur par des opérateurs de babillards électroniques ou par des fournisseurs de services, bien que certains plaidoyers de culpabilité aient été enregistrés. Pour donner lieu à une poursuite pénale, les actes de violation de droits d'auteur commis par un exploitant de babillard électronique ou par un fournisseur d'Internet doivent nécessairement être couverts par l'un ou l'autre des alinéas du paragraphe 42(1) de la Loi. On pourrait facilement concevoir qu'un tel exploitant mette en circulation des exemplaires contrefaits d'une oeuvre encore protégée, soit dans un but commercial, soit de façon à porter préjudice au titulaire du droit d'auteur.[80] Il est également possible que les actes de violation accomplis par un exploitant soient assimilés au fait d'exposer commercialement en public un exemplaire contrefait d'une oeuvre encore protégée.[81]

En vertu de la Loi d'interprétation,[82] les dispositions du Code Criminel relatives aux actes criminels s'appliquent, sauf dispositions contraires dans le texte créant l'infraction, aux actes criminels prévus dans le texte de la Loi, tout comme les dispositions du Code relatives aux infractions punissables sur déclaration sommaire de culpabilité s'appliquent à toutes les autres infractions créées par le texte.[83] Or, la Loi sur le droit d'auteur ne contient aucune disposition qui empêcherait d'appliquer celles du Code Criminel. Par conséquent, une personne pourrait être accusée de violation au droit d'auteur, à titre de participant à l'infraction ou à titre de conseiller. Une personne participe à une infraction lorsqu'elle la commet réellement, lorsqu'elle accomplit ou omet d'accomplir quelque chose en vue d'aider quelqu'un à la commettre ou lorsqu'elle encourage quelqu'un à la commettre.[84] Une personne qui conseille à une autre de commettre une infraction peut être déclarée coupable de cette infraction, lorsqu'elle amène, incite ou encourage cette autre personne à commettre l'infraction.[85] Dans le cas des opérateurs de babillards électroniques et des fournisseurs de services, la condamnation pour participation ou conseil à une infraction demeure une question de preuve.

En ce qui a trait aux recours pénaux, la recommandation du Sous-comité sur le droit d'auteur, voulant que l'exploitant d'un babillard électronique ne soit pas tenu responsable lorsqu'il peut démontrer qu'il ne savait pas et ne pouvait soupçonner que des abonnés portaient atteinte au droit d'auteur, alors qu'il avait pris des mesures raisonnables pour prévenir les abus, ne fait rien de plus que confirmer ce que l'énoncé du paragraphe 42(1) de la Loi sur le droit d'auteur prévoyait déjà, à savoir qu'il s'agit d'une infraction de responsabilité stricte. À notre avis, le texte du paragraphe 42(1) de la Loi est suffisamment clair pour permettre à tous types d'accusés de tenter de se disculper par une preuve de diligence raisonnable. Par conséquent, aucune modification ne devrait être apportée à la Loi de manière à couvrir le cas particulier des exploitants de babillards électroniques et des fournisseurs de services.

Conclusion

En conclusion, la Loi canadienne sur le droit d'auteur semble suffisamment souple pour s'adapter aux nouvelles contraintes posées par l'autoroute de l'information. Comme l'ont démontré les rapports du Sous-comité sur le droit d'auteur et le Comité consultatif sur l'autoroute de l'information, la Loi sur le droit d'auteur n'aura pas à subir de modification majeure pour que les oeuvres qui circulent sur l'autoroute de l'information bénéficient d'une protection adéquate. En effet, les quelques recommandations formulées à l'égard des droits économiques ne visent qu'à éliminer les doutes qui pourraient subsister quant à l'application de la Loi aux actes de reproduction et de transmission au public par télécommunication, dans le contexte de l'autoroute de l'information.

En ce qui a trait aux exceptions, outre les conclusions auxquelles sont arrivés les différents groupes de travail au sujet de l'utilisation équitable et du survol, il conviendra de tenir compte des modifications qui seront apportées à la Loi lors de l'adoption de la seconde phase de la réforme de la Loi sur le droit d'auteur. On s'attend en effet à ce que des exceptions en faveur des écoles, des handicapés, des bibliothèques et des services d'archives soient adoptées lors de la réforme. Il s'agira alors d'évaluer si ces exceptions aux droits exclusifs des titulaires auront un impact particulier sur l'autoroute de l'information.

Le contenu des recommandations des comités d'étude relativement aux recours civils et pénaux ne s'écarte pas sensiblement de l'état actuel de la Loi. La suggestion voulant que la responsabilité civile et pénale des opérateurs de babillards électroniques et de fournisseurs de services soit retenue uniquement lorsque ces derniers ne peuvent démontrer qu'ils ne savaient pas et ne pouvaient soupçonner que des abonnés portaient atteinte au droit d'auteur, alors qu'il avait pris des mesures raisonnables pour prévenir les abus, est conforme au texte de la Loi et à la jurisprudence dominante dans le domaine.

Enfin, seule la question de l'affranchissement des droits semble encore poser certains problèmes d'orientation de politique et de pratique. Il sera intéressant de voir le sort qui sera réservé au projet de tarif de la SOCAN pour la perception des droits d'exécution sur l'autoroute de l'information.

Notes

1. Commission des Communautés Européennes, *Livre vert - Le droit d'auteur et les droits voisins dans la Société de l'Information*, Bruxelles, 19 juillet 1995, COM(95) 382 final, p. 77 (ci-après Livre vert européen); Information Infrastructure Task Force, *Intellectual Property and the National Information Infrastructure - The Report of the Working Group on Intellectual Property Rights*, Présidé par Bruce A. Lehman, Washington D.C., Septembre 1995 (ci-après Rapport Lehman); Ministère de la culture et de la francophonie, *Industries culturelles et nouvelles techniques*, Rapport de la Commission présidée par Pierre Sirinelli, Paris, 1994, p. 69 (ci-après Rapport Sirinelli); Multimedia Committee of the Institute of Intellectual Property, *Exposure '94*, Tokyo, Japon, février 1994, p. 19 (ci-après Exposure '94).
2. Sous-comité sur le droit d'auteur, *Le droit d'auteur et l'autoroute de l'information - Rapport préliminaire*, Ottawa, décembre 1994 (ci-après Rapport préliminaire du Sous-comité). Disponible sur l'Internet: http://www.ic.gc.ca/info-highway/prelim.report/fra/.
3. Sous-comité sur le droit d'auteur, *Le droit d'auteur et l'autoroute de l'information - Rapport final*, Ottawa, mars 1995, p. 1 (ci-après Rapport final du Sous-comité). Disponible sur l'Internet: http://www.nlcbnc.ca/documents/infopol/canada/cihac007.txt.
4. Comité consultatif sur l'autoroute de l'information, *Le défi de l'autoroute de l'information - Rapport final*, Ottawa, Ministère des approvisionnements et services Canada, 1995, recommandations portant sur la Question No. 6 (ci-après Rapport final du Comité consultatif). Aussi disponible sur l'Internet:

http://www.ic.gc.ca/info-highway/final.report/fra/.

5. LRC (1985), c. C-42, modifiée par LRC 1985, ch. 10 (1er suppl.); ch. 1 (3e suppl.); ch. 41 (3e suppl.); c. 10 (4e suppl.); L.C. 1988, ch. 65; 1990, ch. 37; 1992, ch. 1; 1993, ch. 15; ch. 23; ch. 44; 1994, ch. 47 (ci-après Loi sur le droit d'auteur ou Loi).
6. Rapport final du Sous-comité, p. 2.
7. Rapport final du Sous-comité, pp. 11 et 13.
8. NGL Le Groupe Nordicité Ltée, *Étude sur les nouveaux médias et le droit d'auteur*, Ottawa, juin 1994, rapport final préparé à l'intention du ministère de l'Industrie du Canada, p. 29 (ci-après Étude sur les nouveaux médias et le droit d'auteur).
9. Étude sur les nouveaux médias et le droit d'auteur, p. 31.
10. En anglais on désigne cet acte par l'expression *"uploading"*, que l'on peut traduire par télétransmission de fichiers ou téléchargement en amont.
11. En anglais, on désigne cet acte par l'expression *"downloading"*, que l'on peut traduire par téléréception de fichiers ou téléchargement en aval.
12. Loi sur le droit d'auteur, art. 3(1)f, qui se lit comme suit: *"droit exclusif: (f) de communiquer au public, par télécommunication, une oeuvre littéraire, dramatique, musicale ou artistique"*.
13. Loi sur le droit d'auteur, article 2, définition de "télécommunication".
14. Rapport final du Sous-comité, p. 11.
15. Voir: *Canadian Cable Television Association c. Canada (Copyright Board)*, (1993) 46 CPR (3d) 359 (CFA); et *CTV Television Network c. Canada (Copyright Board)*, (1993) 46 CPR (3d) 343 (CFA).
16. Loi sur le droit d'auteur, article 3(1.4).
17. Rapport final du Sous-comité sur le droit d'auteur, p. 12.
18. *Id.*, p. 14.
19. Pub. L. 94-553, 90 Stat. 2541, adoptée le 19 octobre 1976 et codifiée à 17 USC, § 106(3), telle que modifiée.
20. Rapport final du Sous-comité sur le droit d'auteur, pp. 27 et 28.
21. *Canadian Cable Television Association c. Canada (Copyright Board)*, (1993) 46 CPR (3d) 359 (CFA).
22. Rapport final du Sous-comité, p. 12.
23. Loi sur le droit d'auteur, article 3(1)g: *"le droit exclusif de présenter au public lors d'une exposition, à des fins autres que la vente ou la location, une oeuvre artistique — autre qu'une carte géographique ou marine, un plan ou un graphique — créée après le 7 juin 1988"*.
24. 17 USC, § 106(5): *"in the case of literary, musical, dramatic, and choreographic works, pantomimes, and pictorial, graphic, or sculptural works, including the individual images of a motion picture or other audiovisual work, to display the copyrighted work publicly"*.
25. Loi de mise en oeuvre de l'Accord de libre-échange nord-américain - Annexe, LC 1993, c. 44, signé le 11 octobre 1992.
26. Rapport final du Sous-comité, p. 13.
27. Rapport final du Sous-comité sur le droit d'auteur, p. 14.
28. Loi sur le droit d'auteur, article 27(2)a à (2)m.
29. Loi sur le droit d'auteur, article 27(2): *"Ne constituent aucune violation du droit d'auteur: a) l'utilisation équitable d'une oeuvre à des fins d'étude privée ou de recherche; a.1) l'utilisation équitable d'une oeuvre à des fins de critique, de compte rendu ou de préparation d'un résumé destiné aux journaux, à condition qu'il soit fait mention de la source et du nom de l'auteur, s'il figure dans la source"*.
30. Rapport du Sous-comité sur le droit d'auteur, p. 29.
31. Hugues G. Richard et Laurent Carriere, *Canadian Copyright Act Annotated*, Toronto, Carswell, édition à feuilles mobiles, p. 27-14.
32. Consommation et Corporations Canada, *De Gutenberg à Télidon - Livre blanc sur le droit d'auteur*, Ottawa, Ministère des Approvisionnements et Services Canada, 1984, p. 37.
33. Comité permanent des communications et de la culture, *Une charte des droits des créateurs et créatrices - Rapport du Sous-comité sur la révision du droit d'auteur*, Ottawa, Ministère des Approvisionnements et Services Canada, 1985.
34. Loi sur le droit d'auteur, article 27(2)a et a.1.
35. S.R.C. (1970), c. C-30, article 3(2).
36. LRC (1985), c. C-42, art. 4 telle que modifiée par LC 1988, c. 65.
37. Rapport final du Sous-comité, p. 33.
38. Rapport du Comité consultatif, recommandation no. 6.5.
39. Rapport final du Sous-comité sur le droit d'auteur, p. 15.
40. Comité permanent des communications et de la culture, *op.cit.*, *supra*, note 32, p. 45.
41. Loi sur le droit d'auteur, article 3(1.1).
42. Loi de mise en oeuvre de l'Accord de libre-échange nord-américain - Annexe, LC 1993, ch. 44, signé le 11 octobre 1992.
43. *Canadian Admiral Corporation Ltd. c. Rediffusion Inc. et al.*, [1954] Ex. C.R. 382, 20 CPR 75; voir Harold G. Fox, *The Canadian Law of Copyright and Industrial Design*, 2e éd., Toronto, Carswell, 1967, p. 140.
44. Comité permanent sur les communications et la culture, *op.cit.*, *supra*, note 32, pp. 45 et 46.
45. DC NCalif, No. C-95-2009 RMW, du 21 novembre 1995. Voir discussion sur la responsabilité des opérateurs de babillards électroniques et de fournisseurs de services, *infra*.
46. *Religious Technology Center c. Netcom On-Line Communication Services Inc. et al.*, p. 23, note 25.
47. Livre vert européen, p. 77; Rapport Sirinelli, p. 69; Exposure '94, p. 19.

48. Voir: Carolina Saez, "Enforcing Copyrights in the Age of Multimedia", (1995) 21 *Rutgers Computer & Technology L.J.* 351-393, 390; et Fran Smallson, "Soliciting From a Spectrum of Sources", disponible sur l'Internet: http://www.portal.com/~recorder/smallson.html, où l'auteur écrit: *"Repackaging existing works for multimedia requires a "title search" for ownership rights, complicated by the complex relationships within collaborative efforts like music and movies".*

49. Rapport final du Sous-comité, p. 40.

50. Loi de mise en oeuvre de l'Accord de libre-échange nord-américain - Annexe, LC 1993, c. 44, signé le 11 octobre 1992.

51. A noter que le paragraphe 1706(3) de l'Accord, applicable aux droits des producteurs d'enregistrements sonores, se lit dans les mêmes termes, de même que l'article 13 de l'Accord relatif aux aspects des droits de propriété intellectuelle qui touchent au commerce, y compris le commerce des marchandises de contrefaçon, signé à Marrakech le 15 avril 1994. Cet Accord est incorporé dans le droit canadien par la Loi portant mise en oeuvre de l'Accord instituant l'Organisation mondiale du commerce, LC 1994, c. 47, sanctionnée le 15 décembre 1994. Les dispositions relatives à la propriété intellectuelle entrent en vigueur à compter du 1er janvier 1996.

52. Voir aussi: Livre vert européen, p. 77 où la Commission déclare: *"Lors de l'audition des 7 et 8 juillet 1994, les milieux intéressés ont fortement souligné leur aversion quant à l'introduction des licences non-volontaires. La Commission partage pleinement ce point de vue. Non seulement elle ne voit aucune justification valable pour imposer, de manière générale, des licences non-volontaires pour la création d'oeuvres multimédias ou pour l'introduction d'oeuvres et de prestations protégées sur les autoroutes de l'information, mais, de plus, de telles licences non-volontaires, si introduites au niveau national, donneront nécessairement lieu à des problèmes pour la circulation des oeuvres et prestations protégées".*

53. Rapport final du Sous-comité, p. 41.

54. Rapport final du Comité consultatif, recommandation 6.12.

55. Supplément à la Gazette du Canada, Partie I, 30 septembre 1995.

56. *Id.*, p. 31.

57. Rapport final du Comité consultatif, recommandation 6.16; Rapport final du Sous-comité, pp. 17-18.

58. Loi sur le droit d'auteur, article 27(1).

59. Hugues G. Richard et Laurent Carriere, *Canadian Copyright Act Annotated*, Toronto, Carswell, édition à feuilles mobiles, p. 27-6.

60. Voir: *Compco Co. c. Blue Crest Music Inc.*, [1980] 1 RCS 357, aux pages 364, 375 et 378-379.

61. *Canadian Performing Right Society Ltd. c. Canadian National Exhibition Association*, [1934] 4 DLR 154 (Ont. SC); *Falcon c. Famous Players Film Co.*, [1926] 2 KB 474 (CA); *Adelaide Corporation c. Australasian Performing Rights Association* (1928), 40 CLR 481 (Aust. HC)).

62. *CBS Inc. c. Ames Records & Tapes Ltd.*, [1981] 2 All ER 812, à la p. 823: *"... indifference exhibited by acts of commission or omission, may reach a degree from authorization or permission may be inferred. It is a question of fact in each case what is the true inference to be drawn from the conduct of the person..."*; et *Performing Right Society c. Cyril Theatrical Syndicate*, [1924] 1 KB 1.

63. Voir l'article 1463 du Code civil du Québec, qui prévoit que: *"Le commettant est tenu de réparer le préjudice causé par la faute de ses préposés dans l'exécution de leurs fonctions; il conserve néanmoins ses recours contre eux".*

64. *De Tervagne et Société des Auteurs et Compositeurs Dramatiques c. Ville de Beloeil et al.*, Cour fédérale, Division de première instance, T-36-91, 4 mai 1993, Juge Joyal, jugement non rapporté, p. 21 où le juge déclare: *"Soulignons par exemple les arrêts cités par les demandeurs dans les deux cas de Canadian Performing Right Society c. Canadian National Exhibition Association, ainsi que dans l'affaire Canadian Performing Right Society c. Ming Yee. Dans ces trois décisions, le degré de contrôle exercé par les défendeurs sur les personnes ayant commis la violation a été évalué en fonction de la relation maître-serviteur ou employeur-employé qui existait entre les parties. En l'espèce, la ville de Beloeil et les Productions de la Coulisse n'exerçaient aucun contrôle sur le producteur de la pièce, M. Bossac, ou sur sa troupe de théâtre. De plus, la relation de maître-serviteur ou employeur-employé n'existait pas. Il s'agissait plutôt d'une relation strictement d'affaire...".*

65. *Apple Computer c. Mackintosh Computers*, (1987) 8 CIPR 153; et *Performing Rights Society c. Mitchell & Booker*, [1924] 1 KB 762.

66. *Canadian Performing Right Society c. Yee*, [1943] 4 DLR 732.

67. (1975) 49 ALJR 267 (Aust. HC), à la p. 271.

68. 839 F. Supp. 1552 (MD Fla. 1993).

69. Voir le Rapport préliminaire du Sous-comité, p. 16 où il est dit en toutes lettres que le jugement était trop sévère. Cette remarque a cependant été retirée du Rapport final.

70. Rapport final du Sous-comité, p. 18.

71. *Religious Technology Center c. Netcom On-Line Communication Services Inc.*, DC NCalif., No. C-95-2009 RMW, du 21 novembre 1995. Disponible sur l'Internet: http://www.cybercom.net/~rnewman/scientology/ net/whyte-11.21.95.

72. *Id.*, p. 15.

73. *Sony Corp. c. Universal City Studios, Inc.*, 464 US 417 (1984), à la p. 435: *"[t]he absence of such express language in the copyright statute does not preclude the imposition of liability for copyright infringement on certain parties who have not themselves engaged in the infringing activity. For vicarious liability is imposed in virtually all areas of the law, and the concept of contributory infringement is merely a species of the broader problem of identifying the circumstances in which it is just to hold one individual accountable for the actions of another"*; et *Gershwin Publishing Corp. c. Columbia Artists Management,*

Inc., 443 F.2d 1159 (2d Cir. 1971).

74. Voir aussi: *Sega Enterprises Ltd. c. Maphia*, 857 F. Supp. 679 (ND Cal. 1994).

75. À noter que la preuve de ce dernier critère n'est pas requise en droit civil québécois pour entraîner la responsabilité des commettants pour les actes commis par leurs subordonnés.

76. Rapport final du Comité consultatif, recommandation 6.16; Rapport final du Sous-comité, p. 18.

77. Loi sur le droit d'auteur, art. 42 qui se lit comme suit: *"Commet une infraction quiconque, sciemment: a) se livre, en vue de la vente ou de la location, à la contrefaçon d'une oeuvre encore protégée; b) vend ou loue, ou commercialement met ou offre en vente ou en location, un exemplaire contrefait d'une telle oeuvre; c) met en circulation des exemplaires contrefaits d'une telle oeuvre, soit dans un but commercial, soit de façon à porter préjudice au titulaire du droit d'auteur; d) expose commercialement en public un exemplaire contrefait d'une telle oeuvre; e) importe pour la vente ou la location, au Canada, un exemplaire contrefait d'une telle oeuvre".*

78. Voir: *R. c. Laurier Office Mart Inc.*, (1995) 58 CPR (3d) 403 où la Couronne n'a pu prouver hors de tout doute raisonnable que les propriétaires d'un service de photocopies avaient connaissance que les usagers faisaient la reproduction d'oeuvres encore protégées par le droit d'auteur.

79. Sur le principe de la responsabilité stricte en droit criminel canadien, voir: *La Reine c. La Ville de Sault Ste-Marie*, [1978] 2 RCS 1299.

80. Loi sur le droit d'auteur, article 42(1)c.

81. *Id.*, article 42(1)d.

82. LRC (1985), c. I-21, article 34(2).

83. Voir: H.G. Richard et L. Carrière, *op. cit.*, *supra*, note 24, p. 42-9.

84. Code criminel, article 21(1).

85. Code criminel, article 22.

Finland

J. OJALA

1. **Rights which are involved**

Under Finnish law, are the following acts subject to certain economic rights (such as e.g. the reproduction right, distribution right, public performance right, display right, broadcasting right, cable transmission right, etc.)?

1.1. *The storage of a work on a network computer, e.g. in a site on a server ('uploading').*

Storage of a work on a network computer, *e.g.* on a site on a server ('uploading'), is subject to the reproduction right. Storage of a work on a network computer is the same as storing a work on any computer. According to Finnish law, transferring a work on any device by which it can be reproduced, is also regarded as making a copy of the work. By means of a computer it is possible to make a copy of a work first of all in a form readable by a person or otherwise perceivable without technical devices (normally by printing the work). Secondly, an 'output' of a work can be obtained in a machine-readable form by storing the work on a device which serves as a memory linked to the computer, or on a data medium, or by storing it in the memory of another computer. According to the Finnish Copyright Committee, a copy of a work can be made by each of the methods mentioned above.

According to Finnish law, there is, in principle, no difference whether a work is stored temporarily or permanently in a computer's memory. In both cases the work is transferred on a device by which it can be reproduced. The question of momentary storage is, however, unclear: a situation where a work is not in the user's terminal at one time, but only exists in portions in a 'buffer' or another temporary storage device, is formally/technically reproduction. The most extensive interpretation of the reproduction right would lead to a excessively extensive right which covers all possible uses of the work. Therefore, a common understanding on the extent of the notion 'reproduction' should be developed.

1.2. *Making that work available to others. If so, please specify whether it is relevant if it is made available at large or to a restricted group only.*

Making the work available to others on a network computer is subject to the author's exclusive rights if there is a possibility for anyone to access the work. A work that is made available to the public on a network can be subject to either the performance right or the display right.

a. *Public performance of a work*

The following categories of works may be performed to the public: films, radio and tv programmes, videos, musical compositions in a form of sounds, and literary works including computer programmes. According to Finnish law, a performance of a work in the context of economic activities for a comparatively large closed group of people, is also considered to be a public performance. At what point a group of people is considered to be 'comparatively large', is left to the courts to be solved on a case-by-case basis. It has been pointed out that the watershed might be a group of around 20 to 50 persons.

b. *Public display of a copy of a work*

Traditionally, works of fine art (*e.g.* drawings and paintings), photographs and still-pictures of films and videos are regarded as subject to the display right. This also includes printed copies of literary works (*e.g.* newspapers, magazines and books) as well as printed copies of musical works, *i.e.* sheet music. There is no specific provision regarding performance for a comparatively large group of people. Thus there may be some difference in the coverage of rights and in the extent to which acts are coverd by the right. It is not excluded that in some cases there could be an interpretation by analogy with the specific provision regarding public performance. When works are delivered in networks, some right holders may be in a weaker position than others.

c. *Possible solutions*

According to the Copyright Act the distribution right is not applicable to transmissions on a network, because the notion of distribution is confined to the distribution of physical copies. Another question is whether the final result of transfer of 'on demand' services is similar to the result of distribution in the cases when a copy is produced at the receiving end. One possible solution could be to establish a new rule according to which the notion of a transfer of a work is extended to a distribution of a copy, *i.e.* when the work is reproduced at the receiving end or even if there is a possibility to reproduce it.

Another possibility might be to define the existing performance right so that it would also include digital deliveries, possibly even all digital transmissions. Reproduction in the context of digital transmission is, according to the present law, also subject to the reproduction right. For the future, the redefinition of the performance right and applying the right of reproduction seem like the best alternatives because of the possible convergence of radio and tv networks and data networks. It will, however, take several years before analogue transmissions have been transformed into digital ones. Thus the same rules would cover transmission of any copyrighted materials both in analogue and in digital form in traditional radio or tv networks and in digital form in data networks. A revision of the Finnish Copyright Act is considered simultaneously with international solutions.

1.3. *Distribution of the work, e.g. to a newsgroup or a forum.*

'Distribution' of the work, *e.g.* to a newsgroup or forum, is subject to the reproduction right if the work is made available to the public by a performance or display. If the notion 'distribution' is meant here in the sense of copyright, the act is not subject to the distribution right according to Finnish law.

1.4. *On-line consultation of the work,* i.e. *having it displayed on the consulting person's monitor (this will probably also require temporary fixation of that work in the consulting person's computer's internal memory).*

On-line consultation of the work, *i.e.* having it displayed on the consulting person's monitor, will probably also require temporary fixation of that work in the consulting person's computer's internal memory. The question how the output of works on the computer's display is to be assessed from the viewpoint of the Copyright Act, is unclear. The basic principles of copyright have been formulated in such a way that they can be applied not only to known types of works and their technical forms of use, but also to those which will not become known until later. If the transmitting computer is controlling the work on the receiving computer's screen and no fixation (momentary recording) in the receiving computer's internal memory occurs, *i.e.* the work which has disappeared from the screen and can be shown only by receiving it again, there may at least be the act of public display. However, there is a possibility to store the work in the computer's internal memory or another medium. Whether the display is public or not depends for instance on the location of the computer's monitor(s): if it is possible for anyone to see the monitor(s), the work is displayed publicly (ref. to answer 1.2.).

The above-mentioned situation can, in the sense of copyright, be subject either to the display right or the performance right. The Finnish Copyright Committee has concluded that showing a work on a computer's monitor(s) amounts to exhibiting a copy of the work in the sense of copyright legislation, when the physical copy as such is shown on the screen. In other cases the situation should be regarded as performance of the work (ref. to answer 1.2). In any case the situation is regarded as making the work available to the public. The display of a work on a computer's screen is one part of the digital delivery process. The other part would be the transmission of the work. Thus the process would include both the act of reproduction and the act of making available to the public.

1.5. *Copying the consulted work on a hard disc or other media ('downloading').*

Downloading the consulted work on a hard disc or copying it to other media is subject to the reproduction right (a material fixation at the receiving end).

1.6. *Printing the consulted work.*

Printing the consulted work is also subject to the reproduction right.

1.7. Transmission of the work through the network in the course of it being consulted.

Transmission of the work through a network in the course of it being consulted, is regarded as making the work available to the public. It can be the technical part of the performance or the display (ref. to answer 1.4). It is irrelevant at which end the transmission is initiated.

1.8. Making back-ups, perhaps fully automatic, by the services provider.

Making back-ups of a work stored on a server or bulletin board is subject to the reproduction right, irrespective of whether the service provider makes the back-up automatically or intentionally.

2. Exceptions (limitations)

2.1. Will any of the acts, mentioned under 1.1-1.8, although in principle covered by certain economic rights, nevertheless be permissible in some situations under existing restrictions to copyright (e.g. restrictions for educational purposes, or for private use)? If so, please give details.

a. *Introduction*

Yes. The acts, mentioned under 1.1-1.8 are in some cases permitted without the consent of the author. However, the existing limitations have to be tested in practise. According to Finnish law there are certain preconditions for the limitations. Most of the limitation articles only apply if a work has been disseminated or published. A work is considered to be disseminated when it has been lawfully made available to the public (article 8(1)). Thus a work can be disseminated for example by recording it in a database, which may be located on a server connected to the Internet or any public network. One form of dissemination is publication. A work is considered published when copies of it have first been offered for sale or otherwise distributed to the public with the consent of the author (article 8(2)). Thus there are three preconditions for publication in Finnish copyright: (1) a physical copy of a work, (2) which has been made available to the public, (3) with the consent of the author.

In a network environment it has become problematic to define the notion of 'publication' because there is no material copy which could be transmitted. By analogy with the Finnish Copyright Committee's view point, a work is to be regarded published when it is 'uploaded' to a site on a server or other computer, with the consent of the author, and is thus continuously made available to the public so that the receiver can produce copies of the work by printing it (with or without 'downloading' the work). Thus the act of publication and dissemination would sometimes be the same, for example in electronic publishing. According to the Committee, the consent of the author may be manifested in the agreement explicitly or implicitly. A place of publication can be interpreted to be the country where the database is located. The database can, for example, be stored on a server.

The definition of 'public' is left to be determined by the courts on a case-by-case basis. The notion of 'public' is on the one hand related to the definition of 'making available to the public' (article 2) and, on the other, to the definitions of 'dissemination' and 'publication' (article 8). In a network environment a relevant question is whether a work transmitted to a closed network, which for example is used in a small private enterprise, is made available or not.

b. *Examples*

According to the Finnish Copyright Act, the exclusive right of the author has been limited mostly because of the integrity of the private (family/home) circle, social needs or freedom of information. The following examples of the limitations to the exclusive right might *in casu* apply in a network environment to the acts mentioned under 1.1-1.8. Articles listed hereinafter are interpreted more or less according to their written form. The situation is unclear at the moment, due to the lack of case-law. Some special articles concerning radio and tv broadcasts are (based on the interpretation of the articles 11 and 11*bis* of the Berne Convention) not meant to be applied as such to data network originated transmissions in a data network, but some articles, for example those concerning retransmissions of broadcasts, are applicable. In any case, the limitations are interpreted in Finland in favour of the author according to the legislative history.

Reproduction on a network computer ('uploading') (question 1.1)

Free uses

- A disseminated work may be quoted, in accordance with proper usage to the extent necessary for the purpose (article 22).
- Pictures of a disseminated work of art, associated with the text, may be reproduced in a critical or scientific presentation (article 25(1)).
- A work of art included in a collection, or exhibited, or offerd for sale, may be reproduced in catalogues and notices concerning the exhibition or sale (article 25a(1)).
- Freedom of retrieving information from a public document (article 25d(1), (3)).
- A work may be used when the administration of justice or public security so requires (article 25d(2), (3)).

Making available to the public (question 1.2)

(a) Free uses

- Exhaustion of the display right concerns only published works (article 20), *see question 1.4 hereinafter.*
- Right of quotation (article 22).
- A published work, excluded dramatic or cinematographic works, may be publicly performed at divine services and for education purposes. It may also be publicly performed in cases where the performance is not the main feature of an event,

provided that no admission fee is charged and the event is not conducted for profit. A kind of work mentioned above may also be publicly performed in connection with educational programmes and for charitable or other non-profit purposes, provided the performer(s) receive(s) no payment for his/her/their performance. (Article 21.)
- Including a work of art in a critical or scientific presentation (article 25(1)).
- Including a work of art in certain catalogues and notices (article 25a(1)).
- In the reporting of a news event in a radio or television broadcast or a film, a work visible or audible in the current event may be included in the report to the extent required by the purpose of providing information (article 25b).
- Reporting of public statements in a public representation or before an authority or at public meetings concerning public interests. However, opinions as well as writings or similar works, referred to as evidence, may be reported only in connection with an account of the case or the matter in which they were used and only to the extent required by the purpose of such an account. The author shall have the exclusive right to publish a compilation of his statements. (Article 25 c.)
- Publication of public documents and needs for administration of justice (article 25d).

(b) Extended collective licence

Special provisions concerning radio and television transmissions: retransmission of a work included in a radio or tv broadcast (article 25h).

'Distribution' to the public (question 1.3)

(NOTE: 'distribution' is here understood to be a special case of making a work available to the public. It is not distribution in the sense of the distribution right in the Finnish Copyright Act.)

Free uses

- Exhaustion of the display right (article 20), *see question 1.4 hereinafter.*
- Public performing at divine services, in connection with education and certain events (article 21).
- Right of quotation (article 22).
- Including a work of art in a critical or scientific presentation (article 25(1)).
  Including a work of art in certain catalogues and notices (article 25a(1)).
- Reproduction of public statements (article 25c).
- Publication of public documents and needs for administration of justice (article 25d).

Display on a computer's monitor (question 1.4)

Free uses

- It is permitted to engage an outsider to reproduce a few copies which are intended for the private use of the party ordering the copies (with the exclusion of reproduction of musical works, cinematographic works, utility articles or sculptures, or copying of any other work of art by artistic methods of processes, or computer programmes) (article 12(2), (3), (4)). In principle, this could apply if a work has been stored in a computer's internal memory by the transmitting computer.

- A copy of a work may be publicly displayed whenever it, with the consent of the author, has been sold or otherwise permanently transferred, or whenever such work has been published (article 20). Exhaustion of the display right might be relevant in some cases also as to display by means of data network connection. There is no exhaustion of the public performance right in Finnish law. Thus films, tv programmes, musical works and possibly also other works stored in digital form are not allowed to be performed without permission of the right holder. On the contrary, works created in physical form, *i.e.* copies of works, for example works of art and the covers of literary works, may be displayed. The criteria for the exhaustion of the display right is either a transfer of ownership of the copy of the work or the criterias of publication: offering the copy of the work for sale or distributing it otherwise to the public.
- Public performance at divine services, in connection with education and certain events (article 21).
- Reproduction of public statements (article 25c).
- Publication of public documents and needs for administration of justice (article 25d).

Storage (downloading) (question 1.5)

(a) Free uses

- A few copies of a disseminated work, excluding a computer programme, may be produced for own, private use (article 12(1), (4)).
- Right of quotation (article 22).
- Including a work of art in a critical or scientific presentation (article 25(1)).
- Reproduction of public statements (article 25c).
- Publicity of public documents and needs for administration of justice (article 25d).
- Special provisions concerning radio and television broadcasts: of a work included in a news programme broadcasted on radio or tv, a few copies may be made for purposes of internal communication of a public authority, enterprise or some other organization (article 25g(3)).

(b) Compulsory licensing

Minor parts of a literary or musical work or, if such a work is not extensive, the whole work may be incorporated into a compilation work consisting of works of several authors, which is intended for educational use, after five years have passed since the year during which the work was published. In connection with the text, a picture of a work of art may be reproduced. The provisions of the article 18 do not apply to a work created for educational use.

(c) Extended collective licensing

Making copies by audio or visual recording of a disseminated work, included in a radio or television broadcast, is permitted for use in educational activities or in scientific research (article 14(1)).

Printing (question 1.6)

(a) Free uses

- Copying for private use (article 12(1), (4)).
- Right of quotation (article 22).
- Including a work of art in a critical or scientific presentation (article 25(1)).
- Reproduction of public statements (article 25c).
- Needs for administration of justice (article 25d).

(b) Compulsory licensing

Compilation works for educational use (article 18).

Transmission (question 1.7)

(a) Free uses

- Exhaustion of the display right (article 20) might come into question if there was no material fixation (temporary or permanent recording) and temporary recording was not relevant for the reproduction right.
- Public performance at divine services, in connection with education and certain events (article 21).
- Right of quotation (article 22).
- Including a work of art in a critical or scientific presentation (article 25(1)).
- Including a work of art in certain catalogues and notices (article 25a(1)).
- Reproduction of public statements (article 25c).
- Publication of public documents and needs for administration of justice (article 25d).

(b) Extended collective licensing

Special provisions concerning radio and television broadcasts: retransmission (article 25h).

Making back-ups (question 1.8)

(a) Free use

- Copying for private use (article 12(1), (4)).
- Permitted only as far as natural persons are concerned.

2.2. Does Finnish law provide for special exceptions regarding such acts in respect to network use of copyright works? Has there been any discussion about the need to implement such special exceptions? In your opinion, should such special exceptions be developed for certain specific situations?

There are no such exceptions in the Finnish Copyright Act. Some restrictions do apply without greater difficulties. Private copying in the network environment has been under discussion in Finland (ref. to Danish legislative proposal according to which a work in a digital form is not allowed to be reproduced for private use). My own opinion on the need of such exceptions for certain specific situations? The questions concerning private use and exhaustion of rights will probably need special provisions in digital environment. Restrictions, which aim to protect freedom of information or which have their basis in social needs, should be equal in any environment, analogue or digital, transmissions or broadcasts in wire/cable or terrestrial/satellite systems. It must be kept in mind that the technological development goes on rapidly and that its commercial applications are likely follow within a few years. This has significance for instance in radio and tv broadcasting. On the Internet there are already some sound transmissions and within a couple of years there may even be some sort of television broadcasts. In the long run it seems that the convergence of different networks (*e.g.* television might be connected to the Internet) leads to a situation where it is difficult or even impossible to separate networks from each other.

3. Licensing

3.1. Are there special problems for information providers who want to acquire permission to upload and distribute existing works? For example, if the copyright has been transferred to a publisher before networking became possible or feasible, will it be clear whether the networking rights are owned by that publisher or still by the author?

The situation is not clear: it depends on the interpretation of contracts.

3.2. Are there special facilities for information providers who want to acquire permission to upload and distribute existing works? E.g. is there any system of statutory or compulsory licensing that will cover these acts?

The situation is not clear at the moment (ref. to article 25i).

3.3. Are there any systems for collective administration of copyright which deal with these rights? If so, do those systems function in practice and do they have sufficient coverage (that is, will they be applicable for all or most of the works in a certain category of works)?

In Finland, there is no center for 'multimedia' works. At the moment there is no support in Finnish law for it, but something may be established in the near future.

4. **Liability**

It is evident that persons who infringe copyright by up- or downloading will be liable. However, can action for copyright infringement also be taken against the mentioned persons in the following situations?

4.1. *The information provider on whose site a work has been uploaded by an unknown person.*

Criminal liability

The information provider is not liable for such an uploading, unless he, after he was (or should have been) aware of the uploading, intentionally or out of gross negligence stays passive and thus makes himself guilty of a copyright offence. If the information provider stays passive intentionally for purpose of gain, or if for another comparable reason the act has to be regarded as gross, he will have committed a copyright crime.

Civil liability

If the work is used in violation of the Copyright Act or an instruction in a will, a fair compensation for such a use has to be paid to the author (no-fault liability). In addition to the compensation, damages for any other loss, also mental suffering and for other injury, have to be paid also, if such a use is intentional or is negligent (fault liability). If the information provider is, otherwise than by using a work, guilty of a copyright crime or offence, he is obliged to pay the author damages for any loss, mental suffering or other injury caused by the crime (fault liability). The provisions of the Act regarding damages and tort liability apply in cases of fault liability (employer's liability, conciliation, period of limitation).

4.2. *The services provider who owns the server on which a work has been infringingly uploaded by an information provider.*

Liability of the service provider is uncertain. There is a lack of case-law. If we compare the service provider to a telephone operator, would there be any difference in their liabilities? We can also compare some situations to a service by which a copier is offered to the public. Comparisons can also be made to radio and tv broadcasts: an owner of the transmission equipment (terrestrial, cable, satellite) is not responsible for the content of the transmissions; the broadcaster who decides what is going to be broadcasted is responsible. It will, in any case, be taken into consideration what kind of service is provided in the (data)network. Liabilities should be solved on a case-by-case basis.

Criminal liability

First of all, there is no obligation for the service provider to control beforehand the flow of data on his server. Ownership of a server does not in itself constitute criminal liability. The service provider may be implicated in a copyright crime (for which the preconditions are: intention, purpose of gain and gross behaviour) as an offender, if he, for example, takes part in planning or making decisions regarding the infringing act or possibly only as an accessory, if he, for extra benefit, only passively gives his permission for such a use of the work. The activity has to be so extensive that the act is, for that or another comparable reason, to be regarded as gross. Thus a service provider will, in practice, very rarely commit a copyright crime. If some of the above-mentioned preconditions are not met, the service provider may be implicated in a copyright offence (for which the preconditions are: intention or gross negligence) as an offender or as an accessory. Also when he is or he should have been conscious of the infringing act, stays passive without any direct benefit for himself, he may be committing a copyright offence. Normally the service provider does not know (or even has to know) the content of the flow of data.

Civil liability

Committing a copyright crime or offense will also lead to the obligation to pay damages for any loss, mental suffering or other injury caused by the crime or offense. Can the service provider be considered to use the work by letting it be uploaded or used in another manner (question of fault liability and no-fault liability)? The question is relevant, but the answer is unclear.

> ***4.3.*** *Does it make any difference if that services provider makes automatic back-ups which include the infringingly uploaded work?*

It is unclear whether no-fault liability applies when the infringingly uploaded work includes back-ups made by the service provider automatically. Can the service provider be regarded to be using the work?

> ***4.4.*** *Is a service provider required to take certain precautionary measures (such as reminding information providers of their obligations under copyright law, scanning uploaded subject matter for possible infringements, keeping a log on all uploading and consultations, etc.)?*

At the moment, there are no such regulations for the data network environment. Such obligations have to be considered, taking also into consideration existing obligations for traditional radio and tv broadcasting. Those obligations are, however, made for other purposes than the protection of copyright. They have, however, effects on the limitations of copyright.

> ***4.5.*** *The networking services provider, for transmitting the work through the network in the course of it being consulted.*

See 4.2 and 4.3.

> ***4.6.*** *Does it make any difference if that networking services provider has been informed that certain infringements may take place; assuming, moreover, that*

it would be technically feasible to monitor transmissions in order to detect potentially infringing transmissions?

There is no obligation for the service provider to monitor transmissions in order to detect potentially infringing transmissions. The service provider is not the one who should enforce copyrights.

France

P. Sirinelli

1. Les droits concernés

En vertu de votre droit national, les opérations suivantes sont-elles soumises à certains droits patrimoniaux (comme par exemple le droit de reproduction, le droit de distribution, le droit de communication au public, le droit d'exposer, le droit d'émettre, le droit de transmission par câble, etc.)?

1.1. *La numérisation d'une oeuvre sur un réseau informatique, par exemple dans un site sur un serveur* ("uploading").

Le stockage d'une oeuvre se fait par numérisation, laquelle est indiscutablement un acte de reproduction. L'article L 122-3 CPI (anciennement article 28, Loi n° 57-298 du 11 mars 1957) dispose en effet: *"la reproduction consiste dans la fixation matérielle de l'oeuvre par tous procédés qui permettent de la communiquer au public d'une manière indirecte. Elle peut s'effectuer notamment par imprimerie, dessin, gravure, photographie, moulage et tout procédé des arts graphiques et plastiques, enregistrement mécanique, cinématographique ou magnétique (...)"*, tandis que l'article 9 de la Convention de Berne précise que *"(1) les auteurs d'oeuvres littéraires et artistiques protégés par la présente Convention jouissent du droit exclusif d'autoriser la reproduction de ces oeuvres, de quelque manière et sous quelque forme que ce soit"*. On peut également mettre en avant le mémorandum réalisé par l'OMPI (Organisation Mondiale de la Propriété Intellectuelle) à l'intention du Comité d'experts sur l'éventuel protocole additionnel à la Convention de Berne. Ce texte précise clairement que *"le stockage d'une oeuvre dans un système informatique doit être considéré comme une reproduction au sens de l'article 9 de la Convention de Berne"* et s'applique, que la reproduction ait été effectuée pour une diffusion en ligne ou pour une reproduction sur support édité.

Trois précisions me paraissent utiles. *(1)* On ne peut distinguer entre reproduction durable, provisoire, éphémère ou intermédiaire. *(2)* Il est impossible de ne pas prendre en considération la destination de la reproduction pour savoir si elle met ou non en oeuvre le monopole, c'est-à-dire que la quesion 1.1 doit s'articuler sur la question 1.2 ("rendre disponible"). La réponse pourrait être différente s'il y avait numérisation pour soi (on songe alors à l'exception de copie privée). Mais à priori, numériser, stocker sur un site ou un serveur trahit la destination désirée, c'est pour autrui que l'opération est faite. Il n'y a donc pas lieu d'appliquer l'exception de copie privée. *(3)* En amont il y a le plus souvent un autre acte de numérisation (scanner l'oeuvre). Cet acte paraît mettre en oeuvre le monopole (reproduction). L'exception de copie privée paraît tout autant inapplicable pour deux raisons. D'abord si le scanneur est une personne autre que l'usager de la reproduction. En effet, en application de la jurisprudence Rannou-graphie,[1] rendue en matière de photocopie, il y a contrefaçon lorsque le copiste (au sens de gardien du matériel qui permet la photocopie) et l'usager ne sont pas une seule et même personne. En second lieu (et même à supposer que l'on retienne une conception large de la notion de copiste s'attachant à la "personne qui prend la décision d'opérer la reproduction et qui la réalise (elle-même) ou la fait réaliser par un tiers",[2] il faut observer que cette reproduction était faite "en vue" d'un usage public: l'installation sur un site et la consultation par des tiers. Dans les intentions, il n'est pas douteux que la reproduction était destinée à être communiquée au public. Or la loi (article L 122-5-2° CPI) ne tolère que les reproductions "strictement réservées a l'usage privé du copiste". Il est unanimement admis que la lettre et l'esprit de la loi "militent pour l'interprétation la plus favorable au monopole d'auteur, et donc la plus sévère pour le copiste".[3]

1.2. Le fait de rendre cette oeuvre accessible à d'autres personnes. Dans l'affirmative, préciser si le caractère étendu ou restreint du groupe a une incidence éventuelle.

On notera ici la formulation passive de l'opération qui pourrait laisser croire que le responsable du site n'est en rien responsable de la communication. Néanmoins: *(1)* Il y a là un autre acte de communication au public qui met en cause le droit de représentation. En effet, selon l'article L 122-2 CPI, *"la représentation consiste dans la communication de l'oeuvre au public par un procédé quelconque, et notamment (1) par récitation publique, exécution lyrique, représentation dramatique, présentation publique, projection publique et transmission dans un lieu public de l'oeuvre télédiffusée; (2) par télédiffusion. La télédiffusion s'entend de la diffusion par tout procédé de télécommunication de sons, d'images, de documents, de données et de messages de toute nature. Est assimilée à une représentation l'émission d'une oeuvre vers un satellite"*. L'analyse peut, à tort, paraître redondante par rapport à la précédente. Elle n'est pourtant pas indifférente. Ne serait-ce que parce que souvent les titulaires des droits de reproduction et de représentation ne sont pas une seule et même personne. Soit que le créateur ait cédé ses droits à deux (ou plus) personnes différentes. Soit que l'auteur se soit réservé le droit de représentation (hypothèse peu étonnante lors de la conclusion d'un contrat d'édition sur support papier). *(2)* La vraie difficulté ne concerne pas la prise en considération des destinataires. Qu'il s'agisse d'une pluralité de points isolés de réception ou d'un groupe, il y a pour le droit français un public. Voir, pour s'en convaincre, l'admission en jurisprudence de l'idée selon laquelle une pluralité de destinataires uniques (chambres d'hôtel) constitue un public: Cour de cassation (1° Ch. civ., affaire *CNN*), 6 avril 1994 et sur renvoi: Versailles, 20 septembre 1995. Au demeurant la doctrine française admet depuis longtemps le concept de public potentiel (exemple de Desbois à propos d'une salle de théâtre vide où une représentation est offerte au public mais que ce dernier a boudé). Il est vrai que la diffusion point à point sur un réseau privé pourrait poser un problème (cf. *infra*). *(3)* Un débat pourrait exister lorsque l'on envisage la question à l'envers, c'est-à-dire en prenant en considération l'utilisateur qui va chercher l'oeuvre. (On pourrait alors insister à tort sur la prétendue "passivité" du serveur.) Il s'agit là d'un faux raisonnement. Le serveur se comporte comme un libre service électronique. Il y a lieu d'appliquer la jurisprudence *CNN* précitée dans laquelle l'hôtel était aussi prétendument passif puisqu'il se contentait de poser une antenne qui permettait aux clients des chambres de recevoir certaines chaînes de télévision, inaccessibles sans cette antenne. En dépit de sa passivité, l'hotel a été regardé comme commettant un acte de représentation soumis au monopole du titulaire de droit.

Nota: le débat n'est pas que purement théorique. En effet, même si l'on appréhende l'opération globalement et on la contrôle déjà par le biais du droit de reproduction (en cause indiscutablement en amont) la nature du droit en cause (représentation?) à ce moment là a une importance, d'une part parce que le titulaire de ce droit peut être une autre personne, d'autre part, parce qu'il peut y avoir perception d'une nouvelle redevance.

> *1.3. La distribution de l'oeuvre, par exemple à destination d'un groupe d'information ou d'un forum.*

La terminologie est pour les français à la fois intéressante et trompeuse, intéressante parce qu'elle met en avant l'action du serveur, trompeuse parce qu'elle évoque pour nous le droit de reproduction. Or il est clair, conformément à ce qui a été dit *supra*, que c'est le droit de représentation qui est en cause (voir la définition, à la question 1.2).

> *1.4. La consultation d'une oeuvre on-line, par exemple le fait de la diffuser sur l'écran de la personne qui la consulte (ce qui nécessitera aussi vraisemblablement la fixation de cette oeuvre dans la mémoire interne de l'ordinateur de la personne qui consulte).*

Il faut considérer la question en dehors du "transport" de l'oeuvre envisagé en 1.3 et 1.2. L'apparition sur écran peut faire l'objet de plusieurs analyses. On peut la considérer comme *(a)* une reproduction en mémoire vive. On peut alors comparer avec les solutions retenues en matière de logiciel et avec la Directive du 14 mai 1991 qui considère que le monopole est bien en cause mais que l'on doit tolérer l'acte parce qu'il s'agit d'un acte nécessaire pour l'utilisateur légitime. *(b)* Une représentation. Ici, une analyse très fine pourrait conduire à distinguer suivant la nature des oeuvres en cause puisque pour le texte on pourrait considérer que la représentation est la conséquence inéluctable de la reproduction (voir les licences relatives aux programmes d'ordinateur et les clauses *"as a book"*). Néanmoins cette analyse est trop fine et trop complexe en présence d'une oeuvre multimédia qui réunit des créations de tous genres. Par souci de simplification, il faut soumettre tous les éléments au même régime. Il y aurait alors représentation de tous les éléments présents dans le multimédia.

> *1.5. Copier l'oeuvre consultée sur un disque dur ou sur une autre forme de support* ("downloading").

Il s'agit là d'une préoccupation majeure en raison des risques très importants de pertes économiques. Il y a indiscutablement acte de reproduction. Mais deux difficultés pourraient surgir. *(1)* Parfois cette reproduction apparaît comme inévitable (obligation de stocker au moins de façon provisoire en raison des faibles débits). Est-ce alors un acte nécessaire au sens vu *supra*? L'analyse apparaît comme un peu excessive et fait trop dépendre le droit d'auteur de la situation purement technique. *(2)* Du point de vue de l'utilisateur, la reproduction apparaît comme une copie privée. Cependant, une fois de plus, il semble qu'il ne faille pas regarder l'opération sous cet angle mais en prenant en considération la personne qui est à l'origine de l'opération, c'est-à-dire, "l'émetteur". Dans cette approche, il y a transmission en vue d'une reproduction. S'agit-il d'un nouvel acte de reproduction (de la part du serveur), donnant lieu à une nouvelle redevance? Ou ne faut-il pas considérer que cela est compris dans les actes réalisés en amont? Le groupe français a paru divisé sur la question. Si le rapporteur a montré quelques réticences à considérer que le serveur commet un nouvel acte de reproduction en cette hypothèse (alors que la reproduction est réalisée sur un autre site), la majorité du groupe français semble admettre que le champ du droit de reproduction est plus large que les simples actes de reproduction matérielle. Le droit serait en cause sans qu'il y ait lieu de regarder qui fait matériellement la copie en sorte que le serveur serait responsable parce qu'il en fournit l'occasion.

On peut seulement remarquer que la question apparaîtra plus clairement à l'avenir, pour au moins deux raisons. *(a)* D'abord parce que les transmissions pourront s'opérer avec des procédés anticopie. Ainsi, le serveur ne permettra plus un acte de reproduction qui pourrait lui être reproché. *(b)* Ensuite (et en attendant?) parce que l'on peut s'interroger sur l'avenir du droit des utilisateurs à la copie privée, notamment eu égard aux termes de la Convention de Berne. Selon l'article 9(2) *"[e]st réservée aux législations des pays de l'Union la faculté de permettre la reproduction desdites oeuvres dans certains cas spéciaux, pourvu qu'une telle reproduction ne porte pas atteinte à l'exploitation normale de l'oeuvre ni ne cause un préjudice injustifié aux intérêts légitimes de l'auteur"*. À l'avenir on pourrait donc considérer que le copiste matériel commet un acte de reproduction mettant en oeuvre le monopole même si cet acte est accompli sur son propre disque dur.

1.6. L'impression de l'oeuvre consultée.

Il y a indiscutablement un acte de reproduction. Pour s'en convaincre il suffit de constater que cet acte pourrait être concerné par l'article 122-3 CPI (anciennement article 28, Loi n° 57-298 du 11 mars 1957) selon lequel *"la reproduction consiste dans la fixation matérielle de l'oeuvre par tous procédés qui permettent de la communiquer au public d'une manière indirecte. Elle peut s'effectuer notamment par imprimerie, dessin, gravure, photographie, moulage et tout procédé des arts graphiques et plastiques, enregistrement mécanique, cinématographique ou magnétique (...)"*. On remarquera, en outre, que les sorties imprimantes sont concernées par les nouvelles solutions françaises en matière de reprographie.[4] Cependant, il convient d'observer que nous serons assez souvent en présence d'une reproduction à usage privé. Il faudra donc, par application des règles traditionnelles, distinguer entre les copies vraiment privées (libres), celles destinées à l'usage interne ou collectif, et celles destinées à l'usage professionnel ou commercial (soumises au monopole). Reste qu'au delà de l'analyse purement théorique se posera une question de mise en oeuvre de ces solutions: comment appréhender l'opération sur le plan matériel ou s'agissant de la preuve?

1.7. La transmission de l'oeuvre à travers le réseau suite à sa consultation.

Il semblerait que l'on puisse renvoyer aux questions précédentes (1.2, 1.3 et 1.4). Si l'usager prend l'initiative d'un "relai" vers quelqu'un d'autre, il y a de sa part indiscutablement acte de représentation (nouvel acte).

1.8. La réalisation de back-ups, *éventuellement entièrement automatiques, par le fournisseur d'accès.*

Il convient d'abord de s'accorder sur le sens des termes utilisés et de convenir que *"back up"* signifie bien enregistrement à titre de sauvegarde. Cependant, généralement, le terme est surtout utilisé en pratique pour les fichiers que l'on a créés soi-même et non pour les oeuvres créées par autrui. En raison de ce qui a été déjà exposé, il faut admettre qu'il s'agit là d'un acte de reproduction et que, l'oeuvre n'étant pas (entièrement) logicielle (au sens de *software*), il y a lieu de considérer que l'exception de copie de sauvegarde est inapplicable. Celle de copie privée paraît également difficile à retenir au vu des précédents développements.

2. Exceptions

2.1. Les opérations visées aux points 1.1 à 1.8 sont-elles autorisées dans certaines situations, en vertu de dérogations au droit d'auteur, malgré le fait que ces opérations soient soumises en principe à la protection de certains droits économiques (par exemple, les restrictions liées à des fins d'enseignement, ou à l'usage privé)? Dans l'affirmative, prière de bien vouloir détailler.

On peut renvoyer à ce qui a été dit précédemment. Il ressort des différentes analyses. *(1)* Que l'exception de copie privée sera bien rarement admise. *(2)* Que l'exception relative aux représentations privées sera très rarement applicable. En effet, si l'article L 122-5 CPI prévoit que *"lorsque l'oeuvre a été divulguée, l'auteur ne peut interdire: (1°) Les représentations privées et gratuites effectuées exclusivement dans un cercle de famille (...)"*, l'exception est envisagée par la quasi-unanimité de la doctrine comme devant être interprétée de façon restrictive en sorte que l'on peut estimer que la notion de cercle de famille est de toute façon inopérante quand s'interpose un moyen de diffusion. La notion a été conçue pour les représentations dites "primaires" où le public est en contact direct de l'oeuvre.[5] *(3)* Il n'existe aucune exception particulière "pour buts éducatifs" en droit français. Seul le droit de citation pourrait être envisagé mais il ne concerne que des reproductions partielles qui doivent être courtes, respectueuses du droit moral et justifiées par des fins didactiques et que la doctrine répugne à étendre aux oeuvres musicales et artistiques.

2.2. Votre droit national prévoit-il des exceptions spécifiques concernant ces opérations à propos d'oeuvres protégées par le droit d'auteur qui sont utilisées sur réseaux? Y a-t-il eu des discussions sur la nécessité d'introduire de pareilles exceptions spécifiques? A votre avis, pareilles exceptions particulières devraient-elles être appliquées à certaines situations spécifiques?

Il n'existe aucun projet visant à restreindre les droits des créateurs. L'idée répandue en France est plutôt celle d'une éventuelle disparition du droit de copie privée dans l'univers numérique (arg. article 9(2) Convention de Berne; voir *supra* question 1.1).

3. **Licences**

-

4. **Responsabilités**

Il n'existe pour le moment en France aucune jurisprudence et très peu de doctrine sur la question.

> *Il est évident que les personnes qui contreviennent aux dispositions sur le droit d'auteur en transmettant ou en reproduisant des oeuvres sur réseau seront responsables. Cependant, une action pour violation du droit d'auteur peut-elle être intentée à l'encontre des personnes mentionnées dans les situations suivantes?*

> *4.1. Le diffuseur d'informations sur le site duquel une oeuvre a été diffusée par une personne inconnue. / 4.2. Le fournisseur d'accès qui détient le serveur sur lequel une oeuvre a été illégalement diffusée par un diffuseur d'informations.*

Le groupe français a répondu sans hésitation que la responsabilité de ces personnes pouvait être engagée. Il est apparu à tous qu'une vigilance minimale devait être exigée et que ces personnes devaient mettre en oeuvre des moyens de contrôle.

> *4.3. Quelle est l'incidence de* back-ups *qui incluent une oeuvre illégalement diffusée, et qui sont réalisés automatiquement par le fournisseur d'accès?*

Non. Mais il n'est pas sûr que nous ayions compris le sens de la question. Si on a peu de prise sur le serveur, pourquoi pas "le provider".

> *4.4. Un fournisseur d'accès a-t-il l'obligation de prendre certaines mesures de précaution (comme par exemple, rappeler au diffuseurs d'informations leurs obligations résultant de la législation sur le droit d'auteur, examiner les transmissions susceptibles de constituer une infraction aux dispositions sur le droit d'auteur, conserver un relevé de tout enregistrement et consultation, etc.)?*

Le groupe français estime que le système ne sera viable que si l'on responsabilise les personnes. Le fournisseur doit en effet prendre toutes les précautions mentionnées dans la question. C'est son devoir.

4.5. *Le fournisseur d'accès au réseau, pour avoir transmis sur réseau une oeuvre en cours de consultation. /* ***4.6.*** *Quelle est l'incidence du fait que le fournisseur d'accès au réseau a eu connaissance du fait que certaines irrégularités peuvent survenir: considérant, de surcroît, qu'il est techniquement possible de contrôler les transmissions en vue de détecter les éventuelles transmissions illégales?*

A priori, il paraît lourd de faire peser une responsabilité automatique sur le fournisseur d'accès. En réalité tout dépend des situations. Si l'atteinte a lieu dans un *groupe de discussion* (babillards?): en France, le fournisseur d'accès sélectionne les groupes. Il peut donc autoriser ou interdire, et par conséquent, être tenu pour responsable de ce qui s'y passe. Si le fournisseur offre l'accès à un *site d'informations*: généralement le fournisseur se réfugie derrière le fait qu'il ne peut contrôler ce qui passe par ses "tuyaux". Mais il semble que l'analyse doive être différente si le fournisseur est averti de l'existence de l'atteinte. Il ne peut plus prétendre ignorer la situation et rester passif. Dès lors, il pourrait être regardé comme un *diffuseur* (A 335-2 CPI = délit de débit d'oeuvre contrefaisante). Peut-être même comme complice pour fourniture de moyens. Dans cette voie le rôle des sociétés d'auteurs pourrait être prépondérant. Grâce aux contrats de représentation réciproque qui peuvent les lier à des sociétés dans tous les pays, les sociétés sont en mesure de tisser une toile comparable aux réseaux. Ce "filet" permettrait de constater les atteintes, d'avertir les fournisseurs d'accès et d'agir en cas de passivité de ces derniers. Si le fournisseur d'accès veut éviter de voir sa responsabilité engagée, il doit "fermer le robinet" pour le serveur en cause. Techniquement, il suffirait de fermer le numéro d'IP *(Internet Protocol)* qui identifie ce dernier sur le réseau.

Notes

1. Civ. 1°, 7 mai 1984; *RIDA* Juillet 1984, p. 152, *RTD Com.* 1984, 677, obs. A. Françon; *JCP* 1985, II, 20351, note R. Plaisant.
2. En ce sens, A. & H.-J. Lucas, Traité de Propriété littéraire et artistique, Litec, § 288.
3. En ce sens, A. & H.-J. Lucas, Traité de Propriété littéraire et artistique, Litec, § 289. Dans le même sens, A. Françon, note au *JCP* 1975, II, 18163; H. Desbois, Traité, § 243.
4. Article L 122-10 (L. 5 janvier 1995): *"La publication d'une oeuvre emporte cession du droit de reproduction par reprographie à une société régie par le titre II du livre III et agréée à cet effet par le ministre chargé de la culture. Les sociétés agréées peuvent seules conclure toutes convention avec les utilisateurs aux fins de gestion du droit ainsi cédé sous réserve, pour les stipulations autorisant les copies aux fins de vente, de location, de publicité ou de promotion, de l'accord de l'auteur ou de son ayant-droit. A défaut de désignation par l'auteur ou son ayant-droit à la date de la publication de l'oeuvre, une des sociétés agréées est réputée cessionnaire de ce droit. La reprographie s'entend de la reproduction sous forme de copie sur papier ou support assimilé par une technique photographique ou d'effet équivalent permettant une lecture directe. Les dispositions du premier alinéa ne font pas obstacle au droit de l'auteur ou de ses ayants-droit de réaliser des copies aux fins de vente, de location, de publicité ou de promotion. Nonobstant toute stipulation contraire, les dispositions du présent article s'appliquent à toutes les oeuvres protégées quelle que soit la date de leur publication."*
5. En se sens, A. & H.-J. Lucas, Traité de Propriété littéraire et artistique, Litec, § 345.

Germany

O. SCHWENZER

The technical developments, especially in digital transmission systems, pose a challenge for copyright law. The exploitation rights in German copyright law are conventionally strictly divided in material and non-material exploitation (article 15 *UrhG*). Digital publishing and transmission of works through information network systems does not seem to fit in this partition, nevertheless it needs to be observed by copyright law.

1. **Rights which are involved**

Under German law, are the following acts subject to certain economic rights (such as e.g. the reproduction right, distribution right, public performance right, display right, broadcasting right, cable transmission right, etc.)?

1.1. The storage of a work on a network computer, e.g. in a site on a server ('uploading').

Uploading works to a network computer on a site of a server is an act of exploitation. It cannot take place without permission of the right holder. A necessary conversion from analogue to digital data is normally an act of reproduction (article 16 *UrhG*). Digital use can be a new kind of exploitation, which needs to be seperately addressed in licensing contracts. The display right, also called the exhibition right (article 18 *UrhG*), can only be relevant when drawings or photographs are made visible to the public. It is contested whether the term 'public' in article 18 *UrhG* is identical to 'public' defined in article 15(III) *UrhG*. In that definition, 'public' means a group of persons without a personal relationship. Interpreting the term 'public' extensively would make the uploading of unpublished drawings and photographs into an act which is relevant to the display right.

1.2. Making that work available to others. If so, please specify whether it is relevant if it is made available at large or to a restricted group only. / 1.3. Distribution of the work, e.g. to a newsgroup or a forum.

Making works available to others by distributing them to newsgroups or forums, should be treated as broadcasting (article 20 *UrhG*). There certainly are important interests of neighbouring right owners, like performers and record producers, who do not have an exclusive broadcasting right, to prefer an exclusive distribution right (articles 17, 75, 85 *UrhG*). But comparing digital distribution in a network system to material distribution would cause new problems with exhaustion (article 17(II)

115

UrhG). The broadcasting right requires a transmission to the public. The use of an extensive definition of 'public' does not make a difference if the works are distributed to a large or to a restricted group. A transmission between personally related persons is not 'public'.

> *1.4. On-line consultation of the work, i.e. having it displayed on the consulting person's monitor (this will probably also require temporary fixation of that work in the consulting person's computer's internal memory).*

On-line consultation of works, *e.g.* listening to music or watching pictures or news on a screen, is an act of exploitation, which needs to be met with an effective author's right. But traditionally the reception of works on a radio or a television is not a copyright-relevant act for the consumer. Only making works perceivable to the public, *e.g.* by broadcasting, needs the author's permission. Even if on-line consultation of works is not hiring or lending copies, it seems to be a comparable situation, which leads to the conclusion that an analogy with article 27 *UrhG* might be preferred. Temporary fixation on an internal memory might be treated as reproduction, irrespective of the duration. There are special provisions on computer programs which deal with comparable forms of fixation as restricted acts (article 69c(1) No. 1 *UrhG*). Only unavoidable acts to get the information on the screen can be disregarded.

> *1.5. Copying the consulted work on a hard disc or other media ('downloading') / 1.6. Printing the consulted work.*

The downloading process is a subject to reproduction right, immaterial of the problem to control copying the consulted work on digital media like CD-ROM, DAT or diskette. Nevertheless, making single copies for private use, *e.g.* printing the consulted work or recording it on tapes, is allowed (article 53 *UrhG*).

> *1.7. Transmission of the work through the network in the course of it being consulted.*

The transmission of works through the network in the course of it being consulted, asks for a different view. Transmitting works back to the original provider or server without having changed its contents might be a non-relevant act. Making works available to another person or entity must be treated as a transmission by an original information provider, similar to broadcasting (article 20 *UrhG*).

> *1.8. Making back-ups, perhaps fully automatic, by the services provider.*

The making of back-ups by service providers is reproduction. But it might be quite similar to reproduction only for broadcasting by a broadcasting organization (article 55 *UrhG*). An analogy with article 55 *UrhG* leads to the duty to destroy back-ups not later a month after making them. Giving works to official network archives means that the author must be notified without delay.

2. Exeptions

2.1. Will any of the acts, mentioned under 1.1-1.8, although in principle covered by certain economic rights, nevertheless be permissible in some situations under existing restrictions to copyright (e.g. restrictions for educational purposes, or for private use)? If so, please give details.

In general, the conventional limitations on copyright should be valid for digital transmission in network systems under the condition that there is a public interest in restrictions (articles 55-63 *UrhG*). With regard to certain restrictions, *e.g.* for religious or educational use, an equitable remuneration must be considered. Making single copies for private use should be permissible.

2.2. Does German law provide for special exceptions regarding such acts in respect to network use of copyright works? Has there been any discussion about the need to implement such special exceptions? In your opinion, should such special exceptions be developed for certain specific situations?

At present, there is no need to provide for special exeptions with respect to digital network systems. There have been discussions about copyright problems with on-line services in general, but a need to implement special exeptions has hardly been discussed. See for example the position of the Max-Planck-Institute for foreign and international Patent, Copyright and Industrial Property Law to the Green Paper *'Copyright and related rights in the Information Society'*, worked out by the Multimedia Seminar Group (November 1995), and the Symposium of the Institute for Copyright and Media Law, *'Legal problems in international network systems'* (November 1995).

3. Licensing

3.1. Are there special problems for information providers who want to acquire permission to upload and distribute existing works? For example, if the copyright has been transferred to a publisher before networking became possible or feasible, will it be clear whether the networking rights are owned by that publisher or still by the author?

Information providers can only get permission to upload and distribute works from the real right holder. *Bona fide* acquisition of an exploitation right is not possible and the information providers cannot have 'good faith' in networking rights being owned by the publisher. Digitization itself can mean a new kind of exploitation. Therefore, the publisher needs to acquire the rights from the author by means of a seperate, new contract. The holding of digital network rights by the publisher cannot be presupposed.

3.2. Are there special facilities for information providers who want to acquire permission to upload and distribute existing works? E.g. is there any system of statutory or compulsory licensing that will cover these acts? / 3.3. Are there any systems for collective administration of copyright which deal with these rights? If so, do those systems function in practice and do they have sufficient coverage (that is, will they be applicable for all or most of the works in a certain category of works)?

In the present system, collective administration by the collecting societies, using compulsory licensing, is very important, especially in the music industry (GEMA, GVL). For literary works there is the VG Wort. Information providers can get permission from these societies, which have sufficient 'coverage' to cope with the licensing for multimedia works. Of course getting permission from different collecting societies can be difficult. Therefore it might be useful to summarize the ways of administration for digital network use in the future. Even individual administration by big publishing, record or entertainment companies is imaginable, provided that the information providers can get permission regarding sufficient repertoire under equitable conditions. Individual rights could again be centralised by a kind of 'one-stop-shops' or 'clearing houses' to simplify rights management and to make the administration system more transparent. In every case a equitable remuneration for the authors and performers must be guaranteed.

4. **Liability**

It is evident that persons who infringe copyright by up- or downloading will be liable. However, can action for copyright infringement also be taken against the mentioned persons in the following situations?

4.1. The information provider on whose site a work has been uploaded by an unknown person. / 4.2. The services provider who owns the server on which a work has been infringingly uploaded by an information provider.

The question who should be held liable for the infringement of copyright and neighbouring rights in digital netsworks is a matter under discussion at the moment. The biggest problem is the technical impossibility to locate the infringer. An information or service provider can be held liable as an accessory to infringement, depending on the facts of the case.

4.3. Does it make any difference if that services provider makes automatic back-ups which include the infringingly uploaded work?

Strict and careful control of the necessary automatic back-ups, made by the service provider, can be a disproportionate strain on efficient management, but in every instant article 101a *UrhG* must be observed, entailing that a provider may be required by the injured party to give as much technical information as possible on the infringing acts.

4.4. Is a service provider required to take certain precautionary measures (such as reminding information providers of their obligations under copyright law, scanning uploaded subject matter for possible infringements, keeping a log on all uploading and consultations, etc.)? / 4.5. The networking services *provider, for transmitting the work through the network in the course of it being consulted. /**4.6.** Does it make any difference if that networking services provider has been informed that certain infringements may take place; assuming, moreover, that it would be technically feasible to monitor transmissions in order to detect potentially infringing transmissions?*

At present, there is no duty for service providers to take special precautions. Nevertheless, voluntary self-control is desirable as long as there is no danger for data protection and for the freedom of speech. The benefit of reminding information providers of their obligations might be contestable. On the one hand, monitoring transmissions in order to detect potential copyright infringements could benefit copyright interests, on the other, it could entail censorship. It is a challenge to find a reasonable compromise between these interests.

Italie

A. Pojaghi

1. **Les droits concernés**

En vertu de droit italien, les opérations suivantes sont-elles soumises à certains droits patrimoniaux (comme par exemple le droit de reproduction, le droit de distribution, le droit de communication au public, le droit d'exposer, le droit d'émettre, le droit de transmission par câble, etc.)?

1.1. La numérisation d'une oeuvre sur un réseau informatique, par exemple dans un site sur un serveur ("uploading").

Le stockage d'une oeuvre dans un réseau informatique comporte l'exercice du droit de reproduction (article 13 de la Loi sur le droit d'auteur).

1.2. Le fait de rendre cette oeuvre accessible à d'autres personnes. Dans l'affirmative, préciser si le caractère étendu ou restreint du groupe a une incidence éventuelle.

La mise à disposition d'une oeuvre par réseau informatique pourrait constituer un exercice du droit de diffusion à distance (article 16) ou bien du droit de distribution (article 17). La circonstance que la mise à disposition de l'oeuvre ait lieu à l'égard d'un groupe plus ou moins large de personnes n'a pas d'importance, étant donné qu'un telle circonstance concerne le droit d'exécution, représentation et de récitation. En ce qui concerne le droit de diffusion ou de distribution, au contraire, l'étendue du cercle des destinataires n'a pas d'importance, puisque en puissance illimité.

1.3. La distribution de l'oeuvre, par exemple à destination d'un groupe d'information ou d'un forum.

La distribution de l'oeuvre à des groupes d'information ou de débat pourrait constituer un exercice du droit de diffusion ou de distribution.

1.4. La consultation d'une oeuvre "on-line", *par exemple le fait de la diffuser sur l'écran de la personne qui la consulte (ce qui nécessitera aussi vraisemblablement la fixation de cette oeuvre dans la mémoire interne de l'ordinateur de la personne qui consulte).*

La consultation d'une oeuvre *"on-line"*, après sa fixation dans la mémoire, implique l'exercice des droits de reproduction et de diffusion.

1.5. Copier l'oeuvre consultée sur un disque dur ou sur une autre forme de support ("downloading") / *1.6. L'impression de l'oeuvre consultée.*

La copie de l'oeuvre consultée sur support mécanique ou graphique comporte l'exercice du droit de reproduction.

1.7. La transmission de l'oeuvre à travers le réseau suite à sa consultation.

La transmission de l'oeuvre par réseau informatique dans le but de sa consultation devrait comporter l'exercice du droit de diffusion.

1.8. La réalisation de "back-ups", éventuellement entièrement automatiques, par le fournisseur d'accès.

La réalisation de copies de sécurité comporte l'exercice du droit de reproduction.

2. Exceptions

2.1. Les opérations visées aux points 1.1 à 1.8 sont-elles autorisées dans certaines situations, en vertu de dérogations au droit d'auteur, malgré le fait que ces opérations soient soumises en principe à la protection de certains droits économiques (par exemple, les restrictions liées à des fins d'enseignement, ou à l'usage privé)? Dans l'affirmative, prière de bien vouloir détailler.

Parmi les cas de libre utilisation prévus par la loi, il faut mentionner, en ce qui concerne la matière ici considérée, la faculté de reproduction pour usage personnel des lecteurs, faite à mains avec des moyens de reproduction non-destinés à la vente ni à la diffusion (article 68) et la faculté d'utiliser le résumé, la citation ou la reproduction d'une oeuvre dans un but de critique, de discussion ou d'enseignement, à condition qu'ils ne constituent pas une concurrence à l'utilisation de l'oeuvre même (article 70).

2.2. Le droit italien prévoit-il des exceptions spécifiques concernant ces opérations à propos d'oeuvres protégées par le droit d'auteur qui sont utilisées sur réseaux? Y a-t-il eu des discussions sur la nécessité d'introduire de pareilles exceptions spécifiques? A votre avis, pareilles exceptions particulières devraient-elles être appliquées à certaines situations spécifiques?

La loi prévoit une limitation à l'exclusivité du droit d'auteur dans des conditions particulières, en ce qui concerne la faculté de reproduction et de diffusion de la part du service public de radiodiffusion. On a discuté pour savoir si une telle règle peut profiter aux émetteurs privés. Actuellement, n'est pas prévue aucune faculté de libre utilisation de la part de réseaux informatiques. J'estime que la centralisation à l'échelle internationale des services de licence, recouvrement et contrôle, rendra de plus en plus théorique l'exercice du droit de la part de chaque titulaire.

3. **Licences**

3.1. Existe-t-il des problèmes spécifiques pour les diffuseurs d'informations qui souhaitent obtenir l'autorisation de reproduire et de diffuser des oeuvres existantes? Par exemple, dans l'hypothèse où le droit d'auteur a été cédé à un éditeur avant que la numérisation sur réseau ne devienne possible ou réalisable, pourra-t-on déterminer clairement si les droits liés à l'utilisation du réseau sont détenus par cet éditeur ou s'ils appartiennent encore à l'auteur?

Dans le domaine du contrat d'édition, nous connaissons le principe, non-susceptible de convention contraire, selon lequel ne peuvent pas être cédés les droits, attribués par des lois postérieures, qui comportent une protection plus large. Si on reconnaît que l'oeuvre multimédia est un phénomène de fait fondé sur les nouvelles technologies, et pas sur de nouvelles lois, il ne devrait pas subsister de problèmes d'identification de la titularité pour la concession de licences au cessionnaire de l'auteur pour un contrat, même si cela a été stipulé avant l'introduction de telles nouvelles technologies.

3.2. Existe-t-il des dispositions spécifiques permettant aux diffuseurs d'informations d'obtenir facilement l'autorisation de reproduire et de diffuser des oeuvres existantes? Par exemple, existe-t-il un système de licence légal ou contractuel qui couvre ces opérations?

Il y a les organisations traditionnelles d'administration des droits d'auteur, qui agissent sur base statutaire et volontaire et qui, avec les éventuelles nécessaires adaptations, pourront intervenir dans le secteur ici considéré.

3.3. Existe-t-il des systèmes de gestion collective des droits d'auteur qui concernent ces droits? Dans l'affirmative, ces systèmes fonctionnent-ils en pratique et ont-ils une couverture suffisante (ceci étant, s'appliquent-ils à toutes les oeuvres ou à la plupart des oeuvres répertoriées dans une certaine catégorie d'oeuvres)?

L'activité d'intermédiaire dans le domaine des droits de représentation, d'exécution, de récitation, de radiodiffusion et de reproduction mécanique et cinématographique est réservée en exclusivité à la SIAE (article 180). Un tel système permet la représentativité presque totale de la part de la SIAE des auteurs et éditeurs.

4. **Responsabilité**

Il est évident que les personnes qui contreviennent aux dispositions sur le droit d'auteur en transmettant ou en reproduisant des oeuvres sur réseau seront responsables. Cependant, une action pour violation du droit d'auteur peut-elle être intentée à l'encontre des personnes mentionnées dans les situations suivantes?

4.1. Le diffuseur d'informations sur le site duquel une oeuvre a été diffusée par une personne inconnue / 4.2. Le fournisseur d'accès qui détient le serveur sur lequel une oeuvre a été illégalement diffusée par un diffuseur d'informations.

L'*"information provider"* et le *"service provider"* qui ne montrent pas la diligence nécessaire pour éviter d'illicites introductions d'oeuvres dans leurs propres systèmes de la part de tiers, pourraient être responsables, à cause de leur négligence, des préjudices qui peuvent léser les auteurs. En outre, au cas où l'introduction dans le système pourrait inclure l'utilisation des oeuvres de la part de tiers, l'*"information provider"* et le *"service provider"* pourraient être estimés responsables du fait indépendamment de toute négligence.

> ***4.3****. Quelle est l'incidence de* "back-ups" *qui incluent une oeuvre illégalement diffusée, et qui sont réalisés automatiquement par le fournisseur d'accès?*

Pour le même motif, on pourrait estimer responsable le *"service provider"* qui effectue la reproduction, même sans s'en rendre compte, d'oeuvres d'autrui sans autorisation.

> ***4.4****. Un fournisseur d'accès a-t-il l'obligation de prendre certaines mesures de précaution (comme par exemple, rappeler au diffuseurs d'informations leurs obligations résultant de la législation sur le droit d'auteur, examiner les transmissions susceptibles de constituer une infraction aux dispositions sur le droit d'auteur, conserver un relevé de tout enregistrement et consultation, etc.)?*

Le *"service provider"* doit sans faute adopter toute forme nécessaire à éviter des utilisations illicites de la part de tiers du matériel qui lui a été confié.

> ***4.5****. Le fournisseur d'accès au réseau, pour avoir transmis sur réseau une oeuvre en cours de consultation.*

Pour le même motif, on devrait estimer responsable celui qui transmet des oeuvres non-autorisées.

> ***4.6****. Quelle est l'incidence du fait que le fournisseur d'accès au réseau a eu connaissance du fait que certaines irrégularilés peuvent survenir: considérant, de surcroît, qu'il est techniquement possible de contrôler les transmissions en vue de détecter les éventuelles transmissions illégales?*

Au cas où le *"networking service provider"* a été averti de l'existence d'utilisations, il sera dans l'obligation de faire cesser immédiatement le flux.

The Netherlands

D.J.G. VISSER[1]

1. Rights which are involved

1.1. *Introduction*

In the Dutch Copyright Act 1912 ('DCA') the economic or exploitation rights are divided into two categories: a reproduction right *('verveelvoudigingsrecht')* [2] and a right to communicate to the public *('openbaarmakingsrecht')*. The reproduction right covers all kinds of reproductions (as foreseen by article 9 of the Berne Convention). The right to communicate to the public is defined very broadly and covers traditional ways of exploitation such as distribution, public performance, public display and broadcasting but also all other existing and future ways of making a work perceivable to the public.

1.2. *Reproduction right*

General

The Dutch Copyright Act gives no definition of the *'verveelvoudigingsrecht'* in its primary meaning of reproduction right. The explanatory memorandum speaks of 'the making of one or more copies'.[3] The main requirements of a reproduction can be described as durability and perceptibility.

Durability

Reproduction traditionally requires a 'more or less permanent' fixation or storage of the work on a physical carrier of some sort: *'It is only possible to talk of fixation if the connection between the work and the object is more or less permanent'*.[4] The degree of durability is probably one of the most important unresolved issues. Traditionally, the projection on a screen, for instance a television screen, is considered not to be permanent enough to be a reproduction.[5] The durability of the reproduction did not cause any real problems until the advent of computers and computer programs.

Perceptibility

As early as 1912 the Dutch legislator made clear that the reproduction right also applies to reproductions that can not be perceived directly, *i.e.* without the use of some kind of apparatus. In 1912 it was deemed necessary to make this clear in a separate article in the Copyright Act,[6] but there is consensus that it also follows from the broadly defined reproduction right in general.[7]

Software Directive

The definition of the reproduction right in relation to computerprograms is dominated by the description given in article 4 of the Council Directive of 14 May 1991 on the legal protection of computer programs (91/250/EEC) ('Software Directive'). Article 4 (Restricted acts): *'Subject to the provisions of articles 5 and 6, the exclusive rights of the right holder within the meaning of article 2, shall include the right to do or to authorize: (a) the permanent or temporary reproduction of a computer program by any means and in any form, in part or in whole. In sofar as loading, displaying, running, transmission or storage of the computer program necessitate such reproduction, such acts shall be subject to authorization by the right holder; (...)'.* This definition, which has been implemented in article 45i DCA, has given rise to a lot of controversy. One question is whether 'temporary reproduction' includes the temporary storage in the Random Access Memory (RAM) (in the course of loading a program) and/or the transient fixation in the Central Processing Unit (CPU) (in the course of running the program). As in most European countries, the prevailing view seems to be that, according to the Directive, the storage of a computerprogram in the RAM is a reproduction relevant under copyright law.[8] The status of even more transient fixations, such as take place in the course of running the program, is unclear. Another important question is whether the scope of the reproduction right as prescribed for computer programs (by the applicable Directive) does or should influence or even apply to other types of works.[9] There is no case law and no clear view on this issue. If, however, the mere viewing of a work on a screen, or other acts of use, would constitute a reproduction relevant under copyright law, a systematic inconsistency would arise with the right to communicate to the public, because the latter right expressly exempts from copyright acts of use and communication inside a circle of family and friends and thus, of course, mere individual use.

The Dutch Copyright Association, in its reaction to the EC Green Paper on Copyright and Related Rights in the Information Society, has stated the following:[10] *'Extending the Computer Programs Directive definition of reproduction right to the reproduction of copyrighted works other than programs in a digital environment would obliterate the traditional right of private copying and should therefor be reconsidered very carefully. Under such definition the uploading into a network or downloading of a work in the temporary memory of a computer for purposes of projection thereof on a computer screen would constitute an unauthorised reproduction, which is open for question in a system of exploitation where compensation of right holders is eventually calculated* pro rato *of the use of the information concerned. Doubts therefore remain whether the rules related to computer programs in this should be applied to other works in general.'* The reference in this statement to *'pro rato* of the use of the information' relates to another important statement in the reaction of the Copyright Association:[11] *'It is clear that in the marketplace the technologies facilitating and controlling exploitation of copyrighted works in a digital environment are not directed towards facilitating and controlling reproduction, but towards facili-*

tating and controlling access and use of data. Such development of new technologies may lead to a system of pay-per-use with respect to exploitation of copyright and works in a digital environment. Regulators should ensure that such development is not being hindered by legislation.' The message from those two statements is clear: an over-stretched reproduction right (as prescribed by the Software Directive) might well prove to be an obstacle for the development of the exploitation of copyrighted works in cyberspace.

1.3. Communication to the public

General

The Dutch legislator in 1912 saw no need to give a general definition of the *'openbaarmakingsrecht'*, the right to communicate the work to the public, because *'in relation to every kind of literary, scientific or artistic work the word* (i.e. *'openbaar-maken'*, in translation, the phrase 'to communicate to the public') *clearly has its natural meaning'*.[12] In relation to literary and scientific works it means to distribute copies to the public, in relation to paintings and sculptures it means to display publicly. In article 12 DCA a short list is given of activities also covered by the right to communicate to the public. This list includes public recitation, performance or presentation, and (since 1995) rental and public lending, and is not an exhaustive enumeration. For instance, broadcasting is not mentioned in article 12 DCA, but there is no doubt that it is covered by the right to communicate to the public.[13] The *'openbaarmakingsrecht'* is a very broad concept that is meant to cover all existing and future forms of communication to the public.

Circle of family and friends

The main characteristic of a communication to the public is that it is directed to the public or takes place in public. The DCA gives no general definition of 'public' or 'the public', but article 12(4) indicates that: *'[a] recitation, performance or presentation in a closed circle shall be deemed to be a public recitation except if restricted to the family circle, a circle of friends or a circle that may be assimilated thereto if no fee of any kind is charged for admission to the recitation, performance or presentation. This provision shall apply also to an exhibition.'* Consequently, 'public' can be defined as 'outside a circle of family and friends'. The Dutch Supreme Court has ruled in 1993[14] that this 'circle criterion' not only applies to public performance and display, but also to cable redistribution. It is likely that this criterion applies to all forms of communication to the public (except maybe to distribution).[15]

Individual viewing

The right to communicate to the public also applies to the situation where members of the public do not receive or view the work at the same time, nor at the same place. In relation to private video cabins the Court of Appeals in The Hague has ruled that offering the possibility of individual viewing of (pornographic) movies to the public constitutes a communication to the public.[16] The rights to communicate to the public also applies to video-on-demand and other on-demand services.[17]

Rental, lending and exhaustion

As prescribed by the relevant EC Directive, rental and public lending are covered by the right to communicate to the public. The Dutch parliamentary history of the amendment to the DCA to implement this Directive makes clear that electronic delivery services (such as video-on-demand and electronic document delivery), although subject to the *genus* communication to the public, are not covered by *species* rental or public lending.[18] The Dutch Copyright Association has stressed the fact that the application of the Rental Rights Directive to the act of immaterial communication to the public is not appropriate.[19]

The effect of the so-called exhaustion or first sale doctrine is limited to the right to distribute (physical) copies. As in most countries, the rental and lending right is an exception to the principle of exhaustion. Exhaustion does not apply to other forms of communication to the public.

Status of the hyperlink (personal opinion)

A 'hyperlink' enables the visitor of an Internet site to link to another site, possibly on another server, possibly on the other side of the world. By clicking his mouse he gains access to this other site. It has been argued that the presence of such a hyperlink might in itself amount to a communication to the public of the works on the site it 'links' or gives access to. The reasoning behind this point of view is that the hyperlink is an offer to access the contents of the linked site and should therefore be classified as a communication to the public of these contents. The counter argument is that the hyperlink is no more than a footnote which makes the visitor aware of the existence of another site. Although the hyperlink has a lot more impact than a footnote, in the sense that it makes it much easier to access the information it refers to, it does not seem appropriate to classify the hyperlink as a communication to the public.

Hyperlinks seem to be comparable to (references to) addresses of mail-order firms or to radio or television frequencies. Making the public aware of the fact that someone else makes information available to the public does in itself not amount to a communication the public. It might, however, amount to an unlawful act (tort), which might be described as contributory copyright infringement, if someone knowingly and in bad faith creates hyperlinks to sites on which works are made available illegally. Such a situation might be compared to the case in which someone published a leaflet called *The Pirate* which contained the program of illegal television broadcasts in the Amsterdam region. The President of the Amsterdam District Court ruled that this was an unlawful act of 'parasitic competition'.[20]

1.4. Individual questions

Under Dutch law, are the following acts subject to certain economic rights (such as e.g. the reproduction right, distribution right, public performance right, display right, broadcasting right, cable transmission right, etc.)?

1.1. *The storage of a work on a network computer, e.g. in a site on a server ('uploading'). /* **1.2.** *Making that work available to others. If so, please specify whether it is relevant if it is made available at large or to a restricted group only.*

The uploading of a work to a network computer involves permanent storage and as a consequence is covered by the reproduction right. If the work is (consequently) made available to a group of people larger than a circle of family or friends this probably[21] constitutes a communication to the public.

1.3. *Distribution of the work, e.g. to a newsgroup or a forum.*

('Immaterial') distribution of the work to a newsgroup or a forum involves (more or less) permanent storage on a server and is consequently subject to the reproduction right. It is also a form of communication to the public because (or: in so far as) it is accessible to people from outside a circle of family and friends.[22]

1.4. *On-line consultation of the work, i.e. having it displayed on the consulting person's monitor (this will probably also require temporary fixation of that work in the consulting person's computer's internal memory).*

On-line consultation as such is not covered by the right to communicate to the public. However, making the work available to the public for such consultation probably is. The temporary fixation in the consulting person's computer internal memory can be considered a reproduction relevant under copyright if the (arguably overstretched) reproduction concept of the Software Directive is applied. If the traditional and systematic concept that copyright does not cover consumptive acts as viewing or use is followed, this kind of temporary storage should be exempted from copyright, not as an exception but as a rule.[23]

1.5. *Copying the consulted work on a hard disc or other media ('downloading'). /* **1.6.** *Printing the consulted work.*

Downloading results in permanent storage and consequently in reproduction relevant under copyright law. So does printing.

1.7. *Transmission of the work through the network in the course of it being consulted.*

Transmission of the work in the course of its being consulted, is an integral part of the on-line consultation itself (see question 1.4). The transmission itself is not a communication to the public. The making available for transmission in the course of consultation, however, is probably covered by the right to communicate to the public. The temporary fixation in the course of the transmission can be considered a reproduction relevant under copyright if the (arguably overstretched) reproduction concept of the Software Directive is applied. The arguments against this approach are the same as mentioned before in relation to screen display and other acts of use.

1.8. *Making back-ups, perhaps fully automatic, by the services provider.*

Back-ups are stored permanently and are consequently relevant reproductions.

2. Exceptions

2.1. *Existing exceptions*

General

Until recently it was generally understood that the exceptions on the exploitation rights were enumerated exhaustively in the DCA. There was no general fair use or fair dealing exception. The ruling of the Supreme Court in the *Dior v. Evora* case of 20 November 1995[24] may have changed this situation. Following this judgment there might now be room for (more) exceptions outside those listed in the DCA.[25] The existing exceptions in the DCA were never meant for a digital environment and in many cases they do not fit in cyberspace.

Private use copying

It is important to distinguish between private use as such and copying for private use.[26] Mere private use is the viewing, reading and listening, which has traditionally been exempted from copyright altogether, because it does not constitute a communication to the public. *Copying* for private use, however, covers the acts preceding the actual use and is covered by the reproduction right, but may be subject to an exemption to that right. It is unclear whether or to what extent the exceptions relating to copying for private use apply to situations in cyberspace. A private use copying exception does by nature not apply to activities that can be qualified as communication to the public. Therefore, the activities mentioned sub 1.2 and 1.3 are not covered by the private use copying exception.

The existing private use copying exception is different for different kinds of works:
- Copying for private use of computer programs is not allowed at all, following the Software Directive.[27]
- Copying for private use of texts is allowed in relation to short articles and out-of-print works and in relation to small parts of other written works (including sheet music).
- Copying for private use of all other works 'in a few copies' is allowed without any (other) limitations.

Depending on the quantity and the type of work, the activities mentioned sub 1.5 and 1.6, downloading and printing, might be allowed under the present private use copying exception. If the activities mentioned sub 1.4 and 1.7 (activities to do with consultation) have to be qualified as reproduction, they might be covered by the private use copying exception.

A problem of the Dutch private use copying exception is that it does not distinguish (sufficiently) between copying, having copies made, making available for copying and offering the service of sending copies on request (document delivery). All these activities seem to be allowed under the existing private copying exception,[28] but their impact differs considerably. In fact, making available for copying and offering the service of sending copies on request (document delivery) might be considered communication to the public. If private copying exceptions would apply to these activities they would probably constitute a violation of article 9(2) of the Berne Convention.

Internal use

The exceptions relating to reprographic copying (photocopying) for internal use probably do not apply to any kind of electronic copying (including all kinds of dissemination in local area networks). Recently, the Copyright Advisory Committee of the Ministry of Justice has advised against dealing with electronic copying in the framework of the regulation of reprographic reproduction.[29]

Educational exceptions

It is unclear whether or how the exception relating to public recitation, performance or presentation for non-profit educational purposes or the exception relating to educational textbook reproduction and publishing do apply to electronic network situations. Arguably, making a work available in a very small network that would only reach (the equivalent of) one classroom might be covered by the existing educational use exception of article 12(5) DCA.

2.2. (Desirable) special network exceptions

There are as yet no special network exceptions in Dutch copyright law. It is very hard to tell what kinds of exception would be desirable, because it is as yet unknown what the effect on (the possibilities of) 'normal exploitation' by the right holder would be. In fact, nobody knows what the normal exploitation (in the sense of article 9(2) Berne Convention) in a networked environment actually is. Many right holders take the view that private use copying exceptions should be extremely limited, if not abolished.

Private use and browsing

It is very important to distinguish between consumptive activities such as downloading and printing on the one hand and on the other hand operating a service (offered to the public) which either consists of sending (digital) copies on request or making them available on-line for 'private copying' (i.e. downloading). The latter activities should, for obvious reasons, not be covered by a private use copying exception. The personal opinion of the Dutch national reporter is that operating a document delivery service, whether it is in electronic or paper form, has to be qualified as a communication to the public in just the same way as the making available of an on-line database.

It has been suggested that 'mere browsing' on-line should in some way be exempted from copyright in the same way as browsing in a library or in a bookshop is allowed without permission of the right holder.[30] This comparison is flawed, in sofar as it suggests that making available for browsing should not be subject to copyright. Browsing or consulting information on-line is possibly the most important way of satisfying the demand for information in the future. Exploiting this demand will therefore be crucial to the interest of copyright holders. It is, again, important to distinguish between the consumptive activity of browsing and the exploitation by *making (publicly) available for* browsing.[31] The making available is the crucial activity, because it enables the members of the public to browse. It is obvious therefore that it makes much more sense to subject the making available (for browsing) rather than the actual browsing to an exclusive right of the copyright holder.

Other exceptions

There has not yet been any detailed discussion on the need for special network exceptions. In their reactions to the European Green Paper all parties (understandably) stress the interests of their members but do not propose any specific changes to existing law. To give just two examples of comments from different interest groups. The Dutch Foundation for Copyright Interests (*'Stichting Auteursrechtbelangen'*) reacted as follows:[32] *'In how far exceptions can be justified is a matter for (fresh) consideration, not necessarily to be answered along the lines of the tradition that have marked the present situation. It is our belief that each and every proposal for an exception on this reproduction right must be examined and weighed against the provisions of article 9(2) of the Berne Convention.'* The Dutch Federation of Organizations in the Library, Information and Documentation field *(FOBID)* commented in a letter to the Minister of Justice: *'To its unpleasant surprise FOBID has found that in the Green Paper little or no attention is paid to the statutory limitations on copyright, such as library privileges and rules on educational, scientific and private use. Many existing statutory limitations are technology dependent. It has to be examined whether and to what extent these limitations should be maintained or adapted in the digital environment.'*

It might well be true that it is in fact to early to determine what kinds of exceptions are needed in the digital environment. However, it is important to realise that, as a recent comparative analysis of existing limitations has shown:[33] *'[m]any limitations are the results of successful 'lobbying'. Intermediaries and users applying for specific limitations must realise that right owners, who will oppose any limitation as a matter of principle, are generally very well represented at the (national and international) legislative level. Thus, the extent to which copyright limitations will be preserved or extended in the digital environment will eventually be determined by the ability of intermediaries and users to have their voice heard on the political level.'*

Technological side effects (personal opinion)

It is essential to put technological side effects into perspective. If, for instance, we want on-line consultation of a work as such not to be covered by copyright, because we think it would suffice to subject the making available for such consultation to an exclusive right, we should not be distracted by the technological side effect of temporary storage, either anywhere in a network or in the consulting person's computer. Another typical example of what seems to be a technological side effect, or at least a sideline, is the making of back-ups by the service provider as described sub 1.8. If we decide that a provider is under particular circumstances not liable for a copyright infringement which takes place on his server, it would be rather strange hold him liable 'through the back door' of his automatic back-ups. Exploitation rights are meant to give the right holder the possibility to effectively exploit his work, they are not meant to subject every new technological side effect to an exclusive right.

3. **Licensing**

3.1. *General problems*

There are problems for information providers who want to acquire permission to upload and distribute existing works. The first problem is the fact that it is often not clear who holds the electronic rights. Only filmproducers, for whose benefit there is the presumption of transfer of all exploitation rights, can be sure that they do hold all the rights necessary.[34] A complete transfer of all rights relating to all existing and future ways of exploitation is probably possible under Dutch copyright law. However, such a complete transfer hardly ever takes place. Deeds of transfer have to be interpreted restrictively[35] and in many cases it is unclear whether or not future forms of exploitation are part of the transfer. Many publishers take considerable risks in exploiting information on-line without the certainty that they actually hold the rights to do so.

The second problem for information providers is that right holders, even those who are certain they hold the electronic rights, are reluctant to give permission to make their works available on-line. The main reason for this reluctancy is that right holders do not know what the impact of a particular kind of distribution to the public will be on the exploitation value of the work. The fact that it will be available in digital form makes it very easy to copy and distribute further. There are no special (compulsory) licensing facilities for information providers in relation to existing works and it is unlikely that they will be created in the near future. Nobody knows what the impact of certain kinds of network exploitation will be and it seems therefore unreasonable and unjustified to force right holders in existing works to have there works distributed in cyberspace.

3.2. *Internet licensing by Buma/Stemra*[36]

The collecting societies for performing and mechanical rights in musical works, Buma and Stemra, are planning to license jointly the making available of musical works on Internet. They are probably the parties most likely to succeed in any collective licensing and yet there will be many problems. The first problem that arises in many countries in relation to Internet licensing is the fact that making available on-line will imply both a communication to the public and a reproduction will be covered. This problem will be avoided by the fact that Buma and Stemra will cooperate and consequently represent both the performing (communication to the public) rights and the reproduction and distribution rights.

The main problem is whether they actually hold the 'Internet rights'. In relation to their Dutch members this will probably not be very problematic because the deeds of transfer contain a very broad description of the rights covered. Due to the cross-border or rather global character of Internet, another aspect of this problem is whether they have the right to license kinds of communication to the public which will reach every corner of the earth. This could, of course, give rise to conflicts with other collecting societies in other countries. If they want to prove that they have an important role to play in cyberspace, the only practical approach to this seems to be, at least for the time being, for the different national collecting societies not to challenge each other's rights, as far as Internet licensing in the country of origin is concerned. It can be difficult to determine a country of origin, but in many cases it will be comparatively easy. If both the information provider and the service providers are nationals of a particular country and the server is physically located in that same country it may be concluded that it is the country of origin.

Another problem is determining the price and other conditions of the licence. As nobody knows the economic value of the making available of a single musical work on a Web site, the price of a blanket licence is even more of a shot in the dark. The only way forward seems to experiment without long term commitments.

4. Liability

4.1. Present legal uncertainty [37]

General

It is evident that persons who infringe copyright by up- or downloading will be liable. However, can action for copyright infringement also be taken against the mentioned persons in the following situations?

4.1. *The information provider on whose site a work has been uploaded by an unknown person.*

It is likely that the information provider (as defined in the questionnaire) will be held liable for everything that takes place on his 'site'. *(See further hereunder.)*

4.2. *The services provider who owns the server on which a work has been infringingly uploaded by an information provider.*

The same goes for a Bulletin Board Service operator who is actively involved in making available a particular work. The District Court of Rotterdam ruled in its judgment of 24 August 1995:[38] *'The 'downloading' by others was apparently possible because Lenior* [defendant, DJGV] *had changed part of the Title Allocation Table of*

133

the software uploaded by a third party. In doing so Lenior communicated the work to the public and infringed Bridgesoft's [plaintiff's] copyright'. (See further hereunder.)

Questions 4.3 to 4.6 cannot be answered with any degree of certainty because there is no case-law and hardly any literature. These questions are dealt with in part in paragraph 4.2 according the personal view of the national reporter.

Scientology-case

The case brought against a number of service providers and one information provider by the Church of Scientology lead to the first judgment on the liability of service providers in the Netherlands. The text of this judgment is included in this report *(see annexe)*. The court expressed the view that service providers are in principle not liable for copyright infringement taking place on their server. However, they might be liable in cases in which the infringement by an information provider is 'unmistakably clear' and it is reasonable to assume that this is known also by the service provider, for example because he has been informed about it. In such cases the service provider 'might' be required to 'deal with' the information provider concerned. An appeal filed by the Church of Scientology against this judgment is pending.

4.2. *Personal opinion*

In relation to the liability issue the best approach seems to be to have an open mind for the practical needs and consequences. The situation in cyberspace can probably not be solved by simply applying traditional copyright infringement liability rules and standards. In the Netherlands, liability for (contributory) infringement of copyright is covered by tort (*'onrechtmatige daad'*, 'unlawful act') law and the liability rules under Dutch tort law, as laid down in the Civil Code of 1992, are very flexible. Article 162, Book 6 Dutch Civil Code:[39]

'1. *A person who commits an unlawful act toward another which can be imputed to him, must repair the damage which the other person suffers as a consequence thereof.*

2. *Except where there is a ground of justification, the following acts are deemed to be unlawful: the violation of a right, an act or omission violating a statutory duty or a rule of unwritten law pertaining to proper social conduct.*

3. *An unlawful act can be imputed to its author if it results from his fault or from a cause for which he is answerable according to law or common opinion'.*

The rule of article 162(3), Book 6 Civil Code has to be applied to the different kinds of providers in cyberspace and, in this respect, a 'common opinion' has to be developed.

Information provider (question 4.1)

As unknown people cannot be held liable, the information provider who allows works to be uploaded to his site (by people unknown) must probably be held liable for this. Otherwise nobody could be held liable and the end of copyright would be near. This means that the information provider has to constantly monitor the contents of his site and not allow direct uploading without previous screening. Even then the problem would remain that the information provider will not always be able to recognise infringing material. This, however, can probably not be helped and it is the same risk that publishers have to take. It seems advisable that information providers at least do not to allow any anonymous uploading.

Service provider (question 4.2)

The service provider who owns a server on which a work has been infringingly uploaded by an information provider poses a more complex problem. The appropriate degree of liability of the service provider will be sought here by narrowing down from two extremes. The one extreme approach would be to hold the service provider fully liable (together with the information provider). As it is not possible for the service provider to screen the material before it is made available on a site, this is not an acceptable approach. Even if the service provider would constantly monitor all the sites on his server he could never be able to actually prevent an infringement and consequently could never avoid liability. The only thing he could do would be to have the infringing material removed or the site closed, but the infringement would already have taken place and damage would already have been done. The other extreme would be to hold the service provider not liable at all. As it is possible for information providers to remain anonymous (to the outside world) and as the service provider is the only person, apart from the information provider himself, who can stop the infringement by closing the site, this is not an acceptable approach either. Consequently, a service provider should at least be obliged to provide the right holder with the name and address of the information provider[40] and to close the site if the information provider refuses to remove the infringing material after the infringement has been proven in court.

As service providers often have hundreds or even thousands of different sites on their server, it seems practically impossible to require them to constantly monitor all those sites. A requirement of this sort, forced on them by a rather strict liability, would probably put most service providers out of business. This means that they can probably not be held liable for the mere fact that infringing material is present on one of the sites on their server. It would however be an unacceptably grave burden for the right holder to have to prove an infringement in court before a service provider would be obliged to reveal to him the identity of the anonymous information provider and close the site. In fact it seems not unreasonable that the service provider has to reveal the identity of the information provider at the first request of a right holder or take full responsibility for the infringement concerned. Any other approach would make it impossible for a right holder to take swift action against an infringement.

In this respect a comparison could be drawn with articles 53 and 54 of the Dutch Penal Code, relating to the so-called printing offences. Article 53(1) reads as follows: '*In the case of indictable offences committed by means of the printing press the publisher shall not be liable to prosecution if his name and address appear in the publication concerned and the identity of the offender is known or is divulged by the publisher in response to the first admonition to do so after the institution of a preliminary judicial investigation'*.[41] A modern interpretation of this penal liability rule might well be applicable to (copyright in) cyberspace.[42] This obligation on the part of the service provider to reveal the identity of the information provider might, however, not suffice in all cases. One case in which the revelation of the identity of the information provider seems insufficient is the situation in which the information provider lives in another country. He might well live on the other side of the world. This means that it will often take time for the right holder to force this person to remove the infringing material, if he would be able to achieve that at all. In the mean time the material would be present at the site on the server. A solution to this problem would be to hold the service provider liable in all those cases in which the information provider lives abroad.

The parallel with article 53 of the Penal Code continues. Article 53(2) reads: *'The above provision shall not apply if at the time of publication the offender was not liable to prosecution or was officially resident outside the Kingdom* [of the Netherlands] *in Europe'*. As a result of this, service providers would probably have to refuse to allow foreigners to have a site on their server. A less radical solution would be to require service providers to close down sites of foreigners as soon as a right holder has proven to them beyond a reasonable doubt that an infringement is taking place on that particular site. The same would apply to information providers who can not be traced easily or can not be held liable for other reasons, for example because they have given a false name or address to the service provider. If the service provider would refuse to close down a site in such a case he would become fully liable.

Right holders will probably argue that this will still not suffice because infringing material on the Internet can cause enormous damage and it will often not be possible to recoup those damages from individual information providers. They will also argue that the service providers are the professionals who make (a lot of) money out of exploiting their servers and should therefore be held liable to higher degree for what goes on on those servers. This wish could be met in part by requiring service providers to close down sites as soon as a right holder has proven to them beyond a reasonable doubt that an infringement is taking place on that particular site, irrespective of the question whether or not the information provider can be found. In the case of downright piracy this seems to be a reasonable approach, but careful consideration has to be given to the possibility that service providers will close down sites rather quickly just to be on the safe side. This might lead to a situation where right holders or people who just pretend to be right holders will have the possibility to abuse their (pretended) rights rather easily.

Networking services providers and access providers (question 4.5)

Networking services providers and access providers (who make it possible for members of the public to access or to 'surf' on the Internet) should not be held liable for the fact that infringing material is available on servers of other service providers, neither for the fact that this material is accessible through their computers, nor for the fact that the material actually passes trough their computers and is possibly temporarily stored in the process. The fact that they might have been informed that certain infringements may take place does not make a difference as long as there is no reasonable way to prevent this. This might be different if there will be efficient and effective ways to act upon such information. It is impossible for networking and access providers either to prevent or to repress infringements taking place on the millions of 'sites' on other (Internet) servers. It might be possible in some cases for them to deny their own Internet subscribers access to a particular site. The effect of such a measure would, however, be very limited and would not put an end to the infringement itself.

Precautionary measures (question 4.4)

It would be wise for service providers to make clear in their contracts with information providers that the latter will be liable for all copyright infringements that may take place on their sites. This would not exonerate them from liability in situations described above, but it would remind information providers of their responsibility under copyright. Monitoring or keeping a log of activities taking place by the service provider should not be required and would be unnecessary if service providers will only be liable in cases where they have been informed of a particular infringement taking place.

5. **Individual communication** (personal opinion)

Individual communication in cyberspace deserves special attention. The individual transmission between two private individuals is, to a large extent, protected by the right to privacy, as guaranteed by article 8 of the European Convention on Human Rights. Control on individual communication is therefore in principle undesirable. An individual transmission which is not part of a service (offered) to a group of people (which constitutes 'a public'), is not a transmission or communication to the public. Applying the reproduction right in cases of individual communication might lead to the same undesirable result. Copyright should not be extended to situations in which control is either impossible or undesirable.

Footnotes

1. The author would like to thank the following people for their comments on a draft version of this report: dr Erwin J. Arkenbout, Juliette Jonkers, Rob A.E. Stuyt, Prof. dr D.W. Feer Verkade , C.Th. Livia Visser-Fuchs and Willem A.Q. Wanrooij.
2. In the Netherlands the *'verveelvoudiginsgrecht'* also encompasses the right to make adaptations of the work. This right will not be dealt with in this report.
3. The Dutch Neighbouring Rights Act 1993 does give a definition of the reproduction right in article 1c: *'The making of one of more copies of all or part of a recording'*.
4. J.H. Spoor, 'Copies in continental copyright', in: *Copies in copyright*, Alphen a/d Rijn 1980, p. 52. (*Copies in continental copyright*, originally published in Dutch as '*Scripta Manent, De reproduktie in het auteursrecht'* (Groningen 1976) is the 1976 Utrecht thesis of J.H. Spoor.)
5. *'A television screen can show a given picture for a considerable time, but that picture in reality is constantly reformed, it is not fixed: the dots on the screen keep lighting up for just a few hundredths of a second at a time'*, Spoor, *Copies in copyright*, p. 52.
6. Article 14 DCA (as it reads since 1972): *'The reproduction of a literary, scientific or artistic work shall be understood to mean also the recording of all or part of the work on an object intended for causing a work to be heard or seen'*.
7. Spoor, *Copies in copyright*, p. 30.

8. This does, however, not mean that most Dutch scholars agree with this result, it just means that they recognise that this probably is the meaning of the Directive and consequently inevitably the current situation in Dutch copyright law. See *infra* footnote 23.

9. The definition of the reproduction right in article 5 of the Council Directive of 11 March 1996 on the legal protection of Databases (96/6/EC) ('temporary or permanent reproduction by any means and in any form') might indicate that there is a movement in that direction on a European level, or, at least, within the European Commission.

10. Preliminary position of the Dutch Copyright Association to the Green Paper, p. 16.

11. *O.c.*, p. 15.

12. Explanatory memorandum 1912, De Vries (parliamentary history of the DCA), p. 12.3.

13. Following the amendment to implement the Council Directive of 27 September 1993 on the coordination of certain rules concerning copyright and rights related to copyright applicable to satellite broadcasting and cable retransmission (93/83/EEC), broadcasting will be inserted explicitly in article 12 DCA.

14. Supreme Court 24 December 1993, *NJ* 1994, 641. See also: J. Jonkers, 'The Dutch Community Cable case: a Christmas Judgment by the Dutch Supreme Court', *Copyright World* 1994, pp. 43-45.

15. It can be argued that in relation to distribution a wider 'closed circle' applies. (See J.H. Spoor and D.W.F. Verkade, *Auteursrecht*, Deventer 1993, p. 160, note 66.)

16. Court of Appeals The Hague 1 December 1994, *AMI* 1995, p. 51.

17. The Minister of Justice and the Secretary of State for Culture have expressed the view that video-on-demand services are also covered by the right to communicate to the public in a letter of 28 February 1995 relating to the implementation of the EC Rental and Lending Directive (23247, nr. 21, p. 12).

18. See letter mentioned in previous note.

19. Preliminary position of the Dutch Copyright Association to the Green Paper, p. 15.

20. President of the District Court of Amsterdam 25 June 1981, *NBB v. De Piraat*, *RvdW/KG* 1981, 89, *AMR* 1981, p. 85, *BIE* 1983, p. 147.

21. In view of the local area network cable redistribution decision by the Dutch Supreme Court (24 December 1993, *NJ* 1994, 641) it is likely that the the circle of family and friends criterion does apply.

22. Reply to the EC Green Paper prepared by the Dutch Ministry of Justice (relating to section IV; Communication to the public): '*The dissemination of information to news groups on the Internet and of information to and from home pages and bulletin board servers is covered by communication to the public*'.

23. In favour of the latter view: D.W.F. Verkade, 'Computerprogramma's in de Auteurswet 1912: het vierde regime...', *Computerrecht* 1992, p. 87; P.B. Hugenholtz, 'Convergence and Divergence in Intellectual Property Law: The Case of the Software Directive', in: *Information Law towards the 21st century*, Deventer 1992, p. 323: '*Copyright does not, and should not, restrict the reception (consumption) of information*'; D.J.G. Visser, '*Groen papier over auteursrecht van E4@DG15.cec.be*', *Mediaforum* 1995, p. 119.

24. Supreme Court 20 October 1995, *RvdW* 1995, 212 C, *Informatierecht/AMI* 1996, p. 51.

25. See: F.W. Grosheide, *Informatierecht/AMI* 1996, pp. 43-44.

26. In the opinion of the Dutch national reporter, the EC Green Paper on Copyright and related rights in the Information Society (of July 1995) does confuse the two in section IV on Communication to the public (pp. 52-54).

27. Following article 45k DCA and article 5(2) Software Directive the legitimate user is allowed to make a back-up copy if necessary for the intended use of the program.

28. The only exception to this exception is the ordering for private use of copies of audio or audiovisual works.

29. '*Interimrapport over het reprorecht*', Commissie Auteursrecht, February 1996, p. 15.

30. See: P.B. Hugenholtz, *NJB* 1995, p. 516.

31. The irony is that, in a sense, it seems to be the other way round: the person who browses is active and intitiates the transmission to his own computer in the course of consulting the documents, whereas the person who makes available seems passive, because he 'only' makes the information accessible on-line and may not even know who are browsing and what they look at.

32. *Reaction to the Green Paper 'Copyright and Related Rights in the Information Society'*, Stichting Auteursrechtbelangen, Amstelveen, January 1996, p. 16.

33. P.B. Hugenholtz and D.J.G. Visser, *Copyright problems of electronic document delivery: a comparative analysis*, Report to the Commision of the European Communities (DG-XIII), Brussels/Luxembourg 1995, p. 62.

34. Filmproducers do however have the obligation to pay an equitable remuneration for new kinds of exploitation (Article 45d DCA).

35. Article 2 DCA: '*The transfer shall comprise only those rights specifically mentioned in the deed of transfer or which are necessarily implied from the nature or purpose of the agreement*'.

36. See: J. Jonkers and W. Wanrooij, 'Music, copyright and new techniques seen from the perspective of collecting societies', in: *Multimedia deals in the music industry*, MAKLU Apeldoorn 1996, pp. 131-141.

37. See: M. Kennedy and J. Linneman, 'On-line distribution of multimedia works: the perspective of the on-line service and infromation providers', in: *Multimedia deals in the music industry*, MAKLU Apeldoorn 1996, pp. 99-111.

38. *Bridgesoft v. Lenior*, Court nr. 120/94, not yet published.

39. Translation: P.P.C. Haanappel and E. Mackaay, *New Netherlands Civil Code; Patrimonial Law*, Kluwer Deventer/Boston 1990, p. 298.
40. Although the information provider might be anonymous to the outside world, his name and address have to be known to the service provider because they have a contractual relationship.
41. Unofficial translation provided by the Ministry of Justice. Article 54 contains a comparable rule relating to printers.
42. Compare: De Roos, Schuijt and Wissink, 'Uitingsdelicten op de elektronische snelweg', ITeR-rapport, March 1996, chapter 5 and conclusion.

Annexe

The President of the Regional Court of The Hague

Ruling dated 12 March 1996, in the Summary Proceedings instituted at this Court under roll-number 96/160 between:

1. the legal entity registered as a church under foreign law CHURCH OF SPIRITUAL SCIENTO- LOGY, established in Los Angeles, California, USA;
2. the legal entity registered as a church under foreign law RELIGIOUS TECHNOLOGY CENTER, established in Los Angeles, California, USA;
3. the legal entity incorporated under foreign law, NEW ERA PUBLICATIONS INTERNATIONAL ApS, established in Copenhagen, Denmark,
plaintiffs, barrister R. Laret, solicitor R. Hermans,

versus:

1. the private limited liability company DATAWEB BV, statutorily seated in The Hague and having offices at (2593 BS) The Hague, on the Laan van Nieuw-Oost Indië number 269;
2. the foundation STICHTING XS4ALL, statutorily seated in Amsterdam and having offices in Amsterdam on the Prins Hendrikkade number 192A;
3. the foundation STICHTING DE DIGITALE STAD, statutorily seated in Amsterdam and having offices at (1011 TD) Amsterdam, on the Prins Hendrikkade number 193A;
4. the private limited liability company CISTRON INTERNET SERVICES BV, statutorily seated in Alphen a/d Rijn and having offices at (2404 AK) Alphen a/d Rijn, at Hoorn number 186;
5. the private limited liability company INTERNET ACCESS EINDHOVEN BV, statutorily seated in Eindhoven and having offices at (5612 DS) Eindhoven, on the Bisschopsmolen number 18 (...);
6. the company incorporated under foreign law EURONET INTERNET INC., statutorily seated in Wilmington, USA, and having offices at (1012 AC) Amsterdam on the Prins Hendrikkade number 48;
7. the private limited liability company PLANET INTERNET BV statutorily seated in Amsterdam and having offices at (1112 XN) Diemen, at Diemerhof number 26c;
8. the private limited liability company B-ART NOORD NEDERLAND BV, statutorily seated in The Hague and having offices at (9711 RH) Groningen, at Schuitendiep number 88-I;
9. the private limited liability company WIREHUB INTERNET BV statutorily seated in Rotterdam and having offices at (3061 AS) Rotterdam at the Oudedijk number 196;
10. the foundation STICHTING INTERNET ACCESS, statutorily seated in Slochteren and having offices at (9621 AG) Slochteren at Hoofdweg number 113;
11. the foundation STICHTING TELEBYTE, statutorily seated in Nijmegen and having offices at (6532 XE) Nijmegen on the Fleminghstraat number 73;
12. Ronald Walter VERGEER, residing in Leidschendam, the name B-ART MIDDEN NEDER LAND BV I.O. (currently being incorporated), acting and on the grounds of that determined by article 1:14 of the Civil Code of the Netherlands, also opting for residence at (2583 CM) The Hague at the Dr. Lelykade number 64;
13. the partnership incorporated as company LUNATECH RESEARCH, established and having offices at (3039 LH) Rotterdam at the Statensingel number 121a;
14. Michael David PENTOWSKI, partner in the company listed under sub-section 13, residing in Rotterdam and on the grounds of article 1:14 of the Civil Code of the Netherlands also opting for residence at (3039 LH) Rotterdam on the Statensingel number 121a;
15. Peter Firth MUNRO, partner in the company listed under sub-section 13, residing in Workingham, United Kingdom and on the grounds of article 1:14 of the Civil Code of the Netherlands also opting for residence at (3039 LH) Rotterdam on the Statensingel number 121a;
16. Stefan Mark ARENTZ, partner in the company listed under sub-section 13, residing in Schagen and on the grounds of article 1:14 of the Civil Code of the Netherlands also opting for residence at (3039 LH) Rotterdam on the Statensingel number 121a;
17. Peter Alexander KAAS, partner in the company listed under sub-section 13, residing in Odijk, in the municipality of Bunnik and on the grounds of article 1:14 of the Civil Code of the Netherlands

also opting for residence at (3039 LH) Rotterdam on the Statensingel number 121a;

18. the partnership incorporated as a company SPIRIT INTERACTIEVE DIENSTEN BV I.O. (presenting being incorporated as a private limited liability company), established and having offices at (3012 KN) in Rotterdam on the Westblaak number 180;

19. the public limited liability company NV ENECO, partner of the respondent listed under sub-section 18, also residing on the grounds of article 1:14 of the Civil Code of the Netherlands at (3012 KN) Rotterdam on the Westblaak number 180;

20. the private limited liability company ROTTERDAMS DAGBLAD BV partner of the respondent listed under sub-section 18, also on the grounds of article 1:14 of the Civil Code of the Netherlands at (3012 KN) opting for residence in Rotterdam on the Westblaak number 180;

21. the MUNICIPALITY OF ROTTERDAM (DEVELOPMENT COMPANY OF ROTTERDAM), partner of the respondent listed under sub-section 18, also seated in Rotterdam (3011 AD) on the Coolsingel number 40;

22. the private limited liability company METROPOLIS INTERNET BV, statutorily seated in Dordrecht and having offices on the Madame Curiestraat number 2;

23. Karin SPAINK, residing at (1018 LP) Amsterdam on the *[home address - ed.]*; defendants sub-sections 1 up to and including 6 and sub-section 9 and sub-sections 12 up to and including 23: barrister W. Takema, solicitor P.H. Bakker Schut; defendant sub-section 7: barrister W.E. Pors, solicitors messrs. W.E. Pors and J.C.H. van Manen; defendants sub-sections 8, 10 and 11 did not appear.

1. The facts

On the grounds of the documents submitted and that put forward at the Court Session held on 26 February 1996, the following has been determined:

1.1. Defendants in these proceedings are so-called Internet access providers (defendants sub-sections 1 up to and including 22) as well as one of them being an Internet user (defendant sub-section 23). The Internet is a worldwide computer information network. Internet access providers make it possible for their subscribers to use the Internet. People with a subscription can gain access to the various facilities of the Internet like making a so-called home page. A home page is a data-file which is created by a subscriber and which can be consulted by other Internet users.

1.2. Plaintiffs state that defendants infringe their copyright by publishing (making it possible to publish) texts, the copyright of which rests with plaintiff sub-section 1, which texts are certain confidential works written by L. Ron Hubbard who died in 1986. These works concern the theology of and the activities conducted by the Church of Scientology founded by L. Ron Hubbard.

2. The claim, its grounds and the defence

The claim

2.1. Plaintiffs claim, in brief, that the defendants should be required to refrain from making any infringement and should be required to cease and desist from making any infringement of the copyright held by plaintiff sub-section 1.

2.2. Secondarily, plaintiffs claim that in connection with defendants sub-sections 1 up to and including 22, once these defendants have been notified of the presence of documents which constitutes an infringement on their computer systems (or those checked by them), then they should ensure for the immediate removal of said documents. Even more secondarily, plaintiffs claim that defendants sub-section 1 up to and including 22, should deny further access to users. Furthermore, plaintiffs claim that defendants sub-section 1 up to and including 22, in the aforementioned case, should inform them as to the names and addresses of third parties, which or who have published or reproduced the documents constituting the infringement of copyright through their computer systems (or those checked by them).

The grounds

The following was put forward:

2.3. Defendants have infringed copyright. Plaintiff sub-section 1 holds the copyright to a number of confidential and non-confidential works, created by L. Ron Hubbard who died in 1986. Plaintiff sub-section 2 is the exclusive licensee worldwide, aside from the United States of America, of the copyright to the confidential works and is the proxy-holder to ensure these copyrights are upheld and complied with. Plaintiff sub-section 3 is the exclusive worldwide holder of the rights (with the exception of the North America and Latin America) of a number of the non-confidential works for their publication, and is the proxy-holder to ensure these copyrights are upheld and complied with.

2.4. Legal proceedings in the United States conducted in 1993 between the Church of Scientology International and Steven Fishman contained an affidavit called the Fishman Affidavit. An appendix to this affidavit contained a reproduction of a part of the published, non-confidential work *'Ability'* without the permission required for this from the plaintiff and also contained a considerable part of the unpublished, confidential works called *'Operating Thetan'* (hereinafter called: OT) I up to and including VII.

2.5. Plaintiffs noticed that the Fishman Affidavit, which contains a considerable quantity of material taken from the OT works, and from *'Ability'*, was published or reproduced on the Internet. Defendant sub-section 23, as a user, published the texts by processing them and incorporating them into her home page. Other users have hence gained access to the works in question through the auspices of defendants 1 up to and including 22. With this, publication or reproduction has been made of the works, by the users of Internet, in the sense of article 1 of the Netherlands Copyright Act of 1912. Defendants sub-sections 1 up to and including 22, the Internet access providers, infringe copyright by making the works available through and on their systems to third parties. In contrast to that put forward by the defendants, the Internet access providers do not play a passive role in the provision of information. They publish, or at least facilitate publication. In any case, the Internet access providers have been aware of the infringement and have deliberately collaborated in this for some time.

2.6. In order to demonstrate that the works in question have been literally quoted, the plaintiffs have made copies of the documents on the Internet and compared them with the confidential OT works which are registered with the American Copyright Office; these are OT-II and OT-III, and these were then submitted to a civil law notary public. The notary's declaration, dated 16 February 1996, confirmed that certain passages were literally quoted. A comparison made of the non-confidential works also shows that large sections have been literally quoted.

2.7. Defendants have wrongly put forward that there is no infringement of copyright as the Fishman Affidavit is, according to them, part of a ruling given in the sense of article 11 of the Netherlands Copyright Act, or, because the work was published by or due to a public body in the sense of article 15b of the Netherlands Copyright Act, or, because the text is a lawful quotation in the sense of article 15a of the Netherlands Copyright Act, or that dissemination of the works is permissible on the grounds of article 10 of the European Convention on Human Rights.

2.8. Article 11 of the Netherlands Copyright Act has no connection with the Court ruling itself, which in this case is not an issue. Article 15b of the Netherlands Copyright Act does not apply to this case as submitting declarations in legal proceedings did not lead to or cause publication in the sense of the law. The right to quote is not applicable as, according to article 15a of the Netherlands Copyright Act, quoting is solely permissible in connection with works which have been lawfully published, which is not the case here. No quotes were made, as a complete copy of the Fishman Affidavit was originally placed on the Internet. The intention of defendant sub-section 23 is clear: the dissemination of the OT works.

2.9. In conclusion, it has been put forward that the European Convention on Human Rights in no way exercises an effect on or impairs the effectiveness of the Netherlands Copyright Act. The copyright protection appealed to by the plaintiffs exercises no influence on the rights to freedom of speech retained by the defendants.

2.10. Defendant sub-section 23 recently replaced the texts constituting the infringement with new texts. However, this does not diminish the plaintiffs' interest in their claim against the defendants. Defendants do not state that they shall refrain from making any further infringement.

The defence

Defendants mounted their defence as follows:

2.11. The Internet access providers dispute that even if it were to be assumed that a subscriber infringes copyright, they could be made liable for this. They solely concern themselves with infrastructure for communications between users and not with the content of information made available to users. They do not receive, as it were, the message, they are only the messenger. The role of Internet access providers may not be compared to that of a publisher but resembles the role played by the telephone company which connects callers, or inter-connects fax and data transmissions.

2.12. No reproduction, as stipulated in article 13 of the Netherlands Copyright Act, was carried out by Internet access providers. The copy was not made available by the Internet access provider but by the end-user. Nor was publication made, as no processing of or addition to the text was carried out by the Internet access providers. The Internet access providers play a passive role.

2.13. The Internet access providers have not committed an unlawful act against the plaintiffs by deliberately profiting from the infringement of copyright against the holder(s) thereof. They exercise no influence on the content of that which is published or reproduced on and through a home page. They are not able to exercise any control on that which passes through their servers. Such censorship would moreover conflict with the constitutional right of subscribers, pursuant to article 10 of the European Convention on Human Rights.

2.14. That any infringement of copyright has been made is also disputed. The only works in connection with which plaintiffs have been able to make it plausible that copyright exists are those of OT-II and OT-III and the work *'Ability'*. In the meantime, these works have been removed from the Internet by defendant sub-section 23. The aforementioned works are currently only available on the Internet in the form of paraphrases which are non-infringing forms.

2.15. Defendant sub-section 23 appeals, where relevant, to the right to quote pursuant to article 15a of the Netherlands Copyright Act, because included in this there is an assessment, announcement and polemic, as meant by that article. The other conditions of the right to quote have also been met. The OT works have been lawfully published, that is, by publication in legal proceedings. The work *'Ability'* appeared in book form and consequently was also lawfully published. The section quoted forms a subordinate part of the total text, making the quotations made by the defendant sub-section 23 not such as to be deemed to be capitalising on those works.

2.16. In conclusion, defendant sub-section 23 appeals to her rights of freedom of speech. Her texts enjoy the exceptional protection afforded by article 10 of the European Convention of Human Rights. It is vital, according to the defendant sub-section 23, that the texts in question are shown (as a warning) as these texts undermine/overthrow the values underpinning a democratic society. In this case, the rights of free speech prevail above and beyond copyright protection, should the latter be deemed to be extant.

3. **Assessing the dispute**

3.1. In order to reach a decision in this case, the assumption is made that plaintiffs, at least one of them, is the copyright holder of the works OT-I and OT-II, and similarly holds the copyright to *'Ability'*.

Defendant sub-section 23

3.2. It has been determined that until very recently the defendant sub-section 23 had included a number of passages taken from the works in question on her home page on the Internet. It has been similarly determined that this defendant drastically reworked her home page after the plaintiffs had more convincingly substantiated their claims to copyright due to pressure to do this having been brought to bear by the defendants. That she currently infringes any copyright held by the plaintiffs has not been made plausible. Inasmuch as she still literally quotes passages from protected works these quotes are covered by the exception of article 15a of the Netherlands Copyright Act, given the context in which these quotes are made.

Plaintiffs have discoursed that in connection with the works OT-II and OT-III the publication thereof is in any case unlawful, but this argument is rejected. It has been determined that (important parts of) these works have been available as part of the Fishman Affidavit, which was part of legal proceedings conducted in the United States of America, where that affidavit was freely available for being perused for a considerable period of time. There is no reason to take the view that this availability for being perused ought not to be deemed to be publication in the sense of article 15a of the Netherlands Copyright Act. The application of article 11 of the Netherlands Copyright Act requiring, as it does the vital question being answered as to whether or not the Fishman Affidavit should be deemed to be part of a ruling issued by a Court, therefore does not need to be answered.

The foregoing means that the claims submitted against this defendant shall be denied, in which connection, it has been borne in mind that it has not be made plausible that there is a real threat that the defendant shall (yet again) infringe the copyrights held by the plaintiffs.

Defendants sub-sections 1 up to and including 22

3.3. In connection with defendants sub-sections 1 up to and including 22, it has to be assumed that they do nothing more than offer an opportunity to publish and that, in principle, they are unable to exercise any influence on, or even be aware of, that which people (are able to) say on the Internet thanks to the access provided to the Internet by the defendants.

In principle, there is therefore no reason to hold them liable for unlawful acts committed by Internet users, for example, infringements of copyrights held by third parties. Liability could be assumed in a situation in which is it unmistakably clear that a publication of an user is unlawful and in which it may be assumed in all reasonableness that this is also known to the access provider, for example, because the access provider has been informed about this. In such a situation it may well be possible that the access provider could be required to take action against the user in question.

In this present case, the plaintiffs have not made it plausible that one of the defendants sub-sections 1 up to and including 22 ought to have taken action. This also applies, see that considered above under 3.2, to action which might have been taken with regard to defendant sub-section 23.

Against this background there is no reason to grant the primary claim nor to uphold the secondary and even more secondary claims based thereon.

3.4. Defendants 8, 10 and 11 did not appear. As the remaining defendants did appear, the case against the parties which failed to appear shall also be deemed to have failed. That stipulated by article 79, section 1 of the Civil Procedural Code in connection with adjournment and subsequent issue of summonses to defendants who/which did not appear, may not be activated within the constraints imposed by summary proceedings.

3.5. The foregoing leads to the conclusion that the claims should be rejected. Plaintiffs shall be required to pay the costs of these proceedings as the Court has found against these parties.

4. **Ruling**

The President of the Court:

Rejects the claims.

Requires the plaintiffs to pay the costs of these proceedings, estimated until now on the part of the defendants sub-sections 8, 10 and 11 at zero, and on the part of the defendant sub-sections 1 up to and including 6, 9, and 12 up to and including 23, as well as on the part of defendant sub-section 7, at NLG 2,830 each, of which NLG 330 is the court charge for this case having been put on the rolls which is due to be paid to the Office of the Clerk of the Court.

This ruling was issued by A.H. van Delden, and read out loud at the public session of the Court held on 12 March 1996 in the presence of the Clerk of the Court.

Suisse

J. CAVALLI & V. SALVADÉ

1. **Les droits concernés**

L'article 10 LDA dispose que l'auteur a le droit exclusif de décider si, quand et de quelle manière son oeuvre sera utilisée. Il s'agit là d'une clause générale. L'alinéa 2 de cet article précise à titre exemplatif les droits dont bénéficie l'auteur. Le législateur suisse n'a pas voulu se limiter à un certain nombre de droits, tenant compte du caractère imprévisible de l'évolution technique. Cela permet donc de couvrir des utilisations d'oeuvres qui n'étaient pas prévues au moment où la loi a été rédigée. La clause générale permettrait d'éviter le recours à l'analogie. Nous avons tout de même essayé ci-après de procéder à cet exercice en classant les nouvelles utilisations dans les catégories traditionnelles du droit d'auteur (droit d'exécution, droit de reproduction, etc.).

> *En vertu de droit suisse, les opérations suivantes sont-elles soumises à certains droits patrimoniaux (comme par exemple le droit de reproduction, le droit de distribution, le droit de communication au public, le droit d'exposer, le droit d'émettre, le droit de transmission par câble, etc.)?*

> ***1.1.** La numérisation d'une oeuvre sur un réseau informatique, par exemple dans un site sur un serveur* ("uploading").

Application de l'article 10 alinéa 2 lettre a LDA: droit de reproduction.

> ***1.2.** Le fait de rendre cette oeuvre accessible à d'autres personnes. Dans l'affirmative, préciser si le caractère étendu ou restreint du groupe a une incidence éventuelle.*

Application de l'article 10 alinéa 2 lettre d LDA, éventuellement cumulativement à la lettre f, dans la mesure où un large groupe de personnes peut voir et entendre les émissions diffusées ou retransmises.

> ***1.3.** La distribution de l'oeuvre, par exemple à destination d'un groupe d'information ou d'un forum.*

Idem.

> ***1.4.** La consultation d'une oeuvre "on-line", par exemple le fait de la diffuser sur l'écran de la personne qui la consulte (ce qui nécessitera aussi vraisembla-*

blement la fixation de cette oeuvre dans la mémoire interne de l'ordinateur de la personne qui consulte).

Idem. On se référera également au droit de reproduction en cas d'introduction de l'oeuvre dans une banque de données: application de l'article 10 alinéa 2 lettre a LDA. Le droit suisse ne connaît pas d'exception au droit d'auteur pour les copies dites "éphémères".

1.5. *Copier l'oeuvre consultée sur un disque dur ou sur une autre forme de support* ("downloading").

Application de l'article 10 alinéa 2 lettre a LDA: droit de reproduction.

1.6. *L'impression de l'oeuvre consultée.*

Idem.

1.7. *La transmission de l'oeuvre à travers le réseau suite à sa consultation.*

Application de l'article 10 alinéa 2 lettre d LDA.

1.8. *La réalisation de* "back-ups", *éventuellement entièrement automatiques, par le fournisseur d'accès.*

Application de l'article 10 alinéa 2 lettre a LDA, éventuellement de l'article 24 alinéa 1 LDA si cette opération vise à protéger l'original de l'oeuvre.

2. Exceptions

Les restrictions au droit d'auteur sont prévues au chapitre 5 LDA. Nous traitons ci-après des exceptions les plus importantes qui peuvent concerner les utilisations en réseau.

2.1. *Les opérations visées aux points 1.1 à 1.8 sont-elles autorisées dans certaines situations, en vertu de dérogations au droit d'auteur, malgré le fait que ces opérations soient soumises en principe à la protection de certains droits économiques (par exemple, les restrictions liées à des fins d'enseignement, ou à l'usage privé)? Dans l'affirmative, prière de bien vouloir détailler.*

L'utilisation de l'oeuvre à des fins privées est la principale restriction au droit d'auteur. L'article 19 alinéa 1, lettres a, b et c LDA distingue entre trois types d'utilisation à des fins privées, celle visée sous la lettre a étant la plus étroite. Dans l'hypothèse où l'utilisation a lieu à des fins personnelles ou dans un cercle de personnes étroitement liées, telles des parents ou des amis (article 19 alinéa 1 lettre a LDA), aucune rémunération n'est due (article 20 alinéa 1 LDA). En revanche, selon l'article 19 alinéa 1 lettres b et c LDA, toute utilisation d'oeuvres par un maître et ses élèves à des fins pédagogiques, ainsi que la reproduction d'exemplaires d'oeuvres au sein des entreprises, administrations publiques, institutions, commissions et organismes analogues, à des fins d'information ou de documentation, est soumise à un droit à rémunération (article 20 alinéa 2 LDA). Il convient en outre de préciser que l'article 20 alinéa 3 LDA introduit une redevance sur les cassettes vierges même si l'utilisation a lieu dans un cadre strictement privé.

D'après l'article 22 alinéa 1 LDA, le droit de faire voir ou entendre simultanément des oeuvres diffusées ne peut être exercé que par les sociétés de gestion agréées. Cette disposition instaure une restriction au droit d'auteur, en ce sens qu'elle prévoit une gestion collective obligatoire. Elle est susceptible de s'appliquer lorsque l'oeuvre est transmise dans un réseau et consultée par un large groupe de personnes (voir chiffre 1.2 ci-dessus, notamment). L'article 22 alinéa 2 LDA prévoit quant à lui qu'il est licite de retransmettre des oeuvres au moyen d'installations techniques destinées à un petit nombre d'usagers. Le législateur avait surtout en vue le cas des antennes collectives desservant des immeubles plurifamiliaux, qui permettent aux habitants de recevoir des émissions de télévision. Toutefois, on pourrait aussi imaginer que cette exception trouve application lorsque des oeuvres sont diffusées d'une manière ou d'une autre et retransmises par un réseau informatique destiné à un petit nombre de personnes.

Les articles 26 et 28 LDA permettent des restrictions au droit d'auteur concernant les catalogues de musées, d'expositions, de ventes aux enchères ainsi que pour les compte-rendus d'actualité. Dans ces cas, l'utilisation des oeuvres est licite.

> **2.2.** *Le droit suisse prévoit-il des exceptions spécifiques concernant ces opérations à propos d'oeuvres protégées par le droit d'auteur qui sont utilisées sur réseaux? Y a-t-il eu des discussions sur la nécessité d'introduire de pareilles exceptions spécifiques? A votre avis, pareilles exceptions particulières devraient-elles être appliquées à certaines situations spécifiques?*

La législation nationale ne prévoit pas d'exceptions spécifiques concernant la seule utilisation des oeuvres sur un réseau. Il n'y a pas actuellement de discussions en cours à ce sujet. A notre avis, il n'y a pas lieu de développer de telles exceptions dans ce cas particulier, sous peine de voir le droit d'auteur perdre de sa signification face à l'évolution technique.

3. Licences

> **3.1.** *Existe-t-il des problèmes spécifiques pour les diffuseurs d'informations qui souhaitent obtenir l'autorisation de reproduire et de diffuser des oeuvres existantes? Par exemple, dans l'hypothèse où le droit d'auteur a été cédé à un éditeur avant que la numérisation sur réseau ne devienne possible ou réalisable, pourra-t-on déterminer clairement si les droits liés à l'utilisation du réseau sont détenus par cet éditeur ou s'ils appartiennent encore à l'auteur?*

L'article 16 alinéa 2 LDA prévoit que, sauf convention contraire, le transfert d'un des droits découlant du droit d'auteur n'implique pas le transfert d'autres droits partiels.

De même, dans les dispositions de droit transitoire de la loi, l'article 80 alinéa 2 LDA dispose que, sauf stipulation contraire, les contrats relatifs à des droits d'auteur ou à des droits voisins conclus avant l'entrée en vigueur de la loi ne s'appliquent pas aux droits instaurés par la nouvelle législation. En d'autres termes, si le contrat est muet, les droits concernant de nouvelles utilisations restent sous le contrôle de l'auteur.

3.2. Existe-t-il des dispositions spécifiques permettant aux diffuseurs d'informations d'obtenir facilement l'autorisation de reproduire et de diffuser des oeuvres existantes? Par exemple, existe-t-il un système de licence légal ou contractuel qui couvre ces opérations?

Les droits définis sous le chiffre 1 ("Les droits concernés") s'appliquent. Il n'existe pas de facilités particulières, ni de licences obligatoires ou légales à l'égard des nouveaux moyens techniques.

3.3. Existe-t-il des systèmes de gestion collective des droits d'auteur qui concernent ces droits? Dans l'affirmative, ces systèmes fonctionnent-ils en pratique et ont-ils une couverture suffisante (cela étant, s'appliquent-ils à toutes les oeuvres ou à la plupart des oeuvres répertoriées dans une certaine catégorie d'oeuvres)?

Il existe en Suisse cinq sociétés de gestion collective de droits d'auteur et de droits voisins:
- SUISA pour les droits des auteurs d'oeuvres musicales,
- PROLITTERIS pour les droits des auteurs d'oeuvres littéraires et plastiques,
- SUISSIMAGE pour les droits des auteurs d'oeuvres audiovisuelles,
- La Société Suisse des Auteurs (SSA) pour les droits des auteurs d'oeuvres dramatiques ainsi que pour les auteurs d'oeuvres audiovisuelles, et
- SWISSPERFORM pour les droits voisins.
- SUISA représente la quasi-totalité du répertoire musical mondial, alors que les sociétés gérant d'autres catégories de droits ne sont pas forcément dans la même situation. L'article 2 LDA donne une liste exemplative des oeuvres protégées par le droit d'auteur. Il n'existe pas de société spécialisée pour la gestion des droits d'auteur exploités sur un réseau. Les sociétés existantes ont en revanche la possibilité d'intervenir dans la mesure où elles le jugent utile.

4. Responsabilité

Les articles 61 et suivants LDA régissent les actions civiles qui sont à la disposition des auteurs. A noter en particulier que l'article 62 alinéa 2 LDA réserve les actions intentées en vertu du Code des Obligations (CO) qui tendent au paiement de dommages-intérêts, à la réparation du dommage moral ainsi qu'à la remise du gain selon les dispositions sur la gestion d'affaires. Les articles 67 et suivants LDA contiennent des dispositions pénales.

Il est évident que les personnes qui contreviennent aux dispositions sur le droit d'auteur en transmettant ou en reproduisant des oeuvres sur réseau seront responsables. Cependant, une action pour violation du droit d'auteur peut-elle être intentée à l'encontre des personnes mentionnées dans les situations suivantes?

***4.1.** Le diffuseur d'informations sur le site duquel une oeuvre a été diffusée par une personne inconnue.*

En principe, la responsabilité n'est pas engagée. Des cas particuliers pourraient être réservés.

***4.2.** Le fournisseur d'accès qui détient le serveur sur lequel une oeuvre a été illégalement diffusée par un diffuseur d'informations.*

Oui, en principe. Au niveau civil, la responsabilité du *"services provider"* pourrait être engagée solidairement avec celle de l'*"information provider"* (articles 50 et 51 CO). Il faudrait cependant que le *"services provider"* ait commis une faute intentionnelle ou par négligence. Sur le plan pénal, une faute intentionnelle est nécessaire pour que la responsabilité soit engagée.

***4.3.** Quelle est l'incidence de* "back-ups" *qui incluent une oeuvre illégalement diffusée, et qui sont réalisés automatiquement par le fournisseur d'accès?*

Cet élément pourrait encore aggraver la faute.

***4.4.** Un fournisseur d'accès a-t-il l'obligation de prendre certaines mesures de précaution (comme par exemple, rappeler au diffuseurs d'informations leurs obligations résultant de la législation sur le droit d'auteur, examiner les transmissions susceptibles de constituer une infraction aux dispositions sur le droit d'auteur, conserver un relevé de tout enregistrement et consultation, etc.)?*

Dans le droit actuel, on ne trouve, à notre connaissance, aucune disposition réglant cette question.

***4.5.** Le fournisseur d'accès au réseau, pour avoir transmis sur réseau une oeuvre en cours de consultation.*

La responsabilité civile solidaire peut être engagée dans la mesure où la personne concourt à la violation des droits. Au surplus, voir chiffre 4.2 ci-dessus.

***4.6.** Quelle est l'incidence du fait que le fournisseur d'accès au réseau a eu connaissance du fait que certaines irrégularilés peuvent survenir: considérant, de surcroît, qu'il est techniquement possible de contrôler les transmissions en vue de détecter les éventuelles transmissions illégales?*

Ici également, si la personne a été renseignée, cela peut aggraver sa faute en cas de violation des droits (pour autant bien entendu que l'on puisse en avoir des preuves).

United States of America

J.C. Ginsburg & A.G. Kaplan

1. Rights which are involved

Under United States law, are the following acts subject to certain economic rights (such as e.g. the reproduction right, distribution right, public performance right, display right, broadcasting right, cable transmission right, etc.)?

1.1. *The storage of a work on a network computer, e.g. in a site on a server ('uploading').*

Under US law, storage on a network computer is a reproduction subject to the reproduction right in 17 USC § 106(1).

1.2. *Making that work available to others. If so, please specify whether it is relevant if it is made available at large or to a restricted group only.*

Depending on the facts involved, making the work available to others may be a reproduction, the distribution of copies, a public performance or a public display subject to the rights enumerated, respectively, in 17 USC § 106(1, 3, 4, 5). If the work is made available to a restricted group only, the dissemination might not be considered to effect a *public* performance or display; to the extent it would be considered a reproduction, dissemination to a restricted group might, in certain circumstances, be deemed a fair use.

1.3. *Distribution of the work, e.g. to a newsgroup or a forum.*

See response to 1.2.

1.4. *On-line consultation of the work, i.e. having it displayed on the consulting person's monitor (this will probably also require temporary fixation of that work in the consulting person's computer's internal memory).*

This may be a reproduction or a public performance subject to the rights in 17 USC § 106(1) or (4), respectively.

1.5. *Copying the consulted work on a hard disc or other media ('downloading').*

This is a reproduction subject to the reproduction right in 17 USC § 106(1).

1.6. *Printing the consulted work.*

See response to 1.5.

1.7. *Transmission of the work through the network in the course of it being consulted.*

The transmission is probably a public performance (as defined in 17 USC § 101) subject to the public performance right in 17 USC § 106(4). It may also be a reproduction. Pending legislation would clarify that distribution of a work by means of transmission is also an act that comes within the scope of 17 USC § 106(3), the distribution right. See S. 1284 and H.R. 2441, 104th Cong., 1st Sess. (1995) (NII Copyright Protection Act of 1995).

1.8. *Making back-ups, perhaps fully automatic, by the services provider.*

This is the making of a reproduction subject to the reproduction right in 17 USC § 106(1). Depending on the facts, it might be considered a fair use, as described in 17 USC § 107, and therefore not an infringement.

For further discussion of the issues in question 1 above, see Jane C. Ginsburg, *Putting Cars on the 'Information Superhighway': Authors, Exploiters, and Copyright in Cyberspace,* 95 *Columbia Law Review* 1466, 1475-87 (October 1995). See also *Intellectual Property and the National Information Infrastructure: The Report of the Working Group on Intellectual Property Rights* (the US 'White Paper') (September 1995), at 63-72, 213-20 (iitf.doc.gov; http://www.uspto.gov.).

2. Exceptions

2.1. *Will any of the acts, mentioned under 1.1-1.8, although in principle covered by certain economic rights, nevertheless be permissible in some situations under existing restrictions to copyright (e.g. restrictions for educational purposes, or for private use)? If so, please give details.*

Depending on the facts, it is possible that fair use or some of the exemptions of certain performances and displays in 17 USC § 110 will excuse the acts described in question 1. Note that on its face, fair use as codified in 17 USC § 107 could apply to acts beyond reproduction. The Conference on Fair Use (CONFU) has been meeting for approximately 18 months in an attempt to determine 'guidelines' for fair use in the area of on-line education. These guidelines are being negotiated by groups representing libraries, educators and authors. If an agreement is reached, the guidelines would be equivalent in the NII context to those formulated shortly before enactment of the 1976 Copyright Act between rights holders and educational users in relation to several other types of works.

2.2. *Does United States law provide for special exceptions regarding such acts in respect to network use of copyright works? Has there been any discussion about the need to implement such special exceptions? In your opinion, should such special exceptions be developed for certain specific situations?*

No. As of the date of this response, US law does not provide for special exceptions in respect to network use of copyrighted works. There has been some discussion about this. See the US White Paper, at 73-100, 225-28. The Working Group was concerned that the public should be able to browse and study on-line works in schools and libraries as they can browse books. In our opinion, there should be continued discussion as to whether the fair use doctrine should encompass some notion of 'fair browsing' of material disseminated on open computer networks.

3. **Licensing**

3.1. *Are there special problems for information providers who want to acquire permission to upload and distribute existing works?* E.g., *if the copyright has been transferred to a publisher before networking became possible or feasible, will it be clear whether the networking rights are owned by that publisher or still by the author?*

There is a problem defining the exclusive rights in this area and some publishers have taken the position that network rights are part of the grant of first publication rights. This is a very controversial issue in the US as to which there is on-going litigation. See *Tasini v. New York Times*, an action filed in December 1993 by a journalist against a number of primary print publishers. The action is pending in the Federal Court for the Southern District of New York. It should be noted, however, that as a result of the work-made-for-hire doctrine in the United States, all rights in certain types of works are often consolidated in large entities, such as major periodicals or motion picture producers, in contrast to individual authors.

3.2. *Are there special facilities for information providers who want to acquire permission to upload and distribute existing works?* E.g. *is there any system of statutory or compulsory licensing that will cover these acts?*

There are not any special facilities as yet but the US Copyright Office is working on the development of an automated clearance system. The US White Paper did not recommend any new compulsory licenses with regard to these acts.

3.3. *Are there any systems for collective administration of copyright which deal with these rights? If so, do those systems function in practice and do they have sufficient coverage (that is, will they be applicable for all or most of the works in a certain category of works)?*

There are some systems for collective administration of copyright dealing with these rights that are already in place and new systems are being developed. The American Society of Media Photographers has developed a mechanism (the Media Photographers Copyright Agency) to clear rights for the use of photographs on-line, with payment going to the photographers and not to the publishers. The National Writers

151

Union has established a division (the Publication Rights Clearing House), which will be operational soon, to deal with database reprints of texts owned by individual authors. A collective agreement has been signed with the UnCover Company which is being sent to author members of the Union. As of this date, about fifty authors have enrolled. Similarly, the Authors Guild, the American Society of Journalists and Authors, the Dramatists Guild and the Association of Authors' Representatives have announced the formation of The Authors Registry, Inc. to provide a simple accounting system for paying royalties to registered authors. The Registry, established in large part because of the explosion of electronic publishing but also involving royalties for photocopying, will work with the Copyright Clearance Center, the collective licensing organization for photocopying, to provide for compatibility with CCC's system.

With regard to music performing rights organizations, ASCAP and BMI have developed blanket licences covering all of the music in their respective repertories for computer online services, electronic bulletin boards and Internet sites. ASCAP's experimental licence permits a licensee to elect from among four possible rate schedules the one that best meets its needs. SESAC is in the process of developing such a licence which it hopes will be finalized in the spring of 1996.

4. Liability

It is evident that persons who infringe copyright by up- or downloading will be liable. However, can action for copyright infringement also be taken against the mentioned persons in the following situations?

4.1. *The information provider on whose site a work has been uploaded by an unknown person.*

The question posed seems inconsistent with the definition of 'information provider' as set forth in the questionnaire. If it refers to the person exploiting an individual 'site', the rationale of the *Netcom* case, described below, would seem to cover this person as well.

4.2. *The services provider who owns the server on which a work has been infringingly uploaded by an information provider.*

This is the subject of considerable controversy with which the courts are just beginning to grapple. In the recent case *Religious Technology Center v. Netcom On-Line Communications Services*, 907 F. Supp. 1361 (N.D. Cal. 1995) (hereafter *Netcom*), the court held that the operator of a computer bulletin board service (BBS) and an Internet access provider may be contributorily liable for infringement of copyright if they either knew or should have known that copyrighted works were uploaded without authorization and they refused to remove them. But since there was no allegation that the operator of the BBS and the Internet access provider took any affirmative action that resulted directly in the copying of plaintiff's works (other than setting up a system where messages were automatically forwarded onto the

Internet and copies were temporarily stored on the system), they were not directly liable for copyright infringement. With regard to vicarious liability, the court said it would be necessary to show that the defendants (1) have the right and ability to control the infringer's acts and (2) receive a direct financial benefit from the infringement. When a fixed fee is paid by subscribers to the operator of the BBS and the Internet access provider and the amount of the fee is not affected by the content of the postings, the *Netcom* decision held this claim would fail. See also on this subject the US White Paper, at 109-24, and the Ginsburg article, cited *supra* at the end of question 1, at 1492-94. Both of these present arguments in favor of the copyright infringement liability of the service provider which, having a direct relationship with its subscribers, is in the best position to know and stop infringing activities. They recognize, however, that service providers may vary in size, structure and the role they play in the process and therefore no one rule may be appropriate across the board at this time.

> ***4.3.*** *Does it make any difference if that services provider makes automatic back-ups which include the infringingly uploaded work?*

It could be argued that this reproduction strengthens the case for direct copyright infringement. In the *Netcom* case, discussed in section 4.2, it was pointed out that, unlike the BBS in *Playboy Enterprises Inc. v. Frena*, 839 F.Supp. 1552 (M.D. Fla. 1993), *'Netcom does not maintain an archive of files for its users. Thus, it cannot be said to be 'suppl[ying] a product.' In contrast to some of its larger competitors, Netcom does not create or control the content of the information available to its subscribers; it merely provides* access *to the Internet, whose content is controlled by no single entity. Although the Internet consists of many different computers networked together, some of which may contain infringing files, it does not make sense to hold the operator of each computer liable as an infringer merely because his or her computer is linked to a computer with an infringing file. It would be especially inappropriate to hold liable a service that acts more like a conduit, in other words, one that does not itself keep an archive of files for more than a short duration.'* (907 F.Supp. at 1372.)

> ***4.4.*** *Is a service provider required to take certain precautionary measures (such as reminding information providers of their obligations under copyright law, scanning uploaded subject matter for possible infringements, keeping a log on all uploading and consultations, etc.)?*

The *Netcom* decision did not suggest that a service producer must take such precautionary measures. If servers were, for example, *'responsible for screening all messages coming through their systems, this could have a serious chilling effect on what some say may turn out to be the best public forum for free speech yet devised'.* (*Netcom*, 907 F.Supp. at 1377-78.) But see the US White Paper, at 124: *'Implementation of preventative measures, compliance with the law, and development of technological mechanisms to guard against infringement must be encouraged. Service providers should have incentive to make their subscribers more aware of copyright law and to react promptly and appropriately to notice by copyright owner that infringing material is available on their systems. Service providers should make clear that infringing activity is not tolerated on the system and reserve the right to remove infringing material or disconnect the subscriber who participated in the placement of it on the system.'*

4.5. *The networking services provider, for transmitting the work through the network in the course of it being consulted.*

See response to question 4.2.

4.6. *Does it make any difference if that networking services provider has been informed that certain infringements may take place; assuming, moreover, that it would be technically feasible to monitor transmissions in order to detect potentially infringing transmissions?*

This might affect a decision on the issue of contributory infringement. See response to question 4.2.

Contributions des membres du panel

J. Corbet:

Il n'y a pas très longtemps, certains prêchaient le chambardement radical du droit d'auteur pour l'adapter aux besoins de la société de l'information, voire même sa suppression pure et simple. Aujourd'hui les esprits se sont calmés et on se rend compte que le droit d'auteur est parfaitement capable de faire face aux problèmes de la société de l'information, et qu'il suffit d'y apporter quelques adaptations et précisions. Pour ce faire, le point de départ est évidemment l'identification des droits concernés par les nouvelles formes d'exploitation propres à la société d'information. C'est l'objet de cette première séance de travail, pour lequel nous disposons de l'excellent rapport général du professeur Spoor, que nous venons d'écouter, et qui a fait une synthèse remarquable des problèmes qui se posent et des solutions que les différentes législations nationales y apportent ou cherchent encore.

Pour orienter les débats, je vous propose de classer les questions en trois groupes: le droit matériel, les contrats et les sanctions.

Le droit matériel

Un large consensus semble se développer pour considérer:
- que la numérisation d'une oeuvre est une reproduction;
- que le chargement d'une oeuvre dans la mémoire d'un serveur est une reproduction;
- que la transmission de l'oeuvre par le réseau est une communication; et
- que la réalisation d'une copie à la réception, soit électronique, soit graphique, est une reproduction.

Il est vrai qu'aux États-Unis, la transmission semble pouvoir être considérée comme une communication, mais également comme une distribution de copies. Pour clarifier cette situation, le Livre blanc publié par le *Working Group on Intellectual Property Rights* propose de préciser la définition de la transmission de copies équivalente à la transmission d'une communication. Il a déjà été observé que ce raisonnement est quelque peu circulaire, parce que la transmission serait une distribution et une distribution serait, entre autres, une transmission (L. Nemschoff, *"The Shape of Things to Come: US Policy-makers Look at Cyberspace"*, (1996) 3 *Ent. L.R.* 103) mais quoi qu'il en soit, le Livre blanc ne dit pas qu'une transmission n'est pas une communication. Les seuls problèmes qui subsistent dans ce domaine concernent le caractère public de la communication et les exceptions.

Généralement, une communication est publique lorsqu'elle est faite en dehors du cercle de famille. Une transmission accessible à un nombre indéterminé de destinataires, est donc publique. Le fait que les destinataires ne reçoivent pas la transmission simultanément, comme dans le cas de la radiodiffusion, est irrelevant (cfr. La Haye, 1er décembre 1994, *AMI* 1995, 51; Cour Suprême Autriche, 27 janvier 1987, *EIPR* 1987, D-159). En ce qui concerne les exceptions, deux questions doivent retenir l'attention. Le régime de la copie privée, autorisée dans le cadre d'une licence légale, est connu dans la plupart des pays, en tout cas en Europe. Mais ce régime convient-il aux copies réalisées à la réception d'une transmission par réseau? Autre question: faut-il prévoir des exceptions spécifiques pour la transmission par réseau, ou faut-il estimer que les exceptions existantes suffisent?

Les contrats

Il ne sera pas question ici des problèmes de droit international privé, qui feront l'objet d'une autre séance de travail. Les problèmes à examiner sont surtout d'ordre pratique. Comment conclure des contrats, avec qui et à quelles conditions?

Une première question concerne la titularité des droits. Les anciens contrats d'exploitation comportent-ils le droit d'effectuer ou d'autoriser la transmission par réseau, mode d'exploitation inconnu lors de la conclusion des contrats? Dans la plupart des pays, la législation indiquera une réponse négative, mais souvent cette législation est récente et la question restera posée pour les contrats antérieurs. Sans doute la transmission par réseau ne sera pratiquement possible que sous le couvert de licences globales délivrées par des sociétés de gestion collective. Pour être efficace, il faudra que cette gestion soit réellement collective et que l'exploitant puisse s'adresser idéalement à un "guichet unique". L'alternative des licences légales est rejetable; c'est d'autant plus le cas pour la transmission par réseau qu'il est actuellement impossible d'en évaluer les conséquences économiques pour l'exploitation des oeuvres. D'ailleurs, ni le Livre vert de la CCE, ni le Livre blanc du *Working Group* aux États-Unis ne les envisagent.

Les sanctions

C'est dans ce domaine que semblent se poser les problèmes les plus difficiles. Le problème essentiel est celui de la responsabilité des différents opérateurs intervenant dans la transmission par réseau. La responsabilité du fournisseur de matériel, soit qu'il le charge lui-même sur son *site*, soit qu'il en autorise le chargement par des tiers, ne paraît pas faire de doute. Plus délicate est déjà la responsabilité de l'opérateur d'un serveur. Le nombre des sites possible sur un serveur en rend le contrôle difficile, sinon impossible, ce qui incite les opérateurs de serveurs à se déclarer irresponsables. Ils se comparent à des sociétés de télécommunications, lesquelles échappent en principe à toute responsabilité concernant les communications par leurs réseaux.

Cependant, des serveurs ont déjà été condamnés aux États-Unis (*Playboy v. Frena*, 839 F. Supp. 1552 - MD Fla 1993; *Sega v. Maphia*, 857 F. Supp. 679 - ND Cal. 1994). Mais d'autres décisions sont moins claires (*Religious Technology Center v. Netcom*,

907 F. Supp. 1361 - ND Cal. 1995). Le Livre blanc du *Working Group* n'accepte pas l'irresponsabilité du serveur. Il suggère plusieurs solutions que les serveurs pourraient mettre en pratique pour faire face à leurs obligations, telles que des licences collectives, des assurances, des garanties à fournir par les fournisseurs de matériel, la surveillance technique des sites, la fermeture d'un *site* reproduisant du matériel illicite. La concrétisation de telles solutions dans la législation mérite d'être examinée.

La responsabilité du fournisseur d'accès au réseau est encore plus incertaine. Son activité se rapproche le plus de celle d'une société de télécommunications. Leurs possibilités d'action contre des communications illicites sont très limitées. Un aspect de la question de la responsabilité, la responsabilité pénale, mérite l'attention. L'on sait que la responsabilité pénale se différencie de la responsabilité civile par la présence de l'intention doleuse. Aux États-Unis, l'affaire *La Macchia* (871 F. Supp. 535 - D. Mass. 1994) a incité le *Working Group* dans son Livre blanc à proposer de remplacer le critère de l'intention doleuse par le critère de l'importance du préjudice (valeur pénale dépassant les 5.000 USD). Il est clair qu'une telle proposition peut avoir des conséquences considérables, et il faut se demander si cela est souhaitable.

J.M. Gutton:

Ni juriste, ni professeur, je n'ai nulle prétention d'analyser les "droits économiques concernés" en matière de transmissions numériques et au regard des nouvelles possibilités qu'elles offrent.

Je vous laisse donc le soin de vous exprimer sur:
- ces droits économiques,
- les actes concernés,
- le droit de communication publique, et
- la responsabilité des fournisseurs d'accès.

Je dirai néanmoins d'emblée que le droit de communication publique s'applique, selon nous, à la transmission numérique comme il s'applique au domaine analogique. J'exprimerai mon expérience pratique de la gestion des droits au regard des nouvelles techniques numériques et ce pour les seules images fixes, intervenant majeur de ces nouveaux supports. Nous avons, tout à la fois, à faire face à des problèmes, et à des difficultés. Nous avons une pratique et surtout nous disposons, espérons le, d'une solution.

Problèmes

Premier problème: cette conversion des données en langage binaire a pour première conséquence les capacités sans cesse accrues des supports en terme de stockage d'oeuvres protégées, la multiplicité des supports et la multiplicité de l'exploitation

et ce du réseau au multimédia. Il en résulte:
- une dématérialisation, une désacralisation de l'oeuvre par compression, couplage interactivité, d'où un risque de brouillage des frontières classiques et des concepts du droit d'auteur, et
- une exploitation, une commercialisation d'oeuvres sans support tant sur les lieux de ventes qu'à domicile par la transmission en réseau à destination d'ordinateurs, interactivité et *pay-per-view*, téléchargement.

Deuxième problème: le piratage qu'autorisent numérisation, scannage, copie privée etc. semblent bien malmener le droit d'auteur.

Troisième problème: la méconnaissance générale du droit d'auteur par les informaticiens;
- le vrai problème est pour nous, matériellement, d'appréhender, de contrôler,
- le vrai problème est pour nous le respect de l'intégrité de l'oeuvre.
Néanmoins, ces mises à l'épreuve du droit d'auteur n'ont pas, selon nous, de raison d'être: il ne nous apparaît nullement qu'il soit besoin de remettre en cause le système actuel. Ses facultés d'adaptation ont fait et continuent de faire leurs preuves.

Une pratique

Nous sommes depuis plusieurs années confrontés à l'épanouissement des technologies nouvelles et ce, avec un succès très variable. Nous y faisons face avec un décalage dans le temps, certes, car inhérent à la nature des choses, à la nature humaine. Toutefois, en droit, le problème nous semble, excusez m'en, relativement simple. En droit, la protection conférée par le droit d'auteur ne peut, selon nous, en aucun cas être subordonnée ou substituée à des exigences liées au respect des systèmes techniques. Quels que soient les supports, les principes sont les mêmes: toute nouvelle technique (du multimédia aux "réseaux" - Internet ou services commerciaux en ligne) est un nouveau support impliquant:
- une acte de communication publique,
- une reproduction, et
- un accord de l'auteur pour la transmission numérique de l'oeuvre, accord de l'auteur qui exerce son droit exclusif.
La différence, pour nous, tient beaucoup plus au nombre d'oeuvres concernées et à leur *contrôle*.

Transmission en réseau: la grande incertitude

Là, le culturel a bon dos car, à ce jour, tout est libre d'accès, on n'est pas censé vendre de l'information, on a donc pas a payer et, je dois le dire, nous n'avons pas trouvé nos marques en terme financier. Le *WEB* actuellement n'est pas rentable et rien ne se négocie vraiment. Qui plus est, nos sociétés sont contraintes, la plupart du temps, à agir en aval et non en amont.

Les principaux problèmes sont: *la territorialité:* un même site hébergé, abrité par des serveurs différents sur des territoires et législations différentes. *Les interlocuteurs:* il faut les retrouver! Les sites naissent et disparaissent, d'où la nécessité de les fixer physiquement, de savoir à qui s'adresser. *Les recherches:* on doit s'en remettre à des moteurs de recherche pour les sites, ce sur un nom, un concept.

Il est donc difficile de cerner les utilisations périphériques (publicitaires par exemple) car elles ne sont pas identifiées sur les sites (exemple: BMW, Dali). Enfin, si les musées, quant à eux, demandent des autorisations, ils n'ont pas les moyens de payer.

Multimédia: la gestion fonctionne relativement bien

Que le multimédia (CD-ROM) soit une oeuvre collective (cf. *ante* encyclopédie) ou de collaboration (cf. *ante* film) ne change rien pour l'image fixe. Nous ne sommes pas des co-auteurs.

Deux questions se posent. *(1)* Si l'oeuvre préexistante est reproduite sur un nouveau support quand cette oeuvre est déjà reproduite sur papier, faut-il une nouvelle autorisation, et ceci d'autant plus qu'il y a le problème du droit moral, faut-il de nouveaux droits? Pour un CD par exemple. Pour nous, oui, sans ambiguïté. Pour certains, non (cf. Encyclopédie Bordas!). Il est pour moi, je le souligne, fortement étonnant que certains aient écrit qu'aucune autorisation n'est requise. *(2)* Les artistes multimédia (infographistes) sont-ils des co-auteurs? Ce n'est pas de l'image fixe, mais il nous apparaît que ceux-ci peuvent relever de nos répertoires et se voir appliquer le droit d'auteur. On a, à cet effet, deux cas de figure: (a) il s'agit d'une oeuvre collective: on revient à l'image fixe avec une rémunération forfaitaire, (b) il s'agit d'une oeuvre de collaboration: rémunération proportionelle à l'exploitation.

En droit, un problème essentiel est celui du respect du droit moral de l'auteur. Ces technologies permettent toutes les variables - détails, agrandissements, mutilation, juxtaposition. L'autorisation de l'auteur serait donc encore plus nécessaire que sur les reproductions papier, mais ... d'une mise en oeuvre pour le moins difficile. Une solution est en cours face à la nécessité de rationalisation, d'efficacité des mécanismes d'acquisition et de gestion des droits. La réponse est l'opération de regroupement qui s'opère en France (et ailleurs) avec l'aval de la Commission et naturellement du Livre vert. La réponse est dans le renforcement de la gestion collective, dans l'intérêt de tous, utilisateurs et auteurs. La réponse est SESAM: société nouvelle, guichet unique, qui aura mandat de gérer les droits d'auteur des oeuvres préexistantes et originales reproduites sur ces nouveaux supports, en premier lieu, le multimédia. Si nous n'avons pas attendu la mise en oeuvre de SESAM pour agir, mettre au point des barèmes, des contrats images fixes, gérer vis-à-vis de ces nouveaux supports - du *"off-line"* au *"on-line"* pour la mise en oeuvre de quelques sites - , le salut, nous le savions dès le début, passait par l'unité de gestion des auteurs concernés.

A défaut:
- c'était à terme, quelle que soit notre ténacité, une quasi-impossibilité de faire face, pour faire valoir le droit des auteurs dans ce contexte en perpétuel évolution,
- c'était à terme le passage au second plan de la création individuelle et une

destabilisation du droit d'auteur des auteurs.

SESAM est donc pour nous la réponse appropriée. SESAM regroupe les 5 sociétés françaises SACEM, SACD, SCAM, ADAGP et SDRM. Cette unité sera formalisée, dans les prochaines semaines.

SESAM permettra donc:
- de contrôler l'accès et l'utilisation des oeuvres: négocier les droits de la pluralité des auteurs ne sera plus "le parcours du combattant",
- d'identifier les oeuvres préexistantes dans les différents domaines de la création en ayant accès aux bases de données existant dans les sociétés d'auteurs et, demain, dans le fichier commun qui devra être constitué pour faire le lien avec les systèmes de codification. Cela passe par la mise au point, en cours, de systèmes techniques d'identification et de protection: standardisation, normes uniques etc.,
- mise au point également de tarification adaptée et de clés de répartition interso-ciales,
- perception, répartition,
- contrôle à tous les stades - de la fabrication à l'exploitation - de l'utilisation effective des oeuvres, et
- de lutter contre la contrefaçon.

Enfin, SESAM n'entend pas limiter sa représentivité aux seules sociétés d'auteurs françaises. SESAM est ouvert à tous les autres titulaires de droits: éditeurs, agences photos, autres sociétés d'auteurs étrangères etc. SESAM est ouvert à la transmission numérique. Beaucoup reste à faire mais la voie est, désormais, ouverte.

En conclusion

Le Livre vert a engagé une vaste consultation des parties intéressées. Pour ce qui nous concerne il est indispensable que plusieurs principes soient respectés:
- ne pas subordonner le droit d'auteur aux systèmes techniques: le droit de commu-nication publique s'applique à toute transmission,
- rationaliser au mieux les mécanismes d'acquisition et de gestion des droits, et
- éviter que n'apparaissent des réglementations nationales divergentes et incompa-tibles avec les principes du marché.

Interventions

N. Arcomano:

I would like to make the following remark on the question of liability. The service providers take the position that they cannot know what their subscribers are doing. If, indeed, the service providers are therefore deemed exempt from liability, the copyright owners' recourse will be limited to the pursuit of *individual* network users, whose identities are typically known only to the providers of the services to which they subscribe. This could result in a serious problem for the collecting administration organisations in protecting the rights of their affiliated writers and publishers. Unfortunately, certain courts in the United States have found service providers not liable for infringement, either because they were not directly involved in the unauthorized use or they did not know the unauthorized use was occurring.

A. Sterling:

The interpretation of the phrase 'communication to the public' in articles 11 and 11*bis* of the Berne Convention has been the subject of extensive debate over many decades. The questions giving difficulty include those as to the place of communication, the acts constituting communication, and the definition of 'public'. In the modern context, it is no longer practical to divide communications into those taking place solely by wireless broadcasting and those taking place solely by cabling. Furthermore, old definitions of 'public' are unrealistic in relation to modern methods of dissemination of protected material. The author should enjoy an exclusive right of telecommunication of his/her work, wherever and by whatever means the telecommunication takes place, and the right should embrace the acts of the initiator, the conveyor and the recipient of the signal. As with reproduction, exceptions can be incorporated as appropriate. The reproduction right is not limited to 'reproduction by the public': similarly, the telecommunication right should not be limited to 'telecommunication to the public'. Effective protection of the author requires the granting of a general right, one which avoids the necessity of defining 'public', and which does not bring with it the preceding controversies and uncertainties surrounding the phrase 'communication to the public'.

II

Authenticity of authorship and work

*L'authenticité de la qualité d'auteur
et de l'oeuvre*

Authenticity of authorship and work

A. Dietz[*]

Preliminary remarks

Without doubt the title of, and debate about, the subject of this year's ALAI Study Days in Amsterdam, *i.e. 'Copyright in cyberspace'* or, more concretely, *'Copyright and the Global Information Infrastructure'*, owes much to a number of official documents stemming from both sides of the Atlantic Ocean. This is true, in particular, for the preliminary and the final Report of the Working Group on Intellectual Property Rights entitled *Intellectual Property and the National Information Infrastructure*, established under the chairmanship of Bruce A. Lehman,[1] as far as the United States is concerned. It is certainly also true for the *Green Paper on Copyright and Related Rights in the Information Society*, presented in July 1995 by the Commission of the European Communities.[2] These and other documents stemming from other countries and institutions[3] deal with the whole spectrum of copyright questions and with other intellectual property problems connected with the appearance and use of national or global information infrastructures. It is, however, undoubtedly a special merit of the Lehman Report, the preliminary and the final one, to have put forward, formulated and discussed the problem of authenticity of authorship and work in a very clear manner. This was done, understandably, against a US background, so consequently there is not so much attention for the traditional moral rights problems. It is thus the task of this General Report to establish this relationship in order to understand if and how far the problem of authenticity concerns moral rights questions.

In doing this, I was helped by a number of very comprehensive National Reports, which I received as a response to my questionnaire from the following national groups of ALAI: Belgium (Tiene Vanhyfte and Greet van Bosstraeten), Canada (Éric Franchi and Pierre Emmanuel Moyse), Finland (Rainer Oesch), France (Frédéric Pollaud-Dulian), Italy (Mario Fabiani), Switzerland (Paul Brügger), Sweden (Gunnar Karnell) and, finally, the USA (Maria Pallante). I would like to thank all reporters for their valuable assistance for the development of my own ideas on this subject, including especially their problematic aspects.

In view of the pioneer role of the Lehman Report it was only natural that a reference to the passages on authenticity and digital signatures (still in its preliminary version) was given at the beginning of the questionnaire. It is no surprise then that a number

*) Head of Division, Max-Planck-Institut for Foreign and International Patent, Copyright and Competition Law, Munich, Germany

of the national reporters also referred in one way or another to this American government document. Others rightly referred to the European Green Paper as well, which, in contrast to its American counterpart, did not shy away from dealing with moral rights questions. These are made even an express topic in the European Green Paper[4] whereas the Lehman Report[5] only mentions them shortly in the chapter on the international framework. But why do the American pioneer deliberations on authenticity problems, discussing questions of 'signature' of works as well as questions of checking 'unauthorized modifications' of such works - a terminology which sounds very 'moral' to Europeans - do this without any reference to moral rights? Is this a totally new approach or does it mean discussing moral rights protection without naming it, *i.e.* through the back door? Consequently, we have to ask what is the moral rights relevance of the authenticity debate.

The moral rights relevance of the authenticity debate

Let us begin with some quotations from the Lehman Report, but also from the European Green Paper. Already at the beginning of chapter II, entitled 'Technology', the Lehman Report[6] mentions that content providers must have secure and reliable means for delivering information products and services to customers and that this means that content providers must be confident that the systems developed to distribute these works will be secure and that works placed on these systems will remain authentic and unaltered.[7] In addition to that, technological solutions are mentioned and the Report goes on to state:[8] *'These solutions enable copyright owners not only to protect their works against unauthorized access, reproduction, manipulation, distribution, performance or display, but also serve to assure the integrity of these works and to address copyright management and licensing concerns'.* Even more relevant passages can be found in the sub-chapter of that Report on 'Digital Signatures'[9] where we can read the following: *'Mathematical algorithms can also be used to create digital 'signatures' that, in effect, place a 'seal' on a digitally represented work. Generating a digital signature is referred to as 'signing' the work. The digital signature serves as means for authenticating the work, both as to the identity of the entity that authenticated or 'signed' it and as to the contents of the file that encodes the information that constitutes the work. Thus, by using digital signatures one will be able to identify from whom a particular file originated as well as verify that the contents of that file have not been altered from the contents as originally distributed.'* It is certainly not without interest to contrast these important deliberations with the introductory part of the section on moral rights within the European Green Paper[10] where the following is stated: *'The author's moral rights principally protect his entitlement to object to any unauthorised modification of his work and to claim authorship of it. The work must not be modified without the author's consent, at any rate in a way prejudicial to his honour or reputation. The right to claim authorship prevents anyone else from claiming to be the author of the work.'* Are these 'European' words not an exact expression, in traditional terms of moral rights, of what the American deliberations describe as necessary means for authenticating both the identity of the source and the unaltered state of the content of a work? Once more therefore: is the authenticity debate only a disguised form of a moral rights debate or are we talking about totally different things?

In order to clarify the situation, I think we should begin with a distinction between a work and a (cultural) product. Of course, in the context of copyright or, better, authors' right protection, we are accustomed to think in categories of creations of the mind representing a sort of 'intellectual goods' or sometimes even 'spiritual entities'. As such, however, these goods or entities are as a rule - apart, perhaps, from works of fine art - not yet marketable goods or products. Consequently they have to be transformed into such (cultural) products, such as books, phonograms, videos or multimedia products etc., an activity typically of others than the authors, namely producers of all kinds. It is therefore at the production stage - which, in the case of audiovisual works, can be interwoven with the creative process itself - where commercial interests of producers enter the field. Several of the National Reports answering the questionnaire emphasize, indeed, that the authenticity debate within the Lehman Report is written against the background of commercial interests of producers who in many cases are original copyright owners under American copyright law. By the way, from an economic point of view, such commercial authenticity interests should, at least potentially, have been already present in traditional analogue environments. Indeed, the very foundation of copyright has always been legally and in artificially created property rights in specific and identifiable cultural goods or products. Such cultural goods or products can, however, only be sold and otherwise be marketed or licensed when the basic double identity of the good (a) with itself as a specific recognizable entity and (b) with its origin or its (first) owner is guaranteed. The first of the two identity relations concerns, in traditional terms, the integrity of the work, the second its paternity. From this point of view it is rather surprising that the authenticity debate begins only now. This, however, has certainly to do with the fact that digitization makes alteration and manipulation of source and content of works so easy. Nevertheless, it is fascinating to observe that traditional concepts such as the protection of the right of attribution (identity of the entity that authenticated or 'signed' a work) and protection of the integrity of a work (the unaltered contents of a file) are suddenly discovered as a commercial interest; in other words, a sort of quasi-moral right of producers is postulated here. The question, however, is on what legal basis such a right can be or, perhaps, already is established.

Against the background of the traditional concept of inalienable moral rights of authors, we must be aware that such a concept of a quasi-moral right of producers also represents certain dangers, as the Belgian and the French National Reports more than once explain. Such dangers exist not only in the sense that the quasi-moral right of producers could all too easily replace those inalienable rights of authors, but particularly also in the sense that certain technical means to guarantee authenticity demands of producers could have a direct and negative effect on authors' moral rights themselves. As a typical example of case-law the French National Report at this point cites the *tv logo* case, where the inclusion of a tv logo, without consent of the authors of the audiovisual work concerned, has been condemned by a court.[11] Another example also cited by the French reporter, concerns practices of press (picture) agencies who protect themselves against acts of piracy by distributing unfocused, and consequently low quality, pictures first. New methods of digital marking seem to avoid at least the dangers of the second kind. But, apart from these tensions between authors' interests and producers' interests, for which we have also to find solutions, are moral rights for producers a feasible concept?

Moral rights for producers?

Some of you may remember that three years ago, not far from here, I discussed legal principles of moral rights in civil law countries, also in the framework of a General Report for an ALAI Congress.[12] One of the elements introduced in that Antwerp Report was the opposition between the dualistic and the so-called monistic or synthetic interpretations of copyright as a whole as well as the explanation of the relationship between moral rights, on the one hand, and pecuniary rights of authors under both systems, on the other. From a strictly dualistic point of view - and this is once more confirmed by the National Reports stemming from countries with a dualistic tradition such as Belgium, Finland and particularly France, and to a certain degree also Canada - it is a strange idea to relate moral rights' protection to commercial interests of producers, or even authors themselves. Doing this would seem a deviation from the true nature of moral rights, which should be kept pure according to the Finnish report, even if, as the French reporter admits, sometimes a certain utility for the respect of moral rights can be found in the systems of identification and authentification organized by producers.

On the other hand, the so-called monistic - or, better, synthetic - interpretation of copyright, as it prevails in certain Central European countries such as Germany, Austria and Hungary, partly also in Switzerland, starts from the idea that copyright as a whole with all its faculties, comprehensively serves intellectual and moral rights as well as economic interests of authors. It is only a tradition that some of these faculties are called moral rights and others economic or pecuniary rights since, to different degrees depending on different situations, all of these faculties serve all possible interests. As the Swedish reporter sarcastically states: the author's name is that which sells the book.

From this point of view it can easily be understood that protection of authenticity of a work or product intended to guarantee its identity, *i.e.* its source (author/producer) and its integrity, can also be seen as a response to certain pecuniary or commercial interests, basically already of authors themselves. To illustrate this aspect I would like to refer to a very recent case decided by the Munich Court of Appeals in the so-called *Mens' Magazine* case.[13] In that case, parts of a scientific book containing some delicate questions of secret services in Germany, had been reprinted in a mens' magazine with the consent of the original book publisher. So far there was no copyright infringement because the author was no longer owner of the publishing rights. The magazine editors, however, had made a number of very serious and deteriorating changes in the text during the process of selection and editing of the relevant parts of the book; the author was even cited as a 'collaborator' of the magazine. What is of interest here, is that the author did not only get a compensation for so-called immaterial or moral damage, but that the court made the additional statement that a material/pecuniary damage was also highly probable for the career interests of the author as a professional and scientific writer with a reputation of seriousness. In other words, the commercial interests of the author had also been damaged, whereby the compensation was exclusively based on the author's 'moral right' of integrity of the work.

Could it not be that, in a digital world with the potentially much greater dangers of manipulation of works, this kind of case will occur much more frequent in the future? Let us look at what the European Green Paper[14] tells us in this respect: *'Moral rights are thus a powerful component in copyright, and to a lesser extent in the rights of performers. One aspect of the information society is that total digitization of works and other protected matter combined with interactivity over networks means that it is becoming easier and easier to transform works, to colourise them, to reduce them and so on. The time is coming when anyone will be able to change the colours in a film, or replace the faces of the actors, and return the modified film to the network. This capacity to change works in whatever way and to whatever extent one likes, is regarded by some as one of the great advantages of digitization. The creators of works, however, are greatly concerned that this technical possibility will be used to mutilate their works, and are asking for their moral rights to be strengthened.'*

If, however, strengthening of the moral rights of authors and/or performers also means, as demonstrated, strengthening of the protection of their commercial and pecuniary interests, could it not also mean that, in view of the easy digital alteration of works or products, producers are also interested, much more than before, in a correct identification of the source and in integrity of the work or product? The difference between genuine moral rights of authors and quasi moral rights of producers would perhaps only lie in the fact that the commercial interest aspect is, as a rule, only incidental and secondary with authors' moral rights, whereas it represents the very essence of the quasi moral rights of the producer. By the way, at least from a monistic or synthetic point of view, we can and should not exclude that even producers fighting for authenticity sometimes do this also on the basis of intellectual interests which they have as producers. But how can we legally construct such a producer's right?

How to construct moral rights of producers?

It is characteristic that the Lehman Report[15] discusses authenticity questions in the chapter on technology, in particular related to technical means of digital signatures, encryption and other techniques. The Report avoids the mentioning of authenticity rights in the strict sense of the word. It rather seems that protection of commercial interests connected with authenticity is only intended indirectly by way of development of standards and the legal prohibition of devices that defeat technological methods of preventing unauthorised use etc. A direct grant of quasi moral rights of attribution of source and against alteration of products is apparently not intended, at least not in the framework of copyright. The situation in Canada appears to be more or less the same. Certainly the American reporter underlines that section 43(a) of the US Lanham Act should already apply to alteration of authorship or false designations of origin in the digital environment; insofar US producers have already attribution and integrity rights. In addition to that, according to the US reporter, authenticity in the Global Information Infrastructure environment is considered a commerce necessity, which by definition does not favour inherent source rights of individual authors or 'content providers', for whom authentication issues exist by contract with licensees if at all. But apart from that special American situation, are there other positive ways to grant protection for authenticity interests of producers?

One possible way would be the derivative one, based on a concept of restricted alienability of moral rights of authors themselves. Such a somewhat more flexible concept was already suggested in the resolution on moral rights, adopted by ALAI as a result of its Congress of Antwerp in 1993;[16] it could even serve as an element of compromise between the copyright and the *droit d'auteur* systems. In that resolution the Executive Committee of ALAI admits *'that a certain flexibility in the application of copyright law with regards to authors' moral rights may be accepted depending on the types of work in question and the methods of its exploitation, but maintains that in all cases the personality of the author, as reflected in the work, must be protected.'* Furthermore, it believes that, although this flexibility *'should also permit authors to include certain clauses in the contracts which they enter into with users of their works, regarding the exercise of their moral rights subject to strict limits, in specifically-determined cases, a prohibition on assignment of moral rights as well as a global waiver of same must in essence be maintained as the basic corner stone of authors' protection, as guaranteed by the Universal Declaration of Human Rights.'* This aspect of flexibility within a general concept of basic inalienability of moral rights is also confirmed by a number of National Reports, in particular the Belgian, Swedish and Swiss ones. The American Report simply states that inalienability of moral rights is a problem in the US copyright context for which economic concerns are the driving force and, furthermore, that contract language varies from assignability to non-exclusivity, with some author attribution issues arising in the context of general attribution for an entire product, coupled with the licensor's right to change or omit individual components of its product, at its discretion.

For European taste the latter goes, of course, much too far, and compromises still seem to be far away. For the moment, however, we are not so much interested in details of the relationship between author and producer. What we discuss here is the question whether elements of the positive content of the author's moral rights can be transferred to producers in order to be exercised by them against third parties. Indeed, in a traditional analogue environment of utilisation of works it happened more often than not that certain elements of moral rights' protection were exercised by publishers and other producers in the name of authors or even in their own name, *e.g.* in cases of stage productions of operas or dramatic works not respecting the integrity of the underlying work. However, in this case the authors themselves always retain the possibility to assert their moral rights, and there is no true or at least no full transfer of rights, but only a sort of trusteeship. Consequently, this derivative way for the establishment of a moral rights position of producers, as hinted at already in the ALAI Resolution, can only function as long as author and producer agree on the basic elements of the authenticity to be defended, *i.e.* attribution of authorship and source as well as integrity of work and product. On the contrary, this way cannot function without difficulties in cases where the producer unilaterally defines his own standards of authenticity, perhaps even by infringing the moral rights of the author himself. The French reporter has several times mentioned and explained this danger, citing, as already mentioned, the *tv logo* case as well as the example of press agencies fixing certain limits for definition and resolution of images they distribute which entails that certain non-authorized reproductions are necessarily of minor quality. Does this, the French reporter asks, not imply a certain disrespect for the distributed work, it is of limited quality? Other ways, such as digital marking, which do not influence the quality of a presentation of the work, therefore appear to be preferable.

Still, the French reporter admits several times that modern means of identification and authentication of works, if not conceived in particular in the interest of protection of moral rights of authors, can have an indirect utility for a better protection of those moral rights. If that is true, one could also conclude that a direct grant of some quasi-moral rights to producers should not, at least not necessarily, deteriorate the moral rights position of authors and, in many cases, even could help them indirectly. Interestingly enough, the idea of granting specific quasi-moral rights to producers of different kinds is not absolutely new, as is also emphasized in the Italian Report. The Italian Copyright Act of 1941, which was, after the Austrian Copyright Act of 1936, one of the first modern copyright acts in the sense that it introduced a special chapter on neighbouring rights, contains an interesting provision on that question. Apart from the exclusive rights and the remuneration right as granted to the phonogram producer by articles 72 and 73 of the Act, that producer, according to article 74(1), is also empowered to oppose any use of a phonogram under conditions which seriously prejudice his industrial interests. In addition to that, the Austrian Copyright Act of 1936 which, in the field of film works, operates a system of *cessio legis*, grants in parallel to the moral rights of the film authors themselves an express quasi moral rights protection to film producers, directed against alterations in the cinematographic work, its title or the name of the film producer.[17]

Also the German legislator of the Copyright Act of 1965, following a recommendation by Prof. Ulmer, made as early as 1953,[18] has introduced a similar right. This was done in the framework of Part III of the Act, concerning special provisions on films, where article 94 regulaties the neighbouring right of the film producer. Article 94(1), second sentence, provides that the film producer shall have the right to prohibit any distortion or abridgement of the video and audio recording which may jeopardize his legitimate interests.[19] Finally, in France and other countries that know the concept of collective works,[20] the producer of such works is considered as first owner of copyright including the moral rights in the work. Even if, according to the position stressed in the French report, the producer could not use this moral right for purely economic interests, the reporter admits that he could be less interested in the integrity of the work than the author is. This, however, depends on the individual situation, as the whole authenticity debate demonstrates. These and other examples (*e.g.* - according to the Dutch majority opinion[21] - moral rights of employers in case of employed authors in Dutch law)[22] demonstrate that cases of granting a sort of moral right to producers of different kinds, if not very frequent, exist for about 60 years. Could a systematisation of this approach in the final result not be in the interest of both, authors and producers, if the necessary guarantees for the moral rights of authors themselves are given to the latter?

The necessary guarantees for the moral rights of authors

In an ideal world, the fact that producers of all kind begin to discover their own authenticity interest should lead to some reduction of the tensions at the old front line between authors defending their moral rights and producers fighting against them. At least theoretically there could be more comprehension on the producers' side for the fundamental necessity of protection of integrity and attribution of works in the same way as of products in a digital environment. This mutual understanding could even lead to a common front line against the dangers of destruction and manipulation of authenticity of work and origin by third parties.

Unfortunately, such an ideal situation does not exist very often; consequently there is no guarantee for, or automatic way to, more comprehension for inalienable moral rights of authors simply because producers discover their own protection needs. As already mentioned, realisation of the latter interests could even, in certain circumstances, represent dangers for the former. A number of National Reports answering have confirmed that there remain problems;[23] it seems even that a systematic weakening of authors' moral rights could sometimes be the intended result. The American Report makes it very clear that inalienability is a problem in the US copyright context for which economic concerns are the driving force. It quotes at this occasion the following passage of the Lehman Report:[24] *'Even among Berne members, the nature and scope of moral rights varies considerably from country to country, but regardless of their scope and extent, moral rights are typically not transferable and sometimes, may not be waived. The fact that these rights are non-waivable may create difficulties for the commercialisation of works in the GII environment. A current report of the multimedia study committee of the Japanese Institute for Intellectual Property suggests that there may be a need either to permit the specific waiver of the right of integrity or to limit its application in the digital world.'* In addition to that, the American Report mentions that, as a matter of commercial convenience and profit orientation, future plans for digital commerce tend towards wholesale assignability, in keeping with recent entertainment industry experience with non-digital commerce. Moreover, the Report quotes, as an example, language from a digital archive licence for photographers, where not only the right to digitize, use, reproduce and modify etc. is granted, but where it is also provided that, as part of the digitization process, elements may be compressed, cropped and/or retouched including colour correction, cloning, presentation of details, removal of incidental dust and dirt, silhouetting, removal of backgrounds and reversal of flopping. On the other hand, the American Report also states that technical means will likely play a key role in insuring authenticity, quoting another Report[21] where it was stated, *inter alia*, that in an open digital environment, verifying the source of a message or document and assuring that it has not been changed was mentioned as a concern in a number of different meetings.[26]

From a continental European point of view this, of course, represents a curious contradiction. What is strived for as protection for cultural products at the producer level is fiercely denied and fought against at the work/author level. In other words, from the producers' perspective third parties will never be allowed to do with their (the producers') product, what the latter themselves want to be free to do with the authors' work. It is evident that such a consequence is inacceptable from a point of view which defends protection of moral and material interests of authors as a human right. This is perhaps also the reason why, as already mentioned, a number of National Reports, such as the Belgian, the Finnish and the Swiss one, would prefer to remain within a traditional concept of moral rights intended to protect intellectual interests and to avoid deviations and weakening that protection. In Canada moral rights never had a real standing and never were really integrated into the copyright system. It is no surprise, finally, that the French Report, in a particular way, insists on the fact that precisely the digital era and the revolution connected with it demonstraties the absolute necessity of the moral rights and that technical systems could never replace them. Legal concepts like moral rights remain thus indispensible, an opinion which is shared not only by the Report of the Sirinelli Commission, cited several times in the French Report, but which corresponds with a majority position in Continental Europe. Still, some differenciations appear necessary, in particular concerning the right of attribution of authorship, on the one hand, and the right of integrity of the work, on the other. In both cases, however, technical means can play a positive role in the future.

As far as the right of attribution is concerned, we find some remarkable elements in the context of what, within the Lehman Report, is called copyright management information.[27] On several occasions, authorship is mentioned as an element of such copyright management information, as the following quotations demonstrate: *'Systems for managing rights in works are being contemplated in the development of the NII. These systems will serve the functions of tracking and monitoring uses of copyrighted works as well as licensing of rights and indicating attribution, creation and ownership interests. And measures should be studied to ensure that systems established to serve these functions are not readily defeated. To implement these rights management functions, information will likely be included in digital versions of a work (i.e., copyright management information) to inform the user about the authorship and ownership of a work (e.g., attribution information) as well as to indicate authorized uses of the work (e.g., permitted use information). For instance, information may be included in an 'electronic envelope' containing a work that provides information regarding authorship, copyright ownership, date of creation or last modification, and terms and conditions of authorized uses. As measures for this purpose become incorporated at lower levels (e.g., at the operating systems level), such information may become a fundamental component of a file or information object.[28] Under the proposed amendment, copyright management information is defined as the name and other identifying information of the author of a work, the name and other identifying information of the copyright owner, terms and conditions for uses of the work, and such other information as the Register of Copyrights may prescribe by regulation - to provide adequate flexibility in the future.'[29]*

Why should we not take this important general statement as starting point for the

173

formulation of a legal rule providing that the right of attribution (the moral right of authors and performers to be named), shall be guaranteed not only against third parties, but also against the producer? Of course, the Lehman Report itself would not go so far since it makes, in addition, the following statement:[30] *'While the proposed amendment does not recruire copyright owners to provide copyright management information, it does require that when such information is included, it be accurate. However, the Working Group encourages copyright owners to include the information to enable consumers to more easily find and make authorized uses of copyright works.'*

We can even understand that, in an American context, such a legal requirement would have meant the introduction of a general attribution right for authors through the back door. Nevertheless, the distance between an encouragement by the government and a legal right does not seem to be unsurmountable, since, as the Lehman Report suggests, accurateness of information is also a public interest. If the public should be protected from false information about who created the work, why should it not also be protected when true information is being withheld without any justification? The result, corresponding with a moral rights position under the Continental European system, could be that, at least as a rule (subject to certain exceptions) the name of the author of a work or of a performer (at least of featuring artists) should always be identified if the author or performer so wishes. Much will depend, of course, on international standards which are discussed and made at this moment,[31] and professional associations of authors should be aware of the interests at stake.

The question of an inalienable and unwaivable moral right of integrity appears to be much more difficult. Let me once more come back to what I already have discussed at the Antwerp Congress, namely the search for a compromise on the basis of a developed and finely tuned system of balancing of interests. We have already mentioned a certain modern tendency, such as recently realised in the Belgian law[32] and explained by the Belgian reporters, namely to be more flexible in terms of inalienability, where specific waivers for specific concrete acts of use are allowed. In addition to that, in a number of countries, in particular also in Belgium, Canada, Italy, Germany and Sweden, the integrity right is from the outset not granted in an absolute way, but is qualified, more or less in the sense of article 6*bis* of the Berne Convention, by the criterium of 'prejudice to the authors, honour or reputation'.[33] The application of this criterium leads to a concept of balancing of interests as it has been developed in a number of cases, *e.g.* by German courts. It means that changes or modifications in the process of exploitation of a work, which would be solely dictated by artistic and aesthetic convictions and concepts of other persons (especially the user of the work) would not be acceptable, whereas those dictated by the concrete technical, financial and circumstantial conditions of the exploitation of the work would have to be taken into consideration in the process of balancing of interests. This is also recognized even in French law in the special case of adaptations of a work, a situation which, under modern conditions, exists more often than one would expect, since adaptation in the technical but not necessarily creational sense of the word appears rather the rule than the exception. Since the situations in various fields, *e.g.* in the book sector, press, the film industry, theater and opera, design and architecture, and multimedia, are so different, ultimately the balance of interests would also have to differ according to a case-by-case analysis.

In addition to that, especially in case of multimedia and new interactive media, moral rights protection against changes and adaptations will not be available as far as the active intervention of the third user of the work or product corresponds to the purpose of the product itself which has been authorized by the author in the exploitation contract. This is true especially in on-line situations. By the way, interactive use of a medium does not change its constituent elements as such, as long as the user does not go beyond what is implicitly allowed. Finally, as far as off-line situations are concerned, if the user of an individual copy of a multimedia product is a consumer or end user acting in his private sphere, the problem of moral rights protection normally does not arise at all, since - apart from very delicate questions of destruction of unique pieces of art - it was never denied that an end user can dispose, manipulate, modify and destroy his copy of the work as he likes, as long as the results of his activities do not reenter the public sphere.[35] Of course, in a digital and interactive environment, this danger of reentry into the public sphere is much greater. One could consequently question this result of irrelevance of moral rights problems. But, still, infringement of the moral right of integrity would only take place when the altered form of the work is fed back to the system or network. By the way, as in case of general copyright infringement, the question of how such infringements can be discovered and sanctioned, is not an easy one, of course. This remains outside of my deliberations. Let me only quote a nice statement of the Swiss reporter, according to whom we can imagine that one day we will have 'Interpol in the skies' controlling the 'passports' of multimedia works.

The most problematic case probably concerns the relationship between authors and performers, on the one hand, and multimedia producers, on the other. It is here that the modern tendencies of wholesale assignability, as described by the American Report, come to the fore as well as far-going grants of the rights to modify, to combine, to remove etc. as the example of an archive licence for photographers states. As already mentioned, as part of the digitization process this licence would allow the following: *'elements may be compressed, cropped and/or retouched, including color correction, cloning, presentation of details, removal of incidental dust and dirt, silhouetting, removal of backgrounds and reversal of flopping'.* It is precisely here that the system of balancing of interests as proposed should be tested, since neither a simple principle of alienability and waivability nor a simple principle of inalienability and non-waivability represent a convincing solution in that situation. We need criteria for in-between solutions, precisely as result of the balancing of interests. One could even imagine a codification of criteria for such a balancing procedure in the same way as the US legislator had incorporated criteria for fair use within the Copyright Act of 1976 (section 107). One of the criteria should, in my opinion, also be the nature and the artistic rank or class of a work, not of course a judgment of its aesthetic value. Critics of such a concept often forget that copyright laws themselves, in a number of fields such as computer programs, film works and architecture, have already established different standards of moral rights protection for different kinds of works.[36] I think that absolute protection against modification of even single words or syllables is justified, *e.g.* in case of a poem but not in case of a short news article. In the same way colorization should not be accepted in case of a highly ambitieus artistic black and white movie, whereas it can be much more acceptable if applied to a purely scientific film, colorized *post festum* simply in order to achieve a better contrasting effect.

Finally, against the background of article 6*bis* of the Berne Convention, moral rights questions are often presented as a minimal concept, apparently only concerning the integrity right and the attribution right. We must not forget, however, that a number of legislations also grants a divulgation right or dissemination right, *i.e.* the right of the author to decide whether, when and how his work will be released to the public. This right will certainly acquire a fundamental new importance in a digital and GII environment, since in view of globally organized information systems and networks the step from the private sphere to the public sphere will often be irreversible, in particular when individual exploitation of works is replaced by collective licensing systems. The fundamental decision on whether to 'go public' or not is an indispensable element of that human rights position of authors, no matter whether they are employed or self-employed authors. This is another case where legal systems working with work-made-for-hire rules or *cessio legis* rules, according to which the employer 'is considered the author'[37] or 'is the first owner of copyright',[38] have conceptual problems and where a transatlantic compromise can be achieved only with great difficulties. But can we say that human rights end at the door of the business building simply because people are in an employment relationship?

Conclusion

The European Green Paper contains a whole sub-chapter on moral rights. But if it underlines the importance and urgence of moral rights questions in a digital environment, it still remains at a preliminary stage of studying the concrete problems connected with them. On the contrary, the Lehman Report discusses in much more detail a number of questions of a moral rights character, in particular questions of authenticity of source and content of a file document, making interesting proposals for guarantees for such authenticity, without expressly relating them to moral rights questions. It was therefore the main task of this General Report to bring the basic ideas of both documents together in order to demonstrate that authenticity problems are in many cases moral rights problems. If, in addition to that, we were prepared to accept that something like quasi-moral rights of producers could also exist and that the latter would not necessarily be to the detriment of traditional moral rights of authors, a first step to a big compromise could already be made. This, however, is only feasible when the necessary guarantees for authors' moral rights continue to exist, mitigated perhaps by a general system of balancing of interests, based on a number of criteria, in particular the class or rank of the work concerned.

A basic mutual understanding appears to be possible at least in case of the attribution right, since public interests are also to be taken into consideration here. The most controversial case remains the right of integrity. Neither a principle of alienability nor a principle of inalienability seem to do justice to the complex interest situation present here. We have to find in-between solutions; the more we are in the field of art, the less we should tolerate unilateral modifications and manipulations made by producers and other work users, if these are not specifically allowed by the authors or performers. Total and abstract waivability of moral rights in advance can therefore not be a solution.

Footnotes

1. Published in July 1994 and in September 1995, respectively, and cited in the text as *'Lehman Report'*. The quotations are taken from the Final Report.
2. COM(95) 382 final; cited in the text as *'European Green Paper'*.
3. See some examples of comparable reports in other countries such as Australia (Copyright Convergence Group, *Highways to Change - Copyright in the new Communications Environment*, Canberra, August 1994); Canada (*Draft Final Report of the Copyright Sub-committee on Copyright and the Information Highway*, March 1995); France (Rapport-Sirinelli, *'Industries culturelles et nouvelles technologies'*, September 1994); Japan (several reports, in particular the *Report on Discussions by the Working Group of the Subcommittee on Multimedia*, Copyright Council, Agency for Cultural Affairs, Japan, February 1995); Sweden (The Olsson-Report to the Swedish Ministry of Justice, 1994). See also the 'Reports on the Reports', written by Dreier (Australia and France), Heath (Japan) and Von Lewinski (Canada), in *GRUR Int.* 1995, 837 *et seq.*, 840 *et seq.*, 843 *et seq.* and 851 *et seq.*, respectively.
4. See Chapter Two, Part Two, Section VII, p. 65 *et seq.*
5. See p. 133 *et seq.*
6. See p. 177.
7. Emphasis on *'remain authentic and unaltered'*.
8. *Op. cit.*
9. *Op. cit.,* p. 187.
10. *Op. cit.,* p. 65.
11. Tribunal de Grande Instance Paris 29 June 1988, *Marchand v. La Cinq, RIDA* No. 138 (October 1988), p. 328.
12. Published in ALAI (ed.), *Le droit moral de l'auteur/The moral right of the author*, Congrès d'Anvers/Congress of Antwerp, 19-24 September 1993, Paris 1995, p. 25 *et seq.* (French text) and 54 *et seq.* (English text); edited version also published in *Columbia-VLA J. of Law & the Arts* Vol. 19, No. 3-4 (1995), p. 189 *et seq.* as well as in *Copyright Reporter (Australia)* Vol. 11, No. 3 (1993), p. 1 *et seq.*
13. See decision of 23 February 1995, *NJW* 1996, p. 135.
14. *Op. cit.,* p. 65.
15. *Op. cit.,* p. 183 *et seq.*
16. See ALAI (ed.), *op. cit.* (*supra* note 12), p. 561.
17. See article 38(2) subject to article 39(3) as well as article 21(1) of the Act.
18. See Ulmer, *'Consultation sur la cinématographie et le droit d'auteur'*, *Le Droit d'Auteur*, 1953, p. 97 *et seq.*, p. 99 and p. 109; *idem*, 'Rapport complementaire sur la cinématographie et le droit d'auteur', *DdA* 1994, p. 108 *et seq.*, p. 112; Ulmer had introduced at this occasion the expression of *'quasi-droit moral'*.
19. See also Sterling, *Intellectual Property Rights in Sound Recordings, Film and Video*, London, 1992, pp. 125, 233 and 366.
20. See, *e.g.*, article L. 113(5) of the French Intellectual Property Code of 1992; article 8 of the Spanish Act on Intellectual Property of 1987.
21. See the references given by Van Lingen, *Auteursrecht in Hoofdlijnen*, 3rd ed., 1990, p. 94; Van Lingen himself is against that solution, and he is right, since this solution means simply replacing moral rights of authors by those of producers.
22. See article 7 of the Dutch Copyright Act of 1912.
23. See generally also Gendreau, 'Digital Technology and Copyright: Can moral Rights Survive the Disappearance of the Hard Copy?', *Entertainment Law Review* 1995, p. 214 *et seq.*, p. 216 *et seq.*; Grosheide, 'De commercialisering van het auteursrecht', *Informatierecht/AMI* 1996, p. 43 *et seq.*, p. 47 *et seq.*
24. *Op. cit.,* p. 146.
25. The National Information Infrastructure Security Issues Forum Draft Report. NII Security: The Federal Role (June 1995).
26. Emphasis on *'verifying the source of a message or document and assuring that it has not been changed'*.
27. *Op. cit.,* p. 235 and p. 191.

28. *Op. cit.*, p. 191.
29. *Op. cit.*, p. 235.
30. *Op. cit.*, p. 235 *et seq.*
31. The French Report is full of examples of ongoing international negotiations on standard making such as MPEG 2 in the audiovisual field, JPEG in the field of photographs, SPIDER in the field of fixed pictures etc. I want to refer to these valuable explanations, but cannot analyse them in detail here.
32. See article 2 § 2 of the Copyright Act 1994, prohibiting only a *'global waiver of future exercise of the inalienable moral right'*.
33. See generally Dietz, *loc. cit.* (*supra* note 12), p. 74 *et seq.* (English text).
34. See generally Dietz, 'Commentary to article 14 of the German Copyright Act' (Nos. 18 *et seq.*), in: Schricker (ed.) , *Urheberrecht, Kommentar*, Munich 1987, p. 265 *et seq.*
35. I exclude, at this moment, the special problem of computer programmes where, at least in most European countries, the possibilities of allowed private use are very restricted, *e.g.* in case of decompilation in order to establish interoperability with other programs.
36. See Dietz, *loc. cit.* (*supra* note 12), p. 76.
37. See Sec. 201(b) of the US Copyright Act.
38. See Sec. 11 (2) of the British Copyright, Designs and Patent Act 1988.

Questionnaire

1. Are there official documents such as the US Green Paper, drafts of new laws or other documents expressly discussing problems of 'authenticity of works and/or authorship' in the multimedia or Global Information Infrastructure (GII) context?

2. If yes, does the discussion or proposal establish a relation with the traditional concept of moral rights, in particular with the paternity right and the integrity right as covered by article 6*bis* of the Berne Convention?

3. If no, what is probably the reason why this relation is not established? Is the authenticity problem a totally new concept independent of traditional solutions of moral rights?

4. Do traditional elements connected with moral rights protection, such as inalienability and protection of seemingly merely intellectual and personal interests, hinder the development of a modern concept of protection of authenticity of work and/or authorship?

5. Can protection by moral rights also serve more than only intellectual or personal interests, in particular also pecuniary interests? Is such an approach facilitated in your country by doctrinal approaches such as the monistic interpretation of copyright (*i.e.* copyright as a whole with all its faculties serving all interests related to its protection) or others?

6. Can a concept that moral rights also cover and guarantee authenticity of work and authorship, be applied without changes of interpretation of what the function of moral rights is?

7. Are moral rights of 'producers' of any kind, either in the capacity of legal successors of authors or in their capacity of original owners of copyright/neighbouring rights, imaginable and can those rights perhaps be instrumentalized for the protection of their authenticity interests?

8. How can it be guaranteed that moral rights are not totally made 'economic' under a concept of authenticity protection when the necessity of protection of authenticity interests of producers cannot be denied?

9. What will be the role of technical means for insuring authenticity in the future?

10. Can international systems of identifying numbers for works and other objects (such as phonograms) be made legally binding?

11. Do legal provisions which prescribe certain technological methods for the authentification of the work and/or prohibit methods defeating such technical protection systems, already exist?

12. Has a concept of moral rights protection (in particular the paternity right and the integrity right), eventually in extended form, guaranteeing authenticity of work and authorship, a reduced or a more important role to play in future copyright practice?

General remarks

The US Green Paper on *Intellectual Property and the National Information Infrastructure* (*A Preliminary Draft of The Report of the Working Group on Intellectual Property Rights,* July 1994) has initiated a discussion on 'authenticity of works' (authenticating the work) in the context of what is called the National Information Infrastructure and what can also be called the multimedia debate or the digital revolution debate (see p. 113 *et seq.* of the Green Paper).

Without directly mentioning protection of moral rights at this point, the Green Paper shortly discusses ways of 'sealing' digitally represented works, whereby digital signatures are created which can, if verified, ensure that the work has not been modified. If the work is changed, a new seal must be computed on the revised information. The short analysis in the Green Paper of the 'authenticating problem' ends with the following passage: *'Generating a digital signature is called 'signing' the work. Both the digital signature and the public key are often appended to signed copyrighted works (or they may be stored in a header). The signature serves as a 'seal' for the work because the seal enables the information to be independently checked for unauthorized modification. If the seal is verified (independently computed signature matches the original signature), then the copyrighted work is a* bona fide *copy of the original work - i.e., nothing has been changed in either the header or the work itself'* (see p. 114).

It is the task of the General Report and, in preparation of it, of the Questionnaire and the relevant National Reports to identify the problems stemming from such authenticating of the work in a more traditional context of the copyright debate.

Questionnaire

1. Est-ce qu'il y a dans votre pays des documents officieux comme, par exemple, le Livre vert américain, ou des projets de nouvelles lois ou d'autres documents qui discutent, d'une manière expresse, des problèmes de "l'authenticité d'oeuvres et/ou de l'auteur" dans le contexte multimédia ou de l'infrastructure mondiale d'information?

2. Si oui, est-ce que la discussion ou les projets concernés établissent une relation du problème avec le concept traditionnel du droit moral, en particulier le droit à la paternité et le droit à l'intégrité de l'oeuvre, tels qu'ils sont prévus à l'article 6*bis* de la Convention de Berne?

3. Si non, quelle est probablement la raison pour laquelle cette relation n'est pas établie? Est-ce que le problème de l'authenticité est un concept entièrement nouveau et indépendant des solutions traditionnelles du droit moral?

4. Est-ce que des éléments traditionnellement liés à la protection par le droit moral, comme par exemple, son inaliénabilité et la protection d'intérêts apparemment exclusivement intellectuels et personnels, empêchent le développement d'une conception moderne de protection de l'authenticité de l'oeuvre et/ou de l'auteur?

5. La protection par le droit moral peut-elle servir d'autres intérêts à part les intérêts intellectuels et personnels, en particulier aussi des intérêts pécuniaires? Est-ce qu'une telle approche est facilitée dans votre pays par certaines conceptions doctrinales comme l'interprétation moniste du droit d'auteur (c'est-à-dire un droit d'auteur, conçu dans son intégralité avec toutes ses facultés, servant tous les intérêts liés à sa protection) ou d'autres conceptions?

6. Est-ce qu'une conception suivant laquelle le droit moral peut aussi couvrir et garantir l'authenticité de l'oeuvre et de l'auteur peut être appliquée sans changement de l'interprétation des vraies fonctions du droit moral?

7. Est-ce qu'on peut imaginer des droits moraux de "producteurs" de tous genres, dans leur capacité de successeurs légaux des auteurs ou dans leur capacité de titulaires originaux du droit d'auteur ou de droits voisins? Est-ce que ce genre de droits moraux peut être instrumentalisé pour la protection de leur intérêt à l'authenticité?

8. Comment peut-on garantir que le droit moral n'est pas rendu entièrement "économique" sur la base d'une conception de protection de l'authenticité si, en même temps, la nécessité de la protection de ces intérêts d'authenticité des producteurs ne peut pas être niée?

9. Quel sera le rôle des moyens techniques pour assurer l'authenticité à l'avenir?

10. Est-ce que des systèmes internationaux de nombres qui identifient des oeuvres et d'autres objets protégés (comme des phonogrammes) peuvent être prescrits d'une manière impérative?

11. Est-ce qu'il y a des dispositions légales qui imposent certaines méthodes technologiques pour l'authentification de l'oeuvre et/ou qui interdisent que l'on supprime de tels systèmes de protection technique?

12. Est-ce qu'une conception de la protection par le droit moral (en particulier le droit à la paternité et le droit à l'intégrité), éventuellement dans une forme étendue qui garantit l'authenticité de l'oeuvre et de l'auteur, va jouer un rôle plutôt réduit ou plus important dans la pratique future du droit d'auteur?

Remarques générales

Le Livre vert du gouvernement des Etats-Unis sur *"Intellectual Property and the National Information Infrastructure"* (*A Preliminary Draft of The Report of the Working Group on Intellectual Property Rights*, juillet 1994) a initié un débat sur "l'authenticité des oeuvres" (leur authentification) dans le contexte de ce qu'on appelle infrastructure nationale de l'information et de ce qu'on peut aussi appeler le débat sur les multimédias ou le débat sur la révolution digitale (voir p. 113 et suiv. du Livre vert).

Sans mentionner directement, à cet endroit, la protection par le droit moral, le Livre vert discute brièvement des méthodes par lesquelles on "scelle" des oeuvres qui sont exprimées d'une manière digitale, créant ainsi des signatures digitales qui, après vérification, garantissent que l'oeuvre n'a pas été modifiée. Si l'oeuvre est modifiée, un nouveau sceau doit être apposé sur l'information révisée. La courte analyse du problème de l'authentification telle qu'elle est contenue dans le Livre vert se termine avec le passage suivant: *"Generating a digital signature is called 'signing' the work. Both the digital signature and the public key are often appended to signed copyrighted works (or they may be stored in a header). The signature serves as a 'seal' for the work because the seal enables the information to be independently checked for unauthorized modification. If the seal is verified (independently computed signature matches the original signature), then the copyrighted work is a* bona fide *copy of the original work - i.e., nothing has been changed in either the header or the work itself"* (voir p. 114).

C'est la tâche du rapport général et, en vue de sa préparation, du questionnaire et des rapports nationaux y relatifs d'identifier les problèmes créés par l'authentification de l'oeuvre dans un contexte plutôt traditionnel du débat mené dans le domaine du droit d'auteur.

Belgique

G. van Bosstraeten & T. Vanhyfte

La nouvelle infrastructure de l'information a provoqué aussi bien en Belgique qu'ailleurs une vague de réflexions. La problématique des multimédia et des autoroutes de l'information a été posée et parfois vraiment d'une façon pointue. On peut constater par là que son évolution ne laisse plus personne indifférent. Même si on se limite à la question juridique, on ne peut éviter qu'en arrière plan, il y aura toujours une prise de position philosophique qui portera le système juridique et son interprétation, d'autant plus qu'il s'agit d'une évolution profonde - peut être même d'une révolution. A cause des moyens technologiques, il y a une internationalisation, non seulement dans l'accessibilité des oeuvres, mais aussi dans leur création même. Les circonstances dans lesquelles les oeuvres d'art sont faites changent également. Ce qui entraîne une évolution de la "production" d'une pièce dans le cadre d'un contrat de travail, d'un statut ou encore d'un contrat de commande. Donc, il y a une tendance vers une harmonisation internationale. Bien sûr ce mouvement n'est pas nouveau, mais il est devenu de plus en plus présent. C'est là qu'une option doit être prise, car différents intérêts commerciaux rendent possible l'évolution technologique et les intérêts des auteurs. Toutefois il est utile d'en parler. C'est dans ce contexte que se situe la mise en question de ce que sont une oeuvre d'art, un auteur, un ayant-droit et les droits moraux.

Comment la législation belge y répond:

1. Originalité

Déjà il y a vingt ans la doctrine mettait en question la définition d'une oeuvre d'art comme elle-même et la jurisprudence l'avaient définie. En effet, l'oeuvre, obtenue par l'intermédiaire de "la machine" (les oeuvres d'art obtenus par ordinateur et ses moyens) correspond-t-elle toujours à la définition: *"réalisation originale qui témoigne de la personnalité créatrice d'un être humain"*? (Gotzen, F., "L'ordinateur et la propriété intellectuelle, Protection des programmes - Banques de données - Création artistique automatisée", *JT* 1976, p. 89 *et seq*.). La vitesse à laquelle se développent les possibilités technologiques a aiguisé cette mise en question. Bien que le législateur belge eut pu jouer un rôle dans ces évolutions, dans le cadre de la nouvelle loi du 30 juin 1994 relative au droit d'auteur et aux droits voisins et de la loi transposant en droit belge la directive européenne du 14 mai 1991 concernant la protection juridique des programmes d'ordinateur de la même date, il n'a osé aborder la question et a préféré attendre les nouvelles directives européennes. Cette décision prudente fut suggérée par le fait qu'en Belgique il n'existe pas "un livre vert" pour guider le législateur.

Est-ce que les règles, intégrées dans la nouvelle loi belge peuvent être appliquées aux oeuvres d'art dans le contexte multimédia ou de l'infrastructure mondiale d'information? Il nous semble bien que ces oeuvres sont soumises aux dispositions générales de la loi sur le droit d'auteur. On pourrait se demander si les dispositions particulières prises pour les oeuvres audiovisuelles ne pourraient être appliquées aux oeuvres multimédia. Il nous semble que non. La rédaction de l'article nous apprend que le législateur belge n'avait certainement en vue que les films. Il nous paraît également que la nature des oeuvres d'art multimédia ne répond pas forcément à la définition d'une oeuvre audiovisuelle (dans le même sens: Berenboom, A., *Le droit d'auteur*, 1995, no. 173).

Dans la nouvelle loi relative au droit d'auteur et aux droits voisins, on ne donne pas de définition. On doit donc se référer à la doctrine et la jurisprudence qui définissent l'oeuvre d'art comme une idée qui est matérialisée d'une façon concrète et originale. Cette originalité est composée de deux éléments: l'oeuvre est le résultat d'un effort intellectuel d'une personne physique (voir Cass., 27-4-1989, Arr. Cass., 1988-89, 1006 et Cass., 2-3-1993, Ing. Cons., 1993, 145) et porte l'empreinte de la personnalité de l'auteur (voir Cass., 25-10-1989, Arr. Cass., 1989-1990, 272). Par contre, dans la loi transposant en droit belge la directive européenne du 14 mai 1991 concernant la protection juridique des programmes d'ordinateur, l'article 2(1) considère un programme d'ordinateur comme protégé par le droit d'auteur si il s'agit d'une création intellectuelle propre à son auteur. Aucun autre critère ne s'applique pour déterminer s'il peut bénéficier d'une protection par le droit d'auteur. Ceci veut dire que pour les programmes informatiques, on exige seulement l'authenticité. Quand on compare l'exigence d'originalité dans le droit d'auteur avec l'exigence d'authenticité dans la loi sur le programme d'ordinateur, cette dernière ne demande pas l'empreinte de l'auteur (contra: Strowel A., *Vers un droit d'auteur* sui generis: *la loi du 30 juin 1994 sur les programmes d'ordinateur, Ing. Cons.* 1994, 75, pour qui l'exigence d'authenticité dans la loi sur les programmes d'ordinateur est identique à l'exigence d'originalité dans la loi sur le droit d'auteur). Une oeuvre d'art dans les multimédia est donc soumise à des exigences plus contraignantes que les programmes d'ordinateur.

On peut regretter cette évolution, d'autant plus qu'on attribue un statut d'oeuvre littéraire aux programmes informatiques, toutefois en demandant moins à ces dits programmes, et ceci dans le but de pouvoir leur attribuer des droits d'auteur. Selon la loi susmentionnée, l'auteur de programmes informatiques reçoit aussi des droits moraux (droit de paternité et d'intégrité, selon la Convention de Berne). La loi sur les programmes d'ordinateur ne mentionne pas les caractéristiques des droits moraux, ce qui entraîne une interprétation de la loi relative aux droits d'auteur, puisque ce qui n'est pas reglé dans la loi spécifique doit trouver une solution dans la loi générale. (Dans le même sens Malfliet, K., Ponet, B., *Industriële eigendomsrechten*, Biblo., p. 291, *contra*: Strowel, A., *l.c.*, p. 80.) L'exemple de la loi sur les programmes d'ordinateur, montre que, indirectement (ou inconsciemment?) le législateur belge se laisse porter par le mouvement européen: la tendance étant de créer des nouvelles catégories, nommées *sui generis*, in casu, spécifiques à l'utilisation des moyens techniques et/ou au résultat de plus en plus technique obtenu. L'expression de la personnalité de l'auteur diminue.

2. **L'auteur**

L'auteur est celui qui réalise l'oeuvre d'art comme définie ultérieurement. Mais de plus en plus d'oeuvres d'art naissent dans le cadre d'une coopération de différents artistes. Les nouvelles techniques les aident à coopérer d'une façon spécifique. Selon la nouvelle loi en vigueur, on ne parle de coauteurs que si les auteurs ont collaboré dans un esprit commun et dans la mesure où ils apportent à l'oeuvre commune une attribution créative, protégée en soi par le droit d'auteur, ou bien une attribution sans laquelle l'oeuvre n'existerait pas ou montrerait des différences importantes dans sa forme finale (dans ce sens: Brison, F., *Le titulaire du droit d'auteur*, DAOR, 1992, 105). Celui qui exécute sous surveillance et avec les indications concrètes de(s) auteur(s) ne peut être considéré par conséquent comme coauteur (voir Dali-Forani: Cas., 22 mai 1980, *Ing. Cons.*, 1981, 354, note Demeur, M.). A l'aide de la digitalisation et du *"networking"*, les multimédia combinent à la fois textes, images et sons, par l'intermédiaire des systèmes informatiques et de la technologie numérique. On peut donc intervenir directement en modifiant les oeuvres auxquelles l'auteur a accès, en utilisant certains de leurs éléments pour les inclure dans une nouvelle oeuvre. De ce fait peut-on parler de coopération d'artistes ou de coauteurs lorsqu'un auteur s'approprie des fragments d'oeuvres existantes et en fait une nouvelle oeuvre? Est-ce dans ce cas, une reproduction ou une adaptation ou alors une coopération d'artistes? Même si les fragments de ces oeuvres existantes sont minimes, cela peut suffire à les considérer comme un apport essentiel. L'auteur ou les auteurs de ces oeuvres déjà existantes devraient donner leurs consentements. En se référant à leurs droits moraux, ces auteurs auraient toujours un droit de regard sur l'utilisation fragmentaire de leur travail.

La question est: est-ce que cela est voulu par toutes les parties concernées? Il y a controverse entre d'un côté la liberté de pouvoir techniquement s'approprier et manipuler tout ce qui est protégé par le droit d'auteur, et de l'autre des efforts légaux et techniques pour protéger les intérêts de l'auteur et des ayants-droits, afin de les protéger de l'appropriation et manipulation qu'ils perçoivent comme une menace (voir Davies, G., *"The convergence of copyright and author's right - reality or chimera"*, IIPR 1995, no. 6, p. 964 *et seq.*). Dans cette controverse, est-ce possible pour un auteur d'obtenir toutes les autorisations nécessaires, dans la mesure où il n'existe pas de *"clearing houses"* internationales qui peuvent légitimer l'usage que l'on fait d'un travail? Et une fois le consentement obtenu, sera-t-il encore possible pour les auteurs des pièces déjà existantes d'invoquer leurs droits moraux? Dans cette optique un auteur moderne est limité par les droits moraux des autres auteurs et plus spécifiquement les droits moraux seront une restriction à la libre création. La loi belge n'a pas prévu de dispositions spécifiques afin d'obtenir une solution pour les multimédia. De toute façon, il faudra sauvegarder la protection des principes du droit d'intégrité (cfr. article 6*bis* de la Convention de Berne) et de paternité. C'est-à-dire qu'il faudra savoir s'il s'agit d'une oeuvre originale appartenait à l'auteur indiqué.

3. Droits moraux

La définition d'une oeuvre d'art selon la loi belge lie le concept fortement aux droits moraux. Les droits moraux trouvent leur origine dans le lien qu'un auteur a avec son oeuvre. Les droits moraux sont nés du fait que l'on peut retrouver la personnalité de l'auteur dans son oeuvre, ce qui a pour conséquence un lien intime entre l'auteur et son oeuvre. La fonction de ces droits est de protéger ce lien dans tous ses aspects. (Dans ce sens, Corbet, J., *Auteursrecht, APR* 1991, Story-Scientia, p. 46.) Les droits moraux sont donc liés à la personne et sont séparés des droits patrimoniaux. De ce fait, les droit moraux ne peuvent être vus comme économiques - ce système de dualisme qui est défendu en Belgique, ne le permet pas.

Le respect de ce lien intime entre auteur et oeuvre et, par conséquent, ses droits moraux personnels et individuels, est dans la nouvelle loi sur le droit d'auteur affaibli dans certains domaines. L'article 1 par. 2 dispose que l'auteur jouit d'un droit moral inaliénable mais le même paragraphe prévoit aussi que la renonciation globale à l'exercice futur de ce droit est nulle. En interprétant cette deuxième partie, le résultat devient: la renonciation spécifique de l'exercice actuel du droit moral est possible. Dans le développement actuel, un auteur peut très bien accepter de ne pas se référer à l'exercice de son droit d'intégrité pour rendre possible une certaine manipulation d'une de ses oeuvres sans que l'authenticité de cette oeuvre soit atteinte. Ceci à condition qu'il puisse encore prévoir et qu'il soit conscient de l'impact que peut avoir cette renonciation. Selon nous, c'est pour cette raison que le législateur a prévu la deuxième partie de l'article 1 par. 2. L'auteur dans le cadre d'un contrat de travail, d'un statut ou encore d'un contrat de commande, pourra renoncer à l'exercice de ses droits moraux aux conditions soulignées ci-dessus et à condition que ceci soit explicitement prévu dans le contrat (Vanhees, H., *Een juridische analyse van de grondslagen, inhoud en draagwijdte van auteursrechtelijke exploitatiecontracten*, Antwerpen, Maklu, 1993, nr. 986). Il n'est pas inimaginable que l'employé (l'auteur) cède sous une quelconque pression de l'employeur.

L'important dans la loi est que, malgré chaque renonciation à l'exercice de son droit à l'intégrité, l'auteur pourra toujours s'opposer à toute déformation, mutilation ou autre modification de son oeuvre ou à toute autre atteinte à la même oeuvre, préjudiciables à son honneur ou à sa réputation (article 1 *in fine* de la loi relative au droit d'auteur), comme il est prévu dans l'article 6*bis* de la Convention d'Union de Berne. Pour que l'auteur puisse faire appel à ses droits moraux, la législateur belge a choisi finalement le système de la preuve du préjudice. Dans cette optique, la loi belge en vigueur, n'empêche pas le développement d'une conception moderne de protection de l'authenticité de l'oeuvre et/ou de l'auteur. En Belgique, des moyens techniques pour assurer l'authenticité ne sont pas légalement prévus et donc, lorsque l'auteur renonce à son droit d'intégrité, la protection de l'oeuvre originale s'impose, par exemple par le moyen de la signature digitale.

Les possibilités de protection et de contrôle au bénéfice de la protection de l'authenticité d'une oeuvre d'art sont illimitées. Un système de dispositions légales qui impose certaines méthodes techniques pour l'authentification de l'oeuvre est défendu par la Commission Européenne dans le Livre vert. Ceci doit être adopté par l'ensemble des utilisateurs, non seulement au niveau européen, mais également au niveau international. C'est donc, d'après la Commission européenne, à l'industrie de développer les systèmes techniques nécessaires (voir aussi Visser, D.J.G., *"Groen papier over auteursrecht van E4 DG15.ccc.be"*, *Mediaforum* 1995-10, p. 121).

Cependant, l'utilisateur quant à lui pourra dire que les mécanismes de contrôle de ce genre portent inévitablement atteinte à son droit de liberté individuelle. Pourtant ces techniques de contrôle semblent d'autant plus attrayantes qu'elles rendent possibles le recouvrement des droits de l'exploitation dans le plus ample sens du mot au bénéfice des différentes catégories des ayants-droits. Donc en se référant au principe de la protection de l'authenticité de l'auteur et son oeuvre, on offre par un détour à tous les ayants-droits le moyen de garantir leurs droits patrimoniaux. Ainsi la vraie fonction du droit moral est déviée. Les producteurs qui n'ont pas de droits moraux, auront quand même intérêt à prendre les droits moraux de l'auteur à coeur, ne serait-ce que pour servir leurs propres intérêts.

La question est maintenant de savoir si l'on doit leur attribuer explicitement des droits moraux. Dans la loi belge relative au droit d'auteur, la confirmation des droits voisins est nouvelle. Dans cette loi les producteurs de phonogrammes et des premières fixations de films sont notamment visés. Légalement, les producteurs n'obtiennent en aucun cas des droits moraux et le législateur estime nécessaire de disposer dans l'article 33 que les droits, attribués aux titulaires des droits voisins ne portent pas atteinte aux droit de l'auteur. Aucun d'entre eux, ne peut être interpreté comme une limite à l'exercice du droit d'auteur. Les producteurs ne peuvent pas obtenir les droits moraux de l'auteur, mais ils peuvent être les possesseurs de licence de non-exécution de ces droits. Tout ceci se justifie dans la philosophie de la loi qui se veut protectrice de l'auteur et de ses droits. Les producteurs toutefois des droits patrimoniaux, avec la possibilité d'agir contre les infractions faites à leurs propres droits. Cette possibilité leur est donnée directement par la loi même. En dehors du champ du droit d'auteur, la protection peut être recherchée dans le droit de la concurrence déloyale et des pratiques du commerce (Brison, F. et Triaille, J.P., "La directive CEE du 14 mai 1991 et la protection juridique des programmes d'ordinateur en droit belge", *JT* 1991, p. 782).

On peut remarquer cependant (article 16 par. 1) que si la loi ne donne pas de droits moraux aux producteurs, l'oeuvre audiovisuelle est réputée achevée lorsque la version définitive *"final cut"* a été établie de commun accord entre le réalisateur principal et le producteur. Donc, sans l'accord du producteur, l'oeuvre audiovisuelle ne peut être divulguée. Dans ce sens on peut constater que le législateur belge a attribué *de facto* un droit de divulgation limitée au producteur. En attribuant ce droit n'a-t-il pas porté atteinte aux droits moraux de l'auteur? Au regard de cet exemple, il faudra veiller à ce que les droits moraux ne soient pas vidés de leur sens par des droits qui se glisseraient insinueusement dans la loi mais dont l'impact ne serait pas à sousestimer.

Les droits moraux ont une importance cruciale pour contrebalancer les valeurs économiques pour lesquelles l'oeuvre d'art n'est considérée que comme produit économique. Il est donc dangereux, à chaque nouvelle technique, de créer des dispositions *sui generis*. La loi belge sur les droits d'auteur de 1886 a tenu 100 ans grâce à l'interprétation modulable que l'on pouvait en faire. La nouvelle loi de 1994 tiendra-t-elle aussi longtemps? Il faut être conscient que les nouvelles manières de créer ne tombent pas forcément et facilement sous les règles générales conçues dans cette nouvelle loi mais la question concernant les règles que l'on applique aux multimédia, montre que l'instauration de différentes catégories de droits *sui generis* comporte le danger de disparition d'une valeur qu'il faut sauvegarder à tout prix: les droits moraux.

Canada

É. Franchi & P.E. Moyse

Note introductive sur le droit moral canadien

Le Canada est le premier pays de tradition de *copyright* à avoir consacré le droit moral dans sa législation.[1] L'article 14(1) de la Loi sur le droit d'auteur canadienne,[2] qui met en oeuvre l'article 6*bis* de la Convention de Berne, a cependant fait l'objet d'une adoption récente. Il n'y a ainsi pas, au Canada, de tradition du droit moral[3] et l'insertion d'une telle disposition dans un système imprégné des valeurs de *copyright* peut paraître surprenante,[4] d'autant qu'elle permet à l'auteur de renoncer par écrit à l'exercice ultérieur de ce droit.[5] Il a été justement remarqué que: *"that provision was fraught with difficulties for anyone who wanted to rely on it. While they helped to solve most of the problems that were associated with it, the changes that were introduced with Phase I of the copyright revision process continue to reflect the same attitude towards moral rights. In particular, the existence of a waiver provision (...) undermines the* raison d'être *of the moral right system"*.[6]

Parce que le droit canadien hérite des conceptions économiques sous-jacentes aux systèmes de *copyright*, les conflits résultant des atteintes éventuelles à l'oeuvre de l'auteur se règlent avant tout sur le terrain des droits patrimoniaux ou, plus généralement, du droit des obligations. D'ailleurs, et c'est une règle commune à tous les pays de *copyright*, jusqu'à l'adoption de lois consacrant expressément le concept de droit moral, la protection des intérêts extra-patrimoniaux de l'auteur était recherchée par voie contractuelle. Le professeur Dworking fait d'ailleurs cette remarque générale concernant le système de *copyright*: *"in most cases the main difference between the right of paternity in common law and civil law country is that in the former the author's right to accreditation is usually created by contract (...). So also with the integrity right: where an author transfers an interest in his or her work, the express or implied terms of the contract will determine whether and to what extent, the integrity interest is protected."* Cela explique d'une manière certaine que l'auteur puisse renoncer contractuellement à l'exercice de son droit moral. Cette faculté de l'auteur peut conduire à l'extinction pratique du droit moral puisque seuls subsistent alors les droits économiques pour protéger les intérêts des auteurs.

Il n'y a pas vraiment de jurisprudence canadienne sur le droit moral[7] susceptibles de cautionner une protection de l'authenticité de l'oeuvre ou, plus généralement, des droits moraux dans l'environnement numérique. Dans le domaine des oeuvres interactives, nous relevons toutefois l'affaire *Nintendo et al. v. Camerica*,[10] dans laquelle est examinée brièvement la question des droits moraux. Camerica mit sur le marché un logiciel permettant de modifier les paramètres de jeux vidéo produits par Nintendo, notamment la vitesse d'exécution et les couleurs du jeu. Le concepteur du jeu s'était joint à l'action intentée par Nintendo mais la Cour a rejeté son argumentation au motif qu'il ne rapportait pas la preuve de l'atteinte à sa réputation et/ou à son honneur.

> ***1.*** *Est-ce qu'il y a en Canada des documents officieux comme, par exemple, le Livre vert américain, ou des projets de nouvelles lois ou d'autres documents qui discutent, d'une manière expresse, des problèmes de "l'authenticité d'oeuvres et/ou de l'auteur" dans le contexte multimédia ou de l'infrastructure mondiale d'information?*

Le Livre vert du gouvernement des États-Unis intitulé *"Intellectual Property and the National Information Infrastructure"*[9] a initié un débat sur l'authenticité des oeuvres (leur authentification) dans le contexte de l'infrastructure nationale de l'information et du débat sur le multimédia et la révolution numérique.[10] Ce sujet n'a pas fait l'objet d'une réflexion précise au Canada.

Sans évoquer explicitement le droit moral, le Livre vert américain aborde brièvement les méthodes par lesquelles on "scelle" des oeuvres numérisées créant ainsi des signatures électroniques visant à garantir l'intégrité de l'oeuvre et la paternité. En cas de modification de l'oeuvre, un nouveau sceau doit etre apposé sur la nouvelle version. La courte analyse de la question de l'authentification faite dans le Livre vert se conclut comme suit: *"Generating a digital signature is called 'signing' the work. Both the digital signature and the public key are often appended to signed copyrighted works (or they may be stored in a header). The signature serves as a 'seal' for the work because the seal enables the information to be independently checked for unauthorized modification. If the seal is verified (independently computed signature matches the original signature), then the copyrighted work is a* bona fide *copy of the original work - i.e. nothing has been changed in either the header or the work itself."* [11]

Le Canada a pour sa part entrepris, depuis deux ans, une série d'études prospectives relatives à l'application - voire à l'adaptation - des concepts actuels du droit d'auteur canadien à l'environnement électronique dans le cadre plus général de l'autoroute de l'information.[12] Le Sous-comité sur le droit d'auteur a dégagé les principales questions et formulé un ensemble de recommandations au Comité consultatif sur l'autoroute de l'information. Le Rapport final du Comité consultatif sur l'autoroute de l'information constitue ainsi le document de principe au Canada. Il n'y est fait allusion que brièvement à la question du droit moral. *A fortiori* la question plus complexce de "l'authentification de l'oeuvre ou de son auteur" n'y est pas traitée. Tout au plus pouvons-nous relever dans le rapport final un appel à des solutions techniques qui permettraient de faire respecter les droits moraux des auteurs qui estime notamment que "compte tenu de la nécessité de sauvegarder l'intégrité de ces documents, les usagers ne devraient pas être en mesure de les modifier." [13]

> ***2.*** *Si oui, est-ce que la discussion ou les projets concernés établissent une relation du problème avec le concept traditionnel du droit moral, en particulier le droit à la paternité et le droit à l'intégrité de l'oeuvre, tels qu'ils sont prévus*

*à l'article 6bis de la Convention de Berne? / **3**. Si non, quelle est probablement la raison pour laquelle cette relation n'est pas établie? Est-ce que le problème de l'authenticité est un concept entièrement nouveau et indépendant des solutions traditionnelles du droit moral?*

Le problème de l'authentification des oeuvres n'est pas en soi nouveau. Il est à lier à la nature intrinsèque du droit d'auteur, concu à l'origine comme le droit exclusif d'une personne sur une création immatérielle. Cette perception est issue des théories civilistes romaines d'un droit naturel sur la chose *(res)*, théories qui ont servi à définir progressivement le droit intellectuel. Il est donc nécessaire pour reconnaître à ce droit subjectif toute son efficacité que l'on identifie l'auteur de chaque oeuvre. C'est, en pratique, cette exigence qui est posée, en d'autres termes, par le droit de paternité et le droit à l'intégrité. La technologie numérique ayant rendu plus aisée la manipulation des oeuvres, le problème ne se pose aujourd'hui qu'avec plus d'acuité.

L'industrie de l'informatique et de l'information ne semble cependant pas voir dans le droit moral un instrument juridique très utile. La faculté offerte à l'auteur par la Loi sur le droit d'auteur de renoncer à l'exercice de ses droits moraux renforce l'omniprésence et la prépondérance des droits économiques dans le système canadien. De plus, la Loi sur le droit d'auteur comporte un ensemble de dispositions visant à favoriser l'exploitation de l'oeuvre. Par l'effet des dispositions relatives à la création salariée, l'employeur est notamment présumé premier titulaire du droit d'auteur sur les créations de ses employés. On note également la pratique de cessions de droits universelles faites au détriment des créateurs indépendants. Pour ces raisons, l'authentification des oeuvres reste perçue au Canada, non comme une question à rattacher au droit moral, mais comme une solution technique sécurisant l'exploitation économique de l'oeuvre. Cette question n'a pas été soulevée à l'égard des logiciels ou, plus récemment à l'égard des oeuvres multimédia. Cela confirme le fait que la numérisation des oeuvres ne conduit pas à des amendements substantiels de la Loi sur le droit d'auteur canadienne, car ses concepts fondamentaux sont énoncés en termes technologiquement neutres.

On relève, toutefois, dans le rapport final du Comité consultatif, plusieurs suggestions ayant trait à des solutions techniques qui pourront permettre un certain contrôle de l'utilisation des oeuvres dans les réseaux électroniques. La réflexion est abordée, au Canada, sous l'angle des droits économiques, pour garantir une perception et une répartition équitables de la rémunération due aux auteurs et ayants-droit.

*   **4**. *Est-ce que des éléments traditionnellement liés à la protection par le droit moral, comme par exemple son inaliénabilité et la protection d'intérêts apparemment exclusivement intellectuels et personnels empêchent le développement d'une conception moderne de protection de l'authenticité de l'oeuvre et/ou de l'auteur?*

Le droit moral canadien demeure, par tradition, de portée limitée même en théorie. La lettre de la Loi est universaliste. Le Canada possède une tradition de *copyright*, même si certaines dispositions de sa Loi sur le droit d'auteur depuis ses amendements de 1988, paraissent inspirées de conceptions d'Europe continentale. En pratique, le droit moral est rarement exercé par les auteurs ou leurs ayants-droit, car ses conditions d'application sont sévères. L'auteur supporte un double fardeau de preuve d'une atteinte matérielle à l'oeuvre et à son honneur ou à sa réputation. Cette dernière condition, éminemment personnelle, est factuelle, avec toutes les incertitudes que cela suppose. Comme dans la plupart des pays anglo-saxons, c'est par le biais des droits économiques des auteurs que leurs intérêts sont classiquement protégés. Le Rapport canadien du Sous-comité sur le droit d'auteur[14] traduit ce phénomène, puisque les solutions techniques, seules susceptibles de garantir, en pratique, l'authenticité d'une oeuvre, ont été abordées pour garantir les droits économiques, voire contrôler l'utilisation qui est faite des oeuvres afin d'assurer la rémunération des auteurs.

> **5.** *La protection par le droit moral peut-elle servir d'autres intérêts à part les intérêts intellectuels et personnels, en particulier aussi des intérêts pécuniaires? Est-ce qu'une telle approche est facilitée dans votre pays par certaines conceptions doctrinales comme l'interprétation moniste du droit d'auteur (c'est-à-dire un droit d'auteur, conçu dans son intégralité avec toutes ses facultés, servant tous les intérêts liés à sa protection) ou d'autres conceptions?*

Le droit moral canadien reste distinct des autres droits exclusifs de l'auteur mais n'a pas expressément de tradition moniste ou dualiste. Le développement de telles théories se conçoit surtout dans des systèmes d'Europe continentale et c'est essentiellement dans ces systèmes que la nature et le rôle du droit moral ont été examinés. Le droit moral canadien reste donc essentiellement limité à quelques dispositions statutaires qui dénotent cependant une approche plutot dualiste. La pratique canadienne semble nier l'existence de cette dualité. Le droit à l'intégrité de l'oeuvre permet d'empêcher, certes, la reproduction de certains éléments d'une oeuvre, par la simple interprétation littérale de l'article 14.1 de la Loi sur le droit d'auteur. Mais, faute de jurisprudence et de doctrine,[15] il faut conclure, malgré l'évidence d'éléments conceptuels, à l'absence d'arguments concrets pour développer une approche autre que restrictive du droit moral au Canada.

> **6.** *Est-ce qu'une conception suivant laquelle le droit moral peut aussi couvrir et garantir l'authenticité de l'oeuvre et de l'auteur peut être appliquée sans changement de l'interprétation des vraies fonctions du droit moral?*

La fonction théorique du droit moral canadien, est de garantir l'intégrité et la paternité de l'oeuvre qui permet, apparemment, la protection de l'authenticité de l'oeuvre. Nous avons cependant souligné l'inefficacité pratique des droits moraux devant les tribunaux canadiens du fait du fardeau de la preuve qui incombe à l'auteur. Ainsi, au Canada, c'est par l'exercice des droits économiques que sera effectivement protégée l'authenticité de l'oeuvre. A titre d'exemple, l'article 28.1 (2) de la loi canadienne dispose que *"toute déformation, mutilation ou autre modification d'une peinture, d'une sculpture ou d'une gravure est réputée préjudiciable (...)"*. On conçoit difficilement l'application de cet article qui pose une présomption de préjudice dans l'environnement télématique puisqu'il semble, en effet, que seuls les originaux des oeuvres soient concernés par cette disposition, ce que relève le Sous-comité sur le droit d'auteur dans son rapport au Comité consultatif canadien. La protection du droit moral au Canada n'est donc pas automatique. La renonciation à son exercice ultérieur est fréquente et dans de nombreuses hypothèses, le droit moral canadien sera ineffectif dans l'environnement télématique.

> **7.** *Est-ce qu'on peut imaginer des droits moraux de "producteurs" de tous genres, dans leur capacité de successeurs légaux des auteurs ou dans leur capacité de titulaires originaux du droit d'auteur ou de droits voisins? Est-ce que ce genre de droits moraux peut être instrumentalisé pour la protection de leur intérêt à l'authenticité?*

La création salariée est appelée à se développer, notamment dans l'industrie de l'informatique et de l'information multimédia. La loi canadienne contient une présomption de première titularité des droits d'auteur à l'employeur pour les créations salariées.[16] Seuls les droits patrimoniaux appartiennent à l'employeur et, sauf renonciation de sa part, l'employé conserve l'exercice des droits moraux sur son oeuvre. Il n'y a pas, à notre connaissance, de jurisprudence canadienne où le droit moral de l'employé fut invoqué pour limiter l'exploitation de l'oeuvre par l'employeur.

Il reste difficilement concevable que le droit canadien reconnaisse des droits moraux au profit des producteurs; l'article 14.1 de la Loi sur le droit d'auteur fut adopté pour respecter les exigences individualistes de la Convention de Berne. Selon cette conception classique du droit moral, il s'agit d'un droit personnel et extra-patrimonial. On conçoit donc mal comment une telle prérogative entrerait dans l'actif d'une personne morale. Si le titulaire des droits d'auteur n'est pas une personne physique - ce qui est souvent l'hypothèse des logiciels - l'existence d'un droit moral n'est plus justifiée puisque le lien personnel et subjectif du créateur avec l'oeuvre disparaît. Les droits moraux sont donc, au Canada, des droits octroyés exclusivement au profit des personnes physiques. Le droit moral canadien ne peut donc servir à garantir l'authenticité des oeuvres que dans la mesure où il est invoqué par une personne physique. Le législateur canadien n'est pas disposé à accorder un tel droit à des personnes morales, car le droit moral symbolise ici, comme en Europe, une conception personnaliste du droit d'auteur. Cela est confirmé par la place distincte des dispositions sur le droit moral au coeur de la législation canadienne et on ne peut prétendre étendre ce droit aux producteurs sans en méconnaître la nature.

> **8.** *Comment peut-on garantir que le droit moral n'est pas rendu entièrement "économique" sur la base d'une conception de protection de l'authenticité si, en même temps, la nécessité de la protection de ces intérêts d'authenticité des producteurs ne peut pas être niée?*

Si l'on venait à utiliser les droits moraux pour protéger des intérêts exclusivement économiques, tels ceux des producteurs, nous risquerions de voir se développer une jurisprudence relative au droit moral teintée de critères techniques et mercantiles. Cela explique que l'exercice du droit moral soit limité aux personnes physiques. La fonction particulière du droit moral est complémentaire à celle des droits économiques: il permet de contrôler l'exploitation de fractions ou d'extraits modifiés d'oeuvres sans l'accord de l'auteur tout en assurant le respect de sa paternité. Cette protection peut être obtenue par le biais d'autres règles légales notamment par l'exercice des droits de reproduction et de représentation de l'oeuvre au public, essentiellement par télécommunication. La nécessité d'un fondement juridique assurant la protection des intérêts des producteurs ne peut être niée, mais les droits économiques peuvent assurer ce rôle.

Le concept d'authentification de l'oeuvre peut se concevoir comme un ensemble de moyens techniques (codage, immatriculation, signature électronique) qui servent l'exclusivité des droits économiques et moraux. Les solutions logicielles suffisent, en principe, à contrôler les utilisations des oeuvres disponibles dans les réseaux électroniques. En pratique, des licences exclusives combinées à des solutions techniques et contractuelles, offriront une protection efficace contre les exploitations non-autorisées d'oeuvres ou d'extraits, altérés ou non.

> *9. Quel sera le rôle des moyens techniques pour assurer l'authenticité à l'avenir?*

Rendre les copies numérisées d'oeuvres protégées inviolables par l'utilisateur, de sorte que nul ne puisse altérer sans autorisation, les informations contenues sur la copie, notamment la mention de paternité.

> *10. Est-ce que des systèmes internationaux de nombres qui identifient des oeuvres et d'autres objets protégés (comme des phonogrammes) peuvent être prescrits d'une manière impérative?*

Sous réserve du respect des principes de droit international public, rien ne paraît s'y opposer au Canada.

> *11. Est-ce qu'il y a des dispositions légales qui imposent certaines méthodes technologiques pour l'authentification de l'oeuvre et/ou qui interdisent que l'on supprime de tels systèmes de protection technique?*

Pas en ce qui concerne le droit d'auteur, mais il existe diverses dispositions dans le Code Criminel canadien susceptibles de prohiber le contournement de dispositifs de protection technique et notamment:

Article 342.1
(1) Utilisation non autorisée d'ordinateur
Quiconque, frauduleusement et sans apparence de droit:
a) directement ou indirectement, obtient des services d'ordinateur;
b) au moyen d'un dispositif électromagnétique, acoustique, mécanique ou autre, directement ou indirectement, intercepte ou fait intercepter toute fonction d'un ordinateur;
c) directement ou indirectement, utilise ou fait utiliser un ordinateur dans l'intention de commettre une infraction prévue à l'alinéa a) ou b) ou une infraction prévue à l'article 340 concernant des données ou un ordinateur,
est coupable d'un acte criminel et passible d'un emprisonnement maximal de dix ans ou d'une infraction punissable sur déclaration de culpabilité par procédure sommaire.
(2) Définitions
Les définitions qui suivent s'appliquent au présent article:

"Dispositif électromagnétique, acoustique, mécanique ou autre". Tout dispositif ou appareil utilisé ou pouvant être utilisé pour intercepter une fonction d'un ordinateur, à l'exclusion d'un appareil de correction auditive utilisé pour améliorer, sans dépasser la normale, l'audition de l'utilisateur lorsqu'elle est inférieure à la normale.

"Données". Représentations d'informations ou de concepts qui sont préparés ou l'ont été de façon à pouvoir être utilisés dans un ordinateur.

"Fonction". S'entend notamment des fonctions logiques, arithmétiques, des fonctions de commande et de suppression, des fonctions de mémorisation et de recouvrement ou de relevé des données de même que des fonctions de communication ou de télécommunication de données à destination, à partir d'un ordinateur ou à l'intérieur de celui-ci.

"Intercepter". S'entend notamment du fait d'écouter ou d'enregistrer une fonction d'un ordinateur ou de prendre connaissance de sa substance, de son sens ou de son objet.

"Ordinateur". Dispositif ou ensemble de dispositifs connectés ou reliés les uns aux autres, dont l'un ou plusieurs d'entre eux:
a) contiennent des programmes d'ordinateur ou d'autres données;
b) conformément à des programmes d'ordinateur:
    (i) soit exécutent des fonctions logiques et de commande,
    (ii) soit peuvent exécuter toute autre fonction.

"Programme d'ordinateur". Ensemble de données qui représentent des instructions ou des relevés et qui, lorsque traités par l'ordinateur, lui font remplir une fonction.

"Service d'ordinateur". S'entend notamment du traitement des données de même que de la mémorisation et du recouvrement ou du relevé des données.

Article 430
(1.1) Méfait concernant des données
Commet un méfait quiconque volontairement, selon le cas:
a) détruit ou modifie des données;
b) dépouille des données de leur sens, les rend inutiles ou inopérantes:
c) empêche, interrompt ou gêne l'emploi légitime des données;
d) empêche, interrompt ou gêne une personne dans l'emploi légitime des données ou refuse l'accès aux données à une personne qui y a droit.
(...)
(5) Idem
Quiconque commet un méfait à l'égard de données est coupable:
a) soit d'un acte criminel et passible d'un emprisonnement maximal de dix ans:
b) soit d'une infraction punissable sur déclaration de culpabilité par procédure sommaire.
(...)
(5.1) Infraction
Quiconque volontairement accomplit un acte ou volontairement omet d'accomplir un acte qu'il a le devoir d'accomplir, si cet acte ou cette omission est susceptible de constituer un méfait qui cause un danger réel pour la vie des gens ou de constituer un méfait à l'égard de biens ou de données est coupable:
a) soit d'un acte criminel et passible d'un emprisonnement maximal de cinq ans;
b) soit d'une infraction punissable sur déclaration de culpabilité par procédure sommaire.

Article 326
(1) Vol de service de télécommunication
Commet un vol quiconque, frauduleusement, malicieusement ou sans apparence de droit:
(...)
b) (...) se sert d'installations ou obtient un service en matière de télécommunication.
(2) Définition de "télécommunication"
(...) *"télécommunication"* désigne toute transmission, émission ou réception de signes, de signaux, d'écrits, d'images, de sons ou de renseignements de toute nature par fil, radioélectricité, optique ou autres systèmes électromagnétiques.

Article 327
(1) Possession de moyens permettant d'utiliser des installations ou d'obtenir un service en matière de télécommunication
Quiconque, sans excuse légitime, dont la preuve lui incombe, fabrique, possède, vend ou offre en vente ou écoule des instruments ou des pièces particulièrement utiles pour utiliser des installations ou obtenir un service en matière de télécommunication, dans des circonstances qui permettent raisonnablement de conclure qu'ils ont été utilisés, sont destinés ou ont été destinés à l'être à cette fin, sans acquittement des droits exigibles, est coupable d'un acte criminel et passible d'un emprisonnement maximal de deux ans.
(2) Confiscation
Lorsqu'une personne est déclarée coupable d'une infraction prévue au paragraphe (1) ou à l'alinéa 326(1)*b)*, tout instrument au moyen duquel l'infraction a été commise ou dont la possession a constitué l'infraction peut, après cette déclaration de culpabilité et en plus de toute peine qui est imposée, être par ordonnance confisqué au profit de Sa Majesté, après quoi il peut en être disposé conformément aux instructions du procureur général.
(3) Restriction

Aucune ordonnance de confiscation ne peut être rendue en vertu du paragraphe (2) relativement à des installations ou du matériel de communications téléphoniques, télégraphiques ou autres qui sont la propriété d'une personne fournissant au public un service de communications téléphoniques, télégraphiques ou autres ou qui font partie du service ou réseau de communications téléphoniques, télégraphiques ou autres d'une telle personne et au moyen desquels une infraction prévue au paragraphe (1) a été commise, si cette personne n'a pas participé à l'infraction.

***12.** Est-ce qu'une conception de la protection par le droit moral (en particulier le droit à la paternité et le droit à l'intégrité), éventuellement dans une forme étendue qui garantit l'authenticité de l'oeuvre et de l'auteur, va jouer un rôle plutôt réduit ou plus important dans la pratique future du droit d'auteur?*

Le droit moral devrait, au Canada, conserver son rôle actuel, malgré le développement des autoroutes de l'information dans lesquelles les droits économiques prendront une place prépondérante.

Notes

1. Le droit d'auteur canadien connaît la notion de droit moral depuis 1931, date de son adhésion à la Convention de Berne. Elle resta inchangée jusqu'en 1988, date à laquelle le législateur a introduit de plus nombreuses références au droit moral dans le corps du texte de la loi refondue en 1985. Pour les fins de cette étude, nous ferons référence à la codification de 1985. LRC (1985), c. C-42.
2. *"14.1 (1) L'auteur d'une oeuvre a le droit, sous réserve de l'article 28.2 à l'intégrité de l'oeuvre et, à l'égard de tout acte mentionné à l'article 3, le droit, compte tenu des usages raisonnables, d'en revendiquer, même sous pseudonyme, la création, ainsi que le droit à l'anonymat.*
14.1 (2) Les droits moraux sont incessibles, ils sont toutefois susceptibles de renonciation, en tout ou partie."
3. Cf. Y. Gendreau, "Moral Right" dans: G.F. Henderson, *Copyright and Confidential Information Law of Canada*, Toronto, Carswell, 1994, 161.
4. En effet, la question du droit moral n'était pas vraiment à l'ordre du jour de la conférence de Rome de 1931. Les pays anglo-saxons furent surpris de voir à quel point elle était d'intérêt pour le groupe des pays civilistes. Il est à penser que l'enjeu même du débat sur le droit moral n'ait pas réellement été compris. Il n'y eu de ce fait que peu d'objections à l'adoption de l'article 6*bis* actuel de la Convention de Berne. Voir notamment, G. Dworking, *"The Moral Right of the Author: Moral Rights and the Common Law Countries", Columbia-VLA Journal of L. & the Arts* (1995) 229, p. 232.
5. Article 14.2 Loi sur le droit d'auteur (ci-apres "LDA").
6. Y. Gendreau, *"Digital Technology and Copyright: Can Moral Rights Survive the Disappearance of the Hard Copy?", Ent. L.R.*, p. 214 et 217.
7. Cf. cependant *Snow c. The Eaton Center Ltd.* (1982) 70 CPR (2d) 105 et *Gnass v Cité d'Alma*, 30 juin 1973. C.S. Roberval inédite; CA du 30 juin 1977, 09-0000032-745 inédite: la Cour d'appel a décidé que *"ces droits [cession d'une sculpture] sont régis par les dispositions du Code civil. Or, dans notre droit, les deux sources de responsabilité civile sont la violation de la loi et la violation des obligations. D'une part, le propriétaire d'une oeuvre ne viole aucune loi en déformant, en mutilant ou en modifiant cette oeuvre; d'autre part, si le propriétaire ne s'est pas engagé contractuellement à entretenir et à conserver l'oeuvre, il ne peut être recherché en dommages et intérêts."*
8. *Nintendo of America Inc. v. Camerica Corp.*, [1991] 34 CPR (3d.) 173.
9. *"A Preliminary Draft of The Report of the Working Group on Intellectual Property Rights"*, juillet 1994.
10. Cf. p. 113 et suiv. du Livre vert américain.
11. Cf. p. 114.
12. Cf. Rapport préliminaire du Sous-comité sur le droit d'auteur, *Le droit d'auteur et l'autoroute de l'information*, Ottawa, décembre 1994. Cf. aussi l'étude du groupe Nordicity, *Study on New Media and Copyright*, Final Report, Ottawa, Minister of Supplies and Services Canada, juin 1994; le Rapport du Comité consultatif sur l'autoroute de l'information, *Le défi de l'autoroute de l'information*, Ottawa, septembre 1995 et le Rapport final du Sous-comité sur le droit d'auteur, *Le droit d'auteur et l'autoroute de l'information*, Ottawa, mars 1995, disponible sur Internet: http://info.ic.gc.ca/infohighway/copyright2/.
13. Recommandation No. 6.5.
14. Précité.
15. Cf. cependant P.B. Mignault, "La propriété littéraire", [1880] 2 no. 10 *La Thémis* 289; [1880] 2 no. 12 *La Thémis* 367; [1881] 3 no. 1 *La Thémis* 1. Également, Normand Tamaro, "La dissociation de la

propriété du Code civil des droits d'auteur: l'exemple de la saisie", dans *Développements récents en droit de la propriété intellectuelle*, Montréal, Yvon Blais, 1991; A. Perrault, "La propriété des oeuvres intellectuelles (1)", [1924] 3 no. 2 *Revue de droit* 49; [1924] 3 no. 3 *Revue de droit* 107; 2 no. 10 *La Thémis* 294. A. Perrault, "La propriété des oeuvres intellectuelles (I)", [1924] 3 no. 2 *Revue de droit* 57; Y. Gendreau, "La nature du droit d'auteur selon le nouveau Code civil", [1993] 27 *RJT* 85, 87-92 et 94-97.

16. L'article 13(3) LDA règle la titularité du droit d'auteur lorsqu'une création est réalisée par un employé dans le cadre de son contrat de travail: *"lorsque l'auteur est employé par une autre personne en vertu d'un contrat de louage de service ou d'apprentissage, et que cette oeuvre est exécutée dans l'exercice de cet emploi, l'employeur est, à moins de stipulation contraire, le premier titulaire du droit d'auteur"*.

Finland

R. OESCH

1. *Are there official documents discussing problems of 'authenticity of works and/or authorship' in the multimedia of Global Information Infrastructure context?*

No, there are not.

2. *If yes (...)*

-

3. *If no, what is probably the reason why this relation is not established? Is the authenticity problem a totally new concept independent of traditional solution of moral rights?*

According to Finnish law, the moral rights' protection is basically a protection against certain forms of malpractice directed to the personal relationship between the author and his creation (reputation and paternity). Authenticity is not a basic goal of copyright.

Probably it is totally a new concept in this connection. One exceptional thing (outside the *droit moral*) in the Nordic legislation is the so-called protection for classical works. According to article 53 of the Finnish Copyright Act, the Ministry of Education may prohibit a measure if, after the death of the author, a literary or artistic work is subject of a public action in a manner which violates cultural interests (*e.g.* the publishing of a badly abridged translation of a classical work). In principle, the authenticity of works is equally important in an analogue and in a digital environment. Authenticity in itself is a question that has become more important with the development of digital technology. Because making changes and alterations becomes common practice in a digital environment, the question of authenticity has become a topic.

In Nordic copyright the authenticity is linked with the basic economic rights, not with moral rights. The author has the right to control the production of copies of the work, be it in original or altered form (article 2 of the Finnish Copyright Act). Even if copyright has been transferred, the transferee has no right to make alterations unless otherwise explicitly agreed (article 28).

4. *Do traditional elements connected with moral rights protection such as* *inalienability and protection of seemingly merely intellectual and personal interests hinder the development of a modern concept of protection of authenticity of work and/or authorship?*

Authenticity in this sense is in my view not linked with the traditional copyright. It is better to keep the moral rights' protection purely with respect to the author's personality and only in cases of very serious infringements. If copyright is transformed into a 'genuine' right, there is the risk of endangering the free flow of ideas and the risk of introducing a kind of censorship. The free flow of ideas supports creativity, which is one of the basic goals of copyright.

5. Can protection by moral rights serve more than only intellectual or personal interests, in particular also pecuniary interests? Is such an approach facilitated in Finland by doctrinal approaches such as the monistic interpretation of copyright?

From the practical and pragmatic point of view, moral rights can bee seen as a method of strengthening and supporting the economic rights. According to the Nordic doctrine, both rights are separate elements of the same right.

6. Can a concept that moral rights also cover and guarantee authenticity of work and authorship, be applied without changes of interpretation of what the function of moral rights is?

Making changes as such does not normally have any significance as far as moral rights are concerned. The suggested interpretation could not be possible without change in the legislation. However, any change affects the authenticity of the work or at least the economic rights of the author. He has the right to control the public use of the work, whether in original or in an altered form, in translation or adaptation, other literary or artistic form, or by other technical means (article 2 of the Finnish Copyright Act). Also when copyright (economic rights) is transferred, in the absence of agreement to the contrary, the licencee may not alter the work (article 28).

7. Are moral rights of 'producers' of any kind (...) imaginable and can those rights perhaps be instrumentalized for the protection of their authenticity interests?

Moral rights cannot belong to a legal person.

8. How can it be guaranteed that moral rights are not totally made 'economic' under a concept of authenticity protection when the necessity of protection of authenticity interests of producers cannot be denied?

A tendency of this kind of concept is not known in Finland.

9. What will be the role of technical means for insuring authenticity in the future?

Technical means are the only means to ensure the authenticity. An authenticity mark could be an 'a' in a circle, to signify that the product is authentic. But because all technical means can be defeated by other technical means, any technical means of authentification does not eliminate all the problems raised by the use of altered works.

> *10. Can international systems of identifying numbers for works and other objects (such as phonograms) be made legally binding?*

No, not at this stage. Identifying should not be made legally binding. The use of identification should be voluntary.

> *11. Do legal provisions already exist which prescribe certain technological methods for authentification of the work and/or prohibit methods defeating such technical protection systems?*

No.

> *12. Has a concept of moral rights protection (in particular the paternity right and the integrity right), eventually in extended form, guaranteeing authenticity of work and authorship, a reduced or a more important role to play in future copyright practice?*

Maybe it will get some role in the future legislation. But the best thing would be to keep the moral rights 'pure' and create a separate system for protection of authenticity and only if the authenticity is supported by some kind of technical means and if legal policy arguments are further developed and have become more convincing. On the other hand, it is possible to make rules including sanctions against fraudulent changes or removal of the code.

France

F. Pollaud-Dulian

Dans le rapport du groupe de travail sur les droits de propriété intellectuelle, intitulé *"Intellectual property and the National Information Infrastructure"*, présenté sous forme de projet en juillet 1994, puis en septembre 1995 par M. Bruce Lehman aux Etats-Unis, on trouve évoquée la question de l'authenticité de l'oeuvre en rapport avec l'identification des oeuvres.[1] *"Des algorithmes mathématiques peuvent aussi être utilisés pour créer des signatures "digitales" qui, effectivement, placent un "sceau" sur une oeuvre représentée digitalement (...) La signature digitale sert comme moyen d'authentifier l'oeuvre, aussi bien en ce qui concerne l'identité de l'entité qui l'a authentifiée ou "signée", qu'en ce qui concerne le contenu du fichier qui encode l'information qui constitue l'oeuvre. Ainsi, en utilisant des signatures digitales on sera capable d'identifier de qui provient un fichier particulier aussi bien que de vérifier que le contenu de ce fichier n'a pas été modifié par rapport au contenu originellement diffusé (...) Générer une signature digitale, c'est utiliser des techniques cryptographiques, mais ce n'est pas un encodage de l'oeuvre; l'oeuvre peut très bien ne pas être encodée de sorte qu'on puisse y accéder et l'utiliser sans décryptage. En fait, les signatures digitales et l'encodage peuvent être utilisés simultanément pour protéger l'oeuvre. En général, une signature est d'abord calculée pour une oeuvre protégée et ensuite l'oeuvre (avec le sceau) est encodée. Quand on veut utiliser l'oeuvre, l'oeuvre est décodée, puis la signature (c'est-à-dire le sceau) est vérifiée pour être sûr que l'oeuvre n'a pas été modifiée (dans sa version originale ou cryptée). Si l'oeuvre n'est jamais modifiée, le sceau n'a pas besoin d'être retiré ou changé. Si l'oeuvre est modifiée, un nouveau sceau doit être calculé sur l'information révisée (...) la signature digitale est incorporée d'une manière quelconque dans la transmission que constitue l'oeuvre (...) La signature sert de sceau pour l'oeuvre parce que ce sceau permet de vérifier l'information de façon autonome pour les modifications non autorisées.[2] Si le sceau est vérifié conforme (la signature calculée indépendamment correspond à la signature originale), alors l'oeuvre est une copie conforme de l'oeuvre originale - c'est-à-dire que rien n'a été changé dans le document qui constitue l'oeuvre."*

Le questionnaire prend ce texte pour point de départ, afin de déterminer les problèmes qui naissent d'un tel type d'authentification "dans le contexte plus traditionnel du droit d'auteur". Plus précisément, il s'agit de savoir si un tel processus de "signature digitale" et de vérification permet d'être sûr que l'oeuvre n'a pas subi de modification et si, dès lors, il peut y avoir là un aspect intéressant pour la protection du droit moral de l'auteur. Le groupe français regrette toutefois que le sujet soit limité à cet aspect, étant donné que les systèmes d'identification présentent surtout un intérêt capital pour l'avenir des droits patrimoniaux de l'auteur, en rendant possible et efficace la gestion de ces droits dans le "cyberspace".

La réponse aux questions posées suppose de décrire les techniques de signature digitale des oeuvres qui sont envisagées et leurs éventuelles répercussions en droit d'auteur. La difficulté tient à ce que le système de signature envisagé à l'heure actuelle ne correspond pas tout à fait à la description que fait M. Lehman - nous semble-t-il - et n'a, en tout cas, pas vocation directe à protéger les intérêts extra-patrimoniaux des auteurs. Elle tient aussi au caractère très technique[3] et non juridique des réponses préparées par la pratique au problème de l'identification des oeuvres numérisées. Nous nous efforcerons donc de répondre, mais en reconnaissant bien volontiers les limites des connaissances techniques du juriste d'une part et d'autre part en soulignant que les techniques et les projets évoluent constamment, ce qui donne à toute réflexion un caractère à la fois prospectif et précaire.

1. L'identification des oeuvres dans l'univers numérique

Nous évoquerons d'abord les enjeux que représente l'identification numérique, puis les travaux en cours.

a. *Les enjeux*

Pour pouvoir protéger efficacement les auteurs et leurs ayants-droit à l'avenir, il est nécessaire de pouvoir identifier les oeuvres dans les supports électroniques (CD-ROM, CD-I) et dans la diffusion en réseaux, qu'il s'agisse de diffusion par le moyen de la télévison numérique ou "en ligne" sur des réseaux télématiques et informatiques d'échanges de données (utilisant généralement le système "Internet").[4] En effet, la numérisation facilite le stockage et la transmission des oeuvres, l'accès interactif à ces oeuvres et leur modification. Il devient alors difficile, spécialement en cas de transmission "en ligne" de contrôler leur utilisation et de gérer les autorisations et les rémunérations. De plus, le numérique augmente les possibilités de modification, donc de dénaturation de l'oeuvre, notamment parce que ces modifications sont plus faciles à opérer et plus difficiles à détecter.

La numérisation, toutefois, permet aussi de mettre au point de nouvelles techniques de contrôle et de perception des droits. En effet, la numérisation de l'oeuvre peut être assortie d'une numérisation d'éléments d'identification, qui permettent de "retracer" l'oeuvre et d'identifier ses ayants-droit: par exemple, d'identifier l'oeuvre qui circule sur un réseau ou qui est reproduite sur un support d'édition électronique. Grâce au code numérique intégré à la numérisation de l'oeuvre, on peut alors suivre à la trace le code à travers les multiples reproductions ou diffusions de l'oeuvre. On peut ainsi vérifier quand, comment et par qui est diffusée l'oeuvre, ainsi que l'étendue de la diffusion.

La reproduction numérique (et non plus analogique) est connue depuis déjà des années, mais le numérique n'atteignait pas encore le stade de la diffusion, pour des raisons tenant à la capacité des mémoires et à la quantité de mémoire que les oeuvres numérisées nécessitent pour leur diffusion. Ce problème a été résolu par la technique de la compression numérique qui permet de comprimer les informations pour en transporter beaucoup plus sous cette forme avec les mêmes capacités et de les restituer, à l'arrivée, en les décompressant.[5] Ces techniques numériques devraient permettre, en particulier, une multiplication des diffusions sur réseaux, posant ainsi un problème de contrôle des autorisations et de rémunération considérable. Si l'oeuvre comporte un code numérisé, qui y est intégré et la suit donc dans toutes ses diffusions et reproductions, des systèmes de lecture de ces codes permettront de contrôler la circulation des oeuvres sur les réseaux, même partielle, et d'assurer le respect des intérêts économiques des auteurs et des producteurs ou autres ayants-droits.

Encore faut-il que de tels codes soient effectivement intégrés à la numérisation des oeuvres. Le système ne peut être véritablement efficace que si des codes identifiant l'oeuvre sont systématiquement incorporés et accompagnent la transmission des oeuvres qu'ils identifient. Ceci, à son tour, n'est possible que si la numérisation conçue par les industriels de l'informatique et de la télécommunication comporte une petite place pour les informations sur les droits intellectuels. Autrement dit, il faut que quelques "bits" soient laissés à la disposition des ayants-droit pour inscrire le code d'identification de l'oeuvre. Enfin, il faut que les modes de codage soient normalisés au niveau international, que tout le monde s'accorde sur des standards et sur les mêmes numéros d'identification. Ce qui signifie une certaine mondialisation des répertoires, à travers des bases de données universelles ou au moins régionales, en matière d'identification des oeuvres.[6]

b. *Les travaux en cours*

Ces objectifs semblent en bonne voie de réalisation. En effet, les représentants des auteurs et des autres ayants-droits ont réussi à faire monter le droit d'auteur en marche[7] dans le train des nouvelles techniques.[8] Il faut souligner, sur ce point, l'importance des efforts déployés par les sociétés d'auteurs françaises.

A l'origine, les experts représentant les industries des télécommunications, de l'électronique, de l'informatique et de l'audiovisuel ont entrepris d'établir des algorithmes constituant des normes de compression et de décompression des données multimédia pour permettre leur transmission sur les réseaux numériques et leur utilisation, pour les raisons précédemment évoquées. Pour les industriels, il s'agissait de se mettre d'accord sur des normes pour fabriquer et vendre le matériel, c'est-à-dire pour élaborer les encodeurs de données destinés aux diffuseurs et les décodeurs de données destinés aux usagers. Les représentants des ayants-droit ont alors réussi à les convaincre de la nécessité de permettre l'intégration des données d'identification des oeuvres qui seraient ainsi diffusées sur les réseaux numériques. Pour cela, il fallait normaliser l'identification et en systématiser l'utilisation. C'est-à-dire laisser un espace pour le marquage numérique de l'oeuvre, marquage renvoyant, par un numéro d'identification, à une source où l'on trouvera les informations détaillées relatives à l'oeuvre, aux ayants-droit et à la gestion. L'identification suppose que la norme de compression permette l'inclusion d'un code d'identification, qu'un système d'identification par attribution de numéros aux oeuvres soit organisé, qui renvoie à des bases de données comportant des renseignements détaillés sur l'oeuvre et ses ayants-droit.

En matière d'oeuvres audiovisuelles, les industriels ont préparé une norme de compression des images sous forme numérique, baptisée "MPEG-2", [9] qui doit devenir le standard international de compression et de décompression des images animées et du son pour le "CD" et la télévision numérique. Cette norme intègre le principe d'un code d'identification des oeuvres. L'algorithme de compression ou de décompression comporte de la place pour le numéro d'identification, c'est-à-dire plus précisément à trois champs d'informations: existe-t-il des droits de propriété intellectuelle ou non? Quel est le type d'identifiant ou support (c'est-à-dire: livre, disque, ou audiovisuel)? Enfin, quel est le numéro d'identication proprement dit?[10]

En matière de photographies, une norme de compression des images fixes a été établie, sous le nom de "JPEG",[11] qui comporte, elle aussi, de la place pour le numéro d'identification. L'existence de ces deux normes distinctes s'explique par la différence des problèmes techniques de compression posés: en effet, le codage de l'oeuvre audiovisuelle doit résoudre le problème de l'association images/sons. Il faut numériser et coder trois champs, audio, vidéo et systèmes.[12]

Quant à la numérotation, il existe des précédents: les numéros d'"ISBN" pour les livres,[13] l'"ISRC" pour les phonogrammes,[14] l'"ISMN" pour les partitions.[15] Des projets de numérotation sont en cours pour les différents types d'oeuvres, qui devraient faire l'objet d'une normalisation internationale sous l'égide de l'"ISO".[16] En matière audiovisuelle, la structure du numéro d'identification des oeuvres est définie et baptisée "ISAN", et devrait être standardisée, une fois que l'"ISO" l'aura approuvée.[17] Le numéro d'identification sera attribué par le producteur (et non par l'auteur) et géré par l'AGICOA.[18] Une base de données commune aux auteurs, producteurs et, le cas échéant, aux interprètes, est développée par l'AGICOA et la CISAC, à partir de la norme "MPEG-2" pour permettre l'identification des oeuvres audiovisuelles et des ayants-droit.

Ces codes ou signatures sont limités dans leur contenu et renvoient donc à des bases de données plus détaillées où l'on trouve des informations sur les ayants-droit et les possibilités d'utilisation. En ce qui concerne les interprètes, l'élaboration des codes identifiants semble moins avancée.[19] Toutefois, en matière audiovisuelle, le fichier de chaque oeuvre devrait contenir les noms des principaux interprètes, ce qui est conçu comme un moyen de retrouver l'oeuvre, mais laisse ouverte, pour l'avenir, la possibilité d'intégrer ces interprètes au système envisagé.

Nous n'entendons pas présenter en détail les différents systèmes, qui sont en développement et évolueront encore. Nous dirons seulement quelques mots sur l'un d'eux à titre d'exemple, celui qui semble le plus achevé à l'heure actuelle et qui concerne l'identification des images fixes. Un projet de dépôt d'image numérique, dit "projet SPIDER",[20] fondé sur la norme de compression d'images fixes "JPEG" établie par l'ISO, a été présenté en première mondiale en février 1996, au salon du MILIA, à Cannes. Le principe, en matière audiovisuelle,[21] est sensiblement le même, mais la norme de compression est différente de la "MPEG-2", du fait qu'il faut allier images, sons et systèmes.

Le système repose d'abord sur un fichier. A chaque image fixe protégée correspond un fichier. Ce fichier (au format "SPIFF 1") comporte trois parties et surtout des éléments d'identification et d'authentification de l'oeuvre numérisée:
1) une vignette, qui est constituée par une reproduction réduite de l'image (1/16 d'écran);[22]
2) les informations permettant l'identification (titre, description, date et heure de création et version) et des informations sur la nature de l'image (ou "niveau d'authenticité": original, extrait de l'image non modifiée ou modification de l'image originale) et les droits d'autre part (nom de l'auteur de l'image, protection, mention des ayants-droit et numéro du dépôt, identité et adresse de l'autorité d'enregistrement);
3) un authentifiant de l'original numérique.

Le fichier sera transmis dès sa création à l'autorité d'enregistrement nationale (autorité agréée, en France, par l'AFNOR)[23] ou internationale, qui le réceptionnera et délivrera un numéro de dépôt. Par conséquent, le déroulement des opérations est le suivant. L'auteur ou son ayant-droit numérise l'image fixe. L'image numérique originale permet de créer un fichier comportant image réduite et informations, qui est envoyé à l'autorité nationale d'enregistrement et fait l'objet d'un enregistrement par cette autorité qui en assure la conservation. Elle possède un serveur auquel les utilisateurs peuvent accéder. En "cliquant" sur la vignette, on obtient les informations. L'autorité peut se contenter de conserver le fichier pour établir la date du dépôt et son contenu; elle peut aussi ouvrir sa banque de données, c'est-à-dire l'ensemble des images déposées, ce qui permet aux utilisateurs potentiels d'entrer en contact avec les ayants-droit. Elle pourrait même commercialiser le fichier original. Ce cadre technique étant défini, nous pouvons, à présent, apprécier les rapports entre l'identification numérique et le droit moral.

2. Les rapports entre l'identification numérique et le droit moral

Tout d'abord, il convient de souligner que les nouvelles techniques, notamment numériques, rendent le droit moral d'autant plus nécessaire qu'elles peuvent faciliter les utilisations dénaturantes des oeuvres. Comme le souligne le gouvernement français dans sa réponse au Livre vert de la Commission européenne sur le droit d'auteur et les droits voisins dans la société de l'information,[24] *"dans le contexte de la société de l'information où les oeuvres sont davantage exposées à un risque de manipulation et de dénaturation ou à de véritables réécritures, le droit moral, notamment le droit à l'intégrité, est d'autant plus pertinent"*. La même affirmation vaut pour la défense de l'intégrité des prestations des artistes-interprètes. Quelle peut alors être l'influence réciproque du droit moral et de l'identification électronique des oeuvres?

a. *Le rôle des systèmes d'identification dans la défense du droit moral*

Le rôle des systèmes électroniques de "signature" des oeuvres est de permettre l'identification (ou des objets de droits voisins) et de déterminer les ayants-droits. Ces systèmes devraient donc faciliter l'accès aux oeuvres tout en permettant et en améliorant le contrôle des utilisations, ainsi que la gestion des redevances. Ils devraient permettre aussi de lutter contre la piraterie, en retraçant le parcours de l'oeuvre. On remarquera que la prise en compte de la dimension extrapatrimoniale n'est jamais évoquée dans les travaux sur la "signature" électronique: ils ont essentiellement pour objectif d'assurer la gestion des oeuvres, mais apparemment, il n'est pas envisagé de s'en servir comme d'un moyen pour faire respecter l'intégrité de l'oeuvre ou la paternité de son auteur.

D'une manière générale, il est évidemment nécessaire que les fabricants de matériel, les télédiffuseurs et les producteurs mettent ce dispositif en oeuvre en créant les matériels *ad hoc*, en mettant en place l'espace d'identification et en le remplissant effectivement et correctement. Par conséquent, se posera la question de l'effectivité du système d'identification, qui suppose un consensus de l'ensemble de la chaîne qui va de la conception des matériels à la diffusion, en passant par la numérisation et l'identification numérique de chaque oeuvre. Mais, même si l'on peut espérer que ce consensus soit obtenu, une autre difficulté risque de surgir.

La numérotation de l'oeuvre et l'intégration de son code identifiant seront laissées à l'initiative principalement du producteur,[25] qui s'en chargera lors de la numérisation de cette oeuvre. Il y a alors un risque pour l'intégrité de l'oeuvre, voire pour la paternité: c'est que cette numérisation soit faite de façon incorrecte, par exemple que ce soit une oeuvre déjà tronquée, modifiée ou dénaturée qui soit numérisée à l'insu de ses auteurs.[26] Il y a là une difficulté potentielle, qui concerne les rapports entre les auteurs et les producteurs qui procéderont aux opérations. Les règles régissant le droit moral pourront être invoquées par l'auteur contre le producteur ou toute autre personne chargée de la numérisation de l'oeuvre et de l'obtention du numéro d'identification, pour réagir contre la dénaturation de son oeuvre (ou la méconnaissance de sa paternité). Mais lorsque l'auteur n'aura pu réagir qu'après la diffusion de l'oeuvre imparfaitement numérisée, comme c'est le plus probable, la correction des erreurs risque de poser des problèmes pratiques importants. Dans sa réponse au Livre vert sur le droit d'auteur et les droits voisins dans la société de l'information, le gouvernement français soulève au moins indirectement cette question lorsqu'il remarque:[27] *"l'identification est assurée par un système mis en oeuvre par un opérateur (...) Même si l'opérateur a un intérêt commercial à ce que les contenus diffusés soient identifiés et/ou identifiables, il appartient aux titulaires de droits de veiller eux-mêmes à la mise en place correcte de l'identification normalisée."*

Il convient de relever que, dans le domaine du "multimédia", d'autres modes d'identification, plus "primitifs" que ceux que nous avons précédemment décrits, sont parfois utilisés. Il s'agit d'intégrer à l'image couverte par un droit exclusif et qui apparaît dans un "CD-ROM", un signe immédiatement identifiable, c'est-à-dire visible sur l'écran et qui indique que l'oeuvre présentée est la propriété d'une personne. On est à mi-chemin entre la mention de réserve de droits et l'apposition d'une marque. Concrètement, par exemple, des ayants-droit, par exemple des musées, font figurer un sigle sur les reproductions dont ils entendent s'assurer le droit exclusif d'exploitation (par exemple, le logo de la Réunion des musées nationaux, c'est-à-dire un sigle formé d'un "M" dans un cercle).[28] Ce sigle ou logo apparaît dans l'image qui est incluse dans le "CD-ROM" ou qui circule sur un réseau. De la sorte, celui qui consulte l'écran est immédiatement averti de l'existence d'un droit ou, au moins, de la source du document, dans la mesure où il connaît la signification du sigle. De surcroît, la reproduction non autorisée de l'oeuvre à partir de cette diffusion, reproduira sans doute le sigle, sauf à réussir à l'effacer bien sûr. Cette technique toute simple présente deux inconvénients. Le premier, c'est que l'on peut supposer que le sigle peut être matériellement éliminé. Le second nous intéresse plus spécialement: c'est que l'inclusion dans l'image d'un tel sigle ou logo porte, en elle-même, atteinte à l'intégrité de l'oeuvre, puisqu'un élément étranger y est ajouté. Il faut donc l'accord de l'auteur de la photographie et celui de l'auteur de l'oeuvre artistique reproduite. En ce sens, la jurisprudence a eu, naguère, l'occasion de condamner l'inclusion, sans l'accord des auteurs, du logo d'une chaîne de télévision dans les images d'une oeuvre audiovisuelle télédiffusée.[29]

En revanche, les systèmes de signature numérique ne présentent pas ce genre d'inconvénients puisque le code n'est pas perceptible lors de la diffusion de l'oeuvre,[30] un tel code ne pouvant être appréhendé que par une machine et non par le spectateur ou l'auditeur de l'oeuvre. Encore faut-il que l'on ne puisse pas neutraliser le système à moins de coûts exorbitants: en d'autres termes, il faut que le système d'identification soit verrouillé ("plombé", pour reprendre un terme employé en matière informatique). Or, l'inconvénient de tout procédé technique, c'est qu'il suscite des procédés techniques contraires. Certes, en l'état actuel, il sera plus difficile et plus coûteux d'altérer un code numérisé que de supprimer un générique sur une copie analogique d'un film. La reproduction de l'oeuvre numérique implique la reprise du code, mais, comme le souligne un représentant des auteurs:[31] *"dès lors qu'on établit un système de codage ou de marquage, on doit imaginer qu'il y aura des tentatives pour le détourner et s'affranchir des obligations inhérentes au droit des auteurs. On ne peut concevoir de système inviolable, il faut donc qualifier clairement ces tentatives d'actes de piraterie."*

Tout barrage technique suscite des voies de contournement. L'exemple du logiciel l'a bien montré: lorsque l'on a imaginé des techniques de "plombage", c'est-à-dire des procédés destinés à empêcher techniquement la reproduction d'un logiciel, rapidement on a vu surgir des logiciels de "déplombage". La jurisprudence française avait alors admis la validité de la pratique du "plombage" et sanctionné, dans un premier temps, l'incitation à la reproduction illicite que constituait la mise sur le marché de logiciels de "déplombage".[32] Il sera donc indispensable que les violations du système d'identification, notamment les suppressions, altérations ou autres falsifications du code, soient juridiquement sanctionnées, soit par l'action en concurrence déloyale ou, plus généralement, par l'action en responsabilité civile, voire par le recours à la législation sur les fraudes,[33] soit par une conception élargie des actes de contrefaçon, ce qui peut poser davantage de problèmes, ou par des sanctions spécifiques que le législateur aurait à définir.[34]

Dans le même ordre d'idées, le désir de se protéger contre la piraterie peut conduire à d'autres pratiques discutables du point de vue du droit moral: certaines agences de presse fixent, à cette fin, des plafonds à la définition et à la résolution de l'image diffusée, ce qui fait que la reproduction non autorisée sera nécessairement d'une qualité médiocre.[35] Mais, cela n'implique-t-il pas aussi un certain non-respect de l'oeuvre dans la diffusion qui a été autorisée puisqu'elle s'opère sous une forme qui est elle-même de qualité limitée? Là encore, le marquage numérique a l'avantage de permettre de donner la meilleure qualité possible à la présentation autorisée de l'oeuvre, puisque la protection contre la piraterie se situe à un autre niveau et n'affecte pas la perception de l'oeuvre par le public.

Même si la protection des intérêts moraux de l'auteur (ou de l'interprète) ne semble pas avoir particulièrement guidé les travaux sur l'identification des oeuvres, celle-ci présente une utilité indirecte pour contribuer à une meilleure protection des intérêts moraux des auteurs. L'identification permet de retracer les utilisations, même partielles, de l'oeuvre, ce qui pourra aussi permettre à l'auteur de critiquer les utilisations dénaturantes par des tiers, puisque que l'on pourra identifier une oeuvre à partir d'une reproduction ou diffusion seulement partielle, ou encore permettre de faire valoir sa paternité, si elle a été violée. Au moins, sur le terrain de la preuve - preuve de la teneur de l'oeuvre originale numérisée, preuve de la qualité d'auteur, preuve de la contrefaçon - le système pourrait jouer un certain rôle indirect pour la défense du droit moral. Surtout, la présence ou l'absence du signal numérique (du code) permettra de savoir si l'oeuvre a subi des modifications. Pour une oeuvre audiovisuelle numérisée, par exemple, le signal est répété: si, donc, lors d'une diffusion ou dans un support, le code manque partiellement (par intermittences) ou même a totalement disparu, il devient évident qu'une modification a été apportée à l'oeuvre. Il est alors possible de comparer l'oeuvre diffusée sous cette forme à l'oeuvre originaire numérisée pour constater l'étendue des atteintes à l'intégrité. De plus, on peut utiliser le système d'identification pour remonter à la source de la modification et déterminer le responsable.

Mais ce n'est à l'évidence pas dans le but de protection du droit moral que le système d'identification a été conçu. Il en résulte que la conception dualiste du droit d'auteur n'a pas d'influence particulière sur cet aspect des choses. Le système est conçu pour des raisons économiques mais peut avoir des utilités pour le droit moral; mais, de toute façon, la jouissance des droits n'est pas juridiquement conditionnée par le marquage. De ce point de vue, il nous semble que la distinction entre systèmes monistes et systèmes dualistes est indifférente.[36]

Il n'existe, à notre connaissance, aucun document, rapport ou projet qui ait soulevé la question du droit moral dans ce contexte.[37] On ne trouve cette question évoquée de façon aussi rapide que dans le texte de M. Lehman. C'est dire, *a fortiori*, que les implications éventuelles de ces projets de systèmes d'identification conçus comme ayant une portée internationale vis-à-vis de l'article *6 bis* de la Convention de Berne ne sont pas non plus évoquées. La raison de ce silence tient sans doute à l'approche choisie, qui concerne la gestion des oeuvres. Du reste, les travaux ont été conduits d'abord avec des industriels des secteurs informatique, télématique ou électronique et avec les organismes spécialisés dans la normalisation (l'ISO, et, en France, l'AFNOR), dont le droit moral n'est vraisemblablement pas une préoccupation majeure.

En revanche, la question du droit moral de l'auteur de l'oeuvre numérisée (ou du droit moral de l'interprète dont l'interprétation est numérisée) est évoquée par le rapport sur les "Industries culturelles et les nouvelles techniques" établi, pour le Ministère de la Culture, par la Commission présidée par le Professeur P. Sirinelli en 1994.[38] Le rapport relève lui aussi l'intérêt potentiel du système en matière de preuve des atteintes à l'oeuvre. En ce qui concerne, en effet, la pratique de l'"échantillonnage" (ou *"sampling"*), la difficulté à laquelle se heurte la protection de l'auteur réside dans la détermination de l'emprunt opéré, c'est-à-dire la découverte de l'existence même d'un emprunt, de la source de cet emprunt et de son importance. Le codage numérique peut probablement faciliter la recherche de ces emprunts.

Selon le rapport de la Commission Sirinelli: *"un problème pratique posé par l'échantillonnage musical est celui de la preuve des emprunts puisque, par définition, la numérisation permet des manipulations des données numérisées à l'infini. Ici, la technique peut, peut-être, venir à l'aide du droit si tant est qu'on parvienne à élaborer des systèmes de codage ou de marquage des oeuvres ou des supports qui soient assez efficaces pour déceler les emprunts non autorisés. La technique ne doit pas se substituer au raisonnement juridique. La preuve, matérielle (marquage retrouvé), de l'emprunt n'implique pas automatiquement la contrefaçon puisqu'il peut advenir que l'élément emprunté ne soit pas protégé (faute d'originalité). La technique simplifie seulement la recherche d'éléments matériels sur lesquels le juge devra se forger librement une opinion."* Le marquage faciliterait ainsi la découverte et la preuve des emprunts illicites, qui constituent à la fois une atteinte au droit d'exploitation et à l'intégrité de l'oeuvre.

La preuve pourra aussi être facilitée dans de tels systèmes lorsque l'oeuvre originale sera inscrite dans la banque de données à laquelle renvoie le code du marquage, la signature. Dès lors, on pourra vérifier très facilement le respect de l'intégrité de l'oeuvre, en comparant l'objet qui circule sur le réseau télématique à l'original incorporé à la banque de données. En l'absence de vignette dans le fichier de la banque de données,[39] celui-ci donne, de toute façon, les moyens de se reporter à l'original. Il en va de même, bien entendu, pour la paternité, puisque le marquage se réfère aussi à l'auteur et au titre de l'oeuvre. Le même raisonnement vaut pour la défense du droit moral de l'interprète sur son interprétation.

Le rapport de la Commission Sirinelli envisage brièvement aussi cette utilité: *"Les techniques de signature numérique s'appliquent de manière à garantir, au "bit" près, l'intégrité de l'oeuvre originale. Ces techniques (...) comprennent la circulation des clés permettant de vérifier les signatures. Cependant, un seul "bit" erroné fait échouer la vérification de signature."* En ce cas, l'attention est immédiatement attirée sur l'imperfection de la présentation qui est faite de l'oeuvre (ou de l'interprétation) et une confrontation avec l'original suffit ensuite à vérifier si l'intégrité de l'oeuvre est effectivement atteinte de telle sorte que le droit au respect de l'oeuvre trouve à s'appliquer. C'est aussi ce que dit le rapport de la Commission Sirinelli: *"Les techniques de signature et d'horodatage conviennent bien pour enregistrer le dépôt d'une oeuvre afin de pouvoir disposer ultérieurement d'un élément de preuve permettant de faire des comparaisons. Ces dernières peuvent ensuite se faire sur des informa-*

tions imperceptibles dans la représentation sonore ou visuelle, mais dont la présence simultanée dans l'original et dans l'oeuvre contestée apporte une forte présomption de plagiat ou d'atteinte au droit d'auteur." Est-ce à dire que l'authentification de l'oeuvre et l'identification de l'auteur soient, de ce point de vue, des questions entièrement nouvelles?[40] A vrai dire, nous ne le pensons pas. Ce qui est nouveau, ce sont les possibilités démultipliées à l'extrême de diffusion, leur mondialisation et les possibilités de dénaturation que suscitent à la fois la technologie numérique et l'interactivité.

b. *L'influence des systèmes d'identification sur le concept de droit moral*

L'émergence des systèmes permettant l'identification, voire l'authentification de l'oeuvre modifie-t-elle en quelque manière le concept de droit moral? Nous ne le pensons pas. Le concept d'identification et d'authentification n'est pas neuf, même s'il prend ici une dimension accrue.

Identification de l'oeuvre et droit moral

Quant à l'identification des oeuvres, il existe déjà depuis longtemps des systèmes d'identification par numéros, notamment pour faciliter le fonctionnement des bibliothèques, l'archivage et le dépôt légal. On peut rappeler, en ce sens, l'existence des numéros d'"ISBN" ou d'"ISSN".[41] L'existence de tels systèmes de numérotation à des fins bibliométriques ou d'archivage ne pose pas de problème particulier en droit d'auteur. Mais ce type d'identification n'a pas d'effet de droit d'auteur, ni de répercussion sur le droit d'auteur. En tout cas, il est totalement neutre à l'égard du droit moral. En principe, en dehors de leur utilité sur le terrain de la preuve, les systèmes de marquage électronique envisagés n'auront pas d'effet juridique, en ce sens qu'ils ne préjugeront pas de l'existence du droit et ne limiteront pas non plus sa jouissance.

C'est ainsi que l'OMPI, à propos du système international d'identification qu'elle envisage, indique: *"l'utilisation du système de numéros d'identification serait facultative (ce qui signifie, entre autres, que l'attribution des numéros d'identification et la publication des données correspondantes ne conditionneraient pas la jouissance et l'exercice des droits sur les oeuvres et phonogrammes concernés (...) aucun effet juridique ne serait attaché à l'existence ou à l'inexistence d'un numéro d'identification pour une oeuvre ou un phonogramme (ce qui signifie...entre autre, qu'aucune présomption légale ne serait attachée au système de numérotation, cependant, ... les données à partir desquelles les numéros d'identification internationaux sont attribués et la publication de ces données peuvent avoir une certaine valeur probante ...)"*.[42]

Il paraît difficile en effet d'aller beaucoup plus loin, compte tenu du principe fondamental de la protection sans formalité:[43] une oeuvre ne pourrait pas être privée de protection au motif que l'on aurait négligé de lui attribuer un numéro d'identification. En revanche, sa protection et sa gestion deviendraient *ipso facto* plus difficiles en pratique, alors même qu'elles seraient intactes en droit. Cela signifie que l'attribution de numéros devrait être systématique et sans doute obligatoire pour être efficace.

Authentification et droit moral

En ce qui concerne l'authentification de l'oeuvre et l'attribution de sa paternité, la question n'est pas entièrement neuve, puisqu'elle se pose fréquemment dans le domaine des oeuvres d'art. Dans les systèmes d'identification électronique, ce n'est généralement pas l'auteur lui-même qui procède au marquage, mais celui qui numérise l'oeuvre, c'est-à-dire normalement le producteur ou l'agence photogra–phique, par exemple. Ce marquage ne s'apparente donc pas à la signature que l'artiste appose sur un tableau. D'ailleurs, l'auteur serait tout à fait en droit de contester l'attribution de la paternité d'une oeuvre que lui feraient le marquage et la base de données de référence. L'auteur pourrait très bien invoquer son droit moral pour contester une attribution de paternité inexacte (qu'il conteste être l'auteur de l'oeuvre qui lui est attribuée par le marquage ou qu'il revendique une paternité faussement attribuée à une autre personne par ce marquage).

Il pourrait aussi l'invoquer pour contester le titre qui a été donné par erreur à son oeuvre ou encore pour se plaindre d'une atteinte à l'intégrité de son oeuvre, soit que l'oeuvre ait été mal numérisée (par exemple, qu'elle n'ait été numérisée que dans une version partielle ou de mauvaise qualité), soit que la base de données à laquelle renvoie le marquage, comporte une version dénaturée de l'oeuvre. Les différents attributs du droit moral s'appliquent évidemment aux modalités du marquage. Une oeuvre non divulguée ne pourrait pas non plus être marquée sans l'accord de l'auteur. L'exercice éventuel du droit de retrait ou de repentir devrait logiquement conduire à retirer l'oeuvre de la base de données. Les opérateurs devront donc prendre garde au respect du droit moral dans les modalités des opérations de numérisation et de marquage, mais - en elles-mêmes - ces opérations sont neutres. Cette neutralité implique que le droit moral et ses caractères, notamment l'inaliénabilité, ne peuvent en rien gêner le développement du système d'identification.[44]

> *Le concept de droit moral peut-il être appliqué aux questions de détermination de l'authenticité de l'oeuvre et d'identification de l'auteur, ou s'agit-il de notions entièrement différentes, ou encore faut-il adapter le droit moral dans ce domaine?[45]*

L'expérience du secteur des oeuvres d'art

Comme on l'a déjà annoncé, le droit d'auteur connaît déjà depuis longtemps le problème d'authentification et d'identification en matière d'oeuvres d'art. Il s'agit concrètement de savoir si l'authentification et l'attribution d'un tableau relèvent du droit moral de l'auteur ou non. C'est une question assez délicate. L'artiste est, à l'évidence, bien fondé à dire si une oeuvre qui lui est attribuée est authentique ou pas, et bien sûr à critiquer les modifications qui auraient été apportées à une oeuvre originale. Dans la mesure où il est question d'attribuer une oeuvre, le droit au nom ou à la paternité de l'artiste est en cause (article L 121-1 CPI). Il faut signaler que l'apposition d'un nom usurpé ou d'une fausse signature sur une oeuvre constitue aussi le délit spécial de "faux artistique" (loi des 9-12 février 1895).[46] Il est intéressant de relever que le droit moral du CPI vise à protéger l'auteur, tandis que la législation sur le faux artistique tend surtout à assurer la loyauté du marché de l'art, mais, bien sûr, l'auteur et ses ayants-droit peuvent aussi agir sur ce second fondement.

En pratique, la détermination de la personne qualifiée pour authentifier une oeuvre d'art pose des problèmes: l'auteur l'emporte-t-il sur l'avis d'un expert; le titulaire du droit de reproduction est-il qualifié? Un fabricant de copies manuelles peut-il apposer la signature de l'auteur copié?[47] Etc. Si l'on se place sur le terrain de la propriété intellectuelle, à notre avis, l'auteur est toujours fondé à invoquer son droit à la paternité pour faire reconnaître qu'il est bien l'auteur d'une oeuvre ou même que l'oeuvre qui lui est attribuée est un faux.

Il est vrai que l'on pourrait soutenir que ce deuxième cas relève peut-être plutôt de ses droits généraux de la personnalité au nom et à la réputation, puisqu'il ne s'agit pas de défendre la relation de l'auteur à l'une de ses oeuvres. Toutefois, il y a un lien logique évident entre le droit à faire reconnaître sa paternité sur une oeuvre et le droit de faire savoir qu'une oeuvre fait l'objet d'une fausse attribution de paternité. C'est pourquoi, la jurisprudence ne semble pas vouloir s'arrêter à cette distinction sans doute exagérément subtile et inclut dans le droit moral de l'auteur au respect de son nom, le droit de contester sa paternité sur une oeuvre qu'il n'a pas créée.[48] Cela paraît raisonnable et ne modifie pas fondamentalement le sens du droit moral.[49]

Un arrêt rendu par la Cour d'appel de Paris en 1986, dans l'affaire *Utrillo*,[50] a jugé ainsi que le droit de reproduction étant un droit patrimonial, il ne donne pas à son titulaire la qualité pour contester en justice l'authenticité d'un tableau, une telle action relevant du seul droit moral. L'enseignement sur ce point de cet arrêt reste valable bien qu'il ait été cassé sur un autre point.[51] Et, du reste, sur renvoi après cassation, la Cour d'appel de Versailles a jugé, le 3 octobre 1990,[52] que le *"titulaire du droit moral sur l'oeuvre de Maurice Utrillo, était fondé à poursuivre une vérification d'authenticité (...)"*. En l'occurrence, le titulaire du droit moral était donc fondé à opérer une saisie-contrefaçon de tableaux dont il contestait l'authenticité. La même solution se retrouve dans plusieurs autres décisions.[53] Par exemple, dans un arrêt du 23 mars 1992, la Cour de Paris[54] affirmait que: *"l'attribution à Rodin, par l'usurpation de son nom, d'une oeuvre qui n'est pas de lui constitue une atteinte au respect du nom du sculpteur et à l'identité artistique de son oeuvre"*. Le refus d'authentifier l'oeuvre, dans ce domaine, a évidemment aussi des conséquences économiques, puisque l'objet dont l'attribution à l'auteur est refusée perd évidemment une grande partie de sa valeur marchande. Mais ce n'est pas là, bien sûr, l'objet du droit moral, ce n'est qu'une conséquence de son exercice.[55]

> *Quels enseignements peut-on tirer de ces décisions pour l'authentification des oeuvres numérisées?*

D'abord, il faut considérer qu'en dernier ressort, c'est toujours à l'auteur, invoquant son droit moral, qu'il revient de dire si la reproduction ou la représentation de son oeuvre est bien respectueuse de l'intégrité de cette oeuvre et, *a fortiori*, si ce qui est diffusé ou reproduit est bien son oeuvre. Si ce qui est diffusé est conforme à l'information contenue dans la base de données, notamment à la vignette reproduisant l'oeuvre, il a là un élément de preuve utile. Toutefois, l'auteur pourra encore démontrer que la vignette de la base de données, elle-même, est incorrecte et dénature l'oeuvre ou que l'attribution qui lui en est faite dans la base de données est erronée. Ici, l'effet du système de marquage paraît être d'inverser la charge de la preuve, mais pas d'interdire la démonstration par l'auteur de la violation de son droit moral. A l'inverse, si la reproduction dans le CD-ROM ou la présentation en ligne entre en contradiction avec les informations auxquelles renvoie le numéro d'identification, la preuve de la violation du droit moral sera particulièrement aisée et pratiquement impossible à combattre pour le contrefacteur.

En revanche, le fait que l'authentification de l'oeuvre relève essentiellement du droit moral n'interdit pas de confier à un autre que l'auteur, la tâche de réaliser matériellement l'identification et le renvoi éventuel à une reproduction de contrôle dans un fichier.[56] C'est pourquoi il n'y a pas d'objection au fonctionnement du système d'identification qui puisse être fondée sur le droit moral. Tout au plus, peut-on trouver souhaitable que l'auteur soit invité à donner son avis sur la confection des "vignettes" destinées à servir de moyen de consultation et de référence dans la base de données (ou ailleurs), ce qui éviterait aussi bien des contestations ultérieures sur leur caractère dénaturant ou non-authentique, que des erreurs matérielles.

Par conséquent, il nous semble bien que le système d'identification et d'authentification envisagé n'a pas pour objet premier la protection des intérêts moraux de l'auteur. Il peut y contribuer, dans une certaine mesure, sur le terrain de la preuve, mais sa mise en oeuvre pourrait parfois aussi y porter atteinte, quoique d'une façon qui devrait être marginale. La fonction d'authentification de l'oeuvre assurée ainsi n'a donc pas exactement la même portée que celle que l'on a évoquée en matière d'oeuvres d'art. En ce sens, parler de "signature" électronique de l'oeuvre apparaît un peu comme un abus de langage, puisque ce n'est pas l'auteur lui-même qui marque l'oeuvre.

Autres intérêts extrapatrimoniaux en jeu

Quant à savoir si l'on peut imaginer un droit moral pour les producteurs, elle appelle, en France, une réponse nécessairement négative, sauf en ce qui concerne le cas de l'oeuvre collective,[57] hypothèse (malheureuse), où le promoteur est investi du droit moral sur l'ensemble qui constitue l'oeuvre collective (article L 113-5 du CPI).[58] En pareille hypothèse, certes le promoteur exerce le droit moral, mais il ne peut le détourner de son objet pour l'utiliser à des fins purement économiques au lieu de l'appliquer à la protection de l'oeuvre,[59] mais il n'est pas à exclure qu'il soit moins attaché à l'intégrité de l'oeuvre que ne l'est un auteur. Toutefois, l'authentification présente un intérêt en quelque sorte publicitaire pour le producteur, voire pour le diffuseur, dans la mesure où elle leur permet d'assurer au public qu'on lui présente bien l'oeuvre originaire, une oeuvre "authentique" - ce qui a, réciproquement, un intérêt de nature peut-être "consumériste", mais en tout cas culturel, pour le public, qui attend une oeuvre authentique d'un auteur donné, et non des versions déformées ou incomplètes.

Bien entendu, les interprètes ont, eux, de véritables droits moraux, proches de ceux des auteurs, à faire valoir vis-à-vis du numérique et des systèmes d'identification. Il est d'ailleurs envisagé de leur ouvrir l'accès au dispositif d'identification des oeuvres audiovisuelles.

Conclusion

Le questionnaire pose enfin des questions à caractère prospectif. La réponse à ces questions nous servira de conclusion.

Quel sera le rôle des moyens techniques pour garantir l'authenticité dans l'avenir?

Il est difficile de répondre. Sur l'utilité des systèmes d'identification, nous avons dit l'utilité indirecte qu'ils peuvent présenter, spécialement en matière de preuve. Mais, étant mis en oeuvre à l'initiative des producteurs, ils n'élimineront pas le rôle du droit moral exercé par l'auteur. On peut penser que les capacités de mémoire des matériels puissent encore augmenter et que, comme dans le système "SPIDER/SPIFF", les bases de données de référence des autres oeuvres puissent contenir aussi, un jour, une reproduction complète de chaque oeuvre. On peut aussi imaginer que des dispositifs empêchant toute modification de l'oeuvre numérisée (ou même toute reproduction) soient mis au point un jour, ce qui protégerait parfaitement l'intégrité de l'oeuvre. Mais nous n'y croyons pas, d'une part parce que l'on ne voit pas pourquoi les fabricants de matériel et même les producteurs engageraient les dépenses nécessaires à la mise au point éventuelle et à l'utilisation de tels procédés, et d'autre part parce que tout système technique de verrouillage suscite rapidement l'invention de systèmes de déverrouillage.[60]

Une autre interrogation porte sur la possibilité de rendre légalement obligatoires les systèmes d'identification internationale des oeuvres. Il n'existe pas, à l'heure actuelle, de disposition légale rendant le marquage numérique obligatoire. Mais il existe, depuis longtemps, en dehors du droit d'auteur, un système de dépôt légal obligatoire.[61] Ce système obligatoire ne conditionne en rien la protection de l'oeuvre par le droit d'auteur, qui repose sur le principe de la protection sans formalité (article L 111-1 CPI). Mais il est à noter que le Code de la propriété intellectuelle lui-même reconnaît une utilité à ce système sur le terrain de la preuve (cf. article L 123-3 CPI).[62] Si donc, les systèmes d'identification internationale devaient être rendus légalement obligatoires, ce serait à condition que le non-respect de cette obligation ne soit en aucune manière sanctionnée par un refus de protéger l'oeuvre, par une restriction à l'étendue du droit d'auteur ou par une déchéance quelconque. Ni la jouissance, ni l'exercice du droit ne seraient conditionnés à l'enregistrement (dans la conception présentée ci-dessus).

Dans la mesure où ces systèmes n'ont juridiquement aucun effet, si ce n'est de fournir un moyen de preuve parmi d'autres,[63] et servent seulement à faciliter la gestion des droits, il ne nous semble pas que l'on se heurterait au principe de la protection sans formalités posé à l'article 5(2) de la Convention de Berne et à l'article L 111-1 du

CPI.[64] De surcroît, on peut penser que ces systèmes, ainsi conçus, ne devraient pas susciter de divergences entre pays de droit d'auteur et pays de *"copyright"*, puisque les intérêts des producteurs et des auteurs à l'existence d'un tel système d'identification paraissent largement convergents[65] (tant que l'on n'en fait pas une condition juridique de la protection de l'oeuvre toutefois).

Si l'on se place un instant sur le terrain patrimonial, le groupe français estime devoir souligner particulièrement qu'il est nécessaire, pour permettre de sauvegarder les droits patrimoniaux des auteurs et d'en assurer une gestion effective, non seulement de rendre obligatoires ces systèmes, mais aussi de les assortir de sanctions efficaces. Il faudra absolument prévoir d'une part des sanctions efficaces contre les fabricants de matériels qui ne prévoiraient pas l'intégration des systèmes de codage et contre les producteurs ou autres exploitants qui ne mettraient pas en oeuvre le système d'identification;[66] d'autre part, des sanctions dissuasives à l'égard des tiers qui violeraient le système d'identification mis en place.[67] C'est certainement de ces conditions que dépendent non seulement l'effectivité des systèmes d'identification, mais encore l'avenir des droits patrimoniaux des auteurs dans le "cyberspace".

Enfin, quant à l'avenir du droit moral, en particulier le droit à l'intégrité et le droit au nom, y compris dans leur dimension d'authentification de l'oeuvre et d'identification de son auteur,[68] il nous semble que la révolution que constitue le numérique démontre l'impérieuse nécessité de ces prérogatives. On a vu que les systèmes envisagés ne sauraient se substituer au droit moral, ne serait-ce que parce que leur rôle est différent. Par ailleurs, si l'on voit toujours surgir de nouvelles techniques qui permettent ou facilitent des atteintes aux droits des auteurs, il ne faut pas trop miser sur la technique pour protéger sans faille les intérêts des auteurs ou des interprètes, surtout en ce qui concerne leurs intérêts moraux. C'est pourquoi un concept juridique comme le droit moral reste indispensable, quels que soient les espoirs que l'on puisse nourrir, à un moment donné, sur telle ou telle technique. La numérisation des oeuvres et l'interactivité des réseaux risquent de conduire à toutes sortes de violations du droit moral et, plus généralement, du droit des auteurs. Mais comme le relève justement le rapport de la Commission Sirinelli, *"Il convient d'apprécier si la numérisation entraîne une véritable différence de nature plutôt que de degrés. A vrai dire, cette évolution technique ne bouleverse pas les analyses, même si, ici ou là, certains aménagements sont nécessaires. On retrouve aujourd'hui d'éternelles interrogations simplement remises au goût du jour. L'adaptation est pour le moment possible sans modification radicale."* [69]

Plus que jamais peut-être, le droit moral, et un droit moral conçu de façon assez large, a un rôle essentiel à jouer. C'est aussi le sens des réponses données par le gouvernement français ou par notre association, à la section VII du questionnaire du Livre vert de la Commission européenne sur le droit d'auteur et les droits voisins dans la société de l'information.

Notes

1. "Preliminary draft", juin 1994, p. 113; report, sept. 1995, p. 187 - notre traduction du second texte.
2. *"Anyone who has access to an information object, in addition to having access to the work, also has access to the digital signature for the object. Consequently, the digital signature for the object may be recomputed and used to independently confirm the integrity of the object by comparing it to the digital signature appended to the object".*
3. Cf.: L. Laborelli, "Tatouage des images et des sons, techniques cryptographiques d'authentification et contrôle du copyright", *Expertises* décembre 1995, p. 428.
4. Les réseaux de services en ligne offrant des serveurs "Internet", sont à l'heure actuelle: "Compuserve", "America on line" et "Microsoft Network" (Etats-Unis, présents aussi en France). En France, il existe (ou existera bientôt) plusieurs services en ligne d'origine française ou européenne ("Infonie", "Wanadoo", "France en Ligne", "Europe Online") (cf.: *Libération* du 16 février 1996, supplément multimédia) ... sans compter le "Minitel", plus grand réseau au monde par le nombre d'utilisateurs, mais système fermé et à capacités limitées.
5. Cf.: C. Gaillard, "Les défis à la gestion collective", *Le Journal*, 1995, Sacem; p. 18.
6. Pour les oeuvres audiovisuelles, on envisage, à l'heure actuelle, une base de données pour l'Europe et une autre pour l'Amérique du nord, en attendant les autres parties du monde.
7. En particulier, en intervenant *in extremis* au Congrès de l'ISO/MPEG en mars 1994 pour faire réserver un espace d'identification des oeuvres dans la norme "MPEG-2", alors que les personnes intéressées aux questions de droits intellectuels n'avaient pas été consultées jusque-là. Cf.: G. Vercken, "Droits d'auteur et multimédia, quelques réflexions", Digimedia, Genève 27 mai 1994.
8. En matière de diffusion radio-numérique (DAB), toutefois, la norme "MPEG-1" ne comporte pas de champ réservé à l'identification.
9. *"Motion Picture Expert Group".*
10. Cf.: interview de M.Ph. Vincent (SACD), in: *Ecran Total,* n. 115, 7 février 1996 p. 53.
11. *"Joint Photographic Expert Group".*
12. Il faut signaler en outre l'existence d'une troisième norme "MHEG" (*"Multimédia and Hypermedia and information coding Expert Group"*), norme de gestion des objets multi- et hypermédia.
13. Géré par la Bibliothèque Nationale Allemande.
14. Géré par l'IFPI.
15. Géré par la Bibliothèque Nationale Allemande.
16. En outre, pour simplifier la gestion des droits, on peut organiser l'attribution de numéros d'identification aux auteurs (fichier "CAE", "compositeur, auteur, éditeur", de la CISAC) et aux interprètes (projet "International performers database" de la SCAPR, *"Societies council for the administration of performers rights"*), cf.: C. Rodrigues, précitée.
17. *Ibid.*
18. Association de gestion internationale des oeuvres audiovisuelles.
19. Cf.: Réponse du Gouvernement français au Livre vert CEE sur le droit d'auteur et les droits voisins dans la société de l'information, janvier 1996, pp. 18 *et seq.*; Comp.: C. Rodrigues, "Les bases de données multimédia, un pas de plus à franchir pour les artistes-interprètes", Gaz. Pal. 11-12 octobre 1995, p. 20.
20. SPIDER est le nom du logiciel et signifie: "Système de protection des images par la documentation, l'identification et l'enregistrement des fichiers numériques" ou *"System of protection for images by documentation, identification and registration of digital files".*
21. V.: "La SRF et les enjeux de l'identification des oeuvres", Film Français 12-19 mai 1995, p. 40.
22. L'autorité d'enregistrement fournit le logiciel qui permet de créer la vignette.
23. Association française de normalisation.
24. Janvier 1996, spé. p. 13.
25. Pris ici au sens le plus large. Pour les photographies, il pourrait s'agir, par exemple, d'une agence de presse ou de photographies à laquelle l'auteur a cédé ses droits.
26. Ou que l'oeuvre soit numérisée à partir d'un support analogique de qualité insuffisante.
27. P. 24.
28. *Libération* 5 janvier 1996, cahier multimédia, p. II; L. Laborelli, préc., Expertises déc. 1995, p. 428.
29. Tgi. Paris 29 juin 1988, *Marchand c. La Cinq*, *RIDA* octobre 1988, n. 138, p. 328: "seule importe ... l'image qu'elle distribue sur son réseau et qui doit être la reproduction fidèle, sans suppression, ni ajout, sinon expressément autorisés, de l'oeuvre ...".
30. Technique dite "stéganographique", qui consiste à masquer une signature qui n'est lisible que par un ordinateur. Cf.: L. Laborelli, précité.
31. Ph. Vincent, précité.
32. Paris 20 octobre 1988, Cahiers du droit d'auteur juin 1989 p. 20; Cass. com. 22 mai 1991, *Bull. civ.* IV n. 172; JCPG 1992-II-21792, obs. J. Huet; La législation actuelle, précisons-le toutefois, a modifié les termes du débat en matière de logiciel; cf.: Jurisclasseur Propriété littéraire, Fasc. 1246, n. 52 *et seq.*
33. Intégrée au Code de la Consommation.
34. Comparez: l'article L 122-6 du CPI.
35. *Libération* 5 janvier 1996, précité.
36. Questionnaire, point 5.
37. Questionnaire, points 1, 2 et 3.
38. "Industries culturelles et nouvelles techniques", *La documentation française* 1994, spé.: pp. 96 et 100.
39. Pour des raisons tenant à la capacité des mémoires, il ne semble pas possible, à l'heure actuelle,

d'intégrer une reproduction d'oeuvre audiovisuelle dans le fichier, car cela consommerait trop de place par rapport à la capacité du support.

40. Questionnaire, points 3, 2ᵉ phrase; 6; 8.
41. *"International Standard Book Number"* (livres); *"International Standard Serial Number"* (publications en série et périodiques). Il existe aussi un numéro d'identification consacré aux phonogrammes, l'ISRC *("International Standard Recording Code")*; un numéro pour identifier les fabricants de disques compacts (le "SID"). Cf.: OMPI, "Réunion consultative relative à la création d'un système facultatif de numérotation internationale pour certaines catégories d'oeuvres littéraires et artistiques et pour les phonogrammes", 10 janvier 1994, memorandum.
42. Document OMPI, précité, n. 2.
43. CPI, article L 111-1; Convention de Berne, article 5(2).
44. Questionnaire, point 4.
45. Questionnaire, point 6.
46. Article 1er: *"Seront punis d'un emprisonnement (...) et d'une amende (...), sans préjudice des dommages intérêts s'il y a lieu: (1°) ceux qui auront apposé ou fait apparaître frauduleusement un nom usurpé sur une oeuvre de peinture, de sculpture, de dessin, de gravure et de musique. (2°) Ceux qui sur les mêmes oeuvres, auront frauduleusement et dans le but de tromper l'acheteur sur la personnalité de l'auteur, imité sa signature ou un signe adopté par lui"*. Cf.: D. Gaudel, "Droit d'auteur et faux artistiques", *RIDA* janvier 1992, n. 151, p. 103; S. Durrande, "L'artiste, le juge pénal et le faux artistique - plaidoyer pour une loi méconnue", *Revue de Sciences criminelles* octobre-décembre 1989, p. 687; Lyon-Caen, "Le faux artistique", *RIDA* 1959, n. 25, p. 33; J. Fauchere, "Les faux en matière de peinture et d'art", *RIDA* octobre 1975, p. 89 et janvier 1976, p. 3.
47. Cf.: Tgi. (ch. correctionnelle) 9 mai 1995, *RIDA* janvier 1996, p. 282.
48. Sur cette discussion, cf.: Desbois, Traité (1978), n. 424; A. & H.J. Lucas, Traité (1994), n. 407.
49. Questionnaire, point 6.
50. Paris 17 décembre 1986, JCP-G 1987-II-2O899, note B. Edelman; *RIDA* n. 132, avril 1987, p. 66.
51. C'est-à-dire sur les règles de dévolution du droit moral: Cass. civ. I°, 11 janvier 1989, *Bull. civ. I*, n. 9; *RIDA* juillet 1989, p. 256.
52. Versailles 3 octobre 1990, *RIDA* avril 1991, n. 148, p.148, note P.Y. Gautier.
53. En dernier lieu, à propos de l'apposition de la signature de Renoir sur des copies manuelles: Tgi. Paris (ch. correctionnelle) 9 mai 1995, *RIDA* janvier 1996, p. 282, qui affirme que "le droit de l'auteur au respect de son nom et de sa qualité (...) permet aussi à l'auteur de s'opposer à ce que lui soit attribuée une oeuvre qui n'émane pas de lui".
54. Paris (chambre correctionnelle) 23 mars 1992, *RIDA* janvier 1993, n. 155, p. 181 (ajoutez: les jugements cités par A. et H.J. Lucas, précités, p. 330 note (230).
55. Questionnaire, point 5, 6 et 7.
56. En ce sens, on peut mentionner une jurisprudence qui a admis qu'un artiste peut s'engager contractuellement à apposer sa signature sur des reproductions autorisées de ses oeuvres, reproductions qu'il "authentifie" ainsi, et que sa légataire peut être tenue par cet engagement, mais sous réserve de l'exercice du droit moral: Cass. civ. I°, 26 janvier 1994, *Bull. civ. I*, n. 33, p. 25; D. 1995, som. com. 55, obs. C. Colombet.
57. On rappellera que la qualification d'oeuvre collective ne s'applique jamais aux oeuvres audiovisuelles, qui sont qualifiées par la loi d'oeuvres de collaboration: Cass. civ. I°, 26 janvier 1994, *Bull. civ. I*, n. 35, p. 27; *RIDA* octobre 1994, p. 433; Paris 16 mai 1994, *RIDA* octobre 1994, p. 474; *RTDCom.* 1995 p. 124, note A. Francon; D. 1995 som. com. 55, note C. Colombet; Paris 17 janvier 1995, *RIDA* juillet 1995, p. 332.
58. Questionnaire, point 7.
59. Questionnaire, point 8.
60. Questionnaire, point 9.
61. Depuis une loi de 1925, actuellement loi du 20 juin 1992.
62. "Pour les oeuvres pseudonymes ou collectives, la durée du droit exclusif est de cinquante années à compter du 1er janvier de l'année civile suivant celle de la publication (...) La date de publication est déterminée *par tout mode de preuve du droit commun, et notamment par le dépôt légal* (...)".
63. Cf.: les travaux de l'OMPI, précités.
64. Questionnaire, points 10 et 11.
65. Selon, des représentants de la SRF (société des réalisateurs de films), en: *Le Film Français du 12-19 mai 1995,* p. 40: "sans identification des oeuvres, il n'y aura pas de marché. La clé de l'essor du multimédia, c'est qu'il y ait un code-barre pour permettre la gestion automatisée des droits".
66. Les sanctions s'adressant aux exploitants, le principe de la protection sans formalité est respecté.
67. Voir plus haut.
68. Questionnaire, point 12.
69. Précité, p. 103.

Italie

M. Fabiani

1. Est-ce qu'il y a en Italie des documents officieux comme, par exemple, le Livre vert américain, ou des projets de nouvelles lois ou d'autres documents qui discutent, d'une manière expresse, des problèmes de "l'authenticité d'oeuvres et/ou de l'auteur" dans le contexte multimedia ou de l'infrastructure mondiale d'information? / 2. Si oui, est-ce que la discussion ou les projets concernés établissent une relation du problème avec le concept traditionnel du droit moral, en particulier le droit à la paternité et le droit à l'intégrité de l'oeuvre, tels qu'ils sont prévus à l'article 6bis de la Convention de Berne?

En Italie, il n'y a pas encore de documents officieux sur les problèmes de l'authenticité d'oeuvres et/ou de l'auteur dans le contexte multimédia ou de l'infrastructure mondiale de l'information.

3. Si non, quelle est probablement la raison pour laquelle cette relation n'est pas établie? Est-ce que le problème de l'authenticité est un concept entièrement nouveau et indépendant des solutions traditionnelles du droit moral? / 4. Est-ce que des éléments traditionnellement liés à la protection par le droit moral, comme, par exemple, son inaliénabilité et la protection d'intérêts apparemment exclusivement intellectuels et personnels, empêchent le développement d'une conception moderne de protection de l'authenticité de l'oeuvre et/ou de l'auteur?

Le problème de l'authenticité et de l'authentification de l'oeuvre est étroitement lié à la protection du droit de l'auteur à la paternité intellectuelle et à l'intégrité de l'oeuvre. La loi italienne sur le droit d'auteur n. 633 du 1941 reconnaît à l'auteur le droit de revendiquer la paternité de l'oeuvre et de s'opposer à toute déformation, mutilation ou autre modification de l'oeuvre et à toute autre atteinte à l'oeuvre préjudiciables à l'honneur ou à la réputation de l'auteur. Ce droit est attribué à l'auteur indépendamment des droits exclusifs d'utilisation économique de l'oeuvre et même après cession de ces droits. Parmi les droits exclusifs d'utilisation économique de l'oeuvre, l'auteur a le droit exclusif d'apporter à son oeuvre n'importe quelle modification (article 18 de la Loi). Sur la base de la disposition de l'article 62 de la Loi sur le droit d'auteur, les exemplaires d'un disque phonographique ou d'un autre instrument similaire reproducteur de sons ou de voix, sur lequel l'oeuvre de l'esprit a été enregistrée, ne peuvent être mis dans le commerce s'ils ne portent pas, apposés d'une manière indélébile sur le disque ou sur l'instrument, les indications suivantes: (1) le titre de l'oeuvre reproduite, (2) le nom de l'auteur, (3) le nom de l'artiste interprète, et (4) la date de la fabrication.

5. La protection par le droit moral peut-elle servir d'autres intérêts à part les intérêts intellectuels et personnels, en particulier aussi des intérêts pécuniaires? Est-ce qu'une telle approche est facilitée dans votre pays par certaines conceptions doctrinales comme l'interprétation moniste du droit d'auteur (c'est-à-dire un droit d'auteur, conçu dans son intégralité avec toutes ses facultés, servant tous les intérêts liés à sa protection) ou d'autres conceptions? / 6. Est-ce qu'une conception suivant laquelle le droit moral peut aussi couvrir et garantir l'authenticité de l'oeuvre et de l'auteur peut être appliquée sans changement de l'interprétation des vraies fonctions du droit moral?

Si le préjudice à l'honneur ou à la reputation de l'auteur a une incidence sur les droits patrimoniaux, l'auteur peut demander le payement de dommages-intérêts en réparation du préjudice économique causé. Face aux dispositions ci-dessus évoquées, on peut exprimer l'opinion que la sauvegarde de l'authenticité de l'oeuvre et/ou de l'auteur est couverte par la législation actuellement en vigueur.

7. Est-ce qu'on peut imaginer des droits moraux de "producteurs" de tous genres, dans leur capacité de successeurs légaux des auteurs ou dans leur capacité de titulaires originaux du droit d'auteur ou de droits voisins? Est-ce que ce genre de droits moraux peut être instrumentalisé pour la protection de leur intérêt à l'authenticité? / 8. Comment peut-on garantir que le droit moral n'est pas rendu entièrement "économique" sur la base d'une conception de protection de l'authenticité si, en même temps, la nécessité de la protection de ces intérêts d'authenticité des producteurs ne peut pas être niée?

Le droit moral de l'auteur est inaliénable. En outre, la loi italienne donne au producteur de disques phonographiques et instruments similaires le droit de s'opposer à ce que l'utilisation du disque ou instrument similaire reproducteur de sons ou de voix soit effectuée dans des conditions de nature à porter "un grave préjudice à ses intérêts industriels".

9. Quel sera le rôle des moyens techniques pour assurer l'authenticité à l'avenir? / 10. Est-ce que des systèmes internationaux de nombres qui identifient des oeuvres et d'autres objets protégés (comme des phonogrammes) peuvent être prescrits d'une manière impérative? / 11. Est-ce qu'il y a des dispositions légales qui imposent certaines méthodes technologiques pour l'authentification de l'oeuvre et/ou qui interdisent que l'on supprime de tels systèmes de protection technique?

Les moyens techniques devront jouer, à l'avenir, un rôle important pour assurer l'authenticité. En Italie, une nouvelle loi (décret législatif n. 685 du 16 novembre 1994), a introduit, dans le chapitre consacré aux défenses et sanctions pénales de la Loi sur le droit d'auteur, un article (article 171*ter*) qui prévoit la peine à la réclusion de trois mois jusqu'à trois ans et d'une amende pour quiconque vend ou met en location vidéocassettes, musicassettes ou autres supports d'oeuvres cinématographiques ou audiovisuelles ne portant pas le visa de la Société italienne des auteurs et éditeurs (SIAE). L'utilisation éventuelle de ce visa appliqué sous forme de *"digital* *signature"* (v. page 188 du Livre vert américain, septembre 1995) pourra aider l'identification de l'oeuvre et de son auteur. La suppression ou la contrefaçon du visa, en tant que certification d'un établissement de droit public (SIAE), comporte l'application de sanctions pénales sur la base du Code Pénal (article 468 *et seq.* du Code Pénal).

> **12.** *Est-ce qu'une conception de la protection par le droit moral (en particulier le droit à la paternité et le droit à l'intégrité), éventuellement dans une forme étendue qui garantit l'authenticité de l'oeuvre et de l'auteur, va jouer un rôle plutôt réduit ou plus important dans la pratique future du droit d'auteur?*

A mon avis, une conception de la protection par le droit moral (droit à la paternité intellectuelle et à l'intégrité) dans une forme étendue qui garantit l'authenticité de l'oeuvre et de l'auteur ne pourra que jouer un rôle plus important dans la pratique future du droit d'auteur.

The Netherlands

A.A. QUAEDVLIEG

Introductory remarks

The problems stemming from authenticity of authorship and work in a more traditional context of the copyright debate have in the Netherlands hardly been touched so far in the discussions about the emergence of the Global Information Infrastructure.

There is a clear relation between the traditional right of paternity and the right of integrity, and the new right of authenticity of authorship and work, but they are not identical. Therefore, it should be determined where the essential difference lies. The shift from the problem of the integrity and paternity of the work to the authenticity of authorship and work primarily indicates a shift in perspective. It is not so much the legal interest of the original author which is at stake when I speak of authenticity of authorship and work, but the legal interest of the producer or employer.

The Netherlands already have some practical experience with this 'producer perspective', as the articles 7 and 8 at the Dutch Copyright Act 1912[1] open the possibility of regarding employers or corporations as author. Under the articles 7 and 8,[2] the employer or corporation is not just granted the copyright or considered as copyright holder, but they are considered to be the author. As a consequence, it is often assumed that the copyright holder under these articles is also the holder of the *moral* rights, even if this view has been questioned because part of the doctrine which considers it contrary to the logic of moral rights. The Supreme Court has never been called to decide the question.[3] Nevertheless, the existing situation has provided sufficient reason for some Dutch authors to shed their light on the legal consequences of moral rights, when they are exercised not by the actual maker but by employers and producers, often in the form of legal persons, and the difficulties and differences which may result from such a different perspective.

These same difficulties and differences play a role as regards to the right of authenticity. Thus, much of the analysis regarding traditional moral rights in the hands of a producer also proves useful as to the 'right of authenticity'. Therefore, I will will elaborate on this subject in my answers.

Answers to the questionnaire

1. Are there official documents such as the US Green Paper, drafts of new laws or other documents expressly discussing problems of 'authenticity of works and/or authorship' in the multimedia or Global Information Infrastructure (GII) context?

Yes and no. The only official document available at this moment is the reaction of the Dutch Ministry of Justice to the European Commission regarding section VII (Moral Rights) of the Green Paper on Copyright and Related Rights in the Information Society. This reaction dates from 3 January 1996 and has been based on a very careful and comprehensive consultation of all circles concerned. Although the authenticity right is mentioned (page 19), the Reaction is succinct at this issue. Nevertheless it reveals that the importance of authenticity was emphasized from several sides. A solution could be found in technical provisions. *'This does not have to lead to an extension of the list of moral rights'.*

> **2.** *If yes, does the discussion or proposal establish a relation with the traditional concept of moral rights, in particular with the paternity right and the integrity right as covered by article 6bis of the Berne Convention?*

The reaction of the Ministry of Justice to the Green Paper rather implicitly establishes a relation to the traditional moral rights, in submitting that the existing list of moral rights does not need to be extended with a right of authenticity (see above). The problem of authenticity of authorship and work does not seem to be a totally new concept independent of traditional solutions of moral rights. The fact that questions concerning authenticity have, so far, received little special attention, could perhaps be explained by the fact that the Netherlands have a tradition of granting moral rights to employers and legal persons, which has not caused any important practical problems so far. Problems regarding authenticity of authorship and work have right from the beginning been conceived as having a relation to the traditional concept of moral rights as covered by article 6*bis* of the Berne Convention and article 25 of the Dutch Copyright Act. In general, there is confidence that problems regarding authenticity of authorship and work can be solved with the instrument of moral rights. It is not considered as an urgent question and the majority of legal specialists would seem to prefer that, if problems arise, they will be solved gradually by case-law and/or by technical solutions rather than by immediate legal action.

> **3.** *If no, what is probably the reason why this relation is not established? Is the authenticity problem a totally new concept independent of traditional solutions of moral rights?*

Although the Reaction to the Green Paper (see question 2) clearly indicates that the Dutch Government establishes a relation between the traditional moral rights and the right of authenticity, I think that the wording of the answer is rather cautious. By indicating that the list of moral rights does not need to be extended, the Reaction still leaves room - in my view - for the possibility that the content or purport of the existing moral rights could develop in a new direction where it concerns specific requirements of the right of authenticity. Moreover, the Reaction expressly points out that the solution might, in first instance, be sought in technical rather than in legal action.

4. Do traditional elements connected with moral rights protection, such as inalienability and protection of seemingly merely intellectual and personal interests, hinder the development of a modern concept of protection of authenticity of work and/or authorship?

In the Netherlands there is a strong current in favour of a practical and rational application of moral rights.[4] Case-law and doctrine do not conceive moral rights as a protection of merely intellectual and personal interests; from this side, there will be no hindrance to the development of a modern concept of the protection of authenticity of authorship and work.

As far as inalienability is concerned, the following applies. According to article 7 of the Dutch Copyright Act, the employer can be considered as the original author of the work; the same applies to the corporate copyright of article 8. Thus, the majority of case-law considers the employer and/or the corporation as the holder of the moral rights. Consequently, inalienability is no objection to the exercise of moral rights by the employer himself, but it does prevent the employer to transfer his moral rights to third parties. It should, however, be remarked that in order to defend authenticity interests, other legal instruments are available to the employer and his successors in title on the basis of trademark law and the law of unfair competition. I will deal with these below.

The development of a modern concept of protection of authenticity of work and authorship is not hindered by an interpretation of traditional moral rights as merely intellectual and personal interests. Nonetheless, some authors have warned that there is, in essence, an undeniable difference between moral rights in the hands of corporations and employers, on the one hand, and the specific intellectual and personal interests the protection of which is envisaged by the traditional moral rights, on the other. It has been suggested that the exercise of a right of authenticity will be subject to a stronger scrutiny by the courts, *i.e.* to judge whether the exercise is reasonable and fair, whereas the exercise of a right of integrity in the traditional sense by the author himself is, to a greater extent, left to the author's own discretion. Nevertheless, such differences are still seen as a difference in emphasis, but not as an essential difference in legal nature.

Also, it must be emphasised that up to now, the Dutch employers have not seemed to be inclined to effectively exercise the right of integrity. The reason that they are rather eager to keep their position as holders of the moral rights is not that they would have the intention to actually use those moral rights against third parties, but because they want to have absolute legal certainty that the employees will not hinder the employer's clients with claims based on moral rights. Although to my knowledge, no such cases have occurred in the Netherlands as far as it concerns employees as such, there has been a case of two freelancers who had designed Dutch banknotes for the *Nederlandse Bank*, the Dutch National Bank, invoking their moral rights against third parties who used the design of the banknotes for advertising purposes.[5] Although the action was dismissed by the Court of Appeals of Arnhem, this is probably not an idea which will appeal to many employers.

5. *Can protection by moral rights also serve more than only intellectual or personal interests, in particular also pecuniary interests? Is such an approach facilitated in the Netherlands by doctrinal approaches such as the monistic interpretation of copyright (i.e. copyright as a whole with all its faculties serving all interests related to its protection) or others?*

The discussion between the monistic and dualistic approach in the Netherlands has only a limited significance. The law clearly distinguishes between exploitation rights (article 1) and moral rights (article 25); the exploitation rights can be transferred, whereas the moral rights are inalienable. Insofar, the Dutch system may appear as a dualistic one. Nonetheless, all authors agree that moral and economic rights are closely linked.[6] Consequently, there are no objections to the use of moral rights to serve more than only intellectual or personal interests, in particular also pecuniary interests; this seems to be tacitly (but unanimously) accepted in doctrine and in case-law. It is recognized by article 25 section 3 of the Copyright Act, and is accepted practice, that authors waive their moral rights in a contract and against payment, with the exception of the right to object to any distortion or mutilation of, or other derogatory action in relation to, the work which might be prejudicial to the honour or reputation of the maker or to his value as such. This right cannot be waived; neither can the right to object to the publication of a work under a name different from the authors' name be waived. Although the 'commercial value of moral rights' is, in general, limited to modest amounts which will rarely exceed ƒ 5.000,- (± $ 3,000.-), cases are known in which substantial amounts of damages were granted. An architect was allowed damages to the amount of ƒ 70.000,- (± $ 40,000.-) for violation of his integrity right.[7]

6. *Can a concept that moral rights also cover and guarantee authenticity of work and authorship, be applied without changes of interpretation of what the function of moral rights is?*

Case-law and doctrine in the Netherlands do not contain any indication that a moral rights concept which also guarantees the authenticity of work and authorship would bring about a change of interpretation of the function of moral rights. It has, however, been submitted that the claim of producers and employers regarding the authenticity of the work, necessarily implies a shift in accent in the application of this right.[8] For example, concerning its exercise in the private atmosphere of third parties.

I. Changes in the interpretation of the function of the rights of integrity and paternity

Integrity right

Bearing in mind the *Felseneiland mit Sirenen* decision of the German *Reichsgericht*,[9] there is hardly any doubt that the traditional right of integrity can also apply in the more or less private atmosphere. Such an exercise of the 'right of authenticity' by industries and enterprises would, in my view, not be obvious or acceptable. Moreover, it is likely that the exercise of the 'right of authenticity' by producers and employers will be subject to a more serious scrutiny, whether the exercise of the right is reasonable and fair, and whether it takes into account the interests of other participants in the economic field. The idea that this would imply a change in the essence of the moral rights as such is, however, rejected. When it concerns works which are manufactured in mass production for consumptive purposes, a similar shift in accent also occurs in the application of the traditional *droit au respect*. Even when in such a case the moral rights are still with the original authors, the exercise of these rights will be subject to certain limitations, as opposed to the case where unique objects of art are concerned.

Right of paternity

A much more obvious change in the character of the moral right may result from the right of authenticity of authorship. Authenticity of authorship may be involved in two situations. Firstly, when the contents of the work have been tampered with and the new appearance of the work does not correspond anymore to the original intentions of the author. Although this is, in its most typical form, a matter for the integrity right, it can also in some cases be approached from the angle of authenticity of authorship.[10] In cases in which the judges would consider that there was no room for allowing the author to exercise the full extent of his moral rights, there seems to be no reason why Dutch courts would not be willing to at least grant the claim that his name will not be mentioned in relation to the work.[11] This especially is relevant to some authors who consider the integrity right not to be a protection of the author-as-such or the work-as-such, but as a protection of the integrity of the bond between author and work.[12]

Furthermore, article 45e under c of the Dutch Copyright Act grants each (co-)author of filmworks the right to oppose the mentioning of his name on the filmwork, unless such opposition would be unreasonable. Two problems may arise in this context. Firstly, in the internal relation: how is the relation between the producer and the artist working for him, if the artist refuses that this name be mentioned in relation to the product? Does the right of authenticity include a *right* for the producer to disclose the names of the (physical) persons who are the 'authentic' designers of the product (and whose name may represent an important commercial interest)? Secondly, a problem may arise in external relationships: suppose that third parties have revised or reconditioned the right holder's goods; how far stretches the right of authenticity in that case? Won't producers claim that this moral right in this commercial context should enable them to forbid every sale of goods under the 'authentic' name as long as they cannot quarantee the authenticity of authorship and work, thus limiting the right to sell authentic products under the authentic name to the sole authorised dealers?

In the second situation it is the paternity right as such, the moral right to claim that the name of the author be mentioned in relation to the work, which is at stake. It has been submitted that such a right can hardly be upheld in relation to works manufactured in mass production and predestined for mass consumption. In fact, this would create a kind of right to free advertising in favour of the information industry, which would be impracticable and unjustified, as there is no special reason why such a right would be granted to the information industry and not to other branches of industry. Here again, it must be remarked that such a restriction would also, to an extent, apply to the author himself in cases where it concerns works which are manufactured in mass production for mass consumption. It can, for example, not be required that if a presidential candidate wears glasses which as such are eligible for copyright protection, the election posters with the candidate's portrait should mention *'Glasses: copyright 1996 Rohdenstock'* or *'Mr X, designer'*.

II. Is the right of authenticity in essence a copyright problem?

Regarding the question whether the interpretation of the function of moral rights is changed by the adoption of a right of authenticity, it should be remarked that much depends on the situation in which the right is exercised. In some cases producers and employers will have, in exercising their authenticity rights, legal interests which can be very similar to the rights of 'physical' authors. For example, the public will often hold newspapers responsible for their articles, as if they were a kind of real person, and the exercise of a right of authenticity can, under such circumstances, be very similar to the exercise of the traditional right of integrity. On the other hand, one could imagine a producer exercising an authenticity right against the original author, who for good personal reasons would like (for example) to exercise his *droit de repentir*. The author wants to modify the work and the producer objects to that, invoking his moral right. This would be in such a dramatical contradiction to the original principle of moral rights as a protection of authors, that it can hardly be denied that in such a case the exercise of an authenticity right requires a different approach and a different interpretation from the traditional integrity right.

More in general, it would be wise to consider well the fact that moral rights have initially been conceived to protect physical persons in their personal expressions. This also indicates that there is a difference in function at the root of the question. Business life is, and should be, more 'open' to interference by third parties than personal life. Where a strong protection of the personal expression of an artist as such can be very desirable or at least harmless to other people's interest, a protection of the same strength can, in a commercial context, hamper competition and even lead to monopolistic consequences. To the extent that a work has been more explicitly created as or changed into a mass product, market-oriented principles of competition law will be more likely be applied; the moral aspect, and with it the moral right, shrinks in that scenario.

It has therefore been submitted[13] that, in order to protect the legitimate interests of producers and employers with regard to the authenticity of authorship and work, other instruments of intellectual property are available. Instruments which more effectively than copyright take into account the genuine commercial nature of the interests underlying the right of authenticity. Especially trademark law might offer more appropriate ways to afford protection for these interests. Where producers and employers put their name on the product, it is, in the majority of cases, not so much an indication of original authorship but a means of identifying the goods and/or providing an indication of their origin. Moreover, and this brings us closer to the functions of the moral right, such an indication, like a trademark, offers *'a guarantee that all goods bearing it have been produced under the control of a single undertaking which is accountable for their quality'*.[14] One could replace 'control' by the word 'authorship' and 'quality' by 'authenticity of the work' in order to illustrate that these concepts of trademark law and copyright law come, in a way, close together in this case: 'works produced under the *authorship* of a single undertaking which is accountable for the *authenticity of the work'*.

Under the EEC Trademark Directive[15] the trademark holder can supervise the condition of the goods which are sold under his trademark. In principle, the trademark right is exhausted once the goods have been put on the market in the Community by the proprietor of the trademark or with his consent (article 7(1) Trademark Directive). However, according to article 7 section 2, this rule shall not apply *'where there exist legitimate reasons for the proprietor to oppose further commercialisation of the goods, especially where the conditions of the goods is changed or impaired after they have been put on the market'*. Whereas this provision takes into account the interests of the trademark holder, it does not exceed the limits of the commercial field. It grants no protection against changing or impairing goods, if the trademark (*i.e.* 'the name of the producer/employer') is not affixed to the goods. It does not provide protection against use outside the course of trade, and in purely private situations. There is no obligation to mention the trademark in relation to the goods. Even so, the trademark holder enjoys, under modern trademark law, a very good protection which does not give rise to serious complaints. Moreover, favoured by modern theories on the function of the trademark, Benelux trademark law seems inclined to provide a protection of the 'moral rights' of the trademark holder, at least, to the extent that it protects the 'integrity' of the product's image and its trademark.

In the recent case of *Dior v. Evora*,[16] the importance of which can hardly be underestimated and which has led to questions from the Dutch *Hoge Raad* to the Benelux Court of Justice as well as the European Court of Justice, the relation between the integrity right and trademark interests seems to have been drawn even narrower. Evora had advertised Dior's perfumes (Poison, Eau Sauvage, Dune and others) by depicting the packages and bottles in an advertisement brochure for the *Kruidvat* chain, which consists of drugstores of a more unpretentious character than Dior's official dealers. The questions put to the Benelux and European Courts of Justice concern the problem whether Dior can, on the basis of trademark law, oppose the damage thus done to the *psychic* condition of the goods, more in particular the elegant style, the prestigious image and the aura of luxury of its products. Obviously, this is the trademark version of the well-known integrity right case, in which a work is published or presented in a maladjusted or defamatory context.[17]

Therefore, the question is justified whether the protection of authenticity of authorship and work in a commercial context should not in the first place be a task for trademark law, which, historically and intrinsically, is more adapted to the balancing of pure business interests than the moral rights which have been created for 'physical' authors. At any rate, the question can be asked whether a right of authenticity of authorship and work should, in a copyright context, exceed the limits of the intellectual property protection set for the same commercial interests in a trademark context.[18]

7. *Are moral rights of 'producers' of any kind, either in the capacity of legal successors of authors or in their capacity of original owners of copyright/ neighbouring rights, imaginable and can those rights perhaps be instrumentalized for the protection of their authenticity interests?*

a. *Producers as legal successors*

Moral rights of producers in the capacity of legal successors of authors are, from a copyright perspective, not imaginable, as moral rights are inalienable. However, this does not mean that no other legal instruments could be available in order to defend the producers' legal interest in the authenticity of work and authorship. If some product would violate the authenticity of work or authorship, there will be, in all probability, a possibility that the public will be confused or misled, or that other circumstances occur that could give rise to a claim based on unfair competition. The very fact that the producer is the legal successor of the author as far as the economic rights are concerned, legitimizes him in also defending the his interests. Sometimes these interests can be of a nature similar to the moral rights of the author. The fact that the author will keep the 'official' moral rights, does not mean that the producer could not invoke any kind of protection. It is, on the contrary, possible that the analogy of his interests with the moral rights of the author will help him to find protection.[19] Apart from that, the possibility exists that the author gives a power of attorney to the producer, thus enabling the latter to defend the author's moral rights in court.

b. *Producers in the capacity of authors*

As pointed out before, the Dutch copyright system knows situations in which employers, companies or institutions are considered to be the author of a work, and majority of case-law is also in favour of granting them the moral rights.[20] Up to now, the Dutch Supreme Court has not been asked to give a decision concerning this question. As far as the doctrine is concerned, some authors have criticized the idea that moral rights can be vested in another subject than the real author,[21] others seem to accept, although not wholeheartedly,[22] that it is nevertheless the consequence of the Dutch system.

Much attention has been given to the question whether legal persons can enjoy moral rights. As producers will often have the form of a legal entity, this is an element which should also be dealt with here. Although the question had not gone unnoticed in Dutch legal science,[23] the first to give the issue full scientific consideration was one of the most outstanding Dutch specialists in corporate law, prof. Maeijer. With references to the historical development of the concept of the legal entity via the opposing theories of Von Savigny and Von Gierke, Maeijer concludes that in the modern view, a legal entity is not considered as a 'fiction' but as a real and existing legal entity which can, for example, be insulted. Consequently, there is no reason why such a legal person would be excluded from the moral rights of the Copyright Act, when this legal entity is considered to be the author on the basis of the articles 7 and 8.[24] Maeijer's plea was to have a notable echo in copyright circles, in particular in the important handbook of Spoor/Verkade, in its 2nd edition.[25] The handbook takes the view that in situations, in which, according to the general opinion in society and also in terms of responsibility for the work, the work can be 'attributed' to the employer;[26] it is not irrational that the employer exercises moral rights as he can have a clear interest in exercising those powers.[27]

It would, however, be too early to say that the debate has now been decided. Van Lingen[28] puts forward that the question, whether it is *desirable* that the fictitious makers of article 7 and 8 should exercise moral rights (and in his view, it is not), precedes the question whether it is *possible* that legal persons have personality interests. Gerbrandy has, in 1992, extensively answered to Maeijer's view.[29] He objects that Maeijer, on the one hand, favours a moral right in the hands of a legal entity, but on the other, tries to escape from some of the consequences: the immunity of a copyright, which has not yet been assigned by the original maker, to seizure[30] is rejected by Maeijer in the case of insolvency of a legal entity. Gerbrandy's view is supported by Grosheide,[31] who adds that in his view the opinion that a legal entity cannot have moral rights, reflects the present state of Dutch law, although exactly the recent decision of the *Hoge Raad* in *Dior v. Evora* could contain elements indicating that the *Hoge Raad* does not exclude the exercise of moral rights by legal entities. In my view, the question remains, as yet, undecided.

The observation that legal entities can have moral interests, is right, as is the view that they should have the possibility to defend those interests. However, this does not justify that the moral rights should be taken away from someone who has an interest in them, which is no less important, and for whom the moral rights were initially intended: the author.[32] It would be better to grant a distinct and different 'commercial moral right' to producers.

Finally, I refer to what has been put forward above under the answer to question 6: the role of trademark law. The interests which producers have in the authenticity of authorship and work are in many ways similar to the interests that the trademark holder has in the fact that the goods which are offered on the market under his trademark, are 'authentically' his and have not been tampered with. Perhaps this relation between authenticity right and trademark law is, in the essence, closer than the relation between authenticity right and integrity right in the traditional sense of the moral right of the maker. Moreover, as put forward under question 6, the trademark approach could in many ways avoid the legal doubts and questions which inevitably arise in the moral rights approach.

> **8.** *How can it be guaranteed that moral rights are not totally made 'economic' under a concept of authenticity protection when the necessity of protection of authenticity interests of producers cannot be denied?*

The fact that in the Netherlands moral rights can be exercised by producers and employers does not mean that the specific interests playing in the artistic atmosphere are not taken into account anymore. It should not be ignored either that the right of authenticity can represent, for producers as well as for 'physical' authors, a genuinely 'moral' interest which is distinct from the (purely) economic interests of the producer. Therefore, moral rights will, in my view, not be made totally economic under a concept of authenticity protection. Although the problem of moral rights to be exercised by producers is clearly in a very early stage of its development, there seems to be right from the beginning an awareness that the exercise of moral rights by producers can, in several respects, show different characterics than the traditional exercise by the 'physical' author. This awareness is a guarantee that authenticity protection and traditional moral rights will not be confused to the detriment of the idealistic character of the rights, by making them a totally economic right. Rather than characterising the authenticity rights as an *economic* concept of the moral right, I would propose to characterise the difference in such a way that the authenticity right is a more specifically *commercial* manifestation of the moral rights. The difference is, that the moral right can represent an economic interest for the maker, even outside commercial situations, but the right of authenticity seems to represent interests of an inherently commercial nature. The commercial nature of the authenticity rights will also entail specific limitations of that right; this has been discussed under question 6.

> **9.** *What will be the role of technical means for insuring authenticity in the future?*

To my knowledge, up to now there has been no or very few contributions in the Dutch legal literature with regard to technical means which, in the future, can guarantee authenticity.

> **10.** *Can international systems of identifying numbers for works and other objects (such as phonograms) be made legally binding?*

To my knowledge, this question has not yet been discussed in the Dutch legal literature. However, there seems to be no reason why international systems of identifying numbers for works and other objects could not be made legally binding. Of course, as far the *use* of such identifying numbers is concerned, other interests than the copyright interests should also be taken into account, especially where it concerns privacy considerations.

> **11.** *Do legal provisions already exist which prescribe certain technological methods for the authentification of the work and/or prohibit methods defeating such technical protection systems?*

There are no provisions in the Dutch legislation which mandatorily introduce specific methods for the authentification of the work. There are no provisions either, which prohibit methods defeating such technical protection systems. Nonetheless, the Dutch Copyright Act contains provisions of criminal law in article 32a, concerning the putting into circulation or the possession for commercial purposes of any means with the intention to facilitate the unauthorised removal or circumvention of any technical device which may have been applied to protect a computer program. This provision is based on article 7 section (1)c of the Council Directive 91/250/EEC on the legal protection of computer programs. There seem to be no objections against creating a provision prohibiting the circumventions or removal of technical means of protection guaranteeing the authenticity of the work.

> **12.** *Has a concept of moral rights protection (in particular the paternity right and the integrity right), eventually in extended form, guaranteeing authenticity of work and authorship, a reduced or a more important role to play in future copyright practice?*

In the discussions concerning the electronic highway, the moral rights have, so far, certainly not played a leading role in the Netherlands. The fact that most people feel confident that the moral right will find its own place on the electronic highway without too drastic changes, may be the reason that the subject is more or less neglected in the present discussions. This seems unjustified. As far as the paternity right is concerned, one can point at the numerous and creative possibilities for mentioning the name of the author which are offered by the new media, and which may often be of a primary importance for the authors involved in order to, also from a commercial point of view, establish a reputation and make their name known to the public. The position of the *droit au respect* is equally important, because on the one hand, some producers stress the importance of this right in order to guarantee the authenticity of works, but on the other, other producers suggest that in the frame of the new media, conditions should be created which are more favourable to the possibility of using and, in the given case, changing materials in order to be able to create new informational products.

A moral right to which little attention has been paid and the importance of which nevertheless should not be underestimated, most particularly where it concerns the electronic highway, is the publication right or *droit de divulgation*. Sometimes, an author may have a clear and obvious interest that a work of his hand is not published at all. I refer to a case decided by the President of the District Court in Arnhem in 1990.[33] In this case, a father who had been divorced had laid hand on the diary of his daughter, in which he had found passages concerning the conduct of his wife prior to the divorce. The father started to copy and distribute those passages to certain people. The daughter objected and the President found in her favour. Although the decision of the President of the District Court was based on the general personality right, it most certainly could also have been a copyright case with a strong accent on the moral aspect of the *droit de divulgation*.

It cannot be stressed enough that the electronic highway will literally offer a million possibilities for the distribution of texts or other works which the author would have preferred to keep to him- or herself, and that at present no effective legal means seem to be available to effectively stop such a distribution. The fact that this aspect of the matter only represents a very small interest to society as a whole, does not mean that for the people and the authors concerned it does not represent interests of vital importance.

By the way, the question also has a clear commercial side. What if, by means of the electronic highway, copyright protected materials are disclosed to markets for which the official release of the work has only been foreseen for a later time? The European Court of Justice has accepted these interests as being part of the essential function of copyright.[34]

Footnotes

1. For a general overview of Dutch Copyright in the English language see H. Cohen Jehoram's Chapter on the Netherlands in Nimmer/Geller, *International Copyright Law and Practice* (loose-leaf ed.); Gerbrandy, *Kort Commentaar op de Auteurswet 1912*, Arnhem 1988, contains a 'commentaire' in French (p. 453-462).
2. Article 7: *'Where work performed in the service of another person consists in the production of certain literary, scientific or artistic works, the person in whose service they were produced shall be deemed to be the author thereof, unless otherwise agreed between the parties'*. Article 8: *'Any public institution, association, foundation or partnership which makes a work public as its own, without naming any natural person as the author thereof, shall be regarded as the author of the work, unless it is shown that making the work public in such manner was unlawful'*.
3. The Dutch legislator has, at the occasion of the introduction of the law implementing the European Software Directive, taken the position that (in accordance with the Directive), under Dutch law, the moral rights stay with the employee, but this standpoint could predominantly have been inspired by the desire, not to be obliged to start a discussion about article 7; Eerste Kamer 1993-1994, 22531, nr. 636, p. 2.
4. Quaedvlieg, *Auteur en aantasting, werk en waardigheid*, Zwolle, 1992.
5. Court of Appeals Arnhem 2 March 1993, *OHRA v. Oxenaar and Kruit, Informatierecht/AMI* 1993, p. 90-93, note Grosheide.
6. Amongst others: Gerbrandy, *Kort commentaar op de Auteurswet 1912*, Gouda Quint, Arnhem, 1988, p. 2-3, with reference to Ulmer, *Urheber- und Verlagsrecht* (1980), par. 17 and 18; Spoor/Verkade, *Auteursrecht*, 2nd. ed., 1993, p. 4. In *Hoge Raad* 1 July 1985 (*AMR* 1985, p. 112-113, note Verkade) the Dutch Supreme Court found that an author who had been commissioned to make a film for a broadcasting organisation had a moral interest in the film being effectively shown on the television; here the moral interests of the maker have a very clear commercial implication.
7. Rechtbank Assen 17 November 1992, *Abma v. Ruinen, Informatierecht/AMI* 1993, p. 191-192.
8. Grosheide, 'De commercialisering van het auteursrecht', *Informatierecht/AMI* 1996, par. 3, p. 44-46; Quaedvlieg, 'Het belang van de werkgever', *Informatierecht/AMI* 1993, p. 83-86.
9. Reichsgericht, Zivilsenat, 8 June 1912.
10. Cf. the American case of *Gilliam v. American Broadcasting Companies*, 538 F. 14 (1976), where what from a European view would have to be considered as an integrity right, was upheld via an action based on misrepresentation. Dworkin reports this case in the Report of the ALAI Congress in Antwerp (1993), p. 87.
11. Spoor/Verkade, nr. 219, p. 328.
12. Kuypers, 'Droit moral: grondslag en uitwerking', *Informatierecht/AMI* 1988, p. 10 (with reference to Gavin, *Le droit moral de l'auteur dans la jurisprudence et la législation française*, Paris 1960, p. 283); Du Bois, 'Auteursrecht', *AMR* 1984, p. 56; Quaedvlieg, *Auteurs en aantasting, werk en waardigheid*, Zwolle 1992, p. 17 (with reference to Dietz, *Das 'droit moral' des Urhebers im neuen französischen und deutschen Urheberrecht*, München 1968). Maeijer, however, rejects this view ('Rechtspersoonlijkheid, persoonlijkheidsrechten en vatbaarheid voor beslag van het auteursrecht', *BIE* 1990, p. 352-355). Spoor/Verkade is not quite clear on the subject. Legal ground for the moral rights is the wish to protect the personal bond between the author and his spiritual child (p. 298), but as far as the decision is concerned whether the moral rights protect the maker, or the work, the authors make a choice in favour of the maker, without mentioning the bond between maker and work as a separate, third option.
13. Quaedvlieg, 1993, p. 84-85.
14. European Court of Justice, case C-10/89, *CNL-Sucal v. HAG* [1990] ECRI 3711 (*HAG II*) and Case C-9/93, 23 June 1994, *IHT v. Ideal Standard, IIC*, Vol. 25, No. 5, 1994, p. 782-792.
15. First Council Directive of 21 December 1988 to approximate the laws of the Member States relating to trademarks (90/104/EEC), *OJ* 11-2-1989 N° L 40/1.
16. Hoge Raad 20 October 1995, *IER* 1995, 6, p. 223; *AMI* 1996, 3, p. 51-52; also see Grosheide, 'De commercialisering van het auteursrecht', *Informatierecht/AMI* 1996, 3, p. 43-50.

17. Gerbrandy (1988), p. 302-303; Spoor/Verkade, p. 319; Hoge Raad 22 June 1973, *Erven Reijers v. Patrimonium, Nederlandse Jurisprudentie (NJ)* 1974, 61, note Wachter. *'De Handen'*; President District Court Utrecht 22 November 1975, *'Sinterklaas en de hulp-zwarte pieten'*, *NJ* 1976, 481.
18. Also see Grosheide (1996), p. 49.
19. Verkade, *Informatierecht/AMI* 1990, p. 13-14.
20. Court of Appeals Den Bosch 24 May 1978, *BIE* 1985, 99; President District Court Amsterdam 20 August 1987, *Zeinstra v. Van den Hoek*, *Informatierecht/AMI* 1988, 1, p. 18 note Cohen Jehoram; District Court The Hague 27 May 1992, *Gorter and De Vries v. PTT, Informatierecht/AMI* 1993, 5, p. 94-96, note Quaedvlieg; President District Court Leeuwarden 12 July 1988, *IER* 1988, p. 88 note Cohen Jehoram; President District Court Amsterdam 4 December 1986, *IER* 1987, p. 13; Court of Appeals Amsterdam 28 February 1991, *BIE* 1993, p. 128. Different: Court of Appeals Amsterdam 10 February 1970, *NJ* 1971, 130. In the important case of *Perfums Christian Dior v. Evora*: the Amsterdam Court of Appeals 19 May 1994, *IER* 1994, p. 117-124 and the Hoge Raad 20 October 1995, *IER* 1995, p. 223 did *not* rule that the exercise of the moral right by a legal entity is excluded; but as this question does not seem to have been considered expressly by the judges, it is not certain what conclusion can be drawn from the silence of the judges.
21. Gerbrandy (1988), p. 290; Van Lingen, *Auteursrecht in hoofdlijnen*, 3rd. ed., 1990, p. 94-95; Van Lingen, 'Morele rechten van fictieve makers', in: *Qui bene distinguit, bene docet* (Gerbrandy-bundel), Arnhem 1991, p. 198; Kuypers, *Informatierecht/AMI* 1981, 1, p. 11; Wijnstroom en Peremans, *Het Auteursrecht*, Zwolle 1930, p. 60 *et seq*.
22. Cohen Jehoram, 'Grenzen aan de contractsvrijheid in het auteursrecht', *NJB* 1976, p. 521-529; Wichers Hoeth/Mout-Bouwman, *Kort begrip van het intellectuele eigendomsrecht*, 7th ed., Zwolle 1993, p. 269.
23. See Boekman, note under President District Court Leeuwarden 12 July 1988, *Bonnema v. Tietjerksteradeel*, *BIE* 1990, p. 54.
24. Maeijer, 'Rechtspersoonlijkheid, persoonlijkheidsrechten en vatbaarheid voor beslag van het auteursrecht', *BIE* 1990, p. 352-355.
25. Also see Verkade, 'Het beste artikel 7 Auteursrecht', in: Mom/Keuchenius, *Het werkgeversauteursrecht*, Deventer 1992, p. 9-19.
26. Spoor/Verkade, nr. 27, p. 34.
27. Spoor/Verkade, nr. 208, p. 306.
28. Van Lingen, 'Morele rechten van fictieve makers', in: *Qui bene distinguit, bene docet* (Gerbrandy-bundel), Arnhem 1991, p. 191-199.
29. Gerbrandy, *Auteursrecht in de steigers*, Arnhem 1992, p. 60-62.
30. See H. Cohen Jehoram in: *Reports of the ALAI Congress in Antwerp* (1993), p. 183-184.
31. Grosheide, in: *Informatierecht/AMI* 1996, p. 48.
32. Quaedvlieg (1993), pp. 85-86.
33. President of the District Court Arnhem 8 August 1990, *'Diary'*, *Kort Geding* 1991, 14.
34. European Court of Justice 18 March 1980, *Coditel v. CinéVog*.

Suisse

P. Brügger

En Suisse, les problèmes de l'authenticité d'oeuvres et/ou de l'auteur dans le contexte multimédia ne semblent pas être très importants. Une discussion sur le plan législatif n'a pas encore lieu.

Le multimédia est une oeuvre complexe, production et diffusion par l'intermédiaire des logiciels de différentes catégories d'oeuvres (images, graphiques, textes, musiques, films). Il sera en général protégé comme recueil (article 4 LDA) ou oeuvre dérivée (article 3 LDA). Celui qui accorde en licence sa création pour un multimédia concède un droit d'adaptation et de combinaison des oeuvres, droit analogue au droit de cinématographier une oeuvre littéraire. Dans le contexte du multimédia, je ne suis pas en mesure de découvrir des violations potentielles du droit moral autres que dans la réalisation d'un film, comme la contestation de la paternité, l'absence de dénomination, la première divulgation sans consentement, des atteintes non consenties à l'intégrité de l'oeuvre comme par exemple des modifications, adaptations, stockage dans un recueil e.a.

Le droit de faire reconnaître sa qualité d'auteur (article 9 al. 1 LDA) est valable pour toutes les catégories d'oeuvres. Il s'en suit que le droit à la paternité des différents auteurs participant à un multimédia devrait être garanti. Dans la doctrine on trouve des suggestions de créer *"un droit de "référence" qui renforcerait le droit à la paternité et serait plus souple que le droit à l'intégrité"* (voir J. de Werra, *Le multimédia en droit d'auteur, RSPI*, 1995, p. 245). Le problème de l'authenticité d'une oeuvre est une facette de la paternité. Pour les différentes catégories d'oeuvres, il existe différentes mesures pour la garantir, la signature, le sceau, le numérotage pour les copies en fonte des sculptures et les plâtres, le code électronique. Il appartient à l'auteur de décider comment il veut assurer l'authenticité de son oeuvre, mais il est bien clair que les intérêts des consommateurs ou du marché peuvent aussi lui imposer des règles pour assurer l'authenticité, par exemple le fait que seulement six copies en fonte peuvent licitement être déclarées comme sculptures originales.

Les problèmes de l'authenticité dans les multimédias ne sont pas d'une importance extraordinaire. Ils peuvent être résolus dans le cadre de la conception traditionnelle du droit moral. Si le producteur d'un multimédia a reçu une licence exclusive pour utiliser une oeuvre particulière dans une forme définitive et spécifique, il est en droit de défendre - sous le titre du droit dérivé - cette authenticité envers des tiers qui piratent dans ce multimédia créé par lui.

Tandis que le commentaire Barrelet/Egloff (*Das neue Urheberrecht*, 1994, p. 147) caractérise la conception suisse du droit d'auteur comme moniste, Rehbinder (*Urheberrechtsgesetz, N1 zu Artikel 16 LDA*, 1993) comprend le système suisse comme dualiste. Selon lui, les droits moraux ne sont pas transférables, mais on peut y renoncer, même le droit à la paternité ou de la dénomination. Le rapporteur, étant partisan de l'interprétation moniste du droit d'auteur, compare la conception suisse à un fromage d'Emmenthal, de principe moniste, mais avec des trous. Les intérêts moraux étaient presque toujours des véhicules appropriés pour promouvoir aussi les intérêts pécuniaires. L'auteur peut adhérer à une certaine utilisation ou modification de son oeuvre qui touche à ses droits moraux, mais il a toujours le droit de révoquer son accord avec l'effet *ex nunc* (même avis R. Auf der Maur, *Multimedia: Neue Herausforderung für das Urheberrecht*, AJP 1995, p. 437). Si l'auteur a donné son accord pour que son oeuvre puisse être adaptée pour l'intégration dans un produit multimédia, il a quand même le droit de s'opposer à la divulgation du multimédia, s'il doit constater que celui-ci a un contenu fasciste.

Sous cet angle, il sera utile que les auteurs qui licencient la première utilisation de leurs oeuvres en multimédia se réservent un droit de réception de la production multimédia, avant que cette oeuvre complexe ne soit divulguée. Avec un tel droit de contrôle, l'authenticité et l'intégrité de l'oeuvre particulière pourraient être garanties - ou au moins être transformées "en calèche d'or"!

Se penchant sur le droit français (article L 121-7 LPI), qui limite le droit de l'auteur d'un logiciel de s'opposer à son adaptation, il se trouve aussi en Suisse des voix qui se prononcent quant au droit à l'intégrité pour 'quelques restrictions de manière à faciliter la modification du multimédia et sa mise à jour ainsi que l'élimination de certaines bogues' (voir J. de Werra, *op. cit.*, p. 245).

Après avoir donné en Suisse des compétences aux douaniers pour permettre de découvrir des violations du droit d'auteur (voir article 75 *et seq.* LDA), il est imaginable qu'un jour on aura "un Interpole en ciel" qui contrôle "les passeports" des oeuvres multimédias. Mais pour le moment je ne vois pas de nécessité de légiférer d'urgence, soit sur le plan national, soit international, pour prévenir des menaces contre le droit moral des auteurs dans le contexte du multimédia.

Sweden

G.W.G. KARNELL

1. *Are there official documents such as the US Green Paper, drafts of new laws or other documents expressly discussing problems of 'authenticity of works and/or authorship' in the multimedia or Global Information Infrastructure (GII) context?*

Mr Henry Olsson has established a report - which was revised in 1994 - for the Swedish Ministry of Justice regarding the issues relevant to the Global Information Infrastructure (GII). The report does not address the subject here before us in much detail. This official document has not been translated.

2. *If yes, does the discussion or proposal establish a relation with the traditional concept of moral rights, in particular with the paternity right and the integrity right as covered by article 6bis of the Berne Convention?*

The document mentioned above does not contain any particular proposal, but only provides an overview of the relevant problems related to the GII, including those regarding moral rights. The authenticity problem is only addressed shortly and in no detail.

3. *If no, what is probably the reason why this relation is not established? Is the authenticity problem a totally new concept independent of traditional solutions of moral rights?*

It is certainly not a new concept. The Swedish Copyright Act provides in article 3 that *'when a work is reproduced, or when it is made available to the public, the name of the author shall be stated to the extent and in the manner required by proper usage'* and that it *'may not be changed in a manner which is prejudicial to the author's literary or artistic reputation or to his individuality, nor may it be made available to the public in the manner stated'*. The same rules apply to performing artists, otherwise protected by neighbouring rights, under article 45 which directly refers to article 3. Also, regarding the rights of authors, it may be important that a non-mandatory rule in article 28 provides that *'the person to whom a copyright has been transferred may not alter the work or transfer the copyright to others'*. This is not a moral rights rule. It aims to protect the original characteristics of the work. It is generally understood that these provisions, in part, aim to guarantee the authenticity of the manifestation of the work. It has been stated most directly in the sole interest of the author/performer. The authenticity discussion also relates to the interests of consumers and other users of the work/performance. It can, of course, be inferred that there is also an interest on the part of public authorities that documents and other information items which are sent throughout the GII are authentic (for example requests for permissions, appeals, etc.).

> **4.** *Do traditional elements connected with moral rights protection, such as inalienability and protection of seemingly merely intellectual and personal interests, hinder the development of a modern concept of protection of authenticity of work and/or authorship?*

It is understood that 'signing' could not replace proper usage of names, pseudonyms etc. of the authors/performers. Such a replacement can of course be prejudicial to the interests of the right owners. At the end of a communication chain it should always be possible to identify the authors/performers without having to use particular 'keys'. In Swedish law, inalienability is not really an issue in this context. Article 3 of the Swedish Copyright Act provides that moral rights may (with binding effect) be waived, but *'only in relation to uses which are limited as to their character and scope'*. This provision should guarantee adequate protection to the extent that uses can be identified.

> **5.** *Can protection by moral rights also serve more than only intellectual or personal interests, in particular also pecuniary interests? Is such an approach facilitated in Sweden by doctrinal approaches such as the monistic interpretation of copyright (i.e. copyright as a whole with all its faculties serving all interests related to its protection) or others?*

Of course. It is a well known element in the discussion on individually negotiated uses, in particular in the visual arts field, where 'signatures' can be translated into money. In the ghostwriter situation, where the 'author's' name is the name which sells the book, the not-mentioning of the ghostwriter's name may be what he is (partly) paid for. What particular problems relate to this subject in partcular in the context of GII, is not easy to grasp.

> **6.** *Can a concept that moral rights also cover and guarantee authenticity of work and authorship, be applied without changes of interpretation of what the function of moral rights is?*

I believe so.

> **7.** *Are moral rights of 'producers' of any kind, either in the capacity of legal successors of authors or in their capacity of original owners of copyright/ neighbouring rights, imaginable and can those rights perhaps be instrumentalized for the protection of their authenticity interests?*

The problem here seems to be that a producer will not be able to use the moral right of an author/performer as a basis for law suits related to alterations of his product, unless an author's/performer's moral right is at stake at the same time and the latter person(s) agree(s) to back the producer's claim with their rights. It should, however, be noted that rules of a market law character - such as rules on unfair competition - can supplement such rights to the advantage of the producer. It is not conceivable that the producer would be allowed to exercise moral rights under a licence, unless doing it as a representative of the right owner. However, in Sweden a producer will be protected by the non-moral rights rule in article 28, as mentioned above. In cases where no transfer of copyright (meaning anything from divestiture of all economic rights with specified parts of moral rights in accordance with the criteria for waiver in article 3, to a simple licence to use) is at issue, but an infringement, then the non-authentic performance of the work will influence the sanctions (award of damages etc.), *i.e.* increase them.

8. *How can it be guaranteed that moral rights are not totally made 'economic' under a concept of authenticity protection when the necessity of protection of authenticity interests of producers cannot be denied?*

It seems that the main problem would be raised by demands for *absolute* identification. If even the smallest changes would activate a right of the producer, media developments would certainly be hampered and the authors' interests in the dissemination of their works may be negatively affected.

9. *What will be the role of technical means for insuring authenticity in the future?*

This role will possibly depend on considerations within the industrial sector as related to communication and on governmental support, and will have to be based on international standards which are to be developed.

10. *Can international systems of identifying numbers for works and other objects (such as phonograms) be made legally binding?*

Why not? But in practice such binding effects will depend on international agreements regarding the spread of the phenomenon.

11. *Do legal provisions which prescribe certain technological methods for the authentification of the work and/or prohibit methods defeating such technical protection systems, already exist?*

The existing law on the prohibition of sales of decoding devices may, to some extent, play a role here. Article 14 of the new Marketing Act of 1995 (which came into force on 1 January 1996) may also offer some protection against market behaviour which is unfair to consumers or to others engaged in business. Also, in general, withholding information which is of particular importance to consumers - and signs of authentication could possibly, under circumstances, be considered to be such information - can under article 15 of the new Marketing Act be countered by an order to, under a threat of a fine, provide relevant information. On this point, I am stretching the present views on the applicability of the provision a bit. Its wording, however, certainly covers some authenticity situations which can be considered relevant to the GII.

12. Has a concept of moral rights protection (in particular the paternity right and the integrity right), eventually in extended form, guaranteeing authenticity of work and authorship, a reduced or a more important role to play in future copyright practice?

Where the big elephants dance, most authors and performers will be as badly off as they have always been. Technical developments in many fields become too difficult to grasp for the individual author, and the economic forces at his or her disposal are usually negligable in comparison to those of professional users. It may be so that producers and original right owners will have more moral-rights-related interests in common in the GII setting, but it seems somewhat premature to say anything more specific about this in reply to this question.

United States of America

M. PALLANTE

1. Are there official documents such as the US Green Paper, drafts of new laws or other documents expressly discussing problems of 'authenticity of works and/or authorship' in the multimedia or Global Information Infrastructure (GII) context?

* Intellectual Property and the National Information Infrastructure: The Report of the Working Group on Intellectual Property Rights ('The White Paper', September 1995) (iitf.doc.gov.).
* National Information Infrastructure Security Issues Forum Draft Report NII Security: The Federal Role (June 1995) (iitf.doc.gov.) (comment period closed).
* The American Bar Association Draft Proposal on Digital Signature Guidelines (Electronic Commerce Law and Information Technology Division (Science and Technology Division)(1995) (http://www.intermarket.com/ecl/) (comment period closed, draft no longer available, final Paper forthcoming).
* NII Copyright Protection Act of 1995, S. 1284, HR 2441 (pending).
* Digital Performance Right in Sound Recording Act of 1995. Pub. L. 104-39, S. 27, HR 1506 (104th Cong., 1st Sess.)

*2. If yes, does the discussion or proposal establish a relation to the traditional concept of moral rights, in particular the paternity right and the integrity right as covered by article 6*bis *of the Berne Convention?*

None of the above-identified sources establishes an express relationship between authenticity and the traditional concept of moral rights.

3. If no, what is probably the reason why this relation is not established? Is the authenticity problem a totally new concept independent of traditional solutions of moral rights?

In the United States, authenticity has been raised as an economic issue, driven by copyright management needs and the security needs of commercial interests. While it is not a totally new concept (section 43(a) of the US Lanham Act should apply to alteration of authorship or false designation of origin in the GII environment) authenticity in the GII environment is considered a commerce necessity which, by definition, does not favour inherent source rights of individual authors or 'content providers', for whom authentication issues exist by contract with licensees, if at all.

4. Do traditional elements connected with moral rights protection such as inalienability and protection of seemingly merely intellectual and personal interests hinder the development of a modern concept of protection of authenticity of works and/or authorship?

Yes, inalienability is a problem in the US copyright context for which economic concerns are the driving force. Economic concerns poised to subvert such personal interests include the lack of assignability or waivability of moral rights, which has specifically been identified as a 'problem' for digital commerce in intellectual property. The White Paper, for instance, draws upon the like trading partner of Japan for support of waiver: *'Even among Berne members, the nature and scope of moral rights varies considerably from country to country, but regardless of their scope and extent, moral rights are typically not transferable and sometimes, may not be waived. The fact that these rights are non-waivable may create difficulties for the commercialization of works in the GII environment. A current report of the multimedia study committee of the Japanese Institute for Intellectual Property suggests that there may be a need either to permit the specific waiver of the right of integrity or to limit its application in the digital world. See 'Exposure '94: A Proposal for the New Rule of Intellectual Property for Multimedia, Institute of Intellectual Property' (18 February 1994).'* (White Paper, p. 146-147.)

As a matter of commercial convenience and profit orientation, future plans for digital commerce tend towards wholesale assignability, in keeping with recent entertainment industry experiences with non-digital commerce. For now, contract language varies from assignability to non-exclusivity, with some author attribution issues arising in the context of general attribution for an entire product, *e.g.* endorsement, coupled with the licensor's right to change or omit attribution for individual components of its product, at its discretion. In addition, the licensee's rights include options to acquire future works, *e.g.* photographs not yet taken, and spell out the right to modify the licensed work. Note the following language from a Corbis (Microsoft) digital archive license for photographers: *'2. License. Licensor hereby grants Corbis and its representatives, agents and assigns a non-exclusive, worldwide license as follows: (a) Grant. Subject to the Term as defined below, the rights granted herein include the right to digitize,* use, reproduce, modify, translate into any language, and create derivative works based upon the Licensed Elements; to combine Licensed elements with Caption Information** and other materials; to catalog, index, market, advertise, display, perform, distribute, transmit, license, sell, rent or lease copies of the Licensed Elements in any medium whatsoever, whether now known or hereafter devised, including without limitation in advertising and promotional products. The foregoing rights may be exercised by Corbis and Corbis' licensees through Element Licenses or Corbis Product Licenses. Notwithstanding the foregoing, neither Cobis nor its licensees or assigns shall have any obligation to incorporate the Licensed Elements into any product or service whatsoever. (*) 'Digitize' and variations thereof means coverting an Element into Digital (i.e. binary) format such that it can be read, utilized and displayed by a device, machine, or any other technology currently in existence or hereafter developed capable of utilizing digital information. As part of the Digitization process, Elements may be compressed, cropped and/or retouched, including color correction, cloning, presentation of details, removal of incidental dust* *and dirt, silhouetting, removal of backgrounds, and reversal or flopping. (**) Caption Information. Licensor shall provide Corbis with Caption Information related to each Element [in electronic spreadsheet or word processing format] in accordance with Section 5 below. Licensor shall work closely with Corbis to determine the [electronic] format that is most compatible with Corbis' information processing system. Corbis shall have the right, in its sole discretion, to include some or all of the Caption Information with each Licensed Element, to combine Caption Information provided by Licensor with editorial materials from Corbis as well as other sources, and to edit, delete or otherwise change the Caption Information.'*

> ***5.** Can protection by moral rights also serve more than only intellectual or personal interests, in particular also pecuniary interests? Is such an approach facilitated in your country by doctrinal approaches such as the monistic interpretation of copyright (i.e. copyright as a whole with all its faculties serving all interests related to protection) or others?*

Not applicable.

> ***6.** Can a concept that moral rights also cover and guarantee authenticity of work and authorship be applied without changes of interpretation of what the function of moral rights is?*

In the view of the author, the concept of moral rights can be applied in tailored part to authenticity of authorship issues without changing its function. See question 12.

> ***7.** Are moral rights of 'producers' of any kind, either in the capacity of legal successors of authors or in their capacity of original owners of copyright/ neighbouring rights, imaginable and can those rights perhaps be instrumentalized for the protection of their authenticity interests?*

In the United States, producers have attribution and integrity rights, both as creators of original works and as licensees of derivative works. That is, they may have claims under the largely economic trademark and unfair competition laws, particularly section 43(a) of the Lanham Act. To the extent producers are joint authors, they will also have some degree of protection in the exclusive rights provisions of the US Copyright Revision Act of 1976.

> ***8.** How can it be guaranteed that moral rights are not totally made 'economic' under a concept of authenticity protection when the necessity of protection of authenticity interests of producers cannot be denied?*

Not applicable.

> ***9.** What will be the role of technical means for insuring authenticity in the future?*

Technical means will likely play a key role in insuring authenticity. The White Paper states the following: *'Technological solutions exist today and improved means are being developed to better protect digital works through varying combinations of hardware and software. Protection schemes can be implemented at the level of the copyrighted work or at more comprehensive levels such as the operating system, the network or both. For example, technological solutions can be used to prevent or restrict access to a work; limit or control access to the source of a work; limit reproduction, adaptation, distribution performance or display of the work; identify attribution and ownership of a work; and manage or facilitate copyright licensing.'* (P. 178.)

For more detailed discussions of the applications of technology to the protection of copyrighted works, the White Paper cites the following sources:
* Symposium, Technological Strategies for Protecting Intellectual Property in the Networked Multimedia Environment, co-sponsored by the Coalition for Networked Information, Harvard University, Interactive Multimedia Association, and the Massachusetts Institute of Technology (2-3 April 1993).
* M.D. Goldberg & J.M. Feder, Copyright and Technology: The Analog, the Digital, and the Analogy, Symposium, WIPO Worldwide Symposium on the Impact of Digital Technology on Copyright and Neighbouring Rights, 37 (31 March-2 April 1993).

The National Information Infrastructure Security Issues Forum Draft Report states that the entertainment, software and computer service industries are developing adequate technical capability to protect their own products, but that the substantial challenge of a central copyright management system for digital works remains. (Sec. II (C)(1).) The draft report further suggests that in the effort to protect information from unauthorized access, reproduction or modification, the use of cryptography will become widespread. In terms of modification, the draft report states the following: *'In an open digital environment, verifying the source of a message or document and assuring that it has not been changed was mentioned as a concern in a number of different meetings. For example, in electronic payments there is a concern that the correct payment is made to the correct individual. As noted at the meetings, the private sector is actively working on providing this capability and assuring effective protection. The underlying technology for such protection is digital signature.'*

A digital signature is created by applying an encryption algorithm to the information, resulting in a unique 'signature' associated with the information. This signature is encrypted and sent with the information, which may or may not itself be encrypted. By verifying the signature and comparing it with the information, the receiver can verify that the contents of the message were not altered in transit. Of course, such a technique does not prevent or correct alterations, it only detects them. While there are a number of different technical approaches to digital signatures, two are prevalent in the current environment. One, based on the RSA encryption algorithm, is coming into use in the Federal Government. Both require a public key infrastructure to provide a trusted third party, which will allow verification that the signer of a given document is indeed who he or she claims to be. The Draft Report goes on to cite the significance of public key infrastructure in assuring the integrity of transmitted information and in preventing unauthorized copying. (Sec. III (C)(2)(a)(2).)

10. Can international systems of identifying numbers for works and other objects (such as phonograms) be made legally binding?

Basic encryption measures and/or digital signatures computed by a combination of the work, mathematical algorithms, and keys thereto already are legally binding on private parties to the extent the parties agree on use. In the context of regulating the licensing of copyrighted works, the White Paper suggests there may be a need to revise article 2 of the Uniform Commerical Code. See White Paper, p. 59. In addition, identifying numbers can be used to control use of protected works. The Audio Home Recording Act, for example, exemplifies how incorporation of digital codes can be used to limit serial copying by technological means. (See 17 USC Sec. 1002 (Supp. V. 1993).)

11. Do legal provisions already exist which prescribe certain technological methods for the authentication of the work and/or prohibit methods defeating such technical protection systems?

The NII Protection Act of 1995, if passed into law, would prohibit any person from importing, manufacturing, or distributing any device or product, or from offering or performing any service, the primary purpose or effect of which is to circumvent any process, treatment, mechanism, or system which prevents or inhibits the violation of any of the exclusive rights of the copyright owner, without the authority of such owner or the law. It would also prohibit a person from knowingly providing, publicly distributing, or importing for public distribution false copyright management information; removing or altering any copyright management information without the authority of the copyright owner or the law; or distributing or importing for distribution such unauthorized altered information or copies or phonorecords from which such unauthorized altered information or copies or phonorecords from which such information has been removed without authorization. The pending legislation defines 'copyright management information' to mean the name and other identifying information of the author of a work, the name and other identifying information of the copyright owner, terms and conditions for uses of the work, and such other information as the Register of Copyrights may prescribe by regulation. Finally, it sets forth civil and criminal penalties for violations.

12. Has a concept of moral rights protection (in particular the paternity right and the integrity right), eventually in extended form guaranteeing authenticity of work and authorship, a reduced or a more important role to play in future copyright practice?

An extended form of moral rights can play a more important role in copyright practice, if application of moral rights is tailored so that commercial needs can be recognized. The right of integrity may present major complications for multimedia producers whose work is comprised of combining and/or altering pre-existing works of authorship. Rights of integrity present enormous problems to the extent they are non-waivable. However, an increased role suggests itself via an international framework. An international framework could evolve, in which integrity rights are expressly waivable in the context of certain transactions in exchange for certain minimum conditions. Attribution standards should prove less controversial. One hopes that those following a civil law tradition will actively contribute to the enrichment of the laws of predominantly common law countries like the UK and US, if not in whole, than at least in part.

Interventions

P. Brügger:

L'authenticité de l'auteur et de l'oeuvre (paternité définie et intégrité de l'oeuvre) fait partie du droit moral de l'auteur. Sa mise en danger par le cyberspace ne nécessite pas l'introduction d'une nouvelle conception du droit moral. Il suffirait de définir des outils appropriés pour défendre ces facettes du droit moral contre les périls surgis par les techniques du *"open sky"*. La construction d'une signature électronique et sa légitimation internationale apporterait probablement une solution au problème. En Suisse, on discute le modèle d'une signature électronique avec une partie de clé publique (enregistrée et accessible) à combiner avec une clé secrète (connue seulement de l'auteur). Cette signature ne pourrait être activée que par la combinaison des deux parties de la clé. Avec une telle signature, l'auteur pourrait identifier son oeuvre, par exemple intégrée dans une oeuvre multimédia envoyée sur les ondes de l'Internet, et en même temps signaler son consentement à l'intégration de son oeuvre dans le multimédia y concerné. Une motion parlementaire qui demanda une législation d'urgence sur la signature électronique pour la vie économique dans le plus vaste sens du terme s'avéra sans succès. Le gouvernement suisse a réagi prudemment en prenant la position *"wait and see"*, c'est-à-dire d'attendre pour adopter une législation suisse, qu'une solution soit trouvée sur le plan international.

La famille du droit d'auteur devrait être consciente que les problèmes de l'authenticité de l'auteur et de l'oeuvre ne touchent pas seulement les relations entre auteur et producteur. Il existe un troisième cercle qui est hautement concerné par les dévelopements de la transmission et de la distribution des oeuvres par voie électronique vers un système d'informations totales et ubiquitaires. C'est "le droit de l'homme à l'information" qui est menacé par cette "dictature informatisée". Il existe un intérêt fondamental des citoyens, des consommateurs de pouvoir vérifier si les oeuvres par lesquelles ils sont inondés sont "authentiques" dans le sens que M. Dietz a attribué à cette notion. L'intérêt d'une déclaration d'origine et de pureté pour la nourriture de l'esprit est aussi grand que pour les aliments et les médicaments qui sont munis d'un *"Waschzettel"* (description et analyse des produits). Les intérêts dits moraux de l'auteur recouvrent, dans cette question sur l'authenticité, ceux des consommateurs/ citoyens intégralement. Et, parce que les parlements dans tous les pays sont plus sensibles aux intérêts des consommateurs qu'à ceux des auteurs, il est fort probable qu'ils soient plutôt prêts à fournir des outils aux consommateurs qu'aux auteurs. Mais, si ces outils sont appropriés pour protéger les intérêts des consommateurs, ils serviront en même temps aux auteurs, et cette législation de droit public pourrait porter ses fruits dans le cadre du droit d'auteur.

A. FRANÇON:

Je voudrais aborder brièvement deux points. Le premier concerne le rapport de mon ami le docteur Dietz. Comme il s'en doute, j'ai des réserves à faire sur les conclusions de son rapport. Ces réserves rejoignent celles exprimées tout à l'heure par le Professeur Pollaud-Dulian. Aussi je me bornerai à dire à cet égard que je suis inquiet quand j'entends parler d'un quasi droit moral du producteur. Pour moi la notion de droit moral doit être réservée aux créateurs. Or, certes les producteurs méritent une protection, mais ils ne sont pas des créateurs. C'est donc à mon avis une erreur de qualifier de droit moral une telle protection. C'est une dérive. Si l'on n'y prend pas garde, je crains qu'un jour prochain, on en vienne à baptiser aussi "quasi droit moral" le droit *sui generis*/consacré au profit des producteurs par la récente directive sur les banques de données, ce qui serait une aberration.

Mon second point concerne les interventions de M. Brügger et du Professeur Karnell. Le premier a dit que, à côté des intérêts des auteurs et des producteurs, il fallait tenir compte aussi des intérêts des consommateurs et le second s'est étonné de ce que l'on ait fait grief au nom du droit moral à une chaine de télévision d'avoir incrusté son logo sur les écrans de télévision lors de la diffusion d'oeuvres protégées alors que l'on n'avait pas protesté quand la diffusion de ces oeuvres était interrompue par des messages publicitaires. En France, les milieux de droit d'auteur ont critiqué au nom de la protection du droit moral, l'interruption de la diffusion télévisuelle des oeuvres par des messages publicitaires. Mais si en fin de compte, le législateur a quelque peu limité la possibilité de telles coupures, il a mis en avant, non la nécessité de protéger ainsi les auteurs, mais celle que les "consommateurs" d'oeuvres que sont les téléspectateurs puissent voir les oeuvres à la télévision dans de bonnes conditions, c'est-à-dire sans que leur diffusion soit ponctuée d'un trop grand nombre de coupures publicitaires.

R. OESCH:

At first Finland was not so enthusiastic to create new systems for protection to improve the authenticity of works, because we traditionally have a moral rights' protection on continental basis and the right of adaptation as a part of economic rights. But after having heard the illustrative General Report and different new points in the discussion we may give up a little of our reservations towards new forms of protection and we may re-examine our position. If the new kind of protection is intended to protect the authenticity of a work with reference to the contents of a work as such, I'm personally still suspicious. But if a reference is made to the expression of a work, *i.e.* expression of a work when it was published for the first time, then I would have more sympathy for a special kind of authenticity protection. If we prefer to see the authenticity problem in the digital age as a special kind of authenticity problem, a certain authenticity right, and if criteria for the new protection are found and defined in an appropriate manner, then the new protection would be welcome.

F. Pollaud-Dulian:

Le mérite de M. Dietz est triple: d'abord, il a su mettre en lumière cet apparent paradoxe du rapport Lehman, qui soulève apparemment - mais peut-être pas délibérément - une question de droit moral, alors qu'il provient d'un pays de *"copyright"*, tandis que le marquage numérique a été, même en France, surtout envisagé comme un instrument de gestion des droits d'exploitation. Ensuite, M. Dietz a réussi un tour de force en présentant un rapport aussi riche sur une question neuve, pour laquelle M. Dietz et les rapporteurs nationaux ont fait oeuvre de pionniers. Enfin, M. Dietz a su nous ramener à des questions fondamentales déjà abordées il y a deux ans, à Anvers. Ce faisant, il nous a fait retrouver quelques "classiques" de sa vision du droit moral, sur lesquels nous ne sommes d'ailleurs pas toujours de son avis. L'objet de cette table ronde montre bien comme les approches d'un même problème demeurent très différentes selon les systèmes de droit.

En ce qui concerne la position française, il faut souligner, pour simplifier, que la question de l'authentification de l'oeuvre peut se subdiviser en deux: (1) est-ce que les procédés techniques de marquage numérique des oeuvres *("digital signatures")* intéressent le droit moral? (2) Est-ce que l'on doit envisager de modifier le système français du droit moral pour faire face aux problèmes soulevés par le "cyberspace"?

(1) En ce qui concerne la technique, est-il besoin de souligner (mais oui!) que les nouvelles techniques numériques facilitent les utilisations dénaturantes des oeuvres et des interprétations. Le concept de droit moral, comme l'a souligné le récent Livre vert de la Commission européenne est donc d'autant plus pertinent. La numérisation facilite le stockage et la transmission des oeuvres, mais aussi l'accès interactif à ces oeuvres et, bien sûr, leur modification. De surcroît, les modifications sont plus faciles à opérer et plus difficiles à détecter. Mais la numérisation permet aussi de mettre au point des techniques pour gérer les droits et contrôler les utilisations des oeuvres. Pour pouvoir protéger efficacement les auteurs et leurs ayants-droit, ainsi que les interprètes, il est nécessaire de pouvoir identifier les oeuvres utilisées dans les supports électroniques (CD-ROM, CD-I) et dans la diffusion en réseaux, qu'il s'agisse de télévision numérique ou de diffusion en ligne sur des réseaux télématiques et informatiques d'échange de données ("Internet"). Il faut un système d'identification qui permette de suivre les oeuvres à la trace, ne serait-ce que pour savoir si la diffusion a été autorisée et si elle est conforme à l'autorisation. Ceci est possible en introduisant dans la numérisation de l'oeuvre, un code qui l'identifie et la suit où qu'elle aille. Des travaux sont en cours et même très avancés pour mettre au point de tels codes, organiser leur attribution et centraliser les informations pertinentes. Alors, bien sûr, pour les auteurs, les ayants-droit et les interprètes, ces codes apparaissent nécessaires parce que, sans eux, le contrôle risque d'être matériellement impossible. Mais la question est placée sur le terrain de la gestion des

droits d'exploitation, pas tellement sur celui du droit moral. Sur le terrain du droit moral, ces codes pourront servir essentiellement d'éléments de preuve: c'est-à-dire qu'ils serviront à établir la preuve qu'il y a eu modification, altération, fausse attribution, mais ce n'est pas leur objet premier. Par ailleurs, il convient de ne pas trop se faire d'illusions sur les dispositifs techniques en eux-mêmes: une technique de protection suscite toujours une autre technique de piratage.

(2) En ce qui concerne la législation sur le droit moral, au risque de passer pour un affreux conservateur, je persiste à penser que la législation française actuelle n'a pas besoin d'être modifiée, qu'elle a toute la capacité pour s'adapter aux problèmes posés par le "cyberspace". Autrement dit, il n'y a pas de changement de nature dans les problèmes soulevés par les nouvelles techniques, simplement un changement de degré. C'est l'ampleur des modifications et de la diffusion qui est nouvelle, mais les questions relèvent toujours du droit à la divulgation, à la paternité et à l'intégrité. Il est vrai que cette approche se conçoit peut-être plus aisément dans un système dualiste, que dans un système moniste. Je ne partage pas les conclusions de M. Dietz sur la nécessité d'un système de pondération des intérêts, système qui, érigé en règle de droit, me semble comporter des dangers. Je redoute fort l'introduction d'un régime de droit moral qui reposerait sur une distinction impossible et illégitime fondée sur la valeur de l'oeuvre. L'indifférence au mérite et à la destination est une des bases du droit d'auteur français. D'ailleurs, si l'on va dans le sens d'une discrimination fondée sur la valeur de l'oeuvre, il me semble que si l'oeuvre ne mérite pas d'être protégée par un droit moral, elle ne mérite peut-être pas non plus de faire l'objet de droits d'exploitation: autrement dit, si l'on admettait cette logique, il faudrait aller jusqu'au bout et refuser alors tout droit d'auteur. A propos de l'adaptation, il faut dire que c'est un cas très particulier: l'auteur qui autorise l'adaptation de son oeuvre, permet la création d'une oeuvre dérivée, donc différente - ce qui explique qu'il accepte par avance certaines modifications (pas n'importe lesquelles, toutefois!). Adapter est créer une oeuvre seconde, par conséquent s'il s'agit de faire de simples modifications techniques, on n'a pas à pondérer les intérêts: on va rechercher si l'oeuvre a été modifiée, altérée ou dénaturée - ou pas. L'affaire *Asphalt Jungle* montre bien la distinction à opérer: les juges français ont refusé de voir une adaptation dans la colorisation, et l'ont qualifiée de modification dénaturante.

(3) En revanche, il me semble tout-à-fait légitime de prévoir deux sortes de dispositions, dispositions qui ne concerneraient pas spécifiquement le droit moral, mais d'abord les intérêts pécuniaires des auteurs. Il s'agirait de rendre le marquage numérique obligatoire pour les exploitants, en prévoyant des sanctions d'une part, et d'autre part, de prévoir aussi des sanctions à l'égard de ceux qui violeraient ces systèmes de marquage. Ceci serait possible, car le marquage obligatoire ne préjugerait ni de l'accès à la protection ni de la jouissance et de l'exercice des droits de l'auteur sur son oeuvre. C'est la proposition faite par l'OMPI et on a un précédent avec le système du dépôt légal. Du point de vue juridique, le marquage numérique n'aurait d'autre valeur que de constituer un moyen de preuve efficace - rien de plus. Dans ces conditions, je ne vois pas d'utilité à créer un "quasi droit moral" au profit des producteurs. J'y vois surtout des inconvénients! Ce que l'on semble vouloir placer sous cette formule un peu choquante relèverait plutôt d'autres techniques

juridiques, comme la répression des fraudes, le droit des marques ou la concurrence déloyale. Mais surtout, il faut garder un sens et une cohérence au droit moral: le droit moral sert à protéger la personnalité d'un individu dans une expression particulière de cette personnalité. Le droit moral protège la personnalité de l'auteur dans son oeuvre, la personnalité de l'interprète dans son interprétation de l'oeuvre. Mais il n'y a pas d'expression ou d'implication de la personnalité du producteur - souvent personne morale. Par conséquent, on ne peut pas admettre un droit moral ou un quasi-droit moral du producteur, sans vider de son sens le concept de droit moral tel qu'il existe à l'heure actuelle. Et, une fois que l'on aurait introduit cette confusion, rien ne s'opposerait plus à ce que le droit moral passe tout entier au producteur. Il suffirait d'admettre en même temps l'aliénabilité du droit moral de l'auteur. Je le redis, comme à Anvers: l'inaliénabilité du droit moral est un élément essentiel. Un autre argument contre le quasi droit moral du producteur, c'est que l'on ne peut avoir deux droits concurrents de contenu similaire sur le même objet. Or, si le droit moral de l'auteur et celui de l'interprète n'ont pas le même point d'application, quid du quasi droit moral du producteur?

Les techniques du "cyberspace" ne justifient en rien une telle révolution. A mon sens, elles n'imposent pas non plus l'aliénabilité, que je persiste à trouver redoutable. Plus généralement, les nouvelles techniques ne doivent pas devenir l'arbre qui cache la forêt: les modes d'expression et de diffusion classiques demeurent et n'ont sans doute jamais été aussi développés. Il faut donc y réfléchir à deux fois avant de modifier un droit qui a amplement démontré jusqu'ici son adaptabilité et son utilité. L'accroissement des techniques de diffusion ne doit pas se traduire, par une dialectique dénoncée naguère par M. Koumantos, par une réduction des prérogatives des auteurs. En revanche, le "cyberspace" pose des problèmes de droit international privé assez nouveaux et épineux, sur lesquels il faudra se pencher cet après-midi avec un regard neuf.

M. RACICOT:

J'aimerais vous apporter le point de vue d'un praticien nord-américain qui représente surtout les intérêts de concepteurs de logiciels et qui pratique le droit en français et en droit civil dans une mer anglo-saxonne de *"common law"*. Pour certaines oeuvres traditionnelles comme les livres et les oeuvres artistiques, c'est le nom de l'auteur qui fait vendre l'oeuvre ou des exemplaires de l'oeuvre au public. Pour les nouvelles oeuvres électroniques telles que les programmes d'ordinateurs, les jeux vidéo et les oeuvres multimédias, c'est plutôt le nom du producteur qui fait vendre des exemplaires de l'oeuvre au public. Il existe bien sûr un marché primaire pour ces nouvelles oeuvres électroniques où l'auteur non employé d'un producteur va vouloir vendre ses oeuvres aux producteurs. Dans ce seul marché plus restreint et invisible aux yeux du public, c'est alors le nom de l'auteur qui fait vendre le produit. Au niveau de la création, les éditeurs de nouvelles oeuvres électroniques exigent de leurs créateurs, qu'ils soient employés, pigistes ou tiers, qu'ils renoncent à leurs droits

251

moraux avant toute distribution de leurs oeuvres.

La solution pour protéger les intérêts des producteurs et des auteurs nous apparaît non pas dans la cession automatique du droit moral à l'employeur lorsque l'oeuvre est créée par l'employé ni la renonciation automatique au droit moral. En effet, la renonciation au droit moral implique que l'on fasse disparaître ce droit moral, qu'on le tue. La solution qui respecterait davantage les intérêts des producteurs et des auteurs me semble plutôt la possibilité de céder le droit moral et, à cet égard, il faudrait distinguer entre le droit à l'intégrité de l'oeuvre et le droit de paternité. Quant au droit à l'intégrité de l'oeuvre, ce droit étant cédé, le producteur protégera ainsi ses propres intérêts et ceux de l'auteur. Il faudrait à cet égard ne plus limiter ce droit à l'intégrité, comme dans la plupart des législations actuelles, au seul cas où la violation de ce droit porte atteinte à l'honneur ou à la réputation de l'auteur. À notre avis, le droit à l'intégrité de l'oeuvre devrait être absolu. Quant au droit de paternité, dans la mesure où il y aurait cession de ce droit en faveur du producteur, cette cession n'impliquerait pas le droit pour le producteur de remplacer l'"avis de droit d'auteur" de l'auteur comme on l'exige parfois dans certains contrats, notamment en matière d'informatique, mais plutôt en la possibilité d'un ajout d'un deuxième avis de droit d'auteur dans la mesure où le producteur aurait ajouté à l'oeuvre ou l'aurait modifiée. En effet, le remplacement de l'avis original constitue, à mon opinion, une fausse représentation qui peut tromper le public.

F. DE VISSCHER:

Je partage l'avis qu'un droit moral ou quasi-droit moral nouveau en faveur du producteur ne devrait pas être introduit, et ce pour les bonnes raisons qui ont été déjà dites. Pour la protection des intérêts du producteur, il convient d'attirer l'attention sur les moyens juridiques d'action dont il dispose en dehors de la législation sur le droit d'auteur et les droits voisins. Il y a lieu de penser notamment au droit des marques. Ainsi en Europe, la directive d'harmonisation des législations en matière de marque reprend une règle déjà présente dans la Loi Benelux sur les marques, permettant au titulaire d'agir contre tout usage de la marque ou d'un signe ressemblant dans la vie des affaires d'une manière préjudiciable au titulaire. Dans le même ordre d'idées, on se rappellera que la règle de l'épuisement du droit de marque cesse de s'appliquer lorsque le produit ou service est modifié. Il y a lieu de penser également au droit de la concurrence déloyale; dans beaucoup de pays, l'on considérera comme déloyal le fait de mutiler ou dégrader le produit d'un tiers.

Les droits moraux se trouvent chez l'auteur. Si l'on conçoit que celui-ci puisse contracter à ce sujet pour en régler l'exercice, il m'est difficile de concevoir qu'un droit moral, par définition non patrimonial et intimement lié à la personnalité qu'il protège, puisse être cédé en tout ou en partie. La question que je me pose plutôt, est de savoir si l'auteur pourrait donner au producteur un mandat pour exercer en tout ou en partie ses droits moraux. Un tel mandat pourrait-il être irrévocable? Peut-être que non si l'on considère qu'un tel mandat est donné dans l'intérêt exclusif de l'auteur.

En ce qui concerne l'éventuelle obligation de pourvoir l'oeuvre d'une "signature" ou "marquage", il est certain qu'il faut maintenir intacte la règle que le droit d'auteur s'acquiert dès la création et sans formalité. Ceci étant, l'on pourrait inciter, voire obliger, les titulaires à utiliser la signature électronique pour leur rendre plus aisée la réparation de la contrefaçon et la gestion de leurs droits. Vous me permettrez peut-être l'analogie avec la police de la route: si le droit à l'intégrité physique existe sans formalité, il est prévu dans la plupart des pays que si une personne circule en voiture sans mettre sa ceinture de sécurité, ses droits à réparation en cas d'accident sont à tout le moins diminués. Si une oeuvre veut emprunter les autoroutes de l'information, elle pourra avoir intérêt "à mettre sa ceinture de sécurité" pour une meilleure protection; cela ne porte pas atteinte au principe de la protection sans formalité. Il faudra toutefois être prudent. Refuser toute indemnisation à défaut de signature, cela reviendrait en réalité à dénier la protection faute d'une formalité. Il ne faudrait pas cacher cette réalité derrière un simple jeu de mots qualifiant cette formalité comme n'étant qu'un moyen obligé de preuve; il faudra donc que tous les autres moyens de preuve restent disponibles et que le principe de l'indemnisation subsiste.

Un autre point auquel il faudra faire attention, est le cas où l'oeuvre est mise sur le réseau par un tiers sans le consentement de l'auteur: un tel acte de contrefaçon ne peut évidemment pas être opposé à l'auteur pour réduire son droit à indemnisation à l'encontre de tous ceux qui, à la suite de cet acte, procèderont à d'autres reproductions ou communications. Ceci conduit notamment à examiner s'il faut apprécier différemment le comportement d'un utilisateur selon que l'oeuvre porte ou non une signature. A mon avis, à peine de porter gravement atteinte à la règle fondamentale que la contrefaçon doit être sanctionnée même si le contrefacteur est "de bonne foi", il faut admettre que dans tous les cas, qu'il y ait ou non signature, la contrefaçon existe et doit donner lieu à une réparation intégrale du préjudice. Ceci n'empêcherait pas d'envisager que lorsque l'oeuvre porte une signature, le contref-acteur est alors "de mauvaise foi" et dès lors redevable d'une réparation renforcée ou forfaitaire.

III

Private international law aspects

Les aspects de droit international privé

Les aspects de droit international privé

G. Koumantos[*]

I. Introduction

L'ignorance de plusieurs données techniques et leur évolution rapide, l'insuffisance des points de repère dans les conventions internationales et les législations nationales, les principes plus ou moins clairs et les intérêts plus ou moins justifiés qui s'affrontent, bref l'extrême complexité de la matière laissent la science juridique assez perplexe devant les problèmes suscités par ce qui est appelé l'"infrastructure mondiale de l'information". Aussi n'est-il pas pas étonnant que les juristes avancent en tâtonnant et que ce Rapport risque de contenir plus de questions que de réponses.

Le thème du Rapport est limité aux aspects de droit international privé de ce phénomène relativement nouveau qui modifie plusieurs données de base du droit d'auteur, notamment les notions de reproduction et de diffusion. Mais les problèmes de droit international privé relatifs au droit d'auteur ne sont pas créés par les nouvelles techniques. Ces problèmes, compliqués par le caractère immatériel de l'objet de ce droit qui conduit à son ubiquité, existent depuis toujours, même si leur importance pratique était souvent réduite par l'existence des conventions internationales.

Le caractère fondamentalement transfrontalier de l'infrastructure de l'information amène les problèmes de droit international privé au centre de l'intérêt. Mais ils y arrivent sans des études de base suffisantes et sous le poids d'exigences qui dépassent leur fonction. Il était prévisible que la discussion de ces problèmes prête à plusieurs confusions.

Le présent Rapport est basé sur les réponses que plusieurs groupes nationaux de l'ALAI ont donné au questionnaire qui leur a été adressé. Des remerciements sincères sont dus à tous ces groupes. Cependant le rapporteur n'a pas crû devoir se limiter à une synthèse des réponses fournies: il s'est permis d'exposer aussi ses propres thèses même lorsque elle ne trouvaient pas d'appui sur des réponses nationales.

Le présent Rapport commencera par un effort d'écarter, autant que possible, des incertitudes et des confusions qui concernent tant les faits et la terminologie que la notion même de droit applicable (II et III). Suivra un essai d'application des règles en vigueur aux différents rapports juridiques créés par l'infrastructure de l'information

---

[*] Professeur émérite à l'Université d'Athènes

(IV à VII). Enfin, quelques réflexions seront présentées sur ce qui pourrait être le fond des problèmes occultés par la référence au droit international privé et sur quelques conclusions à en tirer (VIII).

II. Les faits et la terminologie

Provenant d'un juriste sans formation technique et pour être accessible à des juristes ayant éventuellement les mêmes lacunes, la description des faits ne peut qu'être réduite à son expression la plus simple. Il suffira, pour les besoins de ce Rapport, de prendre comme point de départ qu'un procédé d'enregistrement, de reproduction et de transmission, appelé "analogique", est en train d'être remplacé par un autre procédé, "numérique" *("digital")*, tandis que les câbles sont, de plus en plus, remplacés par un autre support de la transmission, les "fibres optiques". Ce nouveau procédé et ce nouveau matériel permettent le stockage (grâce à une "compression") et la transmission d'"informations" (terme à examiner par la suite) infiniment plus nombreuses, dans un temps infiniment réduit et d'une qualité infiniment supérieure - tout ceci par rapport au procédé et au support précédemment utilisés. Ces données techniques ont conduit à la création de certains termes qui sont utilisés pour indiquer les nouvelles possibilités qui en découlent. Il serait opportun de formuler quelques réflexions sur trois de ces termes: le ou les "multimédia", l'"interactivité" et, surtout, l'"infrastructure globale [ou mondiale] de l'information".

D'abord sur le ou les "multimédia". Sa composante "-média" conduirait à supposer qu'il s'agit d'un nouveau moyen de communication. Sa composante "multi-" ferait même penser qu'il s'agit d'une combinaison de plusieurs moyens de communication. Or, le terme "multimédia" se réfère à l'oeuvre; c'est l'oeuvre qui est "multiple", composée de plusieurs éléments différents mais fixée sur un seul support (par exemple le CD-ROM) ou transmise par un seul moyen (par exemple la fibre optique). Il serait peut-être plus exact de parler de "multioeuvre unimédia".

S'agit-il d'une nouvelle categorie d'oeuvres, inconnue auparavant, à laquelle au-raient donné naissance les nouvelles techniques? Bien sûr, on connaît depuis longtemps des oeuvres composites fixées sur des supports différents (par exemple un livre et une cassette avec des textes et des sons ou même des images en mouvement destinés aux enfants ou à l'enseignement des langues étrangères). Mais, dans les oeuvres "multimédia", d'une part le support est unique et, d'autre part, la quantité des éléments incorporés est telle que, finalement, la modification quantitative devient qualitative, un résultat connu en dialectique. Une nouvelle catégorie d'oeuvres donc mais qui pourrait être soumise aux catégories juridiques déjà connues comme une combinaison de banques de données, d'anthologie, d'encyclopédie et d'oeuvre audiovisuelle - le tout accompagné d'un programme d'ordinateur. Mais l'oeuvre multimédia a, en plus, une nouvelle caractéristique: elle n'est pas figée. C'est ici qu'intervient la notion d'interactivité, c'est-à-dire la possibilité de l'usager de choisir l'aspect définitif que prendra cette oeuvre au moment où elle s'offrira à sa vue et à son ouie. Bien sûr, l'usager n'a que la possibilité de choisir parmi les éléments qui se trouvent déjà, comme alternatives, dans l'oeuvre. Il ne crée rien - si ce n'est le résultat de son choix.

Le terme d'interactivité est aussi utilisé dans d'autres sens comme pour indiquer la possibilité de chaque usager d'un réseau de ne pas être seulement récepteur des signaux transmis mais aussi émetteur de signaux. Ou encore, dans une forme plus élémentaire, pour indiquer la vidéo sur commande ou les jeux électroniques.

Le troisième terme qui suscite des commentaires est celui de "infrastructure globale [ou mondiale] d'information" qui s'est substitué au terme plus imagé de "autoroutes de l'information". Ce terme se réfère à la communication et notamment à l'existence d'un ou plusieurs réseaux qui permettent une communication de signaux sur l'ensemble du globe terrestre, ouverte à tous les possesseurs de terminaux ayant accès au réseau avec la possibilité technique de transmettre des signaux de point-à-point ou de point-au-public, simultanément et dans les deux sens.

Parmi les trois éléments qui composent ce terme, le mot "global" ne semble pas poser de problèmes. Il est correctement utilisé dans deux sens: d'abord pour indiquer le fait que ce moyen de communication couvre ou peut couvrir l'ensemble du globe terrestre et, ensuite, pour marquer que ce moyen peut véhiculer toute sorte de signaux (textes, images, sons). Le mot "mondial" ne contiendrait que la première de ces indications. L'utilisation du mot "infrastructure" pose certaines questions: s'agissant de techniques qui permettent la communication à un degré jamais atteint auparavant, on est en droit de se demander pourquoi ne pas utiliser un terme qui exprimerait ce nouveau fait, la communication et son contenu, au lieu de donner tant de poids à l'infrastructure, au réseau, finalement aux fibres optiques, qui n'en constituent que la condition matérielle? Pourquoi "infrastructure globale" et non "communication globale"? Le mot "information", troisième composante du terme, est celui qui se prête à des critiques encore plus graves et concernant directement le droit d'auteur. Puisque souvent - et de plus en plus - ce qui est communiqué est une oeuvre, pourquoi réduire le contenu de la communication à des informations? Voudrait-on prétendre qu'un roman n'est qu'une série d'informations sur les agissements et les sentiments de ses héros? Ou qu'une oeuvre musicale n'est qu'une série d'informations sur la succession des notes ou des accords? Ou, pour construire différemment, l'information consisterait à annoncer au public que Proust ou Beethoven aurait créé telle oeuvre (qui suivrait)? La réduction d'une oeuvre à une information est manifestement une absurdité. Mais, en plus, elle présente un danger: les informations circulent et doivent circuler librement au nom de la liberté démocatique, de la science, des droits de l'homme. En acceptant l'assimilation des oeuvres de l'esprit à des informations, on risque de voir les serveurs ou les usagers des réseaux revendiquer la même liberté de circulation pour la diffusion de ces oeuvres ou, sinon, de lourdes limitations au droit d'auteur.

III. Droit applicable: distinctions et précisions

Avant toute recherche du droit applicable selon les règles du droit international privé, une question préalable s'impose: applicable à quoi? Dans le domaine qui fait l'objet du présent Rapport, une première distinction semble s'imposer: il faut bien distinguer entre la création d'une oeuvre multimédia (comportant éventuellement l'utilisation d'oeuvres préexistantes) et la diffusion par réseau (d'une oeuvre "classique" ou d'une oeuvre multimédia). Si la création d'une oeuvre multimédia ne semble pas poser de problèmes spécifiques par rapport à la création de toute autre oeuvre éventuellement intégrant ou modifiant d'oeuvres préexistantes, il en est autrement avec la diffusion d'oeuvres par les réseaux modernes. Ici se posent des problèmes de qualification moins pour la détermination du droit applicable que pour l'application de ce droit (v. ci-dessous, IV). Une deuxième distinction est tout aussi nécessaire: il se peut que le droit applicable soit différent selon qi'il s'agisse de déterminer l'existence d'un droit d'auteur ou la licéité de son utilisation ou, enfin, sa protection contre son utilisation illicite - dans le premier cas, il faudrait appliquer un droit international privé éventuellement spécifique au droit d'auteur, dans le deuxième cas et le troisième cas, faute de droit international privé spécifique, c'est le droit international privé des contrats ou des délits qu'il faudrait appliquer. Une troisième distinction générale s'impose, qu'il est utile de rappeler ici, bien qu'elle n'ait rien d'original: la *lex lata* et la *lex ferenda*, le droit tel qu'il est actuellement en vigueur et le droit tel qu'il devrait éventuellement être modifié pour couvrir les nouveaux faits et les nouveaux besoins auxquels donne naissance l'évolution technique. Parlant de droit en vigueur, les théories et les appréciations ont peu d'importance: il est là, on doit l'appliquer, tout au plus pourrait-on essayer de l'interpréter dans un sens ou dans l'autre.

Une dernière précision est nécessaire: il n'y a pas, à proprement parler, de droit international privé qui soit vraiment international; le droit international privé est un droit national qui contient des règles de conflits que chaque état prescrit à ses tribunaux. Cependant, il existe quelques règles de conflit qui portent sur des points spécifiques et qui sont imposées aux états, d'ailleurs avec leur consentement, par des conventions internationales. Les développements qui suivent - présentés séparément pour le droit d'auteur, les contrats et les délits - se réfèrent au droit en vigueur et sont basés sur des règles de droit international privé plus ou moins communes, contenues (soit explicitement soit par déduction interprétative) dans plusieurs législations nationales et dans la Convention de Berne.

IV. **Droit applicable: droit d'auteur**

Plusieurs questions qui relèvent directement du droit d'auteur peuvent se poser à l'occasion de la création d'une oeuvre multimédia et de la diffusion par réseau de toute oeuvre. S'agit-il d'une oeuvre qui présente les caractéristiques nécessaires pour sa protection par le droit d'auteur? Et les oeuvres éventuellement intégrées, avec ou sans modifications, dans l'oeuvre multimédia étaient-elles protégées par le droit d'auteur? Dans les deux cas, qui était le titulaire, originaire ou dérivé, de ce droit, quels en était le contenu, la durée, les limitations? De quel pouvoir particulier, parmi ceux qui constituent le droit d'auteur, relève la diffusion par réseau avec toutes les possibilités qu'elle offre à l'usager final? Et qu'en est-il du droit moral?

Il est évident que la réponse à toutes ces questions et à d'autres qui pourraient être posées dans ce domaine pourrait être différente selon le droit sur lequel cette réponse serait basée. C'est le droit international privé, avec des règles éventuellement spécifiques pour le droit d'auteur, qui permettra de déterminer le droit applicable. Ces règles sont contenues dans des textes législatifs, comme notamment en Allemagne, en Italie, en Suède et en Suisse, ou elles sont formées par la jurisprudence comme au Canada ou en France.

La règle de conflit admise comme étant le droit en vigueur par l'opinion largement prédominante, aussi bien pour les différents droits nationaux que pour la Convention de Berne, est que, à toutes ces matières, doit être appliqué le droit du pays pour lequel la protection est demandée (v. les réponses des groupes allemand, italien, suédois, suisse; avec quelques réserves ou des opinions minoritaires pour une éventuelle application du droit du pays d'origine, les groupes américain, belge, canadien, finlandais, français). Cette opinion, considérée comme découlant d'un soi-disant "principe de territorialité", conduit pratiquement à l'application généralisée de la loi du pays du délit.

L'auteur du présent Rapport ne partage pas cette opinion. Non que le résultat pratique en soit nécessairement mauvais; ce qui est mauvais c'est que cette opinion ne se fonde que sur un "principe", douteux et à contenu fort imprécis, sans pouvoir invoquer de façon convaincante un fondement sur des textes législatifs ou conventionnels. L'auteur du présent Rapport a déjà eu l'occasion, à plusieurs reprises, de soutenir que les textes, nationaux et internationaux, se prononcent plutôt en faveur de l'application de la loi du pays d'origine de l'oeuvre. Il paraît utile d'ajouter que le droit moral peut être régi par un droit différent de celui applicable au droit d'auteur en général. En effet, si plusieurs pays appliquent le même droit aussi bien au droit patrimonial qu'au droit moral (Allemagne, Suisse et, avec quelques réserves, Italie), il y en a d'autres qui soumettent le droit moral au droit de la nationalité de l'auteur (v. Rapport italien) ou, par le biais de l'ordre public, à la *lex fori* (France; v. aussi Rapport belge).

Il n'y a pas lieu d'insister davantage sur ce point puisque le problème est d'ordre général et ne concerne pas spécialement les multimédia et l'infrastructure globale. On admettra, sur le plan général, l'une ou l'autre des opinions proposées et on l'appliquera par la suite aux problèmes spécifiques, relatifs aux oeuvres et aux moyens de diffusion produits par les nouvelles techniques. Des règles spécialement conçues pour ces oeuvres ou pour ces moyens de diffusion n'existent pas, au moins pas encore (les Rapports nationaux le confirment). Il faut ajouter que la détermination du droit applicable est, d'habitude, faite globalement pour l'ensemble du droit d'auteur sans qu'il y ait lieu de distinguer parmi les différents pouvoirs que celui-ci confère à son titulaire. Il n'est donc pas nécessaire, à ce stade, de procéder à une "qualification" spéciale des activités, qui seront régies par le droit déclaré applicable.

V. **Le besoin d'une qualification au second degré**

Si la distinction parmi les différents pouvoirs qui constituent le droit d'auteur n'est pas nécessaire pour la détermination du droit applicable, elle peut le devenir pour son application. En effet, les législations nationales et la Convention de Berne prévoient, pour certains pouvoirs qui découlent du droit d'auteur, des régimes spéciaux (réciprocité, licences non-volontaires, autres limitations prévues ou autorisées). Pour déterminer le régime particulier éventuellement applicable aux techniques modernes de diffusion par réseau, il est nécessaire de procéder à leur "qualification" pour qu'elles puissent être soumises au régime qui leur convient. Cette qualification, appelée parfois "qualification au second degré", est également nécessaire pour une éventuelle interprétation des contrats lorsqu'il s'agirait de savoir si tel ou tel pouvoir a fait l'objet d'un transfert ou d'une licence. La qualification nécessaire pour l'application des régimes particuliers éventuellement prévus par le droit reconnu comme applicable se fera sur la base et selon les critères de ce droit. Il faut cependant ajouter que, sous l'harmonisation de la Convention de Berne, les législations nationales ne présentent pas d'écarts importants dans ce domaine.

Les faits de la diffusion moderne par réseau ont permis la formulation d'un certain nombre de propositions concernant la qualification juridique de cette activité:
- *radiodiffusion*, pour les législations qui étendent cette notion à la transmission par fil ou lorsque la transmission aurait lieu (au moins en partie) sans fil;
- *transmission publique* à condition d'admettre que le public peut être dispersé non seulement dans l'espace mais aussi dans le temps, ce qui semblerait évident;
- *reproduction* en vue du fait que la diffusion par réseau se fait normalement par un enregistrement dans la mémoire du "serveur", en vue aussi du fait que l'oeuvre diffusée est "reproduite" sur écran et, enfin, en vue des possibilités de reproduction par imprimante offerte à l'usager final;
- *location*, puisque l'oeuvre est temporairement rendue accessible à l'usager, opinion qui semble adoptée notamment aux cas d'utilisation "sur demande".

Un examen critique détaillé de chacune de ces constructions dépasserait le cadre du présent Rapport. Il suffira de dire que, parmi toutes les qualifications proposées, celle qui semble correspondre le mieux aux réalités des faits est une combinaison qui admettrait que la diffusion par réseau relève en même temps du droit de transmission publique et du droit de reproduction. Par conséquent, pour que cette diffusion soit licite, il faut le consentement du titulaire de chacun de ces deux droits; et si elle est illicite, elle constitue une atteinte à chacun de ces deux droits.

VI. Droit applicable: contrats

L'utilisation d'une oeuvre protégée par le droit d'auteur pour la création d'une oeuvre multimédia ou pour sa diffusion par un réseau ainsi que toute utilisation de l'oeuvre multimédia doivent en principe se faire avec le consentement de l'auteur. Donc l'utilisation présuppose un contrat entre le titulaire du droit et l'utilisateur. Le contrat en question peut être un transfert ou un contrat d'exploitation ou une licence. C'est la voie de la légalité - sinon on se trouverait devant une utilisation illicite, éventuellement délictuelle. A partir du moment où il y a un contrat pour l'utilisation de l'oeuvre, ce contrat aura réglé le plus grand nombre des questions qui peuvent surgir dans le cadre des rapports entre titulaire et utilisateur sans qu'il soit nécessaire d'avoir recours à des règles législatives. Le problème du droit applicable se pose cependant pour le contrat lui-même (forme, validité etc.) et pour son interprétation.

Pour ce qui est de la forme, une règle généralement admise consacre l'application du droit du lieu de la conclusion. Pour le reste, toutes les législations nationales contiennent des règles de droit international privé qui déterminent le droit applicable en matière de contrats. Le Code Civil hellénique, par exemple, prévoit dans son article 25 que: *"[l]es obligations contractuelles sont régies par le droit auquel les parties se sont soumises. A défaut, est applicable le droit approprié au contrat, d'après l'ensemble des circonstances particulières".* Plusieurs droits contiennent des règles qui, même si elles ne sont pas identiques, s'inspirent du même schéma (les réponses de tous les groupes nationaux confirment cette constatation). Il s'agit de ce qu'on pourrait appeler une "harmonisation spontanée" qui, maintenant, est confirmée par la Convention de Rome de 1980. Ces règles s'appliquent aux contrats en général et doivent également être appliquées aux contrats d'utilisation d'une oeuvre soit par des moyens "classiques" soit par des moyens de la nouvelle technique (intégration dans une oeuvre multimédia, diffusion par réseau).

La loi applicable au droit d'auteur (v. ci-dessus, IV) détermine si celui-ci peut être transféré ou non puisqu'il s'agit là d'une qualité intrinsèque de ce droit. Mais une fois la transférabilité admise, c'est la loi applicable au contrat qui déterminera si un transfert a effectivement eu lieu ou non. Des questions d'ordre public pourraient, dans certains droits (par exemple en droit français), être posées au sujet de la transférabilité du droit moral.

Il est opportun de souligner que le droit applicable au contrat régit non seulement sa validité mais également son interprétation. Les législations nationales contiennent souvent soit des règles générales sur l'interprétation des contrats soit des règles interprétatives spécialement destinées aux contrats relatifs au droit d'auteur. Toutes ces règles seront appliquées pour déterminer le sens des clauses de chaque contrat. Elles seront également appliquées pour répondre notamment à la question de savoir si un contrat autorise l'utilisation par les techniques nouvelles. Et ici se posent de nouveau les problèmes de qualification qui ont été évoqués plus haut (v. ci-dessus, V).

VII. **Droit applicable: délits**

L'utilisation des oeuvres par les moyens de la nouvelle technologie ne se fait pas toujours avec le consentement de l'auteur; faite sans contrat, elle est illicite. Pour déterminer la loi applicable dans ce cas, on aura de nouveau recours aux règles de droit international privé des législations nationales. Ces règles indiquent, de façon plus ou moins similaire, comme droit applicable la loi du pays où l'acte délictuel a été commis (par exemple France, Italie, Suède). Mais le problème n'est pas pour autant résolu, puisque l'application de cette règle aux nouvelles techniques et, plus particulièrement, à la diffusion par un réseau de l'infrastructure globale d'information crée au moins deux problèmes.

Le premier de ces problèmes, relativement plus facile parce que déjà connu, naît du fait que dans le cadre de la diffusion par réseau, le délit est très souvent (ou, en puissance: toujours) transfrontalier: l'oeuvre est injectée dans (ou rendue accessible par) le réseau dans un pays et reçue dans un autre. Le problème n'est pas nouveau;

depuis des siècles, les spécialistes du droit international privé se sont occupés de certains cas qui présentent des analogies marquantes avec le cas examiné ici: lettre missive injurieuse envoyée ou projectile d'une arme à feu tirée d'un côté de la frontière et provoquant des dommages de l'autre côté. La réponse reste controversée: certains soutiennent que c'est le droit du lieu de l'acte qui doit être appliqué (par exemple Allemagne, Belgique) tandis que d'autres se prononcent en faveur du droit du lieu du résultat (par exemple France, Suisse et USA). Mais les deux solutions sont difficilement applicables dans le cas de la diffusion par réseau. D'abord, parce qu'il est souvent difficile d'identifier le lieu où l'oeuvre est illicitement rendue accessible aux utilisateurs du réseau, donc le lieu de l'acte. Et ensuite parce que le résultat de l'acte se réalise virtuellement dans l'ensemble du globe terrestre puisque le réseau est, par définition, "global". Le lieu de l'acte serait introuvable; le lieu du résultat serait partout.

Il ne faut pas exagérer la portée de ces difficultés, surtout de la première: les "serveurs" ne sont pas inconnus et leurs sources peuvent être localisées déjà dans l'état actuel de la technique. Et rien n'empêche qu'une future réglementation, surtout si elle devait être harmonisée internationalement, impose des mesures techniques qui rendraient beaucoup plus aisée, voire automatique, cette localisation des sources. La seconde difficulté pourrait paraître plus grande au niveau du droit international privé: si le résultat de l'acte délictuel se réalise dans un grand nombre de pays (et, virtuellement, dans le monde entier), faut-il appliquer à ce délit cumulativement l'ensemble des législations de la terre? La confusion qui résulterait d'une telle solution pourrait constituer une raison valable pour donner la préférence à l'autre: application du lieu de l'acte et non du lieu du résultat. Mais, peut-être, faut-il aller plus loin et reconnaître que la difficulté provient ici du fait qu'on demande aux règles de droit international privé la solution des problèmes qui dépassent sa fonction. Il s'agirait alors de découvrir le véritable problème qui se cache derrière les questions de droit applicable.

VIII. **Derrière le droit international privé**

Le problème principal posé au droit d'auteur par les nouvelles techniques est comment sauvegarder les droits des créateurs intellectuels face à des utilisations de leurs oeuvres qu'il est difficile ou même impossible de contrôler? La recherche du droit applicable ne résout pas ce problème, même si on arrivait à localiser le délit, les intéressés arriveraient à trouver un pays qui serait plus laxiste quant à la réglementation ou la protection effective du droit d'auteur pour y installer leurs activités.

Derrière les problèmes de droit international privé, se cache un problème de droit matériel: assurer que les oeuvres ne soient pas utilisées sans le consentement de leurs auteurs, c'est-à-dire sans une rémunération librement fixée et dans le respect du droit moral. Pour l'utilisation d'une oeuvre préexistante dans une oeuvre multimédia, les règles en vigueur semblent suffire puisqu'une telle utilisation constitue une reproduction et, éventuellement, une adaptation de l'oeuvre préexistante. En ce qui concerne la diffusion par réseau, il faut partir du fait que toute injection d'une oeuvre dans le réseau, tout acte qui rend l'oeuvre accessible par le réseau, ouvre la voie à une utilisation virtuellement universelle ("globale"). Par conséquent, il faut que le consentement de l'auteur couvre la totalité du globe terrestre - sinon l'injection dans le réseau serait illicite. Dans l'état actuel des choses, il serait justifié d'admettre que le consentement de l'auteur est présumé avoir cette étendue.

Bien sûr, il ne sera pas facile de faire admettre une telle règle par tous les pays. Le conflit des conceptions juridiques et des intérêts économiques est, dans ce domaine, tel qu'il semble illusoire de faire accepter, surtout au niveau international, une règle claire et cohérente. Mais il appartient au théoricien du droit, avant d'arriver à des compromis qui sembleront inévitables, de proposer les solutions qu'il croit les meilleures. Ne serait-ce que pour offrir un point de départ raisonnable à des négociations dont l'aboutissement probable risque de l'être moins.

La règle que la licéité de l'injection dans un réseau de transmission numérique exige un consentement de l'auteur qui est présumé avoir une portée universelle ne devrait pas créer de problèmes pratiques autres que ceux qui sont liés à l'existence même du droit d'auteur. L'intervention des organismes de gestion collective pourrait aider à la solution de ces problèmes.

Questionnaire

1. What is the legal basis of the determination of applicable law in the field of copyright?

2. What is the applicable law when considering issues which specifically concern copyright (owner, object, contents, duration, limits, etc.)?

3. What is the applicable law when considering issues which regard copyright but which particularly deal with:
(a) moral rights;
(b) contracts;
(c) infringement and sanctions (penal or civil)?

4. More particularly, what is the applicable law in case of:
(a) diffusion covering a number of undefined countries;
(b) infringement on copyright
(aa) when crossing borders,
(bb) when the origin of the work is hard to identify?

5. Are there any rules (legislative or jurisprudential) which particularly deal with the Global Information Infrastructure, or any theoretical proposals?

Questionnaire

1. Quel est le fondement juridique de la détermination du droit applicable en matière de droit d'auteur (si un texte législatif, prière de le citer et de le reproduire)?

2. Quel est le droit applicable aux questions qui relèvent spécifiquement du droit d'auteur (titulaire, objet, contenu, durée, limitations etc.)?

3. Quel est le droit applicable aux questions qui se réfèrent au droit d'auteur mais qui concernent plus spécialement:
   (a) le droit moral;
   (b) les contrats;
   (c) les infractions et les sanctions (pénales ou civiles)?

4. Plus particulièrement, quel est le droit applicable en cas:
   (a) de diffusion couvrant un nombre de pays non-déterminés;
   (b) d'infractions au droit d'auteur
      (aa) transfrontalières,
      (bb) de provenance non-identifiable?

5. Y a-t-il des règles (législatives ou jurisprudentielles) spécialement prévues pour l'infrastructure globale d'information ou, éventuellement, des propositions théoriques)?

Canada

R.G. HOWELL[1]

Introduction

In Canada, authors' rights are protected primarily by copyright law, constitutionally a federal jurisdiction,[2] and wholly statutory since 1 January 1924.[3] From this date all prior copyright enactments in Canada and those the United Kingdom in force imperially in Canada, ceased to have effect. Additionally, 'common law' copyright from the United Kingdom and applicable in the common law provinces of Canada ceased to exist. The juridical nature of copyright law has been the subject of debate,[4] but has been described by Estey J., in delivering judgment by the Supreme Court of Canada, as: *'neither tort law nor property law in classification, but is statutory law. It neither cuts across existing rights in property or conduct nor falls between rights and obligations heretofore existing in the common law. Copyright legislation simply creates rights and obligations upon the terms and in the circumstances set out in the statute.'* [5]

Canada is a signatory to both the Berne and Universal copyright conventions. The legislation effective from 1924 was drafted to incorporate the Berne Convention (Berlin, 1908 and Berne, 1914).[6] Statutory amendment in 1931[7] incorporated the Rome 1928 revisions, particularly as to 'moral rights'. Subsequent amendments have included provisions to give effect to the Canada-United States Free Trade Agreement,[8] the North American Free Trade Agreement (NAFTA)[9] and the TRIPs Agreement under the GATT negotiations leading to the World Trade Organisation (WTO).[10] Overall, these amendments have brought Canada into compliance with the 1971 Paris Revision of the Berne Convention.[11]

Since 1924 international copyright conventions are not directly in force in domestic law in Canada. Domestic compliance is entirely dependent upon implementation in domestic legislation, the terms of which determine the nature and extent of the protections available.[12] However, judicial interpretation of those provisions will involve a consistency of purpose with treaty or convention provisions that the legislation manifests an intention to implement.[13] The Canadian Copyright Act, as a federal enactment, is bilingual - English and French. Both versions are equally authoritative,[14] and either may be looked to when interpreting the enactment and its consistency with the Convention.[15] Some additional or ancillary protection is available to authors by way of interpretation in contract and through various common law and statutory torts concerning privacy, integrity of personality and unfair competition. These matters are essentially within provincial constitutional jurisdiction.

1. What is the legal basis of the determination of applicable law in the field of copyright?

Private international law or conflict of laws in Canada is essentially non-statutory, being determined judicially by application of common law principles in each province, with a unifying influence by way of appeals to the Supreme Court of Canada. The English origin of Canadian common law allows English cases upon conflict of laws to remain persuasive, though not binding.[16] Likewise, the common origin of laws and similarity of approach to conflict of laws in some other Commonwealth common law jurisdictions (*e.g.* Australia and New Zealand), enables decisions from these jurisdictions to also be persuasive, at least in the absence of particular constitutional or legislative provisions.[17]

Canada has been noted as 'unusual' instance of a federal state without express constitutional provisions upon conflict of laws.[18] Provincial legislation may be enacted concerning conflict of laws, but only within the constitutional legislative jurisdiction of the province.[19] Copyright, being an exclusively federal legislative jurisdiction, cannot be dealt with directly by a provincial legislature.[20] No federal legislation or regulation exists concerning conflict of laws and copyright. The protection of 'authors' rights' by means ancillary to copyright - noted earlier to include interpretation in contract and various common law and statutory torts *(delict)* concerning privacy, integrity of personality and unfair competition - are within provincial legislative jurisdiction, but have not been the subject of provincial conflict of laws legislation.

As to constitutional judicial competence, copyright is concurrently federal and provincial. The Supreme Court of Canada is the ultimate appellate authority from both federal and provincial court systems. This unifying feature, together with copyright being a single federal or national law, removes any 'choice of law' issue with respect to copyright in Canada. On the other hand, the ancillary protections of authors' rights, as noted above, are exclusively provincial judicial jurisdiction, subject to appeal to the Supreme Court of Canada. In theory, 'choice of law' issues could arise as provincial jurisdiction is territorial. However, the considerable uniformity or comity, in interpreting common law in these ancillary contexts, has always rendered this unlikely.[21] Recently this has been settled to a considerable extent by the Supreme Court of Canada.[22]

Overall, the only potential conflict of laws issue in an interprovincial context in Canada with respect to authors' rights would arise should any cause for copyright or other infringement be brought in the courts of one province for service upon a defendant in another province - *i.e.* an exercise of *ex juris* authority.[23] Copyright and other categories of Intellectual Property, being established by a state within its territorial jurisdiction, have been described as within the 'territorial principle' of conflict of laws.[24] This reflects that, at most, the international conventions stipulate minimum criteria of protection available to qualified authors and owners in all member jurisdictions and, beyond this, to receive an equality of treatment with nationals under the national law of the states concerned.[25]

National laws of copyright and other intellectual property are limited to the national territory. Copinger and Skone James note in an English context concerning the sovereignty of the state: '*[N]o English court can entertain an action under the [United Kingdom's Copyright enactment] by a plaintiff who is the author of a work entitled to copyright under that Act in respect of acts complained of as being committed in France, even if being committed by a defendant who is within the jurisdiction of the English Court*'.[26] This territorial limitation is reflected in the Canadian Copyright Act, s. 5 providing: '*Subject to this Act, copyright shall subsist in Canada, for the term hereinafter mentioned, in every original literary, dramatic, musical and artistic work*'.[27]

It is also the position presented in Fox, the classical Canadian treatise on copyright, in the following terms: '*A Canadian court [as a result of territoriality under the international conventions] has no jurisdiction, at the instance of the Canadian proprietor of a copyright work, to restrain a threatened infringement by a Canadian citizen in any foreign country comprised in the International Copyright Union*'.[28] Fox continues by referring to the need of the Canadian citizen to take action '*in the courts and according to the law of [the country in which the infringement has occurred]*'.[29] Copinger and Skone James, however, continue their commentary with a conclusion that action for infringement outside of the United Kingdom (hypothetically, in France): '*can only proceed in [an] English court, if at all, on the basis that the plaintiff establishes the infringement of such rights as may be granted to him under French law*'.[30] This contemplates a proceeding in England for a copyright infringement in France upon essentially private international law criteria. The authors elaborate earlier in their treatise.[31] This is discussed later in this paper. For the moment, it is noted that there is no expressly similar Canadian initiative.

However, the Federal Court of Canada may have accepted this possibility without reference to the issue or any discussion as to jurisdiction or conflict of laws. In *Preston v. 20th Century Fox Canada Ltd.*,[32] the plaintiff, a Canadian resident (and probably a citizen), claimed to be the holder of a literary copyright in a script entitled, *Space Pets* and a fictitious, non-human character in that script described as an 'Ewok'. The plaintiff alleged he had, through a script writer, sent the script in 1979 to Lucasfilm Ltd., the California company of which George Lucas, the well-known motion picture producer of the *Star Wars* trilogy (*Star Wars*, *The Empire Strikes Back* and *Return Of The Jedi*) is Chairman.[33] The plaintiff alleged infringement of the script and character in various mediums by Lucas, especially the motion picture *Return Of The Jedi* and a television series *Ewok Adventure*. The plaintiff's action was dismissed on its merits. The character 'Ewok' was found not in itself to have copyright protection[34] and the evidence was found to be insufficient to establish that the defendant's motion picture was a reproduction or adaptation of the script alleged to be the plaintiff's.[35] The Federal Court of Appeal affirmed in a brief judgment.[36]

Upon what basis did the Federal Court of Canada take jurisdiction? The proceeding involved a lengthy trial and lengthy reasons for judgment. The substantive law was Canadian copyright law. George Lucas travelled to Canada to give evidence. The following 'connections' with Canada are noted: (1) the plaintiff was currently resident in Canada, (2) the plaintiff's alleged script was said to have been created in

Canada and mailed from Canada to the defendant in California, (3) of the three defendants, George Lucas, Lucasfilm Ltd. and Twentieth Century-Fox Canada Ltd., only the latter is located in Canada (in Alberta, the *situs* of the trial), the first two defendants were located in California, and (4) the defendant, Twentieth Century-Fox Canada Ltd. is a branch of its Los Angeles' parent. It is the Canadian distributor of the motion pictures of its parent.[37] Importantly, the allegation of infringement focused upon copying or reproducing in California. This involves an issue of jurisdiction and conflict of laws. Upon the classic territorial principle of private international law this proceeding should have been brought in the United States and upon United States' copyright law. If the focus had been the distribution in Canada by the corporate defendant located in Canada, an infringement may have involved a public performance or an authorisation of such by that defendant. This would then have been territorial - an infringement(s) in Canada. This does not, however, appear to have been in issue in the proceeding. The case stands as involving an alleged (not proven) infringement by reproduction in California.[38]

There are relevant English precedents. The 1899 case, *Baschet v. London Illustrated Standard Company,*[39] involved an English defendant infringing in England the French plaintiff's work entitled to copyright in France. English copyright law provided a greater quantum of penalty than that available in France. The following principle was stipulated: (1) a person cannot sue in England for infringement of a work published in the country of origin (France) unless there is proof of entitlement to protection in the country of origin, and (2) once entitlement is established in the country of origin, the remedies of the country hearing the suit *(lex fori)* apply.[40] The second case is *Jonathan Cape Ltd. v. Consolidated Press Ltd.,*[41] involving an English copyright partially assigned to the English plaintiff throughout most of the British Commonwealth including Australia, where the defendant infringed the copyright. Jurisdiction was not discussed.[42] Infringement was found. It is not clear if service *ex juris* was involved. The defendant appears to have had a presence in the United Kingdom.

A property approach

These two English cases and *Preston* in Canada might suggest a focus upon country of origin *(lex situs)* for intangible copyright as a proprietary chose in action. Conflict of laws rules for choses in action have developed in the context of debt and securities, but could equally be applied to intangible intellectual property, especially if *situs* were established by registration.[43] If the copyright were found to be within the jurisdiction, no difficulties would arise if the defendant were not in the jurisdiction as the rules for service *ex juris* would likely be met.[44]

Tort (delict) approaches

Copinger and Skone James submit: *'where the defendant is within the jurisdiction and, as in the case of a Berne Convention country, the nature of the wrong is similar under both sets of laws, an action may be maintainable [in that jurisdiction]'.*[45] Inherent in this submission is some identify or similarity of substantive copyright law. This minimises any issue as to choice of law, a matter otherwise not resolved in the submission of Copinger and Skone James. The implication, however, is *lex fori*. This approach would accommodate the position in *Preston* only if the corporate defendant, *i.e.* the distributor of the motion pictures in Canada, were connected with the alleged reproduction or copying in California. The two California defendants were not resident in Canada, although they submitted to the jurisdiction. Furthermore, as between Canada and the United States there is no such identity of copyright laws, notwithstanding the accession of the United States to the Berne Convention in 1988. Stewart makes a broader submission. Relying also on universality or similarity of substantive laws (within the Berne or Universal conventions), he suggests: *'it is arguable that an action can be maintained if the infringement has taken place in that country'.*[46] His choice of law is *lex loci delicti* - where the infringement occurred. This would not accommodate *Preston*. The Canadian Federal Court would have had to have invoked United States copyright law as any infringement by way of reproduction or copying in *Preston* would have occurred in California.[47]

What approach should Canada take?

The absence of any judicial analysis renders the issue of any Canadian position to be pure speculation. The European position is reported as allowing both the jurisdiction of the defendant and the jurisdiction in which the infringement occurred.[48] Stewart has noted courts in the United States to have traditionally declined jurisdiction for extra-territorial infringement on the ground that the United States' courts ought not rule on the validity of a 'foreign right'.[49] This may not necessarily represent the present position. Nimmer, writing in 1995, acknowledges the territorial principle rendering the US Copyright Act 'clearly inoperative' with respect to extra-territorial activities, but nevertheless, notes that courts in the United States may 'arguably' have jurisdiction: *'If the plaintiff has a valid cause of action under the copyright laws of a foreign country, and if personal jurisdiction of the defendant can be obtained in an American court'.*[50] Nimmer theorises that copyright infringement is of a transitory nature, meaning that the transaction that constitutes the wrong could occur anywhere, rather than having to occur only locally, or within a particular jurisdiction.[51] Earlier instances involving patent and trade mark infringement are noted to have involved 'administrative acts undertaken by foreign officials',[52] essentially the granting of the patents or trade marks. This is not the position with respect to copyright. The latter is relatively automatic, or free from 'administrative formalities'.[53] It is suggested that this reflects the more universal, or at least transnational, nature of copyright protection, as discussed earlier. Protection is territorial, yet transnational protection is provided through the mechanism of 'national treatment' to authors and owners within jurisdictions belonging to the Conventions.[54]

If this trend is followed in the United States, the close economic and trading relationship between Canada and the United States, now significantly enhanced by the North American Free Trade Agreement, will provide Canadian courts with further reason to contemplate exercising extra-territorial jurisdiction. Yet even at this fledgling stage there is an important difference between the suggested direction in the United States and that implicit in *Preston* in Canada, where the Federal Court (albeit without analysis) was quite prepared to take jurisdiction with respect to an alleged extra-territorial infringement and to apply Canadian copyright law. Canada was the jurisdiction of origin of the copyright as intangible property or chose in action,[55] but not the location of the defendant who did the alleged copying. This would suggest *lex situs* of the copyright. It involved no assessment of foreign law. The suggested direction in the United States, however, would appear to contemplate *lex loci delicti* - the law of the jurisdiction where the infringement occurred. Nimmer notes, however, that: *'[i]t remains to be seen whether this [trend] may prove to be a means of enforcing the European* droit moral *in American courts'*.[56]

The recently published Lehman Report (September 1995) in the United States clearly contemplates the potential of American courts applying foreign copyright law in appropriate circumstances for which conflict of laws rules will develop. In an electronic informational global context, the Report poses the following question: *'For instance, users in country A, where certain actions are not considered copyright infringements, may use works located on servers in country B, were such actions are. Which country's law controls the resolution of a copyright infringement dispute - the country from which a copyrighted work is uploaded or to which it is downloaded, or the country where the host server is located? In the case of direct transmissions, which country's law applies - the country of origin of the transmission or the transmitter, or the country of the reception?'*. The Report continues by speculating that in this scenario *'[i]t may be that rights of the copyright owner are exercised in each country'* - *i.e.* the country from which the work is uploaded, the country to which the work is downloaded, and the country where the host server is located.[57] It is likely that future legal developments in these respects in the United States will be similarly applied in Canada.

Copinger and Skone James, as well as Stewart, rely upon the conflict of laws rule in *Chaplin v. Boys*,[58] establishing jurisdiction *lex fori* when the territory has *in personam* jurisdiction over the defendant, and: (a) the alleged wrong (tort) by the defendant would have been actionable in the domestic (forum) territory had it have taken place in that territory, and (b) the alleged act was not justifiable under the law of the place of the tort.[59] These criteria would have been met in *Preston*,[60] and *Chaplin v. Boys* has been recognised and applied in Canada,[61] although recently the Supreme Court of Canada in *Tolofson v. Jensen* expressly moved away from British precedents, including *Chaplin v. Boys* and the historical preference for *lex fori*. Instead, La Forest J. in delivering the majority opinion, stipulated that *lex loci delicti* was now the firm preference in Canadian choice of laws in a tort or *delicti* context.[62] This would bring Canadian choice of law closer to the position noted in the United States,[63] but it is not an absolute rule in an international context, La Forest J. noting: *'because a rigid rule on the international level could give rise to injustice, in certain circumstances, I am not averse to retaining a discretion in the court to apply [Canadian] law to deal with such circumstances. [He could] however, imagine few cases where this would be necessary'*.[64] Sopinka and Major JJ. concurred with respect to international choice of law.[65] Given then the continued possibility of *Chaplin v. Boys* applying internationally, the two limbs of that authority will be examined in the present context.

Historically, the territorial limits upon copyright and other categories of intellectual property have inhibited extra-territorial proceedings on the basis that a territorially declared right cannot be violated by an extra-territorial act.[66] The first limb of the test does not, however, ask whether the actual extra-territorial infringement is itself actionable domestically. The answer would be negative. Domestic laws apply only within the territory. The proper focus is upon the hypothetical[67] of that same act occurring *within* the territory and asking whether it would be a wrong upon that hypothetical within the territory. More difficulty might occur with the second limb, concerning justification under the law of the place of the alleged tort. For example, suppose in *Preston* the alleged infringement was to the defendant's *moral rights* in his alleged works. Moral rights are recognized in Canada (meeting the first limb) but not to any considerable extent in the United States.[68] The act would have been justified (*i.e.* legally innocent)[69] in the United States and therefore would have failed under the second limb. This may well illustrate that as between Canada and the United States, the substantive law of copyright is not as similar in detail as perhaps may be the position in Europe. It presents Nimmer's speculation of the possible enforcement of 'European *droit moral* in American courts'.[70]

In this regard it may be further asked whether, in a conflict of laws context, a Canadian court is likely to draw a distinction drawn between economic rights and moral rights. In one sense, there ought to be no distinction. The rights under the Canadian Copyright Act have, as noted, been characterized as simply 'statutory rights'.[71] However, moral rights have recently been described by a federally appointed Sub-committee, reporting on copyright and the Information Highway, as being in the nature of the tort of defamation.[72] Upon such a characterisation, it may be asked whether such rights can be said to be 'property' or a chose in action. This may accordingly preclude a proprietary conflict of laws theory[73] being applied with respect to moral rights. Conversely, since 1988 moral rights are inheritable upon a succession formula stipulated in the Copyright Act.[74] The answer to the question posed must await judicial determination.

Contractual Matters

Section 13(4) provides: *'The owner of the copyright in any work may assign the right, either wholly or partially, and either generally or subject to territorial limitations, and either for the whole term of the copyright or for any other part thereof, and may grant any interest in the right by licence, but no assignment or grant is valid unless it is in writing signed by the owner of the right in respect of which the assignment or grant is made, or by his duly authorized agent'.*[75] This raises issues of rights not only of a proprietary nature, but also a contractual nature in a transborder, or conflict of laws, context as noted by Ulmer.[76] No Canadian authority exists. Nor does there appear to have been any discussion of this issue from a Canadian conflicts of law perspective.

The English decision in *Campbell Connelly & Co. Ltd. v. Noble*[77] is therefore likely to be influential in Canada. It is also found by Ulmer to fit within his broader European analysis that: *'For certain aspects - including in particular the question whether and to what extent the author may assign or grant to another person the rights to which he is entitled - the law of the protecting country is decisive, whilst in other respects the agreement is to be interpreted uniformly according to the law of contract'.*[78] The plaintiffs were musical publishers who had in 1934 obtained from the defendant, band leader and composer, the worldwide copyright in the musical composition *The Very Thought Of You.* In the United States copyright had two terms, the first for 28 years from the date of publication, together with (if the author was alive at the commencement of the 28th year) a right of renewal for a further period of 28 years. The defendant renewed his copyright after the first period, but denied the plaintiff's right to claim through the earlier assignment, rights to this renewal period. He purported to assign it to another. The issues were first, whether the renewal right was in itself assignable in advance; and secondly, whether it had been so assigned in the particular contract. Wilberforce J. found the first matter to be established by United States' copyright law.[79] As to whether the particular contract had actually assigned the renewal copyright, this was a matter of interpretation of *'a purely English contract and must plainly be interpreted according to English law'.*[80] An assignment was found despite authorities in the United States requiring a specific reference to the renewal copyright if it is to be successfully assigned.[81] Copinger and Skone James summarise the result as: *'[the judge] was entitled to look at American law to ascertain the nature of the renewal right, but not to enable him to construe the assignment'.*[82]

It may be speculated that the division of jurisdiction presented in this case will be of considerable importance with respect to (1) an extra-territorial license and a determination of its juristic nature, being probably a matter of the domestic law of the jurisdiction of use; and (2) issues of applicable law with respect to the nature and registration of security interests in extra-territorial assignments or licensing agreements and priorities among persons interested in these transactions.

> **2.** *What is the applicable law when considering issues which specifically concern copyright (owner, object, contents, duration, limits, etc.)?*

The law in Canada for matters specific to authors' rights is the federal Copyright Act.[83] (Note: as question 3 asks specifically as to moral rights, the answers under this part are focused on economic rights.)

(i) Title holder

The author is ordinarily the first owner of copyright. However, the economic rights in a work completed in the course of the author's employment under a contract of service or apprenticeship, vests in the employer.[84] An owner may also assign or licence interests in the copyright.[85]

(ii) Object/Contents

The economic rights of copyright are set out in section 3 of the Act. As yet, there is no case-law specifically concerning the Global Information Infrastructure. However, in March 1995 a federally appointed Sub-committee on Copyright and the Information Highway submitted its Final Report.[86] Given the Committee's broad conclusion that no specific new law, or *sui generis* category of protection, should be enacted to deal with the Information Highway or Global Information Infrastructure,[87] the Committee gave attention to those existing economic rights most relevant to this medium.

These included:

(a) The reproduction of a work or 'a substantial part thereof in any material form whatever' (s. 3(1)). A work downloaded from the Internet to a hard drive or disk would constitute a reproduction in a material form. The Sub-committee envisaged this to be so for any downloading from a Bulletin Board Service (BBS).[88] The writer, however, queries whether the placing of a work in a BBS known to have unrestricted public access, and with knowledge that downloading occurs extensively, might amount to an implied consent to copy that work.[89] The Sub-committee also recommended that 'browsing' works on the Internet be considered to amount to a reproduction. Although there was divergent evidence before the Sub-committee as to the meaning of 'browsing', the act of browsing involves a work being 'accessed', which the Sub-committee considered constituted a reproduction, *'even if it is a temporary or ephemeral fixation'*.[90] A 'fair dealing' defence may well be available in particular instances.[91]

(b) The communication 'to the public by telecommunication' of a work (s. 3(1)(f)). Radio, cable, satellite and telephone transmission is included within the definition of 'telecommunications' as follows: *'any transmission of signs, signals, writing, images or sounds or intelligence of any nature by wire, radio, visual, optical or other electromagnetic system'*.[92] The Internet or information highway is within this definition. The Sub-committee correctly notes that a communication 'to the public' would include placing a work (without the consent of the copyright owner) on a Bulletin Board where it can be read by 'the public' (to 'communicate' does not necessarily involve any copy being made).[93] The meaning of the expression 'to the public' is yet to be judicially determined. The Sub-committee suggested that it will not include 'point-to-point e-mail' between specific individuals, but that it will likely include a Bulletin Board, probably even if members of the public access the Board at different times. The Sub-committee has recommended that any narrowing of this by judicial interpretation be corrected by legislation.[94] The writer suggests that encoded communication to specifically defined groups (*e.g.* between members of a corporation or private club) is not likely to constitute a communication 'to the public'.[95]

(c) The performance in public (s. 3(1)) of a work may also occur on the Internet. However, the definition of 'performance' is narrow. It is essentially an 'acoustic' representation or a visual representation of only a 'dramatic work'. The representation can be by a radio or television receiving set or any 'mechanical instrument'.[96] The expression 'in public' is broader than the earlier noted 'to the public' test. It can mean anything that is not essentially 'private'.[97] However, beyond the above acoustic representation and visual representation of a dramatic work, the act of communicating a work to the public by telecommunication (s. 3(1)(f)) - (say, a digital communication or a non-acoustic visual representation of a literary work) - is not a perfor-

mance in public. Section 3(4) provides that: *'the act of communicating a work to the public by telecommunication does not constitute the act of performing or delivering the work in public, nor does it constitute an authorisation to do the act of performing or delivering the work in public'*.[98]

(d) The publication of a work is a right exclusive to the copyright owner. It is constituted generally by making copies of the work available to the public.[99] There must be a sufficient number to meet reasonable demand.[100] An unauthorized publication does not constitute a publication in law.[101] Performance, exhibition or delivery (of a lecture) does not constitute publication,[102] nor does 'the communication of a work to the public by telecommunication'.[103] The latter would include a communication on the Internet. Does it preclude 'publication' by the Internet? Probably not. A distinction might be drawn between mere 'display' (like 'performance'), which would *not* constitute a publication, and actual downloading, amounting to copies being available to the public, which might constitute publication. The Sub-committee concluded (without giving reasons) that 'electronic transmissions resulting in the making of copies available to the public' would be a publication.[104]

(e) The Sub-committee finds an 'important role' for the public exhibition on the Internet of an artistic work (other than a map, chart or plan) created after 7 June 1988.[105] This right of the copyright owner is expressed as follows: *'to present at a public exhibition, for a purpose other than sale or hire, an artistic work created after 7 June 1988, other than a map, chart or plan'*.[106] There has been no judicial interpretation of the exhibition right. In particular, the phrase 'a public exhibition' may be narrower than simply 'public exhibition'. Possibly a curated or designated event is necessary.[107] If this interpretation is applied, the scope for this right on the Internet may be more limited. However, the Sub-committee further suggests that this right might be extended legislatively to a 'public display' right as found in the United States.[108]

(f) Rental rights for copyright owners of computer programs[109] and sound recordings[110] are not considered to be within the technology of the Internet or information highway which concern accessing and reproducing, rather than renting.[111]

(g) Providers of Internet facilities may infringe the authorisation right of the copyright owner (s. 3(1)). However, section 3(1.3) of the Copyright Act provides expressly that merely 'providing the means of telecommunication' is not itself communicating that work under s. 3(1)(f). Likewise, s. 3(4), noted above,[112] provides that telecommunication to the public does not 'constitute an authorization to do the act of performing or delivering the work to the public'. A breach of the separate authorisation right might, nevertheless, still occur if, for example, an organization were to set up a communications network for use by members of the organisation. If copying is encouraged or, perhaps, if no warning is given to not copy by way of infringement, by the organiser, an infringement might occur. There is little judicial authority in Canada and conflicting positions have been taken as between the Australian High Court and the English House of Lords upon the scope of the authorisation right.[113] Probably an organiser would need some measure of control over users before being found to have authorized an infringement. However, the position may be within s. 3(1.4)(b) providing that a person who is part of a *'programming undertaking whose operations result in the communication of works to the public'* by another person is jointly and severally liable with that person, the work of the two being deemed 'a single communication'.[114]

(h) The copyright owner has the right to control importation of copies of works that would constitute an infringement if reproduced in Canada. This matter is, however, dealt with under question 4 below.

(iii) Duration

The duration of copyright is generally the life of the author, the remainder of the calendar year in which the author dies and a period of fifty years from the end of that calendar year,[115] subject to limited exceptions.[116]

(iv) Limitations

Limitations upon copyright include: *(a)* The need for the work to be original (s. 5).[117] *(b)* Various defences as set out in section 27(2)(a)-(m). The most significant defence is that of fair dealing in section 27(2)(a).[118] The Sub-committee gave attention to this defence, considering it to offer adequate protection to users of the information highway especially with respect to the 'private study' and 'research' categories. The Sub-committee recommended, however that government should review on a regular basis the appropriateness of these provisions to new forms of technology.[119] *(c)* There is a three year limitation period upon commencing proceedings actions for infringement (s. 41).[120]

> **3.** *What is the applicable law when considering issues which regard copyright but which particularly deal with:*

> *a. moral rights*

Canada first provided for the protection of moral rights in 1931.[121] Until 1988 the Copyright Act stipulated these rights in a manner closely following the terms of Article 6 *bis* of the Berne Convention (Rome 1928).[122] Statutory amendments in 1988 enhanced the position.[123]

The present rights are:
(a) A right of integrity in the work.[124] This comprises situations where an infringement constitutes 'prejudice of the honour or reputation of the author' and (i) the work is 'distorted, mutilated or otherwise modified'; or (ii) the work is 'used in association with a product, service, cause or institution'.[125] For a 'painting, sculpture or engraving' the requisite prejudice to the author's honour or reputation is deemed to have occurred merely upon such 'distortion, mutilation or other modification of the work'.[126] In all other situations, prejudice must be established. It expressly cannot be established simply and solely from: '(i) change in the location of a work; (ii) the physical means by which a work is exposed; (iii) the physical structure containing a

work; or (iv) steps taken in good faith to restore or preserve the work';[127] and

(b) A right of association (paternity) in the work. The exercise of this right must be 'reasonable in the circumstances'. It is expressed as a right 'to be associated with the work as its author by name or under a pseudonym'; and

(c) A right 'to remain anonymous'.[128]

Moral rights cannot be assigned. They may be waived.[129] They subsist for the same term as copyright.[130] A waiver does not occur merely upon the assignment of the copyright in a work[131] and the Copyright Act provides a formula for the descending of moral rights upon the death of the author.[132]

There is little judicial interpretation of these provisions but a number of commentaries exist.[133] The leading authority is *Snow v. The Eaton Centre Ltd.*,[134] where a sculptor succeeded in preventing a large mall, who had acquired his sculpture, from placing Christmas decorations on the sculpture - red bows around the necks of Canada geese in a sculpture known as 'Flight Stop' and artistically displayed hanging beneath a glass roof of the mall. The court interpreted the provisions as allowing a certain measure of 'subjectivity' on the part of the author in determining whether what had occurred would cause prejudice to his honour or reputation.[135] On the other hand, there is judicial recognition of some limitation on the enforcement of moral rights when the work has a utilitarian as well as an artistic function.[136]

The relationship between moral rights and the Internet or Information Highway was considered by the Copyright Sub-committee. The comparative ease of manipulation and alteration of information in digital format, with consequent infringement of the moral right of integrity of authors, is acknowledged. The conflict between public access to, and use of, digital technology - including the ability to manipulate and change - and the need to preserve the integrity of the author, was expressly addressed by the Committee. The interest of the author was seen in the nature of injury to honour and reputation, similar to the objectives sought to be protected by the tort of defamation. This would allow some modification to be made. The test of 'honour and reputation' is suggested as setting the balance. In this respect, the presumption of prejudice from any modification to a 'painting, sculpture or engraving'[137] was seen as more appropriately limited to modifications to an original work, rather than to a copy, digital or otherwise. The interest sought to be protected by the presumption was given as the preservation of the history of art. The Sub-committee recommended that this be the subject of legislative amendment.[138] The Sub-committee also considered the difficulty of detecting infringement of, and enforcing compliance with, moral rights in a digital medium, but concluded: *'removing or altering the legal framework because technological development may prevent the enforcement of rights in practice, is pushing the issue in the wrong direction'.*[139]

Systems such as 'sampling, blanket licenses or full-fledged monitoring' were seen as being effective to protect creators, yet still balance the rights of users.[140] These methods are, of course, equally useful with respect to protecting infringement of economic rights. The Sub-committee rejected any distinction being drawn between economic and moral rights, specifically, that the Internet technology did not warrant identifying categories of work that would be denied economic rights but be covered by moral rights.[141]

b. contracts

In addition to the statutory principles discussed above, interpretation of the nature or terms of contracts involving authors' rights, reflects a trend to reconcile moral rights with the purpose of a contract. First, in contracts involving the supply of works that will require repair or maintenance: *'a term must be implied in the contract permitting repairs, involving alteration to copyright material if need be, to ensure the use of the [work] for the purpose for which it was intended as well as to ensure public safety and to prevent public concern'.*[142]

Secondly, with respect to contracts between authors and publishers, Fitzpatrick CJC held in 1911, before any moral rights provisions were included in the Copyright Act in Canada (these were inserted in 1931), that: *'what is called literary property has a character and attributes of its own and that [a contract relating to it] must be interpreted and the rights of the parties determined with regard to the special nature of the thing'.*[143] He considered that apart from any economic interest, the author retained *'a species of personal or moral right in the product of his brain'*,[144] and that the assignment of the manuscript did not permit a publisher to (1) publish the manuscript *'with such emendations or additions as might perchance suit his political or religious views and give them to the world as those of [the author]'*; (2) deny the author *'the right to make corrections, in dates or otherwise, if such corrections were found to be necessary for historical accuracy'*; (3) publish the manuscript *'in the name of another'*,[145] or (4) to retain, yet refuse to publish the manuscript.[146]

Presumably, the Chief Justice assumed that the contract also assigned to the publisher the copyright, as well as the manuscript, as only the copyright holder has the right to publish in any circumstance.[147] The proceeding concerned the fourth point - the publisher retaining the manuscript, yet refusing to publish. The author having tendered the return of the contract payment for the manuscript, the majority ordered the return of the manuscript, the only value of which was in publication.[148] The two judges (Davies and Duff JJ.) joining the Chief Justice in the majority, did not adopt the 'moral rights' analysis of the Chief Justice, but found publication to be the essence of the contract and upon failure to undertake publication *'no property in the manuscript passed [to] and no right to retain the rejected manuscript remained [in the publisher]'* (Davies J.);[149] or that 'suppression' of the manuscript would defeat the contractual intention giving rise to a resulting trust in favour of the author (Duff J.).[150] Dissenting, Idington J. found no distinction between contracting for supplying a literary work and any other product. He declined to imply a condition that would return the manuscript upon non-publication.[151] Anglin J. found similarly[152] and expressly noted the contract to have vested in the publisher the copyright - including the right to publish or to refrain from publishing.[153]

Recently, in almost identical circumstances, the unique rights of an author in a manuscript as found by Fitzpatrick CJC were approved and applied.[154] However, in this case it was important that the copyright had not, under the terms of the contract, passed to the publisher. If it had, then the implication is that the publisher could have retained the manuscript unpublished.[155]

c. infringement and sanctions (penal or civil)

Infringement of the copyright owner's economic rights occurs when any person: *'without the consent of the owner of the copyright, does anything that, by [the Copyright] Act, only the owner of the copyright has the right to do'*.[156] The economic rights relevant to this Report are set out earlier under question 2. Infringement of an author's moral rights is provided for in section 28(1) as follows: *'Any act or omission that is contrary to any of the moral rights of the author of a work is, in the absence of consent by the author, an infringement of the moral rights'*.[157]

Civil remedies are provided for infringement of both economic rights[158] and moral rights.[159] They include injunction, damages, accounts *'and such other remedies that are or may be conferred by law for the infringement of a right'*. An infringer is liable for both damages for loss sustained by an owner and an account of profits made by the infringer.[160] If a defendant proves that at the time of infringement *'he was not aware and had no reasonable ground for suspecting that copyright subsisted in the work'*, civil relief is limited to an injunction, but registration of a copyright is sufficient to overcome this limitation.[161] A deemed 'conversion' remedy is available to the copyright owner with respect to all infringing copies of any work.[162] With respect to the Internet or Information Highway, the Sub-committee has recommended that 'statutory damages based on the US model' be introduced.[163]

Penal provisions are stipulated in sections 42 and 43 and 43.1.[164] Note should also be made of civil indirect infringement provisions in section 27(4) and (5).[165]

4. More particularly, what is the applicable law in case of:

a. diffusion covering a number of undefined countries

There are no provisions in the Copyright Act that provide specifically for transborder transmissions on the Information Highway. However, a significant issue in this context is the prohibition against importation of copies made out of Canada of any work in which copyright subsists in Canada.[166] Is a transborder digital transmission within this provision? Will it constitute an importation? Submissions made to the Sub-committee on Copyright and the Information Highway requested clarification of the position. The Sub-committee, however, responded: *'In the view of the Sub-committee, electronic importation is not possible, as a practical matter, since the transmission of a work from point A to point B constitutes the making of an additional copy with the original or a different copy of the work remaining at point A'*.[167]

The writer does not view the technology to be so obviously outside of the importation prohibition. The retention of an original or a different copy outside of Canada could also be the position with a manual reproduction and importation. The essential focus of the importation prohibition is, surely, that a new copy (or copies) has arrived in Canada. This can certainly occur electronically. However, there is a further matter to be considered. The Copyright Act requires that the '[c]opies be made out of Canada'.[168]

Where is the copy made in respect of an electronic digital transmission? This could be outside of Canada (in a transborder context) when it is entered and stored in the computer unit prior to transmission. Alternatively, it might be at the point of receipt *i.e.* when it is received into the hard drive of the receiving computer unit or displayed on the screen of that unit. It is suggested that a copy would be made in both places. It is further suggested that if this is part of an exercise to make a copy available in Canada, then an importation has occurred. This issue, however, must await judicial determination. For completeness, note should also be made than an owner of copyright wishing to invoke the importation prohibition must have given notice to Canadian customs authorities. Furthermore, significant exceptions exist.[169]

Specific provisions do exist with respect to the retransmission of telecommunication signals in the nature of terrestrial radio and terrestrial television signals. Section 28.01 provides that the communication of copyright works through such signals will not infringe copyright if (1) the signal is retransmitted by a cable retransmission system, (2) 'the signal is retransmitted simultaneously and in its entirety' (except as otherwise may be permitted under law), and (3) if it is a 'distant' - as opposed to a 'local'[170] - signal the retransmitter has paid a royalty, as determined by the Copyright Board each year.[171] Regulations define, in technical terms, the meaning of 'local' and 'distance' signals. Essentially, a 'local' signal is limited to an 'area of transmission' of 32 kilometres.[172] In a North American transborder context, transmissions are either 'local' or 'distant' depending upon the proximity of centres of population to the border. In setting royalties for distant signals transmitted to and within Canada, the Copyright Board must consider certain specified aspects, including 'royalties paid for the retransmission of distant signals in the United States under the retransmission regime in the United States'.[173]

b. infringement on copyright when the origin of the work is hard to identify

There are provisions in the Copyright Act referring to works in respect of which the identity of the author is unknown. However, such provisions are limited to the following contexts, that have no special significance to the Global Information Infrastructure.

(i) Term of copyright: Section 6.1[174] provides, with effect from 1 January 1994 (the NAFTA amendments), that where the author of a work is unknown (essentially concerning anonymous or pseudonymous works) the term of copyright shall be the earlier of (1) the remainder of the calendar year of first publication, followed by fifty years, or (2) the remainder of the calendar year of the making of the work, followed by seventy-five years. If during this term the identity author 'becomes commonly known', the regular term of copyright is applicable. This position applies similarly to works by joint authors, whom are all unknown. However, where the identity of one or more of the authors 'becomes commonly known', the term of copyright is determined by reference to the surviving, 'commonly known' author's life and the regular term applies.[175] The expression 'commonly known' suggests a focus on 'public awareness' as opposed to individual awareness or awareness by a private or small group of persons.

(ii) Where an owner cannot be found: Section 70.7[176] enables a person seeking a licence to 'use' (in a sense that would otherwise involve an infringement of an economic right of copyright) a published work in which copyright subsists, but who cannot locate the owner, to apply to the Copyright Board for a licence. The Board must be satisfied that 'reasonable efforts' have been made by the applicant to locate the owner, but that these have not been successful. the Board may then issue to the applicant a non-exclusive licence and may impose terms and conditions, including a royalty fee. The owner of the copyright has five years from the expiration of the licence to collect the royalties.

> ***5.*** *Are there any rules (legislative or jurisprudential) which particularly deal with the Global Information Infrastructure, or any theoretical proposals?*

There are no copyright provisions or rules (legislative or judicial) specially designed for the Global Information Infrastructure. However, theoretical propositions have been presented by the Copyright Sub-committee in its report to the Information Highway Advisory Council Secretariat in March 1995. These propositions, where applicable, have been presented and discussed throughout this paper. There are no conflict of laws provisions or rules (legislative or judicial) specially designed for the Global Information Infrastructure.

Footnotes

1. I thank my Research Assistant, Mr Steve McKoen (U.Vic. 1997), and Mrs Sheila Talbot for secretarial assistance.
2. Section 91(23), Constitution Act, 1867 (UK), 30 & 31 Vict. c. 3 (originally enacted as the British North America Act, 1867 and re-named by the Constitution Act, 1982 (UK) (Schedule, Item 1)).
3. See currently Copyright Act, RSC 1985, c. C-42, section 63. (Originally enacted as s. 44 Copyright Act, 1921, SC 1921, c. 24.)
4. See Roberts, *'Canadian Copyright: Natural Property or Mere Monopoly'* (1979), 40 CPR (2d) 33 and Keyes & Brunet, *'A Rejoinder to 'Canadian Copyright: Natural Property or Mere Monopoly"* (1979), 40 CPR (2d) 54.
5. See *Compo Co. Ltd. v. Blue Crest Music Inc.*, [1980], 1 SCR 357 at 372-73, 45 CPR (2d) 1.
6. See Copyright Act, s. 65 and Schedule II until 31 December 1993. Repealed with effect from 1 January 1994, see North America Free Trade Agreement Implementation Act, 1993, SC 1993, c. 44, s. 69.
7. See Copyright Amendment Act, 1931, SC 21-22 Geo. V., c. 8 (1931).
8. Canada-United States Free Trade Agreement Implementation Act, 1988, SC 1988, c. 65, ss. 61-65.
9. North America Free Trade Agreement Implementation Act 1993, SC 1993, c. 44, ss. 52-80.
10. World Trade Organisation Agreement Implementation Act, SC 1994, c. 47 (Canada assumed international obligations with respect to these provisions with effect from 1 January 1996).
11. Compliance with Paris 1971 was required by Article 1701(2)(b) of the North America Free Trade Agreement. In addition to these 'trade-related' amendments, significant other amendments to the Copyright Act were: the Copyright Amendment Act, 1988, RSC 1985 (4th Supp.), c. 10; the Integrated Circuit Topography Act, 1990, c. 37, s. 33; the Copyright Amendment Act, 1993, SC 1993, c. 23; and the Intellectual Property Law Improvement Act, S.C. 1993, c. 15. In addition, as a consequence of the World Trade Organisation Agreement Implementation Act, 1993, SC 1993, c. 44, ss. 58-60 and 62-66

(concerning performers' rights) (in effect from 1 January 1996) and a further regime concerning performers' performances, sound recordings and broadcasters' signals contained in Bill C-32 tabled in April 1996 in the Parliament of Canada and, at the time of writing, at Second Reading (public hearings), Canadian legislation will, upon the passing of Bill C-32, also comply with the International Convention for the Protection of Performers, Producers of Phonograms and Broadcasting Organisations, Rome, 1961.

12. See *Louvigny de Montigny v. Cousineau*, [1950] SCR 297, 10 Fox Pat. C. 161 describing the Berne Convention as merely identifying the countries the citizens of which are entitled to protection, with actual protection in Canada being exclusively by the terms of the Copyright Act [today, section 5]. Prior to 1924, the imperial copyright legislation of the United Kingdom, in force in Canada, included the International Copyright Act, 1886, 49-50, Vic. C. 33 (UK) implementing the Berne Convention (1886). By Order in Council in the United Kingdom the terms of the Convention were made part of the municipal law of the United Kingdom and of the municipal law of British Dominions (including Canada). See *Durand v. La Patrie Publishing Company Ltd.*, [1960] SCR 649 at 655. See also H.G. Fox, *The Canadian Law of Copyright and Industrial Designs*, 2d ed. (Toronto: Carswell, 1967) at 547-548 and N. Tamaro, *The Annotated Copyright Act 1992* (English translation, C. McGuire) (Toronto: Carswell, 1992) at pp. 15-16.

13. See *Composers, Authors and Publishers Association of Canada Ltd. v. CTV Television Network Ltd.*, [1968] SCR 676; 55 CPR 132 at 138 (SCC) noting that when a provision in the Copyright Act is not clear, then, as a matter of interpretation, the entire Act, including the schedules containing the Conventions, is to be considered. For example, prior to 1 January 1994, there was some uncertainty in the interpretation of [section 5] of the Copyright Act concerning the qualification of extra-territorial authors for protection in Canada. Judicial determinations considered interpretation issues between the Convention and the legislation. See *Ludlow Music Inc. v. Canint Music Corp. Ltd.*, (1967), 35 Fox Pat. C. 114 at 122 (Ex. Ct.) and *Milliken & Co. v. Interface Flooring Systems (Canada) Inc.*, (1994), 52 CPR (3d) 92 at 96-97 (FCTD). See also H.G. Fox, *ibid.*

14. Section 18(1), Constitution Act, 1982 (UK) being Schedule B to Canada Act, 1982 (UK) Stats. UK 1982, c. 11.

15. See *e.g. Milliken & Co. v. Interface Flooring Systems (Canada) Inc., supra*, note 12 at 95-97.

16. See J.-G. Castel, *Canadian Conflict of Laws*, 3rd ed. (Toronto, Butterworths: 1994) at s. 8 discussing the sources of Canadian conflict of laws. Canadian common law will in this context include international customary rules.

17. See *e.g.* Swan, '*The Canadian Constitution, Federalism and the Conflict of Laws*', (1985), 63 Can. Bar Rev. 271 at 281, 288 and 307 comparing and contrasting some aspects of Canadian and Australian conflict of laws.

18. Swan *ibid.* at 272.

19. See Castel, *supra* note 15 at para. 8 referring to federal and provincial legislation as a potential source of conflict of laws rules 'within their respective fields of competence'.

20. Of course, in any 'division of powers' classification there will be instances which require to be 'characterized' as to whether they are within one category (federal) or another (provincial). For example, since 1988 the Canadian Copyright Act (federal) has included in section 14.2(2) a statutory formula concerning the 'devolution' or 'succession' of moral rights upon the death of an author. Yet, 'succession' in general is a provincial jurisdiction. If, for example, the constitutional validity of s. 14.2(2) of the Copyright Act were to be challenged, then the court would have to decide whether the provision was in 'pith and substance' a matter of 'copyright' (federal) or 'succession' (provincial). For a general treatment of 'characterization' in Canadian constitutional law, see P.W. Hogg, *Constitutional Law of Canada*, 3rd ed. (Toronto: Carswell, 1992) s. 15.5. As a province has a constitutional jurisdiction in relation to 'The administration of Justice in the Province' (s. 92(14) Constitution Act, 1867), and is entitled judicially to determine issues of copyright upon provincial rules of procedure, there may be an opening for some provincial conflict of laws rules to affect matters of copyright. This, however, is unlikely.

21. See generally Castel, *supra*, note 15 at s. 9(a) and s. 9(d).

22. See *Tolofson v. Jensen*, [1994] 3 SCR 1022 discussed *infra* text accompanying notes 61-64.

23. See generally Castel, *supra* note 15 at s. 123.

24. See *Dicey and Morris on The Conflict of Laws*, 9th ed., J.H.C. Morris (London: Stevens & Sons Ltd., 1973) at pp. 952-953. See also E. Ulmer, *Intellectual Property Rights and the Conflict of Laws*, Kluwer/Commission of the European Committee, Luxembourg, 1978 (Originally published in German, translated to English, 1976) at 8-9.

25. See S.M. Stewart, *International Copyright and Neighbouring Rights*, 2nd ed. (London: Butterworths, 1989) at ss. 3.14-3.18.

26. *Copinger and Skone James on Copyright*, 12th ed. (London: Sweet & Maxwell, 1980) at s. 1017.

27. Copyright Act, RSC 1985, c. C-42, s. 5(1). The current s. 5(1) is that substituted by s. 57(1), World Trade Organisation Agreement Implementation Act, SC 1994, c. 47 (in effect from 1 January 1996).

28. H.G. Fox, *supra*, note 11 at 548.

29. *Ibid.*

30. Copinger and Skone James, *supra*, note 25.

31. Copinger and Skone James, *ibid.* at s. 619.

32. *Preston v. 20th Century Fox Canada Ltd.* (1990), 33 CPR (3d) 242 (FCTD) affd (1994), 53 CPR (3d) 407 (FCA).

33. The report indicates that the script was mailed to 'George Lucas in care of 20th Century Fox Film

Corp. in Los Angeles'. *Ibid.*, at 246 and 250.

34. *Ibid.* at 277.

35. *Ibid.* at 274.

36. *Preston v. 20th Century Fox Canada Ltd.* (1994), 53 CPR (3d) 407 (FCA).

37. See *Preston, supra* note 31 at 245. The court noted 'The defendants together are the producers and distributors'.

38. *Ibid.* at 272. The entire reasons for judgment concern only the reproduction right. Pre-trial attempts to argue breach of contract and trademark infringement were discontinued. See *ibid.* 244-245 (in a footnote to the report).

39. *Baschet v. London Illustrated Standard Company,* [1900] 1 Ch. 73 (Ch. 1899).

40. *Ibid.* at 78.

41. *Jonathan Cape Ltd. v. Consolidated Press Ltd.,* [1954] 1 WLR 1313 (QB).

42. *Copinger and Skone James, supra,* note 25 at s. 619, rely upon this authority as an example of extra-territorial jurisdiction by the English courts and note that the copyright law in force in Australia at the time of the infringement was the United Kingdom's Copyright Act, 1911, the same enactment then also in force in the United Kingdom. The law between Australia and the United Kingdom was, therefore, identical.

43. See Castel, *supra*, note 15 at ss. 292-301 pointing out that under Canadian conflict of laws, choses in action (intangible proprietary rights) are treated as having a *situs* and are subject to the same conflict of laws rules as 'movables'. Intellectual property rights are not discussed, but jurisdiction of origin would be justifiable. Registration of copyright is not required in Canada (being a Berne jurisdiction) but is available and if completed, provides procedural advantages to the registrant. See Copyright Act, ss. 54-59. If a grant or interest, either by assignment or license, is not registered, it will lose priority to any *'subsequent assignee or licensee for valuable consideration without actual notice'* (s. 57(3)).

44. See Castel, *ibid.* at s. 123 listing the categories in Canadian law for *ex juris* service, including 'personal property in the jurisdiction'.

45. Copinger and Skone James, *supra*, note 25 at s. 619.

46. Stewart, *supra*, note 24 at s. 3.28.

47. As noted, *supra*, text accompanying note 37, the corporate defendant located in Canada was involved in distributing the motion pictures and may be said to have contributed to any public performance of the alleged copyright in Canada or, perhaps, be found to have authorised such performance.

48. See Stewart, *supra*, note 24 at s. 3.28. For a detailed survey of the European position see Ulmer, *Intellectual Property Rights and the Conflict of Laws, supra,* note 23 especially at pp. 11-14.

49. See Stewart, *ibid.* at s. 3.28, n. 6.

50. *Nimmer on Copyright,* (M.B. Nimmer, D. Nimmer) (Matthew Bender, NY 1996) at s. 17.03.

51. *Ibid.*

52. See Nimmer, *ibid.* noting *Vanity Fair Mills v. T. Eaton & Co.*, 234 F. 2d 633, 647 (2nd Cir., 1956) and *Packard Instrument Co Ltd.. v. Beckman Instruments, Inc.*, 346 F. Supp. 408, 410 (ND Ill. 1972).

53. Nimmer, *ibid.*

54. See *supra* text accompanying notes 23 and 24.

55. See *supra*, note 42 and accompanying text.

56. See Nimmer, *supra*, note 49 at s. 17.03.

57. See *Intellectual Property and the National Information Infrastructure*, (The Report of the Working Group on Intellectual Property Rights), Chair: Bruce A. Lehman, Submitted to the Secretary of Commerce, Information Infrastructure Task Force, Washington DC, September 1995 at p. 147.

58. *Chaplin v. Boys*, [1971] AC 356 (HL).

59. This rule is derived from the classic authority of *Phillips v. Eyre* (1870), LR 6 QB 1 (CA). See Castel, *supra*, note 15 at s. 499.

60. The allegations were not, however, established on their merits. See *supra* notes 33 and 34 and accompanying text.

61. See Castel, *supra*, note 15 at s. 501.

62. *Tolofson v. Jensen, supra*, note 21 at 1046-1055. See also Kincaid, *Jensen v. Tolofson and the Revolution in the Tort Choice of Law* (1995), 74 *Can. Bar Rev.* 537.

63. See *supra* text accompanying note 55.

64. *Tolofson v. Jensen, supra* note 61 at 1054.

65. *Ibid.* at 1078. Sopinka and Major JJ. would have retained a discretion of either *lex fori* or *lex loci delicti* with respect to choice of law issues between the provinces of Canada. Instead, the Court (judgment given by La Forest J.) stipulated that in a tort context, as between provinces in Canada *lex loci delicti* is an absolute rule.

66. The territorial principle is predicated upon the jurisdictional limitation of statutory conferment of rights. See *supra* notes 20-28 and accompanying text.

67. See Castel, *supra*, note 15 at s. 500, n. 34, commenting with respect to the first limb: *'Although the events are to be considered on the hypothesis that they occurred in the [jurisdiction] where the action is brought, due regard will still be given to the actual foreign context, e.g., in respect of the rule of the road in traffic cases'.*

68. Moral rights are recognised federally in the United States in the Visual Artists Rights Act 1990, PL No. 101-650, 104 Stat. 5128, 17 USC 101 (1990). To some extent, state laws concerning unfair competition, passing off, right of publicity, privacy and defamation might also assist. In effect, this presents a traditional approach of a common law jurisdiction to the question of moral rights. In this

respect, the very early adoption in Canada of a specific moral rights provision in copyright legislation was somewhat unique, although most common law countries have, in recent times, moved to enact specific provisions. See Ricketson, *US Accession to Berne: An Outsider's Appreciation (Part 2)* (1993), 8 [Can.] *IPJ* 87 at 99-105.

69. See Castel, *supra*, note 15 at s. 501, p. 640. For a proceeding to meet the requirements of the second limb, the activity must have been either a breach of a criminal or penal statute in the jurisdiction of the alleged wrong; or there must be a civil liability between the parties (rather than in some abstract sense) under the law of that jurisdiction at the time of the alleged wrong (*ibid.* at pp. 640-641).

70. See *supra* text accompanying note 55.

71. See *supra* note 4 and accompanying text.

72. See *infra* text accompanying notes 133-137.

73. This approach is discussed *supra* text accompanying notes 42 and 43.

74. See s. 14.2(2) Copyright Act. See *supra* note 19.

75. S. 13(4) Copyright Act.

76. See Ulmer, *supra*, note 23 at p. 45.

77. *Campbell Connelly & Co. Ltd. v. Noble*, [1963] 1 WLR 252 (Ch. 1962).

78. Ulmer, *supra*, note 23 at p. 45, describes *Campbell Connelly & Co. Ltd. v. Noble (ibid.)* as 'convincingly express[ing]' this principle.

79. See *Campbell Connelly & Co. Ltd. v. Noble, supra*, note 76 at 257-258 to the effect that United States law: 'establishes not only that the renewal copyright is capable of assignment but that it may be made the subject of a contract to assign it, entered into at the same time as the original copyright is assigned, which will be effective when the renewal copyright has been secured'.

80. *Ibid.* at 254.

81. See *ibid.* at 259-261 for analysis of the contractual intent and interpretation according to English law principles of interpretation. See also *Copinger and Skone James on Copyright, supra*, note 25 at s. 1458.

82. Copinger and Skone James, *ibid.* at s. 1185.

83. Copyright Act, RSC 1985, c. C42 (as amended).

84. S. 13(3).

85. S. 13(4). The assignment may be either wholly or partially; either generally or subject to territorial limitations; and either for the whole term or for part of that term.

86. *Copyright and the Information Highway, Final Report of the Copyright Sub-Committee,* Information Highway Advisory Council Secretariat, Ottawa, March 1995.

87. Sub-Committee Report, pp. 6-7.

88. *Ibid.*, at p. 10.

89. Section 27(1) establishes infringement if the specified act is done 'without the consent of the owner of the copyright'. Consent may be oral or presumed from the circumstances. See Fox, *supra*, note 11 at 339-340. Section 13(4) Copyright Act provides that *'no assignment or grant [of any interest in the copyright by licence] is valid unless it is in writing signed by the owner of the [copyright] in respect of which the assignment or grant is made'*. Permission to copy does not involve an assignment. It is certainly a licence, but it might not be a 'grant of any interest in the [copyright] by licence' in terms of s. 13(4). The latter would need to be in writing. However, even if a strict legal interpretation required an effective consent to be in writing, an oral or implied consent could be recognised in equity as creating some rights in the consentee.

90. Sub-Committee Report, *supra*, note 85 at p. 14.

91. *Ibid.*, at p. 15.

92. S. 2 Copyright Act.

93. Sub-committee Report, *supra*, note 85 at p. 10.

94. *Ibid.* at p. 11.

95. Some comparison might be made to the established context of 'publication' of a work and the test of making copies available 'to the public'. Distribution to private or selected persons is not 'to the public'. See *Oscar Trade Mark,* [1980] FSR 429, 435-439 (Ch. 1980).

96. The term 'performance' is defined in s. 2 Copyright Act as am. S. 56, World Trade Organisation Agreement Implementation Act, SC 1994, c. 47.

97. See Fox, *supra* note 11 at 392-393 and more generally, pp. 391-399.

98. S. 3(4) Copyright Act inserted with effect from 1 January 1994 by the North America Free Trade Agreement Implementation Act, SC 1993, c. 44, s. 55(3).

99. S. 4(1)(a) Copyright Act as am. S. 56, North America Free Trade Agreement Implementation Act, SC 1993, c. 44. The construction of an architectural work and the incorporation of an artistic work into an architectural work is also publication (s. 4(1)(b) and (c)).

100. The classic authorities are *Francis, Day & Hunter v. Feldman & Co.*, [1914] 2 Ch. 728, 732-733 (Ch.) affd. 733 (C.A.); apld in *Oscar Trade Mark, supra*, note 94 at 437-438. See now s. 5(1)(c)(i) of the Copyright Act as inserted by s. 57 (NAFTA) and s. 57 (WTO) amendments, incorporating this test.

101. S. 4(2) Copyright Act as am.

102. S. 4(1), (d), (e) and (g) Copyright Act as am.

103. S. 4(1), (f) Copyright Act as am.

104. Sub-committee Report, *supra*, note 85 at p. 11.

105. *Ibid.*, at p. 11.

106. S. 3(1)(g) Copyright Act as am. S. 55 (NAFTA Implementation Act).

107. See C. Brunet, 'Copyright: The Economic Rights' in: *Copyright and Confidential Information Law*

of Canada, G.F. Henderson (a.o., ed.) (Carswell, Scarborough, Ont.: 1994) at p. 152.

108. See *Nimmer on Copyright, supra*, note 49 at S. 8-20[A] for a discussion of this right first provided for in s. 106(5) of the 1976 Copyright Act.

109. S. 3(1)(h), (2) and (3) Copyright Act introduced by s. 55(2) and (3) NAFTA Implementation Act.

110. S. 5(4)(c), (5) and (6) Copyright Act inserted by s. 57(2) NAFTA Implementation Act.

111. See Sub-committee Report, *supra*, note 85 at p. 12.

112. *Supra*, text accompanying note 97.

113. See *University of New South Wales v. Moorhouse* (1975), 133 CLR 1; 6 ALR 193 (HCA) (where merely facilitating infringement by providing the equipment was sufficient) and *CBS Songs Ltd. v. Amstrad Consumer Electronics plc*, [1988] 1 AC 1013; 2 All ER 484 (HL) (where merely selling the equipment was insufficient and some control over the infringers was considered to be necessary). See generally, Brunet, *supra* note 106 at pp. 152-153.

114. See s. 3(1.3) and (1.4) Copyright Act.

115. S. 6 Copyright Act as am s. 58, NAFTA Implementation Act.

116. See ss. 6.1 to 11.1 Copyright Act as am.

117. S. 5 Copyright Act as am. by s. 64, NAFTA Implementation Act.

118. S. 27(2)(a) Copyright Act.

119. See Sub-committee Report, *supra*, note 85 at pp. 30-31.

120. S. 41 Copyright Act as am. s. 9, Copyright Amendment Act 1988, RSC 1985 (4th Supp.) c. 10.

121. Copyright Amendment Act, 1931, SC 21-22 Geo. V. c. 8 (1931), s. 5.

122. See s. 12(7) Copyright Act, RSC 1970, c. C. 30.

123. Copyright Amendment Act, 1988, RSC 1985 (4th Supp.) c. 10, s. 4.

124. Now section 14.1 of the principal act - Copyright Act, RSC 1985, c. C. 42.

125. S. 28.2(1).

126. S. 28.2(2).

127. S. 28.2(3)(a) and (b).

128. S. 14.1(1). These rights of association and anonymity in the author are stipulated as being applicable when any act mentioned in s. 3 (*i.e.* an exercise by the owner of the economic rights of the copyright) occurs.

129. S. 14.2(2).

130. S. 14.2(1).

131. S. 14.1(3).

132. S. 14.2(2). See *supra* note 19.

133. See, *e.g.*, Gibbens, *The Moral Rights of Artists and the Copyright Act Amendments* (1989), 15 Can. Bus. LJ 441; Vaver, *The Canadian Copyright Amendments of 1988* (1989), 4 [Can.] IPJ 120 at 127-132; Vaver, *Authors Moral Rights - Reform Proposals in Canada: Charter or Barter of Rights for Creators* (1987), 25 *Osgoode Hall LJ* 749 and (for a general treatment of the concept of moral rights), Berg, *Moral Rights: A Legal, Historical and Anthropological Reappraisal* (1991), 6 [Can.] *IPJ* 341.

134. *Snow v. The Eaton Centre Ltd.* (1982), 70 CPR (2d) 105 (Ont. HC).

135. *Ibid.* at 106.

136. See *John Maryon International Ltd. v. New Brunswick Telephone Co. Ltd.* (1982), 141 DLR (3d) 193 at 248-249 (NBCA).

137. See *supra* note 125 and accompanying text.

138. See Sub-committee Report, *supra*, note 85 at pp. 18-19.

139. *Ibid.*, at p. 20.

140. *Ibid.*

141. *Ibid.*, at p. 21.

142. See *John Maryon International Ltd. v. New Brunswick Telephone Co., supra*, note 135 at p. 248. The work in this case was an architectural work (a tower). The court considered the position in this respect to be consistent with a 'European interpretation' of the scope of moral rights.

143. See *Morang v. Le Sueur* (1911), 45 SCR 95 at 98.

144. *Ibid.*, at 97-98.

145. *Ibid.* at 97.

146. *Ibid. at 98.*

147. At common law there was a (disputed) view that a gift of a manuscript '*would in the absence of words indicating a contrary intention carry with it the ownership of the incorporeal property recorded in it'*. This consequence has also been attributed to s. 3 of the Literary Copyright Act 1842 (UK). See *In re Dickens*, [1935] Ch. 267, 274-275 (Ch. 1934); 288-290, 301-302 (CA 1934).

148. See *ibid.* at 98 where Fitzpatrick CJC noted '*[the author] can have no value without publication ... [t]he only way in which the [author] can legitimately recoup himself for his expenditure must be by publication of the manuscript, and in this I find an additional reason for holding that publication was an implied term of the contract'*.

149. *Ibid.* at 102.

150. *Ibid.* at 119.

151. *Ibid.* at 108-109.

152. *Ibid.* at 120-121 and 123.

153. *Ibid.* at 124-126. It is not clear whether this was by way of 'assignment' or 'employment'. Anglin J. would seem to have extended the employment rule (copyright vesting in the employer) to a 'person for whom the work has been executed' (*ibid.* at 125). See *supra* text accompanying note 146. It is settled today (upon the repeal of the Literary Copyright Act 1842 (UK) and common law copyright) that any

general assignment of a manuscript does not of itself also involve an assignment of the copyright and vice versa. See *In re Dickens*, [1935] 1 Ch. 267, 290, 297, 306-307 (CA 1934) and *Moorhouse v. Angus & Robertson (No. 1) Pty Ltd.*, [1980] FSR 231, 236 (SC NSW).
154. See *Tedesco v. Bosa* (1992), 45 CPR (3d) 82 at 88-89 (Ont. Ct. (GD)).
155. *Ibid.* at 89-90. The court found the meaning of the contract to be *'that the copyright and the manuscript would pass to [the publisher] upon payment of the fees provided for in the contract and upon completion of the editorial process leading to a manuscript in a publishable form'* (at 89). The latter stage had not been reached. The contract payment had, however, been made and was not reclaimed by the publishing society.
156. S. 27(1) Copyright Act.
157. S. 28.1 Copyright Act.
158. S. 34(1) Copyright Act.
159. S. 34(1.1) Copyright Act.
160. S. 35 Copyright Act. In April 1996, Bill C-32, Copyright Amendment Act was introduced in the Canadian Federal Parliament. Part V of Bill C-32 will strengthen the remedies available upon an infringement. At the time of writing, Bill C-32 had passed Second Reading in the House of Commons. Public hearings at Committee level are proceeding. See *supra*, note 10.
161. S. 39 Copyright Act. See also s. 40 noting that if an infringement consists in 'the construction of a building or other structure' an injunction or order of demolition is not available. In effect, relief in this context is limited to damages and accounts.
162. S. 38 Copyright Act.
163. See Sub-Committee Report *supra*, note 85 at pp. 12-13. The concept of 'statutory damages' operates independently, and in lieu of, actual damage or accounts. It may be elected by a plaintiff and will be beneficial to a plaintiff who has suffered little actual loss. The statute specifies a minimum account ($ 250) and a maximum amount ($ 10,000). The court awards an amount 'as the court considers just' within this range. See *Nimmer on Copyright, supra*, note 49 at s. 14.04 *et seq.* Bill C-32 (*supra* note 159) currently before the Canadian Parliament would introduce 'statutory damages' into Canadian copyright law.
164. Ss. 42, 43 and 43.1 Copyright Act.
165. S. 27(4) and (5) Copyright Act.
166. S. 44 Copyright Act.
167. See Sub-committee Report, *supra*, note 85 at p. 12.
168. The opening portion of section 44 reads: *'Copies made out of Canada of any work in which copyright subsists that if made in Canada would infringe copyright'*.
169. See s. 44 Copyright Act requiring 'notice in writing to the Department of National Revenue that the owner desires that the copies not be so imported into Canada'. For exceptions, see ss. 45(3), (4) and (5). Bill C-32 (*supra*, note 159), currently before the Canadian Parliament, would significantly enhance the import restrictions, particularly with respect to 'books'. See clause 26 of Bill C-32 that would insert several new provisions concerning remedies.
170. See s. 28.01(2)(a)-(d) Copyright Act.
171. See ss. 70.61 - 70.67 Copyright Act.
172. See Local and Distant Signal Regulations (Regulations defining local signal and distant signal for the purposes of section 28.01(2) of the Copyright Act), SOR 89/254 (Canada) (r. 2(a)).
173. See Retransmission Royalties Criteria Regulations (Regulations respecting criteria for establishing a manner of determining royalties for the retransmission of distant signals), SOR 91/690 (Canada) (r. 2(a)).
174. S. 6.1 Copyright Act inserted by s. 58, NAFTA Implementation Act.
175. S. 6.2 Copyright Act inserted by s. 58, NAFTA Implementation Act.
176. S. 70.7 Copyright Act.

Finland

R. OESCH

The private international law questions on the global *'Infobahn'* are extremely difficult and important questions. The choice of law is always of primary importance. Regrettably at this stage I cannot give any detailed answers to the questions, but I can set out some starting points of the private international law principles from the Finnish point of view.

1. What is the legal basis of the determination of applicable law in the field of copyright?

The Finnish private international law principles govern what law is to be applied in questions with an international dimension. There is no general legislation regarding this subject, but there are for example:
* a special Act on law applicable to contracts of international character (law of 27 May 1988/466) (see Buure-Hägglund, *IPRax* 1989, Heft 6, 407-409); the act includes general choice-of-law rules and some specific contracts (*e.g.* consumer contracts, licencing contracts), and
* a special Act on law applicable to sale of goods with an international character (26 June 1964/387).
The written sources of private international law are incomplete (except for the law of contracts). There has not been much research activity recently.

The Finnish Copyright Act contains provisions concerning the geographical applicabilty of the Act; *work protection:* nationality criteria or residence criteria (article 63), *holders of neighbouring rights:* varying criteria (articles 64, 64a) (Act 446/95), *EU adaptations:* national criteria apply to EEA citizens. Berne Convention article 5 paragraph 2; *country where protection is claimed:* this applies only to questions concerning scope of protection and means of protection. The Berne Convention article 14*bis*(2)a gives limited help when it comes to the solving the problems of private international law: it points to the law of the country where protection is sought in questions of ownership of copyright in cinematographic works only.

As for choice of law in a network environment, I distinguish between two major issues: firstly copyright contracts and secondly copyright infringement. Put first and foremost: all the principles of a country's international private law apply. Regarding copyright contracts there is the freedom of contracts; it is up to the parties to choose the applicable law. If there is no agreement on this point, the nearest connecting point is decisive, for example the country of the place of business of the publisher. As for copyright infringements, the place of business of the defendant or the place of the activity (*e.g.* the location of the server) are possible starting points. But there are other possibilities as well, *e.g.* the place of infringement (which again includes several alternatives, for example the place where the consequences of infringement materialize), the 'source' country (from where the infringing material is coming), country of origin, or a combination of several criteria.

   2. *What is the applicable law when considering issues which specifically concern copyright (owner, object, contents, duration, limits, etc.)?*

-

   3. *What is the applicable law when considering issues which regard copyright but which particularly deal with:*

a. *moral rights*

-

   b. *contracts*

The Act on law applicable to contracts of international character of 1988 (1988/466) states that if there is an explicit reference to a special law, than that law has to be applied. If there is no such a reference, the relevant laws are the law of the nearest point of attachment, the *lex loci debitoris* (place of business of the debitor, if his effort is essential to the relationship) (article 5 of the Act), or other laws (like the *lex loci solutionis* or the *lex loci contractus*).

   c. *infringement and sanctions (penal or civil)*

Although the country of origin is a obvious starting point, it does not lead to satisfactory results. The laws of all the countries where consequences of the infringements can be found, should be possible. As regards criminal and civil liability, the *lex locus delicti* (place of infringement) is a possibility, with the additional possibility to use the law of the country where the consequences are (to be) realized.

   4. *More particularly, what is the applicable law in case of:*

a. *diffusion covering a number of undefined countries*

-

   b. *infringement on copyright* (aa) *when crossing borders* (bb) *when the origin of the work is hard to identify*

-

5. *Are there any rules (legislative or jurisprudential) which particularly deal with the Global Information Infrastructure, or any theoretical proposals?*

There are no official proposals so far regarding the choice of law and copyright in a network environment in Finland. Some preliminary reflections have been given in a report concerning multimedia and copyright, published on 2 May 1996 by the Copyright Institute (Publication N° 9/1996) and written by Mrs Kristiina Harenko. Possibilities mentioned in this report are: the law of the country of origin (transmittor country) or the law of the country where relevant acts have been carried out. The definition of 'country of origin' creates difficulties in a network environment. For a judicial framework other possibilities than the country of origin (country of first publication) should be created. Because 'free ports' should be avoided, the law of other countries where relevant acts have been carried should also be possible.

The applicability of the Finnish Copyright Act is connected with the act of first publication in Finland. The revision of this criterion is needed within the network environment, because the notion of publication is connected to the production and distribution of copies.

France

P.Y. GAUTIER

Le rapporteur français se permettra de synthétiser et ordonner les questions posées par le rapporteur général, selon un plan "à la française".

Il y a deux situations bien distinctes, qu'on décrira à travers deux hypothèses de travail: voici un serveur, utilisant les services d'un fournisseur d'accès aux réseaux numériques ("Internet", la plus grande "toile"), établi (à supposer qu'on puisse le localiser) dans un pays étranger; il transmet "en ligne" des oeuvres au titre desquelles il n'a reçu aucune autorisation, ni n'a versé aucune rémunération aux ayants-droit. Quelle est la loi applicable? *Situation délictuelle (I)*. Voici au contraire un autre serveur, soucieux de se mettre en règle avec les auteurs, qui voudrait conclure un contrat général de "communication publique". Avec qui, selon quel droit? *Situation contractuelle (II)*.

I. **Situations délictuelles**

Dans un ordre très classique, on envisagera la détermination de la loi applicable à la situation litigieuse (a), avant d'aborder son domaine (b).

a. *Détermination de la loi applicable*

Un mot des sources, tout d'abord: le droit international privé français, dans son volet "conflits de lois", est à quelques exceptions près essentiellement fondé sur les constructions intellectuelles des juges, tout spécialement de la Cour de Cassation (v. H. Batiffol et P. Lagarde, *Droit international privé*, T. I, 8è éd., LGDJ 1993, n°s 271 *et seq.*). Qui dit droit prétorien, dit donc extrême souplesse du règlement conflictuel. On peut donc parfaitement envisager, pour notre sujet, une règle portant solution du conflit de lois, spécialement adaptée à notre matière et que nos juges forgeraient de toutes pièces. De la sorte, on ferait l'économie d'une disposition législative, requérant l'intervention du Parlement (à l'instar, par exemple, du fameux article 310 du Code Civil), outre qu'on préserverait le futur, pour modifier, adapter, affiner la règle ainsi dégagée, selon les besoins qui s'en feraient sentir et l'expérience que la pratique va sans le moindre doute révéler, dans les années qui viennent.

Dans notre discipline, il y a cependant la Convention de Berne, dont l'article 5(2) est communément interprété comme désignant la loi locale "du pays où la protection est réclamée"; mais la souplesse reste grande, car une fois qu'on est d'accord pour ne pas laisser place, au moins pour le règlement de la question principale d'illicéité (sur les questions préalables, v. *infra*, b) à la loi du pays d'origine de l'oeuvre, il reste à savoir quelle est donc cette loi locale. Et c'est ici que les difficultés commencent. En effet, en matière de réseaux numériques, la diffusion des oeuvres ne se produit pas en un ou quelques points uniques, voire pour une région (câble) ou un continent (satellite), mais partout où un usager peut se connecter, à partir d'un simple micro-ordinateur, c'est-à-dire au même moment, dans des millions de points.

Pour conserver un "instrument de navigation" familier, dans ce monde nouveau, on peut utiliser le traditionnel choix entre lieux d'émission et de réception. Donnera-t-on compétence à la loi du lieu d'émission, en d'autres termes du lieu où le serveur est établi et "injecte" les oeuvres sur le réseau? L'identification du site pourrait être facilitée par le repérage à l'aide d'un logiciel de navigation approprié, des oeuvres, munies d'un code. (Ainsi, même l'usage de relais ou "miroirs" serait déjoué.) C'est dans cette direction que se dirigent les autorités communautaires (Livre vert de la Commission, p. 41 *et seq.*) et américaines. Et l'on pense aussitôt à la solution analogue et déjà de droit positif, retenue par la Directive européenne sur le satellite, du 27 septembre 1993 (article 1). Si l'on se réfère aux tendances actuelles du droit international privé, désignant la loi du pays où se concentre la substance de situation litigieuse, il est clair qu'ici, la "proximité" est celle du point de départ de la transmission en ligne, unique, avant l'éclatement en millions de points.

Pourtant, dans sa réponse au questionnaire de la Commission européenne, faisant suite au Livre vert, le gouvernement français a fermement répudié toute méthode analogique, pour des motifs techniques (le responsable ne sera pas toujours facile à attraper), mais surtout de délocalisation. Et si le pays d'émission est une sorte de "paradis numérique" où les droits des auteurs sont ignorés? (P. 5 *et seq.*) Dans sa propre réponse, l'AJIFPIDA a développé une même argumentation, empreinte de méfiance devant de tels dérapages (p. 4 *et seq.*). Le risque existe, évidemment. Mais n'écartons pas trop vite ce rattachement, qui est tout de même solide.

Trois solutions de secours pourraient être envisagées.

(1) Prévoir une règle de conflit alternative et partiellement substantielle (v. P. Mayer, *Précis de droit international privé*, 5è éd., Domat 1994, nºs 140 et 610; D. Holleaux, J. Foyer et G. de la Pradelle, *Droit international privé*, nº 355), à double détente: le droit à la protection de l'auteur serait soumis à la loi du serveur, mais si celle-ci est impossible à déterminer ou s'avère insuffisante, on pourrait consulter celle du pays où est établi le *prestataire de services*. Et si celle-ci est de la même trempe, alors, on ira consulter une des quelques 200 législations potentiellement applicables! Car il faut être bien clair: il y a autant de lois de réception éventuellement compétentes, que notre planète compte de pays - village global. Ou alors, pour ne pas trop céder au vertige, on se contentera tout bonnement de la *lex fori*, du pays où la protection est demandée devant notre juge local (soit un de nos 181 Tribunaux de grande instance: il y aura toujours un usager ou un *"cyber-café"* dans leur ressort).

(2) Dans le même ordre d'idées, la loi d'émission, désignée par une sorte de présomption simple, pourrait être écartée par la voie d'une "clause échappatoire ou de sauvegarde", qui, prenant en compte le caractère insuffisamment protecteur du

droit élu en premier, fait finalement régir la situation par une autre loi, plus appropriée (sur ce mécanisme, v. B. Audit, *Droit international privé*, Economica 1991, n° 103); cette technique est de plus en plus souvent utilisée en droit international privé conventionnel (et la Commission semble bien la connaître). Ici, ce pourrait être la loi du fournisseur d'accès ou celle du pays où le préjudice subi par les auteurs est le plus important, etc.

(3) Enfin, on peut tout simplement faire jouer l'exception d'ordre public, dont c'est à la vérité la fonction même d'évincer les mauvaises lois étrangères. Telle était l'opinion de votre rapporteur, jusqu'à une date récente. Cependant, pour des raisons de simplicité et de prévention de la fraude à la loi (décourager par avance les contrefacteurs, et une récente affaire en France vient de l'illustrer de façon inquiétante), on acceptera finalement (sans enthousiasme) la compétence virtuelle des lois de réception, des quelques 185 droits. Toute la question étant de savoir à quelle proportion s'arrêter. De sorte que l'on va se trouver devant une nouvelle alternative à trois branches, également classique en DIP (presse et vie privée). Avant de le vérifier, il faut souligner un point capital: alors qu'en droit international privé, les compétences législatives et juridictionnelles sont normalement distinctes, dans certaines matières, elles peuvent exceptionnellement coïncider: tel est le cas en matière délictuelle, le juge du lieu du délit étant bien souvent compétent en vertu du même rattachement que la *lex loci delicti*.

Ou bien, pour une simple diffusion illicite sur le "Net" à un moment donné, l'avocat de l'auteur ou de la société de gestion collective intente son action devant un des 181 TGI français et sollicite l'application de notre Code prop. int., pour réparer l'intégralité de son dommage. Par exemple un serveur en Birmanie, qui n'a pas demandé d'autorisation, accessible sur le "Net" dans le monde entier, notamment en France (une fois de plus il y aura toujours une compétence virtuelle du droit français: au moins un usager peut ou a pu se connecter). Mais la loi locale risquerait de se voir ainsi dotée d'une sorte d'extra-territorialité absolue. Ce ne serait pas raisonnable. Ou bien un de nos tribunaux se déclare compétent et simultanément déclare la loi française compétente pour réparer d'abord le dommage subi en France; ensuite, après que l'avocat du demandeur lui ait produit la teneur de tout ou partie des lois étrangères, il procède à l'application distributive de chacune d'entre elles, pour assurer l'entière réparation du préjudice matériel et moral subi par son client (sur ce mécanisme, v. P.Y. Gautier, *Propriété littéraire et artistique*, PUF 1991, n°s 125 et 309). Une compétence aussi large devrait justifier, au minimum, un rattachement très sérieux à la France (par exemple par le lieu d'établissement du serveur ou en tout cas du fournisseur d'accès).

De ce point de vue, on dispose d'un arrêt européen récent, rendu dans la matière connexe des délits de presse, la diffusion internationale d'un écrit diffamatoire (CJCE 7 mars 1995, *Fiona Shevill*, D. 1996.61, note G. Parléani, qui souligne l'intérêt de la solution pour le conflit de lois): compétence étendue du for de l'édition litigieuse. Le demandeur aura préalablement eu recours aux techniques d'identification, permettant de savoir, pays par pays, combien d'usagers se sont connectés au serveur litigieux. Et s'il ne l'a pas fait, le juge pourra toujours ordonner une mesure de constatation, confiée à un *"cyber-huissier"*. (Pourquoi pas par requête, sur le fondement de l'article 145 NCPC.) Ou bien, plus sagement et dans la philosophie même de la Convention de Berne (loi du pays où la protection est requise), surtout si ni le serveur ni le fournisseur n'ont leur établissement en France, le juge se contente d'appliquer la loi locale/*lex fori* pour ce qui nous concerne, les articles L 335(2) *et seq.* du Code de la prop. int. - après que l'avocat du demandeur ait établi, dans les mêmes conditions, la preuve de la quantité exacte d'abonnés français s'étant connectés au serveur, entre telle et telle date.

Cette option revient à limiter doublement l'étendue de la réparation et la compétence du juge saisi, au dommage souffert sur son territoire. C'est ce qu'a décidé la CJCE dans son arrêt préc. *Fiona Shevill*: on compte le nombre d'exemplaires illicites distribués au for, comparé au nombre total, dans les autres pays; et le juge du for assoit sa propre compétence et celle de sa loi sur cette seule fraction. Transposée aux réseaux numériques, cette solution suppose que l'on identifie précisément les connexions individuelles auprès du serveur (rien d'impossible techniquement).

Il semble au rapporteur français que cette dernière solution soit la meilleure et assure l'harmonie la plus forte entre droit d'auteur et droit international privé.

b. *Domaine de la loi ainsi désignée*

C'est elle qui posera l'existence même du droit et qualifiera la transmission numérique au regard des catégories juridiques préexistantes (par exemple "communication publique", rappr. article L 122(2) Code prop. int., 11*bis* Conv. Berne). Tout comme elle aura compétence pour indiquer si elle lui attribue un caractère exclusif ou si elle entend l'assortir de licences légales; ou encore, s'il y a place pour la gestion collective, obligatoire ou facultative, etc. De même, c'est elle qui est en droit de poser les exceptions aux droits exclusifs, ainsi du droit de citation. Ou réglementer la copie privée de l'oeuvre téléchargée (sur le disque dur ou sur une imprimante).

Quant aux sanctions, la généralité du Code prop. int. devrait permettre de sanctionner en France toute contrefaçon numérique (y compris par voie de saisie-contrefaçon); les responsables étant, en application des critères classiques du droit pénal, le serveur, personne morale et/ou physique (auteur, coauteur ou complice, selon les hypothèses), ainsi que les sites "miroirs" (toute personne qui retransmet sur le réseau, à l'intention du public, voire en *"e-mail"*); et le fournisseur d'accès (complice ou débitant, selon les cas). C'est encore le droit local qui dira s'il y a lieu ou non de faire jouer les redoutables présomptions de mauvaise foi (qui existent ainsi en droit français). Que les délinquants soient éventuellement établis à l'étranger n'ôte rien à la compétence du droit français et de ses juges; tout comme d'éventuels défauts de comparution; tout au plus les difficultés surgiront-elles au stade de l'exécution. En bref, comme le résume un auteur, *"la loi locale affiche clairement sa compétence pour régler toutes les questions ressortissant au contenu et au régime du droit"* (J. Raynard, *Droit d'auteur et conflits de lois*, Litec 1990, n°s 501, 507 *et seq.*, 520 *et seq.*, spéc. 527). Voilà qui vaut pour les droits patrimoniaux (y compris ceux des artistes-interprètes).

Qu'en est-il du droit moral? La Cour de Cassation, dans son célèbre arrêt *Huston*, a décidé *"qu'en France, aucune atteinte ne peut être portée à l'intégrité d'une oeuvre litteraire ou artistique, quel que soit l'état sur le territoire duquel cette oeuvre a été divulguée pour la première fois"* (Civ. 1è 28 mai 1991, rev. crit. DIP 1991.752, note P.Y. Gautier, avec les réf. aux décisions du fond, *JCP* 1991 II 21731, obs. A. Francon, D. 1993.197, note J. Raynard, *Clunet* 1992.133, note B. Edelman, chron. Sirinelli et Ginsburg à la *RIDA* oct. 1991.3 et sur renvoi, Versailles 19 déc. 1994, *ibid.* avr. 1995.389, note Kerever). Ici, toute mise "en ligne" sur le réseau étant par définition susceptible d'être captée en France, notre loi de police prend une vocation "universelle", sous réserve des distinctions que nous venons d'exposer, relativement aux droits patrimoniaux, sur l'étendue du dommage. Cela étant, le questionnaire se réfère à un certain nombre de questions préalables, c'est-à-dire qui justifient que le juge les règle avant d'aborder le point principal, contrefaçon alléguée d'une oeuvre protégée; par exemple l'oeuvre est-elle encore protégée (durée)? Le demandeur est-il bien titulaire des droits (qualité pour agir)? Etc. Le rapporteur français soulignera qu'à son avis, il n'y a guère de spécificité relative à la Société de l'information sur ce point et que les solutions du droit d'auteur international contemporain ont vocation à s'appliquer.

Ainsi, quant à la durée, l'article 7(8) de la Convention de Berne sur la comparaison des délais, prend en compte la durée de protection, telle que déterminée dans le pays d'origine, sous réserve d'un accueil plus favorable dans le pays où la demande en justice est introduite (rappr. le nouvel article L 123(12) Code prop. int.). Ainsi encore, quant à la titularité, on rappellera la nouvelle alternative. Soit, conformément au raisonnement classique du DIP et à la jurisprudence dominante, on interroge la loi d'origine (essentiellement contractuelle, rapport auteurs/entreprise), pour connaître les titres de propriété dont se prévaut en France le demandeur (v. par exemple Paris 14 mars 1991, *Almax*, *JCP* 1992 II 21780, obs. J. Ginsburg, *Clunet* 1992.148, note F. Pollaud-Dulian, *Titularité des droits sur un modèle italien de mannequins;* sur l'ensemble, v. F. Pollaud-Dullan, *J. Cl. droit int.*, fasc., n° 563-60, n°s 59 et 67). Soit, de façon beaucoup plus simple et neuve, on confie également à la loi locale le droit de le déterminer. C'est ce qu'a fait, au demeurant, l'arrêt préc. *Huston* (l'auteur n'est que le créateur/personne physique, point final), certes rendu en matière de droit moral, mais selon un raisonnement qui pourrait sans doute être transposé aux droits patrimoniaux. A cet égard, notons que c'est ce que n'hésite pas à faire désormais notre code lui-même (par exemple nouvel article L 311(7) sur la répartition de la redevance pour copie privée), tout comme les Directives européennes (v. par exemple article 1-5° de la Directive satellite et câble du 27 septembre 1993).

En outre, il convient de faire état d'une nouvelle jurisprudence qui semble transposer à la matière internationale une *"présomption de possession"* régulière des droits, au bénéfice de l'entreprise en demande, qu'elle a forgée pour le droit interne (Paris 9 février 1995, *Tortues Ninja*, *RIDA* octobre 1995, 310; et surtout Civ. 1è 9 janvier 1996, *Dalloz Aff.* 1996.300: pas besoin de se référer au contrat italien d'origine des droits). Cela étant, il convient d'être prudent, car le sujet est délicat et les enjeux, très importants.

II. **Les situations contractuelles**

On raisonnera comme précédemment: détermination (a), domaine (b) de la loi applicable. Précisons qu'on ne traitera que du droit applicable au fond du contrat; quant à sa forme, on sait que le libéralisme de la Convention de Rome sur les obligations contractuelles du 19 juin 1980, article 9, est notable, offrant, dans une optique de *favor validitatis*, un éventail de lois conduisant au résultat recherché, contrat valablement formé (v. par exemple Gautier, *op. cit.*, n° 179). N'est-ce pas après tout le sens de l'arrêt *Le kid*, pionnier en la matière et précisément rendu en droit d'auteur? (Civ. 1è 28 mai 1963, *Grands arrêts du DIP*, d'Ancel et Lequette, 2è éd., Sirey 1992, n° 41.)

a. *Détermination de la loi applicable*

Ici, nous disposons de règles de conflit codifiées et obligatoires en France depuis 1991: la Convention de Rome susvisée. Simplement, leur domaine est-il très général, ce qui ne les empêche pas d'être applicables, selon la doctrine spécialisée, aux contrats internationaux d'exploitation des droits d'auteur et donc aux réseaux numériques. On rappellera brièvement que le principe constitue la liberté de choix de la loi applicable, article 3 (v. par exemple Josselin-Gall, *Les contrats d'exploitation en DIP*, Joly 1995, n° 304); dans sa réponse au questionnaire de la Commission, le gouvernement français a au demeurant réaffirmé son attachement au principe d'autonomie de la volonté (p. 6). Cependant, si l'une des parties usait de sa position dominante lors des négociations, pour désigner une loi par trop complaisante ("paradis numérique"), la théorie de la fraude à la loi pourrait être utilisée; ou encore, l'exception d'ordre public, opposée (article 16).

Au cas où aucune loi n'a été désignée, le juge devra rechercher la loi du pays où se localise objectivement le contrat avec lequel il *"présente les liens les plus étroits"* (article 4(1)). A cet égard, la Convention de Rome pose une présomption (suscep- tible de tomber devant la preuve contraire, v. ci-dessous): son centre de gravité sera normalement localisé au lieu d'établissement de la partie qui fournit *"la prestation caractéristique"* (article 4(2)). C'est parfait dans la vente, le mandat, le bail, etc., mais pour le droit d'auteur, le critère peut laisser perplexe: qui fournit l'obligation essentielle du contrat, l'auteur ou son partenaire? (v. Gautier, *op. cit.*, n° 124, F. Pollaud-Dullan, très sceptique, fasc. réc., n°s 84 et 85). La solution la plus sage sera de le rechercher dans chaque hypothèse. Ainsi, si l'on applique cette méthode aux réseaux numériques, contrat d'utilisation entre le représentant de l'auteur ou de l'artiste et le serveur, la localisation du contrat doit-elle se faire au lieu d'établissement du serveur? Ou de l'établissement de la société de gestion collective autorisant la transmission en ligne (à supposer qu'elle soit à "guichet unique", car on imagine la multiplicité des ayants-droit pour un serveur "multimédia")? C'est à débattre. S'il y a vraiment "guichet unique", il faut choisir le titulaire des droits. Mais si les autorisations sont fractionnées, ce devrait être le serveur, faute de quoi les situations de "dépeçage" (morcellement d'une situation normalement homogène) seront légion.

Mais si cette dernière loi est insuffisamment protectrice? On pourrait alors être tenté de revenir aux "clauses échappatoires", la plus connue étant précisément l'article 4(5), Conv. Rome, qui permet au juge d'écarter la loi de prestation caractéristique, *"lorsqu'il résulte de l'ensemble des circonstances que le contrat présente des liens plus étroits avec un autre pays"*. On pressent comment un magistrat avisé pourra en user (v. par exemple Josselin, thèse préc. n° 331). Dans son Livre vert préc. sur la société de l'information, la Commission UE s'est au demeurant souciée de cet aspect d'éviter l'application de contrats trop complaisants pour les exploitants (v. spéc. p. 43).

Cependant, outre qu'elle détruit la prévisibilité des solutions conflictuelles, une telle clause échappatoire devrait normalement être indifférente au résultat obtenu, ne jouant que sur l'étroitesse des rattachements "neutres" en concurrence (v. par exemple P. Mayer, *op. cit.*, n° 725; P. Lagarde, Commentaire, *rev. crit. DIP* 1991, 310). C'est sans doute trop lui demander (rev. B. Audit, *passim*). Et il est assez significatif que la première application en France de l'article 4(5) ait résidé dans la volonté du juge de sauver un contrat nul, en vertu de la loi normalement applicable, mais valable selon une autre loi (Versailles 6 février 1991, *rev. crit. DIP* 1991, 745, note P. Lagarde, qui souligne la recherche manifeste du résultat substantiel, il s'agissait de la validité d'un cautionnement; *JDI* 1992.125, note J. Foyer, D. 1992, 174, note J.D. Mondolini).

Il ne faudrait pas que l'exception devienne la règle, ou que le juge utilise le critère de prestation caractéristique, lorsqu'il conduirait au pays d'établissement de l'auteur ou de l'artiste ou de leur ayant cause, et fasse jouer la clause échappatoire, dans les cas où la présomption ne pourrait raisonnablement jouer (ce qui n'est pas exclu, en matière de "multimédia", ainsi qu'on l'a vu). Aux juges de se montrer raisonnables.

b. *Domaine de la loi applicable*

Il est clairement énoncé dans l'article 10 de la Convention de Rome: notamment nullité, interprétation, inexécution, résolution, dommage réparable, prescription, caractère licite et effets des clauses de toutes sortes qui le garnissent, etc. (v. par exemple P. Lagarde, commentaire préc., p. 332 *et seq.*; P. Mayer, *eod. loc.*, n°s 740 *et seq.*). Appliqué à l'autorisation de mise sur réseaux numériques, on y rangera notamment d'une part l'éventuelle nullité pour inobservation des conditions de fond, d'autre part, le contrat supposé valable, tout ce qui touche aux droits et obligations respectifs des parties - ainsi: la rémunération des auteurs, les modalités de contrôle de l'exploitation, la durée de la concession, les clauses résolutoires et pénales, l'exécution forcée, les garanties conventionnelles souscrites, etc. En revanche, tout ce qui a trait au contenu et à l'existence même du droit d'auteur (moral et patrimonial), source du contrat, entre dans le domaine de la loi à laquelle ressortit sa protection, selon les distinctions qui ont été établies *supra*, en I.

La conclusion du rapporteur français est, qu'hormis d'éventuelles retouches des règles de procédure (spéc. saisies à l'encontre des *"cyber-contrefacteurs"* et des fournisseurs d'accès), une réforme d'envergure manquerait d'utilité. En revanche, la coopération internationale des états (police, justice) sera capitale.

Germany

TH. DREIER

1. What is the legal basis of the determination of applicable law in the field of copyright?

The German Copyright Act of 1965 (last amended on 23 June 1995) does not contain any conflict of laws provisions. Rather, § 120 *et seq.* merely contain provisions defining the scope of application of German copyright law as regards the persons affected. At best, one might conclude that German copyright law contains a conflict of laws rule pointing to the applicability of the law of the country for which protection is sought, since §§ 121(2), 125(5), 126(3) and 127(3) refer to the contents of international conventions to which Germany is a party. It follows that the general conflict of law rules as laid down in the Introduction Law to the German Civil Code (*EGBGB*, as reformulated in 1986) are applicable to copyright. However, these rules also do not contain provisions which specifically address copyright questions. Worth mentioning seem to be articles 6 *(ordre public)*, 11 (requirement as to the form of legal acts), 27 *et seq.* (choice of law and applicable law in contractual matters), which also include regulations regarding employment contracts (article 30) and the application of imperative provisions on the law, and finally 38 (torts). As regards the EC Directive 93/83 on cable and satellite, which has not yet been implemented in German Copyright Law, see below, answer to question 4.

2. What is the applicable law when considering issues which specifically concern copyright (owner, object, contents, duration, limits, etc.)?

German case-law recognizes the principle of territoriality as the basis of international copyright protection (see *e.g.* Federal Supreme Court, *GRUR Int.* 1975, 361 - *August Vierzehn*; *GRUR* 1994, 798 - *Folgerecht bei Auslandsbezug*; Constitutional Court, *GRUR* 1990, 4318 - *Bob Dylan*). This view is shared by the vast majority of German legal copyright doctrine, and to an increasing extent also by conflict of laws specialists (for reference, see Katzenberqer, in: Beier *et al.* (eds.), *Urhebervertragsrecht*, Munich 1995, p. 241). From this, it is deduced that first ownership, object of protection, contents, scope and duration of protection are governed by the law of the country for which (not: in which) protection is sought. The theory of universality, which tends to apply only one law (namely the law of the country of origin) to a given work throughout the world, is a highly minoritarian view in Germany.

3. What is the applicable law when considering issues which regard copyright but which particularly deal with:

a. *moral rights*

Since moral rights form part of the contents or scope of German copyright law, the applicable law regarding questions of moral rights is the law of the country where protection is sought (for contractual arrangements regarding moral rights prerogatives see below, b).

b. *contracts*

According to article 27 *EGBGB*, the parties to a contract have the freedom of choice of law applicable to the contract. This may include the law of a country which does have no connection with the contract in question. However, if the contract only has contact with one state, any choice of the law of a foreign country cannot overrule the applicability of mandatory legal rules of this state. If the parties have not made a choice of law governing the contract, according to article 28(1) the contract will be governed by the law of the country with which it has the closest contact. Unless the circumstances show a different result (article 28(5)), it is presumed that the closest contact of a contract is with the country in which the party who effects the characteristic performance is domiciled at the time when the contract is concluded (article 28(2)). It is said that the 'characteristic performance' is the grant of a use right (according to monistic German copyright doctrine, the copyright cannot be transferred or assigned in whole or in part; rather it is possible to grant exclusive or non-exclusive use rights, *'Nutzungsrechte'*; § 31 of the German Copyright Act) if the other party only has an obligation to pay royalties, whereas it is the exercise of the use right granted, if the user has a legal obligation to exploit the work (as is the case under a publishing agreement).

In case of an employment relationship, absent a choice of law and absent any circumstances which point to another country, the employment contract is governed by the law of the country where the employee usually works (or where the employer has his place of business, if the employee usually works in more than one state); article 30(2). However, a choice of applicable law may not result in withholding the employee the protection granted to him by mandatorily applicable rules of the country the law of which would be applicable had no choice of law been made by the parties to the contract (article 30(1)). In addition, the party against whom general terms and conditions of business are used cannot be deprived by choice of law from the protection of the German law on general terms and conditions, provided he has his domicile or habitual residence in Germany and makes his declaration of intention in Germany (§ 12 No. 2 *AGBG*).

Most important, however, even where foreign copyright law is the proper law of the contract, and even where no mandatory German legal provisions apply according to what has been said so far, and even before invoking the German *ordre public* (article 6 *EGBGB*), on the basis of article 34 *EGBGB* the majority of German doctrine favours the application of a limited number of provisions contained in the German Copyright Act which protect the author as the weaker party, to cases which have a close contact to Germany (such as is the case when protection is sought for

Germany). These provisions include:
- the nullity of contracts and grants of use rights regarding future uses which were unknown at the time when the contract was concluded (§ 31(4));
- the so-called purpose-of-grant rule as laid down in § 31(5), according to which absent anything to the contrary, only those use rights are deemed to have been granted which are necessary for the purpose of the contract;
- the right to participate in disproportionate unexpected gains (§ 36);
- the right of authors to terminate contracts regarding future works (§ 40(1), (2)); and
- the termination rights because of non-exercise of the use right granted and of changed conviction (§§ 41 and 42) (for reference see again Katzenberger, *op. cit.*, p. 255 *et seq.*).

In addition, the intransferability of moral rights (§ 29 second sentence) will always be judged according to German law, since it forms an integral part of fundamental German copyright doctrine.

Another question results from the fact that in German civil law contractual agreements and the transfer (or assignment) of rights made on the basis of a contractual agreement are treated as legally separate and independent acts (so-called principle of separation and of abstraction). Consequently, some conflict of laws authors have suggested that only contractual matters should be governed by the law of the contract, whereas questions regarding the transfer and/or assignment of rights should be governed by the law of the country for which protection is sought (the so-called '*Spaltungstheorie*'). However, since most copyright scholars agree that the principle of abstraction does not apply regarding copyright transactions (for references see Schricker, *Urheberrechtsgesetz*, Munich 1987, vor §§ 28 ff. para. 61), it follows that according to the majority view, both contractual questions and questions regarding transfer/assignment are governed by the law of the contract (with the exception of the limitations described above).

c. legal consequences

According to the territoriality principle, legal consequences - both civil and criminal - are once more governed by the law for which protection is sought, quite like first ownership, object of protection, contents, scope and duration of protection.

> **4.** *More particularly, what is the applicable law in case of* (a) *diffusion covering a number of undefined countries, and* (b) *infringement on copyright* (aa) *when crossing borders,* (bb) *when the origin of the work is hard to identify?*

According to the theory of the applicability of the law of the country for which protection is sought, the exploitation of use rights and the infringement of copyright are both governed by the law of the country where the exploitation takes place. Where the exploitation takes place is determined by the substantive law of this country. Under the traditional approach, it seems that there is a difference whether transborder diffusion (taken to amount to an activity of communicating protected works to the public via broadcasting, §§ 15(2) and 20 of the German Copyright Act, *i.e.* either wireless or by wire) uses cable or not.

In case a transborder cable system is used (such as, for example, the Internet), it seems that an act relevant to copyright occurs in each country where the cable runs, provided, of course, that the work can be accessed in this particular country by members of the public and that it is not merely 'in transit' (such as in the case of running through telephone lines) nor re-transmitted by a third party who himself is liable for copyright (such as in the case of cable retransmission of broadcasts). However, when transborder communication to the public is made by wireless means, the traditional view has been that since mere reception of the signals is copyright free, it only is an act relevant to copyright in the country where the signal is emitted (see for example Ulmer, *Die Immaterialgüterrechte im internationalen Privatrecht*, Cologne 1975, p. 15). From this a similar choice of law rule has been deduced, namely that the only law applicable to a wireless transborder transmission is the law of the country where the technical emission of the signals takes place. It is well known that in view of the protection deficits which such an approach would lead to in practice (which is due to the absence of sufficient international harmonization of the public communication/broadcasting right; mention should only be made of the possibility contained in article 11*bis*(2) BC allowing Member States to subject the primary broadcasting right to a legal licence), a theory has been developed according to which the applicable law in a wireless transborder broadcast would be the laws of all countries in which the signals could be received (for references see Katzenberger, in: Schricker, *op. cit.*, vor §§ 120 para. 89). This theory later became known as the Bogsch-theory, and was subsequently modified in several respects (namely to provide only for a subsidiary application of the laws of the countries of reception where the law of the state in which the signals were emitted, did not provide for adequate protection).

German courts have so far adopted views similar to the Bogsch-theory (see OLG München, 25 November 1993, *ZUM* 1995, 328: held that the emission of signals aimed at a country other than the emmission state is an infringement of the exclusive broadcasting licence granted for this country; 26 January 1995, *ZUM* 1995, 792: held that the grant of a broadcasting licence also covers the emission state; and the only decision regarding satellite transmission: LG Stuttgart, 21 april 1994, *GRUR Int.* 1995, 412).

It should be noted, however, that the EC Directive on cable and satellite (93/83) adopted another view. Although it leaves the question of applicable law untouched, it harmonizes Member States substantive law to the effect that in a transborder wireless broadcasting the act relevant to copyright only takes place in the emitting state (defined in article 1(2)(a) and (b) as the social rather than the technical act of emission). This leads to the result that - irrespective of which choice of law theory will be applied - at least as regards transmissions originating in one EU Member State (including EEA states and Eastern European states linked to the EU by a so-called Europe Agreement, and certain emissions from outside as long as certain subsidiary points of attachment are fulfilled, see Directive article 1(2)(d)(i) and (ii)), the rights will only have to be acquired for the emitting state, and any unauthorized transmission only violates substantive copyright provisions in the country of emission.

Together with many scholars (see *e.g.* Dreier, in: Möhring *et al.* (eds.), *Quellen des Urheberrechts* (loose-leaf), Frankfurt 1994, Europ. GemeinschaftsR/II/3, p. 9), the first ministerial draft of implementing legislation is of the opinion that this solution adopted for transmissions originating within the EU does not preclude the application of the Bogsch-theory to transmissions originating from outside.

> **5.** *Are there any rules (legislative or jurisprudential) which particularly deal with the Global Information Infrastructure, or any theoretical proposals?*

At present, there are no legal copyright rules which have been specially designed in order to meet the needs and particularities of the global information structure. A Report commissioned by the Chancelor on the Information Society has been published in December 1995. This Report also addresses copyright questions regarding the future digital and networked context (*Rat für Forschung, Technologie und Innovation: Informationsgesellschaft - Chancen, Innovationen und Herausforderungen*, Copyright part at p. 27 *et seq.*). However, it should be noted that choice of law rules have not been discussed in this Report. Legal discussion has, of course, been lively in Germany at numerous conferences, although it should be noted that so far the choice of law issue has so far attracted little attention in legal literature (there is, however, a doctoral thesis under way at the Max-Planck-Institute). Quite like in other countries as well, some discussants favour the simplicity of a solution modelled after the EC Satellite Directive 83/93 (a solution often called 'country-of-origin solution'); others are more cautious in stressing that one should not all too hastily throw traditional solutions overboard, especially since it may lead to serious problems of underprotection which might hinder the development of the Global Information Infrastructure. Yet, others voice the serious concern that it might indeed be difficult, if not impossible, to localize a particular copyright relevant transmission activity within a global network.

Here, some remarks seem to be called for. First, if one looks to the 'country of origin' of a transborder transmission, one looks for the place where a certain exploitation takes place. Such a 'principle of origin' is therefore based on the principle of territoriality, and may may not be confused with what has traditionally been called 'universality principle' (*i.e.* that a particular work is governed throughout the world - universally - by the rules of its country of origin in all, or at least in some respects), and which also speaks of the country-of-origin principle. Second, in judging the (non-)appropriateness of traditional country of protection principle in a transborder digital transmission context, it seems absolutely necessary to differentiate between issues of (first) ownership, content, duration and content (exploitation rights). Furthermore, in order to find an adequate solution, advantages and disadvantages will have to be judged from the sides of both authors/right holders, users and end-users. Third, as an example, necessary thoughts in relation to choice of law principles regarding exploitation rights would again have to differentiate between the acquisition of rights and infringement problems.

As regards the acquisition of rights, the following would have be taken into consideration. Regarding non-split rights, there seems to be no problem since an on-line service provider has to locate and negotiate with a particular right holder for the storage right anyway (this person can grant all the rights out of the bundle of national copyrights necessary against payment of one single remuneration). Regarding split rights which are collectively administered by collecting societies: here the extent of the problem depends on the collecting societies' ability to offer netwide 'one-stop' licensing. Regarding split rights licensed by individual right owners (either territorially split, or split of exploitation rights, *e.g.* film distribution, video, tv rights, merchandising rights): here it seems indeed difficulty for a user to trace and contract all rights owners. In addition, there is a risk of excessive cumulative payments to be made which may render the whole transaction economically unfeasable, but which can hardly be controlled by general antitrust legislation. However, it should not be forgotten that especially in this respect, right holders have a particular and, as it seems, mostly justified interest in not seeing the exploitation of their respective territorial/market segment impaired by the application of only one national law. *In sum*, as regards the acquisition of rights, problems seem relatively limited and/or may eventually be overcome.

As regards infringement of rights, both the appropriateness of the country of protection system and of the country of origin system have to be seen together with questions of jurisdiction, nature of remedies, national scope of remedies granted by the courts, and execution of foreign remedies (which cannot be described here in all detail). For example: do courts in country A accept a case where the infringement of copyright in country B is the subject? Do they award damages/grant injunctions regarding acts done in country B? If so, can such judgments be executed in B, even if there was no jurisdiction over the defendant in country B? If this is the case, we will end up with problems of forum shopping as long as the rules and practices regarding remedies are not harmonized. However, the harshness of this analysis seems to be softened by one additional - technical - consideration: apparently, it seems impossible to control any movement of data in a network (*i.e.* the way which data take in the Internet is highly arbitrary). Therefore to have the law apply of any country where the lines run does not seem to be appropriate. Rather, the emitting server and the host/terminal of the receiver seem to be the only points of possible attachment. Eventually, however, technical solutions will be found which will enable the right holder to effectively control his material in a network environment (such as programs blocking certain countries, not taking material from certain servers etc.). Yet, it seems that we are quite long away from such technical solutions, especially since once material has been digitized and put on the Net, it is extremely difficult to control further re-uses being made by third parties. It follows that this already limits the laws applicable, so that the - eventually - unwanted effect of too many laws to apply is reduced from the outset. Likewise, this reduces the need to deviate from the country of protection principle.

Fourth, contrary to what is often claimed, there are also several disadvantages in adopting a country-of-origin rule. A country-of-origin rule which is not limited to the question where the infringement takes place would interfere with the legitimate national regulatory aim to maintain certain policy rules with regard to acts having an effect within the national territory (such as, for example, first ownership, scope of rights to be granted, protecting the weaker contract party, organize rights management, etc.). As already mentioned above, likewise the legitimate interests of split right owners may be unduly impaired. Furthermore, there is a danger of dislocation of copyright relevant activities as long as there is any single country with low level protection (outsider country). Moreover, as long as rules of international jurisdiction lead to a forum other than the country of origin, courts will have to apply foreign laws. Last but not least, a country of origin rule is not limited to the public communication/ transmission right, but is defined as a general principle covering all exploitation acts regarding a transmission coming from another state, would seem to be too broad and entail all the negative consequences of the so-called universality principle.

Fifth, why has the EU satellite solution then been possible? The answer is that some of the disadvantages are just not felt when it comes to program transmitting activities within the EU. For example, as regards first ownership, continental European models of presumed transfer of most use rights to the film producer basically lead to the same result as the British film producer's copyright or the French model of a collective work. As regards copyright contracts, the problem to protect the weaker party is not so urgent, since the parties are mostly producers and commercial users. Split rights, which mainly exist in the film area, have largely been accomodated by the exception for co-productions. As far as split rights are administered by collecting societies, collecting societies are able to devise an appropriate EU-wide licensing system. There are hardly any other rights but film rights and rights administered by collecting societies (radio apart, where in addition the publishers may have a say). Furthermore, the activity to be regulated is not a global one, but is - supported by technical possibilities of limiting a satellite's footprint, and due to language barriers - mainly European in nature. Ultimately, dislocation to outsider countries has been barred by subsidiary points of attachment and the possibility to adopt the Bogsch-theory for all or certain third-country transmissions.

It follows that any analogy of the EU satellite solution (be it implemented by harmonizing material law or by adopting a unified conflict of laws rule) does not seem to be appropriate (at least not for the time being) as long as harmonization of the points mentioned (first ownership, exact scope of rights - it is still unclear whether or not on-line dissemination amounts to a public communication or not, or whether it has to be treated like the distribution of material copies -, copyright contract rules, collective administration of rights) has not been achieved, and as long as the possibility for each right holder to effectively control the exploitation of his or her protected material and to receive an appropriate remuneration for the use of his or her protected material, has not been secured.

In sum, a successful and appropriate solution for the problem posed by digital transborder transmission would most likely be a combination of harmonization of material rules coupled with appropriate conflict of law rules which complement the system regarding areas where harmonization has not yet been achieved, and which deal with transmissions emanating from countries which only provide for a substandard level of protection.

Italie

M. Fabiani

1. *Quel est le fondement juridique de la détermination du droit applicable en matière de droit d'auteur (si un texte législatif, prière de le citer et de le reproduire)?*

La loi du 31 mai 1995, n. 218, sur le système italien de droit international privé, prévoit, en son article 54 concernant les droits sur les biens immateriels, que ceux-ci sont régis par la loi de l'état d'utilisation de l'oeuvre.

2. *Quel est le droit applicable aux questions qui relèvent spécifiquement du droit d'auteur (titulaire, objet, contenu, durée, limitations etc.)?*

D'après l'article 185 de la loi sur le droit d'auteur de 1941, n. 633, la loi italienne est applicable à toutes les oeuvres d'auteurs italiens, quel que soit le lieu de leur première publication. Cette disposition s'applique à l'oeuvre cinématographique, au disque phonographique ou instrument similaire, aux droits des artistes-interprètes pour autant qu'il s'agisse d'oeuvres ou de produits réalisés en Italie ou qui peuvent être considérés comme nationaux. La loi italienne est applicable également aux oeuvres d'auteurs étrangers domiciliés en Italie, dont la première publication a eu lieu en Italie. Si ces conditions ne sont pas remplies (par exemple oeuvre non-publiée), les oeuvres d'auteurs étrangers sont protégées sous condition de réciprocité et sous réserve de l'application des conventions internationales. L'Italie est liée à la Convention de Berne, Acte de Paris, et à la Convention Universelle sur le droit d'auteur.

3. *Quel est le droit applicable aux questions qui se réfèrent au droit d'auteur mais qui concernent plus spécialement:*

a. *le droit moral*

L'article 24 de la loi de 1995, n. 218, prévoit que l'existence et le contenu des droits de la personnalité sont régis par la loi nationale du sujet. Dans la loi sur le droit d'auteur du 1941, n. 633, le droit moral de l'auteur est reglé dans un chapitre dont le titre est *"Protection des droits sur l'oeuvre pour la défense de la personnalité de l'auteur"*. Si, par contre, l'on considère le droit moral comme une partie du droit d'auteur (théorie dualiste: droit patrimonial et droit moral), le droit applicable est celui prévu par l'article 185 de la loi et par les dispositions des conventions internationales auxquelles l'Italie est liée.

b. *les contrats*

Les obligations contractuelles de droit d'auteur sont régies par la Convention de Rome du 19 juin 1980, ratifiée par l'Italie le 18-12-1984 (article 57 de la loi du 1995, n. 218).

c. *les infractions et les sanctions*

Les effets d'une infraction (responsabilité civile délictuelle) sont régis par la loi de l'état où l'événement (fait auquel vient aboutir la situation dangereuse) a eu lieu. Cependant, la personne qui a subi le préjudice peut demander l'application de la loi où le fait qui a causé le dommage s'est déroulé. Si l'action délictuelle concerne plusieurs ressortissants d'un même état, la loi de cet état s'applique (article 62 de la loi du 1995, n. 218). Le procès civil en Italie est régi par la loi italienne. Sanctions pénales: en principe s'appliquent les sanctions prévues par la loi du lieu où le fait est commis.

4. *Plus particulièrement, quel est le droit applicable en cas:*

a. *de diffusion couvrant un nombre de pays non-déterminés*

La question n'est pas réglée par la législation actuellement en vigueur.

b. *d'infraction au droit d'auteur*

Si l'infraction est destinée à avoir des effets préjudiciables en Italie, c'est la loi italienne qui s'applique, sauf le recours à la règle de l'article 62 de la loi de 1995, n. 218 (v. 3, lettre c). Si l'infraction en Italie est destinée à avoir des effets préjudiciables à l'étranger, les dispositions de l'article 62 de la loi n. 218 et de l'article 16 de la Convention de Berne seront applicables.

5. *Y a-t-il des règles (législatives ou jurisprudentielles) spécialement prévues pour l'infrastructure globale d'information ou, éventuellement, des propositions théoriques)?*

The Netherlands

J.M.B. SEIGNETTE

1. What is the legal basis of the determination of applicable law in the field of copyright?

Dutch law does not provide specific rules for the determination of the applicable law in copyright matters. The applicable law is determined by international copyright treaties or, if these treaties do not provide a solution, by means of the general principles of Dutch private international law.

Copyright protection in the Netherlands arises either from the Dutch Copyright Act (s. 47) or from bilateral or international treaties to which the Netherlands are party. If a work qualifies for protection under several national copyright laws (*e.g.* work created by a German author and simultaneously published in Germany, Belgium and the Netherlands), the Berne Convention (BC) tells us which law to apply. Article 5(3) of the Berne Convention provides that the protection in the country of origin is determined by the national law of that country. If the author is not a national of that country, he enjoys the same rights as the authors of that country. The 'country of origin' is the country of first publication, or in case of simultaneous publication, the country with the shortest term of protection (article 5(4) BC). If a work has not been published in the sense of article 3(3) BC (making available of copies), the country of origin is the country of which the author is a national, or if it is a cinematographic work, the country of domicile of the producer, or if it is an architectural work, the country where the building is located (article 4(b) BC). The dissemination of a work on a digital network probably does not constitute 'publication' in the sense of article 3(3) BC.

If the country where protection is sought is not the country of origin, the applicable law must be determined otherwise. The Berne Convention provides a minimum standard of protection for all works to which the Convention is applicable. To determine the exact scope of protection beyond the minimum standard accorded by the Convention, we have to look at the applicable national copyright law. The Berne Convention provides that the scope of protection and the remedies available are to be determined by the law of the country where protection is sought (article 5(2) BC; see also Supreme Court of the Netherlands, 13 February 1936, *NJ* 1936, 443, annotation E.M. Meijers).

2. What is the applicable law when considering issues which specifically concern copyright (owner, object, contents, duration, limits, etc.)?

a. *Authorship and first copyright ownership*

Although, as a basic rule, authorship and copyright ownership vest in the actual creator of the work, alternative solutions can be found in the various national copyright laws depending on the type of contract pursuant to which the creative contribution has been made (employment contract, audiovisual production contract, work made for hire contract, etc.). The international treaties do not define 'author', nor specifically provide which law must be applied to determine authorship and first copyright ownership.

In many cases, the (possible) existence of a conflict of laws with respect to 'authorship' is ignored by the court and Dutch law is applied without further motivation. In those cases in which the courts do recognize the existence of a conflict of laws, various principles of Dutch private international law are applied to determine the applicable law. In most cases, courts attach to the law of the country of origin of the work or, if the work has been made in the course of employment, the law applicable to the employment contract. This is also the solution which is generally preferred in Dutch doctrine. Application of the law of the country of origin does not provide a solution if the work has not been published in the sense of article 3(3) BC, because the country of origin in that case is the country of which the 'author' is a national (article 5(4) BC).

The Berne Convention provides a special rule for determining copyright ownership in cinematographic works: the law of the country where protection is sought determines who will own the copyright in the cinematographic work (article 14*bis*(2)(a) BC). If that law provides that ownership is vested in the authors who contributed to the work, they cannot object to certain acts of exploitation (article 14*bis*(2)(b) BC). The question whether an agreement to contribute to the creation of a work must be in writing, must be determined by the law of the country of domicile of the producer, unless the government of the country of protection has expressed to the Director-General that the agreement must be in writing (article 14*bis*(2)(c) BC).

Since article 14*bis* BC does not specifically provide which law is applicable to determine who the 'author' of the cinematographic work is, it is not clear whether the provision also provides a solution if the law of the country of protection and the law of the country of origin (or the law applicable to the agreement pursuant to which the contribution is made) identify different persons as being the 'author' of the cinematographic work. EC Council Directives 93/98/EEC and 93/98/EEC provide that the director shall be considered the 'author'. In implementing the Directives, the Dutch legislator did not consider it necessary to amend the Dutch Copyright Act on this point, which means that the provision that the employer is considered 'author' of a work made by an employee in the course of employment (s. 7 Dutch Copyright Act) remains applicable to contributions made by directors in the course of employment (s. 45a Dutch Copyright Act). In view of the convergence of different categories of works in cyberspace, article 14*bis* BC is likely to create more confusion than certainty. Which law is applicable to determine copyright ownership with regard to multimedia works?

b. *Subject matter of protection*

If protection is sought in the country of origin, the subject matter of protection is determined by the law of that country of origin (article 5(3) BC). If the country where protection is sought is not the country of origin, the subject matter of protection is determined by the law of that country (article 5 BC). See also Supreme Court of the Netherlands, 27 January 1995 (*NJ* 1995, 669, annotation J.H. Spoor): the Berne system implies that the questions of whether there is a work and whether a work deserves protection, must be answered according to the law of the country for which territory protection is invoked.

c. *Scope of protection*

If protection is sought in the country of origin, the scope of protection (including limitations) is determined by the law of that country of origin (article 5(3) BC). If the country where protection is sought is not the country of origin, the scope of protection is determined by the law of that country (article 5(2) BC). The Dutch Supreme Court has held that the question whether a reproduction constitutes an infringement, must be determined according to the law of the country where the reproduction has been made (Supreme Court of the Netherlands, 27 January 1995, *NJ* 1995, 669, annotation J.H. Spoor).

d. *Term of protection*

The term of protection is determined by the law of the country where protection is sought. The term of protection shall not exceed the term of protection provided for in the country of origin of the work (article 7(8) BC). Section 42 of the Dutch Copyright Act also provides that the term of protection shall not exceed the term of protection in the country of origin. An exception is made for works of which the country of origin is a member state of the European Union.

3. *What is the applicable law when considering issues which regard copyright but which particularly deal with:*

a. *moral rights*

The means available to enforce the moral rights listed in article 6*bis*(1) of the Berne Convention are determined by the law of the country where protection is sought (article 6*bis*(3) BC). Article 6*bis*(2) BC furthermore provides that the persons entitled to exercise the moral rights after the death of the author shall be determined by the law of the country where protection is sought.

The Dutch Copyright Act provides that the moral rights after the author's death belong to the person whom the author has appointed by will or codicil. If the author does not appoint someone by will or codicil, the moral rights protection provided by the Copyright Act expires upon the author's death. Under German law, the moral rights automatically pass on to the author's heirs. In a case about a work by German

311

composer Carl Orff, the President of the District Court of Amsterdam applied the *locus regit actum* rule (hence: German law) to determine whether Orff's widow had validly acquired the moral rights and whether she had validly transferred the moral rights to the plaintiff/publisher (President District Court of Amsterdam, 24 February 1992, *Informatierecht/AMI* 1992, p. 112). See also 3b below.

The Berne Convention does not say which law is applicable if the 'author' according to the law of the country where moral rights protection is invoked is not the same person as the 'author' according to the law of the country of origin or the law of the employment contract pursuant to which the work has been made. See 2a above.

b. *contracts, copyright transfers*

If the identity of the first copyright owner is not at issue or has been established (see 2a above), conflicts of laws may still arise as to the validity, scope, exclusivity, term and territory of copyright transfers, the legal position of the assignee or licensee (power of suit, right to sublicense, right to renewal term, etc.) and the interpretation of other contract terms.

A choice of law in a contract in principle will be recognized by the courts if the contract has an international aspect and the choice of law can be justified by the actual situation (Supreme Court of the Netherlands, 13 May 1966, *NJ* 1967, 3; article 3 European Agreement on the Law Applicable to Contractual Obligations). The parties cannot set aside, however, domestic conflict rules which do not allow a choice of law, domestic rules of priority (rules of immediate application) and priority rules in other legal systems. A choice of law in a contract furthermore probably cannot set aside provisions in international treaties prescribing which law is exclusively applicable, as is the case with respect to:
- the scope of protection and remedies available: law of the country where protection is sought (article 5(2) BC);
- the protection in the country of origin: domestic law (article 5(3) BC);
- the means of redress for safeguarding the moral rights granted by article 6*bis*: law of the country where protection is sought (article 6(2) BC);
- the term of protection: law of country where protection is sought (article 7(8) BC);
- the copyright ownership of cinematographic works: law of the country where protection is sought (article 14*bis*(2)(a) BC).

It is not clear under Dutch law to what extent a choice of law regarding authorship, first copyright ownership, transferability and the scope of transfers would be recognized. If no choice of law has been made, courts have to determine the applicable law otherwise. It has been argued[1] that a distinction should be made in this respect between:
(1) purely contractual matters (interpretation of contract terms): to be determined by the law of the country which is most connected with the contract. This is presumed to be the country of domicile of the party which obligation is the most characteristic one, unless attachment to that country is not realistic in view of the specific circumstances of the case (cf. article 4 European Treaty on the Law

Applicable to Contractual Obligations as interpreted by the Supreme Court, 25 September 1992, *NJ* 1992, 75);

(2) transferability and scope of transfer: to be determined by the law of the country where protection is claimed;

(3) formality requirements: law of the country where the transfer is executed. According to article 9 of the European Agreement, the law applicable to the form of the contract is (a) in case both parties are in one country, the law of that country or the law of the country where the transfer is executed or (b) if the parties are in different countries, the law which is applicable to the contract in general or the law of one of these countries.

The first and third rule seem to be generally followed in case-law and doctrine (cf. the *Orff* case discussed in par. 3(a) above). The solution suggested for the second type of question has been applied by the Supreme Court in a few old cases,[2] but has met criticism in doctrine, especially in respect of transfers which are not restricted to a particular territory. In more recent cases, lower courts have applied the law of the country where the transfer had been executed to determine whether the copyright had been validly assigned to the plaintiff (*e.g.* District Court of Leeuwarden, 28 January 1988 and 16 March 1989, *IER* 1989, p. 51).

c. *injunctions and sanctions*

If protection is sought in the country of origin, the means of redress are determined by the law of that country of origin (article 5(3) BC). If the country where protection is sought is not the country of origin, the means of redress are determined by the law of that country (article 5(2) BC). If an injunction is sought in several countries, the question arises whether the court in one country can issue an injunction for other countries as well. See 4b(aa) below.

4. *More particularly, what is the applicable law in case of:*

a. *diffusion covering a number of undefined countries*

The general rule of article 5(2) BC implies that the question whether the dissemination of a work in several countries constitutes a relevant act in a particular country, must be determined according to the law of that country. This means that it must be determined on a country-by-country basis whether the dissemination constitutes a relevant act and, if so, what the scope of protection and remedies are. It also means that dissemination requires the permission of the right holder in each country where the dissemination constitutes a relevant act under the national copyright law. According to the Dutch Supreme Court, the act of communication to the public (*'openbaarmaking'*, s. 12 Dutch Copyright Act) requires that the work is made available to the public in one way or another (Supreme Court, 27 January 1995, *NJ* 1995, 669, annotation J.H. Spoor). Transportation in the Netherlands of copies for the purpose of making that work publicly available outside the Netherlands, without making the work available to the public in the Netherlands, does not constitute an *'openbaarmaking'* under Dutch law.

With respect to satellite broadcasting, EC Council Directive 93/83/EEC provides that the act of communication to the public by satellite occurs solely in the Member State where, under the control and responsibility of the broadcasting organization, the program-carrying signals are introduced into an uninterrupted chain of communication leading to the satellite and down to the earth. Satellite broadcasting therefore constitutes a relevant act only in the country where the signals are introduced in the transmission chain. If a work is broadcast by satellite in country X without permission of the right holder, the question arises whether the court in the country of reception can enjoin the broadcast. See 4b(aa) below.

b. *infringement on copyright*

(aa) *when crossing borders*

The question whether a copyright infringement occurs in several countries, must be answered for each country according to the law of that country (article 5(2) BC). If infringement in several countries has been established, it is in principle possible under Dutch law to obtain an injunction for the territory of these countries (Supreme Court of the Netherlands, 24 November 1989, *NJ* 1992, 404, annotation D.W.F. Verkade). The underlying idea is that right holders should not be obliged to sue in each separate country in case of transfrontier infringements. Courts will be reluctant however to impose an injunction for the territory of another country if they feel they are not in a position to determine whether an infringement has taken place in that other country.

In a case about imitation furniture cloth designs sold by a Dutch company in the Netherlands from its wharehouse in Germany, the Court of Appeals of Arnhem denied an injunction for the German territory. Since the plaintiff had announced that the defendant would also be sued before a German court and because the court was not certain whether the designs would qualify for copyright protection under German law, the court thought it best to avoid contradictory judgments and leave it up to the German court to decide. According to the court, the injunction for the Dutch territory did, however, include the production and storage outside the Netherlands of goods for the Dutch market (Court of Appeals of Arnhem, 29 June 1993, *BIE* 1995, 440).

In order for a Dutch court to impose an injunction or hear a claim for damages, it must of course be competent. Pursuant to the European Execution Treaty (EEX), a Dutch court is competent to hear a tort case if the defendant has its domicile in the Netherlands (article 2) or if the act which caused the damage occurred in the Netherlands and the defendant has its domicile in an EEX country (article 5(3)). In respect of unlawful acts which cause damage in another country than the country where the act takes place, the European Court of Justice has held that article 5(3) also creates competency for the court of the country where the damage has occurred (judgment of 30 November 1976, case 21/76).

In a defamation case, the European Court of Justice applied this interpretation of article 5(3) by deciding that if a defamating article has been published in several countries and the plaintiff alleges to have suffered damage in these countries, the court of each of these countries is competent to hear a claim with respect to its own country. If the plaintiff wants a court to hear a claim with respect to damage suffered in all countries, she will have to go to the court of the country from which the article originated or the court of the country of domicile of the publisher. The question whether there is damage and what evidence is required to prove the existence and scope of the damage, must be determined according to the law applicable according to the rules of private international law of the forum country, provided these rules do not undermine the advantageous effects of the Treaty. (7 March 1995, case C-68/93, *Ars Aequi* 44 (1995) 11, p. 880, annotation P. Vlas.) It may be concluded from this decision that Dutch courts are competent to hear copyright infringement cases dealing with works put on a global network in another country by or under the responsibility of a domiciliary of an EEX country other than the Netherlands, albeit that the court in that situation can only decide on a claim for damages with respect to damage suffered in the Netherlands. Whether this decision curtails the power of Dutch courts to impose injunctions for the territory of other countries, is unclear.

Pursuant to article 24 of the European Execution Treaty, Dutch courts may order preliminary or conservatory measures even if a foreign court would be competent to hear the case. Which preliminary or conservatory measures can be taken in respect of a particular country, must be determined according to the law of that country (article 5(2) BC). If it is unlikely that a preliminary or conservatory measure can actually be executed in a particular country, the court must refrain from ordering that measure in respect of that country.

(bb) *when the origin of the work is hard to identify*

If the source cannot be identified, a right holder may seek to hold another person in the transmission chain responsible and/or have that other person reveal the source. The question whether the acts of a service or access provider constitute a copyright infringement, must be determined according to the law of the country where protection is sought (article 5(2) BC). The question whether the service or access providers can be held liable for their involvement in or knowledge of a copyright infringement, probably must be determined as follows: first, it must be determined whether the act of making the work available on the net constitutes a copyright infringement. This question must be answered according to the copyright law of the country where protection is sought (article 5(2) BC). If an infringement is established, it must be determined whether the involvement or knowledge of the service or access provider creates liability. Pursuant to the Dutch rules of private international law regarding torts (unlawful acts), this question would have to be answered according to the *lex loci delicti*. The only exception to the *lex loci delicti* rule is when the unlawful act takes place in another country than the country where both parties are domiciled and where the legal consequences are felt. In that case, the law of the country of domicile of the parties applies. (Supreme Court, judgment of 19 November 1993, *NJ* 1994, 622, annotation P. van Schilfgaarde.)
In the following case, the Supreme Court endorsed a broad interpretation of the *loci*

delicti' in this case about the dumping of heavily polluted plaster on Dutch dumping sites, the appellate court applied Dutch law to determine whether the German company who had produced the plaster and had sold it to the Dutch company who had ordered the dumping, was co-liable for the dumping. The Supreme Court held that the court's application of Dutch law was justified because the activities of the German company, although mainly performed in Germany, found their completion in the Netherlands in the sense that they led to the unlawful situation in the Netherlands which the plaintiffs sought to end. (Judgment of 14 april 1989, *NJ* 1990, 712, annotation J.C. Schultsz.)

> **5.** *Are there any rules (legislative or jurisprudential) which particularly deal with the Global Information Infrastructure, or any theoretical proposals?*

Dutch copyright law does not contain any provisions specifically aimed at the Global Information Infrastructure. Case-law regarding the liability of bulletin board and Internet providers is developing (see contribution by D.J.G. Visser). In its *Green Paper on Copyright and Related Rights in the Information Society*, the European Commission suggested that a 'country of origin' rule similar to that provided for in the Satellite Directive (see 4a above) could be applied in respect of digital point-to-point dissemination. The applicable law would then be the law of the Member State from which the service originates.

Although application of this country-of-origin rule would seem to provide a solution for the fact that information on global networks can be retrieved all over the world, this rule can only be really effective if copyright and neighbouring rights laws are harmonized on a worldwide basis. As long as this is not the case, the country-of-origin rule will stimulate country-shopping. Application of the country-of-origin rule therefore would at least require that additional measures are taken to prevent country-shopping, *e.g.* by providing that the law of the country of origin only applies if it is established (either by the user or the right holder) that it meets a certain minimum protection standard (*e.g.* BC, TRIPs, Rome, EC Council Directives, Berne Protocol, New Instrument), and if this has not been established, that the uploading is presumed to constitute a 'communication to the public' in each country where the data are made available to the public.

Further complications of the 'country-of-origin' rule:
- Definition of the relevant act: what is meant by 'service' and where does it 'originate'? Is it the transmission of data from the content provider to the service provider or the upload from the server on to the net? What if a work is uploaded from different servers simultaneously or successively?
- If digital transmission only constitutes a communication to the public in the country from which the service originates, the right holder can only invoke protection in that country. Protection cannot be invoked in another country, because the transmission is not considered a communication to the public under the law of this country (which is applicable pursuant to article 5(2) BC). This means that the right holder has to sue in the country from which the server originates, unless the court in the country of reception is competent to judge whether an

infringement has taken place in the country from which the service originates and can actually issue injunctions for that country.
- In the course of digital point-to-point dissemination, reproductions take place in multiple countries. Reproduction rights therefore still have to be cleared in accordance with the laws of each country where such reproduction is made.
- The country-of-origin rule cannot solve the problem that the content provider cannot always be identified.
- Application of the law of the country-of-origin may prove unacceptable in the country of reception. Cf. the decision of the French *Cour de Cassation* in the *Huston* case that certain French provisions regarding a creator's right to invoke the right of integrity were considered *'loi d'application imperative'*.
- The country from which the service originates is not necessarily the 'country-of-origin' as defined in article 5(4) of the Berne Convention.
- How to deal with existing contracts?
- Moral rights: it is doubtful whether the country-of-origin rule can determine the law applicable to moral rights protection, because subsection 3 of article 6*bis* BC provides that the means of redress shall be governed by the legislation of the country where protection is claimed. This is not necessarily the country from which the service originates.
- Authorship and copyright ownership: conflicts of laws regarding ownership cannot be solved by the country-of-origin rule, because the law applicable for determining ownership is not (necessarily) attached to the country where the relevant act/infringement takes place. Solving conflicts of laws regarding ownership requires either harmonization of ownership provisions or special rules determining the law applicable to ownership.

For the time being, the best approach probably would be to reduce the negative side-effects of the principle of territoriality by supporting, where necessary by means of legislation, the development of identification, encryption, copy protection and rights management systems suited to digital transmission. Furthermore, the issue of liability of the various persons involved in the transmission chain has to be addressed. Obviously, the development of a uniform set of substantive rules for the dissemination of works on the GII would eventually seem the best solution.

Footnotes

1. Th.M. de Boer, Aanknoping in het internationaal auteursrecht, *WPNR* 1977, 5414, p. 705.
2. Supreme Court of the Netherlands, 13 February 1936, *NJ* 1934, 443, annotation E.M. Meijers; 25 March 1949, *NJ* 1940, 643, annotation D.J. Veegens.

Suisse

P. BRÜGGER

1. Quel est le fondement juridique de la détermination du droit applicable en matière de droit d'auteur (si un texte législatif, prière de le citer et de le reproduire)?

La loi fédérale du 9 octobre 1992 sur le droit d'auteur et les droits voisins (LDA) ne contient pas de dispositions concernant le droit international privé. C'est la loi fédérale du 18 décembre 1987 sur le droit international privé (LDIP) qui régit cette matière, pas spécifiquement pour le droit d'auteur, mais en général pour "la propriété intellectuelle" qui englobe le droit d'auteur. Quant au droit applicable c'est l'article 110 LDIP qui statue ce que suit:

"1. Les droits de la propriété intellectuelle sont régis par le droit de l'Etat pour lequel la protection de la propriété intellectuelle est revendiquée.

2. En ce qui concerne les prétentions consécutives à un acte illicite, les parties peuvent toujours convenir, après l'événement dommageable, de l'application du droit du for.

3. Les contrats portant sur la propriété intellectuelle sont régis par les dispositions de la présente loi relatives aux contrats (art. 122)."

Pour les contrats touchant au droit d'auteur, l'article 122 LDIP dispose ce qui suit:

"1. Les contrats portant sur la propriété intellectuelle sont régis par le droit de l'Etat dans lequel celui qui transfert ou concède le droit de propriété intellectuelle a sa résidence habituelle.

2. L'élection de droit est admise.

3. Les contrats passés entre un employeur et un travailleur, qui concernent des droits de propriété intellectuelle sur des inventions que le travailleur a réalisées dans le cadre de l'accomplissement de son travail, sont régis par le droit applicable au contrat de travail; ce contrat de travail est régi par le droit de l'Etat dans lequel le travailleur accomplit habituellement son travail."

2. Quel est le droit applicable aux questions qui relèvent spécifiquement du droit d'auteur (titulaire, objet, contenu, durée, limitations etc.)?

Puisque l'LDIP ne différencie pas le terme de la propriété intellectuelle, les dispositions générales citées s'appliquent sans réserve aussi aux questions relevant spécifiquement du droit d'auteur.

3. Quel est le droit applicable aux questions qui se réfèrent au droit d'auteur mais qui concernent plus spécialement:

a. *le droit moral*

La conception du droit d'auteur en Suisse selon la LDA de 1992 peut être comprise de principe comme moniste (avis contraire: M. Rehbinder, *Urheberrechtgesetz 1993, N1 zu Art. 16*). Pour le droit applicabie il ne joue aucun rôle si des droits moraux ou des droits pécuniaires sont touchés.

b. *les contrats*

Pour les contrats en matière de droit d'auteur (contrats de licence, mandats e.a.) l'article 122 LDIP précité est décisif. Quand l'oeuvre en cause a été créée sous le régime d'un contrat de travail, l'article 121 LDIP est applicable:
"1. Le contrat de travail est régi par le droit de l'Etat dans lequel le travailleur accomplit habituellement son travail.
2. Si le travailleur accomplit habituellement son travail dans plusieurs Etats, le contrat de travail est régi par le droit de l'Etat de l'établissement ou, à défaut d'établissement, du domicile ou de la résidence habituelle de l'employeur.
3. Les parties peuvent soumettre le contrat de travail au droit de l'Etat dans lequel le travailleur a sa résidence habituelle ou dans lequel l'employeur a son établissement, son domicile ou sa résidence habituelle."

c. *les infractions et les sanctions (pénales ou civiles)*

Le choix du for pour les actes illicites est défini à l'article 129 LDIP:
"1. Les tribunaux suisses du domicile ou, à défaut de domicile, ceux de la résidence habituelle ou de l'établissement du défendeur sont compétents pour connaître des actions fondées sur un acte illicite.
2. Lorsque le défendeur n'a ni domicile ou résidence habituelle, ni établissement en Suisse, l'action peut être intentée devant le tribunal suisse du lieu de l'acte ou du résultat.
3. Si plusieurs défendeurs peuvent être recherchés en Suisse et si les prétentions sont essentiellement fondées sur les mêmes faits et les mêmes motifs juridiques, l'action peut être intentée contre tous devant le même juge compétent; le juge saisi en premier lieu a la compétence exclusive."

Quant au droit applicable les parties peuvent convenir le droit du for (article 110 al. 2 LDIP). A défaut d'élection de droit, l'article 133 LDIP est décisif.
"1. Lorsque l'auteur et le lésé ont leur résidence habituelle dans le même Etat, les prétentions fondées sur un acte illicite sont régies par le droit de cet Etat.
2. Lorsque l'auteur et le lésé n'ont pas de résidence habituelle dans le même Etat, ces prétentions sont régies par le droit de l'Etat dans lequel l'acte illicite a été commis. Toutefois, si le résultat s'est produit dans un autre Etat, le droit de cet Etat est applicable si l'auteur devait prévoir que le résultat s'y produirait.
3. Nonobstant les alinéas précédents, lorsqu'un acte illicite viole un rapport juridique existant entre auteur et lésé, les prétentions fondées sur cet acte sont régies par le droit applicable à ce rapport juridique."

Quant au droit pénal, la plupart des délits contre le droit d'auteur ne sont poursuivis que sur plainte du lésé (voir article 67 LDA). Le juge suisse se déclare en principe compétent pour la poursuite pénale si l'acte criminel a été commis sur le territoire suisse ou si le résultat d'un acte criminel commis à l'étranger (punissable selon le droit suisse) a eu lieu en Suisse.

> **4.** *Plus particulièrement, quel est le droit applicable en cas*
> *a) de diffusion couvrant un nombre de pays non-déterminés;*
> *b) d'infractions au droit d'auteur*
> > aa) *transfrontalières,*
> > bb) *de provenance non-identifiable?*

Quant aux infractions au droit d'auteur visées dans cette question, le juge suisse du lieu où le résultat de l'acte illicite s'est manifesté sera compétent, par exemple le juge tessinois si la diffusion incriminée peut être reçue seulement dans ce canton. Et il appliquera le droit suisse parce qu'il partira de la conviction que l'auteur de la diffusion devrait prévoir que le résultat se produira en Suisse.

> **5.** *Y a-t-il des règles (législatives ou jurisprudentielles) spécialement prévues pour l'infrastructure globale d'information ou, éventuellement, des proposi-tions théoriques)?*

Pour le moment, il n'existe pas, à ma connaissance, de nouveaux projets législatifs sur l'infrastructure globale d'information. En la doctrine, on trouve aussi en Suisse des souhaits de voir le multimédia bénéficier d'une réglementation légale expresse (voir J. de Werra, *Le multimédia en droit d'auteur, RSPI* 1995, p. 256).

Sweden

G.W.G. KARNELL

General remarks

Although the questionnaire is in French, this reply is given in English, being the second working language of the Swedish Group. Also, instead of answering each question as put, I prefer - in order not to cause repetitions and hoping that my explanations will become more consistent - to give a short presentation of Swedish law, as it stands in the domain indicated by the questionnaire.

Some background

Swedish statutory law, articles 60 and 62 of the Copyright Act (1960:724; texts are annexed to this Report), as well as the International Copyright Regulation (1994:193; also extending it to works of some international organisations), where rights are extended in accordance with the Berne and Universal Copyright Conventions as well as the Rome Convention of 1962 and the European Television Agreement of 1960 with its additional protocols of 1965 and 1983, determines whether and how the Copyright Act protects foreign works by copyright and other foreign productions by neighbouring rights. (The text of the Regulation is not annexed, because it just lists the countries to which Swedish law protection is extended because of the specific international instruments.) Also the non-discrimination principle in article 6 of the Rome Treaty (after Maastricht; earlier article 7) applies. Subject matter and right pretenders not covered by the rules mentioned, do not at all enjoy protection under Swedish law. As of 1 January 1996, additions may be made to include TRIPs countries. So far I have given the basic content of law, on which claims can be based by the initial right holder. The law also determines that such a right holder can transfer or license within limits stated therein.

The international private law issue

Now to the international private law issue specifically. Any question about the inception of a Swedish copyright, original right holder, legal content or existence (duration etc.) as well as the prerequisites for lawful transfer of rights (moral rights cannot be transferred, only waived in relation to uses which are limited both as to their character and scope) will in Sweden, by a Swedish court, be decided in application of Swedish law. The same goes for any infringement of the copyright law and neighbouring rights. The rules on the application of Swedish law to criminal acts committed within or outside Sweden are very complicated and supplemented by the provisions of the European convention of 15 May 1972, transformed into Swedish law by the Act (1976:19) on international co-operation regarding legal enforcement (the word may be badly translated from Swedish) against criminal acts. Basically, the Criminal Law Statute *(Brottsbalken)* of 1962 contains in its chapter 2 article 1 a presumption that if it cannot be ascertained if a criminal act - a copyright infringement is such an act - has been committed in Sweden or elsewhere, Swedish law will be applied by Swedish courts to any act about which there is reason to believe that it has been committed in Sweden. Article 2(1) of the same chapter provides that a crime committed abroad will be adjudicated under Swedish law by Swedish courts if committed by a Swedish citizen or by a foreigner having habitual residence in Sweden, by other foreigners who have become Swedish citizens or taken habitual residence in Sweden after the crime or are found in Sweden, being citizens of any other Nordic country, or are other foreigners found here and having committed a crime punishable by imprisonment of more than six months. Article 2(1) does not apply if the act is committed where it is not considered to be criminal or somewhere where no particular country's law applies (space), if Swedish law does not punish it more severely than by a fine. Article 2(2) adds cases of crimes committed against Sweden or any Swedish public body and some more specific cases of no practical relevance in this context. To the extent that foreign rights are at stake, and that the case can at all be tried in Sweden - which is a matter of procedural law and not subject to the request for answers in the questionnaire - a Swedish court will apply the law of the foreign country for which protection is sought *('Schutzland')*.

The rules presented until now apply without regard to contractual stipulations. In other respects contractual stipulations about applicable law will usually be applied by the courts (exceptions may relate to frauds, *ordre public* etc.). Whereas there are no contractual dispositions about other questions than the ones mentioned, the courts must rely upon case-law and legal doctrine for guidance. There is no statutory law to be applied. Also, case-law, as reported, does not give much guidance. There is much disagreement about which is the most suitable rule for various types of conflicts. Swedish courts will, typically, look for the law of the country with which the contract can be said to have its closest connection. The law of the country of the publisher has been proposed for publishing contracts, the country for which protection is sought for others, as well as the country of the transferor. Lack of published case-law makes it very difficult to know which law will apply when parties have left the choice of law open to the courts. This will prove to be particularly difficult in cases involving simultaneously the laws of many countries, as may be a common case in the GII. Regarding only the right to the creations and performances etc. of employees, the law is reasonably predictable: the law of the country that regulates the employment relation, *i.e.* usually the law of the country where the work is performed. There are no special rules intended to cover the GII in particular.

Annexe

Articles 60 and 62 of the Swedish Copyright Act (1960:724)

Applicability of the Act

Article 60

The provisions of this Act concerning copyright apply to:
1. works of Swedish citizens or persons who have their habitual residence in Sweden,
2. works first published in Sweden or simultaneously in Sweden and abroad,
3. cinematographic works the producer of which has his headquarters or habitual residence in Sweden,
4. works of architecture constructed here,
5. works of fine arts incorporated in a building here or in some other way permanently fixed to the ground.

For the purposes of the application of the first paragraph, item 2, a simultaneous publication shall be considered to have taken place if the work has been published in Sweden within thirty days from its publication abroad. For the purposes of the application of the first paragraph, item 3, the person whose name appears on a cinematographic work shall, in the absence of a proof to the contrary, be deemed to be the producer of the said work.

The provisions of Articles 50 and 51 shall apply to all literary or artistic works regardless of their origin.

Article 62

On condition of reciprocity, the Government may provide for the application of this Act in relation to other countries. The Government may also provide for the application of the Act to works and photographic pictures first published by an intergovernmental organization and to unpublished works and photographic pictures which such an organization may publish.

United States of America

J.C. GINSBURG

1. What is the legal basis of the determination of applicable law in the field of copyright?

28 USC § 1338(a) provides for the exclusive jurisdiction of the federal courts in actions arising under the federal copyright law, 17 USC § 101 *et seq*. Section 301(a) of the federal copyright act provides for the exclusive application of the federal copyright law to actions involving the subject matter of federal copyright, and seeking to vindicate rights equivalent to the exclusive rights under federal copyright. These provisions, however, essentially concern the relationship of federal to state law within the US federal system; they do not directly address the problem of international conflicts of copyright (or related) laws. 28 USC § 1338(a) provides: *'The [federal] district courts shall have original jurisdiction of any civil action arising under any Act of Congress relating to patents, plant variety protection, copyrights and trademarks. Such jurisdiction shall be exclusive of the courts of the states in patent, plant variety protection and copyright cases'*. 17 USC § 301(a) provides: *'On and after January 1, 1978, all legal or equitable rights that are equivalent to any of the exclusive rights within the general scope of copyright as specified by section 106 in works of authorship that are fixed in a tangible medium of expression and come within the subject matter of copyright as specified by sections 102 and 103, whether created before or after that date and whether published or unpublished, are governed exclusively by this title. Thereafter, no person is entitled to any such right or equivalent right in any such work under the common law or statutes of any State'*. Because the US copyright act provides for national treatment of qualifying foreign works, US law would apply to a US-based infringement of a foreign work to the same extent that US law applies to a US-based infringement of a US work. § 104 accords national treatment to all unpublished works, regardless of the author's nationality, and to published works whose authors are nationals or domiciliaries of a foreign nation with which the US has copyright relations, or which were first published in such a nation.

2. What is the applicable law when considering issues which specifically concern copyright (owner, object, contents, duration, limits, etc.)?

a. *'Contents, limits ...'*

The general rule of national treatment set forth in § 104 results in the application of US copyright law to alleged acts of infringement committed in the US, regardless of the national origin of the work infringed. This means that the scope of protection - including limitations on protection, such as fair use - will be the same for foreign as for US works.

b. *Duration*

§ 104 also has the effect of extending the US-law period of copyright term to foreign works, without regard to the copyright duration in the country of origin. In other words, the US does not apply the rule of the shorter term. (Compare, Berne Convention, article 7(8).)

c. *Object*

US courts have interpreted § 104 to apply US law to determine the copyrightability of a work of foreign origin. US copyright protection thus does not depend on availability of protection for the work in its country of origin. For example, in *Hasbro Bradley. Inc. v. Sparkle Toys Inc.*, 780 F.2d 189 (2d Cir. 1985), the court rejected defendant's argument that the absence of copyright protection for plaintiff's toys in their country of origin (Japan) should preclude copyright protection in the US Because the toys were 'pictorial, graphic or sculptural works' within the meaning of the US copyright law, they were copyrightable in the US. The court stated: '*Although the toys enjoyed no copyright protection under Japanese law, they fell within the class of "pictorial, graphic, and sculptural works" covered by § 102(a)(5) of the [US Copyright] Act. Since the toys were authored by a Japanese national and first 'published' (i.e. sold) in Japan, they enjoyed copyright protection under United States law from the moment they were created, by virtue of both § 104(b) of the Act and Article II(1) of the UCC*'. (At the time, the US had not yet joined the Berne Convention.)

d. *Copyright ownership*

(i) *Initial ownership*

§ 104 does not directly address the law applicable to determine ownership of copyright in a work of foreign origin. The recently-enacted provision on 'Copyright in restored works', 17 USC § 104A(b), however, specifies: '*OWNERSHIP OF RESTORED COPYRIGHT. A restored work vests initially in the author or initial rightholder of the work as determined by the law of the source country of the work*'. § 104A(h)(8)(C) defines the 'source country' of a published work as (i) the eligible country in which the work is first published, or (ii) if the restored work is published on the same day in 2 or more eligible countries, the eligible county which has the most significant contacts with the work. § 104A(h)(7)(A) defines a 'right holder' as the person '*who, with respect to a sound recording, first fixes a sound recording with authorization ...*'. It is not clear whether § 104A(b) simply codifies the prior approach of US copyright law, or if it signals a departure from US choice of law practice. Judicial discussion of the issue is scant. While in some instances US courts have analyzed assertions that a work of foreign origin was a work-made-for-hire under US law, without considering the ownership status of the work in the country of origin, it appears that the parties did not raise the question whether US law should apply. See, e.g., *Aldon Accessories Ltd. v. Spiegel Inc.*, 738 F.2d 548 (2d Cir.), cert. denied, 469 US 982 (1984) (statuettes commissioned from artists in Taiwan); *Syema Photo News Inc. v. Globe Intl. Inc.*, 616 F.Supp. 1153 (SDNY 1985) (photographs commissioned in UK).

Compare *Schmid Bros. Inc. v. W. Goebel Porzellanfrabrik KG*, 589 F.Supp. 497 (EDNY 1984). In this case, the court rejected defendant manufacturer's argument that statuettes created by Sister Hummel belonged to the convent as 'works for hire'. The court did not consider whether, under German law, a convent is a nun's 'employer', and, if so, whether the convent would therefore own the copyright in the nun's artistic productions. Nonetheless, the court held that the course of dealings between Sister Hummel and her convent made clear that she was the copyright owner.

(ii) *Transfer of ownership*

As a general matter, US courts recognize that a US grantee of rights under copyright cannot claim greater rights than the foreign transferor granted. See, *e.g.*, *Gilliam v. ABC*, 538 F.2d 14 (2d Cir. 1978) (US television broadcaster could not exercise right to adapt work when its grantor, the BBC, had not acquired adaptation rights from the UK authors). It is not clear, however, whether courts consider whether the law of the work's country of origin (or the law of the contract) limits (or broadens) the scope of the grant of rights to the US co-contractant. For example, in *Bartsch v. MGM*, 391 F.2d 150 (2d Cir. 1968), the German plaintiff had acquired from the German composer and lyricist the rights to make and exhibit a film based on *Maytime*, a German musical comedy. That contract, executed in 1930, was probably governed by German law. That same year, the plaintiff granted the rights to make and exhibit the *Maytime* film to MGM. New York law governed that contract. Later, the question arose whether plaintiff's 1930 contract with MGM should be interpreted to include television broadcast rights. The court applied New York law to conclude that the contract did extend to rights in new technological means of exhibiting films, even if those means were not yet in use at the time of the contract.

It appears that no one raised the question whether the plaintiff's German contract with *Maytime*'s composer and lyricist could be interpreted to have granted those new technology rights to the plaintiff. If, under German law, the contract did not convey those rights, then perhaps the court would not have interpreted the plaintiff's contract with MGM to have transferred to the US producer rights never acquired from the German authors. Alternatively, it may be that US courts do not look to the law of the country of origin (or of the contract) because they assume that US law will govern the scope of a grant of US copyright. One recent decision makes this assumption explicit. In *Corcovado Music Corp. v. Hollis Music Inc.*, 981 F.2d 679 (2d Cir. 1993), Brazilian composer Antonio Carlos Jobim assigned to a Brazilian publisher worldwide rights for the full term of copyright. Brazilian law governed the contract. At the end of the first term of US copyright, Jobim renewed the US copyright, and granted the US renewal term rights to another publisher. The first publisher claimed that Jobim's contract had transferred all rights for the whole world, including the US, for the full duration of all copyrights, and that Jobim therefore had no remaining rights to transfer to another publisher. The US court acknowledged that Brazilian law governed the contract, but stressed that US copyright law ruled the determination of whether the Brazilian contract conveyed the US renewal term rights. In other words, the US court viewed the transfer of renewal term copyright as a matter of substantive US copyright law, rather than as a matter of Brazilian contract law. Under US copyright law, a transfer of the renewal term copyright is not effective unless the contract specifies that it covers 'all renewals and extensions'; simply granting rights for 'the full term of the copyright' does not suffice.

Synthesis: With respect to transfers of copyright ownership, the law applicable to determine the scope of the grant may depend on whether the US court characterizes the question as one of substantive US copyright law, or as a matter of contract interpretation governed by the law of the contract.

3. *What is the applicable law when considering issues which regard copyright but which particularly deal with:*

a. *moral rights*

Apart from a special provision covering 'works of the visual arts', US law includes no specific protections for moral rights. As a result, claims seeking redress in the US for alterations of a work, or for failure to attribute authorship credit to the author, would be governed by the US copyright and trademark laws to the same extent as other claims. With respect to 'works of the visual art' (as narrowly defined in 17 USC § 106A), the rule of national treatment applies.

b. *contracts*

See response to 2d(ii), above. For contracts executed as of 1978, the right to terminate a transfer of copyright 35 years following the contract's execution, and, for works published before 1978, the correlative right to terminate the 19-year 'extended renewal' term, see 17 USC §§ 203, 304(c), are available to the authors (or statutory successors) of any work protected by the US copyright act, whether of US or foreign origin. The termination covers only US rights, see 17 USC §§ 203(b)(5), 304(c)(6)(E). The US copyright act reinforces the termination right by specifying that *'Termination of the grant may be effected notwithstanding any agreement to the contrary ...'.* § 203(a)(5); see also § 304(c)(5). The prohibition on formal waivers of the US termination right should apply to all works, regardless of national origin, and regardless of the law that otherwise governs the contract. As a result, a foreign-law contract that purported to grant worldwide rights in a non-US work for the full term of copyright, and all renewals and extensions thereof, still would be subject to termination of the US rights, under the terms of the US copyright act.

c. *infringement and sanctions (penal or civil)*

See response to 2a, above. In addition, the rights under US copyright include the right to exclude the unauthorized importation of foreign-made pirated copies, see 17 USC § 602(b). The US copyright owner's rights also include the right to prevent unauthorized importation of foreign-made copies, even if those copies were lawfully made abroad. See § 602(a). The rule of national treatment applies here as well. As a result, if a French composer authorized the production of phonorecords of her music in the EC, but did not authorize their importation to the US, she could prevent their entry into the US, even though the phonorecords were lawfully made in the European Community. (Obviously, she could also block entry into the US of pirated phonorecords.)

4. *More particularly, what is the applicable law in case of:*

a. *diffusion covering a number of undefined countries*

When the infringing act originates in the US, some US courts have applied US law to the entire series of infringing acts, including those culminating outside the US. See, *e.g.*, *Update Art Inc. v. Modiin Pubs.*, 843 F.2d 67 (2d Cir. 1988) (unauthorized publication in Israeli newspaper of photograph allegedly first copied in the US, then sent to Israel); *Gasté v. Kaiserman*, 863 F.2d 1061 (2d Cir. 1988) (awarding damages for public performances inside and outside US of infringing song). Other courts, however, have held that the US copyright is territorial, and can only govern acts of infringement occurring within the US. See, *e.g.*, *Subafilms Ltd. v. MGM-Pathé Communications Inc.*, 24 F.3d 1088 (9th Cir.), cert. denied, 115 S.Ct. 512 (1994) (US law does not reach manufacturing and distribution of videocassettes in Mexico).

b. *infringement on copyright*

(aa) *when crossing borders*

See responses to 3a and 4a, above.

(bb) *when the origin of the work is hard to identify*

(I assume this question addresses the origin of the diffusion, rather than the origin of the work. See French-language original.) In this instance, US courts would probably limit the application of US law to those acts occurring within the US. In the GII context, this might mean any acts of downloading occurring within the US. It might also mean US acts of distribution, for example, via US-based servers. As a result, a US on-line service provider might be liable under US law for distributing infringing copies (or for furthering unauthorized public performances or displays), even if the infringing material had been uploaded from abroad.

5. *Are there any rules (legislative or jurisprudential) which particularly deal with the Global Information Infrastructure, or any theoretical proposals?*

There are no current GII-specific rules in the US; there is no pending legislation, and courts have yet to address the question explicitly. In its Report, the Working Group on Intellectual Property rights of the Information Infrastructure Task Force (hereafter, 'NII White Paper') recognizes that international conflicts of law may become a problem for distribution of works over the GII. The White Paper makes no specific legislative proposal, but urges global harmonization. The relevant pages of the White

Paper are annexed.

As for theoretical proposals, see, *e.g.*, Ginsburg, *Global Use/Territorial Rights: Private International Law Questions of the Global Information Infrastructure*, 42 *J. Copyr. Soc.* 318, 338 (1995):

'*Infringements alleged to occur in multiple territories:*

In the absence of an applicable treaty supplying a substantive rule, the law applicable to determine the existence and scope of copyright protection, as well as available remedies, shall be the law of the forum country, if that country is also either
- the country from which the infringing act or acts originated; or
- the country in which the defendant resides or of which it is a national or domiciliary; or
- the country in which the defendant maintains an effective business establishment.
For the purposes of this provision, the 'country in which the infringing act or acts originated' includes the country from which an unauthorized copy of the work was first communicated, including by any means of transmission.'

Annexe

(From: *Intellectual Property and the NII*)

(...)

H. *Conflict of laws*

Conflict of laws issues may arise in GII-related copyright infringement actions. Resolution of these issues determines what country's law the court should apply. If the infringer and the infringement are in the United States, the US Copyright Act would apply. However, different situations may present themselves which will raise conflict issues. For instance, users in country A, where certain actions are not considered copyright infringements, may use works located on servers in country B, where such actions are. Which country's law controls the resolution of a copyright infringement dispute - the country from which a copyrighted work is uploaded or to which it is downloaded, or the country where the host server is located? In the case of direct transmissions, which country's law applies - the country of origin of the transmission or the transmitter, or the country of the reception? It may be that rights of the copyright owner are exercised in each country. These issues however, may be no more problematic than the current conflict issues that arise due to the use of telephones, fax machines or modems in international commerce.

I. *Harmonization of international systems*

There is little dispute that worldwide high-speed digital communications networks will have an enormous effect on the way in which works of authorship will be created, stored, communicated to the public, distributed and paid for. The communication revolution is now bringing new opportunities and new challenges to creators and users of intellectual property. The full implementation of the NII and the GII will have an immense effect on our economy, and implementation of such systems internationally will have an equally broad impact on worldwide commerce. The United States must be committed to finding the means to preserve the integrity of intellectual property rights in the materials that will flow in the commerce created in this environment. This is a daunting challenge in the context of the US domestic market. It is an even greater challenge to lay an international groundwork which will ensure adequate and effective protection throughout the world.

As we move toward a world where dissemination of entertainment and information products through on-demand-delivery services operating through interactive digital information communications networks is the norm, it may be necessary to harmonize levels of protection under disparate systems of copyright, authors' rights and neighbouring rights, and consideration should be given to ways to bridge the gaps among these systems. If the GII is to flourish, then the intellectual property rights that mill undergird the economic structure supporting these infrastructures must unequivocally be granted in national legislation fully on the basis of national treatrnent for *all* rights and benefits. However, there is some controverse over the scope of the national treatment obligation under the Berne Convention and its application to what some may regard as newly created rights and subject matter. Similar questions arise under other international copyright and neighbouring rights conventions as will be later discussed. The United States is committed to making progress in WIPO toward improving international protection for works protected by copyright and authors rights and the subject matter of neighbouring rights. Such progress is essential, especially in view of the needs to deal with the intellectual property issues associated with the emerging GII. The transition into a world-wide information society demands both a narrowing of the focus on specific issues in the cases of the Berne Protocol and the New Instrument, and the expansion of the WIPO efforts to encompass the digital world in both areas.

In the emerging world of the GII with its digital distribution systems and multimedia works, distinctions among the rights of authors, producers and performers that are the basis for the separation of copyright and neighbouring rights are rapidly becoming irrelevant. This new world of information superhighways will mean economic growth, jobs, and exports for all economies to the benefit of authors, producers and performers. Governments need to consider carefully the implications of the inevitable development of the GII for their national economies and their copyright systems. The work in WIPO is relevant to the rapidly emerging digital world of the GII in order to set sound policy, and select the essential elements of the present Berne Protocol and New Instrument texts and work toward reaching international agreement on them. Discussions on a Berne Protocol and New Instrument afford an opportunity to consider what enforcement norms, beyond the broadly applicable disciplines clearly established in the TRIPs text, will be necessary if rightsholders are to be adequately protected in the NII/GII environment. Thus, rather than replicate the TRIPs enforcement provisions - which would be redundant and would create the very real possibility of conflicting norms - work on a Berne Protocol and New Instrument should focus on issues not addressed in TRIPs, such as protection of rights management information, the use of technical security measures and the prohibition of devices and services whose primary purpose or effect is to defeat technical security measures.

One of the most important issues for international norm setting is to define the nature of a dissemination of a work or a transmission of a work in digital form. Is it a public performance of the work or a reproduction and distribution? Can it be all at the same time? How do rules concerning the right of importation apply in a digital environment? Just as these questions are critical in the domestic context, they are equally acute in the context of international treaties and harmonization of levels of protection. The right to distribute copies of a work by transmission should be included both in the Berne Protocol and the New Instrument, perhaps as a separate right, as an aspect of a distribution right, as part of a right of communication to the public, or an aspect of the reproduction right. While this is an issue that needs much further discussion, the United States believes that such a right is an important part of the Berne Protocol and New Instrument which would be aimed at meeting the needs of the emerging GII. Provisions to prohibit decoders and anti-copy prevention devices and services also should be included in the Berne Protocol and the New Instrument. The Protocol and the New Instrument should also include a prohibition of the fraudulent inclusion of rights management information and the fraudulent removal or alteration of such information.

To permit the effective development of the GII, national treatment must be the basis for protection in any intellectual property agreement. At an absolute minimum, national treatment must apply to the minimum obligations established in any agreement in WIPO. The author or rights holder should be able to realize fully the economic benefits flowing from the free exercise of his or her rights in any country party to the Protocol or New Instrument. The United States continues to believe that, in respect of any work, this is required by article 5 of the Berne Convention. To do otherwise in either a Berne Protocol or another agreement on copyright protection would be contrary to article 20 because it would be a derogation of rights existing under Berne and would not be an Agreement to 'grant to authors more extensive rights than those granted by the Convention, or contain other provisions not contrary to this Convention' as provided for under Article 20.[1] To the extent that it has been agreed that the principles of the New Instrument should follow those of the Berne Convention, to do otherwise in respect of related rights would be contrary to the letter and the spirit of the Convention.

US copyright legislation has granted rights that some other nations may regard as new rights beyond those set forth in the Berne Convention - for example, rental rights in computer programs, sound recordings, and musical works embodied in sound recordings - and has done so exclusively on the basis of national treatment. The United States has instituted a system of royalties on blank digital audio recording media and digital audio recorders. Benefits from these rights have all been granted on the basis of full national treatment. The United States believes that this is consistent with our obligations under the Berne Convention and other international intellectual property and trade treaties and agreements.

The author or rights holder should be able to realize fully the economic benefits flowing from the free exercise of his or her rights in any country participating in a GII. This is required by article 5 of the Berne Convention. To do otherwise in either a Berne Protocol or another agreement on copyright protection would be contrary to article 20 because it would be a derogation of rights existing under Berne and not be an Agreement to 'grant to authors more extensive rights than those granted by the Convention, or contain other provisions not contrary to this Convention' as provided for under article 20. To protect new works or to grant new rights in respect of new or presently protected works on the basis of reciprocity, would be contrary to the letter and the spirit of the Convention.

As the GII continues to develop through the international interconnection of NIIs, rules must be formulated to protect the economic rights of providers of entertainment and information products. Such rules should be based on principles of national treatment along the lines of the following:
1. Each country participating in the GII must accord to nationals of another country participating in the GII no less favorable treatment than it accords to its own nationals with regard to all rights and benefits now, or hereafter, granted under its domestic laws in respect of literary and artistic works or fixations[2] embodying such works.
2. Benefits must include the same possibility to exploit and enjoy rights in the national territory of a country participating in the GII as the respective country grants to its own nationals.
3. No country participating in the GII may, as a condition of according national treatment, require rights holders to comply with any formalities in order to acquire rights in respect of literary and artistic works or fixations embodying such works.

In addition to these issues of general concern, there are issues that are applicable specifically to the Berne Protocol and to the New Instrument. Following the Supreme Court decision in the *Feist* case there is increasing concern that many valuable, factually-oriented databases may be denied copyright protection or that courts may determine infringement in ways that severely limit the scope of copyright protection for databases. Providing for a *sui generis* unfair extraction right to supplement copyright protection may prove to be useful in view of legal developments in various national laws and should be given serious consideration. How a right, such as the unfair extraction right proposed in the EU Database Directive, could protect such databases should be carefully evaluated. Additionally, the issue of multimedia works will take on an important international dimension. If these are regarded at the international level as works in a new, separate category, the issue of their coverage under the existing conventions and the rule of national treatment will be open to debate. If, however, as current discussions seem to indicate, they are subsumed into the existing categories of works, establishing meaningful rules internationally will be simplified.

Further study to determine what existing rights should be clarified or what other rights may need to be adapted to the emerging digital environment are underway both in domestic and international fora. However, some issues merit identification here, and one of those is the level of protection to be accorded to sound recordings. Many believe that the time has come to bring protection for the performers and producers of sound recordings into line with the protection afforded to the creators of other works protected under the Berne Convention. This includes providing high-level standards for rights and benefits granted on the basis of national treatment. This is necessary for a number of reasons. First, there is no just reason to accord a lower level of protection to one special class of creative artists. Second, the extent of international trade in sound recordings makes it imperative that standards of protection be harmonized at a high level. Third, and perhaps most importantly, the digital communications revolution - the creation of advanced information infrastructures - is erasing the distinctions among different categories of protected works and sound recordings and the uses made of them. Concerns also have been raised over the extent and scope of moral rights in the world of digital communications. Some believe that the ability to modify and restructure existing works and to create new multimedia works makes strengthening international norms for moral rights more important than ever before. Others take the view that any changes to international norms for the protection of moral rights must be carefully considered in the digital world. The United States agrees with this view. Careful thought must be gaven to the scope, extent and especially the waivability of moral rights in respect of digitally fixed works, sound recordings and other information products.

There are issues such as digital fixation, storage and delivery that will need to be taken into account in the New Instrument. There are also questions concerning the scope of rights and the right owners that might be covered by the New Instrument. To the extent possible, definitions in the New Instrument should be identical to those in the Berne Protocol. Otherwise, differences in phrasing could lead to differences in interpretation, and jeopardize the 'bridging' of the New Instrument with the Berne Convention and the Protocol. Many of these issues are critical to the United States and other countries.

To attain the needed level of protection internationally, ways to span the differences between the continental *droit d'auteur* and neighbouring rights systems and the Anglo-American copyright systems must be developed. An essential element of this effort will be to harmonize levels of protection by establishing standards that can be implemented through either system.

(...)

Footnotes (renumbered)

1. Article 20 states: *'The Governments of the countries of the Union reserve the right to enter into special agreements among themselves, in so far as such agreements grant to authors more extensive rights than those granted by the Convention, or contain other provisions not contrary to this Convention. The provisions of existing agreements which satisfy these conditions shall remain applicable.'*
2. This reference to fixations includes the subject matter of neighbouring rights related to works and their performance.

Contributions panelists

Hypothetical case for discussion by the panel

Former French President François Mitterand died in January 1996. Within a few days of his death, his former personal physician published a memoir, titled *Le grand secret (The big secret)*. The doctor disclosed that the cancer that ultimately killed Mitterand had already metastasized at the time that Mitterand first assumed the presidency. Indeed, the doctor claimed that, toward the end of his second seven-year term, Mitterand was no longer in condition to exercise the functions of his office. The book's publication drew Mitterand's family's ire. The family invoked the late President's post-mortem right of privacy under French law to obtain a court order against the book's dissemination. Within days of its publication, the book was withdrawn from circulation.

However, before every copy disappeared from the bookstore shelves, the entrepreneur of a 'cyberspace café' in a provincial French city acquired a copy, scanned all 190 pages, and posted the image files to a French internet site. Patrons of his café could log onto the site, as could remote users elsewhere in France who dialed in to an access number. Faced with threats from Mitterand's family, the entrepreneur declared that if pursued, he would simply send his files to a bulletin board in the US.

Suppose that the French entrepreneur did send the files to a US server. The website at issue is available on the Internet, and customers the world over who do not enjoy direct access to the Net (for example via their universities), can subscribe to the World Wide Web. Many of these services have their principal place of business in the US, but have local offices in many countries around the world, including in your countries. Now suppose the French publishers wish to enforce the copyright in *Le grand secret*. How well would they fare, and against whom, if they sought to bring the claim in your country's courts? Would it make a difference if the publisher and/or the original oploader were a resident of your country? Suppose that, instead of pursuing unlicensed users, the publishers wished to enter into contracts licensing the communication of *Le grand secret* over digital networks. How do private international law considerations affect the drafting of the contracts?

J.M.B. SEIGNETTE:

Potential plaintiffs:
1. the French publisher,
2. the owner of the publishing rights for the Dutch territory, and
3. the owner of the publishing rights in other countries (extraterritorial injunctions).

Potential defendants:
1. French entrepreneur of the Cyberspace café,
2. Internet access provider France,
3. Internet access provider US, and
4. local access providers (on-line services) Netherlands.

Jurisdiction

In order the find out whether the court has jurisdiction, we have to look at the European Execution Treaty (EEX) or the jurisdiction rules of the Dutch Code of Civil Procedure. Jurisdiction in respect of the *local access providers in the Netherlands* is established by the main rule of the Treaty that defendants have to be sued before the court of the country of their domicile (article 2). To determine whether the providers are domiciled in the Netherlands, we have to look at the Dutch law (article 53 EEX: domicile is seat of the corporation. Law of forum determines the seat). Section 2:10 Civil Code provides that a legal entity has domicile in the place of incorporation.

In respect of the *French entrepreneur* and the *French Internet access provider*, jurisdiction may probably be established by articles 5(3) and perhaps also by article 6(1) of the Treaty. Article 5(3) provides that, in case of an unlawful act (act of tort), the defendant who has domicile in a Treaty country can be sued before the court of the country in which the act that caused damage took place (*'lieu ou le fait dommageable s'est produit'*). The European Court of Justice has held that this provision also creates jurisdiction for the court of the country where the damage occurs if the unlawful act takes place in a different country (judgment of 30 November 1976, case 21/76). It is not fully clear however whether this also creates jurisdiction in case of injunction proceedings aimed at preventing damage from occurring. Article 6(1) provides that, if there is more than one defendant, the defendants may be sued before the court of the country of domicile of one of these defendants. This provision may also create jurisdiction in respect of the claims of the French entrepreneur and provider. However, according to the European Court of Justice, it is necessary that the claims against the defendants are connected in the sense that separate procedures against the defendants would lead to irreconcilable judgments (judgment of 27 September 1988, case 198/87). The question is whether this is the case here, where the involvement of the Dutch access providers is of a different nature than the involvement of the French access providers.

Can the *US Internet access provider* be sued before a Dutch court? If the provider is incorporated in the US, we have to look at the Dutch Code of Civil Procedure to determine whether the court has jurisdiction. Section 126(3) of the Code might perhaps serve to create jurisdiction. According to this provision, a plaintiff with domicile in the Netherlands can sue a foreign company before a Dutch court. If the Dutch licensee of the French publishers is willing to act as co-plaintiff, section 126(3) j° 126(5) might create jurisdiction. However, given the trouble of summoning a US company before a Dutch court, and also of enforcing the judgment in the US, the publishers may decide not to sue the US access provider at all, at least not if they seek for a quick remedy.

Aside from the above, the Dutch court in principle is competent to take conservatory or preliminary measures (article 24 EEX). This means that Dutch courts can impose preliminary injunctions or grant permission for seizure even if a foreign court would have jurisdiction under the normal rules. Note that the scope of article 24 EEX in respect of summary proceedings in the Netherlands *('kort geding')* is presently before the European Court of Justice, following questions from the Dutch Supreme Court (*Hoge Raad* 8 December 1995, *RvdW* 1995, 262C). If it is unlikely that a preliminary or conservatory measure can actually be executed in a particular country, the court must refrain from ordering that measure in respect of that country. In addition, section 764 j° 767 Code of Civil Procedure creates jurisdiction for Dutch courts to hear cases in which the plaintiff has laid attachment in the Netherlands in respect of a claim against a foreign party.

Is it worthwhile to litigate before a Dutch court?

Injunctions

If infringement in several countries has been established, it is, in principle, possible under Dutch law to obtain an injunction for the territory of these countries (Supreme Court of the Netherlands, 24 November 1989, *NJ* 1992, 404, annotation D.W.F. Verkade). The underlying idea is that right holders should not be obliged to sue in each separate country in case of transfrontier infringements. However, courts will be reluctant to impose an injunction for the territory of another country if they feel they are not in a position to determine whether an infringement has taken place in that other country. In case of summary proceedings, courts furthermore will have to refrain from imposing injunctions for other countries if it is unlikely that they can actually be enforced.

Wavin/Pipe Liners: plaintiff wants injunction for all sister companies arguing that if the injunction would only extend to the Dutch territory, the companies in the other countries would continue the unlawful activities. Court: injunction for the Netherlands, Germany, England, France, Denmark, Norway, Sweden and Austria justified in view of the relationship between the defendants, their related activities, and the fact that all parties are domiciled in Brussels Convention countries (Court of Appeals, 16 January 1992, *BIE* 1993, 9). In a case about imitation furniture cloth designs sold by a Dutch company in the Netherlands from its wharehouse in Germany, the Court of Appeals of Arnhem denied an injunction for the German territory. Since the plaintiff had announced that the defendant would also be sued before a German court and because the court was not certain whether the designs would qualify for copyright protection under German law, the court thought it best to avoid contradictory judgments and leave it up to the German court to decide. According to the court, the injunction for the Dutch territory did, however, include the production and storage outside the Netherlands of goods for the Dutch market (Court of Appeals Arnhem, 29 June 1993, *BIE* 1995, 440).

In this (hypothetical) case, the plaintiffs will want the court to order the defendants to take the work from the Net. This in fact would mean a worldwide injunction. The question is whether courts are willing to grant such a worldwide injunction for Internet.

Damages

In this case, in which the work is not made available to the public from a location in the Netherlands, it is doubtful whether the Dutch court would consider itself competent to decide on a claim for recovery of damage suffered in other countries. I refer to a decision of the European Court of Justice in a defamation case. The European Court of Justice held that if a defamating article has been published in several countries and the plaintiff alleges to have suffered damage in these countries, the court of each of these countries is competent to hear a claim with respect to its own country. If, however, the plaintiff wants the court to hear a claim with respect to damage suffered in all countries, he or she will have to go to the court of the country from which the article originated or the court of the country of domicile of the publisher. The court added that the question whether there is damage and what evidence is required to prove the existence and scope of the damage, must be determined according to the law applicable according to the rules of private international law of the forum country, provided these rules do not undermine the advantageous effects of the Treaty. (7 March 1995, case C-68/93, *Ars Aequi* 44 (1995) 11, p. 880, annotation P. Vlas.)

Applicable law

How will the Dutch court decide whether the acts of the defendants are unlawful and, consequently, whether there is cause for an injunction and/or damages? To determine whether the act of making the work available on the Net constitutes a copyright infringement, the Dutch court will have to take into account article 5(2) of the Berne Convention: the scope of protection and the remedies available must be determined according to the law of the country where protection is claimed. Which is the country where protection is claimed in this case? Is it the Netherlands as country of reception or is it France or the US as countries of transmission? I would argue that the country of protection is the country where the plaintiff does not want the work to be made available to the public. If this is the Netherlands, Dutch law must be applied.

If copyright infringement has been established, the question arises which of the defendants can be held responsible for it (*i.e.* directly in the sense that they actually performed the copyright infringement, or indirectly in the sense that their acts contributed to the infringement taking place). This question must be answered according to the general rules of Dutch private international law regarding torts. The general rule in this matter is that the *lex loci delicti* applies. (See Supreme Court of the Netherlands, judgment of 19 November 1993, *NJ* 1994, 622.)

What is the *locus delicti* in this case? This question depends on what the alleged unlawful act is. This must be answered for each defendant individually.

Contractual arrangements

To enhance security, the parties can make a choice of law in their contract. This choice of law will, in principle, be recognized by the Dutch court. However, the choice of law cannot set aside domestic rules of priority (rules of immediate application). It furthermore is unclear whether a choice of law can set aside provisions in the Berne Convention prescribing which law is exclusively applicable, as is the case with respect to:
- the scope of protection and remedies available: law of the country where protection is sought (article 5(2) BC);
- the protection in the country of origin: domestic law (article 5(3) BC);
- the means of redress for safeguarding the moral rights granted by article 6*bis*: law of the country where protection is sought (article 6(2) BC);
- the term of protection: law of country where protection is sought (article 7(8) BC);
- the copyright ownership of cinematographic works: law of the country where protection is sought (article 14*bis*(2)(a) BC).

It furthermore is unclear under Dutch law to what extent a choice of law regarding authorship, first copyright ownership, transferability and the scope of transfers would be recognized.

Scope of protection

Where does the relevant act take place? Anywhere in the world? This would mean that the parties have to take into account the copyright laws of all countries.

Interventions

W. CORNISH:

Whatever the scope of the territoriality principle in solving conflicts of law concerning intellectual property, one reason for its near universal acceptance is that it provides an approach which can be applied as much to industrial property (patents, trademarks and so on) as to authors' rights and neighbouring rights. Of course, it would be conceivable that conflict rules should vary from one type of intellectual property to another; and the margins it may be possible to draw upon the differing rationales of the rights in order to do exactly that. But for the most part, in all legal systems they are likely to be treated alike. Since in some cases (notably patents) they are concerned with the encouragement of national economic growth, they are likely to be the subject of intense national rivalries. The territoriality principle, which ties liability for infringement strictly to the place of action, has a moderating effect on their jealousies. The importance of that needs to be kept clearly in mind.

Recognition of the virtue of territoriality has long had a place in the private international law of British Commonwealth countries. Traditionally, they followed a conflicts rule for the whole field of torts which required a demonstration of actionability, both in the territory where the wrong was committed, and under the *lex forum*. The ultimate purpose of this strict choice of law rule was to allow application of the local law to events which occurred outside the jurisdiction. In the field of intellectual property this was in principle an abrogation of strict territoriality, and to hold it in check some courts added a separate jurisdictional limitation: actions for infringements of patents, trademarks and copyright were in character local, rather than transitory, and so could be litigated only in the country where the wrong occurred.

It should be noted that, at least in the United Kingdom, the choice of law rule leased upon double actionability has now been replaced by a presumptive rule favouring the application of the *lex loci protectionis* (Private International Law (Miscellaneous Provisions) Act 1995, Part III). That reinforcement of the prime significance of territoriality comes at a vital juncture. What remains quite uncertain is how far the 'local action' impediment to jurisdiction remains operative, particularly when the countries concerned are subject to the Brussels or Lugano Conventions. The question is now extremely lively, given the propensity of Dutch courts to grant cross-border injunctions in *kort geding* proceedings, and the possible willingness of other countries to enforce these orders. Given the sensitivities which I have already alluded to, there is good reason to doubt the wisdom of the juridical bravado in the field of intellectual property.

G. Koumantos:

J'ai demandé le parole pour clarifier un point et pour en souligner un autre. Le point qui je voudrais clarifier est le suivant. Je n'ai jamais soutenu que, en cas de délit, il faudrait appliquer le droit du pays d'origine. J'ai dit que ce droit est applicable aux questions qui relèvent spécifiquement du droit d'auteur (titularité, transmissibilité, durée, limitations etc.). En ce qui concerne le délit, ses conditions et ses conséquences, c'est la loi du lieu du délit (acte délictueux ou dommages).

Le deuxième point est plus important. Il serait bien sûr difficile d'appliquer à un délit les quelques 180 ou 200 droits qui existent dans le monde. Mais il ne faudrait pas exagérer la portée de cette difficulté. En effet, les différentes lois nationales ne different pas tellement sur la réglementation des délits. Ce qui est beaucoup plus difficile, voire même impossible, c'est le calcul du dommage subi dans l'ensemble des pays du monde. Comment voulez-vous savoir quel dommage subit en Malaisie ou à Singapour un auteur par l'injection de son oeuvre dans un réseau? Mais ce problème est beaucoup plus général car l'évaluation du dommage subi, même si elle est limitée à un seul pays et même si ce pays est le pays du juge, est extrêmement difficile et cette difficulté peut annuler la protection prévue par la loi. C'est pourquoi l'ALAI devrait inventer un système de dédommagement forfaitaire pour les atteintes aux droits d'auteur. Je pense que ce problème mérite d'être examiné de façon plus approfondie et, peut-être, faire l'objet d'une réunion de l'ALAI qui conduirait à des propositions concrètes. Si mon regard est tourné vers le président de l'ALAI, c'est pour attirer son attention sur cette suggestion.

IV

Provisions on circumvention of technical protection devices

Les dispositions tendant à interdire les appareils à contourner les mesures techniques anti-copie

Le droit d'auteur et protections techniques

A. Lucas[*]

L'intitulé du rapport *("Les dispositifs tendant à interdire les appareils à contourner les mesures techniques anti-copie")* apparaît, à la reflexion, trop étroit. D'abord, les protections techniques ne se limitent pas aux mesures anti-copie (précision qui n'apparaît d'ailleurs pas dans le titre en anglais, qui vise les *"technical protection devices"*). Ensuite, le concept même de protection est probablement un peu réducteur. Il fait penser spontanément aux interdictions ou restrictions que doit souffrir le "consommateur", quant à l'accès à l'oeuvre ou quant à son utilisation. Mais, à côté de cette police "défensive", il y a toutes les autres applications tendant à l'amélioration de la gestion de l'information relative aux oeuvres et aux droits. Enfin, il ne s'agit pas seulement, en dépit de ce que peut laisser supposer l'intitulé du sujet, de décrire et d'analyser les dispositions existantes ou futures concernant le contournement des dispositifs de protection. Il s'agit aussi, au-delà, de mesurer l'incidence de ces protections techniques sur le droit d'auteur. C'est donc cette approche large qui sera retenue dans le présent rapport.

Précisions que si l'accent est mis sur le droit d'auteur, la plupart des observations qui suivent valent, sauf précision contraire, pour les droits voisins. L'idée de protéger par des moyens techniques les oeuvres littéraires et artistiques n'est pas nouvelle (les chaînes cryptées de télévision ne datent pas d'hier). Elle a pris une ampleur particulière avec le Livre blanc américain de septembre 1995[1] et constitue l'un des thèmes essentiels des négociations actuellement en cours sur l'éventuel protocole relatif à la Convention de Berne ainsi que sur l'éventuel instrument relatif à la protection des droits des artistes interprètes ou exécutants et des producteurs de phonogrammes.

Bien entendu, la réflexion menée s'inscrit dans un contexte plus large. La sécurité des réseaux n'intéresse pas seulement la propriété intellectuelle. Elle est l'affaire de tous les opérateurs et de tous ceux qui, à un titre quelconque, traitent d'informations "sensibles": les militaires, les policiers, les banquiers, et même les médecins et les avocats.[2] C'est qu'en effet la volatilité de l'information, de toute information, la rend vulnérable. Si l'on n'y prend garde, le constat peut d'ailleurs compromettre le succès du grand chantier des autoroutes de l'information. Il est clair par exemple que le grand public n'acceptera d'y circuler que si les opérateurs sont capables d'assurer la confidentialité des communications privées, sans se contenter du pari optimiste que le flot des informations diffusées suffit à en garantir l'anonymat. Plus important encore, le développement des réseaux passe par une sécurité des moyens de

---

[*] Professeur à la Faculté de droit de Nantes

paiement qui n'est pas encore acquise. La Commission européenne a pris la mesure de ces enjeux dans le Livre vert qu'elle a spécialement consacré, en mars 1996, à la protection juridique des signaux cryptés.

Même en s'en tenant à la diffusion des oeuvres, les intérêts des titulaires de droits ne sont pas seuls en cause. Il faut tenir compte en effet de ceux des "fournisseurs de services", qui ne sont pas nécessairement les mêmes. Les titulaires souhaitent obtenir une maîtrise juridique aussi complète que possible, alors que, comme le note le rapport français, les fournisseurs de services se préoccupent surtout de "fidéliser" leur clientèle (à quoi peut contribuer, comme le note le rapport canadien, le cryptage), afin de conjurer le risque d'une évaporation de leurs investissements, et se soucient moins du sort de l'oeuvre, dès lors qu'ils ont l'assurance que leur client fera encore appel à eux.[3]

Les deux aspects sont souvent mélangés, la propriété intellectuelle étant présentée comme le moyen juridique de protéger les investissements des fournisseurs de services. Même si elle n'est pas toujours clairement exprimée, l'idée sous-jacente est que le droit d'auteur protège le service de lui-même, envisagé comme un "produit informationnel". C'est une confusion regrettable. Certes, une fois numérisées, toutes les oeuvres se présentent sous la forme de données brutes. Mais le droit d'auteur saisit les oeuvres elles-mêmes, dans leur réalité analogique, non des données, dans leur état numérique, ni des produits informationnels.[4] Or, toutes les informations ne sont pas des oeuvres et ce n'est que par une approche exagérément réductrice qu'on peut ramener les oeuvres à des informations.[5]

Il n'est évidemment pas possible, dans le cadre de ce rapport, de décrire par le menu les techniques mises en oeuvre. Elles sont diverses, faisant appel surtout au logiciel, éventuellement "encapsulé" dans du matériel. Les rapports nationaux attestent au demeurant d'un véritable bouillonnement qui incite à la prudence celui qui se hasarde à rendre compte d'une réalité aussi évolutive.[6] Le principe de base est celui du codage de l'information, à partir duquel peuvent être déclinées d'innombrables applications.

L'essentiel, pour le juriste, est de profiter du très relatif répit que donnent les expériences actuelles pour mener une rélexion critique sur le nouveau paysage du droit d'auteur que dessinent les protections techniques en voie d'être mises au point et sur les solutions juridiques à imaginer pour que ce paysage s'ordonne harmonieusement.

La problématique est toute simple: la technique menace le droit d'auteur (constat classique), mais elle peut venir à son secours (constat également classique), tout en le transformant (idée plus neuve qui mérite d'être creusée), à condition d'être encadrée par le droit en général et par le droit d'auteur en particulier. Je montrerai donc successivement comment les protections techniques sont mises au service du droit d'auteur (I) et comment le droit doit se mettre à leur service (c'est-à-dire quel régime juridique il convient de leur appliquer) (II).

I. **Les protections techniques au service du droit d'auteur**

Une première question s'impose qui est de savoir quelles sont les possibilités offertes par la technique (a). Mais, au-delà de ce bilan, une autre vient à l'esprit qui est d'imaginer quelles seront les incidences de ces innovations sur le droit d'auteur (b).

a. *Les possibilités offertes par la technique*

Les rapporteurs nationaux[7] ont été d'abord invités à décrire ce qui a été fait jusqu'à maintenant chez eux. La moisson a été abondante. Il est impossible d'en rendre compte de manière exhaustive dans ce rapport. Une telle description serait d'ailleurs fastidieuse. Le rapporteur général est davantage dans son rôle en tentant une synthèse. Ce qu'on appelle "protection" doit, on l'a vu, être pris au sens large et, ramené au champ du droit d'auteur et des droits voisins, renvoie à deux séries de préoccupations: il s'agit d'abord de réduire la liberté de mouvement de l'utilisateur (du "consommateur" dans la terminologie détestable à la mode) des oeuvres en organisant la police de l'accès ou de l'utilisation, il s'agit ensuite de mieux gérer les droits en traitant l'information pertinente dans de bonnes conditions de sécurité. Les deux choses sont évidemment liées, mais la distinction reste utile.

(1) *La police de l'accès ou de l'utilisation*

Le titulaire des droits peut d'abord contrôler l'accès à l'oeuvre. Par exemple, il subordonnera cet accès à la fourniture d'un mot de passe ou à l'observation d'autres procédures d'identification et d'authentification. Ou bien encore il utilisera des techniques de cryptage.[8] Celles-ci sont elles-mêmes diverses. Dans le système à clé privée, c'est la même clé qui est utilisée pour à la fois crypter et décrypter. On parle de cryptographie symétrique. Dans le système de clé publique, la donnée est cryptée avec la clé publique qui est disponible pour les souscripteurs, mais seule une personne ayant la clé privée peut décrypter. On parle de cryptographie asymétrique. On peut même imaginer un système à clés multiples réparties entre des dépositaires différents. Ces techniques permettent aussi de limiter l'accès, par exemple à certaines heures, à certaines parties des oeuvres ou à certaines personnes.[9]

Le titulaire des droits peut par ailleurs souhaiter limiter la liberté de mouvement de l'utilisateur ayant accédé à l'oeuvre. Il s'agira par exemple d'interdire la copie ou de limiter le nombre de copies,[10] ou plus généralement de limiter l'usage de l'oeuvre.[11] Il s'agira aussi d'authentifier et de garantir l'intégrité des oeuvres. Tel est le but de la "signature digitale", combinaison de procédés d'identification de l'expéditeur et de vérification de l'intégrité de son message qui va servir à authentifier une oeuvre, à la fois quant à l'identité de celui qui a authentifié et quant au contenu authentifié.[12] La cryptographie peut, là encore, être mise à profit.[13] A défaut de limiter directement l'usage, il sera ainsi au moins possible d'en conserver une trace.

Le bilan, on le voit, est riche. Mais il faut s'interroger sur l'opportunité de cette "police technique". Deux objections viennent à l'esprit. D'abord, l'efficacité des techniques citées n'est pas à l'abri des attaques des maniaques du "déplombage".

Certaines n'offrent même qu'une sécurité illusoire. Le rapport américain relève par exemple à juste titre que le contrôle de l'accès par le mot de passe n'est pas très sûr, dès lors qu'on ne peut savoir qui connaît ledit mot de passe. De plus, on peut s'attendre à ce que les utilisateurs ne voient pas d'un bon oeil ces marques de défiance. Le rapport allemand cite à cet égard le précédent des logiciels (et notamment l'expérience Lotus en 1989), qui montre que les consommateurs n'aiment pas être traités en pirates potentiels. Le rapport canadien se montre pour cette raison réservé sur les limitations d'accès.[14]

Ces objections, qui expliquent les réticences exprimées lors des auditions organisées sur ce thème par la Commission européenne en janvier 1996,[15] ne sont peut-être pas, à vrai dire, décisives. D'une part, on peut répondre avec les rapporteurs belges que même si la protection technique n'est pas imparable, l'important est qu'elle décourage les pirates, en compliquant leur besogne, et limite ainsi les risques. D'autre part, il faut souhaiter que les utilisateurs eux-mêmes comprennent que, dans un environnement numérique qui accroît la volatilité des informations, la diffusion des oeuvres passe par ces parades.

Il reste que l'arme doit être utilisée avec discernement. D'ailleurs, toutes les techniques citées ne sont pas promises au même avenir. Seules s'imposeront celles qui rallieront les suffrages de l'ensemble des intéressés (ayants-droit, fabricants de matériels, diffuseurs et opérateurs de réseaux). Il semble que l'unanimité soit facile à réaliser sur les dispositifs permettant de limiter le nombre de copies. Mais d'autres solutions peuvent prêter à discussion. Le rapport canadien indique par exemple que le Sous-comité compétent a suggéré un système anti-copie faisant diminuer la qualité à chaque copie.[16] On peut toutefois se demander si le remède, qui consiste au fond à utiliser les ressources des techniques numériques pour revenir aux imperfections du monde analogique, ne risque pas de provoquer un nouveau mal en mettant en cause l'intégrité de l'oeuvre.

(2) La gestion des droits

Il faut commencer par identifier les oeuvres (ainsi que les prestations et les enregistrements) par un codage interne (inséparablement lié à l'oeuvre, dès l'origine) ou externe (rajouté postérieurement). Beaucoup de travaux sont menés dans cette voie, dont font état les rapports nationaux. L'ambition, affichée notamment par le Livre vert européen, est d'aboutir à une identification systématique, en partant de l'expérience acquise pour l'identification des supports tels que les livres (numéro ISBN) et les phonogrammes (numéro ISRC). La France pour sa part a déjà fait admettre, en association avec les milieux professionnels et avec l'Association internationale de normalisation (ISO), le principe d'une inscription de caractères identifiants dans deux normes: la norme JPEG *(Joint Photographic information coding Experts Group)* pour l'image animée en qualité télévision.[17] Sur cette base, elle suggère l'adoption d'un système d'identification "universelle et univoque". Le projet de codification le plus avancé est le CIS *(Common Information System)*, mis en oeuvre par la CISAC en liaison avec d'autres organisations internationales de titulaires de droits, qui a l'ambition d'identifier de façon uniforme au niveau mondial et de repérer les oeuvres, les ayants-droit et les supports d'oeuvres. Une fois l'oeuvre identifiée, il est possible de suivre à la trace les "consommations" et d'automatiser la gestion des droits, le cas échéant en offrant aux utilisateurs la possibilité d'utiliser les systèmes de facturation mis en oeuvre sur le réseau.[18]

Les techniques utilisées peuvent faire appel, là encore, au cryptage. Mais il n'est même pas forcément nécessaire de crypter le message (pour le rendre inintelligible), il suffit de le marquer (pour le rendre imperceptible). Tel est l'objet de la stégano-graphie qui permet d'attacher à l'information un message concourant à garantir l'authentification.[19] Il s'agit de coder l'information numérisée avec des attributs qui ne peuvent pas être dissociés du fichier qui contient cette information. On s'est aussi référé au concept de *"digital fingerprinting"* ou de *"digital watermarking"*.[20] Grâce à ces techniques, il est possible d'incruster des messages cachés dans les données numérisées. Le message, sorte de "bruit subliminal",[21] n'est pas affecté par les manipulations qu'implique la circulation sur le réseau (compression, décompres-sion, codage). Il est donc difficile à contourner, ce qui explique qu'on ait pu l'assimiler à un "tag indélébile".[22] L'accord est, cette fois, unanime sur l'intérêt pour les titulaires de droits de ces techniques. C'est par elles que passe notamment la rénovation de la gestion collective, ce qui explique que la CISAC joue un rôle décisif dans ce domaine.

Il y a cependant un parti à prendre sur la nature des informations à faire circuler. Le Livre blanc américain paraît assez ambitieux sur ce point puisqu'il envisage de renseigner l'usager sur la paternité, la titularité des droits, la date de création, la dernière version, les usages autorisés, les contreparties exigées.[23] Le Livre vert européen est plus circonspect, qui se borne à constater[24] que la question est controversée, certains plaidant pour une limitation de l'information aux oeuvres elles-mêmes, à l'exclusion de l'identification des ayants-droit et des conditions de licence. Cette prudence n'est pas sans fondement. Il faut en effet s'assurer que l'information fournie reste pertinente, faute de quoi le remède serait pire que le mal.[25] On peut donc se demander s'il ne serait pas plus réaliste, en l'état de la technique, de se contenter d'un code universel unique sommaire renvoyant pour de plus amples informations sur les droits à des bases de données qui pourraient, elles, être mises à jour. Cela bien entendu ne dispenserait pas les exploitants d'indiquer le nom de l'auteur lors de tout acte d'exploitation (afin de respecter le droit moral).

b. *Les incidences sur le droit d'auteur*

Les protections techniques sommairement analysées ci-dessus vont changer le paysage du droit d'auteur, non seulement en facilitant son exercice, mais aussi en transformant son contenu.

(1) *L'exercice du droit*

L'effet principal, le plus spectaculaire, des protections techniques est de renforcer l'exclusivité juridique par une exclusivité technique, bref de garantir l'effectivité du droit exclusif. L'observation vaut d'abord pour les droits patrimoniaux. Les restrictions à l'accès ou à l'utilisation permettent de faire coller le fait au droit. La possibilité de suivre les oeuvres à la trace en rapportant plus facilement la preuve des violations va dans le même sens. Ceci est évidemment de nature à rassurer les titulaires de droits qui répugnent, comme le note le rapport canadien, à donner le "chèque en blanc" qu'implique a priori, en l'état, l'exploitation numérique.

Mais la technique vient également au secours du droit moral, lui-même menacé par les techniques numériques. La fonction "signature électronique" pourra, par exemple, garantir l'exercice effectif du droit à la paternité et du droit au respect de l'oeuvre. La modernisation de la gestion concourt aussi à l'effectivité du droit exclusif en même temps qu'elle peut contribuer à réduire les coûts de transaction.[26] De plus, la meilleure connaissance des utilisations devrait normalement permettre une tarification plus "fine", ce qui ne peut que renforcer la légitimité du droit.

Il est bien difficile de prévoir quelle sera l'incidence des protections techniques sur le mode de gestion. Les systèmes d'identification et de marquage des oeuvres peuvent permettre un contrôle individuel plus efficace. Mais les perspectives de reproduction et de diffusion subséquentes rendent problématique la gestion individuelle, de sorte qu'il est raisonnable de prévoir qu'un nouveau champ s'ouvre à une gestion collective renouvelée.

(2) *Le contenu du droit*

Au-delà de ces considérations pratiques, il est opportun d'examiner les incidences sur le droit d'auteur lui-même des protections techniques (qui ne peuvent être complètement neutres). On écartera sans hésitation la thèse selon laquelle la conjonction des protections techniques et des contrats annonce la mort du droit d'auteur.[27] Outre que toute protection technique est fragile, le contrat ne peut être opposé aux tiers. Pour conjurer le risque de la dissémination, la meilleure solution reste celle de la propriété intellectuelle, c'est-à-dire du droit exclusif. Les rapports allemand, canadien et néerlandais se prononcent clairement en ce sens.

En revanche, la question se pose par exemple de savoir s'il n'est pas opportun de revenir sur des exceptions consenties à regret sous l'empire de nécessités techniques qui n'apparaissent plus de mise dans l'environnement numérique. Dans les systèmes de droit d'auteur continental, on se demandera par exemple si l'exception de copie privée mérite d'être maintenue à partir du moment où la technique permet d'exercer un contrôle efficace sur toutes les copies réalisées. La raison de douter vient de ce que ces exceptions devraient, en toute logique, être d'interprétation stricte au regard du principe qu'est l'exclusivité du droit. Le problème, il est vrai, se pose en des termes différents dans les systèmes de *copyright* dans lesquels les droits des utilisateurs sont conçus dans une optique moins restrictive et peuvent même avoir une dimension constitutionnelle.

Il semble bien aussi que les réseaux conduisent à affiner la distinction traditionnelle entre sphère privée, soustraite à l'emprise du droit exclusif et sphère publique. Par exemple, on peut se demander s'il n'y a pas quelque artifice à assimiler un courrier électronique non crypté à une correspondance privée relevant de ce que le droit français[28] et le droit américain[29] appellent le "cercle de famille" apparaît à cet égard bien venue. Certes, on admet traditionnellement en France qu'elle ne doit pas être prise au pied de la lettre, ce qui permet d'étendre la dérogation à des représentations organisées pour des amis sans lien de parenté, mais à condition qu'il s'agisse de "familiers".[30] C'est-à-dire qu'il ne suffit pas qu'une communication soit privée au sens du droit des télécommunications pour qu'elle puisse s'affranchir du droit d'auteur. Et il n'y a pas de raison de rompre avec cette logique d'interprétation restrictive. Bien avant l'ère des réseaux, Desbois[31] dénonçait la tentation d'utiliser le "cercle de famille" pour "des manoeuvres obliques, sous le prétexte de l'inviolabilité des domiciles ou des lieux privés". L'avertissement vaut pour l'inviolabilité des correspondances. On ne saurait tolérer que les "Internautes" prétendent appartenir à une même "famille" pour tenir en échec le droit exclusif. En réalité, le vecteur utilisé n'implique ni véritable confidentialité ni familiarité.

On peut également regarder d'un oeil neuf le problème de la loi applicable à l'acte de diffusion sur les réseaux. On sait qu'en matière de satellite, la solution retenue par la Directive européenne du 27 septembre 1993 consiste à appliquer la loi du pays d'injection, c'est-à-dire du pays dans le territoire duquel est émis le signal montant vers le satellite. L'un des arguments décisifs en faveur de cette solution est que la radiodiffusion par satellite correspond à un "processus unique" qu'il est logique de localiser au lieu où il débute, solution d'ailleurs plus réaliste que celle consistant à imposer le respect des lois de tous les pays de l'empreinte du satellite.[32] Mais la situation est différente si la technique permet une interactivité "modulant" à volonté la diffusion du signal, comme cela semble devoir être le cas sur les autoroutes de l'information, et l'on n'a donc plus de raison de systématiser l'application de la loi du pays d'injection, dont on sait qu'elle porte en germe le risque de "délocalisations" redoutables pour la cause des auteurs et des titulaires de droits voisins.[33]

II. **Le droit au service des protections techniques**

Comme l'observe le rapport allemand, la technique peut aider à résoudre les problèmes qu'elle pose, toute l'histoire du droit d'auteur témoignant de cette interaction. Que peut-on attendre du droit en pareille matière? D'abord, une certaine neutralité, qui laisse sa chance à la technique (a), ensuite un encouragement à travers un encadrement juridique adéquat (b).

a. *La neutralité du droit*

Le moins qu'on puisse attendre est que le droit n'entrave pas la mise en oeuvre des protections techniques. Cela suppose en premier lieu que les moyens de cryptage ne soient pas pourchassés comme illicites, c'est-à-dire qu'ils soient de libre utilisation (à tout le moins pour ce type d'application). Tel n'est pas le cas actuellement dans certains pays, comme les États-Unis et la France où ils font l'objet de restrictions.[34] La raison de cette méfiance est toute simple. Le pouvoir pratique le secret, mais apprécie peu que les particuliers se mêlent de jouer la même partition indéchiffrable, et appelle spontanément à la rescousse l'ordre public. Cela ressemble fort, à vrai dire, à un combat d'arrière-garde.[35] Beaucoup pensent en effet que les nécessités de la répression pénale seraient suffisamment prises en compte par le dépôt de clés auprès de tiers autorisés (même si ce système de "notariat électronique" est pratiquement difficile à mettre au point). Il y a fort à parier, dans ce contexte, que les restrictions légales ne tarderont pas à disparaître. C'est ce qui est annoncé en tout cas pour les États-Unis et la France.[36] Cela ne signifie pas bien sûr que les utilisateurs de ces procédés puissent s'affranchir de toute contrainte juridique. Le risque d'une atteinte à la vie privée découlant de systèmes retraçant très (trop) fidèlement les consommations a par exemple été souligné,[37] et il appartiendra aux intéressés de prendre les mesures propres à éviter les dérives. Au moins doit-il être clair que les techniques en cause sont de libre utilisation (sous réserve, bien sûr, des droits de propriété intellectuelle que peuvent eux-mêmes invoquer les concepteurs).[38] Il convient également que le contournement ne soit pas légitimé par le droit.

Deux moyens peuvent être opposés à la mise en oeuvre de protections techniques: le droit à l'information et le droit d'auteur lui-même (ou plutôt les droits reconnus, directement ou indirectement, à l'utilisateur par la loi sur le droit d'auteur). Sur le premier point, il n'est pas question de soutenir que le droit à l'information interdit par principe les protections techniques.[39] A ce compte, la diffusion de programmes cryptés serait intrinsèquement illicite.[40] Le problème ne se poserait que si l'exploitant était le seul à pouvoir diffuser l'information en cause. Ce n'est pas inimaginable.[41] Il en résulterait une position dominante dont l'exercice abusif pourrait être critiqué sur le terrain du droit de la concurrence.[42] Mais c'est un cas particulier. D'ailleurs, si l'on distingue bien oeuvre et information, on doit pouvoir concilier la protection des oeuvres et l'accès à l'information. Car la liberté d'accéder aux informations n'implique pas le libre accès aux oeuvres. Un tableau, par exemple, ne saurait sans artifice être ramené à une information à laquelle on pourrait par principe exiger d'accéder.

Pour ce qui est du droit d'auteur, la question se pose du fait que son champ d'application est limité et qu'il tolère, en toute hypothèse, des exceptions. En résulte-t-il des droits que les utilisateurs potentiels pourraient faire valoir pour paralyser licitement les protections techniques? Ou peut-on admettre au contraire que des protections techniques restreignent l'accès à des oeuvres (ou à des parties d'oeuvres) que ne sont pas protégées (ou que ne le sont plus, la protection étant arrivée à son terme), ou qu'elles paralysent les dérogations légales? Tout dépend en vérité du parti que l'on rend sur le fondement de la réglementation applicable aux protections techniques. La question sera pour cette raison traitée plus loin.

b. *L'encouragement du droit*

Une bonne façon d'oeuvrer au développement des protections techniques serait de les rendre obligatoires. Le précédent de l'*Audio Home Recording Act* américain de 1992, imposant aux fabricants de matériel d'enregistrement numérique audio et d'interface audio d'incorporer le système SCMS,[43] mérite à cet égard d'être cité. On notera également que l'article 59 de la loi grecque sur le droit d'auteur de 1993 prévoit que des décrets peuvent fixer des normes applicables aux appareils ou à tout matériel de reproduction, de façon à empêcher ou à limiter leur utilisation à des fins portant atteinte à l'exploitation normale du droit d'auteur ou des drois voisins.[44] Le rapporteur néerlandais va plus loin en n'écartant pas l'idée de refuser le droit d'agir en justice au titulaire qui aurait négligé de prendre ces mesures à la portée de tous. Cependant, l'opinion dominante est que l'introduction des systèmes de protection doit se faire sur une base volontaire de la part de l'industrie et des titulaires de droits.[45] Certains rapports nationaux ont mentionné le rôle que pouvait jouer à cet égard l'OMPI.[46] Mais il n'est pas dit que des solutions plus contraignantes ne verront pas le jour. Le Livre vert de la Commission européenne ne l'exclut pas, précisant[47] que le défaut d'harmonisation des législations des États-membres dans ce domaine est de nature à susciter des entraves aux échanges.

La question essentielle est celle des sanctions à édicter contre ceux qui contourneraient les protections techniques. L'opportunité de ces sanctions n'est pas discutée par les rapports nationaux. Tous les projects vont en ce sens. Mais on ne peut faire l'économie d'une réflexion préalable sur le fondement de ces sanctions. Il y a, on l'a vu, deux approches possibles: celle qui fonde l'intervention du législateur sur la nécessité de protéger le droit d'auteur et les droits voisins, et celle qui tient que les protections techniques doivent être défendues par la loi en dehors de toute référence à la propriété intellectuelle. La première thèse est très majoritaire. C'est elle qui est retenue par le projet américain,[48] qui suggère d'insérer dans la loi sur le droit d'auteur un article 1201 ainsi conçu: *"No person shall import, manufacture or distribute any device, product, or component incorporated into a device or product, or offer or perform any service, the primary purpose or effect of which is to avoid, bypass, remove, deactivate, or otherwise circumvent, without the authority of the copyright owner or the law, any process, treatment, mechanism or system which prevents or inhibits the violation of any of the exclusive rights of the copyright owner under section 106"*.[49]

C'est également sur ce terrain que se situe la proposition de la Commission européenne et des États-membres dans le cadre des négociations sur l'éventuel protocole relatif à la Convention de Berne:[50] *"Contracting Parties shall make unlawfull, and provide for appropriate remedies against the manufacture, distribution and possession for commercial purposes of any device, means or product, by any person knowing or having reasonable grounds to know that it is primary purpose or primary effect is to remove, deactivate or circumvent, without authority, any process, mechanism or system which is designed to prevent or inhibit the infringement of any of the rights under the Berne Convention or this Protocol"*.[51] Dans l'un ct l'autre cas, il est bien clair que les sanctions ne sont encourues que si le contournement permet de violer le droit d'auteur ou les droits voisins. Ainsi, la proposition américaine prend soin d'en écarter l'application en présence d'une autorisation du titulaire des droits ou de la loi.[52] Le texte suggéré par la Commission aboutit, semble-t-il, au même résultat en précisant que seul est incriminé le contournement réalisé *"without authority"*.[53] C'est bien en ce sens que se prononcent les rapports allemand, américain, canadien, italien et néerlandais.

Deux arguments de valeur inégale peuvent être avancés à l'appui de cette analyse. D'abord, on peut être tenté de faire valoir que l'utilisateur de la loi sur le droit d'auteur a le droit d'accéder librement à ce qui n'est pas (ou qui n'est plus) protégé, ou même à ce qui est protégé dans la mesure où il peut se prévaloir d'une dérogation au droit exclusif. Il est probable que beaucoup de ceux qui se prononcent pour un lien entre la propriété intellectuelle et la future législation sur les protections techniques sont sensibles à un tel argument.[54]

Celui-ci n'est pourtant pas imparable. Le lien établi entre les deux aspects peut en effet paraître abusif. Ainsi, le fait qu'il n'y ait pas (ou qu'il n'y ait plus) de protection privative au titre du droit d'auteur ou des droits voisins n'interdit pas à celui qui diffuse l'oeuvre ou la prestation de recourir à des protections techniques.[55] Ce n'est donc pas parce qu'une oeuvre est dans le domaine public qu'un utilisateur peut contraindre un fournisseur de service à lui en garantir l'accès et la libre utilisation.[56] De même, le fait que le titulaire des droits doive souffrir des exceptions ne saurait l'obliger à prêter la main à l'exercice de la faculté qui en découle pour l'utilisateur.[57]

Le problème ne se poserait que si l'exploitant était le seul à pouvoir diffuser l'oeuvre en cause. Il en résulterait, là encore, une position dominante dont l'exercice pourrait dégénérer en abus. Dans le même ordre d'idées, la dérogation spécifique prévue pour la décompilation des logiciels par l'article 5(3) de la Directive européenne du 14 mai 1991[58] ne devrait pas, en tout état de cause, pouvoir être paralysée par des protections techniques.[59]

Mais, en dehors de ces hypothèses exceptionnelles, rien n'autorise à ériger en principe que l'utilisateur tire un droit au libre accès à l'oeuvre du fait que celle-ci n'est pas (ou n'est plus) protégée ou que l'utilisation est couverte par une dérogation. Ce principe serait particulièrement contestable dans les systèmes de droit d'auteur continental, qui, à la différence des systèmes de *copyright*, récusent l'idée de conférer aux utilisateurs de véritables droits opposables aux auteurs, préférant ramener les dérogations à des simples permissions.

En revanche, l'avantage du lien établi avec le droit d'auteur est qu'il donne une légitimité plus grande à l'intervention du législateur. Cela est particulièrement important si l'on songe à édicter des sanctions pénales. En effet, le principe de ces sanctions pourrait en lui-même être discuté. Après tout, la loi pénale n'a pas à venir au secours de tous les intérêts privés, même s'il est vrai que le nécessaire développement des autoroutes de l'information intéresse la collectivité. De ce point de vue, brandir le drapeau du droit d'auteur et des droits voisins permet de réintroduire dans le débat des considérations d'ordre public, puisque la loi fournit déjà des sanctions pénales dans ce domaine.

Malgré tout, la solution liant la question des protections techniques à celle du droit d'auteur (et des droits voisins) n'est pas facile à mettre en oeuvre. On prétend qu'il est possible de concilier les deux impératifs en concevant des protections techniques permettant le libre accès et la libre utilisation dans des conditions conformes aux lois sur le droit d'auteur et sur les droits voisins.[60] Mais on peut se demander si cela ne risque pas de compromettre l'efficacité de la répression. Comment par exemple pourrait-on organiser une protection technique assez rigide pour dissuader des utilisateurs malveillants, et assez souple pour se prêter à l'exercice des facultés, aux contours souvent incertains, reconnues aux utilisateurs au titre du *"fair use"*, de l'exception de citation, de la parodie, etc.? Le juriste veut bien faire confiance au technicien, mais n'est-ce pas la quadrature du cercle?

Le rapport belge ajoute que se cantonner au domaine de la loi sur le droit d'auteur conduirait à trop limiter le champ d'application des sanctions, lesquelles, par exemple ne seraient pas applicables lorsque le contournement des protections techniques aurait permis d'accéder à des informations couvertes par le droit sui generis prévu par la Directive communautaire du 11 mars 1996.

De ce point de vue, l'autre solution, consistant à prohiber par principe le contournement des protections techniques, indépendamment du point de savoir si les oeuvres ou prestations protégées donnent prise à un droit exclusif, est plus simple et plus efficace. Le rapport belge se prononce en ce sens, estimant que mieux vaut bien distinguer les sanctions applicables en cas de violation du droit d'auteur et celles visant le contournement, étant précisé qu'il peut y avoir cumul. La démarche apparaît effectivement cohérente. Il y des précédents. C'est généralement sur cette base, sans avoir égard à l'existence d'un droit de propriété intellectuelle, qu'est sanctionnée la réception frauduleuse de programmes cryptés, dans des lois nationales[61] comme dans des textes internationaux,[62] ou l'intrusion dans des systèmes informatiques.[63]

Il reste en toute hypothèse à prendre parti sur la nature des sanctions susceptibles d'être édictées. Les avis sont partagés sur l'opportunité de sanctions pénales,[64] dont la proposition américaine retient le principe, alors que la proposition de la Commission laisse la porte ouverte, se bornant à prévoir l'adoption de mesures "appropriées". Les avis sont également partagés sur le point de savoir si les dispositions pertinentes doivent être insérées dans la législation sur le droit d'auteur et les droits voisins (solution qui recueillera logiquement les suffrages de ceux qui fondent les sanctions sur la défense du droit d'auteur ou des droits voisins),[65] ou au sein de la législation relative aux télécommunications, ou encore du droit pénal général.[66]

Il reste aussi à déterminer ce qu'il convient précisément d'incriminer. La proposition américaine, on l'a vu, ne prohibe que les dispositifs, les produits ou les services dont le but ou l'effet premier est de contourner les protections techniques. La proposition de la Commission européenne reprend les mêmes termes.[67] Le rapport belge observe à juste titre que le critère de l'effet premier prête à discussion,[68] mais il convient que le texte perdrait beaucoup de sa portée s'il n'était applicable qu'aux mécanismes ayant pour "seul but" de contourner la protection technique, comme le prévoit pour les programmes d'ordinateur l'article 7(c) de la Directive européenne sur les programmes d'ordinateur du 14 mai 1991.[69]

Les rapports belge et canadien considèrent en tout cas que le contournement lui-même ne devrait être réprimé que s'il est effectué dans un but commercial, faute de quoi, précise le premier, les sanctions pénales seraient disproportionnées et d'ailleurs inapplicables. C'est l'approche retenue par la Directive européenne précitée dont l'article 7(c) impose aux États-membres de prendre des mesures appropriées à l'encontre de ceux qui mettent en circulation ou détiennent "à des fins commerciales" les moyens prohibés.

Quant à l'intention criminelle, elle ne paraît pas exigée par la proposition américaine qui subordonne seulement les sanctions au constat que le moyen importé, fabriqué ou distribué, ou le service proposé a essentiellement pour objectif ou pour effet de contourner la protection technique. Le texte de la Commission et des États-membres exige quant à lui que l'intéressé ait su ou ait eu des raisons de savoir que le but ou l'effet premier du moyen ou du service était le contournement.

Notes

1. *Intellectual Property and the National Information Infrastructure, The Report of the Working Group on Intellectual Property Rights,* Information Infrastructure Task Force, septembre 1995, cité infra *NII White Paper.*

2. *NII White Paper,* p. 196

3. Et qu'ils les paiera...., ce qui rejoint la question de la sécurité des moyens de paiement.

4. V. en ce sens *NII White Paper,* préc., p. 14.

5. V. en ce sens F.W. Grosheide, *Paradigms in Copyright Law,* en: *Of Authors and Origins,* sous la direction de B. Sherman et A. Strowel, Clarendon Press Oxford, 1994, p. 203, à la p. 232. "Roméo et Juliette", la Venus de Milo, le Boléro de Ravel sont-ils des "informations"? V. cependant, mettant en avant la "nature informationnelle" du concept d'oeuvre, P.B. Hugenholtz, *Auteursrecht op informatie,* Deventer, 1989, résumé en anglais, p. 181.

6. Pour une description complète de l'état de la technique en 1995, v. *NII White Paper,* préc., note 1, p. 177 *et seq.*

7. Le présent rapport a été élaboré sur la base des rapports allemand (Prof. Lehmann), américain (M. Smith), autrichien (M. Walter), belge (Mme Ledger et M. Triaille), canadien (MM. Franchi et Moyse), finlandais (Dr. Oesch), italien (M. Pojaghi), néerlandais (Prof. Grosheide), suisse (M. Govoni).

8. On parle aussi de cryptographie. Dans le passé, où les chiffres ont souvent servi de code, on parlait de chiffrement. L'article 28 de la loi française du 29 décembre 1990 sur la réglementation des télécommunications vise quant à lui les "prestations de cryptologie", entendues comme *"toutes prestations visant à transformer à l'aide de conventions secrètes des informations ou signaux clairs en informations ou signaux inintelligibles pour des tiers, ou à réaliser l'opération inverse".* Si l'on peut hésiter sur le terme, la chose, elle, est connue depuis longtemps. Les militaires et les diplomates en ont abondamment usé. Jules César nous a même laissé une méthode. La nouveauté est que la cryptographie se démocratise. En témoigne le logiciel PGP *(Pretty Good Privacy),* adopté par les mordus d'Internet (où il est offert en libre-service), qui vantent son efficacité, déjà testée contre les spécialistes des "écoutes légales".

9. V. *NII White Paper,* préc., note 1, p. 178 *et seq.*

10. V. par ex. sur le système SCMS *(Serial Copy Management System)* limitant les copie séquentielles à la copie de première génération, imposé par la loi américaine de 1992 relative à l'enregistrement sonore numérique privé *(Audio Home Recording Act), NII White Paper,* préc., p. 189-190.

11. Seulement voir ou entendre, par exemple, ou encore limitation du nombre de manipulations, *NII White Paper,* préc., p. 190.

12. *NII White Paper,* préc., p. 187 *et seq.*

13. C'est d'ailleurs la deuxième fonction assignée par la loi française précitée de 1990 aux "prestations de cryptologie". Ainsi le sceau classique devient-il signature numérique et le filigrane se prolonge-t-il dans un tatouage plus indélébile que les meilleures encres.

14. Comp. le rapport français, pour qui la protection physique n'est pas un objectif recherché dès lors que l'on se trouve dans un "univers de bonne foi".

15. Dont fait état le rapport néerlandais (p. 3-4).

16. V. aussi le mémorandum du Bureau international de l'OMPI pour la 4e session du Comité d'experts sur un éventuel protocole relatif à la Convention de Berne: *Dr. auteur* 1994, p. 214, n. 98(a)(i).

17. V. pour une présentation d'ensemble, la réponse du Gouvernement français au questionnaire du Livre vert, janvier 1996, p. 17 *et seq.* L'ISO a confirmé son accord lors d'une réunion plénière tenue à Dallas le 15 novembre 1995. Pour préciser les modalités de mise en oeuvre de la procédure dans l'Union européenne, le Comité européen de normalisation a installé en février 1996 un groupe de travail spécifique.

18. Livre vert, p. 79. V. aussi *NII White Paper,* préc., note 1, p. 191 *et seq.*

19. *NII White Paper,* préc., p. 188-189.

20. Le rapport allemand indique que l'Institut Frauenhoher à Darmstadt travaille précisément sur un

projet *"Watermarking"*, visant à établir la paternité et à retracer l'utilisation des oeuvres.

21. *NII White Paper*, préc., note 1, p. 189.

22. *Ibid.*

23. *NII White Paper*, préc., p. 191-192.

24. P. 82.

25. Le rapporteur néerlandais fait état sur ce point (p. 7) des réticences exprimées par la *Stichting Auteursrechtbelangen (SAB)* dans sa réaction au Livre vert de la Commission.

26. *NII White Paper*, préc., note 1, p. 235.

27. P. Samuelson, *Droit d'auteur, données numériques et utilisation équitable dans les environnements numériques en réseaux*, en: *Les autoroutes électroniques, Usages, droit et promesses*, sous la direction de D. Poulin, P. Trudel et E. Mackaay, Ed. Yvon Blais, Québec, 1995, p. 159, estimant que le droit d'auteur n'aurait plus à jouer que le rôle de *"deus ex machina"* justifiant l'utilisation de ces moyens techniques et contractuels.

28. C. propr. intell., article L 122-5-1°.

29. Article 101 de la Loi sur le droit d'auteur.

30. Desbois, *Le droit d'auteur en France*, Dalloz, 3e éd., 1978, n. 275*bis*.

31. *Op. cit.*, n. 276.

32. Sur la controverse, v. A. et H.-J. Lucas, *Traité de la propriété litéraire et artistique*, Litec, 1994, n. 940 *et seq.*

33. Et aussi plus faciles à mettre en oeuvre, tant il est vrai qu'un ordinateur se déplace plus facilement qu'une station émettrice.

34. V. pour le contrôle à l'exportation le rapport américain, p. 17. V. aussi *NII White Paper*, préc., note 1, p. 194, notant que la réglementation pénalise les fabricants américains dans la concurrence internationale. V. pour la France la loi précitée du 29 décembre 1990 sur la réglementation des télécommunications soumettant les services de cryptologie à déclaration préalable (lorsqu'il s'agit d'authentifier une communication ou d'assurer l'intégrité du message transmis), ou même à autorisation préalable (lorsqu'il s'agit par exemple d'assurer la confidentialité des correspondances). Sur les restrictions de l'expertation en droit communautaire, v. le rapport allemand.

35. S. Bortmeyer, *Pour la libéralisation du chiffrement en France*, Le Monde 27 février 1995, observant qu'en l'état du droit positif, les logiciels de cryptage ne profitent qu'aux militaires et aux banquiers.

36. V. le rapport américain, p. 18, et le rapport français, p. 9.

37. *NII White Paper*, préc., note 1, p. 193.

38. *NII White Paper*, p. 200, qui réserve l'éventualité d'abus susceptibles d'être combattus sur la base de la législation *anti-trust*.

39. V. cependant, critiquant les propositions du Livre blanc américain relatives aux protection techniques comme limitant abusivement le droit à l'information, J. Boyle, *Overregulating the Internet*, *The Washington Times* 14 novembre 1995.

40. Ce qu'a écarté à juste titre la Cour de cassation néerlandaise, comme l'indique le rapport néerlandais, p. 10.

41. Rapport néerlandais, préc., p. 4.

42. On pense évidemment à l'affaire *Magill*. Comp. le rapport belge, évoquant (p. 14) la possibilité, pour éviter les abus, de reconnaître un droit d'accès pour certaines informations, le cas échéant contre le rémunération.

43. V. *supra* note 10.

44. L'article 60 de la même loi précise que des décrets peuvent imposer l'usage d'appareils ou de dispositifs permettant de déterminer les oeuvres reproduites ou utilisées ainsi que l'étendue et la fréquence de la reproduction ou de l'utilisation, pour autant que cela ne porte pas atteinte de manière injustifiée aux intérêts légitimes des utilisateurs.

45. V. en ce sens les rapports allemand et belge. La Directive européenne du 14 mai 1991 sur les programmes d'ordinateurs s'inscrit dans cette optique.

46. V. en ce sens les rapports allemand, belge et canadien.

47. P. 82.

48. V. en appendice au Livre blanc.

49. Un amendement en ce sens est discuté au Sénat (S. 1284) et à la Chambre des Representants (H.R. 2441). Un article 1202 permettrait également de réprimer les atteintes au système d'information sur les droits. Le public serait ainsi protégé contre les fausses informations sur la paternité, la titularité et les usages autorisés.

50. BCP/CE/VII/1-INR/CE/VI/1, 20 mai 1996.

51. Le texte propose aussi également d'incriminer sous les mêmes conditions *"the offer or performance of any commercial service"*. La même rédaction est suggérée pour les droits voisins dans le cadre de l'éventuel instrument relatif à la protection des droits des artistes interprètes ou exécutants et des producteurs de phonogrammes.

52. Dans la proposition faite par les États-Unis dans le cadre des négociations menées sous l'égide de l'OMPI (BCP/CE/VI, 10 janvier 1996), le texte se borne à dire que les sanctions sont applicables dès lors que l'intéressé n'est "habilité". Ces précautions n'ont pas désarmé les critiques de ceux qui pensent qu'il est plus facile d'appliquer ces moyens techniques réduisent en fait la propositions du Livre blanc américain relatives aux protections techniques réduisent en fait la portée de l'exception de *"fair use"*. V. par exemple J. Boyle, *op. cit.* C'est pour réclamer une solution plus équilibrée que s'est constituée en groupe de pression, en novembre 1995, la *"Digital Future Coalition"*.

53. Le rapport néerlandais estime toutefois (p. 11) que cette lecture ne s'impose pas dans le cas de la

proposition de la Commission et il suggère d'en modifier la rédaction pour dissiper l'équivoque.

54. V. clairement en ce sens le rapport allemand, notant que le *"fair use"* n'est pas menacé par un simple marquage, mais que les restrictions d'accès posent effectivement, à cet égard, un problème.

55. V. en ce sens le rapport belge, p. 14, qui fait valoir qu'à raisonner autrement, les musées ne seraient pas fondés à faire payer les visiteurs. V. cependant le rapport allemand, évoquant la difficulté suscitée par le fait qu'une oeuvre protégée tombe ensuite dans le domaine public. Comp., hésitant, le rapport belge précité, p. 17. Le problème se poserait dans les mêmes termes dans le cas où l'auteur voudrait renoncer à son droit exclusif (rapport américain, p. 25).

56. V. en ce sens *NII White Paper*, préc., note 1, p. 232, observant que l'oeuvre elle-même peut être reproduite par d'autres voies, par exemple par voie de citation ou de copie manuelle.

57. V. en ce sens *NII White Paper*, p. 231.

58. La jurisprudence américaine aboutit à un résultat voisin sur la base du *"fair use"*. V. *Sega Enterprises Ltd. v. Accolade Inc.*, 977 F.2d 1510 (9th Cir. 1992).

59. V. en ce sens le rapport canadien, estimant que la liberté de décompiler devrait rester entière et donc être réservée par le dispositif de protection technique. Le rapport allemand suggère, comme une solution de compromis, l'institution d'un dépôt permettant de fournir les informations nécessaires.

60. Par exemple en utilisant des clés qui ne soient opérationnelles que pour des oeuvres encore protégées (rapport américain, p. 27). On peut aussi songer à identifier les oeuvres et prestations faisant partie du domaine public, par exemple par la mention DP, comme le suggère l'ALAI dans sa réaction au Livre vert.

61. V. le rapport belge, citant pour la Communauté française le décret du 17 juillet 1987 et pour la Communauté flamande le décret du 4 mai 1994. V. aussi les articles 297 à 299 du *Copyright, Designs and Patent Act* anglais de 1988, les articles 79-1 *et seq.* de la loi française du 30 septembre 1986 (réd. loi 16 déc. 1992), l'article 62 de la loi grecque de 1993. A. Chaubeau, *Le décodage illicite des signaux de télévision cryptée et la protection des auteurs et des producteurs d'oeuvres audiovisuelles*, *Dr. auteur* 1990, p. 385.

62. V. l'article 1707(a) de l'ALENA. V. aussi le mémorandum précité du Bureau International de l'OMPI, *Dr. auteur* 1994, p. 214, n. 98(c)(ii).

63. V. par exemple les articles 326, 327, 342.1 et 430 du Code criminel cités par le rapport canadien, le *Computer Security Act* de 1987 et le *Computer Fraud and Abuse Act* de 1986, cités par le rapport américain, les articles 323-1 *et seq.* du Code pénal français.

64. V. le rapport néerlandais, p. 4, faisant état des auditions organisées par la Commission européenne en janvier 1996 de la Commission.

65. En faveur de cette approche, retenue par la proposition américaine précitée, v. les rapports allemand et canadien.

66. Comp. les rapports autrichien et finlandais, laissant la porte ouverte à toutes les solutions, et préférant laisser à chaque loi nationale le soin de choisir.

67. Comp. le mémorandum précité du Bureau International de l'OMPI, *Dr. auteur* 1994, p. 214, n. 98(a)(i): "spécialement ou essentiellement conçu".

68. Pour une critique de cette formulation, considérée comme dangereuse en raison de son imprécision, v. P. Samuelson, *Regulation of Technologies to protect Copyrighted Works, Forthcoming Communications of the ACM*, juillet 1996.

69. Qui vise *"tout moyen ayant pour seul but de faciliter la suppression non autorisée ou la neutralisation de tout dispositif technique éventuellement mis en place pour protéger un programme d'ordinateur"*. V. cependant en ce sens les commentaires du group ECIS *(European Committee for Interoperable Systems)* sur le Livre vert européen.

Questionnaire

1. State of realizations, studies and projects

a. *State of techniques*

1.1. Are there any activities in your country concerning the technical protection of works, especially in the digital environment?

1.2. In the affirmative, what is the extent of this technical protection (identification of works and authors, authentification of the author and the contents of the work, restricted access to the work or restrictions to the possibility of making copies of the work, information on the right holders and conditions for use)?

1.3. To your knowledge, which technical bases are covered in order to resolve the problem (hardware or software, internal codes inseparably connected with the original work, or external codes which are applied after the creation of the work)?

1.4. Who are the participants in the activities (public authorities, collection societies, hardware/software producers, information providers)?

b. *State of legislation*

1.5. Do any legislative provisions exist in your country that generally sanction circumvention of technical protection devices?

1.6. If no, are there precedents, for example in the domain of encrypting television broadcasts?

1.7. Are use, distribution or export of encryption devices subject to particular restrictions?

2. Critical assessment

2.1. Is, in your opinion, the preparation of sanctions against the circumvention of technical protective devices worthwhile? Will these provisions be efficient? Does the aim justify the substantial investments required?

2.2. Should the sanctions be directed against those who provide users with the means to circumvent protective devices? In the affirmative, should they be limited to those means which are specifically meant to circumvent protective devices, analogous to article 7(1)c of the 1991 Software Directive, or is it preferable, like in the American White Paper, to prohibit means of which one of the aims or most important effect is to circumvent protective devices?

2.3. Do you think that it would be necessary to consider a harmonization of legislations, to prevent distortions in competition? Is it possible to find a uniform standard? How and by whom should this standard be developed?

2.4. What should be the bases of regulations in this field? Is the aim to guarantee security in light of improving the diffusion of works for the benefit of the public? In that view, should regulations lead to compulsory technical protection, analogous to American law (Audio Home Recording Act), imposing an obligation upon the producers of digital sound recording equipment to apply devices limiting copying to copies of the first generation? Or is it an additional protection which is meant to guarantee the rights of the author, which he can renounce?

2.5. Should the injunction to circumvent technical protective devices be part of copyright law or a separate law? In the first case, should it be an act which is a violation of copyright only or is there an act of exploitation, subject to the exclusive rights? In the second case, what is the legal basis? Should the neutralization of a device, for instance, be considered a reproduction in the sense of copyright legislation?

2.6. If the sanctions are limited to the hypothesis that there is an infringement of copyright if technical protection devices are circumvented which leads to access to a work, should these sanctions be limited to the case that the user knew (or should have known) that he was infringing?

2.7. Do you think criticism of the injunction to circumvent technical protective devices is justified, in view of the fact that the access to works which are in the public domain is or could be limited? Or because the traditional limitations on copyright (like fair use or private use) are not respected? Do considerations which are in the interest of the public justify that the technical protection is neutralized by the authorities? In the affirmative, is it imaginable that this neutralization is ordered by using several keys?

2.8. Is it possible to reconcile the general injunction on the circumvention of technical protective devices with the special rules covering the decompilation of software, like those resulting from the Software Directive mentioned before, or with the case-law developed in the United States on the basis of fair use?

2.9. What could be the effect of legislation as has been elaborated upon above on the future of copyright? Do you agree with the hypothesis which says that technical protection, in combination with contracts, means the decline or the end of copyright? Or should we consider the exclusive right of the author an indispensable weapon in the digital environment?

2.10. Other observations?

Questionnaire

1. Bilan des réalisations, études et projets

a. *Bilan technique*

1.1. A-t-on mené dans votre pays des travaux sur la protection technique des oeuvres, spécialement dans l'environnement numérique?

1.2. Dans l'affirmative, quelles sont les finalités qui ont été assignées à cette protection (identification des oeuvres et des auteurs, authentification de l'auteur et du contenu, restrictions à l'accès aux oeuvres ou à la copie de celles-ci, informations sur les ayants-droit et les conditions d'utilisation)?

1.3. A votre connaissance, sur quelles bases techniques est-il envisagé de résoudre le problème (matériel ou logiciel, codage interne, inséparablement lié à l'oeuvre dès l'origine, ou codage externe, ajouté postérieurement à la création)?

1.4. Quels sont les partenaires associés à ces travaux (autorités publiques, sociétés de gestion collective, constructeurs de matériels, fournisseurs de "contenus")?

b. *Bilan législatif*

1.5. Des dispositions législatives existent-elles dans votre pays pour sanctionner de façon générale le contournement de dispositifs de protection technique?

1.6. Dans la négative, existe-t-il des précédents, par exemple dans le domaine du cryptage des émissions de télévision?

1.7. L'usage, la diffusion ou l'exportation des techniques de cryptage sont-ils soumis à des restrictions particulières?

2. Appréciation critique

2.1. Est-il opportun, selon vous, de prévoir des sanctions contre le contournement des dispositifs de protection technique? Ces dispositifs peuvent-ils être efficaces? Les enjeux justifient-ils les investissements importants qui sont nécessaires?

2.2. Les sanctions doivent-elles à votre avis permettre d'atteindre ceux qui mettent à la disposition des utilisateurs les moyens visant à réaliser ce contournement? Dans l'affirmative, faut-il les limiter à la commercialisation de moyens ayant le contournement "pour seul but", à l'instar de l'article 7(1)c de la Directive communautaire de 1991 sur les programmes d'ordinateur, ou peut-on aller, comme dans la proposition du Livre blanc américain, jusqu'à prohiber les moyens dont le but ou l'effet premier est le contournement?

2.3. Pensez-vous qu'il faille envisager une harmonisation des législations, afin d'éviter des distorsions de concurrence? Peut-on concevoir une norme unique? Comment et par qui cette norme devrait-elle être élaborée?

2.4. Quel devrait être selon vous le fondement d'une règlementation dans ce domaine? S'agit-il de garantir la sécurité en vue d'améliorer la diffusion des oeuvres au bénéfice du public? Dans cette optique, peut-on aller jusqu'à rendre obligatoire la protection technique, à l'instar de la loi américaine *(Audio Home Recording Act)* imposant que les fabricants de matériel d'enregistrement sonore numérique incorporent des dispositifs limitant les copies séquentielles à la copie de première génération? S'agit-il plutôt d'une protection complémentaire destinée à garantir la propriété de l'auteur, à laquelle celui-ci pourrait renoncer?

2.5. L'interdiction de contourner les dispositifs de protection technique doit-elle à votre avis trouver place dans la loi sur le droit d'auteur ou dans une loi distincte? Dans la première hypothèse, le contournement doit-il être seulement "assimilé" à une violation du droit d'auteur ou faut-il y voir un véritable acte d'exploitation soumis en tant que tel au droit exclusif? Dans la seconde hypothèse, sur quelle base juridique fonder cette analyse? La neutralisation d'un dispositif doit-elle par exemple s'analyser comme une reproduction au sens de la législation sur le droit d'auteur?

2.6. Si les sanctions sont limitées aux hypothèses dans lesquelles le contournement des dispositifs de protection technique vise à permettre l'accès à une oeuvre donnant prise au droit d'auteur, doivent-elles être subordonnées à la preuve que l'utilisateur savait (ou aurait dû savoir) qu'il violait ce droit d'auteur? Seront-elles encourues lorsque le contournement aura permis d'accéder à des parties non-originales de l'oeuvre?

2.7. L'interdiction de contourner les dispositifs de protection technique peut-elle selon vous être critiquée comme restreignant (ou risquant de restreindre) abusivement l'accès au domaine public? Ou comme paralysant le jeu des dérogations limitant traditionnellement la portée du droit d'auteur (*"fair use"* ou usage privé)? Des considérations d'intérêt public peuvent-elles justifier que la protection technique soit neutralisée par les autorités? Dans l'affirmative, peut-on, pour limiter les risques, imaginer que cette neutralisation soit commandée par la mise en oeuvre de plusieurs clés?

2.8. Comment l'interdiction généralisée de contourner les dispositifs de protection technique pourrait-elle être conciliée avec les règles spéciales gouvernant la décompilation des programmes d'ordinateur, telles qu'elles résultent de la directive communautaire précitée, ou avec la jurisprudence développée aux Etats-Unis sur la base du *"fair use"*?

2.9. Quelle sera l'incidence d'une législation telle que celle envisagée ci-dessus sur l'avenir du droit d'auteur? Faut-il accorder du crédit à l'hypothèse selon laquelle la protection technique, complétée par les contrats, signifie le déclin, voire la mort du droit d'auteur? Ou doit-on considérer que le droit exclusif reste une arme indispensable dans l'environnement numérique?

2.10. Autres observations?

Remarques générales

La question de la protection technique des oeuvres littéraires et artistiques n'est pas totalement nouvelle. Il existe déjà dans certaines législations des dispositions interdisant sous peine de sanctions pénales le fait de contourner ou d'inciter à contourner des dispositifs de protection, par exemple pour les émissions cryptées de télévision (notamment en France et au Royaume Uni; v. aussi l'article 1717(a) de l'ALENA) ou pour la limitations des copies "sous une forme électronique" (au Royaume-Uni).

Elle a pris une ampleur particulière dans l'environnement numérique, spécialement depuis le Livre blanc américain de septembre 1995 *(Intellectual Property and the National Information Infrastructure)*, qui a suggéré d'insérer dans la Loi sur le droit d'auteur un article (1201) ainsi conçu: *"No person shall import, manufacture or distribute any device, product, or component incorporated into a device or product, or offer or perform any service, the primary purpose or effect of which is to avoid, bypass, remove, deactivate, or otherwise circumvent, without the authority of the copyright owner or the law, any process, treatment, mechanism or system which prevents or inhibits the violation of any of the exclusive rights of the copyright owner under section 106".*

Cette préoccupation a également trouvé un écho au Canada dans le Rapport du Comité consultatif sur l'autoroute de l'information (septembre 1995), qui recommande au gouvernement fédéral d'encourager "la mise au point et la standardisation de techniques permettant de contrôler l'utilisation d'oeuvres protégées, qui soient acceptables par les usagers", et qui est d'avis que "l'altération ou le contournement des mesures de protection de toutes sortes, telles que le chiffrement ou les procédés anticopie, doivent être assimilés à un acte criminel en vertu de la Loi sur le droit d'auteur".

La Commission européenne est bien consciente de l'acuité du sujet, déjà abordé dans la directive sur les programmes d'ordinateur (article 7(1)c). C'est ainsi qu'elle finance dans le cadre du programme ESPRIT le projet CITED *(Copyright in Transmitted Electronic Documents)*. Dans le Livre vert de juillet 1995 sur *"Le droit d'auteur et les droits voisins dans la société de l'information"*, elle annonce un autre livre vert spécialement consacré à la protection juridique des signaux cryptés et évoque (p. 82) la possibilité pour la Communauté d'intervenir "afin de rendre obligatoire de façon harmonisée les systèmes techniques de protection lorsque ceux-ci auront été mis au point et acceptés par l'industrie".

La tâche du rapporteur général est d'abord d'identifier l'état de la technique et des recherches, ainsi que l'état des législations ou des propositions législatives dans ce domaine. La question étant encore débattue, le bilan, à ce jour, se révèlera sans doute maigre. Il reste à profiter du répit pour mener une réflexion critique sur les solutions possibles et souhaitables ainsi que sur leurs incidences.

Allemagne

M. Lehmann

1. **Bilan des réalisations, études et projets**

a. *Bilan technique*

1.1. *A-t-on mené en Allemagne des travaux sur la protection technique des oeuvres, spécialement dans l'environnement numérique?*

En Allemagne, l'Institut Frauenhofer pour le traitement des données graphiques à Darmstadt travaille depuis quelque temps sur différents projets nationaux et internationaux dans le domaine de la protection technique du droit d'auteur. En ce moment, il travaille sur un projet *Watermarking* pour la protection technique d'oeuvres digitales. Le responsable en est le Dr. Eckhard Koch (Ekoch@igd.fhg.de). En outre, il existe une série d'entreprises et d'institutions qui s'occupent en général de la sécurité et du contrôle de l'accès.

1.2. *Dans l'affirmative, quelles sont les finalités qui ont été assignées à cette protection (identification des oeuvres et des auteurs, authentification de l'auteur et du contenu, restrictions à l'accès aux oeuvres ou à la copie de celles-ci, informations sur les ayants-droit et les conditions d'utilisation)?*

Le marquage utilisé par l'Institut Fraunhofer permet l'intégration des informations souhaitées dans les données multimédias:
- numéro d'identification de l'oeuvre,
- nom de l'auteur,
- signature digitale de l'auteur,
- poinçon de contrôle pour la preuve de l'authenticité du document,
- nombre des copies autorisées, et
- informations sur les droits et les licences.
Le marquage n'empêche cependant pas la réalisation de copies illégales. Ce n'est pas non plus son but. Son but est de pouvoir ramener une preuve de la paternité et, le cas échéant, de pouvoir retracer le chemin de l'utilisation ultérieure des oeuvres.

1.3. *A votre connaissance, sur quelles bases techniques est-il envisagé de résoudre le problème (matériel ou logiciel, codage interne, inséparablement lié à l'oeuvre dès l'origine, ou codage externe, ajouté postérieurement à la création)?*

Les techniques suivantes entrent en ligne de compte pour la protection technique des oeuvres:

- *Le contrôle de l'accès:* observation pour savoir si l'utilisateur peut avoir en principe accès à un système (logiciel ou matériel, par ex. "cartes chip").

- *"Restrictive use":* contrôle de l'utilisation des données, par ex. nombre des copies, des impressions, etc. Cette possibilité technique n'est cependant réalisable qu'au moyen d'appareils d'édition spéciaux et par conséquent difficile à introduire sur le marché.

- *Codages internes:* marquages ou signaux liquides, inséparablement liés à l'oeuvre, constituent une composante supplémentaire de la protection. Ces marquages peuvent être aussi insérés postérieurement dans l'oeuvre digitale.

Nous considérons l'installation de codages internes comme préférable.

> *1.4.* *Quels sont les partenaires associés à ces travaux (autorités publiques, sociétés de gestion collective, constructeurs de matériels, fournisseurs de "contenus")?*

A côté de l'Institut Frauenhofer qui envisage un propre projet avec des fournisseurs de contenus (photographes) dans le domaine des images digitales, quelques sociétés de gestion collective (VG Wort, Bild-Kunst, GEMA) ainsi que le Ministère de la Justice se préoccupent de cette problématique. Un système technique de protection du droit d'auteur nécessite la participation de beaucoup: fournisseurs de "contenus", fournisseurs de services, sociétés de gestion collective, instances indépendantes *(trusted third parties)*. Une sorte de *controller, registrar and watermarker* doivent être encore éventuellement ajoutés.

> b. *Bilan législatif*

> *1.5.* *Des dispositions législatives existent-elles dans l'Allemagne pour sanctionner de façon générale le contournement de dispositifs de protection technique?*

Indépendamment du contournement de dispositifs de protection technique, les §§ 98 et 99 de la Loi sur le droit d'auteur et les droits voisins *(UrhG)* donnent au titulaire du droit auquel il a été porté atteinte la faculté d'exiger la destruction ou la mise hors d'état des exemplaires fabriqués de façon illicite qui sont la propriété ou en la possession de l'auteur de l'atteinte, ainsi que celle des dispositifs dont celui-ci a la propriété, utilisés ou destinés exclusivement ou presque exclusivement à réaliser ces exemplaires. Le § 69f, al. 1, 1ère phrase *UrhG* va, pour les logiciels, au-delà du § 98 al. 1 *UrhG*, dans la mesure où il donne le droit d'exiger la destruction même à l'encontre du propriétaire ou possesseur d'exemplaires qui n'est pas l'auteur de la contrefaçon. Le § 69f al. 2 *UrhG* donne le droit de réclamer la destruction ou la mise hors d'usage des moyens qui sont uniquement destinés à faciliter la suppression ou le contournement illicite de mécanismes techniques de protection du programme. Comme exemple de moyens de ce genre, les motifs du projet de loi[1] citent des programmes de copie qui sont destinés à éteindre le système de protection contre les copies du programme protégé par le droit d'auteur.

Récemment, les tribunaux ont sanctionné à nouveau le contournement de dispositifs de protection technique sur le fondement de la clause générale qu'est le § 1 de la Loi sur la concurrence déloyale *(UWG)*. En outre, ils ont admis l'atteinte à "l'organisation et l'exercice de l'entreprise" au sens des §§ 823 al. 1 et 1004 du Code Civil *(BGB)*. La Cour d'appel *(Oberlandesgericht)* de Frankfurt am Main a ainsi décidé dans son arrêt du 13-6-1995 (6 U 14/95) que la vente des fameuses "cartes pirates" qui permettaient de recevoir décryptés des programmes de télévision payante codés, sans utilisation de la carte de décodage originale, constitue une gêne contraire au droit de la concurence, au sens du § 1 *UWG*, du distributeur légal des systèmes de décryptage et en même temps une atteinte à l'exercice et à l'organisation de son entreprise (§§ 823 al. 1 et 1004 *BGB*).[2] La Cour Suprême *(Bundesgerichtshof)* a, dans sa décision *Auto-CAD* du 9-11-1995 (I ZR 220/95) considéré la vente d'un programme (prix: 900 DM), qui permettait entre autres le contournement de la protection "Dongle" contre les copies du programme Auto-CAD, "original" au moins selon le droit de la concurrence (prix: 7000 DM), comme une entrave au sens du § 1 *UWG*. Comme sanctions pénales, les §§ 269 et 270 du Code Pénal *(StGB)* sont à prendre en considération.

1.6. *Dans la négative, existe-t-il des précédents, par exemple dans le domaine du cryptage des émissions de télévision?*

Pour le cryptage des émissions de télévision, voir l'arrêt *Piratenkarten* cité ci-dessus sous 1.5.

1.7. *L'usage, la diffusion ou l'exportation des techniques de cryptage sont-ils soumis à des restrictions particulières?*

L'usage de techniques de cryptage de données n'est soumis jusqu'à présent en Allemagne à aucune restriction.[3] Selon le droit de l'Union européenne, il n'existe pas non plus de restrictions d'utilisation.[4] L'exportation de logiciels de cryptage de données hors d'Allemagne est en revanche limité selon l'annexe AL de l'ordonnance pour l'économie extérieure *(Aussenwirtschaftsverordnung)*.[5] Ces limitations sont cependant largement en accord avec celles de l'Union européenne.[6] L'ordonnance *Dual use* de l'Union européenne réglemente l'exportation, hors des États-membres, de biens avec double but d'utilisation. Elle est valable, depuis le 1-7-1995 pour tous les États-membres de l'Union européenne. Conformément à cette ordonnance, l'exportation de systèmes et d'appareils de la "sécurité de l'information" hors de l'Union européenne est soumise à autorisation. Les programmes de cryptage de données sont également soumis à cette réglementation puisque la définition de "la sécurité de l'information" inclut aussi les éléments cryptographiques. En outre, l'annexe 1 de l'ordonnance inclut aussi les logiciels qui possèdent les qualités des appareils saisis ou qui exécutent ou simulent leurs fonctions.

2. **Appréciation critique**

2.1. *Est-il opportun, selon vous, de prévoir des sanctions contre le contourne-ment des dispositifs de protection technique?*

Oui, la condamnation du contournement des dispositifs de protection technique est nécessaire pour pouvoir s'opposer efficacement aux dangers auxquels sont soumises du fait de la digitalisation les oeuvres et prestations protégées (par le droit d'auteur et les droits voisins). Cette technique facilite de façon importante la sauvegarde, l'accès, les utilisations, et par là même malheureusement la piraterie. Le développement et l'installation de systèmes de protection technique doit servir a rendre la tâche plus difficile aux pirates, si ce n'est totalement impossible. Dans l'intérêt d'une protection efficace du droit d'auteur, le simple contournement de ces systèmes doit pouvoir être sanctionné comme action préparatoire à une éventuelle lésion du droit d'auteur ultérieure. Dans l'hypothèse future où des systèmes de protection technique seraient installés pour une comptabilisation et une facturation simplifiée de l'utilisation de l'oeuvre, il semble également nécessaire de prévoir des sanctions pour la protection d'un tel système.

Ces dispositifs peuvent-ils être efficaces?

Les systèmes de protection technique n'offrent - ainsi que le montrent les expériences de l'industrie informatique - pas de sécurité à 100%. Ils sont cependant adaptés pour rendre plus difficile la reproduction illicite d'oeuvres et de prestations protégées. Les consommateurs ne sont cependant pas toujours prêts à accepter un tel obstacle. L'entreprise Lotus en a fait l'expérience. Lorsque, en 1989, elle ajouta à la version DOS 1.0a de son logiciel Lotus 1-2-3 une protection contre les copies, son chiffre d'affaires chuta de façon dramatique. De plus, la protection utilisée contre les copies ne permettait même pas de faire des copies de sauvegarde des disquettes originales. Lotus a par conséquent abandonné l'utilisation de tels systèmes de protection. On peut de toute façon se demander si la situation de l'industrie des logiciels est comparable avec celle des autres objets de protection. En effet, sur le marché du logiciel, il peut être utile d'autoriser des copies ou de prendre consciemment en considération des copies pirates pour favoriser la distribution de ses propres produits et y habituer l'utilisateur. L'argent est alors gagné avec les nouvelles versions *("updates")*.

Les enjeux justifient-ils les investissements importants qui sont nécessaires?

C'est l'industrie, et donc finalement le marché, qui doit répondre à cette question.

> ***2.2.*** *Les sanctions doivent-elles à votre avis permettre d'atteindre ceux qui mettent à la disposition des utilisateurs les moyens visant à réaliser ce contournement? Dans l'affirmative, faut-il les limiter à la commercialisation de moyens ayant le contournement "pour seul but", à l'instar de l'article 7(1)c de la Directive communautaire de 1991 sur les programmes d'ordinateur, ou peut-on aller, comme dans la proposition du Livre blanc américain, jusqu'à prohiber les moyens dont le but ou l'effet premier est le contournement?*

Dans l'intérêt d'une protection efficace du droit d'auteur, il apparaît conseillé d'étendre aussi les sanctions aux personnes qui mettent à disposition des moyens pour la réalisation du contournement. Il devrait cependant être indifférent que la vente de tels dispositifs soit faite ou non dans le cadre d'une activité commerciale. Comme le montre le cas *United States v. LaMachia*,[7] même s'il concerne une autre hypothèse, un agissement non commercial peut également entraîner d'importants dommages. Dans le droit d'auteur allemand actuellement en vigueur (§ 69f al. 2 *UrhG*), le seul but des moyens employés déclenche l'action contre les tiers, indépendamment d'un agissement de nature commerciale.

2.3. Pensez-vous qu'il faille envisager une harmonisation des législations, afin d'éviter des distorsions de concurrence? Peut-on concevoir une norme unique? Comment et par qui cette norme devrait-elle être élaborée?

Une rapide harmonisation des dispositions légales dans le cadre de l'Union européenne apparaît indispensable pour éviter des distorsions de concurrence dans le marché intérieur commun. Les réseaux digitaux à l'échelle mondiale comme Internet rendent cependant souhaitable un accord international par l'OMPI ou l'OMC. En effet, l'augmentation des capacités de transmission et l'amélioration des standards de transmission rendent l'envoi d'oeuvres et de prestations protégées sous forme digitale dans le réseau de plus en plus attirant. Le développement de moyens anonymes de paiement pour le réseau *("digital cash")* donne à penser que des pirates professionnels découvrent aussi ce moyen de distribution pour eux, ce en quoi augmente la menace constituée par les pays dont la législation comporte des lacunes. Il apparaît pour le moins douteux que le développement de la responsabilité de l'exploitant du réseau et sa sensibilité par là même accrue pour les procédés dans le réseau puissent y changer quelque chose.

Quel devrait-être selon vous le fondement d'une règlementation dans ce domaine? S'agit-il de garantir la sécurité en vue d'améliorer la diffusion des oeuvres au bénéfice du public?

Le fondement d'une telle règlementation devrait être le droit d'auteur. Il protège l'auteur dans ses liens spirituels et personnels avec son oeuvre et dans l'utilisation de l'oeuvre (§ 11 *UrhG*) et sert ainsi aussi bien ses intérêts moraux que matériels et ainsi en même temps les intérêts de la collectivité. Le droit moral, le droit exclusif d'exploitation et les autres droits de l'auteur lui octroyent un droit d'exclusivité sur sa propriété intellectuelle, et l'incitent ainsi à créer et à rendre accessible à d'autres les résultats de sa création. Ce système d'encouragement existe et disparaît avec son efficacité. Qu'apporte un droit à l'auteur s'il ne peut pas l'exercer? Des systèmes techniques de protection peuvent faciliter pour l'auteur la mise en oeuvre de ses droits et ainsi participer à l'amélioration de la distribution d'oeuvres pour le bien du public.

Dans cette optique, peut-on aller jusqu'à rendre obligatoire la protection technique, à l'instar de la loi américaine (Audio Home Recording Act) *imposant que les fabricants de matériel d'enregistrement sonore numérique incorporent des dispositifs limitant les copies séquentielles à la copie de première génération? S'agit-il plutôt d'une protection complémentaire destinée à garantir la propriété de l'auteur, à laquelle celui-ci pourrait renoncer?*

Au premier *"hearing"* de l'Union européenne sur le Livre vert *Droit d'auteur et droits voisins dans la société de l'information*, le 8-9 janvier 1995 à Bruxelles, une grande majorité du cercle des intéressés y participant s'est prononcé pour que l'introduction d'un système de protection de toute technique se fasse seulement sur une base volontaire.[8] La question de savoir si on ne devrait pas malgré tout en arriver à une obligation légale dans l'intérêt d'une protection du droit d'auteur plus efficace, semble devoir être encore à examiner. En tout cas, il convient, dans l'hypothèse d'une décision, de prendre en considération les expériences des USA et les intérêts de toutes les parties intéressées (auteurs et titulaires de droits voisins, exploitants de l'oeuvre, industrie et utilisateurs).

> **2.5.** *L'interdiction de contourner les dispositifs de protection technique doit-elle à votre avis trouver place dans la loi sur le droit d'auteur ou dans une loi distincte?*

L'interdiction de contourner les dispositifs de protection des droits d'auteur et de titulaires de droits voisins appartient, selon la conception allemande, à la Loi sur le droit d'auteur et devrait y être insérée aux §§ 96 *et seq. UrhG*. La norme générale de la Loi sur la concurrence déloyale, § 1 *UWG*, peut aussi, comme le montre la jurisprudence actuelle, être appliquée à titre de complément.

> *Dans la premiere hypothèse, le contournement doit-il seulement être "assimilé" à une violation du droit d'auteur ou faut-il y voir un véritable acte d'exploitation soumis en tant que tel au droit exclusif? Dans la seconde hypothèse, sur quelle base juridique fonder cette analyse?*

Le contournement peut, en tant qu'acte préparatoire, être seulement "assimilé" à une violation du droit d'auteur, mais ne consiste pas en lui-même en un véritable acte d'exploitation.

> *La neutralisation d'un dispositif doit-elle par exemple s'analyser comme une reproduction au sens de la législation du droit d'auteur?*

Non, il s'agit d'un acte de violation particulier.

> **2.6.** *Si les sanctions sont limitées aux hypothèses dans lesquelles le contournement des dispositifs de protection technique vise à permettre l'accès à une oeuvre donnant prise au droit d'auteur, doivent-elles être subordonnées à la preuve que l'utilisateur savait (ou aurait dû savoir) qu'il violait ce droit d'auteur?*

Non, puisque pour une action en cessation de l'atteinte, la simple violation objective du droit suffit. La faute n'est requise que pour l'action en dommages-intérêts.

> *Seront-elles encourues lorsque le contournement aura permis d'accéder à des parties non-originales de l'oeuvre?*

Oui, car si l'on veut sanctionner, en vue d'une protection efficace de l'auteur, le contournement de dispositifs de protection technique comme acte précédant une éventuelle violation ultérieure du droit d'auteur, on ne doit pas distinguer entre les parties de l'oeuvre protégées selon le droit d'auteur et celles qui ne le sont pas.

2.7. *L'interdiction de contourner les dispositifs de protection technique peut-elle selon vous être critiquée comme restreignant (ou risquant de restreindre) abusivement l'accès au domaine public?*

Quand des oeuvres qui sont déjà dans le domaine public arrivent sur le marché, elles ne nécessitent aucune protection technique contre les copies. Il n'y a alors pas de danger de contournement et donc pas de risque de sanction, et par conséquent pas de risque de restreindre l'accès aux oeuvres. L'accès aux oeuvres n'est en effet pas restreint par la nécessaire protection de l'intégrité de l'oeuvre et de la paternité, c'est-à-dire par un système technique pour la protection contre des modifications. Quand, à l'inverse, des oeuvres protégées qui arrivent sur le marché avec un système de protection contre les copies, tombent par la suite dans le domaine public à l'expiration du délai de protection, il peut alors y avoir un risque de restriction de l'accès aux oeuvres.

Ou comme paralysant le jeu des dérogations limitant traditionnellement la portée du droit d'auteur ("fair use" ou usage privé)?

Cela dépend de l'organisation du système de protection. Le marquage des oeuvres est certainement moins problématique qu'une limitation technique des utilisations possibles. Mais la systématique détaillée des exceptions au droit d'auteur des §§ 45 *et seq. UrhG* doit être sûrement examinée sous l'angle de sa nécessité et sa conformité.[9] Les dispositions relatives aux revues de presse (§ 49 *UrhG*) et à la reproduction par reprographie à usage privé (§§ 53 et 54 *UrhG*) semblent problématiques. Une nouvelle formulation des §§ 45 *et seq. UrhG* ne doit cependant porter atteinte ni à une exploitation normale de l'oeuvre, ni aux intérêts légitimes des auteurs et autres titulaires de droits (article 9 al. 2 de la Convention de Berne et article 13 *TRIPs*).

Des considérations d'intérêt public peuvent-elles justifier que la protection technique soit neutralisée par les autorités? Dans l'affirmative, peut-on, pour limiter les risques, imaginer que cette neutralisation soit commandée par la mise en oeuvre de plusieurs clés?

Oui. Selon le système d'exceptions actuellement en vigueur (§ 45 al. 2 *UrhG*), les tribunaux et autorités publiques peuvent, par exemple pour des impératifs d'administration de la justice et de sécurité publique, reproduire ou faire reproduire des portraits. Si on laisse persister cette exception (ce qui serait souhaitable), le contournement d'une interdiction de copie est nécessaire pour la reproduction d'une oeuvre protégée et devrait donc être aussi autorisée. Compte tenu des dangers que de telles autorisations emportent pour le système en général, il doit cependant y avoir des garanties. La mise en oeuvre d'un système de plusieurs clés est ici envisageable, comme le propose le Livre blanc américain.

2.8. Comment l'interdiction généralisée de contourner des dispositifs de protection technique pourrait-elle être conciliée avec les règles spéciales gouvernant la décompilation des programmes d'ordinateur, telles qu'elles résultent de la Directive communautaire précitée, ou avec la jurisprudence développée aux États-Unis sur la base du "fair use"?

Une solution technique semble préférable selon laquelle les informations nécessaires à la mise en oeuvre de l'interopérabilité sont exlues d'une protection allant au-delà du simple marquage. Dans l'hypothèse où une solution technique ne serait pas possible ou souhaitable, on pourrait envisager de mettre en place un bureau de dépôt par lequel on pourrait obtenir les informations nécessaires, sous réserve de certaines conditions, telle que la preuve d'un intérêt légitime.

2.9. Quelle sera l'incidence d'une législation telle que celle envisagée ci-dessus sur l'avenir du droit d'auteur? Faut-il accorder du crédit à l'hypothèse selon laquelle la protection technique, complétée par les contrats, signifie le déclin, voire la mort du droit d'auteur? Ou doit-on considérer que le droit exclusif reste une arme indispensable dans l'environnement numérique?

Les nouvelles techniques digitales d'exploitation d'oeuvres et de prestations protégées placent le droit d'auteur devant une série de problèmes. Les systèmes de protection technique peuvent aider à résoudre ces problèmes, mais en apportent d'autres avec eux. L'histoire du droit d'auteur est en général un processus de réactions juridiques aux défis de la technique.[10] Aujourd'hui encore des adaptations et améliorations de la loi sur le droit d'auteur sont nécessaires, sans que ses principes de base doivent cependant être touchés. Il n'existe en particulier aucun motif pour remettre en question le système des droits exclusifs. Ceux-ci seront même renforcés par l'introduction de systèmes de protection technique. Ils devraient également constituer dans le futur un instrument adapté pour la protection des auteurs et des utilisateurs des oeuvres, sans pour autant empêcher l'utilisation de nouvelles technologies.

2.10. Autres observations?

Aucune.

Notes

1. BT-Drucksache 12/4022 du 18-12-1992, p. 15.
2. NJW 1996, 264f.
3. Kuner, NJW-CoR 1995, 413, 414.
4. Comp. la recommandation de la Commission européenne du 19-10-1994 relative aux aspects juridiques de l'échange de données, Annexe 2 *(Europäische EDI-Mustervereinbarung/Rechtlinie Bestimmungen/Kommentar)*, Article 7.3, *ABIEG* Nr. L 338/98 du 28-12-1994.
5. 88e ordonnance du 17-2-1995 portant modification de la liste d'exportation, *Bundesanzeiger* N° 110a du 14 juin 1995, § 5A002.
6. Kuner, *op. cit., loc. cit.*
7. 871 f. Supp. 535 (D.Mass.1994).
8. Comp. point I.D des conclusions de la Commission.

9. Le Conseil pour la recherche, la technologie et l'innovation s'est prononcé en faveur d'un tel examen dans sa vingtième recommandation relative à la protection de la propriété intellectuelle dans la société de l'information de décembre 1995.
10. Schricker, *Urheberrecht*, Introduction, no. 1.

Annexe

Jurisprudence allemande sur le contournement des systèmes de protection technique

OLG Stuttgart 10 fevrier 1989 (Feilhalten von Hardlock-Entfernen), CR 1989 685: Il est contraire au droit de la concurrence, selon le § 1 *UWG*, de porter atteinte à un concurrent (producteur de logiciels) par l'offre de *"Hardlock-Entfernen"* (systèmes de suppression de verrouillage du *hardware*) de telle façon que celui-ci ne peut pratiquement plus écouler ses logiciels sur le marché.

OLG München 3 novembre 1994 (UNPROTECT), CR 1995, 663: La vente illimitée et faite sans *"Auflagen"* d'un programme d'ordinateur destiné à contourner ou supprimer la protection contre les copies installées dans des programmes d'ordinateur, est contraire au § 1 *UWG*, en ce qu'elle constitue une entrave à la libre concurrence.

LG München 1 décembre 1994 (DONGLE), CR 1995, 669: La vente d'un programme destiné au contournement d'un système de protection contre les copies est contraire au § 1 *UWG* en ce qu'elle constitue une entrave à la libre concurrence. Cela vaut également lorsque le programme contient d'autres parties indépendantes dont la vente ne constitue aucune violation du § 1 *UWG*.

LG Mannheim 20 janvier 1995 (DONGLE), CR 1995, 542: La suppression ou le contournement d'une *"Dongle-Abfrage"* est justifié par le § 69d *UrhG* lorsque le programme, à la suite de la *"Abfrage"*, ne fonctionne pas sans perturbation.

OLG Frankfurt am Main 13 juin 1995 (Piratenkarten), NJW-Cor 1996, 56: La vente de cartes pirates qui permettent de recevoir des *"pay-tv-programme"* décryptés sans utilisation de la carte de décodage originale constitue une entrave contraire au droit de la concurrence du distributeur de systèmes de cryptage et une atteinte à l'organisation et à l'exploitation de son entreprise.

BGH 9 novembre 1995 (Dongle-Umgehung), CR 1996, 79: Le créancier a un intérêt prépondérant à l'exécution forcée d'un jugement qui a ordonné la cessation et la remise de l'information contre un débiteur ayant vendu un programme d'ordinateur destiné au contournement du système de sécurité d'un autre programme d'ordinateur.

M. Lehmann, note sous BGH 9 novembre 1995, CR 1996, 81: Bien que cette décision de la première Chambre de la Cour Suprême[1] ait été rendue seulement sur le fondement du § 719 al. 2, 1ère phrase, du Code de Procédure Civile *(ZPO)* et concernait en premier lieu un problème d'exécution forcée, elle contient cependant deux déclarations de droit matériel éminemment importantes: *(1)* Les programmes d'ordinateurs sont en principe protégés sur le fondement du § 1 *UWG*[2] par le droit de la concurrence. *(2)* Les programmes de contournement qui peuvent également supprimer une protection technique contre les copies ne doivent pas être proposés sur le marché ni vendus.

> *1. § 1 UWG: La protection des programmes d'ordinateur selon le droit de la concurrence*

La Cour justifie en une seule phrase le fait que le programme d'ordinateur AutoCAD soit protégé sur le fondement du § 1 *UWG*: la demanderesse ne doit pas être entravée dans la vente de "son programme original au moins selon le droit de la concurrence". Ainsi est confirmé pour la première fois par la Cour Suprême ce qui est depuis longtemps défendu en doctrine:[3] les programmes d'ordinateurs qui présentent une qualité *"wettbewerbliche"* sont protégés selon le § 1 *UWG* contre la reprise directe d'un de leurs éléments. Cette protection selon le droit de la concurrence n'exclut pas une éventuelle protection par le droit d'auteur, puisque le *BGH* renvoie lui-même expressément au § 69g al. 1 de la Loi sur le droit d'auteur *(UrhG)*. Le principe de cumulation[4] est ainsi confirmé. Si ce jugement avait été prononcé plus tôt, cela aurait épargné beaucoup d'encre à la doctrine et la pratique du droit informatique aurait pu, avant même l'entrée en vigueur le 24 juin 1993 de la nouvelle protection par le droit d'auteur, se protéger nettement plus efficacement contre le vol intellectuel. La Cour n'ayant fait aucune observation supplémentaire sur les conditions de l'existence d'une "qualité *wettbewerbliche*", il convient de penser que la détermination de ce critère devra se faire selon les principes généraux de la doctrine et de la jurisprudence. Hefermehl énonce par exemple à ce propos:[5] *"La qualité* wettbewerblich *existe dans un programme d'ordinateur par le seul fait qu'il donne au producteur d'origine une avance dans la concurrence".* En tout cas, lorsqu'un programme d'ordinateur a été développé moyennant beaucoup

371

d'efforts, de temps, et d'argent, l'existence d'une qualité *"wettbewerblich"* doit être reconnue. Dans le cas d'un programme d'ordinateur hautement différencié comme Auto-CAD, cela ne fait pas de doute; mais même de coûteux et simples programmes d'ordinateur ou aussi des jeux peuvent en principe remplir ces conditions pour la protection selon le § 1 *UWG*.

2. *Le contournement de moyens techniques de protection*

La vente d'un programme de contournement pouvant entre autres supprimer une protection technique contre les copies pour des programmes d'ordinateur, constitue une violation du § 1 *UWG* sous la forme d'une entrave à la concurrence. Cette déclaration du BGH est d'une importance économique considérable puisqu'elle doit être envisagée dans le cadre de la discussion internationale actuelle sur la nécessité du développement et de la protection juridique d'une protection technique contre les atteintes à la propriété intellectuelle. Le Livre blanc américain de septembre 1995 *"Intellectual Property and the National Information Infrastructure"* contient par exemple une proposition d'insérer dans la loi américaine sur le droit d'auteur un article 1201 ainsi rédigé: *"No person shall import, manufacture or distribute any device, product, or component incorporated into a device or product, or offer or perform any service, the primary purpose or effect of which is to avoid, bypass, remove, deactivate, or otherwise circumvent, without the authority of the copyright owner or the law, any process, treatment, mechanism or system which prevents or inhibits the violation of any of the exclusive rights of the copyright owner under section 106"*. Des dispositions comparables pour la protection des programmes d'ordinateur se trouvent déjà dans l'article 7 al. 1c de la Directive 91/250/CEE et au § 69f al. 2 de la Loi sur le droit d'auteur.

Dans les nouveaux domaines des informations sous forme digitale, en particulier des produits multimédias, cela peut devenir une sorte de question de survie pour le droit d'auteur et particulièrement pour tous les auteurs. En effet, les nouvelles techniques excluent pratiquement pour le produit la détermination de celui qui est l'original et celui qui est une copie illégale. La Commission européenne a par conséquent elle aussi, dans son Livre vert sur *"Le droit d'auteur et les droits voisins dans la société de l'information"* (du 19-7-1995), accordé une large place à ces questions des systèmes techniques d'identification et de protection. Avec cette jurisprudence du *BGH*, le terrain économique est déjà préparé d'un point de vue de droit de la concurrence, dans la mesure où ces nouveaux instruments de protection pourraient être *"eingepflanzt"*: celui qui supprime ces mesures de protection ou propose sur le marché des systèmes supprimant une telle protection agit en violation des règles du droit de la concurrence.

Il faut espérer, mais aussi attendre, que le *BGH* confirmera encore par jugement ces deux propositions très importantes pour les industries de l'informatique et des multimedia dans la procédure de révision engagée.

Notes

1. Bundesgerichtshof = BGH.
2. *"Wer im geschäftlichen Verkehre zu Zwecken des Wettbewerbes Handlungen vornimmt, die gegen die guten Sitten verstossen, kann auf Unterlassung und Schadensersatz in Anspruch genommen werden"*.
3. Cf. v.Gamm, *WRP* 1969, 100; pour un résumé, Lehmann, *Rechtsschutz und Verwertung von Computerprogrammen*, 2e ed. 1993, p. 391 *et seq.*
4. Cf. Lehmann, *GRUR* 1995, 250.
5. Baumbach/Hefermehl, *Wettbewerbsrecht*, 18e ed. 1995, § 1 UWG, no. 519.

Canada

É. Franchi & P.E. Moyse

1. Bilan des réalisations, études et projets

a. *Bilan technique*

1.1. *A-t-on mené en Canada des travaux sur la protection technique des oeuvres, spécialement dans l'environnement numérique?*

Oui, notamment dans le rapport rendu en septembre 1995 par le Comité consultatif canadien sur l'autoroute de l'information qui recommande non seulement d'encourager *"la mise au point et la standardisation de techniques permettant de contrôler l'utilisation d'oeuvres protégées, qui soit acceptable par les usagers"* mais encore que *"l'altération ou le contournement des mesures de protection de toutes sortes, tel que le chiffrement ou les procédés anti-copie, doivent être assimilés à un acte criminel en vertu de la Loi sur le droit d'auteur"*. Par ailleurs, le Sous-comité sur le droit d'auteur et l'autoroute de l'information canadienne présente, dans un rapport remis au Comité consultatif, une analyse détaillée des solutions techniques envisagées au Canada.

1.2. *Dans l'affirmative, quelles sont les finalités qui ont été assignées à cette protection (identification des oeuvres et des auteurs, authentification de l'auteur et du contenu, restrictions à l'accès aux oeuvres ou à la copie de celles-ci, informations sur les ayants-droit et les conditions d'utilisation)?*

Le Comité consultatif canadien a souligné l'importance de la protection technique selon son opinion. La pertinence des principes fondamentaux du droit d'auteur n'est pas remise en cause, leur efficacité pratique doit être assurée à l'aide de procédés techniques dans l'environnement numérique. Le Sous-comité sur le droit d'auteur a notamment relevé la banalisation des oeuvres numérisées et souligné l'importance du piratage et de la copie privée. Il a aussi présenté un certain nombre d'analogies avec *"l'expérience acquise dans le domaine de la copie des programmes informatiques et de la reproduction des enregistrements musicaux et des vidéos"* ainsi que *"du piratage des émissions diffusées par satellites"*.[1] Dans cette perspective, le Sous-comité sur le droit d'auteur canadien a présenté quatre solutions techniques susceptibles de protéger les droits exclusifs des auteurs et ayants-droit lors d'exploitations d'oeuvres numérisées: le cryptage des signaux numériques radiodiffusés par satellites, dans le but de faire échec au piratage des émissions: un programme empreintes digitales, système de codage numérique de chaque oeuvre protégée; un procédé de marquage des oeuvres par l'insertion d'*"un avis de* copyright *ou un autre message dans une oeuvre protégée pour avertir l'usager lorsqu'une copie illégale de l'oeuvre a été faite et distribuée".* Le marquage pourrait aussi, selon le Sous-comité, comporter le nom et le numéro d'enregistrement de l'usager et apparaître sur l'oeuvre de la même façon que les avertissements à insérer dans les émissions télévisées: enfin, un système de conversion/procédé anti-copie qui *"consiste à transformer l'oeuvre numérisée sous une forme intermédiaire, d'une façon à ce que l'information brute ou le contenu ne puisse être modifié ou dénaturé. Cette technique décourage la reproduction non-autorisée de l'oeuvre, puisque la qualité de l'oeuvre diminue avec chaque copie".*[2] Tout en présentant une piste de solution pour le respect des droits moraux des auteurs. La finalité des solutions techniques est avant tout d'assurer la protection des droits économiques.

La substance de ces principes est reprise dans le rapport final du Comité consultatif sur l'autoroute de l'information[3] et on sent de l'analyse de ces deux travaux que les intérêts des auteurs ne peuvent être efficacement protégés dans l'environnement numérique qu'à l'aide de solutions techniques qui viendront assurer le respect des principes légaux. Le Comité consultatif affirme cette conviction en précisant que "pour être efficace dans un univers numérique, l'exercice des sanctions civiles requièrent des technologies permettant de contrôler la distribution des copies et d'identifier les titulaires des droits d'auteurs".[4] Le Sous-comité suggère pour sa part des peines plus sévères, y compris des amendes, mais souligne que *"pour être efficaces, ces sanctions exigeraient la mise en place de technologies permettant de retracer les copies et d'identifier les titulaires des droits d'auteur"*, ce qui traduit une fonction supplémentaire aux solutions techniques, confirmant leur caractère universel dans la perspective canadienne. Le Sous-comité sur le droit d'auteur suggère enfin trois solutions éprouvées en matière de logiciels, dont l'une est exclusivement informatique: des sanctions renforcées lors de violations de droits d'auteur; des technologies de diffusion qui assurent la confidentialité de l'information à l'aide de procédés techniques comme le cryptage; et l'éducation générale du public au respect du droit d'auteur.

On peut en déduire que les solutions techniques seront, dans un proche avenir, prépondérantes pour garantir les intérêts tant matériels que moraux des auteurs et ayants-droit d'oeuvres numérisées. La technique, source des questions juridiques que soulève l'autoroute de l'information sera à l'origine de leur solution, tant à l'égard du droit d'auteur qu'à celui de la sécurité des transactions électroniques et de la protection des données tant confidentielles que personnelles dans les réseaux numériques.

> ***1.3.*** *A votre connaissance, sur quelles bases techniques est-il envisagé de résoudre le problème (matériel ou logiciel, codage interne, inséparablement lié à l'oeuvre dès l'origine, ou codage externe, ajouté postérieurement à la création)?*

Si l'on part de la conviction que les principes juridiques sont adaptés à l'environnement numérique et que la difficulté pratique ne tient qu'au respect des principes juridiques, toutes les solutions techniques envisageables, connues ou à venir, doivent être explorées. C'est à cette philosophie que semble adhérer le Sous-comité canadien sur le droit d'auteur, puisqu'il suggère, sans volonté exhaustive, un procédé de cryptage, un procédé de tatouage - le programme empreintes digitales qui est, en même temps, un procédé de codage et de référence pour la gestion collective - et un système de conversion/anti-copie par transformation des copies d'oeuvres numérisées. La plupart de ces solutions sont informatiques et se matérialisent par le traitement de l'information numérique. Ce sont, pour le moment, les seuls moyens techniques présentés au Canada pour garantir les intérêts des auteurs dans les réseaux numériques.

> *1.4. Quels sont les partenaires associés à ces travaux (autorités publiques, sociétés de gestion collective, constructeurs de matériels, fournisseurs de "contenus")?*

Du fait de la rapide émergence des technologies de l'information, le Canada présente encore un système ouvert, et les travaux sur le sujet restent embryonnaires. Ce sont ainsi les producteurs, les fournisseurs de contenus, les interconnecteurs et plus généralement l'ensemble des prestataires de services de l'industrie des télécommunications qui développent, sans normes réelles, des systèmes pour sécuriser leurs transactions électroniques. La sécurité des réseaux reste, de fait, un facteur clé du développement des réseaux et fait l'objet de recherches approfondies de la part de l'ensemble des acteurs de l'industrie. Au Canada, les sociétés d'auteurs devraient prendre en charge la gestion collective des droits d'auteur dans l'environnement numérique, peut-être au moyen d'un guichet unique. Par ailleurs, une norme internationale de type ISO devrait offrir des standards de référence et de cryptage à l'industrie à l'aide desquels des systèmes de perception et de répartition effectifs pourraient être mis en place par les organismes de gestion collective.

b. *Bilan législatif*

> *1.5. Des dispositions législatives existent-elles dans votre pays pour sanctionner de façon générale le contournement de dispositifs de protection technique?*

Il n'existe pas, au Canada, de disposition expresse dans la Loi sur le droit d'auteur, alors que le Code criminel canadien prohibe expressément le contournement de nombreux dispositifs de protection techniques:

Article 342.1
(1) Utilisation non-autorisée d'ordinateur
Quiconque, frauduleusement et sans apparence de droit:
a) directement ou indirectement, obtient des services d'ordinateur;
b) au moyen d'un dispositif électromagnétique, acoustique, mécanique ou autre, directement ou indirectement, intercepte ou fait intercepter toute fonction d'un ordinateur;
c) directement ou indirectement, utilise ou fait utiliser un ordinateur dans l'intention de commettre une infraction prévue a l'alinéa *a)* ou *b)* ou une infraction prévue à l'article 340 concernant des données ou un ordinateur,
est coupable d'un acte criminel et passible d'un emprisonnement maximal de dix ans ou d'une infraction punissable sur déclaration de culpabilité par procédure sommaire.
(2) Définitions
Les définitions qui suivent s'appliquent au présent article:
"Dispositif électromagnétique, acoustique, mécanique ou autre". Tout dispositif ou appareil utilisé ou pouvant être utilisé pour intercepter une fonction d'un ordinateur, à l'exclusion d'un appareil de

correction auditive utilisé pour améliorer, sans dépasser la normale, l'audition de l'utilisateur lorsqu'elle est inférieure à la normale.

"Données". Représentations d'informations ou de concepts qui sont préparés ou l'ont été de façon à pouvoir être utilisés dans un ordinateur.

"Fonction". S'entend notamment des fonctions logiques, arithmétiques, des fonctions de commande et de suppression, des fonctions de mémorisation et de recouvrement ou de relevé des données de même que des fonctions de communication ou de télécommunication de données à destination, à partir d'un ordinateur ou à l'intérieur de celui-ci.

"Intercepter". S'entend notamment du fait d'écouter ou d'enregistrer une fonction d'un ordinateur ou de prendre connaissance de sa substance, de son sens ou de son objet.

"Ordinateur". Dispositif ou ensemble de dispositifs connectés ou reliés les uns aux autres, dont l'un ou plusieurs d'entre eux:

a) contiennent des programmes d'ordinateur ou d'autres données:

b) conformément à des programmes d'ordinateur:

(i) soit exécutent des fonctions logiques et de commande,

(ii) soit peuvent exécuter toute autre fonction.

"Programme d'ordinateur". Ensemble de données qui représentent des instructions ou des relevés et qui, lorsque traités par l'ordinateur, lui font remplir une fonction.

"Service d'ordinateur". S'entend notamment du traitement des données de même que de la mémorisation et du recouvrement ou du relevé des données.

Article 430

(1.1) Méfait concernant des données

Commet un méfait quiconque volontairement, selon le cas:

a) détruit ou modifie des données;

b) dépouille des données de leur sens, les rend inutiles ou inopérantes;

c) empêche, interrompt ou gêne l'emploi légitime des données;

d) empêche, interrompt ou gêne une personne dans l'emploi légitime des données ou refuse l'accès aux données à une personne qui y a droit.

(...)

(5) Idem

Quiconque commet un méfait à l'égard de données est coupable:

a) soit d'un acte criminel et passible d'un emprisonnement maximal de dix ans:

b) soit d'une infraction punissable sur déclaration de culpabilité par procédure sommaire.

(...)

(5.1) Infraction

Quiconque volontairement accomplit un acte ou volontairement omet d'accomplir un acte qu'il a le devoir d'accomplir, si cet acte ou cette omission est susceptible de constituer un méfait qui cause un danger réel pour la vie des gens ou de constituer un méfait à l'égard de biens ou de données est coupable:

a) soit d'un acte criminel et passible d'un emprisonnement maximal de cinq ans;

b) soit d'une infraction punissable sur déclaration de culpabilité par procédure sommaire.

Article 326

(1) Vol de service de télécommunication

Commet un vol quiconque, frauduleusement, malicieusement ou sans apparence de droit:

(...)

b) (...) se sert d'installations ou obtient un service en matière de télécommunication.

(2) Définition de "télécommunication"

(...) *"télécommunication"* désigne toute transmission, émission ou réception de signes, de signaux, d'écrits, d'images, de sons ou de renseignements de toute nature par fil, radioélectricité, optique ou autres systèmes électromagnétiques.

Article 327

(1) Possession de moyens permettant d'utiliser des installations ou d'obtenir un service en matière de télécommunication

Quiconque, sans excuse légitime, dont la preuve lui incombe, fabrique, possède, vend ou offre en vente ou écoule des instruments ou des pièces particulièrement utiles pour utiliser des installations ou obtenir un service en matière de télécommunication, dans des circonstances qui permettent raisonnablement de conclure qu'ils ont été utilisés, sont destinés ou ont été destinés à l'être à cette fin, sans acquittement des droits exigibles, est coupable d'un acte criminel et passible d'un emprisonnement maximal de deux ans.

(2) Confiscation

Lorsqu'une personne est déclarée coupable d'une infraction prévue au paragraphe (1) ou à l'alinéa 326(1)*b)*, tout instrument au moyen duquel l'infraction a été commise ou dont la possession a constitué l'infraction peut, après cette déclaration de culpabilité et en plus de toute peine qui est imposée, être par ordonnance confisqué au profit de Sa Majesté, après quoi il peut en être disposé conformément aux instructions du procureur général.

(3) Restriction

Aucune ordonnance de confiscation ne peut être rendue en vertu du paragraphe (2) relativement à des installations ou du matériel de communications téléphoniques, télégraphiques ou autres qui sont la propriété d'une personne fournissant au public un service de communications téléphoniques, télégraphiques ou autres ou qui font partie du service ou réseau de communications téléphoniques, télégraphiques ou autres d'une telle personne et au moyen desquels une infraction prévue au paragraphe (1) a été commise, si cette personne n'a pas participé à l'infraction.

1.6. Dans la négative, existe-t-il des précédents, par exemple dans le domaine du cryptage des émissions de télévision? / 1.7. L'usage, la diffusion ou l'exportation des techniques de cryptage sont-ils soumis à des restrictions particulières?

Il est, au Canada, illégal de décoder sans autorisation des signaux codés de télévision par satellite et de recevoir et/ou retransmettre des signaux codés, décodés sans autorisation. Il existe, au Canada, trois types de réception non-autorisée ou illégale, faite, soit à l'aide d'antennes paraboliques, soit à l'aide de décodeurs, autorisés ou non. D'une part, un signal codé peut être décodé illégalement à l'aide d'un décodeur auquel on a ajouté un circuit intégré ou auquel on a modifié un circuit existant. Cela permet à un individu de décoder les signaux de services de programmation sans avoir à les payer. Par ailleurs, certains utilisent des décodeurs tout simplement illégaux, qui permettent de décoder des signaux de programmation sans payer les frais d'abonnement aux réseaux. Enfin, la troisième forme de réception non-autorisée se fait à l'aide d'un décodeur en dehors du territoire où il est autorisé à décoder le signal d'un service de programmation.

Aux termes de la nouvelle législation sur la radiodiffusion et les télécommunications canadiennes, telle qu'amendée respectivement en 1991 et 1993, il est illégal de posséder ou d'utiliser un décodeur permettant de décoder sans autorisation les signaux codés de télévision par satellite, car cela revient à décoder des signaux sans payer de frais d'abonnement aux services de programmation. Par ailleurs, le fait de décoder un signal codé de programmation sans autorisation, de même que le fait de capter un signal codé, décodé illégalement ou encore le fait de retransmettre des signaux codés et décodés sans autorisation constituent clairement des infractions à la législation canadienne. En outre, la fabrication, la modification ou le commerce de matériel pouvant servir au décodage non-autorisé de signaux codés est prohibé, que cela soit fait par des particuliers ou des entreprises commerciales. Toute personne possédant des intérêts dans la programmation codée ou qui fabrique, fournit ou vend des décodeurs légitimes, peut ainsi entreprendre des recours civils contre les contrevenants. De la même façon, les auteurs et ayants-droit des programmes et émissions possèdent des recours contre les utilisations non-autorisées de leurs oeuvres.

Les contrevenants peuvent être poursuivis pour dommages et intérêts, mais aussi par le biais d'injonctions ou de tout autre recours approprié. Les principales infractions et peines prévues sont les suivantes:
- *pour fabriquer, importer, distribuer, louer, offrir de vendre, vendre, installer, modifier, posséder ou exploiter un décodeur illégal:* 5.000 $ d'amende par jour maximum, avec éventuellement une peine d'emprisonnement jusqu'à un an s'il s'agit d'un particulier; une amende d'un montant maximum de 25.000 $ par jour, s'il s'agit d'une entreprise;
- *pour décoder sans permission un signal codé:* s'il s'agit d'un individu, une amende

d'un maximum de 10.000 $ par jour et/ou une peine d'emprisonnement pouvant aller jusqu'a six mois. S'il s'agit d'une entreprise, une amende allant jusqu'à 25.000 $ par jour;

- *pour capter un signal codé qui a été décodé sans permission:* s'il s'agit d'un individu, une amende pouvant atteindre 10.000 $ par jour et/ou une peine d'emprisonnement allant jusqu'à six mois. S'il s'agit d'une entreprise, une amende d'un montant maximal de 25.000 $ par jour:

- *pour ré-émettre un signal codé qui a été décodé sans permission,* un individu risque une amende de 20.000 $ par jour et/ou une peine de prison pouvant aller jusqu'à une année. Une entreprise peut, pour sa part, être condamnée à une amende allant jusqu'à 200.000 $ par jour.

2. **Appréciation critique**

2.1. Est-il opportun selon vous de prévoir des sanctions contre le contournement des dispositifs de protection technique? Ces dispositifs peuvent-ils être efficaces? Les enjeux justifient-ils les investissements importants qui sont nécessaires?

La protection technique risque être un élément clé pour la protection du droit d'auteur dans l'environnement numérique et son développement devrait être favorisé par des sanctions substantielles en matière de droits d'auteur comme dans les domaines connexes que sont le droit criminel, le droit de l'information et le droit de la radiodiffusion. Les principes actuels du droit d'auteur suffisent apparamment à assurer la rémunération des auteurs et ayants-droit pour les utilisations de leurs oeuvres dans les réseaux électroniques.

Le principe du droit exclusif ne doit pas être remis en cause mais en pratique, il est difficile d'identifier chaque utilisation pour chaque oeuvre. C'est ici que les dispositifs techniques prennent toute leur importance puisqu'ils permettent:
- la comptabilisation de l'ensemble des utilisations;
- la qualification de chaque utilisation;
- l'authentification de chaque copie licite;
- le respect des droits moraux.

Malgré cette perspective, il faut convenir que la sécurité des solutions techniques reste aléatoire puisqu'à tout système de protection correspondra inéluctablement un système de neutralisation. En ce sens, nous doutons de l'efficacité de ces dispositifs lorsqu'ils visent à empêcher la copie ou une forme d'utilisation des oeuvres.

2.2. Les sanctions doivent-elles à votre avis permettre d'atteindre ceux qui mettent à la disposition des utilisateurs les moyens visant à réaliser ce contournement? Dans l'affirmative, faut-il les limiter à commercialisation de moyens ayant le contournement "pour seul but", à l'instar de l'article 7(1)c de la directive communautaire de 1991 sur les programmes d'ordinateur, ou peut-on aller, comme dans la proposition du Livre blanc américain, jusqu'à prohiber les moyens dont le but ou l'effet premier est le contournement?

L'influence du système de copyright rend la proposition du Livre blanc américain[5] acceptable et s'inscrit dans la logique du système canadien.[6] Une sanction généralisée aurait des effets dissuasifs évidents.

> **2.3.** *Pensez-vous qu'il faille envisager une harmonisation des législations, afin d'éviter des distorsions de concurrence? Peut-on concevoir une norme unique? Comment et par qui cette norme devrait-elle être élaborée?*

Sur l'harmonisation des législations repose le respect effectif du droit d'auteur dans les réseaux numériques qui sont, par définition, supranationaux. Il est néanmoins délicat de déterminer l'opportunité d'un instrument juridique universel élaboré dans un proche avenir, vu l'évolution rapide des réseaux. A long terme cependant, le rôle normatif devrait être confié à l'Organisation Mondiale de la Propriété Intellectuelle qui a traditionnellement juridiction pour les traités internationaux et étudie actuellement leur révision. Au plan technique, il existe des organismes de réglementation comme l'*International Standard Organisation (ISO)* dont le rôle naturel est la mise au point de normes de sécurité, de codage, de tatouage et de communication.

> **2.4.** *Quel devrait être selon vous le fondement d'une règlementation dans ce domaine? S'agit-il de garantir la sécurité en vue d'améliorer la diffusion des oeuvres au bénéfice du public? Dans cette optique, peut-on aller jusqu'à rendre obligatoire la protection technique, à l'instar de la loi américaine* (Audio Home Recording Act) *imposant que les fabricants de matériel d'enregistrement sonore numérique incorporent des dispositifs limitant les copies séquentielles à la copie de première génération? S'agit-il plutôt d'une protection complémentaire destinée à garantir la propriété de l'auteur, à laquelle celui-ci pourrait renoncer?*

Les technologies numériques de diffusion ont pour conséquence le risque de perte de contrôle, pour les auteurs et ayants-droit, sur les utilisations faites de leurs oeuvres. Ce risque se traduit par une certaine réticence des auteurs et ayants-droit à autoriser les formes d'exploitation télématique. Le principe du droit exclusif est, à lui seul, inefficace pour contrer, en pratique, les risques de cette technologie et aujourd'hui, l'autorisation donnée par un auteur d'exploiter son oeuvre sous une forme numérisée dans un réseau, équivaut à une perte de contrôle sur sa création. Pour cette raison, de nombreux auteurs et ayants-droit réservent leurs autorisations en attendant que la législation ou les techniques aient évolué (cf. par exemple l'Association des producteurs de disques et vidéo du Québec, dont les membres refusent, pour le moment, d'autoriser les exploitations télématiques de leurs enregistrements sonores). Pour cette raison, nous pensons qu'un dispositif technique aurait pour vocation première de protéger les droits économiques et moraux des auteurs en limitant, d'une part, la copie de leurs oeuvres et, d'autre part, leur réutilisation (notamment par rediffusion) à des fins commerciales. Il est évident qu'une législation qui protégerait ainsi les auteurs et ayants-droit favoriserait, à terme, les membres du public qui verraient ainsi l'accès aux oeuvres offert à un moindre coût. En outre, ce n'est pas tant dans le matériel de lecture et de reproduction des oeuvres numérisées (le *"hardware"*) que les solutions techniques doivent se trouver, mais beaucoup plus, dans l'oeuvre elle-même (*i.e.* code numérique indélébile d'immatriculation ou ISBN numérique). Ce code informatique devrait notamment permettre d'authentifier et d'identifier les utilisateurs de l'oeuvre.

> **2.5.** *L'interdiction de contourner les dispositifs de protection technique doit-elle à votre avis trouver place dans la loi sur le droit d'auteur ou dans une loi distincte? Dans la première hypothèse, le contournement doit-il être seulement "assimilé" à une violation du droit d'auteur ou faut-il y voir un véritable acte d'exploitation soumis en tant que tel au droit exclusif? Dans la seconde hypothèse, sur quelle base juridique fonder cette analyse? La neutralisation d'un dispositif doit-elle par exemple s'analyser comme une reproduction au sens de la législation sur le droit d'auteur?*

La violation du dispositif technique devrait à tout le moins être "assimilée" à une violation du droit d'auteur, car elle constitue souvent un acte de reproduction ou de représentation. Selon nous, les sources de législation pertinentes aux contournements de dispositifs de protection technique sont multiples au Canada. Les sanctions et leurs fondements peuvent être recherchés dans le droit d'auteur, le Code Criminel ou les lois sur la radiodiffusion et les télécommunications canadiennes. Nous avons vu qu'au Canada, c'est dans ces trois derniers textes que l'on trouve ce genre de dispositions. Le contournement d'une protection technique pourrait cependant s'analyser comme un acte de contrefaçon lorsqu'il est fait dans un but commercial ou aux fins de diffusion, voire de reproduction. Une disposition spécifique dans la Loi sur le droit d'auteur ne serait donc pas sans objet.

> **2.6.** *Si les sanctions sont limitées aux hypothèses dans lesquelles le contournement des dispositifs de protection technique vise à permettre l'accès à une oeuvre donnant prise au droit d'auteur, doivent-elles être subordonnées à la preuve que l'utilisateur savait (ou aurait dû savoir) qu'il violait ce droit d'auteur? Seront-elles encourues lorsque le contournement aura permis d'accéder à des parties non-originales de l'oeuvre?*

Pour être efficaces, les sanctions ne doivent pas dépendre d'un élément psychologique de la part de l'utilisateur. C'est l'acte technique, matériel, qui doit être sanctionné, à l'instar d'une contravention pénale. Dans cette logique retenue par le système canadien, la sanction est indépendante de l'originalité des informations auxquelles le contournement aura donné accès. La numérisation permet la constitution de banques de données ou de compilations multimédia dont de nombreuses portions seront constituées de données factuelles. Il est important que les investissements nécessaires à la constitution de ces compilations soient protégés et des sanctions contre le contournement technique fondées sur des critères objectifs nous paraissent, dans cette perspective, les plus appropriées.

> **2.7.** *L'interdiction de contourner les dispositifs de protection technique peut-elle selon vous être critiquée comme restreignant (ou risquant de restreindre) abusivement l'accès au domaine public? Ou comme paralysant le*

jeu des dérogations limitant traditionnellement la portée du droit d'auteur ("fair use" ou usage privé)? Des considérations d'intérêt public peuvent-elles justifier que la protection technique soit neutralisée par les autorités? Dans l'affirmative, peut-on, pour limiter les risques, imaginer que cette neutralisation soit commandée par la mise en oeuvre de plusieurs clés?

Malgré la possibilité de critiques théoriques, nous sommes d'avis que même si des données sont du domaine public, leur exploitation télématique suppose des investissements substantiels. Ainsi, l'utilisateur a-t-il le choix d'accéder "en ligne" à des banques de données présentant à la fois des oeuvres protégées et des informations du domaine public. Il a aussi la possibilité de rechercher seul les sources de ces compilations. Dans le second cas, la protection technique n'a pas lieu de s'appliquer; l'accès aux informations du domaine public étant libre. Cependant, pour l'utilisateur, cet accès est long et fastidieux, parfois onéreux. Ainsi, le recours à un service d'information en ligne constitue une alternative qui justifie le paiement d'une rémunération. La neutralisation de la protection technique par des autorités publiques est envisageable dans l'hypothèse où les données sont cryptées. En effet, les autorités publiques peuvent vouloir exercer un certain contrôle sur les messages diffusés afin d'en vérifier le contenu (propagande haineuse, jeu, prostitution). Dans cette perspective, un système dans lequel les autorités publiques auraient accès à des codes permettant le décryptage des messages, ne devrait pas être critiqué, dans la mesure où cet accès est limité aux autorités publiques et peut éventuellement être contrôlé par des clés. Il n'y a cependant pas eu de débat précis sur ce point au Canada, contrairement aux États-Unis.

2.8. Comment l'interdiction généralisée de contourner les dispositifs de protection technique pourrait-elle être conciliée avec les règles spéciales gouvernant la décompilation des programmes d'ordinateur, telles qu'elles résultent de la directive communautaire précitée, ou avec la jurisprudence développée aux États-Unis sur la base du "fair use"?

Les dispositifs de protection technique et les principes gouvernant la décompilation des programmes d'ordinateur ont deux objets différents: la protection technique vise à limiter la reproduction privée et commerciale ainsi que la rediffusion par un utilisateur d'une oeuvre protégée à laquelle il aura eu préalablement accès. L'exception de décompilation a pour objet l'analyse de la structure d'un programme informatique afin de permettre la création indépendante d'un programme présentant des fonctions identiques tout en étant d'une structure distincte. En ce sens, nous croyons que le dispositif de protection technique limite l'accès et *certaines* utilisations des oeuvres, ce qui ne devrait pas remettre en question la liberté de décompilation. La solution se trouve peut-être dans le dispositif de protection technique lui-même qui devra permettre la décompilation, tout en limitant d'autres utilisations.

2.9. Quelle sera l'incidence d'une législation telle que celle envisagée ci-dessus sur l'avenir du droit d'auteur? Faut-il accorder du crédit à l'hypothèse selon laquelle la protection technique, complétée par les contrats, signifie le déclin, voire la mort du droit d'auteur? Ou doit-on considérer que le droit exclusif reste une arme indispensable dans l'environnement numérique?

Le droit exclusif doit rester l'un des fondements essentiels du droit d'auteur, même dans l'environnement numérique. Les solutions techniques doivent être considérées comme un complément aux règles légales pour permettre l'exercice effectif du droit exclusif des auteurs. Il est cependant à craindre qu'une protection technique généralisée favorise l'institution d'un système de licences obligatoires, selon les solutions techniques retenues. La protection technique et les contrats n'impliquent cependant pas le déclin du droit exclusif des auteurs. Les solutions techniques et contractuelles sont transitoires, destinées à pallier aux ambiguïtés législatives et à l'incertitude jurisprudentielle. Par ailleurs, la protection technique est une solution indissociable de l'environnement numérique et assure un complément pratique aux principes de la Loi sur le droit d'auteur. L'objet des solutions techniques devrait cependant être clairement défini, de sorte qu'elles puissent:
- interdire l'accès gratuit aux oeuvres protégées;
- interdire la copie illicite des oeuvres faite sans rémunération des auteurs et ayants-droit;
- contrôler l'altération des oeuvres et la rediffusion non-autorisées des oeuvres par les membres du public.

2.10. Autres observations?

-

Notes

1. Cf. *Le droit d'auteur et l'autoroute de l'information*, rapport préliminaire du Sous-comité sur le droit d'auteur, groupe d'étude sur la culture et le contenu canadien, Comité consultatif sur l'autoroute de l'information, décembre 1994, p. 22.
2. *Id.* , p. 33.
3. Cf. Rapport final du Sous-comité, mars 1995 et *Le défi de l'autoroute de l'information*, rapport final du Comité consultatif sur l'autoroute de l'information, Ministère des approvisionnements et services Canada, septembre 1995.
4. *Id.*, p. 34.
5. Proposition d'un article 1201 à insérer dans le *Copyright Act* de 76: '*No person shall import, manufacture or distribute any device, product or component incorporated into a device or product, or offer or perform any service, the primary purpose or effect of which is to avoid, bypass, remove, deactivate, or otherwise circumvent, without the authority of the copyright owner or the law, any process, treatment, mecanism or system which prevents or inhibits the violation of any of the exclusive rights of the copyright owner under Section 106*'.
6. Cf. nos réponses 1.5 et 1.7.

Finland

R. Oesch

1. State of realization studies and projects

a. *State of techniques*

1.1. *Are there any activities in Finland concerning the technical protection of works, especially in the digital environment?*

The Finnish Copyright Committee (Ministry of Education) has published a preliminary Report (*Copyright in an Information Society*; 1995:13), in which the Committee discusses at a preliminary level problems raised by digital technology and possible solutions. The Report gives a summary of the material published about this topic. No extensive and detailed national report has been published so far (January 1996) concerning the technical protection of copyrighted material, but a more detailed report with possible suggestions for alterations in the copyright legislation will probably be published in the course of 1996.

1.2. *In the affirmative, what is the extent of this technical protection?*

-

1.3. *Which technical bases are covered in order to resolve the problem?*

-

1.4. *Who are the participants in the activities?*

-

b. *State of legislation*

1.5. *Do any legislative stipulations exist in Finland with regard to general sanctions?*

At the moment there is no general clause in Finnish law to protect technical methods for protection. The only article of importance at the moment is article 58 of the Finnish Copyright Act, according to which in an infringement case a court may prescribe that the special devices used for infringement shall be destroyed or that such property shall be altered in specific ways. It seems quite clear that the provisions of article 58 do not meet the current need for protection. The inclusion of provisions on technical systems of protection and identification is to be welcomed. These issues have been objects of action within European integration as well. There are a number of questions which need closer examination. The basic goal should be the increased effectiveness of technical protection systems. Sanctions should be connected to clearly defined actions. Such acts as manufacturing, importing, distributing and possession should be covered. It should also be considered whether the rules should also cover the use of devices or services.

1.6. If no, are there precedents, for example in the domain of encrypting television broadcasts?

There have been encrypted television broadcasts and copy-protected computer programs in the market. Precedents are very few. It must be pointed out in this context that the Penal Code in its 38th chapter (Crimes in Information and Communication) forbids different forms of offences against telecommunication and information (communications offence or hacking).

1.7. Are use, distribution or export of encryption devices subject to particular restrictions?

2. Critical assessment

2.1. Is the preparation of sanctions against the circumvention of technical protective devices worthwhile in your opinion? Will these devices be efficient? Does the aim justify the substantial investments required?

Yes, it is absolutely necessary to create new supporting forms of protection in order to avoid misbehaviour towards technical forms of protection. Production costs of the works justify technical protection.

2.2. Should the sanctions be directed against those who provide users with the means to circumvent protective devices? In the affirmative, should they be limited to those means which are specifically meant to circumvent protective devices, analogous to article 7(1)c of the 1991 Software Directive, or is it preferable, like in the American White Paper, to prohibit means of which one of the aims or most important effect is to circumvent protective devices?

The scope and focus of the legislation should be defined (especially which Acts are covered). I cannot yet offer a qualitative view on the question, whether the regulation should cover devices/services which are intended for piracy, or the sole purpose of which is circumvention of technical protection systems. Not only copyright legislation but also civil and penal sanctions and remedies should be considered.

2.3. Do you think that it would be necessary to consider a harmonization of legislations, to prevent distortions in competition? Is it possible to find a uniform standard? How and by whom should this standard be developed?

In fact a precondition of introducing any legal rule should be that such systems/ devices/services can be developed which are widely used and generally acceptable. Harmonizing the possible legal principles is most important, because different levels of protection may cause different preconditions for competition.

2.4. What should be the bases of regulations in this field? Is the aim to guarantee security in light of improving the diffusion of works for the benefit of the public? In that view, should regulations lead to compulsory technical protection, analogous to American law (Audio Home Recording Act), impo- sing an obligation upon the producers of digital sound recording equipment to apply devices limiting copying to copies of the first generation? Or is it a complementary protection which is meant to guarantee the rights of the author, which he can renounce?

At this stage we cannot yet be sure which kind of regulation would be feasible.

2.5. Should the injunction to circumvent technical protective devices be part of copyright law or a separate law? In the first case, should it be an act which is a violation of copyright only or is there an act of exploitation, subject to the exclusive rights? In the second case, what is the legal basis? Should the neutralization of a device, for instance, be considered a reproduction in the sense of copyright legislation?

In protecting technical means one cannot be sure whether the protection is for the authors, transmitters and/or public. Obligations for protection (as in the American Audio Home Recording Act) may turn out to be inconvenient. As for the place for the provisions - this is a question of taste and legal tradition. Criminal sanctions against copyright infringements are traditionally placed in the Penal Code in a special chapter for intellectual property rights, where sanction clauses may be included because of the close connection with the contents of copyright.

2.6. If the sanctions are limited to the hypothesis that there is an infringement of copyright if technical protection devices are circumvented which leads to access to a work, should these sanctions be limited to the case that the user knew (or should have known) that he was infringing?

It is difficult to see that these different forms of acts are comparable, at least in the sense that they are regarded equal for the purposes of the indecency in the society to be regulated in the Penal Code. For the liability the infringer must have some degree of fault, *i.e.* some knowledge or some reason to believe that the device is meant for circumvention of protection (subjective preconditions for liability).

2.7. Do you think criticism of the injunction to circumvent technical protective devices is justified, in view of the fact that the access to works which are in the public domain is or could be limited? Or because the traditional limitations on copyright (like fair use or private use) are not respected? Do considerations which are in the interest of the public justify that the technical protection is neutralized by the authorities? In the affirmative, is it imaginable that this neutralization is ordered by using several keys?

This is a possible (serious) problem that is in fact a political one. The limitations (exceptions) of copyright are always there to fulfil the needs of the public.

2.8. Is it possible to reconcile the general injunction on the circumvention of technical protective devices with the special rules covering the decompilation of software, like those resulting from the Software Directive mentioned before, or with the jurisprudence developed in the United States on the basis of fair use?

The decompilation is made by professionals and most probably the technical protection systems are the smallest problems in the microchip and computer program industry.

2.9. What could be the effect of legislation as has been elaborated upon above on the future of copyright? Do you agree with the hypothesis which says that technical protection, in combination with contracts, means the decline or the end of copyright? Or should we consider the exclusive right of the author an indispensable weapon in the digital environment?

Life will continue as analogue phenomenon and digital systems will not completely replace analogue systems for a long time to come. Legal rules and exclusive rights are indispensable also in the digital era.

2.10. Other observations?

France

G. VERCKEN

Remarques préliminaires

Des réponses ont été apportées à la première partie du questionnaire ("Bilan des réalisations, des études et des projets"). Nous ne nous estimons pas compétents pour répondre aux difficiles questions posées dans la seconde partie ("Appréciation critique"). Le présent questionnaire porte sur la protection technique des oeuvres. Le terme générique de "protection technique des oeuvres" peut recouvrir de nombreuses facettes. Il apparaît donc nécessaire avant de faire état des réalisations, études et projets en cours de réalisation, de resituer la question de la protection technique des oeuvres dans un contexte plus général.

Introduction

En matière de sécurité, la définition d'un moyen de protection s'effectue au regard d'un double critère:
- l'étendue du risque encouru, et
- les moyens à mettre en oeuvre pour couvrir ce risque.

Une protection technique est adéquate quand les moyens mis en oeuvre sont proportionnés au risque encouru. Poser la question de la définition d'un système de protection des oeuvres, c'est donc en premier lieu apprécier les risques encourus par les oeuvres dans l'environnement numérique. L'environnement numérique se caractérise par une absence de limitation du volume des oeuvres diffusées, par la dématérialisation, qui rend la copie extrêmement aisée et identique à l'original, et par la décentralisation complète de la diffusion (possibilité de diffusion du "tous vers tous", et non plus du "un vers tous", expression utilisée par Monsieur le Conseiller Kerever lors du colloque annuel de l'ALAI à Paris en septembre 1995).

Par rapport à ces caractéristiques, les risques se situent à deux niveaux différents:
(1) la gestion des oeuvres et des droits y afférents, et
(2) le piratage des oeuvres et des droits y afférents.

(1) La gestion

Pour la gestion, il convient de définir des nouveaux outils afin de permettre de contrôler la diffusion, c'est-à-dire essentiellement d'être des oeuvres diffusées. A ce niveau, les moyens traditionnels de collecte de l'information (par exemple programmes papiers) ne sont plus adaptés au regard de la multiplication des oeuvres diffusées et des diffuseurs. Ces nouveaux outils doivent donc permettre d'identifier facilement et automatiquement les oeuvres, de pouvoir vérifier la bonne mise en place de l'identification, afin de rendre le système cohérent, de gérer l'information suite à l'utilisation de cette identification dans la chaîne de diffusion des oeuvres de l'auteur au diffuseur final, à tous les échelons (auteur, société d'auteur, producteur de services, fournisseur de service, transporteur de service, utilisation final).

C'est la première étape des travaux: assurer l'identification et la gestion de l'information. L'étape suivante et complémentaire en matière de gestion consiste à développer les systèmes de gestion contractuelle par les réseaux, afin que l'acte de prise de connaissance de l'oeuvre puisse être simultané à l'acte de délivrance de l'autorisation (systèmes dits ECMS pour *Electronic Copyright Management System*). Ces outils de gestion sont destinés essentiellement à fonctionner dans un univers de "bonne foi", et la présence de moyens techniques de protection n'apparaît pas indispensable. En matière de gestion des droits, la protection physique de ces outils n'est pas déterminante au regard des buts qui leur sont assignés. Par contre, pour que ces outils fonctionnent, il faut qu'ils soient univoques et universels, ce qui peut donc amener à les rendre obligatoires.

(2) Le piratage

Le deuxième niveau de risque concerne le piratage des oeuvres. Ce piratage est rendu aisé par les caractéristiques décrites prédédemment. Dans la chaîne qui mène de l'auteur à l'utilisateur final, il apparaît possible dans l'environnement numérique de maîtriser une première diffusion. Il est essentiel de noter à ce niveau l'existence de moyens de protection technique mis en place par les acteurs de la chaîne, moyens qui n'ont pas pour but de maîtriser la diffusion des oeuvres, mais de maîtriser l'accès aux services offerts. Ainsi, le fournisseur de service met en oeuvre des systèmes de contrôle d'accès qui lui permet de connaître l'utilisateur final, et, surtout, de pouvoir lui faire payer le service. C'est déjà le cas pour toutes les chaînes à péages (CANAL+, chaînes thématiques du câble), et pour tous les services sur réseaux (INFONIE, COMPUSERVE, AMERICA-ON-LINE, EUROPE-ON-LINE, etc.).

Ce qui distingue les fournisseurs de service des titulaires de droit est donc la finalité de la protection. Les fournisseurs ne sont intéressés par les systèmes de protection que par rapport à ce premier aspect, et ensuite, éventuellement, par la maîtrise de la communication afin d'empêcher que l'utilisateur soit dispensé de revenir vers le fournisseur pour un service identique. Pour illustrer le propos, on peut prendre l'exemple de la vidéo à la demande. Le fournisseur dès lors qu'il facturera l'utilisateur au nombre de diffusions de film, souhaitera maîtriser l'utilisation finale. Si, par contre, il estime que la première diffusion de l'oeuvre auprès de l'utilisateur ne l'empêche pas de "vendre" d'autres oeuvres ensuite, l'utilisation finale de l'oeuvre ne le concerne pas car elle ne porte pas atteinte à ses intérêts. Tel est le cas également si ce fournisseur a facturé l'utilisateur en tenant compte dans la fixation du prix du fait que celui-ci détiendra, après la première utilisation, une copie de l'oeuvre qui le dispensera, pour cette oeuvre, d'utiliser de nouveau le service. Il est donc essentiel de mettre en exergue le fait que les fournisseurs de service sont intéressés uniquement par les systèmes d'accès conditionnel, et non pas directement par la protection du contenu de ses services, sauf de manière indirecte.

De plus, la sécurisation des transactions financières est une priorité absolue pour tous ces services (voir en cette matière: cf. rapport *"Information Transaction in the Global Information Market"* de Anne C. Leer, Oxford, Information Engineering ELPUB 102, Commission Européenne DG XIII). Cette sécurisation repose sur la cryptologie. La cryptologie est un moyen de protection correspondant aux besoins de confidentialité et d'authentification, qui nécessite un rapport direct entre l'utilisateur et le fournisseur d'accès ou de service pour l'acquisition et la gestion des clés (protection du type "carte bleue").

La sécurisation de l'accès par ces moyens passe donc nécessairement par un contrat personnel entre l'utilisateur et le fournisseur de service, contrat qui permet d'assurer le contrôle. La logique de sécurisation pour les oeuvres est différente. Il s'agit d'organiser alors la sécurisation de chaque oeuvre, et d'établir ainsi un contrôle d'accès oeuvre par oeuvre qui prend en compte la spécificité de la diffusion des oeuvres, ce qui est beaucoup plus complexe. Car dès lors que la copie numérique est à la disposition de l'utilisateur final, celui-ci peut à son tour exploiter l'oeuvre, et en raison de la facilité technique de diffusion, devenir lui-même fournisseur de service. Cette nouvelle activité peut être effectuée à titre artisanal, ou au contraire à grande échelle.

Il y a alors perte de contrôle de l'utilisation de l'oeuvre pour les titulaires de droit, ce qui risque de créer un préjudice considérable pour toute la profession (auteurs, sociétés, producteurs de services). C'est pour lutter contre cette perte de contrôle potentielle que la mise en place de systèmes de protection technique s'avère plus particulièrement nécessaire. Une protection efficace des oeuvres dans l'environnement numérique nécessite de décomposer en plusieurs étapes le processus afin d'identifier les finalités de la protection assignée à chaque étape. Le processus comprend trois étapes: *(1)* l'identification de l'objet à protéger, *(2)* la protection de cet objet ou/et de son identifiant, et *(3)* la gestion de la relation entre le fournisseur de l'objet et l'utilisateur.

Pour répondre à ces finalités, plusieurs modalités de protection peuvent être proposées *(a)* protection directe de l'oeuvre, *(b)* protection indirecte de l'oeuvre par la protection de l'identifiant de l'oeuvre, ou *(c)* protection directe de l'exploitation par l'impossibilité technique d'accomplir certains actes (par exemples multicopie). Cette classification sera retenue afin d'ordonner les réponses au questionnaire dans sa première partie.

1. Bilan des réalisations, études et projets

a. *Bilan technique*

1.1. *A-t-on mené dans votre pays des travaux sur la protection technique des oeuvres, spécialement dans l'environnement numérique?*

De nombreux travaux ont été réalisés en France, ou initiés à partir de la France et repris dans un cadre international. En effet, au regard de la dimension mondiale des questions posées, ces travaux doivent s'insérer dans le cadre international: d'autres rapports nationaux ne manqueront certainement pas dès lors de faire état de ces travaux.

(1) L'identification de l'objet à protéger

La protection technique des oeuvres passe en premier lieu par la possibilité de les identifier. C'est la première étape préalable et nécessaire. Des travaux sont donc menés pour (a) mettre en place des systèmes d'identifiants des oeuvres, et (b) les insérer dans les normes techniques. L'efficacité des ces identifiants nécessite qu'ils soient univoques et universels, et qu'ils soient repris et respectés dans toute la chaîne de diffusion.

Mise en place des systèmes d'identifiants

Actuellement, il n'existe pas de système unifié d'identification des oeuvres et des auteurs. Il existe certains systèmes d'identifications, mais qui n'ont pas pour objet d'identifier des oeuvres, mais des exploitations spécifiques (l'ISBN pour l'édition de livres, l'ISSN pour l'édition de publications périodiques, l'ISRC pour l'enregistrement sonore).

Les travaux de la CISAC

La CISAC a mis en place un plan d'action, baptisé CIS *(Commun Information System)*, destiné à uniformiser et à créer des types d'identifiants pour les différentes catégories d'oeuvres: *"Le CIS répond à un besoin des auteurs et des ayants-droit d'identifier de façon uniforme au niveau mondial et de repérer les oeuvres, les ayants-droit et les supports d'oeuvres. Ce numéro d'identification est commun à tous les types d'oeuvres (oeuvres musicales, audiovisuelles, littéraires et artistiques). Le plan CIS prévoit l'adoption par toutes les sociétés concernées de numéros d'identification uniques, pour tout type d'oeuvres, pour les ayants-droit, les enregistrements sonores et les contrats. Ces codes uniques seront ensuite soumis à l'ISO pour adoption. Chaque société saisira les données relatives à son territoire et aura un accès direct aux données de ses sociétés soeurs, qu'elle pourra réutiliser immédiatement, sans transformation ou recodage."* Ce système crée ainsi une banque de données internationale virtuelle permettant à un utilisateur d'avoir accès à des données, peu importe leur emplacement sur le réseau.

Actuellement, la CISAC a arrêté le principe de deux codes; l'ISAN *(International Standard Audiovisual Number)*, identifiant les oeuvres audiovisuelles. La mise en place de ce numéro est issue d'une collaboration entre auteurs (CISAC) et producteurs audiovisuels (AGICOA), et l'ISWC *(International Standard Work Code)*, élaboré pour les oeuvres musicales mais adaptables à d'autres types d'oeuvres.

Les travaux de l'APP

L'APP (Agence pour la Protection des Programmes) a présenté un projet de codification internationale des oeuvres informatiques dont l'extension à toute oeuvre numérisée est envisageable. Ces travaux, développés un moment dans le cadre d'une collaboration avec l'OMPI, sont en cours.

Normalisation

Deux aspects complémentaires et distincts sont à relever: (a) la reconnaissance des identifiants dans les autres normes de diffusion des services, et (b) la normalisation des identifiants.

(a) *La reconnaissance des identifiants*

Le développement des techniques de production et de diffusion numérique entraîne la mise en place de normes techniques permettant aux industriels de se mettre d'accord sur les principes essentiels de standardisation de leurs outils techniques. La normalisation technique est de la compétence de l'ISO *(International Standardization Organization)*. Les travaux de l'ISO ont conduit à la prise en compte, dans les réseaux numériques de la nécessité de l'identification dans les contenus aux fins de protection des ayants-droit concernés.

Deux normes internationales intègrent dors et déjà des dispositions répondant à cet impératif: (1) la norme MPEG-2 *(Moving Pictures Information coding Experts Group)*, concernant la compression numérique des images animées et du son en qualité *"broadcast"*, c'est-à-dire autorisant la diffusion en temps réel vers l'utilisateur final, et (2) la norme JPEG *(Joint Photographic Information coding Experts Group)*, concernant la compression numérique des images fixes de nature photographique. JPEG, qui est la norme de base pour la compression et la transmission de l'image fixe, spécifie dans le format d'échange "SPIFF" *(Still Picture Interchange File Format)*, les dispositions permettant la mise en place des éléments nécessaires à l'identification. Les normes de compression numérique JPEG et MPEG-2 prévoient donc l'espace pour le numéro d'identifiant. Sur la base des normes de compression, d'autres normes en aval doivent fixer les standards des futurs décodeurs. A la première strate de norme s'ajoutera d'autres strates. Tel est l'objet notamment du groupe de travail composé des industriels concernés, dans le cadre de DAVIC *(Digital Audiovisual Information Council)*.

(b) *La normalisation des identifiants*

Les projets de numérotation (comme l'ISAN ou l'ISWC) sont soumis aux procédures de l'ISO afin qu'ils deviennent "normalisés". Cette normalisation signifie principalement que ces systèmes d'identifiants seront disponibles pour toute personne, indépendamment de leur appartenance à une société membre de la CISAC.

(2) La protection de cet objet ou/et de son identifiant

Une fois inscrit dans le train numérique, l'identifiant va être utilisé pour la gestion (cf. ci-après). Afin de répondre à ces objectifs de gestion et de s'assurer de l'authenticité de l'identifiant, des travaux sont en cours pour protéger l'identifiant. Pour la protection des sons, certaines sociétés proposent aujourd'hui des systèmes de marquage (CYBERTECH, DIGIPRO, EURODAT) par exemple. La commercialisation de ces systèmes est encore au niveau du service spécifique, et non du "prêt-à-utiliser". Le marquage de l'image, qui pose des problèmes plus complexes que celui du son, est en cours d'élaboration et fait l'objet d'un ambitieux programme communautaire financé par la DG XIII, TALISMAN *(Tracing Authors Rights by Labelling Image Services and Monitoring Access Network)*. Le premier objectif de TALISMAN est de créer un outil permettant de lier de manière indélébile le contenu de l'image à son identifiant par un algorithme de cryptologie. Le résultat du calcul de l'algorithtme est déposé. Des contrôles sont effectués, en réalisant "en sens inverse" l'opération. Le changement du résultat signifie qu'a été modifié, soit l'image, soit l'identifiant. Le deuxième axe de travail de TALISMAN est d'inclure l'identifiant dans la trame de l'image par filigrane. Ces travaux sont très complexes, car ils obéissent à un cahier des charges contraignant: les outils doivent être performants, faciles d'installation et d'utilisation, offrir un excellent niveau de sécurité, et être peu coûteux.

La difficulté réside également dans la définition des critères d'alarme: à partir de quand une image est-elle modifiée? A partir de quel degré de changement y-t-il atteinte aux droits d'auteur? Notions subjectives pour le juriste que l'informaticien doit pouvoir traduire en requêtes objectives.

(3) La gestion de la relation entre le fournisseur de l'objet et l'utilisateur

La gestion de toutes les opérations de la chaîne de diffusion dans le numérique est au centre de nombreux travaux.

Intégration des identifiants

Les sociétés d'auteurs ont présenté au MILIA 1996, le système SPIDER, développé par la société française AVELEM qui est un système opérationnel d'inscription du numéro pour JPEG. L'inscription de l'identifiant est réalisée par un logiciel qui insère le numéro dans un espace réservé à cet effet. Gestion des relations entre le titulaire de droits et l'utilisateur. De nombreuses réalisations sont opérationnelles dans la gestion du contrôle d'accès et de la sécurisation des transactions financières. Pour la gestion des droits de propriété intellectuelle, des réalisations concrètes sont à l'étude dans le cadre des programmes communautaires de la DG III: CO-PEARMS, COPYSMART, et IMPRIMATUR. Deux programmes spécifiques à certains secteurs d'activité intègrent de manière significative la gestion des droits de propriété intellectuelle: TISSUS et HYPERTOUR. Sur le plan juridique, des travaux sont également menés sur les trois axes définis ci-dessus.

(a) *Identifiant protection de l'identifiant*

La protection indirecte de l'identifiant doit d'abord être assurée par une protection juridique. Dans sa réponse au *Livre vert sur droits d'auteurs et droits voisins dans la société de l'information*, le gouvernement français a proposé à la Commission qu'une initiative communautaire et internationale soit prise afin de mettre en place un dispositif législatif fixant un cadre obligatoire pour l'identifiant, pour interdire toute atteinte aux identifiants, et éventuellement rendre obligatoire la présence de ces numéros dans les trains binaires.

(b) *Gestion*

Une composante juridique est essentielle pour assurer la sécurité sur les réseaux: la procédure pénale. Celle-ci doit s'adapter au nouvel environnement, et les règles traditionnelles doivent être modifiées pour faciliter la mise en oeuvre des procédures de constitution de preuve, de saisie-contrefaçon. Une recommandation du Conseil de l'Europe du 26 septembre 1995 relative aux problèmes de procédure pénale liés à la technologie de l'information a fixé les grandes lignes des réformes à entreprendre sur ce sujet.

> *1.2. Dans l'affirmative, quelles sont les finalités qui ont été assignées à cette protection (identification des oeuvres et des auteurs, authentification de l'auteur et du contenu, restrictions à l'accès aux oeuvres ou à la copie de celles-ci, informations sur les ayants-droit et les conditions d'utilisation)?*

Les finalités générales ont été décrites précédemment (gestion et lutte contre la piraterie). Les travaux en cours portent essentiellement sur l'identification, l'authentification, et les conditions d'utilisation des oeuvres et des identifiants. Les travaux visant à restreindre l'accès aux oeuvres, par exemple par des dispositifs anti-copie, ne sont pas prioritaires. Les expériences en matière de reprographie ou de copie privée ont démontré qu'il était difficile de limiter le progrès technique et de figer celui-ci pour empêcher de nouvelles utilisations des oeuvres et limiter leurs diffusions. Il est préférable d'accompagner le progrès plutôt que de le freiner.

> *1.3. A votre connaissance, sur quelles bases techniques est-il envisagé de résoudre le problème (matériel ou logiciel, codage interne, inséparablement lié à l'oeuvre dès l'origine, ou codage externe, ajouté postérieurement à la création)?*

Le numérique étant basé sur du numérique (0/1), tous les outils se basent sur du logiciel. La question se pose de savoir si dans un deuxième temps, ce logiciel doit être inséré dès l'origine dans les matériels, ou s'il doit être intégré dans la chaîne ensuite. Pour une meilleure protection des oeuvres, il est théoriquement évident que la mise en place des systèmes de protection doit se faire le plus possible en amont, soit dès que le fichier informatique de l'oeuvre existe (soit dès la numérisation pour une oeuvre issue de l'analogique, soit dès la création pour une oeuvre uniquement numérique). Les efforts portent donc sur l'insertion des dispositifs dès la création du fichier informatique. Pour l'insertion de l'identifiant, des contacts ont ainsi été pris par les ayants-droit avec les fabricants d'appareils photographiques et de caméras pour l'intégration de logiciels permettant la mise en place et la gestion de l'identifiant dès la naissance de l'oeuvre.

> *1.4. Quels sont les partenaires associés à ces travaux (autorités publiques, sociétés de gestion collective, constructeurs de matériels, fournisseurs de "contenus")?*

Une des caractéristiques sociologiques centrales de ces travaux est la rencontre entre de nombreux partenaires qui jusqu'à présent s'ignoraient. Les travaux sont donc menés par tous les partenaires concernés: sociétés de gestion collective des titulaires de droits, industriels des télécommunications et de l'informatique, centres de recherche, et institutions publiques.

b. *Bilan législatif*

> *1.5. Des dispositions législatives existent-elles dans votre pays pour sanctionner de façon générale le contournement de dispositifs de protection technique?*

Il n'existe pas de textes permettant de sanctionner de façon générale les détournements, mais des textes sanctionnent soit des actes précis, soit des actes périphériques. Une première initiative, encore timide puisqu'elle ne vise que la publicité ou notice d'utilisation d'oeuvres et qu'elle n'instaure qu'une obligation de mention, doit être soulignée. Un texte récent a été inséré dans le code de la propriété intellectuelle par la loi du 10 mai 1994 lors de la transposition de la Directive programmes d'ordinateur en droit français (article L 122(6)2, Loi no. 94-361 du 10 mai 1994): *"Toute publicité ou notice d'utilisation relative au moyen permettant la suppression ou la neutralisation de tout dispositif technique protégeant un logiciel doit mentionner que l'utilisation illicite de ces moyens est passible des sanctions prévues en cas de contrefaçon. Un décret en Conseil d'État fixera les conditions d'application du présent article"*.

Il existe par ailleurs des dispositifs dans le droit pénal général et dans le droit pénal de l'informatique, qui peuvent trouver à s'appliquer de manière périphérique si une personne accomplit les actes incriminées ayant pour motif de contourner les dispositifs. Le droit sanctionne alors les circonstances dans lesquelles ces dispositifs sont contournés, et non pas l'acte lui-même de contournement. Les textes pénaux applicables sont les suivants. Droit pénal général: (Vol, Escroquerie) abus de confiance, recel, violation du secret professionnel, divulgation du secret de fabrique, destruction, dégradation d'un bien appartenant à autrui. Droit pénal de l'informatique (loi no. 88-19 du 5 janvier 1988, dite loi Godfrain. Cf. articles 321(1) et suivants du code pénal): accès ou maintien frauduleux dans un système informatique, entrave au fonctionnement d'un système de traitement automatisé, introduction frauduleuse de données, suppression ou modification des données d'un système de traitement automatisé de données.

> *1.6. Dans la négative, existe-t-il des précédents, par exemple dans le domaine du cryptage des émissions de télévision?*

Il existe une législation particulière pour protéger les programmes télédiffusés réservés à un public déterminé qui y accède moyennant une rémunération versée à l'exploitant du service, législation prise à l'origine pour protéger CANAL+ contre la reproduction de ses décodeurs. L'article 79(1) de la loi no. 86-1067 du 30 septembre 1986 modifié par la loi no. 92-1336 du 16 décembre 1992, punit de deux ans d'emprisonnement et de 200.000 francs d'amende la fabrication, l'importation, en vue de la vente ou de la location, l'offre à la vente, la détention en vue de la vente, la vente ou l'installation d'un équipement matériel, dispositif ou instrument conçu, en tout ou partie, pour capter frauduleusement des programmes télédiffusés réservés. L'article 79(2) punit la publicité faisant directement ou indirectement la promotion des systèmes mentionnés. L'article 79(3) réprime l'organisation de la réception par des tiers en fraude de l'exploitant du service. L'article 79(4) sanctionne l'acquisition ou la détention des ces systèmes.

1.7. L'usage, la diffusion ou l'exportation des techniques de cryptage sont-ils soumis à des restrictions particulières?

La réponse est positive.

Les textes applicables sont les suivants:
- Décret du 18 avril 1939 modifié fixant le régime des matériels de guerre, armes et munitions,
- Loi no. 90-1170 du 29 décembre 1990, et notamment l'article 28(1),
- Décret no. 92-1358 du 28 décembre 1992,
- Décret no. 93-190 du 10 février 1993,
- Décret no. 93-190 du 10 février 1993, et
- Arrêté du 15 février 1993.

La régime est le suivant. Soit une déclaration préalable, lorsque le moyen ou la prestation de cryptologie ne peut avoir d'autre objet que d'authentifier une communication ou d'assurer l'intégralité du message transmis. Soit une autorisation préalable du Premier Ministre, dans tous les autres cas. Cette législation est amenée à évoluer rapidement, car elle ne correspond plus au développement des activités dans l'environnement numérique, et elle est en décalage avec les législations des pays voisins.

2. Appréciation critique

-

Italie

A. Pojaghi

1. Bilan des réalisations, études et projets

a. *Bilan technique*

La matière de la protection technique des oeuvres multimédia est à présent l'objet d'approfondissement à plusieurs niveaux, aussi en ce qui concerne les rapports avec l'administration publique. En ce moment toutefois, on n'est pas encore arrivé à une définition accomplie et officielle du problème. L'intervention de l'administration publique a concerné, en particulier, les consultations que le Ministère des Affaires Etrangères a effectuées auprès des catégories intéressées afin de répondre aux questions posées au siège de l'Union Européenne dans le cadre des travaux prépara-toires d'un document unitaire (Livre vert sur le droit d'auteur et les droits voisins dans la société de l'information).

b. *Bilan législatif*

Il n'existe pas de dispositions législatives à cet égard. En ce qui concerne le système des émissions cryptées de télévision, une loi a été récemment promulguée en Italie: la loi du 6 février 1996 n. 52 qui, à l'article 16 (ci-joint; v. annexe), prévoit la mise à exécution de la Directive 93/83/CEE du Conseil, en demandant au gouvernement de publier dans le délai d'un an le décret législatif contenant les normes nécessaires.

2. Appréciation critique

2.1. Est-il opportun, selon vous, de prévoir des sanctions contre le contourne-ment des dispositifs de protection technique? Ces dispositifs peuvent-ils être efficaces? Les enjeux justifient-ils les investissements importants qui sont nécessaires?

Il est sans doute opportun de prévoir des sanctions contre le contournement des dispositifs de protection technique.

2.2. Les sanctions doivent-elles à votre avis permettre d'atteindre ceux qui mettent à la disposition des utilisateurs les moyens visant à réaliser ce con-tournement? Dans l'affirmative, faut-il les limiter à commercialisation de moyens ayant le contournement "pour seul but", à l'instar de l'article 7(1)c de la directive communautaire de 1991 sur les programmes d'ordinateur, ou peut-on aller, comme dans la proposition du Livre blanc américain, jusqu'à prohiber les moyens dont le but ou l'effet premier est le contournement?

Il semble opportun d'étendre la prévention jusqu'à limiter la commercialisation des moyens de contournement.

2.3. *Pensez-vous qu'il faille envisager une harmonisation des législations, afin d'éviter des distorsions de concurrence? Peut-on concevoir une norme unique? Comment et par qui cette norme devrait-elle être élaborée?*

Une harmonisation des législations de la part de l'Union européenne est sans doute souhaitable. Dans ce domaine on pourra évaluer s'il vaut mieux établir une discipline unitaire ou bien des dispositions différentes en relation à chaque problème local.

2.4. *Quel devrait être selon vous le fondement d'une règlementation dans ce domaine? S'agit-il de garantir la sécurité en vue d'améliorer la diffusion des oeuvres au bénéfice du public? Dans cette optique, peut-on aller jusqu'à rendre obligatoire la protection technique, à l'instar de la loi américaine* (Audio Home Recording Act) *imposant que les fabricants de matériel d'enregistrement sonore numérique incorporent des dispositifs limitant les copies séquentielles à la copie de première génération? S'agit-il plutôt d'une protection complémentaire destinée à garantir la propriété de l'auteur, à laquelle celui-ci pourrait renoncer?*

Le vrai danger de la communication multimédia est représenté par la possibilité d'éluder les droits d'auteur et les droits voisins utilisés. La seule façon efficace de prévenir la violation consiste à établir des barrières insurmontables au respect desquelles l'usager multimédia sera formellement tenu, indépendamment de toute concession de l'une des parties, qui pourrait être obtenue en profitant de la faiblesse de la partie contractante plus faible.

2.5. *L'interdiction de contourner les dispositifs de protection technique doit-elle à votre avis trouver place dans la loi sur le droit d'auteur ou dans une loi distincte? Dans la première hypothèse, le contournement doit-il être seulement "assimilé" à une violation du droit d'auteur ou faut-il y voir un véritable acte d'exploitation soumis en tant que tel au droit exclusif? Dans la seconde hypothèse, sur quelle base juridique fonder cette analyse? La neutralisation d'un dispositif doit-elle par exemple s'analyser comme une reproduction au sens de la législation sur le droit d'auteur?*

On pense qu'une disposition législative d'interdiction, dans la matière considérée, doit trouver place dans la même loi sur le droit d'auteur, étant donné qu'il faut considérer l'acte élusif comme étant assimilé à la violation du droit d'auteur, et pas comme acte d'utilisation.

2.6. *Si les sanctions sont limitées aux hypothèses dans lesquelles le contournement des dispositifs de protection technique vise à permettre l'accès à une oeuvre donnant prise au droit d'auteur, doivent-elles être subordonnées à la preuve que* *l'utilisateur savait (ou aurait dû savoir) qu'il violait ce droit d'auteur? Seront-elles encourues lorsque le contournement aura permis d'accéder à des parties non-originales de l'oeuvre?*

Les sanctions devraient être fondées sur la circonstance objective de l'acte élusif, indépendamment de la nécessité de la preuve de la conscience de la violation de la part de l'utilisateur.

2.7. L'interdiction de contourner les dispositifs de protection technique peut-elle selon vous être critiquée comme restreignant (ou risquant de restreindre) abusivement l'accès au domaine public? Ou comme paralysant le jeu des dérogations limitant traditionnellement la portée du droit d'auteur ("fair use" ou usage privé)? Des considérations d'intérêt public peuvent-elles justifier que la protection technique soit neutralisée par les autorités? Dans l'affirmative, peut-on, pour limiter les risques, imaginer que cette neutralisation soit commandée par la mise en oeuvre de plusieurs clés?

La protection de l'oeuvre protégée a une portée prioritaire à l'égard de l'utilisation de l'oeuvre qui n'est plus protégée. La limitation de la faculté d'effectuer des copies privées est une conséquence inévitable et nécessaire du système de protection des droits. Il n'y a pas de raison d'établir des dérogations, au détriment des droits subjectifs, au profit de l'administration publique.

2.8. Comment l'interdiction généralisée de contourner les dispositifs de protection technique pourrait-elle être conciliée avec les règles spéciales gouvernant la décompilation des programmes d'ordinateur, telles qu'elles résultent de la directive communautaire précitée, ou avec la jurisprudence développée aux États-Unis sur la base du "fair use"?

Les atténuations nées simultanément à la protection du software se justifient seulement à l'égard de telles oeuvres et il n'y a donc aucune raison d'établir une atténuation analogue, dans le domaine multimédia, à la protection des droits.

2.9. Quelle sera l'incidence d'une législation telle que celle envisagée ci-dessus sur l'avenir du droit d'auteur? Faut-il accorder du crédit à l'hypothèse selon laquelle la protection technique, complétée par les contrats, signifie le déclin, voire la mort du droit d'auteur? Ou doit-on considérer que le droit exclusif reste une arme indispensable dans l'environnement numérique?

L'exclusivité du droit, même si elle est tempérée en fait par une gestion collective, reste une arme indispensable pour sauvegarder le droit d'auteur.

2.10. Autres observations?

-

Annexe

Legge 6 febbraio 1996, n. 52 - Disposizioni per l'adempimento di obblighi derivanti dall'appartenenza dell'Italia alle Comunità europee - legge comunitaria 1994:

(...)

Art. 16

(Dirotto d'autore e diritti connessi nella radiodiffusione via satellite e ritrasmissione via cavo: criteri di delega)

1. L'attuazione della direttiva 93/83/CEE del Consiglio sarà informata ai seguenti principi e criteri direttivi:
a) sarà disciplinato l'esercizio del diritto esclusivo dell'autore di autorizzare mediante contratto la comunicazione al pubblico via satellite o via cavo delle opere protette;
b) saranno emanate disposizioni per estendere nei casi di comunicazione al pubblico via satellite la protezione prevista dalla legge 22 aprile 1941, n. 633, ai diritti degli artisti interpreti ed esecutori, nonché dei produttori di fonogrammi e degli organismi di radiodiffusione;
c) saranno emanate disposizioni che prevedano un equo compenso a favore degli artisti interpreti ed esecutori che abbiano svolto le loro interpretazioni in opere cinematografiche e audiovisive per l'utilizzazione delle stesse nelle emittenti televisive che trasmettono via etere, via cavo e via satellite;
d) l'equo compenso di cui alla lettera *c)* è riconosciuto anche agli autori delle opere cinematografiche e audiovisive in caso di cessione al produttore dei diritti exclusivi e qualora vi sia utilizzazione delle stesse nelle emittenti televisive che trasmettono via etere, via cavo e via satellite;
e) dovranno essere introdotte disposizioni tese ad assicurare che il diritto del-l'autore e dei titolari dei diritti connessi di autorizzare un cablodistributore alla ritrasmissione via cavo sia esercitato esclusiva-mente per il tramite di una società di gestione collettiva. Da tali disposizioni saranno esonerati gli organismi di radiodiffusione per le proprie emissioni;
f) dovranno essere previste disposizioni transitorie in conformità dell'articolo 7 della direttiva 93/83/CEE.

(...)

The Netherlands

F.W. GROSHEIDE

1. Introduction

1.1. *Law and technique*

The development of technology certainly has an effect on the development of the law. In fact, the relation between technology and law is rather paradoxical. On the one hand, technology forces the law to deal with all sorts of new phenomena such as electronic shopping, Internet, or computer software that makes it necessary to rethink notions like payment, freedom of the press and property of information. On the other hand, existing law by its very nature is the framework in which technology should fit.[1] The legal regulation of the information infrastructure is a striking example of this paradox. After its advent, and to a certain extent ever since, the new information technology is far ahead of the law. *'Perhaps, one day,'* someone wrote not later than 1982, *'in a fully automated brave new world, the optical copier will instantly identify and debit my bank account, and identify and credit the author's, whenever I copy his work - as already partly happens with electronic Prestel and is technically possible with magnetic media also'* - and what will be the law's answer to that?[2] What the author describes as the forseeable future is normal practice today, but the law has still not given a satisfactory answer. In the beginning, attention has been focused on how to incorporate the newly created protectable interests within the existing legal system.[3] It seems that tort law, copyright law and *sui generis* legislation are the most appropriate to serve that aim. Until now, emphasis has been laid on how these new interests should be protected. It appears that technology offers all sort of devices that can be used in this respect. And again it is up to the law to develop legal instruments that effectively protect against the circumvention of these technical devices.

1.2. *Infringement and enforcement*

Due to the situation described in paragraph 1.1, copyright holders to date have great difficulty in securing civil remedies that compensate them adequately for infringements in a digitalised environment. A high procentage of the infringements is hardly detectable and even then they will already have had their damaging effects both with respect to the pecuniary and the moral interests of the copyright holders. Besides, the cost of detecting infringement and bringing court cases is rarely recovered. These problems with current copyright remedies tend to discourage right holders from enforcing their rights. Therefore, developing appropriate legal instruments for the prevention and the deterrence of infringement is prominently placed on the agendas of (inter)governmental and non-governmental bodies that strive for the protection of copyright law. Two of those bodies in particular concentrate their efforts on the enforcement of copyright law and intellectual property rights in general: the World Trade Organisation (WTO) and the World Intellectual Property Organisation (WIPO).

Within the framework of the WTO, the GATT Agreement on trade-related aspects of intellectual property rights, including trade in counterfeit goods (TRIPs Agreement) deals extensively with the problem of enforcement (Part III, articles 41 to 61).[4] Accordingly, WIPO has drafted a Provisional Document holding questions concerning a possible Protocol to the Berne Convention (BC), Part IX of which is devoted to the enforcement of rights. In doing so, the Provisional Document also deals with the protection against unlawful circumvention of technical devices.

Its reading is as follows:

96. *Accordingly, the Committee is invited to identify what technical adjustments are needed in the enforcement provisions of the TRIPs Agreement (articles 41 to 61 of the Agreement) to adapt them to the context of the protocol.*

97. *The Committee is also invited to consider the inclusion of provisions on the abuse of technical devices, provisions the scope of which would differ from that of the above-mentioned enforcement provisions of the TRIPs Agreement.*

98. *In this respect, it is proposed that any country party to the protocol be obliged*
(a) to provide for the same sanctions, to be applied by judicial authorities, as the ones provided for in case of infringement of copyright under the provisions referred to in paragraph 96, above, in case of manufacture or importation for sale or rental or the distribution by sale or rental, of
> *(i) any device specifically or predominantly designed or adapted to circumvent any device intended to prevent or restrict the making of copies of works or to impair the quality of copies of works or to impair the quality of copies made (the latter device herinafter referred to as 'copy-protection or copy-management device');*
> *(ii) any device that is capable of enabling or assisting the reception of an encrypted program, broadcast or otherwise communicated to the public, by those who are not entitled to receive the program;*
(b) to provide that, in the application of provisional (conservatory) measures, civil remedies, criminal sanctions and border measures provided for according to the provisions referred to in paragraph 96, above, any illicit device mentioned in item (a) (i) and (ii), above, is assimilated to infringing copies of works;
(c) to provide that the author of, or other owner of copyright in, a work shall be entitled to damages provided for according to the provisions referred to in paragraph 96, above, in the same way as in a case where his or its copyright is infringement, where
> *(i) copies of the work have been made by him or it, or with his or its authorisation, and offered for sale or rental combined with a copy-protection or copy-management device, and a device specifically or predominantly*

> *designed or adapted to circumvent the said device is made or imported for sale or rental or is distributed through sale or rental;*
> *(ii) the work in which he or it has a right is included in an encrypted program, broadcast or otherwise communicated to the public by him or it, or with his or its authorisation, and a device enabling or assisting the reception of the program by those who are not entitled to receive the program is made or imported for sale or rental or is distributed through sale or rental.*

Also in the European Union (EU) it is generally accepted that technical devices are needed in the domain of copyright law to enforce it adequately and that circumvention should be sanctioned. An example of this awareness can be found in article 7 par. 1 sub c EC Directive on computer programs, requiring Member States to provide in accordance with national legislation for appropiate remedies against a person committing *'any act of putting into circulation, or the possession for commercial purposes of any means the sole intended purpose of which is to facilitate the unauthorised removal or circumvention of any technical device which may have been applied to protect a computer program'.*[5]

It is very likely that in the future, similar provisions will be inserted in European legislation as a result of the recently published Green Paper on copyright and related rights in the Information Society. Section IX ('Technical systems of identification and protection') of this document - taking into account that digitisation allows works and other protected matter to be identified, tattooed, protected and automatically managed, provided the appropriate systems are installed - finds it necessary for these systems to be introduced and accepted at an international level if the information society is not to operate to the detriment of right holders.[6] According to the Green Paper, the indicated situation calls for technical devices of protection that go alongside with the informational systems themselves as well as for proper legal remedies to fight circumvention of the protecting techniques.[7]

Since the publication of the Green Paper, the EC has taken further action. In the beginning of 1996 it organised a hearing on certain aspects relating to technical systems for identifying and protecting copyright and related rights, as well as the acquisition and management of these rights in the information society.[8] Of the conclusions to which this hearing came, the following are worthwile quoting. *'A very large majority of participants spoke out in favour of technical systems of identification and protection and their effective implementation in due time. Their main function should be to allow for the identification of works and other protected matter and possibly the respective right holders. The aim of the systems should mainly be to improve the monitoring of access to and use of works and other protected matter. They could also lead to the administration of the remuneration of right holders. They should also make it possible to combat piracy by facilitating more rapid and reliable identification of works and related matter. (...) As far as the management of systems is concerned, participants indicated that these technical systems should be managed as close as possible to the source of the creation. The possibility of international private agencies being entrusted with coordination was not ruled out. A significant number of participants voiced an interest in technical systems of protection against unauthorised digital copies. (...) The majority of participants spoke in favour of developing and applying such systems on a voluntary basis. (...) A large majority of participants were in favour of the adoption of legislative measures to protect the integrity of identification and protection systems once they have been voluntarily agreed upon by interested parties. Most participants considered that acts to circumvent, violate or manipulate these systems should be subject to sanctions (civil and/or administrative) under the law provided for at Community level. A few participants even though that criminal measures would be appropriate. Harmonisation of these issues at international level was also requested. The Commission would like to see an international agreement reached soon on these issues. It considers that current work in the WIPO provides such an opportunity.'*

As early as February 1996 the EC drafted a non-paper to be discussed in the Council Working Group on technological measures on protection of anti-copy devices and copyright management information. In its revised text of May 1996 this non-paper reads as follows. *'Proposal as regards Technical Protection Devices (to be included in both the Protocol to the Berne Convention and the New Instrument for the protection of Performers and Producers of Phonograms). Contracting Parties shall make unlawful, and provide for appropriate remedies against, the manufacture, distribution and possession for commercial purposes of any device, means or product, by any person knowing or having reasonable grounds to know that its primary purpose or primary effect is to remove, deactivate, without authority, any process, mechanism or system which is designed to prevent or inhibit the infringement of any of the rights under the Berne Convention or this Protocol. Contracting Parties shall make unlawful, and provide for appropriate remedies against, the offer or performance of any* [commercial] *service, by any person knowing or having reasonable grounds to know that its primary purpose or primary effect is to remove, deactivate, or circumvent, without authority any process, mechanism or system which is designed to prevent or inhibit the infringement of any of the rights under the Berne Convention or this Protocol.'* [9]

Given the fact that in the near future technical and legal protection will presumably go hand in hand, a question may be raised as to the way in which legislators should fulfil their legislative task: in a specific or in a general way? Should they draft specific provisions for specific purposes to be inserted in special legislation for a particular field of law (*e.g.* the protection of computer programs), or should they provide for a set of legal instruments to be used indifferently of the field of law? It is advocated here that a general approach should be taken to avoid the fragmentation of the enforcement instruments, which would be to the detriment of copyright owners and other owners of intellectual property rights. Maybe the best solution here would be to create some special form of unfair competition law. In addition to this, a caveat should be made however. According to their very nature, technical devices operate indiscriminately of the legal environment in which they are introduced. So, for instance, the same mode of encryptology can be used to protect personal data or computer programs. In addition to this, it should be stressed that any prospective legislation may not be dictated by present-day technology. Dependency on technology will make legislation obsolete in no time. As a consequence, an introduction of tortious liability on a general basis for decoding encrypted information will also have an effect in those instances in which the freedom of information is involved or a lawful user is committing reverse engineering. Articulated for copyright and related rights: technology may not be used as a pretext to reanimate protection for subject matter that belongs already to the public domain. It is obvious that fine tuning of the law in this respect is of the utmost importance.[10]

Finally, it should be noted here that the development and use of technical devices for protection and the legal implication thereof, not being limited to the domain of copyright law (the same is true for instance for the protection of the privacy or that of commercial know-how) the solutions and experiences from one domain, can be beneficial also in another domain.

2. State of the art

2.1. Technique

Until now, studies either by governmental or by non-governmental agencies with respect to technical protection of intellectual efforts in a digital environment are scarce.[11] The same is true for the protection of vital personal data or valuable commercial know-how for the safety and integrity of which technical protection can be helpful. The only thing that may be said in this respect is that, in relation to the protection of computer systems, the *Nederlands Normalisatie Instituut* has issued a Code for the protection of information that is stored in a computer system.[12] In this Code - which has been drafted with a close look to a similar Code published by the British Standards Institution (BSI) - it is advocated that physical security instruments should be installed on the sites where computer systems are operating.[13] However, social and contractual instruments play a major role in this Code. It is advised for example to make sure that the supplier of some particular set of application software, assuring the confidentiality, integrity and availability of the information to be applied by the software is critical to the business, provides the customer with a product which meets generally accepted security principles.

In addition, the reactions to the Green Paper submitted by the *Stichting Auteurs-rechtbelangen* (SAB) and the Dutch Copyright Association (DCA) in the beginning of 1996 should be mentioned.[14] Dealing with Section IX on technical systems of protection and identification of the Green Paper, SAB's and DCA's answers to questions 1-7 are as follows.

Question 1: *Do you think the Community, in co-operation with the Member States, should make provision for legal measures which guarantee compliance with: identifying tags; standards for protection against private digital copying; other technical systems of identification or protection against private digital copying? What would be your view if these had been introduced and accepted by industry?*
SAB: *The Community should provide for regulations to ensure that systems are complied with which make it possible to identify works ('tattooing'), to control 'private copying', and to administer and monitor uses that in law entitle right owners to receive*

a remuneration for the authorised delivery of creation/information by electronic means (for public performance, and for private use/copying). It is to be recalled that the Standards should be industry-standards. Technical systems for controlling the use of the artistic contents, that are introduced by the (software) industry, whether or not in conjunction with hardware counterparts, deserve protection. Maybe the protection should be restricted to industry-standards, that is, standards adopted by a substantial part of a certain industrial sector for general use in (on line or machine readable) publication. Technical systems that moderate, restrict or prevent private copying may ask for a somewhat different approach. Insofar as such systems are only software based, they should be protected against distortion of their functioning by way of 'black boxes' (special equipment, services and processes). Insofar as such systems involve their being made part of consumer electronics configurations, in addition to their being embodied in the software, they should be established by way of negotiations between hardware manufacturers, telecommunication service operators and 'content providers' (a cold description for holders of intellectual property rights!). They are likely to be specified in regulations of public law (as opposed to the first mentioned group of systems) that should command compliance.

DCA: *The technologies controlling access to information and UDID systems, not only for files but for separate bits of information, are being developed much slower than the technologies facilitating exploitation of copyrighted works in the digital environment. Apart from technological reasons, this is also due to some parts of the media industry not realising the potential risks involved in the delayed development of such technologies and standardisation thereof. Such industry-wide and worldwide standardised technologies should be developed as soon as possible for an effective pay-per-use system to work. Although the development of such standardised technologies should in first instance be market-driven, the EC should provide an active platform and measures for discussion and research, in order to enchance, promote and maintain the development of these technologies and the compliance with the standards so set.*

Question 2: *What sort of information should the identifying contain: identification of the work or other protected matter; identification of the original right holders; identification of the work or other protected matter, of the original right holders, of licensees and other managing parties; licence terms for possible future assignees of the licence?*

SAB: *The identifiers should indicate the identity of the works (i.e., extended to whatever the nature is of the creative contribution in question) and of the original right owners. Extension to the identity of licensees and to the applicable licensing conditions would mean a burden for all parties concerned and would lead into great difficulties for the mere reason that this very kind of information is usually subject to frequent changes. The latter kind of data could better be made available to information clearing houses or databases, with which parties interested to obtain a license can get in touch, and which can refer such interested parties to the respective right owners. In this connection one can thing about the future responsibilities of collecting societies. The task of the Community in this respect would only be to give a minimum of information necessary to identify the works. But a vital part of its task would lie somewhere else: it should protect the integrity of the identification, which by or on behalf of the right owner was enclosed in subcodes. This protection must extend to materials on line, in* *machine readable form, when downloaded (with or without the authorisation by the right owners), when transmitted or retransmitted, and irrespective as to whether it was received, retrieved or adapted in computers.*

DCA: *The minimum information that UDID systems should tag to bits of information is the identification of the work. Additional information could concern the source of the work (where to get permission).*

Question 3: *In your opinion, should works and other protected matter originating in third countries be prevented from entering the Internal Market if it does not incorporate systems of identification compatible with those recognised in the Community?*

SAB: *Although one's first impulse may be a positive reaction, there are a few possible drawbacks. Let us take the hypothesis that the principle, laid down as an underlying element in the thought leading to this question, would have as a result an elaborate, formal set of identification requirements. Let us further suppose that these were to be adhered to so strongly that market access would be difficult for material equipped with identifiers that are not entirely identical to the standards but do not materially differ from them. In that case, the overall effect would be a blessing in disguise. For, since for the kind of creation/information transported in the ways that are at issue here, national borders are no barriers to consumption. Therefore the use of it is world wide. Consequently, as a rule, the standards and systems under consideration in this Section must be global. If the above meant policy in its application leads to impediments to market access, the remedy is no better than the disease. Maybe it is a safer method to protect such identifiers as are chosen by the right owners themselves, instead of prescribing extensive and detailed minimum requirements as compulsory. These choices of systems should be made Industry-wise, in negotiations to be conducted jointly with other right owners. At a later stage, when de facto standards emerge out of the market place, it may be considered to extend the legal minimum requirements. One may doubt why the (European) border should remain closed to works originating from countries outside the Union, which works do not formally conform to (European) standards, but do not materially differ.*

DCA: *A UDID system, the application of which is limited to the EU, will not serve the purposes and will not allow the Commission to reach the goals, set out in this Green Paper. Any identification system should be universal.*

Question 4: *To the extent that technical systems of protection against private digital copying can be developed and applied, what other legislative measures in respect of those systems would it be necessary and possible to adopt?*

SAB: *So-called 'black boxes', circumventing or disabling methods or devices, must be forbidden. The provisions for protection of these methods or devices, embodied in software only are to include such prohibition, confirmed by civil and criminal sanctions; these should be directed against manufacture and importation of and trade in such mechanisms or equipment. To extent the restricting methods or devices are embodied in both hardware and software together, intended to implement information as regards the possibility or impossibility to make copies, they should come to existence by way of negotiations between right owners and hardware manufacturers. Such systems may require public law specifications, and entrance to the Internal Market may then have to be made conditional upon the compliance with these specifications.*

Because the relevant industries are global, the systems should be agreed upon between right owners and hardware manufacturers and be tested against the public interest by the Community, and by other governments of the countries outside the Union. The same principle, in fact, applies if Question 6 is to be answered.

DCA: *If and to the extent it is desired that systems preventing or limiting private digital copying are applied, regulation could be implemented under which aparatusses circumventing such copying limitations are forbidden.*

Question 5: *If a technical system of protection against private digital copying were introduced on a harmonised basis, do you think that the marketing and importation of any equipment not containing such systems of protection should be forbidden?*

SAB: *For obvious reasons, the answer is yes.*

DCA: *It is not unreasonable that, if a technical system to prevent or limit private digital copying were introduced on a harmonised basis, the marketing and importation of any equipment not containing such systems of protection were forbidden.*

Question 6: *Do you consider that the eventual effectiveness of technical systems of protection against private digital copying depends upon the creation of international standards?*

SAB [no comment]

DCA: *It is imperative that international standards are developed, not only for equipment limiting or preventing private digital copying, but more importantly and in first instance, in particular for equipment identifying information and equipment controlling and monitoring access to and use of information, including but not limited to equipment controlling the uplink and downlink of information.*

Question 7: *How should it be determined whether works and other protected matter are in the public domain? How could it be guaranteed that protection of works and other protected matter by intellectual property law does not hinder or restrict access to data in the public domain?*

SAB: *The principle attached to this question may look the task of finding an answer as being more complicated than it really is. It is evident, that technology may not be used as a pretext to reintroduce protection for material that is nog longer protected under copyright law. But the matter at issue is not so much the question, whether in the case of works belonging to the Public Domain the relevant material is to be made available free of charge, as the statement that establishing conditions for the dissemination are no longer the (exclusive) prerogative of the (original) right owner. The very exceptional case that the material discussed here does completely belong to the Public Domain does in our view not justify the burden of distinguishing between Public Domain and protected material, when applying technical systems.*

DCA [no comment]

As a conclusion of this paragraph it could be said, paraphrasing Clark, that the answer to the machine is, at least partly, *in* the machine.[15] Partly and not completely, because it does not seem very likely that it will be possible to introduce technical means of protection that, in the long run, will not be disabled by using the same technology. However, taking for granted that the majority of (potential) users of protected subject matter are law-abiding and will live up to the standards of protection, a combination of social, technical and legal remedies against improper use of such protected matter will suffice.

2.2. Law

In Dutch law, a series of provisions exist that sanction unauthorised access by infringing the security and integrity of information of all kind that has been stored electronically. Such provisions can be found in the Penal Code *(Wetboek van Strafrecht, WvSr)*; articles 138a and 350 a-b for example sanction what can be labelled as a trespass to a computer system and disablement of electronically stored data by changing, erasing, or otherwise afflicting them.[16] Also article 441 *WvSr* is relevant in this respect, sanctioning the publication of a non-public message that has been transmitted by telegraph or telephone and is illegally intercepted. This provision, inserted in the *Wetboek van Strafrecht* in 1922, gives the exclusiveness of a semi-copyright to news messages and in doing so prohibits other news agencies to take advantage of the gathering of information by the transmitting agency.[17] *Idem* with respect to the *Wet Persoonsregistraties (WPR)*, applicable to electronical and non-electronical registration of indicated personal data. This statute sanctions for example the gathering as well as the distribution of information beyond the purpose of a particular database containing personal information.[18] Also relevant is the *Wet op de Telecommunicatievoorzieningen (WTV)*; article 50 par. 3 of this statute sanctions so-called manipulation, *i.e.* unauthorised use by way of a technical device of any telecommunication infrastructure.[19]

Specific provisions that sanction circumvention of technical devices for protection can only be found in the *Auteurswet (Aw)*.[20] Article 32a *Aw*, following article 7 par. 1, sub c EC Directive on the protection of computer programs, sanctions any person who knowingly publicly offers for distribution, in the course of his business possesses for reproduction, distribution or importation into the Netherlands, or has in consignation any device whose exclusive purpose is to remove, circumvent, or facilitate the removal or circumvention without the permission of the copyright owner of technical means to protect a computer program.

At this moment, no special legislation exists or is in preparation that deals with the coding or decoding of information of any kind. This is true for the use, the dissemination and the exportation of technical devices for encrypting information alike. However, with reference to the initiatives of the European Commission mentioned in paragraph 1.2, it is very likely that legislation will be enacted in the near future to implement European regulations on this point.

In addition, a mention should be made of some case-law that comes to terms with the decoding of information. In *FilmNet v. Planken* and *Esselte v. Ten*, making available to the public of devices, the sole purpose of which without reasonable doubt is to provide the public with a means to decode pay-tv-programs, has been brought under tortious liability.[21] In *Groeneveld v. Television Distribution Systems NV (TDS)*, the Dutch Supreme Court ruled that the freedom to receive information, guaranteed by article 10 ECHR, might not be invoked to claim free reception of television broadcasts that had been previously encrypted by the distributor aiming at limiting the reception of these broadcasts to the subscribers of his distribution system who had to pay duties for their reception. In the case at hand, TDS was transmitting television programs of American television stations for which it had to pay licence fees. These programs, after having been encrypted, were transmitted by TDS to its subscribers who got a special wire *cum annexis* and a decoder to assure proper reception.[22] In a case comment it is rightly said that under other circumstances, such as a complete monopoly of information with the distributor of television programs, the free flow of information argument may break through civil law and copyright law barriers to assure that the public at large has access to the particular information.

3. **Critical assessment**

Unauthorised circumvention of technical devices for the protection of rights granted under the BC and the RC is a serious infringement of these rights, which should be sanctioned by national and international law. However, the question may be raised what exactly is meant by unauthorised circumvention and whether the design, manufacturing and distribution of such devices already constitute civil or criminal offenses. In the proposed provisions in the Protocol to the BC and the non-paper of the EC, the condition is made that such devices are specifically or predominantly designed or adapted or have as their primary purpose or effect to circumvent the installed protection. Drafted this way, such provisions will also apply to those devices that are designed or adapted for the sole purpose of circumvention but in the course of lawful acts such as reverse engineering.

The indicated situation is not unknown; it has already come up with respect to photocopying devices. It is obvious that a copier may be used to make legal and illegal photocopies. As a consequence, it is advocated here to modify the language of the proposed or any other provisions to make it clear that what is sanctioned, is the unauthorised use of the circumventing device. In addition the designer, manufacturer, distributor, and the like may be said to be under tortious liability in those instances in which he/she should have refrained from doing so, because he/she knew or should have known that the devices would be used for illegal purposes.

In the same line of reasoning it seems appropriate to prescribe by law that those who are professionally dealing with the design, manufacturing or distribution of circumvention devices are bound to keep a register of customers, so that illegal users can be traced. It should be open for discussion whether only commercial activities with respect to the trade in hacking devices should be taken into account. At this moment, considering that relevant experiences with improper use of intellectual property rights in digital environments such as Internet/World Wide Web are still lacking, it seems impossible to answer this question. Referring to what already has been stated in paragraph 1, it is repeated here that both sanctions of a civil and criminal law nature preferably should be enacted in a general way (Civil Code or Criminal Code).

It follows from what has been said so far, that developments such as those under discussion in this Report are not considered to be the causes for the decline and fall of the existing system of copyright and neighbouring rights law. On the contrary, it seems likely that the introduction of new legislation as indicated above together with technical means for protection will provide the appropriate remedies against infringement of intellectual property rights in general and those granted by the BC and the RC in particular.

In addition, the following observations should be made. Firstly, it is necessary to standardize the technical specifications with respect to the devices under consideration since such a standardisation is a prerequisite for the legal harmonisation of the EU copyright law and neighbouring right law. Secondly, taking into consideration that the technical protection measures of the rights in question are not very difficult to install, it should be a matter of further concern whether a right holder who abstains from proper measures on this point is himself at fault. If the answer is affirmative, it may be appropriate, in any case when an infringement of rights is made in a professional capacity, to deny such a right holder a claim for damages and to restrict him to injunctive relief.

Footnotes

1. H. Gibbons, *The relationship between law and science*, *IDEA* 1981, Vol. 21, nr. 1; Vol. 22, nr. 2, p. 3; E. Denninger, *Neue Rechte im technologischen Zeitalter?*, *Kritische Justis* 1989/2, pp. 147-156.
2. P. Sieghart, *Information technology and intellectual property*, Opinion 1982, 7 *EIPR*, pp. 187-188.
3. F.W. Grosheide, *Paradigms in copyright law*, in: Sherman/Ströwel, *Of Authors and Origins*, Oxford 1994, pp. 203-233.
4. WIPO, Provisional Document, *Questions concerning a possible protocol to the Berne Convention*, Geneva 29 April 1994. See also WIPO, Committee of Experts on a possible protocol to the Berne Convention, Sixth Session, Geneva 1-9 February 1996, Report Paragraph VIII, which gives a broad record of the different views on technological measures and rights management information of the represented countries and organisations (pp. 48-58). A similar protocol is drafted with respect to the neighbouring rights granted by the Rome Convention (RC).
5. EC Directive 14 May 1991 on the legal protection of computer programs (91/250/EEC), *Official Journal* no. L 122/42 (17-5-1991).
6. EC Documents, COM (95) 382 final Green Paper - Copyright and Related Rights in the Information Society, Brussels 19-7-1995.
7. Green Paper, note 6, p. 82: '*The Community may find it advisable to act in order to make technical systems of protection compulsory, on a harmonised basis, once they have been developed and accepted by industry*'. The problems that are indicated here play also a major role with respect to satellite broadcasting and distribution by cable as regulated by EC Directive 93/83/EEC, 27-9-1993. In particular, attention is given here to the unauthorised production, import and distribution of decoders.
8. European Commission, Conclusions of the hearing of 8 and 9 January 1996 on Technical systems of identification and protection and Acquisition and management of rights, Brussels 27 February 1996.
9. European Commission, *Non-paper on technological measures on protection of anti-copy devices and copyright management information*, 22 April 1996.
10. How fundamentally opposing the views of interested parties might be, can be illustrated by the following two interventions taken from the Report mentioned in footnote 4. '*213. The representative of BSA pointed out that the software industry had much experience in technological methods of protecting works, and indicated that the effectiveness of the actual technology, and the consumer acceptance of it, were important factors in its success. He believed that the final treaty provisions must be technology-neutral, otherwise it would fossilise systems, which would become irrelevant in a short period of time. The provisions must not discriminate between national and foreign works, and there must be no formalities. The representative remarked that the commercial purposes distinction raised in previous interventions was unnecessarily narrow, since, in a point-to-point world, what was commercial and what was private was increasingly difficult to separate. He observed that, with technical-protection-defeating devices, one had to look not only to the intent of the designer or the producer or the manufacturer, but also to how the product was actually used.' 215. The representative of JEIDA expressed concern over the proposals for technocolgical measures and rights management information, and the view that the issues require further*

study at this point due mainly to the fact that they are so new, and there is not much research or information available at this point. Using the proposal of the United States on technological measures as an example, the representative pointed out that the proposal did not specify that it did not affect any legitimate use of copyright. The primary purpose or effect test was too broad and vague, in that many computer-related products could be used both for legitimate and illegal purposes. The representative preferred the sole intended purpose test, and a requirement for actual knowledge of illegal use. With respect to copyright management information, the representative felt that it was extremely difficult to determine the information to be covered, and if the information was not determined, how it would be difficult to regulate its fraudulent use. He urged WIPO to conduct further studies. He also pointed out that much fraudulent conduct was already regulated by federal and fair trade practice law'.

11. Registratiekamer, Advies Beveiliging van persoonsregistraties (1994); Registratiekamer, *Privacy-enhancing technologies - The path to anonimity* (Volume I and II) (1995).
12. Nederlands Normalisatie Instituut, Code voor Informatiebeveiliging 1994, initiated by a group of governmental agencies, non-governmental agencies and members of the Dutch Industry.
13. The BSI is in force since February 1995.
14. Stichting Auteursrechtbelangen, *Reaction to the Green Paper 'Copyright and Related Rights in the Information Society'*, Amstelveen January 1996. SAB is a foundation that coordinates the activities of organisations of interest groups in the field of copyright and related rights.
15. C. Clark, *The answer to the machine is in the machine*, in: *The future of copyright in a digital environment*, P.B. Hugenholtz (ed.), Deventer 1996, pp. 139-145.
16. *WvSr* refers to the Criminal Law Statute. These articles amongst others are inserted in the *WvSr* following legislative proposal 21551, TK 1989-1990 (hacking) and entered into force on 1-3-1993.
17. Comp. Spoor/Verkade, *Auteursrecht*, Deventer 1993, pp. 87-88 (nr. 63). See also President District Court The Hague 14 May 1923, *NJ* 1923, p. 970 *(news telegrams)* and Dutch Supreme Court 27 June 1986, *NJ* 1987, 191.
18. *WPR* refers to the Statute on personal data registration.
19. *WTV* refers to the Statute on the telecommunication infrastructure.
20. *Aw* refers to the Copyright Statute.
21. President District Court The Hague 20 January 1986, *KG* 1986, 92 *(FilmNet v. Planken)* and Court of Appeal Amsterdam 2 May 1991, *Mediaforum* 1991, p. B73, note Van Engelen, p. 94, *Informatierecht/ AMI* 1992, p. 70, note Verkade.
22. Dutch Supreme Court 17 December 1993, *NJ* 1994, 274, note Alkema.

Suisse

C. GOVONI

1. Bilan des réalisations, études et projets

a. *Bilan technique*

1.1. *A-t-on mené dans votre pays des travaux sur la protection technique des oeuvres, spécialement dans l'environnement numérique?*

Non.

1.2. *Dans l'affirmative, quelles sont les finalités qui ont été assignées à cette protection (identification des oeuvres et des auteurs, authentification de l'auteur et du contenu, restrictions à l'accès aux oeuvres ou à la copie de celles-ci, informations sur les ayants-droit et les conditions d'utilisation)?*

-

1.3. *A votre connaissance, sur quelles bases techniques est-il envisagé de résoudre le problème (matériel ou logiciel, codage interne, inséparablement lié à l'oeuvre dès l'origine, ou codage externe, ajouté postérieurement à la création)?*

-

1.4. *Quels sont les partenaires associés à ces travaux (autorités publiques, sociétés de gestion collective, constructeurs de matériels, fournisseurs de "contenus")?*

-

b. *Bilan législatif*

1.5. *Des dispositions législatives existent-elles dans votre pays pour sanctionner de façon générale le contournement de dispositifs de protection technique?*

Non.

1.6. *Dans la négative, existe-t-il des précédents, par exemple dans le domaine du cryptage des émissions de télévision?*

Non.

1.7. L'usage, la diffusion ou l'exportation des techniques de cryptage sont-ils soumis à des restrictions particulières?

Non.

2. **Appréciation critique**

2.1. Est-il opportun, selon vous, de prévoir des sanctions contre le contournement des dispositifs de protection technique? Ces dispositifs peuvent-ils être efficaces? Les enjeux justifient-ils les investissements importants qui sont nécessaires?

Oui.

2.2. Les sanctions doivent-elles à votre avis permettre d'atteindre ceux qui mettent à la disposition des utilisateurs les moyens visant à réaliser ce contournement? Dans l'affirmative, faut-il les limiter à la commercialisation de moyens ayant le contournement "pour seul but", à l'instar de l'article 7(1)c de la directive communautaire de 1991 sur les programmes d'ordinateur, ou peut-on aller, comme dans la proposition du Livre blanc américain, jusqu'à prohiber les moyens dont le but ou l'effet premier est le contournement?

Première question: oui. Deuxième question: plutôt proposition américaine.

2.3. Pensez-vous qu'il faille envisager une harmonisation des législations, afin d'éviter des distorsions de concurrence? Peut-on concevoir une norme unique? Comment et par qui cette norme devrait-elle être élaborée?

Oui.

2.4. Quel devrait être selon vous le fondement d'une règlementation dans ce domaine? S'agit-il de garantir la sécurité en vue d'améliorer la diffusion des oeuvres au bénéfice du public? Dans cette optique, peut-on aller jusqu'à rendre obligatoire la protection technique, à l'instar de la loi américaine (Audio Home Recording Act) imposant que les fabricants de matériel d'enregistrement sonore numérique incorporent des dispositifs limitant les copies séquentielles à la copie de première génération? S'agit-il plutôt d'une protection complémentaire destinée à garantir la propriété de l'auteur, à laquelle celui-ci pourrait renoncer?

Il s'agit à notre avis plutôt d'une protection complémentaire concernant le droit d'auteur.

2.5. L'interdiction de contourner les dispositifs de protection technique doit-elle à votre avis trouver place dans la loi sur le droit d'auteur ou dans une loi distincte? Dans la première hypothèse, le contournement doit-il être seulement "assimilé" à une violation du droit d'auteur ou faut-il y voir un véritable acte d'exploitation soumis en tant que tel au droit exclusif? Dans la seconde hypothèse, sur quelle base juridique fonder cette analyse? La neutralisation d'un dispositif doit-elle par exemple s'analyser comme une reproduction au sens de la législation sur le droit d'auteur?

Droit d'auteur.

2.6. Si les sanctions sont limitées aux hypothèses dans lesquelles le contournement des dispositifs de protection technique vise à permettre l'accès à une oeuvre donnant prise au droit d'auteur, doivent-elles être subordonnées à la preuve que l'utilisateur savait (ou aurait dû savoir) qu'il violait ce droit d'auteur? Seront-elles encourues lorsque le contournement aura permis d'accéder à des parties non-originales de l'oeuvre? / 2.7. L'interdiction de contourner les dispositifs de protection technique peut-elle selon vous être critiquée comme restreignant (ou risquant de restreindre) abusivement l'accès au domaine public? Ou comme paralysant le jeu des dérogations limitant traditionnellement la portée du droit d'auteur ("fair use" ou usage privé)? Des considérations d'intérêt public peuvent-elles justifier que la protection technique soit neutralisée par les autorités? Dans l'affirmative, peut-on, pour limiter les risques, imaginer que cette neutralisation soit commandée par la mise en oeuvre de plusieurs clés? / 2.8. Comment l'interdiction généralisée de contourner les dispositifs de protection technique pourrait-elle être conciliée avec les règles spéciales gouvernant la décompilation des programmes d'ordinateur, telles qu'elles résultent de la directive communautaire précitée, ou avec la jurisprudence développée aux États-Unis sur la base du "fair use"? / 2.9. Quelle sera l'incidence d'une législation telle que celle envisagée ci-dessus sur l'avenir du droit d'auteur? Faut-il accorder du crédit à l'hypothèse selon laquelle la protection technique, complétée par les contrats, signifie le déclin, voire la mort du droit d'auteur? Ou doit-on considérer que le droit exclusif reste une arme indispensable dans l'environnement numérique?

A l'heure actuelle il nous n'est pas possible de donner un avis bien fondé parce qu'il manque de temps pour étudier et discuter ces problèmes d'une manière approfondie.

2.10. Autres observations?

Sweden

G.W.G. KARNELL

Regrettably there is very little to say from a Swedish point of view in reply to the questionnaire. In Swedish law there is only article 57a of the Copyright Act: '*Anyone who, in cases other than those referred to in Article 53, sells, leases or offers for sale or possesses for sale, lease or other commercial purposes a device intended solely for facilitating unauthorised removal or circumvention of a device placed in order to protect a computer program against unauthorised reproduction, shall be punished by fines or imprisonment for not more than six months*'. This means that an infringing person, according to this article, cannot be taken into custody awaiting a final session in court; for that there must be a maximum penalty of two years, as is provided for copyright infringement in general.

We have not been able to have a group meeting on the questions addressed in the questionnaire. Work is going on in ministries and governmental bodies, but little is known and little is as yet established with any reasonable amount of certainty. We do not want to speculate here, but we will return to speculations during the Study Days.

United States of America

N.A. Smith

1. State of realizations, studies and projects

a. *State of techniques*

1.1. Are there any activities in the USA concerning the technical protection of works, especially in the digital environment? / 1.2. In the affirmative, what is the extent of this technical protection (identification of works and authors, authentification of the author and the contents of the work, restricted access to the work or restrictions to the possibility of making copies of the work, information on the right holders and conditions for use)? / 1.3. To your knowledge, which technical bases are covered in order to resolve the problem (hardware or software, internal codes inseparably connected with the original work, or external codes which are applied after the creation of the work)? / 1.4. Who are the participants in the activities (public authorities, collection societies, hardware/software producers, information providers)?

The answers to the above four questions have been divided into technological subject area subgroups, in which each subject is discussed with regards to the four questions asked.

Technical security, as distinguished from organizational and administrative security, is generally classed into three broad categories of security techniques: communications and electronic exposure, hardware and encryption, and software. (See generally, Philip E. Fites, Martin P.J. Kratz, and Alan F. Brebner, *Control and Security of Computer Information Systems* (1989).) The widespread use of technical security with computer software and data has arisen more as a result of the often critical necessity of keeping certain information confidential than the inherent difficulties and inefficiencies associated with the enforcement of copyright owner's rights under the Copyright Act. Various techniques, most importantly encryption, are described below. The assertion has been made that only encryption can provide adequate protection of information contained in computer databases and software. (*Id.* at 192.) In general, this type of encryption is directed toward situations where the information is kept from those not authorized to access the information. In contrast, 'Copyright in cyberspace' seems to be directed beyond limiting access to limiting use and/or further distribution or copying of protected information.

Physical security

Communications in the form of signals sent on a wire, or over the air, such as by microwave, or by satellite, or optical fiber, including voice communications utilizing computer processing, are exposed to various security problems. These problems can occur at the originator, the transmission medium or at the receiver. Electromagnetic leakage from the internal components of the computer system and its peripherals can permit unauthorized interception of information processed by the computer. One solution is to 'shield' any vulnerable components with faraday shields to thereby block electromagnetic signals. Shielding may also be accomplished by placing metal around entire computer rooms to block external signals and around vulnerable components such as power supplies, chips and other signal emitters within the system. The Department of Defense uses 'Tempest' equipment which protects its equipment at a very high standard. (See *id.* at 184.) Computer systems which utilize optical fibers are not subject to leaking electronic signals and electronic interference (to and from the optical portions of such computers) from outside sources and are therefore less susceptible to interception or wire-tapping.

'Value-added communications', especially in 'Open System Interconnections' (OSI) which are generally accessible by the outside world, such as the Internet, are especially susceptible to electronic exposures because the shielding must have intentional gates to allow desired signals to be sent and received. (See Stephen T. Walker, *Network Security: The Parts of the Sum*, Proceedings of 1989 IEEE Symposium on Security and Privacy (1994), p. 4.) Value-added communications are those that add value to the work being performed. (Frites, *supra*, at 185.) Some examples include telecommunications, electronic mail, city traffic light coordination systems, and the list goes on *ad infinitum*. 'Local Area Networks' (LANs) are less susceptible than OSIs to security risks because they do not extend beyond a limited area. Typically LANs are useful only for intra-office communication.

Any measures taken to minimize noise and interference may nonetheless not protect a computer system from memory resident or introduced 'viruses' and 'worms' that often accompany the accessing and downloading of freeware and public domain programs from bulletin boards or the Internet. Viruses and worms are memory algorithms that can degrade an operating system, destroy data files, and generally do damage to the information a computer works with. (*Id.* at 186.) Viruses intricately attach themselves to a computer's operating system and worms move more freely about the system. Unauthorized persons may intercept, or read, a communication and may replace it with another of his choice whenever communications are sent out via an open system. The potential presence of such viruses and worms means that screening and identification functions are often included in computer communication systems. These are also useful functions to prevent copying and to identify copiers.

The most feasible solution, however, to this security problem is often encryption. The International Standards Organization (ISO) comprises the national standards for the OSI's of many countries. The ISO/OSI framework comprises seven levels including: the application layer where the system interacts with the end-user application, the presentation layer which prepares the information for the application, the session layer which establishes the communication link between network nodes, the transport layer which translates requirements from higher layers into a protocol that can be used by the network, the network layer which establishes the logical transmission path through a switched network, the data link layer which performs functions necessary to move data through an electrical connection, and the physical layer which describes the physical and electrical connections in the network. (Walker, *supra*, at 4; Fites, *supra* at 189-90; Jane Sinclair, *Considering the Common Criteria: Introduction to Panel Discussion*, IEEE Computer Security Foundations Workshop Proceedings, 148 (September 1995), describing the Department of Defense Trusted Computer Security Evaluation Criteria (TCSEC or 'Orange Book') prescribed by the United States Computer Security Center. TCSEC describes seven levels of security rating, from D to A1, each with increasingly stringent requirements.)

Encryption

Encryption is the process of changing text that is easily read by a user, or 'plaintext', into unreadable 'ciphertext' by applying to the plaintext an encryption procedure controlled by a 'key'. (See generally Per Christofferson *et al.*, *Crypto User's handbook* (1988); Jerome Lobel, *Foiling the System Breakers* (1986); Abrams, *Tutorial: Computer and Network Security*, 17 (1987); Information Infrastructure Task Force, *Intellectual Property and the National Information Infrastructure: The Report of the Working Group on Intellectual Property Rights* ('White Paper', September 1995), II.C.2.) An unauthorized user cannot interpret ciphertext without the key. A key consists of a preset number in binary of bits containing a string of zeroes and ones. A security algorithm formula is presumed to be more secure the greater the number of bits. Encrypting data or communications protects the confidentiality of the information represented by the data, but does not prevent unauthorized access to it and/or consequent copying, alteration or destruction of it. (See Abrams, *supra*, at 18.) However, it is believed that controlling access is important to controlling copying. This (1) prevents many infringements from ever taking place and (2) it is easier to control copying by authorized, known users, either by contract or by identification of the duplicated copy.

Public key and private key are the two basic encryption systems in use today. In the private key system, only one key is used to both encrypt and decrypt. In the public key system, different keys are used to encrypt and decrypt. Normally, data is encrypted with the public key which is readily available to subscribers, but only a person holding the private key can decrypt it. The security of the encryption method thus relies heavily on the system's ability to protect the keys. (See Steven Levy, *Wisecrackers*, *Wired*, March 1996, describing attempts, successful and unsuccessful, to 'crack' encrypted security systems.) For example, the most recent US government development and method of protecting its critically important databases such as defense and the treasury, the Encryption Escrow System, see *infra*, requires two keys for decryption. One key is held with the Department of the Treasury and the other with the Department of Commerce.

The National Security Agency (NSA) handles security for classified data within the United States government (50 USC § 401-32 (1988 & Supp. V 1993); 'National Security Act of 1947'). The US Department of Commerce is authorized to control and create processing standards for unclassified but sensitive data (40 USC § 759(f); 'Brooks Act'). The Department of Commerce delegates this duty to the National Institute of Science and Technology (NIST). NIST develops Federal Information Processing Standards (FIPS). FIPS are the mathematically determined standards of security of encryption systems. (See Note, *Personal Data Security: Divergent Standards in the European Union and the United States*, 19 *Fordham Int'l L.J.* 1995, 142.) The current United States national standard is the private key system known as the Data Encryption Standard (DES), utilizing a 64-bit key. (See Fites, *supra*, at 197.)

Another encryption device developed in the private sector is the public key system known as Rivest-Shamir-Adelman (RSA), utilizing 129-bit keys. Although RSA is more secure than DES, NIST's desire to issue royalty-free FIPS prevents it from endorsing RSA. The United States government's current data security system is the Escrowed Encryption Standard (EES) which was approved by NIST in February of 1994. (See Note, *supra*, at 143.) It is currently believed that the government wants to make EES the *de facto* encryption standard in the United States. (See Jaleen Nelson, *Sledge Hammers and Scalpels: The FBI Digital Wiretap Bill and Its Effects on Free Flow of Information and Privacy*, 41 *UCLA* 1994 1139, 1140.) EES is comprised of two tamper-proof components which utilize the 80-bit algorithm 'Skipjack'. One is the Clipper Chip, which encrypts high-speed data transmissions, and the other is the Capstone Chip, which encrypts low speed data and voice transmissions. Each EES chip possesses an identification number that constitutes the chip-unique key. (See Note, *supra*, at 164, quoting Clinton C. Brooks, Special Assistant to the Director, NSA.) Each chip unique key is broken into two components. One component is escrowed with the Department of Treasury and the other with the Department of Commerce. Constructing the chip-unique key necessary to decrypt the data requires the retrieval of the key's components from both escrow agents.

Trusted authentication servers

Another security system is the use of Trusted Authentication Servers. Two entities which share no secret keys can securely communicate with each other using the assistance of a third party 'Trusted Authentication Server'. (L. Chen, D. Gollmanm and C. Mitchell, *Key Distribution Without Individual Trusted Authentication Servers*, IEEE Computer Security Foundations Workshop Proceedings (1995), 30.) Typically this third party is an authentication server who provides an authentication service including distributing a secure session key with each authentication to these entities as clients. The security of such a key distribution protocol depends on the assumption that the authentication server is trustworthy, or secure.

Digital signatures

Just as handwritten signatures verify personal checks and personal documents, so do digital signatures authenticate electronic transactions and works. (*White Paper* at

II.C.3.) The sender encrypts the message or work with its own unique set of binary digits and private key and the receiver can then decrypt the message or work with a private or public key. Particular authors can use their personal digital signature on all of their works and can further assign unique bits to individual messages or works. Digital signatures identify the author and act as a seal, making it possible to verify that the contents of the file containing the author's work have not been altered.

Command scripts

Command scripts are programs written by one user which act on the writer's behalf when another user executes the script. (Trent Jaeger and Atul Prakash, *Implementation of a Discretionary Access Control Model for Script-based Systems*, IEEE Computer Security Foundations Workshop Proceedings (1995), 70.) Mosaic, the information server for the World Wide Web, for example, uses command scripts to define server actions when a client wants to access information from the server. The user owns a process which runs on the user's machine and the command script is executed with the user's access rights. Generally, security is provided by the use of two interpreters: a trusted and an untrusted interpreter. (*Id.* at 71.) The untrusted interpreter limits the ways in which command scripts can be used, but the system allows for input and output (I/O) capability of building applications that perform I/O. By their very nature, command scripts are vulnerable to mischievous users.

Steganography

Steganography is a method for encoding digital information with attributes that cannot be disassociated from the file that contains the information. (*White Paper* at II.C.4.) A party can embed hidden messages in digitized visual or audio data. The embedded information does not interfere with the quality of the work but stamps the work with a verifiable 'watermark'. An example of this technique is modulating noise with the information contained in the message or work and distributing this 'subliminal noise' throughout the entirety of the work.

Server and file access controls

Access control is affected through user identification and authentication (*i.e.* user name and password) procedures that deny access to unauthorized users to a server or to particular information on a server. (*Id.* at 115; see Fites, *supra*, at 214.) The system stores each user's password for comparison with the password presented by the user. (Abrams, *supra*, at 17.) The problem with this system is the user's maintenance of the secrecy of the password is unreliable. Another method of authentication involves a machine-readable object possessed by the user, such as a card or a badge. Such objects are susceptible to being lost, stolen or forged, however.

Security kernels

Most government operating systems including that used by the Department of Defense contain a security kernel (see Abrams, *supra*, at 16; Fites, *supra*, at 208). The kernel is a small module, a portion of the operating system (Fites, *supra*, at 208). All references to information and all changes to authorizations must pass through the kernel. The kernel mediates all accesses to the system and is presumably tamper proof (Abrams, *supra*, at 16). The kernel is also verifiable in order to demonstrate that it correctly implements the system's security policy and that the programs of the kernel correctly implement the design of the system.

Multilevel secure systems

Multilevel security (MLS) is concerned with protecting information with respect to a multilevel hierarchy (*e.g.* unclassified, secret, top secret). (Paul F. Syverson and James W. Gray III, *The Epistemic Representation of Information Flow Security in Probabilistic Systems*, IEEE Computer Security Foundations Workshop Proceedings (1995), 152.) The additional security provided by such systems is derived from the separability of users at different levels in the security hierarchy. (A. Zakinthinos and E.S. Lee, *The Composability of Non-Interference*, IEEE Computer Security Foundation Workshop Proceedings (1995), 2.)

Non-interference captures the intuitive notion that system security is preserved whenever high level users are prevented from influencing the behavior of low-level users. The MLS system makes use of the standard engineering procedure of constructing large complex systems from a standard set of smaller systems that can be verified independently. The practice leads to a more reliable and cost-effective system. The elimination of illicit communication between processes at different classification levels is often facilitated by using a system of hardware and software that makes probabilistic choices (*e.g.* by consulting a random number generator) during its execution. (Syverson, *supra*, at 152.) Such probabilistic choices introduce noise to eliminate the illicit communications between levels.

Other securitization methods

Many other ways of providing computer system security are used in various ways for varying purposes. Some of these include Traffic Padding, Routing Control and Notarization. (See Walker, *supra*, at 5, describing ISO security services and mechanisms and scrutinizing TCSEC's non-inclusion of many such services and mechanisms.)

b. *State of legislation*

1.5. Do any legislative provisions exist in the United States that generally sanction circumvention of technical protection devices?

Yes. The two most important United States statutes governing computer security are the Computer Security Act of 1987 (Pub. L. No. 100-235, 101 Stat. 1724, 1988) and the Computer Fraud and Abuse Act of 1986 (18 USC § 1030, 1988 & Supp. V 1993, prohibiting unauthorized access to computer networks). (Richard D. Marks, Symposium: Legal Issues in the Information Revolution; article: *Security, Privacy, and Free Expression in the New World of Broadband Networks*, 32 *Hous. L. Rev.* (1995)

501.) The Computer Fraud and Abuse Act is a criminal statute aimed at prosecuting individuals who perpetrate fraud and related activities in connection with computers. (*Id.* at 505.) The statute prohibits unauthorized access to computer networks resulting in various forms of harm and extends to private interests as well as national security. (*Id.*; *United States v. Morris*, 928 F.2d 504 (2d Cir.) cert. denied 502 US 817 (1991), *United States v. Brady*, 820 F. Supp. 1346 (D. Utah 1993); *United States v. Riggs*, 739 F. Supp. 414 (ND 111, 1990).) The United States Court of Appeals for the Second Circuit found criminal jurisdiction under the statute to prosecute a private individual who gained authorized access to the internet but did unauthorized irreparable harm to private computer systems by releasing a worm. *(US v. Morris, supra.)* Jurisdiction can be had under the statute if there is some effect on a federal computer, *unauthorized access of protected information*, or damage exceeding $ 1,000. (Marks, *supra*, at 509, citing 18 USC § 1030(a).)

Interception, disclosure and use of electronic communications are prohibited under 18 USC §§ 2510-2521 (1988 & Supp. V 1993). Section 2511(2), however, provides for certain exceptions including incidental access by employees of the service provider and actions pursuant to the official duty of an agent of the United States charged with electronic surveillance. In the former case, the service provider may disclose the contents of the communication to law enforcement (§ 2511(3)(b)(iv)). Civil and criminal penalties are further provided for unauthorized access to stored wire and electronic communications records (§§ 2701-2711). Section 2701(c) exempts certain parties including communications service provider and law enforcement officials, and permits the service provider to disclose the information to law enforcement. Congress passed the Communications Assistance for Law Enforcement Act in October of 1994 to preserve the ability of law enforcement agencies to monitor ('wiretap') communications over the new digital communications infrastructure (Pub. L. No. 103414, 108 Stat. 4279 (1994)).

The United States copyright law also provides criminal, as well as civil, penalties for wilful acts of infringement (17 USC §§ 504, 506 and 18 USC §§ 2319, 2319A). The difficulty in the digital age is that copying identical copies, and their movement over the information highway, the Internet, or other transmission, is easy, inexpensive, and can often be accomplished without identification of the original, from which the copy was made, or identification of the copier, and there are no limits to the number of identical copies which can be made. As a result, manufacturers or copyright organizations have recommended including identification information in digital copies or media to identify and control the number or nature of copies that can be made.

The White Paper's recommendation to amend the Copyright Act to protect such identification or copy control or limitation of information or features is supported by similar existing provisions in US law. For example, see 17 USC § 1002(c) (Supp. V 1993), prohibiting circumvention of any program or circuit that implements a serial copy management system or similar system included in digital audio recording devices and digital audio interface devices; and 47 USC § 605(e)(4) (1988) prohibiting unauthorized decryption of satellite cable programming; and NAFTA, at article

1707(a) (HR Doc. No. 159, 103d Cong., 1st Sess. (1993)) prohibiting manufacture, import, sale or lease of satellite signal decrypting devices. The United States has proposed introducing new language into the Copyright Act to specifically prohibit the circumvention of technical protection devices. (White Paper at IV.A.6.) Current legislation is being considered to implement the recommendations of the US White Paper (S. 1284 and H.R. 2441, 104th Cong., 1st Sess. (1995)). The United States has also proposed that the same language be added to the Berne Convention Treaty which governs most of the international law of intellectual property. (World Intellectual Property Organization, Committee of Experts on a Possible Protocol to the Berne Convention, Sixth Session, article 7 (1-9 February 1996).)

Many computer crimes can be prosecuted in the United States under one or more statutes relating to theft and/or fraud. (See, *e.g.*, 18 USC §§ 641 (theft), 1341 (mail fraud), 1343 (wire fraud), 1001 (deceptive practices) cited in Michael C. Gemigiani, *A legal Guide to EDP Management*, 140-43 (1989).) Moreover, almost all states have criminal statutes dealing specifically with computer crime. (See Gemigiani, *supra*, at 143-4, reprinting a list of state computer crime statutes compiled by the National Center for Computer Crime Data in 1986; see, *e.g.*, *State v. Rowell*, 895 P.2d 232 (NM 1995), prosecuting under the New Mexico Computer Crime Act (NMSA 1978 § 30-45-1-7 (Repl. Pamp. 1989).) However, under current United States law, criminal copyright violations can only be prosecuted if undertaken for profit or gain. Altruistic copying or even knowingly making copyrighted works available for copying by others without an intent to profit by the infringement, cannot be prosecuted criminally. (See *United States v. LaMacchia*, 871 F. Supp. 535 (D. Ma. 1995).) The US White Paper and the above pending legislation allow criminal prosecution where a threshold amount of copying is accomplished.

While United States civil law cases have not specifically dealt with defeating devices for serial copy management systems or other legislatively created protection for devices, several cases have found liability under contributory copyright infringement theories and enjoined the sale of distribution of copying devices. In *Sega v. MAPHIA* (857 F. Supp. 679, 685 (N.D. Cal. 1994)), the court enjoined a computer bulletin board operator from selling and distributing copying devices which are *'used for the making of unauthorized copies of Sega's video game programs and some purchasers use them so as to avoid purchasing Sega's game cartridges from Sega'*. Contributory copyright infringement is found under United States law where *'[o]ne who, with knowledge of the infringing activity, induces, causes or materially contributes to the infringing conduct of another'*. (*Id.* at 686.)

Finally, a recent debate has resulted in the United States concerning implementation of inclusion of a mandated 'V-chip' in television receivers for cable television. The V-chip would allow parents to selectively screen out what they didn't want their children to watch. This would replace current controls on broadcasters' television content.

In a recent case concerning the constitutionality of the Public Telecommunications Act of 1992, the dissent argued that prohibiting indecent broadcast at hours other than from 10 p.m. to 6 a.m. was not the least restrictive way to serve the compelling interests of protecting youth and allowing parents to proscribe their children's viewing of certain types of programming. (*Action for Children's TV v. FCC, en banc,* 58 F.3d 654 (D.C. Cir. 1995).) The dissent argued that such forthcoming technologies as the V-chip which are much less restrictive and facilitate rather than preempt parental supervision, render the statute unconstitutional. In the United States, constitutional considerations often depend upon the nature of the restrictions. Similar technology could be wed, in combination with copy management functions and information, to control access to or duplication of copyrighted works.

NIST was created to develop standards and guidelines for cost-effective security and privacy of sensitive information in federal computer systems and to propose means to strengthen security (15 USC § 278g-3(a)(1)-(5) (1988)). Congress also created the Computer System Security and Privacy Advisory Board to advise NIST and the Secretary of Commerce on security and privacy issues pertaining to federal computer systems (§ 278g-4(a), (b)(1)). However, NIST's existing guidelines provide direction to owners and users of computer networks generally (§ 278g-3(b)(1)). NIST's guidelines are therefore mandatory for federal government computers and voluntary for nonfederal government computers. (See Marks, *supra,* at 504.)

In the field of cable television security systems, the Telecommunications Act of 1995 was proposed to amend 47 USC § 544 A(B)(2) to withhold authority from federal, state, and franchising agencies to prohibit a cable operator's use of security systems, such as scrambling, encryption, traps and interdiction. The amendment would allow the use of such systems wherever necessary to prevent the unauthorized reception of basic service tiers. (S. 652, 104th Cong., 1st Sess. (1995); HR 1555, 104th Cong., 1st Sess. (1995).) The pending US Anticounterfeiting Consumer Protection Act of 1995 would extend to computer programs, and computer program documentation, and packaging existing prohibitions and penalties applicable to trafficking in counterfeit labels affixed or designed to be affixed to audiovisual works such as motion pictures and phonorecords, including compact disks. (S. 1136, 104th Cong., 1st Sess. (1995); HR 2511, 104th Cong., 1st Sess. (1995).) The Act would make such counterfeit labelling a predicate offense under the Racketeer Influenced and Corrupt Organizations Act.

> *1.6. If no, are there precedents, for example in the domain of encrypting television broadcasts?*

-

> *1.7. Are use, distribution or export of encryption devices subject to particular restrictions?*

Yes. For United States security purposes, encryption export control is strictly regulated by the Bureau of Export Administration of the Department of Commerce. The Bureau maintains the Commerce Control List which governs export control of all items (commodities, software, and technical data) subject to the Bureau's export controls. (White Paper at II.F, citing 15 CFR § 799.1(a) (1994).) United States entities are currently prevented from exporting software and hardware with certain types of encryption technology. Currently, software can be exported with encryption key sizes no larger than approximately 40 bits. (Levy, *supra*, at 196.) This is due to an export licensing system developed to limit proliferation of encryption technology that could hinder efficient intelligence gathering and effective law enforcement. (See The Export and Administration Act of 1979, 50 USC app. §§ 2401-2420 (1988 and Supp. V 1993); 22 CFR §§ 120.1(c), 120.2 (1994), requiring a license to export software containing encryption technology; Marks, *supra*, at 505.) There is pressure from US software manufacturers to relax export controls and allow them to compete with foreign companies that currently incorporate strong encryption technology in their products.

Legislation has been proposed that is presently before Congress that would ease these restrictions on the exportation of their goods. (See *Wall Street Journal* 26 February 1996, B5.) The United States Congress is studying the international market for computer software for encryption purposes, and the impact of US export controls on encryption hardware and software on the international competitiveness of the United States computer industry in light of those controls. (See HR 361, 104th Cong., 1st Sess. (1995).) Possibly in response, the Working Group on Intellectual Property Rights has expressly given its support to efforts to work with industry on key-escrow encryption technologies and other encryption products which could be exported without compromising US intelligence gathering and law enforcement. (White Paper II.F.)

Technical protection devices

Technical protection devices may be broadly classified into two categories:
a) those devices - hardware and/or software - which are intended to prevent interception by unauthorized recipients of data (*i.e.* financial data, trade secrets), programs, and/or electronic forms of copyrightable works, (*i.e.* motion pictures distributed on a pay-per-view basis), and
b) those devices - hardware and/or software - which are intended to limit the uses and/ or further distribution of data, programs, and/or other electronic forms of copyright-able work by those persons/entities authorized to use (on a limited basis) such data, programs and/or other forms of copyrightable works. Examples are the Serial Copy Management Systems included with US digital audio tape recorders and digital audio tape cassettes (DAT).

2. **Critical assessment**

***2.1.** Is, in your opinion, the preparation of sanctions against the circumvention of technical protective devices worthwhile? Will these provisions be efficient? Does the aim justify the substantial investments required?*

Protection of an author's exclusive rights under the US Copyright Act or other laws is believed worthwhile because it promotes the Constitutional purpose of the progress of the useful arts. (US Const., article I, § 8, cl. 8.) Revision of the US

Copyright Act of 1976 was in response to significant changes in technology that took place after the enactment of the 1909 Act, and further revision should be made from time to time when new technology requires it. (See White Paper, Introduction, fn 26.) Technical protective devices are widely used because of the difficulty and inefficiency of enforcing authors' exclusive rights under the US Copyright Act for digital or digitized works contained in computer software and systems. For the same policy reasons that technical protection is encouraged (or necessary), sanctions against methods of circumvention are justified. The efficiency of protective devices depends on the manner in which they are implemented and their circumscription proscribed. Implementation of EES, the administration's solution, would provide a solid means of maintaining law enforcement, even though it raises concerns with possible privacy deprivation. Especially in the area of national security, it seems that substantial investment is justified considering the potential repercussions that compromising government computer systems would entail. Thus many of the sanctions against circumvention even have national security value as well.

Sanctions against circumvention are also justified on the grounds that it is often the direct intent of intruders of computer systems to violate the rights of copyright owners. Tremendous efforts to prevent violations of the law are often justified in other areas such as in felonious criminal prosecutions and probably are justified in this case. Obviously, the extent of investment required depends upon the technology. In the United States, civil and, particularly, criminal laws may deter investment in copy protection defeating devices and technology.

> *2.2. Should the sanctions be directed against those who provide users with the means to circumvent protective devices? In the affirmative, should they be limited to those means which are specifically meant to circumvent protective devices, analogous to article 7(1)c of the 1991 Software Directive, or is it preferable, like in the American White Paper, to prohibit means of which one of the aims or most important effect is to circumvent protective devices?*

To the extent that providers of the means to circumvent technical protective devices are contributory infringers of the exclusive rights of copyright owners, sanctions should be directed at those individuals or entities in proportion to the violations of the actual direct circumventors. However, if another effect of such sanctions is to inhibit lawful actions or purposes, then a line needs to be drawn as to how much of the lawful rights of these providers can and should be curtailed in conjunction with prevention of the purposes and effects of their unlawful conduct. The White Paper, the most recent policy statement on this issue, is probably the authority that should be looked to for guidance. The White Paper recommended: *'[T]hat the Copyright Act be amended to include a new Chapter 12, which would include a provision to prohibit the importation, manufacture or distribution of any device, product or component incorporated into a device or product, or the provision of any service, the primary purpose or effect of which is to avoid, bypass, remove, deactivate, or otherwise circumvent, without authority of the copyright owner or the law, any process, treatment, mechanism or system which prevents or inhibits the violation of any of the exclusive rights under Section 106'*. (White Paper, IV.A.6.) Such an amendment to the

Copyright Act has now been proposed in bills pending in the United States Senate (S. 1284) and in the House of Representatives (H.R. 2441). Also, Constitutional concerns such as first amendment rights and the associated policy behind them should be considered. It is extremely difficult to draw a line when conduct has both legal and illegal (infringing and non-infringing) purposes and uses. However, it is believed that United States courts are experienced at deciding difficult balancing and policy questions.

> *2.3. Do you think that it would be necessary to consider a harmonization of legislations, to prevent distortions in competition? Is it possible to find a uniform standard? How and by whom should this standard be developed?*

The question seems to be speaking to the disparity of encryption protections provided by US software exporters and those of other countries with less limited restrictions than current US export control law allows. The debate is raging and is currently being taken up by the US Congress. The protocol to the Berne Convention would implement some uniformity in standards recognized by all of its signatories. The administration's efforts to implement EES is also an attempt to provide US software exporters the authority to utilize greater encryption protection (without blocking law enforcement - the governments hold the keys!) to provide uniformity. International law is often a less efficient means to protect the interests of a nation than implementation of its own standards.

Certainly it would be desirable to have harmonization. If hardware or software or other mechanisms are used to prevent control copying, they will be of little value if circumvention devices are available in other countries. Given the different security consensus of nations, encryption mechanism harmonization will be most difficult. Copy protection mechanisms directed toward preventing copying of copyrighted works are directed toward protecting investments and encouraging investments of efforts and money in creating such works. Unfortunately, different nations have differing views about protecting intellectual property, depending upon whether it is good or bad for that nation's economy. Harmonization will be very difficult as a result.

> *2.4. What should be the bases of regulations in this field? Is the aim to guarantee security in light of improving the diffusion of works for the benefit of the public? In that view, should regulations lead to compulsory technical protection, analogous to American law (Audio Home Recording Act), imposing an obligation upon the producers of digital sound recording equipment to apply devices limiting copying to copies of the first generation? Or is it an additional protection which is meant to guarantee the rights of the author, which he can renounce?*

Compulsory technical protection provides greater security for the rights of authorship, but the public may have less access to works in the public domain as well as to uses of copyrighted works that would otherwise be allowed under the doctrine of fair use under United States law. Furthermore, when an author can choose to renounce rights under the United States Copyright Act, the public gains the benefit of

427

increased access to the work and the author presumably gains whatever benefit that prompted the renouncement (such as input). It should also be noted that many authors may not have the resources to enforce their copyrights, so mandatory technical protection provides them some benefits in controlling or discouraging copying the authors could not enforce against.

Compulsory technical protection is very restrictive. The basis of regulation should be to promote the progress of the useful arts as mandated by the United States Constitution and compulsory protection may not be the least restrictive way to promote that progress. Thus, United States law may discourage it. However, given the ease with which identical digital copies can be made at little cost and without detection, it is likely in the reporter's view that the United States may adopt legislation and technology for compulsory technical protection. Renouncement of copyrights by authors is not used very often in the United States, and, presumably, the technical protection mechanism could have a 'pass through' identification code identification for authors who wish to permit copying, similar to 'disclaimers' or 'permission to copy granted' statements made by the authors.

> *2.5. Should the injunction to circumvent technical protective devices be part of United States Copyright Law or a separate law? In the first case, should it be an act which is a violation of copyright only or is there an act of exploitation, subject to the exclusive rights? In the second case, what is the legal basis? Should the neutralization of a device, for instance, be considered a reproduction in the sense of copyright legislation?*

In the reporter's view, the United States Copyright Law would be appropriate law for such an injunction. The United States law is well developed to weigh intent and purpose issues. For example, in the United States law case, *Sega Enterprises Ltd. v. MAPHIA Bulletin Board* (857 F. Supp. 679 (N.D. Cal. 1994)), the court weighed a similar argument about the purpose for which copying devices were used in granting an injunction against the sale of copying devices. Under United States law, it would be consistent with contributory copyright infringement law principles to hold that the neutralization of an autocopying device would be contributory copyright infringement for which an injunction and damages would be available to the copyright owner.

> *2.6. If the sanctions are limited to the hypothesis that there is an infringement of copyright if technical protection devices are circumvented which leads to access to a work, should these sanctions be limited to the case that the user knew (or should have known) that he was infringing?*

In the reporter's view, the user's knowledge, or that the user should have known of the purpose of the circumvention, is an appropriate requirement. Usually, this will be shown without difficulty. Manufacturers and facilitators of circumvention devices should be on notice. Only sellers of such devices may be innocent of their purpose if included in a product with other purposes and uses, such as a DAT audio recording device. The United States law has special limitations of remedies for innocent printers of items infringing intellectual property, and it would be appropriate to have the remedy different, and limited to an injunction, under United States law.

> *2.7. Do you think criticism of the injunction to circumvent technical protective devices is justified, in view of the fact that the access to works which are in the public domain is or could be limited? Or because the traditional limitations on copyright (like fair use or private use) are not respected? Do considerations which are in the interest of the public justify that the technical protection is neutralized by the authorities? In the affirmative, is it imaginable that this neutralization is ordered by using several keys?*

Certainly, there may be criticism of broad injunctions against the manufacturer or sale of devices which have as their purpose the circumvention of protection devices, because such devices can also be used for copying public domain works or making 'fair use' of copyrighted works. It may be possible, technically, as mentioned above, to limit the protection device's use by use of several keys and have codes in copyrighted works which last only as long as their copyrights remain valid, to limit the over broad effect of such an injunction. The question of whether circumvention of protective devices for the purpose of gaining access to works not protected by copyright law should be declared unlawful under the Copyright Act does raise the issue of whether this appears to contradict the Act's purposes. To provide penalties under other statutes or legal doctrine, such as those mentioned above in 2.5, may be an effective, non-contradictory means of deterring circumscription without contradicting copyright policy. However, it may be difficult beyond relying upon national security threatening content or theft prevention to find a basis for such a law in the United States.

> *2.8. Is it possible to reconcile the general injunction on the circumvention of technical protective devices with the special rules covering the decompilation of software, like those resulting from the Software Directive mentioned before, or with the case-law developed in the United States on the basis of fair use?*

It would not be easy to reconcile a general injunction against the circumvention of technical devices with the rights of others to copy portions of protected works under the fair use defense. The prohibition is a blanket one; fair use is a defense depending upon the circumstances, particularly, the purpose for which the copy was made. In only certain law cases, will the ultimate use, for which a copy of a copyrighted work has been made, ever be known.

> *2.9. What could be the effect of legislation as has been elaborated upon above on the future of copyright? Do you agree with the hypothesis which says that technical protection, in combination with contracts, means the decline or the end of copyright? Or should we consider the exclusive right of the author an indispensable weapon in the digital environment?*

As mentioned above, copyright law would be changed dramatically if circumvention of protective devices becomes a *per se* violation of the Copyright Act. It should be remembered that it is the specific circumstances of computer software and digitization of works, and the inherent inefficiency of enforcement of the Copyright Act for works which are in this form, that has prompted the widespread use of protective devices (and thus this debate about their prescription). The rest of copyright law should remain unaffected. Protection of the exclusive rights of the author under the Copyright Act as it stands today should be complemented by and not replaced with new legislative protections concerning computer software and digital works. This is not the decline of copyright, only a new challenge for law makers to balance the interests of authors and users.

Interventions

M. RACICOT:

What lesson can we learn from the Michelangelo story of Professor Lehman? The lesson that I personally learn is that the answer comes from the market, from the necessity. As we say in French: *'la nécessité est la mère de l'invention'*. Michelangelo was not dictated by some form of higher authority to put his name on the work. It was his response to the market. Other authors of masterpieces, most notably those who conceived the cathedrals in the Middle Ages, chose to remain anonymous. Consequently, in my opinion, the role of the law should be to support the technical protection of the works but not to inhibit it or prevent the work from being protected by copyright if it is not protected technically. Such support from the law should restrict itself to making it illegal to tamper with or circumvent technical means of protection but without any restriction in relation to the existence of copyright.

It is the market that should develop uniform technical means (and in this regard we can remember the VHS/Betamax situation), which should not be imposed by legislators or some other authority. The uniformization should come from the base, not from the top. Undoubtedly, in order to achieve uniformity, there must be some multilateral forum to establish these standards on basis of consensus. I suggest that a forum such as ISO is a very appropriate forum for such purposes, but the role of such a forum should not be to impose but to facilitate the establishment of uniform standards. In my opinion, the most effective harmonized technical specifications are those that come from the market, such as those applicable to the telecommunication networks or the TCP/IP standard applicable to electronic communications, such as on the Internet.

TH. VINJE:

I agree with the observations of those who have stated that the process on the front of technical protection systems is moving too fast, and that it is premature to include any provision on this issue in the Berne Protocol. Many difficult questions remain to be discussed and resolved. It is not easy to craft a provision that will prohibit 'circumvention divices' without altering the existing balance in copyright law. We must carefully consider the impact on the public domain and existing copyright exceptions.

One topic that deserves but has not yet received detailed attention, is software

431

reverse engineering. Sometimes the interface information necessary to create inter-operable computer products, is not readily available. Therefore, the EU Software Directive and US case law have carved out an exception to the reproduction/translation rights for the software reverse engineering, necessary to obtain interface information. The problem that arises in this context is that software producers can include in their computer programs technical mechanisms, designed to prevent reverse engineering. These mechanisms might constitute 'technical protection systems' within the meaning of the proposals on this topic made by the US and the EU. Indeed, even the distribution of computer programs in object code form (as opposed to source code) might be deemed a technical protection system. Reverse engineering might be seen to constitute a means of 'circumventing' this 'protection', and divices designed to defeat anti-reverse engineering mechanisms might be considered to be 'circumvention devices'. We must therefore carefully consider this issue, so that any legislation adopted on 'technical protection systems' does not unwittingly undermine the law that wisely permits reverse engineering for interoperability purposes.

V

Protection of and vis-à-vis databases

La protection en faveur des et vis-à-vis des banques de données

Protection of and vis-à-vis databases

W.R. Cornish[*]

I. Introduction

This General Report is made in the light of National Reports from our host country, the Netherlands, and from Belgium, Canada, Finland, France, Germany, Italy, Switzerland and the United States. Seven of the nine Reports thus come from member states of the EC. Given the fact than on 11 March 1996, the EC's Directive to its member states to harmonise their national copyright and other laws on database protection in certain distinctive ways, was adopted, those Reports describe the landscape as Noah began to build the Ark. In some of them, however, that description also incorporates a vision of life after 1998, by which time the Directive's flood ought to have been absorbed. Of the other Reports, that from Switzerland stands as an example of independent development within the authors' right tradition. Whereas Canada and the United States emerge as islands in the common law gulfstream, each with its own distinctive vegetation.

I shall refer briefly to the various approaches which we find exemplified in inherited national laws. The speakers who will follow are better able to say something of their national experience, and the condition in which protection of and vis-à-vis databases finds itself today in their law. But the completed Directive is an event of structural significance, not only for EC states but for all countries of the world, which may take it as a model. Accordingly, I consider that this General Report should comment mainly on its characteristics, so that may form a major part of the ensuing discussion.

The ALAI has been in the forefront in examining the problems of protection set by databases. At its 1989 Congress in Quebec, it identified the need for protection of the information collections. At that time they were already becoming commonplace in a world of electronic communication and they were plainly open to full-scale misappropriation. At the same time, it was becoming clear that on a world basis, copyright protection was unlikely to provide an adequate answer to the problem. So Professor Lucas concluded in his General Report (see ALAI, *L'informatique et le Droit d'Auteur, Actes du 57e Congrès* (1990), pp. 313-348). Intervening events have shown how right he was.

There have been three principal ways in which legal systems have been able to answer the demand for protection of information collections.

---

[*] Herchel Smith Professor of Intellectual Property Law, Cambridge University

(i) The first is by copyright. It is possible, by taking the generous view that there is sufficient originality in any literary expression if it is itself not copied. Famously or infamously, the United Kingdom and the countries of its Commonwealth have for a long time accepted this approach and have accordingly used copyright to protect the content of all sorts of mundane material like TV programme listings, horse-race fixtures and street directories (see the Canadian Report). The Dutch have reached a result by the interpretation placed by the *Hoge Raad* on the copyright protection of 'other writings' (see the Netherlands Report). A convenient route to sufficient and certain protection, if you can accept the undoubted element of pragmatism involved; if you cannot, a denial of all principle, an unstoppable hole in the dike.

Many countries have considered that copyright can pertain to a data collection only if the person making the collection acts as an author, *i.e.* there must be an element of personal judgment which affects the manner in which the collection is expressed as a literary or other work. Any protection is accordingly 'thin' in two senses of that ambiguous concept: there will be no protection at all if there is no element of personal judgment; and any protection there may be will go only to the element of ordering or selection which the collector provides. The result, of course, is that the more complete the collection, the less likely it is to attract copyright.

(ii) The second mode of protection is through a law of unfair competition. This is possible where a country extends liability for unfair competition beyond misleading statements to the misappropriation of information in order to protect the value amassed from collecting the information. If unfair competition has been formulated with the sweep that is to be found in the modern Swiss law (as the Swiss Report demonstrates) then this alternative route may provide much of the necessary answer. It is of course the absence of such a doctrine which turned common law countries in the direction of 'sweat-of-the-brow' copyright.

(iii) A special regime, more or less in the nature of a neighbouring right, can be annexed to copyright law, as with the Scandinavian protection of catalogues (as described in the Finnish Report) and the Dutch protection of non-personal writings; about these we shall hear something more from our moderator and our local reporter.

Since Professor Lucas reported in 1989, courts in different countries of the world have indeed exhibited a hostility towards 'sweat-of-the-brow' copyright which have underlined the percipience of his warning. The Dutch Supreme Court, in the case of *Van Dale v. Romme*, described in the Netherlands Report, has reasserted the basic importance of personal expression as the touchstone of literary copyright. The US Supreme Court, in *Feist v. Rural Telephone*, has drawn the law of that country away from other common law systems, so as to leave the range of protection for databases in a possibly parlous condition (see the US Report).

II. **Protection of databases under the EC Directive**

The Directive has elements within it which are related to all three types of protection which I have just mentioned. It requires recognition of copyright related to databases, but insists that this be limited to elements in the arrangement of the collected material which constitute the author's personal expression. It creates a separate right to object to extraction and re-utilization of the contents of the database, which exists to protect the organiser's investment in establishing the database. And because this right is confined to databases which satisfy certain minimum criteria, this separate *sui generis* right can be regarded as following in the Scandinavian (and indeed the Dutch) tradition of special legislative solutions.

(1) *Database*

As several national reports suggest, the concept of a database is not a finite thing. The root idea is a collection of information of some sort and we can all think of obvious cases: lists of writings, music and art, records of births, deaths and marriages, land registry entries and summaries of land transactions, telephone, street and business directories and catalogues, information about entertainments, and so on and on. The ability to store information digitally vastly increases both the type of information which can be held and the range of it. But if legal attributes are to be conferred on databases alone, then it becomes necessary to decide whether one is concerned only with electronic storage, and an attempt has to be made to define the minimum content which will suffice to bring the legal principles into play. Accordingly, the Directive defines 'database' as 'a collection of independent works, data and other materials arranged in a systematic or methodical way and individually accessible by electronic or other means' (article 1(2)).

(2) *Copyright under the Directive*

The Directive adopts the standard view in authors' right countries that copyright can arise in a database to the extent that the selection or arrangement of its contents express literary or artistic judgment. The nearest analogy is perhaps to a *catalogue raisonné* of the works of an artist or a critical edition of the works of a writer. The subject matter of the database copyright is the confined to the contribution made by the cataloguer. It does not extend to the data itself (just as it does not prejudice any copyright which may exist in individual works which are incorporated into the database) (article 3(2)). The crucial criterion is 'the author's own intellectual creation' (article 3(1)). Only a natural person or group of natural persons can be this author or authors (article 4(1)). While the Directive itself requires nothing in respect of moral rights, a Recital (28) conserves their existence and application under current national laws, whatever they may be.

Thanks to the Directive, the Dutch, the Irish and the British will be obliged to give up their 'sweat-of-the-brow' copyright so far as it extends to the information collected together in a single source, where that source constitutes a database. As a consequence, those countries will have to decide whether to adhere to their former rules concerning originality in relation to material which is not within the definition of database. They too will have to join in the unending hunt for identifiable meaning behind the maxim *There is no copyright in facts*. They may be reluctant, both within the Directive and beyond it, to take any markedly new attitude over what suffices for originality. After all, in many Continental systems, courts are prepared to give 'thin' copyright to 'small change'. In that way, they too avoid the embarrassment of categorically disqualifying material from protection on the basis of their personal instinct for what should be regarded as creative work.

Beyond this, the Directive contains a definition of the exclusive rights which are to arise in database copyright and also provisions on the limits to their scope (remedial rules remain a matter for national law; see article 12). The list of restricted acts is unsurprising, covering as it does reproduction, adaptation, distribution and public communication but not imposing particular answers to any of the precise issues now dominating discussion of digital servicing (article 5). Reproduction may be temporary as well as permanent, but we are not told how temporary. Distribution is subject to the standard formula excepting internal market exhaustion without specifying what rule shall apply to initial marketing outside the EEA. The nature of rights in transmissions on demand is not advanced; there is for instance no resolution of the question whether public communication must be for the public as a whole at a given time.

As to the exceptions, whatever is currently part of national law is to a large extent preserved (see article 6). However there are three positive requirements of the Directive to note:

(i) *Private use.* Any exception for private use must be confined to database copyright which is non-electronic. This modifies older understandings about private use which have applied to most *droit d'auteur* systems. (One consequence may be that it ceases to be permissible to introduce into this sphere a levy system for loss of royalties for home use.) However, more limited exceptions are still permitted. These include 'use for the sole purpose of illustration for teaching or scientific research, as long as the source is indicated and to the extent justified by the non-commercial purpose to be of achieved'.

(ii) *Public uses.* The other permitted exceptions cover (a) public security and administrative and judicial procedure, and (b) other 'traditionally authorized exceptions', such as that allowing the free use of public documents, including law reports and patent specifications. As we shall see, this second category is not included in respect of the *sui generis* right.

(iii) *Scope of licence.* The lawful user of a database must be treated as licensed to have access to the contents and to use them as is normal (article 6(1)). This requirement may not be abnegated by contract (article 15). Nevertheless, other provisions of the law still pertain, and these include 'laws on ... unfair competition trade secrets, security, confidentiality, data protection and privacy, access to public documents' as well as the law of contract (article 13). Accordingly, the same riddles surround the effectiveness or otherwise of restrictive terms in the database use contracts as occur with computer program licences under the EC Directive on that subject. Courts ought not to use obligations to respect trade secrets or confidence in order to sidestep mandatory limits which have been placed upon contractual powers. Whether they will not, remains to be seen.

(3) *The* sui generis *right: a neighbouring right for the database producer*

The *sui generis* right will protect those who invest in the production of databases, *i.e.* makers who take the intiative and risk of investing, rather than any subcontractor (see Recital 41). The protection, moreover, will be of the substantive content, rather than just of the underlying organisation of the material (article 7(1)).

The protected content of the database may consist of works of the copyright type, but equally it may be made up of factual information beyond the range of copyright; or it may even comprise other material: one thinks, perhaps, of a compilation of recordings of the noises that steam trains or racing cars make. Content is protected not, as it is with copyright, for the expression of intellectual activity; it is protected for the sweat of assembling it, however inspired, however mundane that process may actually be. Thus it fulfils Professor Lucas' desideratum.

Let us note six basic characteristics of the new right.

(i) To receive *sui generis* protection the database has to be the product of substantial investment, which may involve the obtaining, verification or presentation of the contents. 'Substantial investment' is to be measured qualitatively as well as quantitatively, which presumably imports some judgment upon the intrinsic value of the enterprise. Just what is a mystery. Recital 19 tells us, by way of example, that the collection together of - say - musical performances on an ordinary CD is not of itself sufficient. But beyond that, what? May a collection of recordings by Benjamin Britten qualify at a smaller and cheaper level than a collection of recordings by the Beatles?

Inescapably, the new right imports the kind of equitable assessment of unfairness which arises in unfair competition laws when they are extended to any form of misappropriation, such as, for example, slavish imitation. It is not the sole factor which invites a court to make a balanced assessment of the case for protection against the activity of the particular defendant. As with copyright in all systems, the test of infringement of the right will turn upon a qualitative and a quantitative evaluation of whether there has been extraction and or re-utilisation of substantial parts of the whole content. In other words, as with copyright, there will be scope for protection which stretches from thin to thick depending upon the intrinsic merit of the protected material. But the introduction of a preliminary threshold of sufficient investment before a database acquires any claim to protection surely identifies it as a trade value important enough to warrant protection against misappropriation: a form, in other words, of unfair competition protection. Its proximity to the position in Switzerland again deserves to be emphasised.

(ii) The owner of the *sui generis* right acquires two types of exclusive protection (article 7(1),(2)).

(a) In respect of extraction, which means permanent or temporary transfer of content to 'another medium' (I have difficulty with what may be implied by this undefined concept).

(b) More importantly, in respect of re-utilisation, which means 'any form of making available to the public all or a substantial part of the contents of a database' by distribution of copies, renting, on-line and other transmission. While copies are subject to the usual EC provisions of exhaustion of right by first authorised sale (the question of first importation into the EC being left for judicial interpretation), it is accepted that on-line provision is not subject to these rules (see Recital 33).

Given the impressive capacity of digital technology to alter, adapt and reclassify material, there is always a danger that the idea/expression dichotomy of copyright law may be taken as the appropriate touchstone and that it will have too limiting an effect. This could indeed be so even in respect of a 'sweat-of-the-brow' copyright, as well as or a compiler's copyright in personal arrangement. However, in the Canadian Report Mr Sookman suggests that this is not very likely under the current state of British Commonwealth law. The definitions of extraction and re-utilisation are intended (as Recital 38 makes clear) to avoid the idea/expression concept being imposed in this new territory. How far this will be successfully achieved in the laborious process of transposing Directive into national law in a form which courts actually understand, is guesswork. In any case, the broader intention again emphasises how the Directive launches national law into the seas of unfair competition liability. It certainly gives a pietistic ring to Recital 45, which intones that no copyright is being given to mere facts or data.

(iii) The right will normally endure for a period of fifteen years from the database becoming available to the public - anywhere in the world, or so it would appear (article 10). (It will last for fifteen years from making in the unusual case that it is not made publically available within that time.) However, further substantial investment in additions, deletions, alterations or even verification, will start time running afresh. There will be some databases so complete from the outset that there can be no call to change them - but these are surely exceptional. The major question is whether the degree of alteration needed to transform *sui generis* right into indeterminate protection is equivalent to that required initially to acquire the right. Presumably the answer is yes, but perhaps this is a point at which qualitative considerations can lead to a generous view of what is a sufficient refresher. In practical terms, the issue will likely be: has a sufficient cumulative change been undertaken within the last fifteen years? In other words, it will not be enough to show that, of a series of changes, the last took place within that period. It certainly behoves a database owner to keep scrupulous records of the treatment of content over time.

(iv) The EC Directive imposes a test of material reciprocity before non-EEA countries of origin can benefit from the *sui generis* right (article 11). This has a special

resonance, give the paucity of protection which currently pertains in US law. Nothing in TRIPs specifically inhibits this prerogative, since that Agreement requires only that copyright be accorded in original arrangements of databases (article 10(2)). But TRIPs requires observance of substantive provisions of the Paris Industrial Property Convention (article 2(1)), and article 10*bis* of that venerable treaty requires protection to be accorded against unfair competition on the basis of national treatment between Union states. Can we therefore be so sure that strict reciprocity for the *sui generis* database right is internationally in order?

(v) The *sui generis* right may be subjected by individual member states to limited exceptions but these are narrower in one crucial respect than those which may affect copyright in a database. While equivalent exceptions are allowed in the case of extractions for private purposes, illustration for teaching or scientific research; and in the case of both extraction and re-utilisation for public security, and administrative or judicial procedure, there is no permitted exception on grounds traditionally allowed for copyright. Thus national law may not apply any public domain exception to the *sui generis* right in databases comprising patent documentation. This represents a profound shift in public policy for many EC states, and provides a proprietary basis (as distinct from only purely contractual) on which public services can charge for the provision of most governmental information. The implications of this have barely been appreciated yet. They make highly significant the controls discussed in the next paragraph.

(vi) The *sui generis* right is not subject to explicit compulsory licensing arrangements in cases where the data comes from a sole source and others are therefore precluded from collecting it afresh and offering their version in competition. Such an express limitation was part of previous drafts, and database producers lobbied hard to secure its removal. In the course of the Directive's evolution, the European Court of Justice decided the *Magill* case (*Radio Telefis Eireann v. EC Commission* [1995] 4 CMLR 718) and this provided a general anti-trust basis for objecting to oppressive use of the *sui generis* right.

The case was brought in consequence of a British decision that 'sweat-of-the-brow' copyright exists in the programme listings of a television station (*BBC v. Time Out* [1984] FSR 64). The station and its associates accordingly had power to protect their own listings magazine against competition from listings in daily newspapers and elsewhere. Under the Rules of Competition of the Rome Treaty an abuse of dominant position is treated as a form of unlawful monopolisation (article 86). It was held that the refusal to grant more than a restricted licence for listings amounted to such an abuse, which could be rectified only by ordering the compulsory licensing of the material. This general limitation on the powers of intellectual property owners to extract full economic value from their apparently exclusive right is said by the Court to operate only in exceptional cases. But where a right is conferred directly to protect investment, as is the avowed purpose of the right in database contents, it should not be allowed to become a barrier against access to information. The social interest in being able to obtain information of many kinds at a reasonable, rather than a monopolist's, price may rather readily be regarded as paramount. 'Exceptional', after all, means meriting an exception; in this context it should imply nothing more.

III. Protection vis-à-vis databases

As already noted, the EC Directive is careful to acknowledge the continuance of copyright in works and neighbouring rights in material upon their transference into digital form, which is not to be affected by the *sui generis* right (see Recital 26 and article 8(3)). But the Directive goes no further in enhancing or guaranteeing either the moral or the material rights of these pre-existing authors. Not all National Reports responded to an invitation to reflect upon the relationship between author and database assembler. However, the French report by Mr Kerever pulled no punches on the matter. May I quote from it in slightly adapted form: 'Clearly publishers and producers of databases want the maximum freedom to collect and assemble data, as well as strategic control over exploitation of their databases. In France that effort has already been crowned with partial success in the *Microfor* decision (where the *Cour de Cassation* gave a liberal interpretation to the 'citations' exception to the reproduction right, by allowing the adoption of titles and headwords for individual data). Certainly these interests play upon the fascination inherent in new technologies in order to justify certain 'softenings' of the rigour of copyright, which are said to be necessitated by the spread of technical progress'.

Now the Directive's grant of an extraction right for the benefit of database producers should help to persuade them to accept their obligations in respect of the rights of authors. No doubt that is a sentiment that will be widely, if not indeed universally, shared in this Meeting. The complex New Deal which the Directive provides as an EC solution and proffers on terms to the rest of the world is, in practical terms, as generous to database constructors as the solution which the British Commonwealth countries reached with a minimum of fuss by adaptation of copyright. But nowhere in the world, least of all under that British solution, has it therefore been denied that those who contribute works to the pile should be obliged to do so on terms other than those which recognise their exclusive right. The ALAI will undoubtedly wish to urge that it should remain so.

Questionnaire

I. Protection of databases themselves

1. Does protection in any form turn on a distinction between electronic and non-electronic databases?

2. (a) Are databases treated as copyright?

(b) What type of work or other subject matter do they constitute?

(c) What test (of 'originality' or other characteristic) determines whether they qualify for copyright?

(d) Who is the initial owner of this copyright? What is its duration? Is the database a collective work?

(e) What scope of protection attaches to this copyright? How far can it be used to protect a datum or data incorporated in the base?

(f) What limitations may apply particularly to this copyright? Can these limitations be overridden by a contractual term?

(g) What additions to the database will constitute a second work?

3. (a) Are databases protected by trade secret, unfair competition and *sui generis* law?

(b) Is any such protection cumulative with copyright where the latter also applies?

(c) Who is entitled to the right or rights? How long do they endure? What further additions to the database would add to the period of protection?

(d) What is the scope of protection? How does it enable a datum or data to be protected?

(e) What limitations may apply to these rights? May the limitations be overridden by contract?

II. Protection for copyright works included in databases

1. In what circumstances does a copyright work require to be authorised in order for it to be stored in a database? How far is the cataloguing of titles and other identifying data, abstracts and other summaries allowed without needing permission?

2. What extractions of copyright data constitute infringements of economic rights?

3. In what circumstances could extractions and manipulations of copyright data constitute a breach of moral rights? In practice, what contractual or other arrangements exist to allow material to be used without acknowledgement of authorship, or after alteration of content?

III. **Impact on database operations**

1. Are there considerable numbers of database operators in your country? How actively are they pressing the case for greater legal protection through copyright or other intellectual property protection? Will they be satisfied by legal reforms which may currently be under consideration?

2. What other economic factors deserve to be given consideration in achieving adequate legal solutions to database problems?

Questionnaire

I. **Protection des banques de données elles-mêmes**

1. Existe-t-il une distinction entre banques informatisées et banques analogiques?

2. (a) Les banques sont-elles traitées comme des oeuvres protégées par le droit d'auteur?

(b) Quel type d'oeuvres ou d'autres objets de protection constituent-elles?

(c) A quel test d'originalité ou d'autres caractéristiques est subordonnée la protection des banques par le droit d'auteur?

(d) Quel est le titulaire initial du droit d'auteur? La banque est-elle une oeuvre collective? Quelle est la durée du droit d'auteur?

(e) Quelle est l'étendue de la protection attachée au droit d'auteur? Dans quelle mesure cette protection peut-elle être utilisée pour protéger une ou plusieurs données incorporées dans la banque?

(f) Quelles sont les limitations spécifiques au droit d'auteur applicables aux banques de données?

(g) Quels ajouts à une banque peuvent aboutir à une seconde oeuvre?

3. (a) Les banques de données sont-elles protégés par le secret d'affaires, la concurrence déloyale et le droit *"sui generis"*?

(b) Est-ce qu'une telle protection peut se cumuler avec celle du droit d'auteur là où cette dernière s'applique aussi?

(c) Qui est titulaire du ou des droits? Quelle est leur durée? Peut-on prolonger la période de protection de la banque de données?

(d) Quelle est l'étendue de la protection? Quel est son objet?

(e) Quelles limitations peut-on appliquer à ces droits? Les limitations peuvent-elles être contournées par des clauses contractuelles?

II. **Protection des oeuvres incluses dans les banques de données**

1. Le stockage d'une oeuvre protégée dans la banque doit-il être autorisé? Dans quelle mesure le cataloguage de titres, de données identifantes, d'abstracts et autres résumés peut-il être incorporé sans autorisation?

2. L'extraction de données protégeables constitue-t-elle une atteinte aux droits patrimoniaux?

3. Dans quelles circonstances les "extractions" et manipulations d'oeuvres constituent-elles une atteinte au droit moral? En pratique, quelles sont les mesures contractuelles ou autres qui permettent d'utiliser du matériel sans reconnaissance du droit d'auteur, ou après modification de son contenu?

III. Impact sur les opérations des banques de données

1. Y a-t-il de nombreux opérateurs de banques de données dans votre pays? Tentent-ils activement de faire adopter une plus grande protection légale par le droit d'auteur ou un autre droit de propriété intellectuelle? Seront-ils satisfaits par des réformes légales qui sont actuellement prises en considération?

2. Quels sont les autres acteurs économiques à prendre en considération pour élaborer un cadre juridique adéquat aux activités de banques de données?

Belgique

J.P. Triaille

I. **Protection des banques de données elles-mêmes**

1. *Existe-t-il une distinction entre banques informatisées et banques analogiques?*

Pour pouvoir bénéficier de la protection par le droit d'auteur, il est nécessaire que l'oeuvre soit non seulement originale mais également *"coulée dans une forme particulière qui la destine à être communiquée"* (Berenboom, A., *Le nouveau droit d'auteur et les droits voisins*, Larcier, 1995, p. 54, n° 33); la forme choisie (le support, la technique: *on-line/off-line*) importe peu (Berenboom, A., *ibidem*, p. 55). La protection est accordée, pourvu qu'elles soient originales, aussi bien aux banques de données "sur papier" qu'aux banques de données électroniques (par exemple sur CD-ROM) (comp. Brison, F., *Het auteursrechtelijk statuut van databanken in België, Computerrecht* 1990, n° 2, p. 71).

Au niveau des *règles*, il n'y a donc aucune distinction à faire entre ces types de banques de données du point de vue de leur protection par le droit d'auteur. Au niveau des *applications*, certains ont cependant observé que l'originalité d'une banque de données (en ce qu'elle résulterait de la disposition originale) se vérifierait plus aisément pour les banques de données électroniques que pour les supports papiers (Triaille, J.P., *La protection juridique des bases de données, Revue de droit de l'U.L.B.*, 1994 - 1, Bruxelles, Bruylant, p. 23). Au niveau des *sanctions*, un accès illicite à une banque électronique serait susceptible de constituer un délit particulier: ainsi, dans un arrêt du 24 juin 1991, la Cour d'Appel de Bruxelles a condamné pénalement des prévenus pour *"détournement de communications confiées au réseau public des télécommunications"* (Bruxelles, 24 juin 1991, *Rev. dr. pén. crim.* 1992, pp. 340 *et seq.*)

2. *(a) Les banques sont-elles traitées comme des oeuvres protégées par le droit d'auteur?*

Oui, à condition qu'elles soient originales (voir ci-après).

(b) Quel type d'oeuvres ou d'autres objets de protection constituent-elles?

Une oeuvre littéraire ou artistique au sens de l'article 1er, § 1er de la Loi du 30 juin 1994 relative au droit d'auteur et aux droits voisins (ci-après: la loi). Le droit belge ne connaît pas de catégories spécifiques d'"oeuvres de compilation" ou d'"oeuvres d'informations" (Triaille, J.P., *La protection juridique des bases de données*, p. 16). Lorsque les données rassemblées dans la banque se constituent d'oeuvres littéraires ou artistiques protégées, d'une manière, qui par le choix ou la disposition des matières, constitue une création intellectuelle individuelle (voir *infra*), la banque de données sera considérée comme un "recueil" au sens de l'article 2, § 3 de la Convention de Berne (Acte de Bruxelles, auquel la Belgique a adhéré).

> *(c) A quel test d'originalité ou d'autres caractéristiques est subordonnée la protection des banques par le droit d'auteur?*

Comme toute oeuvre, les banques de données doivent, pour être protégées par le droit d'auteur, être originales. La Cour de Cassation a prononcé plusieurs arrêts récents sur la notion d'originalité. Par un arrêt du 27 avril 1989, la Cour a affirmé que pour bénéficier de la protection légale il est nécessaire mais suffisant que l'oeuvre (une photographie) soit l'expression de l'effort intellectuel de celui qui l'a réalisé, ce qui constitue une condition indispensable pour donner à l'oeuvre le caractère individuel à travers lequel une création existe (Cass., 27 avril 1989, *Pas.* 1989, I, 908). Les commentateurs en ont déduit qu'il fallait un effort intellectuel (Strowel, A., *L'originalité en droit d'auteur: un critère à géométrie variable, J.T.*, 515) quelle que soit l'importance de cet effort (Gotzen, F., *Het Hof van Cassatie en het begrip oorspronkelijkheid in het Belgische auteursrecht. Van foto's en catalogi naar computerprogramma's en databanken?*, *Computerrecht* 1990, n° 4, 161).

Mais un effort même important ne suffit pas: encore faut-il l'expression d'une personnalité. C'est en ce sens qu'il faut lire l'arrêt du 25 octobre 1989 de la Cour de Cassation qui retient comme critère le fait que l'oeuvre doit être marquée par la personnalité de son auteur en manière telle qu'elle revêt un caractère original (Cass., 25 octobre 1989, *Pas.* 1990, I, 238). La doctrine en a conclu qu'il fallait deux éléments pour parler d'originalité: d'une part une activité intellectuelle (même faible) et d'autre part une forme propre marquée du sceau d'une personnalité. Dans le deuxième arrêt cité, la Cour de Cassation a confirmé une décision qui considérait comme sans pertinence les multiples efforts accomplis par le prétendu créateur dès l'instant où ces efforts n'aboutissaient pas à une forme personnelle. Il va de soi que l'originalité doit porter sur la forme et non sur le contenu (Strowel, A., 515). Le critère de la possibilité d'un choix entre plusieurs formes est un critère nécessaire mais non suffisant (Gotzen, F., *ibidem, eo. loc.*); encore faut-il que le choix adopté ne soit pas évident (pas banal), c'est-à-dire révèle la personnalité (*ibidem*, p. 162).

Transposés au domaine des banques de données, ces notions se traduisent comme suit. Il faut, pour qu'une banque de données soit l'expression d'une personnalité, que la sélection des données ou l'arrangement de ces données soit l'effet d'un choix personnel. La doctrine a fait observer à cet égard que si l'ensemble des données était exhaustif (en manière telle qu'il n'y avait pas de choix personnel) et si l'arrangement ne correspondait qu'à une logique fonctionnelle (et n'était donc pas caractérisé par un choix arbitraire) il ne pouvait y avoir d'originalité (Triaille, J.P., *La protection juridique des bases de données*, p. 23). Cette dernière situation ne sera pas exceptionnelle; la doctrine semble se montrer pessimiste à cet égard.

(d) Quel est le titulaire initial du droit d'auteur? La banque est-elle une oeuvre collective? Quelle est la durée du droit d'auteur?

Le titulaire originaire du droit d'auteur est la personne physique qui a créé l'oeuvre (article 6, alinéa 1er de la loi). Les personnes morales ne sont que titulaires du droit d'auteur de manière dérivée: après une cession en leur faveur par le titulaire originaire, personne physique. La loi prévoit cependant des présomptions de titularité. Ainsi est présumé auteur, sauf preuve contraire, quiconque apparaît comme tel sur l'oeuvre du fait de la mention de son nom ou d'un sigle permettant de l'identifier (article 6, alinéa 2 de la loi). La doctrine admet que les personnes morales peuvent également bénéficier de cette présomption (Strowel, A. et B., *La nouvelle législation belge sur le droit d'auteur, J.T.* 1995, 121). De même, l'éditeur d'un ouvrage anonyme ou pseudonyme est réputé, à l'égard des tiers, en être l'auteur (article 6, alinéa 3 de la loi).

Le droit d'auteur se prolonge pendant 70 ans après le décès de l'auteur (personne physique, cfr. *supra*), au profit de la personne qu'il a désignée à cet effet ou à défaut de ses héritiers (article 2, § 1 de la loi). Pour les oeuvres anonymes ou pseudonymes, la durée du droit d'auteur est de 70 ans à compter du moment où l'oeuvre est licitement rendue accessible au public; acte de distribution d'un support, communication au public, etc.

Lorsque la banque de données est le produit d'une collaboration, le droit d'auteur existe au profit de tous les ayants-droit jusque 70 ans après la mort du dernier co-auteur survivant (article 2, § 2, alinéa 1er de la loi). Les règles susénoncées transposent la Directive communautaire du 29 octobre 1993. La loi ne fait aucune distinction, en ce qui concerne la durée légale de protection, entre les droits patrimoniaux et le droit moral de l'auteur (l'importance du droit moral dans le domaine des banques de données doit toutefois être relativisée).

Il arrivera très fréquemment que la banque de données à considérer comme une oeuvre soit le produit d'une collaboration. La loi belge ne connaît pas la notion d'oeuvre collective, au contraire du droit français (au sens où celui qui prend l'initiative de la création, la dirige, la contrôle et l'organise, serait titulaire de tous les droits *ab initio*). En droit belge, l'auteur originaire reste les personnes physiques qui ont créé l'oeuvre en collaboration. Le fait que ces personnes ont créé la banque de données en exécution d'un contrat de travail ou en exécution d'un contrat de commande n'y change rien (la seule incidence de ce dernier fait se situe sur le plan de la souplesse des conditions de cession en faveur de l'employeur ou en faveur de celui qui a placé la commande).

(e) Quelle est l'étendue de la protection attachée au droit d'auteur? Dans quelle mesure cette protection peut-elle être utilisée pour protéger une ou plusieurs données incorporées dans la banque?

(f) Quelles sont les limitations spécifiques au droit d'auteur applicables aux banques de données?

Les limitations de protection particulières aux banques de données résultent tout d'abord de l'objet même (limité) de la protection: le droit d'auteur éventuellement attaché à la banque de données protège sa forme mais non son contenu (Triaille, J.P., *La protection des banques de données*, p. 24). La limitation de l'objet entraîne évidemment la limitation du champ de protection: sous réserve de ce qui sera dit après (concurrence parasitaire, clauses contractuelles, droit exclusif *de lege feranda*), l'exploitation des informations elles-mêmes n'enfreindra pas le droit d'auteur si cette exploitation recourt à une autre forme que la forme protégée (qui se caractérise par une sélection ou un arrangement personnels).

Pour le surplus, les droits attachés à une banque de données sont soumis aux exceptions générales en matière d'oeuvres littéraires (dont les plus significatives pour les banques de données sont: la communication dans le cercle de famille, la copie privée ou pour usage didactique).

Les clauses contra elles peuvent être utiles pour compenser les faiblesses de la protection par le droit d'auteur ou la renforcer et neutraliser certaines exceptions légales (copie privée). Ainsi, des clauses peuvent (1) limiter le nombre de reproductions autorisées, et (2) confirmer que les utilisations sont strictement réservées aux besoins propres de l'entreprise; interdire de "vider" la banque, la reconstituer pour la commercialiser; communiquer des données à des tiers; interdire le télédéchargement (transfert sur d'autres supports informatiques permettant des manipulations et la constitution d'une banque concurrente) (sur ces questions: Dalcq, Ch., *La protection des banques de données et le droit des contrats*, Rev. droit de l'ULB, 1994, 83).

La faiblesse des clauses contractuelles réside dans leur effet relatif: elles ne seraient, par exemple, pas opposables à un tiers acquéreur d'un CD-ROM (Triaille, J.P., *La protection juridique des bases de données*, p. 38). Cette faiblesse est partiellement compensée par la théorie de la tierce-complicité (qui suppose que le tiers connaissait la clausse contractuelle) et par le mécanisme de porte-fort ou stipulation pour autrui (le co-contractant du producteur de la banque s'engage à imposer à son tour les clauses restrictives aux tiers acquéreurs).

(g) Quels ajouts à une banque peuvent aboutir à une seconde oeuvre?

La question peut être examinée d'un double point de vue: les adjonctions donnent-elles lieu à une nouvelle oeuvre (qui s'ajoute à la première) digne de protection? Les adjonctions donnent-elles lieu à une oeuvre différente de la première (qui ne doit rien à celle-ci) en manière telle qu'elles ne portent pas atteinte aux droits d'auteur attachés à la première ?

Pour que les adjonctions donnent lieu à une oeuvre nouvelle (dérivée) protégeable par le droit d'auteur, il faut que ces adjonctions confèrent une originalité nouvelle et différente de la première originalité à l'ensemble: il s'agira d'une oeuvre dérivée faisant l'objet d'un droit d'auteur propre. Des lors que les adjonctions consistent en une adaptation de la banque de données premières (ce qui veut dire qu'il y a un emprunt de l'originalité de l'oeuvre première), l'autorisation du titulaire du droit sur la banque de données première devra évidemment être accordée (il s'agit du droit d'adaptation: article 1er, § 1er, alinéa 2 de la loi).

Ces "adjonctions" pourraient consister dans des sélections (arbitraires) de données complémentaires ou de créations de nouvelles subdivisions dans l'arrangement des données. En revanche, si les adjonctions sont telles qu'elles correspondent en réalité à une nouvelle originalité qui ne doit rien à l'originalité de l'oeuvre première (modifications globales de la sélection des données et de leur arrangement), il ne s'agira plus d'une adaptation mais de la création d'une oeuvre nouvelle. En effet, dès l'instant où seule la forme est protégée, la reprise des données sous une autre forme n'est pas une atteinte au droit d'auteur.

> **3.** *(a) Les banques de données sont-elles protégés par le secret d'affaires, la concurrence déloyale et le droit* "sui generis"?

En droit belge, il n'existe pas d'interdiction générale légale de divulguer des secrets d'affaires (Triaille, J.P., *La protection des idées*, *JT* 1994, 804). La protection de ces secrets relève éventuellement du droit commun de la responsabilité ou de la concurrence déloyale (voir ci-après). Il existe bien une disposition spécifique dans la loi sur le contrat de travail, à charge du travailleur: il est interdit au travailleur tant en cours de contrat qu'après la cessation de celui-ci de divulguer les secrets de fabrication ou d'affaires dont il aurait eu connaissance dans l'exercice de son activité professionnelle. Cela suppose en l'espèce que la banque de données soit confidentielle au départ. De même, le travailleur ne pourra être inquiété après la cessation de son contrat de travail s'il reconstruit une banque de données à partir des informations qui appartiennent à ses connaissances et son expérience. En revanche, il serait évidemment interdit à l'ancien travailleur d'emporter avec lui un support comprenant la banque de données pour l'exploiter ou la communiquer: il y aurait à la fois un vol, une atteinte à un droit d'auteur ou, à défaut, de concurrence déloyale.

A défaut d'une protection par le droit d'auteur, la banque de données pourrait bénéficier d'une certaine protection en vertu de la théorie de la concurrence parasitaire. De même, cette théorie pourrait permettre le pillage du contenu de cette banque (sans qu'une forme protégeable ne soit reproduite). Cette doctrine n'est pas unanimement admise. En outre, ses conditions pour une sanction sont très incertaines. Il semble, en résumé, qu'une protection soit possible sous les conditions suivantes: la banque de données copiée doit avoir représenté des investissements importants en travail et/ou en argent; elle doit représenter une valeur commerciale; la copie de son contenu ne peut être coupable que s'il s'agit d'un pillage systématique; le pillage, pour être coupable, doit procurer au copieur un avantage disproportionné par rapport au préjudice souffert par le titulaire de la banque pillée; le copieur doit être dans l'incapacité de justifier objectivement la copie.

Contrairement à ce que pouvait laisser espérer la doctrine (Triaille, J.P., *La protection juridique des bases de données*, p. 33) la jurisprudence belge la plus récente ne semble plus particulièrement réceptive à la doctrine du parasitisme (en matière de banque de données: voir Prés. trib. comm. Bruxelles, 19 juillet 1995, à paraître dans *Auteurs & Médias*). Il n'existe pas encore dans la loi belge de protection *sui generis*. Son introduction en application de la directive communautaire se révèle dès lors souhaitable sinon indispensable pour interdire l'extraction de la totalité ou d'une partie substantielle du contenu de la banque de données, vu l'insuffisance et l'incertitude du droit commun (concurrence déloyale).

(b) Est-ce qu'une telle protection peut se cumuler avec celle du droit d'auteur là où cette dernière s'applique aussi?

Le droit commun de la concurrence déloyale ne vient que compenser les faiblesses de la protection par le droit d'auteur. Dans le cas ou celui-ci s'applique, il s'applique à titre exclusif. La loi en matière de concurrence déloyale prévoit d'ailleurs expressément que la procédure spécifique dans ce domaine ne s'applique pas aux actes de contrefaçon sanctionnés par la Loi sur le droit d'auteur (article 96 de la Loi 14 juillet 1991 sur les pratiques du commerce et sur l'information et la protection du consommateur).

(c) Qui est titulaire du ou des droits? Quelle est leur durée? Peut-on prolonger la période de protection de la banque de données?

Les questions relatives à la titularité des droits jurisprudentiels (concurrence déloyale) et de leur durée restent des questions ouvertes (Triaille, J.P., *La protection juridique des bases de données*, p. 36). Pour ce motif d'ailleurs, une certaine doctrine s'oppose à l'application des principes de la concurrence déloyale pour compenser le défaut de protection par le droit d'auteur. S'agissant du titulaire d'une protection par le droit commun, il nous semble que cette notion devrait recouvrir tout utilisateur légitime de la banque. S'agissant de la durée, en ce qui concerne l'obligation pour le travailleur, après la cessation de son contrat d'emploi, divulguer des secrets d'affaires, cette obligation n'est pas soumise à une restriction dans le temps (Triaille, J.P., *La protection des idées*, *JT* 1990, p. 802).

Par ailleurs, on serait en droit d'exiger que dans l'hypothèse où un tribunal accepte de protéger dans le cadre de la concurrence déloyale une banque de données non protégée par le droit d'auteur, il devrait préciser à tout le moins que cette protection ne peut excéder un certain délai; en particulier, il ne serait plus contraire aux usages honnêtes en matière commerciale d'exploiter sans autorisation une banque de données après l'écoulement d'un délai égal au délai prévu par la loi dans le cas d'un droit exclusif; dans l'attente d'un droit exclusif *sui generis*, ce délai devrait, nous semble-t-il, être raisonnablement fixé à quinze ans.

(d) Quelle est l'étendue de la protection? Quel est son objet?

La question du champ de protection dans le cadre du droit commun en application de la concurrence déloyale est également une question ouverte. Dans l'hypothèse où les tribunaux admettent de faire application de la doctrine de la concurrence parasitaire, ils ne la sanctionneront que dans le cas de copies serviles et de pillages systématiques. L'objet de la protection dans ce cadre (contrairement au cadre du droit d'auteur) ne réside pas seulement dans la forme mais également dans le contenu (pillage systématique). Il s'agirait d'une anticipation jurisprudentielle sur un droit *sui generis* à venir.

> *(e) Quelles limitations peut-on appliquer à ces droits? Les limitations peuvent-elles être contournées par des clauses contractuelles?*

Les droits étant eux-mêmes incertains, on peut difficilement parler de "limitations" à ces droits; il est encore plus difficile de préciser le rôle de clauses contractuelles qui organiseraient ces droits imprécis (Triaille, J.P., *La protection juridique des bases de données*, p. 36). Soulignons encore que les contrats par lesquels des tiers s'interdiraient d'exploiter des banques de données non-protégées par le droit d'auteur sont soumis aux règles de concurrence quant à leur validité. L'effet de ces contrats est de toute façon relatif.

II. Protection des oeuvres incluses dans les banques de données

> *1. Le stockage d'une oeuvre protégée dans la banque doit-il être autorisé? Dans quelle mesure le cataloguage de titres, de données identifantes, d'abstracts et autres résumés peut-il être incorporé sans autorisation? / 2. L'extraction de données protégeables constitue-t-elle une atteinte aux droits patrimoniaux?*

L'article 1er, § 1er de la loi donne à l'auteur de l'oeuvre le droit exclusif de la reproduire ou d'en autoriser la reproduction de quelque manière et sous quelque forme que ce soit. La doctrine considère de manière unanime que le stockage de l'oeuvre dans une banque de données constitue une reproduction de cette oeuvre soumise au consentement du titulaire du droit d'auteur (Brison, F., *o.c.*, p. 72). Il en va ainsi encore pour tous les autres actes qui impliquent une reproduction, comme l'extraction. Cela suppose évidemment que l'oeuvre soit (encore) protégée et que sa reproduction ne soit pas légalement autorisée, ce qui ne sera pas le cas en particulier pour les actes offficiels (loi, règlement), l'usage privé (la copie privée) (mais non pas la copie par les fabricants de banques de données: Brison, F., *o.c.*, p. 174, n° 2a), certains discours publics.

La règle du consentement préalable du titulaire vaut évidemment pour tout acte de reproduction de l'oeuvre totale ou partielle. La loi prévoit toutefois que la reproduction d'un extrait de l'oeuvre en vue de la confection d'une anthologie *destinée à l'enseignement* n'est pas soumise au consentement des ayants-droit de l'auteur après le décès de celui-ci moyennant paiement d'une rémunération équitable (article 21, alinéa 3 de la loi); il s'agit d'une licence obligatoire; il semble bien que cette licence vaut pour tout type d'oeuvres. En revanche, avant le décès de l'auteur, son autorisation reste nécessaire pour la reproduction même de simples extraits de son oeuvre en vue de la confection de l'anthologie que constitue la banque de données, même lorsque celle-ci est destinée à l'enseignement.

Qu'en est-il des citations (qui sont plus brèves que des extraits), des titres, des résumés et sommaires? La loi prévoit (article 21, alinéa 1er) que l'autorisation préalable de l'auteur n'est pas requise lorsqu'il s'agit de courtes citations tirées d'une oeuvre licitement publiée effectuées dans un but de critique, de polémique ou d'enseignement ou dans des travaux scientifiques conformément aux usages honnêtes de la profession et dans la mesure justifiée par le but poursuivi.

En dehors des buts strictement déterminés par la loi, l'exception ne s'appliquera pas (ce qui sera très souvent le cas); cette exception ne permet que de courtes citations (ce qui représente moins qu'un extrait); elle oblige l'exploitant à indiquer la source et le nom de l'auteur. Cette dernière précision confirme si besoin en était que l'indication des références bibliographiques, c'est-à-dire la reproduction notamment du titre de l'oeuvre (qui lui-même est parfaitement susceptible d'être protégé par le droit d'auteur: Berenboom, A., o.c., n° 48, p. 73) sans l'autorisation de l'auteur non seulement est licite mais s'impose même dans les cas d'exceptions susvisés.

En ce qui concerne les résumés, des l'instant où ceux-ci ne font que reprendre des idées, c'est-à-dire le contenu, mais non la forme de l'oeuvre résumée, leur exploitation ne requiert pas l'autorisation préalable du titulaire du droit; il en va a fortiori ainsi des sommaires (Brison, F., o.c., p. 73). Il va de soi que si le résumé est lui-même la reproduction d'un résumé original effectué par un tiers, l'autorisation de ce dernier est requise. Par ailleurs, si le résumé ne se contente pas de reproduire des idées, mais reproduit également la forme (expressions et/ou compositions), autrement qu'à titre de citations autorisées, le consentement préalable de l'auteur sera également requis (la doctrine a souligné à juste titre l'aspect délicat de la distinction entre le résumé libre et le résumé - adaptation de l'oeuvre préexistante: Brison, F., o.c., p. 73; Triaille, J.P., *La protection juridique des bases de données*, p. 14). La rédaction et l'exploitation de "abstracts" et de mots clefs ne nécessitent pas l'autorisation préalable du titulaire du droit d'auteur dès l'instant où il n'y a pas d'emprunt à la forme. A cet égard, la doctrine admet la liberté d'"indexation", qui entrame, nous semble-t-il, la reproduction des titres (Berenboom, o.c., n° 176).

> **3.** *Dans quelles circonstances les "extractions" et manipulations d'oeuvres constituent-elles une atteinte au droit moral? En pratique, quelles sont les mesures contractuelles ou autres qui permettent d'utiliser du matériel sans reconnaissance du droit d'auteur, ou après modification de son contenu?*

Les reproductions, extractions et manipulations d'oeuvres préexistantes, en tout ou en partie, sont évidemment susceptibles de constituer des modifications de ces oeuvres. L'article 1er, § 2, alinéa 6 de la loi prévoit que l'auteur peut s'opposer à *toute* modification de son oeuvre. L'auteur peut contractuellement accepter le principe de la modification de son oeuvre; la loi ne déclare en effet nulle que la renonciation globale à l'exercice futur du droit moral. La question de savoir si l'auteur peut accepter par avance le principe de *toute* modification (sans en connaître les détails) est controversée. De plus la loi prévoit qu'après renonciation, l'auteur conserve encore le droit de s'opposer à toute déformation, mutilation ou autre modification de son oeuvre ou à toute autre atteinte à la même oeuvre préjudiciables à son honneur ou à sa réputation.

III. **Impact sur les opérations des banques de données**

1. Y a-t-il de nombreux opérateurs de banques de données dans votre pays? Tentent-ils activement de faire adopter une plus grande protection légale par le droit d'auteur ou un autre droit de propriété intellectuelle? Seront-ils satisfaits par des réformes légales qui sont actuellement prises en considération?

2. Quels sont les autres acteurs économiques à prendre en considération pour élaborer un cadre juridique adéquat aux activités de banques de données?

Canada

B.B. Sookman

1. Introduction

The storage of works, whether literary, artistic, musical or otherwise and other materials such as text, sounds, images, numbers, facts and data in a computer memory is now common place. Technologies for scanning and digitizing works and other forms of electrocopying have made it possible to transfer works in all forms of traditional media to computer memories almost as easily as photocopying works in printed form. These sophisticated and powerful new technologies together with innovative new distribution media including fibre optics, direct broadcast satellites, CD-ROMs and the Internet are dramatically changing the way Canadians and others can access, utilize and interact with works stored on computer systems. Information in machine readable forms can be downloaded from a database to a local computer with ease, readily copied, manipulated and redistributed to others over electronic networks, or uploaded onto bulletin boards, or web sites to be further copied, accessed, used, manipulated, and redistributed by others.

There can be little doubt that inter-connected worldwide high-speed digital communications networks will have an enormous impact on the way in which machine readable works will be created, stored, communicated to the public, otherwise distributed and paid for. This 'Global Information Infrastructure' or 'GII'[1] - this seamless web of communications networks, computers, databases and consumer electronics - will put vast amounts of information at users' fingertips. The development of the GII with the attendant on-line access to vast amounts of information will raise significant issues for copyright laws both in Canada and elsewhere. Although governments in Canada[2] and elsewhere[3] have begun the daunting task of reviewing the adequacy of their copyright legislation to meet the challenges of the 'information super highway', the worldwide process is only beginning and changes to meet the challenges have barely begun.

What is a database?

There is no uniform definition of the term 'database' in the computer or legal literature. A simple definition of a database *'is any collection of information held in a computer memory'*.[4] Various other definitions of the term are possible. For example, under the European Common Position on a Council Directive on the Legal Protection of Databases the term 'database' is defined to mean *'a collection of works, data, or other independent materials arranged in a systematic or methodical way and capable of being individually accessed by electronic or other means'*. The preamble to

456

the Directive explains that the term should be understood to include collections of works, whether literally, artistic, musical or other, and other material such as text, sounds, images, numbers, facts and data which are systematically or methodically arranged and whose arrangement, storage and access is performed by means which include but are not limited to electronic, electromagnetic or electro-optical processes or analogist processes. The term is understood there to mean as well materials necessary for the operation or consultation of databases such as the thesaurus and indexation systems.

The notion of a 'database' is sometimes used in a narrower sense, to only mean 'electronic database' - an aggregate of information which is systematically arranged and stored in a computer system. It has now come to be recognized that the term 'database' should not be limited to computer storage of information, but that all compilations of information should be considered 'databases' irrespective of whether they exist in print, in computer storage units or in other forms.[5] For example, under the TRIPs Agreement article 10(2) provides that: *'compilations of data or other material, whether in machine readable or other form, which by reason of the selection of arrangement of their contents constitute intellectual creations shall be protected as such. Such protection, which shall not extend to the data or material itself, shall be without prejudice to any copyright subsisting the data or material itself.'*

For the purpose of this Report, the term database will be considered in its broadest sense to include both compilations of existing works, and collections of information, data and facts irrespective of whether the embodiment thereof exists in print, writing, in a computer memory, or in any other form from which the said materials can be perceived by the human eye, or with the aid of a machine or device.

Statutory definition of compilation

Prior to January 1994 the *Copyright Act*[6] contained no definition of the term 'compilation'. To implement Canada's obligations under the North American Free Trade Agreement (NAFTA) the Act was amended to expressly include a definition of the term compilation.[7] Under the Act a 'compilation' is defined to mean (a) a work resulting from the selection or arrangement of literary, dramatic, musical or artistic works or parts thereof, or (b) a work resulting from the selection or arrangement of data.

As the above definition indicates, the term 'compilation' is intended to embrace both the selection and arrangement of existing categories of works and works resulting from the selection or arrangement of data. Compilations of literary works are protected as such. Compilations consisting solely of artistic, dramatic or musical works are protected in the same way. The mere fact that a work is included in a compilation does not increase, decrease or otherwise affect the protection conferred by the Act in respect of the copyright in the work or the moral rights in respect of the work.[8]

A compilation containing two or more of the categories of literary, dramatic, musical or artistic works is deemed to be a compilation of the category making up the most substantial part of the compilation.[9] The Act does not expressly state which category of work a work resulting from the selection or arrangement of data falls into. Presumably, the legislative intent is to protect a selection and arrangement of data as a literary work where such data can be assimilated to the category of literary works. Similarly, where the data is expressed in a visual medium it will most likely be produced as an artistic work,[10] and so on with respect to selections and arrangements of data which can be assimilated to musical or dramatic works.

Electronic and non-electronic databases

The Act does not expressly distinguish between compilations in electronic form and those in non-electronic form. There is little doubt that a work, whether literary, dramatic, musical or artistic in traditional form which is copied without the authorization of the owner of the copyright into a tangible computer memory will infringe the reproduction right which grants to the owner of a copyright in Canada *'the sole right to produce or reproduce the work or any substantial part thereof in any material form'*.[11] Therefore, the act of keying, scanning or digitizing an original compilation, or a substantial part thereof, existing in non-electronic form into a computer database, or the printing out of all or any substantial part of a protected compilation into a printed document or other material form, can also infringe the reproduction right.[12]

There currently is some doubt in Canada as to the protection of a compilation which results solely from the selection or arrangement of data created and stored only in a computer memory. For example, it has yet to be decided in Canada whether works stored only in the Random Access Memory (RAM) of a computer are sufficiently permanent in order to satisfy the fixation requirement for copyright protection.[13] As well, for literary works other than computer programs,[14] there is still some doubt as to whether the work must originally exist in print or in writing to be protected or whether it is sufficient that there exists only a means by which the work in machine readable form can be reproduced in visible form or in some other way made to be perceptible.[15]

Some recent decisions of the Canadian Radio-television and Telecommunications Commission (CRTC) have held that information in a database of directory information in machine readable form is capable of being protected under the Act.[16] Further, on this issue, in *Dun & Bradstreet Ltd. v. Typesetting Facilities Ltd.,*[17] Mr Justice Harman of the English High Court, in a case involving the subsistence of copyright in a computer database, made the observation that it was established by practise and by decisions of the Court that copyright is capable of subsisting in works in machine readable form, even if these works are not capable of examination by the ordinary eye. *'This is a case in which the plaintiff, a very well known name, Dun & Bradstreet Limited, allege that they have a copyright compilation kept, I would say unhappily, but they would say necessarily, upon computer. I say unhappily because of course the court is then faced with a copyright in something which no ordinary judge is, and certainly I am not able to look at, read, examine and compare with any alleged copy of it. That makes copyright cases in computer matters peculiarly difficult. However, there is no doubt that it has been established by practice and by decisions* sub silentio *that the courts do treat computer material as having the necessary qualities to come within the Copyright Act and indeed the 1988 Act makes specific provisions for that matter. I must therefore proceed on the basis that I can envisage the original, I suppose literary work, which is contained not in writing on paper capable of examination by the ordinary eye but in electronic blips hidden within the tapes, disks or other data storage systems in the plaintiff's computers.'*

Originality requirement

Under the Act, only 'original' compilations are entitled to be protected.[18] The question of what is 'original' is a question of fact and degree depending on the amount of 'skill, judgment or labour' that has been involved in making the compilation.[19] In most cases compilations of existing works where the selection or arrangement is more than negligible will result in a protected database. Since only a low level of originality is required, copyright may subsist to the extent of the original creative efforts of the author,[20] or in the literary substance or sense which the selection or arrangement is designed to convey.[21] If only commonplace matters are put together or arranged without the exercise of more than negligible work, labour or skill, then no protectable interest can arise.[22] Further, merely copying an existing compilation in printed or other non-electronic form into electronic form itself will not confer originality on the database, as generally copying of a work, however much labour and skill may be devoted to the process, cannot make an original work.[23]

The term 'compilation' in the Act expressly states that it must result from 'the selection or arrangement' of one or more categories of works or of data. A compilation of data will be regarded as original, therefore, if the author thereof has exercised the requisite degree of originality in the selection or arrangement of the information. For example, in the *Dun & Bradstreet* case,[24] Justice Harman accepted that a computer database consisting entirely of information in the public domain could be protected if it is 'sorted, arranged, and disciplined so as to be available in a defined form'. There he stated the following: '*The material thus stored is alleged by the plaintiffs to be a copyright body of material because, it is said, it is a compiled (to use another word), edited, co-ordinated and cross-referenced version of a mass of material otherwise in large part at least available in the public domain and are the direct authorship, I suppose is the word, although it sits slightly unhappily with computers, of servants (I use the word simply as a technical description of their position and occupation, in a non-derogatory sense), of the plaintiff. There is no doubt that a compilation put together in a particular order - again it is hardly appropriate to say by the sweat of anyone's brow when they are typing matters into a computer or writing a computer program - by the labour and skill, above all skill, of those who operate these arcane machines from information contained in public sources is properly called, as Mr Carr said, a compilation of material. That is so notwithstanding that the great majority of the items of information are available from a public source, because the body of material so sorted, arranged, and disciplined so as to be available in a defined form is capable of being a copyright work.*' In a similar vein, the CRTC recently expressed the view that copyright could attach to an electronic compilation of basic non-confidential listing information as a result of the sorting, arrangement or classification of that information.[25]

There is still uncertainty whether factors other than selection or arrangement of data, or of literary, dramatic, musical or artistic works, can give rise to a protectable interest. Prior to the January 1994 amendments to the Act, the originality requirement was capable of being satisfied by a more than negligible expenditure of labour, time and expense in assembling facts, or in the skill, judgment, knowledge, ingenuity or mental effort involved in selecting or arranging them, or both.[26] Labour and expense alone have been held in England to be a sufficient basis for copyright to subsist in a compilation.[27]

The definition of the term 'compilation' in the Act did not expressly recognize that acts of labour alone could give rise to a protected interest. Accordingly, there is some doubt as to whether the January 1994 amendments to the Act changed the law to restrict the types of databases that are capable of subsisting under the Act. It is submitted that Parliament had no intention of restricting the types of databases that can be protected. The object of the amendments was to ensure that compilations would be protected in Canada so that Canada's obligations under the North American Free Trade Agreement would be complied with. That treaty did not require Canada to harmonize its laws with that of the United States. It required only that Canada establish minimum standards for protection of compilations and expressly authorized stronger protection of works beyond the standard established by the agreement, provided that such protection is not inconsistent with the agreement.[28]

In view of the relative consistency of the case-law under the Act before the amendments to protect compilations based on factors that included 'sweat-of-the-brow' criteria, the amendments would most likely not be interpreted in a manner as would lessen the scope of protection of compilations. In this regard, the amendments will most probably be interpreted as merely codifying the existing law with reference to the protection of compilations of information. As such, the statutory terms 'selection or arrangement' could be interpreted as terms of art, long understood in Anglo-Canadian copyright law, to embrace the traditional criteria sufficient to support the Act's originality requirement for compilations and other works. Such a conclusion would be consistent with the long tendency to apply the language of the Act in a practical manner, consistent with the needs of the time, the then current concepts, and mindful of advances in technology. Such a construction of the Act would also be consistent with one of the Act's predominant purposes, which is to prevent persons from unfairly availing themselves of the work of others.

Some difficult questions still remain to be resolved with respect to computer databases which are created by computer programs which select, manipulate and format data without the expenditure of identifiable human skill or effort in the completed work, other than in the creation of the computer program. A great deal of financial, statistical, meteorological, seismic and geological information is now collected, analyzed and put into a form valuable to its owners without the necessity for human involvement in the process. New and emerging technologies are being used and have been announced for use on the information highway to develop compilations of information through the use of intelligent 'robots' or 'agents'. These are sophisticated computer programs which can electronically sift through masses of information in a short period of time and produce very valuable collections of data.[29] Work is also under way on natural language processing systems to enable computer systems to scan documents in a database and produce written abstracts of the documents in response to users' queries. Research is also being conducted on machine-generated translations of documents from one language to another.[30] In these cases there is human involvement insofar as someone has invested the capital and human resources to create the computing machines that produce the desired results. The human effort, skill, and judgment involved in the particular work may, however, fall short of the labour, skill, time, ingenuity, selection, or mental effort that is required for attribution of authorship under the Act.[31]

Making the subsistence of copyright in a computerized database dependent on selection and arrangement could well leave many databases containing raw information unprotected. Concerns have been expressed that given the capacity of the user or computerized robots to select information from a computerized database is so powerful, that making protection of such databases depend on their originality by reason of the selection and arrangement of the data ignores the reality that the user, not the database creator, makes the desired selection of material to suit the user's needs. All the operator has to do is ensure that the database is comprehensive and up to date.[32]

Owner of copyright

Ordinarily, the author of a work is the first owner of the copyright therein.[33] Where the author of a work was in the employment of some other person or under a contract of service and the work is made in the course of his employment by that person, the person by whom the author was employed is ordinarily, in the absence of any agreement to the contrary, the first owner of the copyright.[34]

Difficult questions of ownership can arise with respect to databases created over computerized networks where there has been on-line collaboration by two or more individuals. Computer networks, such as bulletin boards, facilitate the creation of composite works by many individuals, some of whom may be identified and some who may be anonymous or impossible to identify. The databases may go through a series of modifications, the authors of which may be unknown, or may be foreign persons not entitled to copyright protection under the Act. As a result of this co-operative effort, it will often be unclear which author has a claim to ownership in the work and who is the author and owner of which part. Under the Act, an author has the moral rights to the integrity of the work and, where reasonable in the circumstances, to be associated with the work as its author by name or under a pseudonym, and the right to remain anonymous.[35] How is this right to be respected in the circumstances?

Under the Act, copyright can subsist in a 'work of joint authorship'. A 'work of joint authorship' is defined to mean *'a work produced by the collaboration of two or more authors in which the contribution of one author is not distinct from the contribution of the other author or authors'*.[36] Accordingly, for a work to be a 'work of joint authorship' under the Act, there must be both a work produced with the collaboration of two or more authors, and the work in which the contribution of one author is not distinct from the contribution of the other author.[37]

The Act does not specifically address the degree of collaboration that must exist between the authors of the work for the work to qualify as a 'work of joint authorship'. Case-law has established, however, the requirement that there must be some working together in the furtherance of a common or preconcerted joint design to produce the work.[38] The requirement for collaboration may be met in the creation of a written work where there is active collaboration in the writing or compiling of the work such as by substantial editing, alterations, additions, omissions and corrections of the work,[39] but minor alterations or additions with or without the concurrence of the other authors does not give rise to joint authorship.[40]

For a work to qualify as a 'work of joint authorship', the contribution of each author must not be distinct from the contribution of the other authors. The Act does not specifically define the degree to which the contributions of each author must be distinct in the completed work. Clearly if the contributions of the authors are merged into inseparable parts of a unitary whole, then the work will be capable of being a 'work of joint authorship'.[41] Also, the requirement of distinctiveness might be met if there is agreement upon a general design and structure for the work and parts are worked on separately by the authors provided that there is co-operation in the common design.[42]

For many databases of on-line information neither the owner of the computer facilities upon which the data is stored nor the various contributors to the database will be sufficient to constitute their contributors authors of a 'work of joint authorship'. If the owner of a computer facility does not contribute towards the writing of the work, such person cannot be regarded as an 'author' for copyright purposes. The contributions of the numerous contributors may be regarded as collaborative. However, the requirement that there be some working together in furtherance of a common or preconcerted joint design to produce the work will often be missing.

If an on-line database is produced by the collaboration of two or more authors and if the contribution of each is distinct from the other, then each contribution will be considered as a separate work in which copyright may subsist. Such a work could be a 'collective work' in which a separate copyright may exist if it is written in distinct parts by different authors.[43] A 'collective work' might exist if works or parts of works of different authors are incorporated together into the work.[44] Ordinarily, separate copyrights will exist in works written in distinct parts by the different authors as well as in the effort and judgment involved in selecting and arranging the parts previously created by the others.[45] In the case of distinct contributions made by many individuals to a computer database, it may be difficult to ascribe any copyright to the collective work as a whole where the owner of the computer system upon which the database resides does not take any active role in selecting, arranging or organizing the contributions of the others.

Scope of protection

Reproduction

As stated above, the reproduction of a protected database into another material form such as another computer memory or a computer printout will ordinarily infringe the reproduction right if all or a substantial part of the database is copied.[46] Since the Act expressly protects the original 'selection or arrangement' of materials forming the compilation, it would be infringement to reproduce all or any substantial part of the selection or arrangement of the materials in the database.[47]

Of critical importance to owners of databases, particularly electronic databases which are easily accessible over networks, is whether protection will also extend to the extraction of data from the database without any copying of the selection or arrangement of the information in the database.[48] Historically it had been considered infringement of copyright in Canada and in other countries of the Commonwealth to extract, rearrange and republish all or a substantial part of the information in a compilation.[49] Facts included in an original compilation were protected from appropriation by a subsequent compiler, even if the language employed was different, or the order of the material was altered, if an undue amount of the skill and judgment or labour of the original compiler was made use of.[50]

As a result of the January 1994 amendments to the Act, there is some uncertainty as to whether the extraction of raw data from a database without the reproduction of all or a substantial part of the selection or arrangement thereof will infringe copyright. If, as indicated above, the January 1994 amendments to the Act did no more than confirm that compilations are protected under the Act, then the extraction and rearrangement of a substantial part of a database composed of data will continue to be an infringing act. However, in the event the amendments substantially altered the law in Canada to protect only the selection and arrangement of data in a compilation, then such acts will not infringe copyright. If such should prove to be the case, there might well be the need in Canada to introduce a right to prevent the unauthorized extraction and reutilization of the contents of the database, similar to the European Common Position on a Council Directive on the Legal Protection of Databases.

An unresolved question in Canada is whether database users are able electronically to view and read the works and data contained in a database. This issue is of central importance to database owners, as the on-line access to materials contained in an electronic database may reduce the market for purchasing a copy of the material available on-line.[51] The display of information on a computer screen could result in a reproduction if the part of the work displayed on the screen is reproduced in a video memory or other memory of a computer, or if the data necessary to display the work is reproduced in such memory, or if the materialization of the work itself on a video display unit itself constitutes a reproduction of the protected work in a material form. In the English case *Bookmakers' Afternoon Greyhound Services Ltd. v. Wilf Gilbert (Staffordshire) Ltd.*[52] it was held that the display of images on a video display unit in private constituted a reproduction in a material form on the basis that the words 'material form' under the United Kingdom statute were wide enough to embrace 'materialization on a television monitor'. In the United States it is well established that copying of all or a substantial part of a work into Random Access Memory may infringe the reproduction right under its copyright legislation.[53]

It is arguable, however, that the act of browsing a work contained in a database is analogous to reading a book or hearing a musical work and that such acts should not be regarded as reproductions of the work.[54] Further, browsing of only a part of a large database may, even if technically a reproduction of the part looked at, be considered to be insubstantial and therefore not infringing. Where the person accessing the database has been given permission by the owner of its contents to use same, an implied licence to reproduce the database in the course of its use may be presumed from the circumstances in which access is granted.[55] Where a copy of a database is sold, such as where a database recorded on a CD-ROM is sold, the owner of the copyright may be unable to contend that the reproduction of the database in the normal course of its use infringes the reproduction right if to do so would derogate from the grant of rights made in the course of such a transaction.[56]

Lastly, the reproduction of the database may not infringe the reproduction right if it constitutes a fair dealing with the work for the purposes of private study or research.[57] However, for this exemption from infringement to apply, the conduct must be capable of being characterized as 'private study' or 'research' and there must be a fair dealing for either of those purposes.[58]

In the Final Report of the Information Highway Advisory Council, the Council expressed the view that it should be left to the copyright owner to determine whether and when browsing should be permitted on the information highway. There it was recommended that the Act be amended to provide a definition of browsing along the following lines: *"Browsing' means a temporary materialization of a work on a video screen, television monitor or similar device, or the performance of the audio portion of such a work on a speaker or a similar device by a user, but does not include the making of a permanent reproduction of the work in any material form'.*

Communicate to the public

It is infringement of copyright to communicate any literary work, including a compilation of literary works, or any dramatic, musical or artistic work, to the public by telecommunication without the permission of the owner of the copyright in the work.[59] The term 'telecommunication' is broadly defined in the Act to mean *'any transmission of signs, signals, writings, images or sounds or intelligence of any nature by wire, radio, visual, optical or other electromagnetic system'.*

The above provision makes it clear that the transmission of a database work to the public in general without the authorization of the copyright holder is capable of being infringing. It is unclear, however, in the context of various types of electronic transmissions where the concept of 'to the public' begins and where it ends. For example, a transmission from a point-to-point basis will be unlikely to be considered as a 'communication to the public'. An on-demand service made generally available to the public also may not be caught. In the Final Report of the Information Highway Advisory Council, the Council expressed the opinion that the right to communicate a work to the public by telecommunication embraced the communication of material to the public, regardless of whether or not that material is made available on an on-demand basis. It went on to state that if further consideration establishes that this is not clear, the *Copyright Act* should be amended to clarify that a communication offered to the public by means of telecommunications is subject to the authorization of the copyright owner, even where such communication is made on demand to separate individual users.

Originality requirement for additions

In order for an updated database to be the subject of a separate copyright, it must be so enlarged and improved as to constitute in reality a new work, or it must impart to the work a true and real value over and above the first work.[60] To constitute an original work the additions to the database must result in some material alteration or embellishment that suffices to make the totality of the work an original work, as the period of statutory protection will not be prolonged by the periodic reproduction of the original work with minor alterations.[61]

Database materials often are in a state of flux, with material being deleted and new material added all the time. In principle, if sufficient alterations and updates of the database are made to meet the Copyright Act's relatively low threshold of originality, separate copyrights can exist in each version of the database. This issue was commented upon by Mr Justice Harman of the English High Court of Justice in *Dun & Bradstreet Ltd. v. Typesetting Facilities Ltd.*,[62] wherein he stated the following: '*But in my judgment the evidence is sufficient to show direction, compilation, distillation of material and adding of material to warrant an assertion that the plaintiff has an original copyright work. There may be, I suspect there are, difficulties in identifying that original copyright work at differing times, in that it seems to me probable that there are, as it were - again the analogy is imperfect - successive editions of the information as it is substantially altered, updated, and weeded. From time to time parts are rejected as obsolete, unsatisfactory or out of date in some other way, other items of information are added as new companies are formed, new classifications of industrial activity are thought of, new names are given to old companies, and similar changes are made. It seems to me likely that there may well be an original copyright work in the edition extant on 1 February 1988 and substantially different original copyright work in the edition extant on 1 August 1991. Nonetheless, each of those would be an original copyright work which the plaintiff would be entitled to protect from having copied.*'

465

Other forms of protection of databases

Computer databases gathered with the expenditure of time and money by a commercial enterprise for the purpose of a business may be protectable pursuant to the laws related to trade secrets.[63] However, because of the intangible nature of confidential information, it is not considered to be property capable of being stolen for criminal law purposes in Canada.[64] Since information that is collected and compiled is often accessible to the public, trade secret protection of computer databases can usually not be relied upon for databases which are made generally available to the public. Copyright protection in no way pre-empts actions for breach of confidence[65] and there may well be circumstances in which actions for infringement of copyright may fail, but an action for misappropriation of confidential information contained in a database would succeed.[66]

Protection of copyright works included in databases

The Act makes it clear that the mere fact that a work is included in a compilation does not increase, decrease or otherwise effect the protection conferred by the Act in respect of the copyright in the work or the moral rights in respect of the work.[67] Accordingly, the owner of the copyright in a work has the right to authorize its reproduction as part of a compilation. Further, the inclusion of a work in a compilation does not derogate from the copyright owner's right to restrain the reproduction of the work by others.

Footnotes

1. The term Global Information Infrastructure or 'GII' refers to the global information highway initiative put forward by the United States to the G7 Countries. See *The Challenge of the Information Highway: Final Report of the Information Highway Advisory Counsel*, September 1995 ('*IHAC Report*').
2. See the *IHAC Report*, Issue 6, pp. 112-120 and '*Copyright and the Information Highway' Final Report of the Sub-committee on Copyright*, March 1995.
3. See *Australia: Computer Software Protection: Copyright Law Review Committee*, 1995 (hereinafter '*Australia Copyright Law Report*'), *Highways to Change: Copyright in the New Communications Environment: Report of the Copyright Conversions Group*, August 1994, *United States Intellectual Property in the National Information Infrastructure: The Report of the Working Group on Intellectual Property Rights*, September 1995 (hereinafter referred to as the '*Lehman Report*').
4. Laddie *et al.*, *The Modern Law of Copyright*, 2nd ed., Butterworths, 1995, p. 843.
5. See World Intellectual Property Organization (WIPO): Memorandum prepared by the International Bureau prepared by a Committee of Experts on a Possible Protocol to the Berne Convention for the Protection of Literary and Artistic Works, November 1991.
6. RSC 1985, c. C-42 as amended (hereinafter referred as the Act).
7. SC 1993, c.44.
8. Section 2.1(2).
9. Section 2.1(1).
10. See *DRG Inc. v. Datafile Ltd.*, (1987) 17 CIPR 136 (Fed. T.D.), affirmed (1991), 35 CPR (3d) 243 (Fed. CA) in which Justice Reid of the Federal Court held that the term 'artistic work' in Canada is used as a general description of works which find expression in a visual medium.
11. Section 3(1).
12. See *Waterflow Directories Ltd. v. Reed Information Services Ltd.*, *The Times* 11 October 1990; *Roland Corp. v. Lorenzo and Sons Pty Ltd.*, (1992) 23 IPR 245 (Aust. Fed. Ct.).
13. *Canadian Admiral Corp. Ltd. v. Rediffusion Inc.*, [1954] Ex. CR 382 (Ex. Ct.); *Warner Brothers Seven Arts Inc. v. CESM-TV Ltd.*, (1971) 65 CPR 215 (Ex. Ct.); *Grignon v. Roussel*, (1991) 38 CPR (3d) 4 (Fed. TD); *FWS Joint Sports Claimants v. Canada (Copyright Board)*, (1991) 36 CPR (3d) 483 (Fed.

CA), leave to appeal to SCC refused (1992), 88 DLR (4th) vi (note), 140 NR 210 (note) (SCC).

14. Computer programs are clearly protected as literary works regardless of whether they exist only in print or in writing as under the Act the term 'computer program' is defined to mean 'a set of instructions or statements, expressed, fixed, embodied or stored in any manner, that is to be used directly or indirectly in a computer in order to bring about a specific result'.

15. Several cases have canvassed the requirement that a literary work be in written or printed form to be protected. In the computer program context see *Apple Computer Inc. v. Mackintosh Computers Ltd.*, (1986) 28 DLR (4th) 178 (Fed. T.D.), varied (1987) 44 DLR (4th) 74 (Fed. CA) per MacGuigan J. (CA), affirmed [1990] 2 SCR 209; *Apple Computer Inc. v. Computer Edge Pty Ltd.*, [1984] FSR (246) (Aus. Fed. Ct.), reversed [1984], FSR 481 (Aus. Fed. F.C.), reversed in part [1986] FSR 537 (Aus. HC).

16. *Provision of Directory Database Information and Real-Time Access to Directory Assistance Databases*, Telecom Decision CRTC 95-3, 8 March 1995; *Bell Canada - Directory File Service*, Telecom Decision CRTC 92-1, 3 March 1992.

17. [1992] 19 FSR 320, (Ch.D.) at p. 325.

18. Section 5(1).

19. *Ladbroke (Football) Ltd. v. William Hill (Football) Ltd.*, [1964] 1 All ER 465 (HL).

20. See for example, *John Richardson Computers v. Flanders*, [1993] FSR 497 (Ch.D.) (copyright held to subsist in dose codes contained in computer program); *Titan Linkabit Corp. v. SEE. See Electronic Engineering Inc.*, 48 CPR (3d) 62 (Fed. TD) (serious issue to be tried established that copyright subsisted in unit seeds forming part of security system); *Prism Hospital Software Inc. v. Hospital Medical Records Institute*, (1994) 57 CPR (3d) 129 (BCSC) (collection of public domain ICD-9 codes which had been changed and truncated and included in a program were held to be protectable on the basis of the changes and truncations made); *Euclid Industries Canada Ltd. v. Reg. Holloway Sales Inc.*, (1989) 25 CIPR 290 (Fed. TD) (copyright in alpha-numeric codes).

21. *Morgan v. Australian Consolidated Press Ltd.*, [1964-1965] NSWR 247.

22. *Ladbroke (Football) Ltd. v. William Hill (Football) Ltd.*, [1964] 1 All ER 465 (HL); *Canadian Admiral Corp. Ltd. v. Rediffusion Inc.*, [1954] Ex. CR 382 (Ex. Ct.); *G.A. Cramp & Sons Ltd. v. Frank Symthson Ltd.*, [1944] AC 329 (HL); *FWS Joint Sports Claimants v. Canada (Copyright Board)*, (1991) 36 CPR (3d) 483 (Fed. CA), leave to appeal to SCC refused, (1992) 88 DLR (4th) vi (note) (SCC).

23. *Interlego A.G. v. Tyco Industries Inc.*, [1988] 3 All ER 949 (PC). It has been suggested, however, that the transformation of the work into one which can be searched electronically at high speed in a convenient manner would be sufficient to confer originality upon the electronic database. See Laddie, *The Modern Law of Copyright*, p. 844.

24. *Dun & Bradstreet v. Typesetting Facilities Limited*, [1992] 19 FSR 320 (Ch.D.)

25. *Provision of Directory Database Information and Real-Time Access to Directory Assistance Databases*, Telecom Decision CRTC 95-3, 8 March 1995; *Bell Canada - Directory File Service*, Telecom Decision CRTC 92-1, 3 March 1992.

26. *B.C. Jockey Club v. Standen Winbar Publications*, (1985) 22 DLR (4th) 467 (BCCA); *Underwriters Survey Bureau Ltd. v. American Home Fire Assur. Co.*, [1939] 4 DLR 89 (Ex. Ct.); *Cuisenaire v. South West Imports Ltd.*, (1967) 54 CPR 1 (Ex. Ct.), affirmed, (1968) 57 CPR 76 (SCC); *Fourgons Transit Inc. v. Fourgons Ramco Inc.*, (1989) 22 CIPR 165 (Fed. TD); *Hogg v. Scott*, (1874) LR 18 Eq. 444.

27. *Scott v. Stanford*, (1867) LR 3 Eq. 718; *Football League Ltd. v. Littlewoods Pools Ltd.*, (1959) 1 Ch. 637 (Ch.D.).

28. Article 1702.

29. See *Business Week* 27 February 1995, p. 82.

30. 'Intellectual Property Rights in an Age of Electronics and Information', US Congress, Office of Technology Assessment, 1986, p. 76.

31. See John E. Appleton, 'Computer-Generated Output - The Neglected Copyright Work', [1986] 8 *EIPR* 227.

32. *Australia Report on Computer Software Protection*, p. 250.

33. Section 13(1).

34. Section 13(3).

35. Section 12.1.

36. Section 2.

37. Robic-Leger, *The Canadian Copyright Act, Annotated* (Carswell) at s. 5.3.

38. *Levy v. Rutley*, (1871) 24 LT 621 (CP), *Heptulla v. Orient Longman Ltd.*, [1989] FSR 589 (High Ct. India).

39. Lahore, *Copyright Law* (Butterworths) s. 3.8.30.

40. *Copinger and Skone, James on Copyright* (Sweet and Maxwell) p. 154.

41. Robic-Leger, *The Canadian Copyright Act, Annotated* (Carswell) at s. 5.5.

42. *Levy v. Rutley*, (1871) 24 LT 621 (CP).

43. Section 2, *Eighteen Music Publishing of Canada Ltd. v. Rogers Radio Broadcasting Ltd.*, (1982) 35 OR (2d) 417 (Ont. HC).

44. Section 2.

45. William Hayhurst, 'Copyright Subject Matter', in: *Copyright Law of Canada*, A.D. Henderson (ed.) (Carswell: 1994) at p. 50.

46. Section 3(1).

47. *Underwriters Survey Bureau Ltd. v. American Home Fire Assurance Co.*, [1939] 4 DLR 89 (Ex. Ct.); *Slumber-Magic Adjustable Bed Co. v. Sleep-King Adjustable Bed Co. Ltd.*, [1985] 1 WWR 112 (BC SC); *Garland v. Gemmil*, (1887) 14 SCR 321; *National Film Board v. Bier*, (1970) 63 CPR 164 (Ex. Ct.);

467

Editions Hurtubise HMH Ltée v. Cegep André-Laurendeau, (1989) 24 CIPR 248 at 269 (CS Qué.).

48. It is clear in the United States that the scope of protection for a database extends only to the selection, co-ordination and arrangement of the data in the database. Accordingly, subsequent database compilers can use facts contained in another database in producing another database as long as the selection and arrangement of the compilation is not copied. See *Feist Publications Inc. v. Rural Telephone Service Co.*, 111 S. Ct. 1282.

49. *British Columbia Jockey Club v. Standen*, (1985) 22 DLR (4th) 467 (BCCA); *Universal Press Pty Ltd. v. Provest Ltd.*, (1989) AIPC 90-593 (Aus. Fed. Ct.); *Euclid Industries Canada Ltd. v. Reg. Holloway Sales Inc.*, (1989) 25 CIPR 290 (Fed. T.D.); *Demerera Turf Club Ltd. v. Phang*, (1963) 6 WIR 177 (British Guyana SC).

50. *British Columbia Jockey Club v. Standen*, (1985) 22 DLR (4th) 467 (BCCA); *Elanco Products Ltd. v. Mandops (Agrochemical Specialists) Ltd.*, [1979] FSR 46 (CA); *Euclid Industries Canada Ltd. v. Reg. Holloway Sales Inc.*, (1989) 25 CIPR 290 (Fed. TD); *Morgan v. Australian Consolidated Press Limited*, [1964-1965] NSWR 247; *National Film Board v. Bier*, (1970) 63 CPR 164 (Ex. Ct.).

51. See *Australia Report on Computer Software Protection*, p. 261.

52. [1994] FSR 723 (Ch. D.).

53. *MAI Systems Corp. v. Peak Computer Inc.*, 26 USPQ 2d 1458 (9th Cir. 1993); *Triad Systems Corp. v. Southeastern Express Co.*, 31 USPQ 2d 1239 (ND Cal. 1994); *Advanced Computer Services of Michigan, Inc. v. MAI Systems Corp.*, 30 USPQ 2d 1443 (ED Va. 1994).

54. *Autodesk Inc. v. Dyason*, (1990) 18 IPR 109 (Aust. Fed. Ct.), reversed, (1992) 173 CLR 330 (Aust. HC) per Sheppard J.

55. See *North American Systemshops Ltd. v. King*, (1989) 68 Alta LR (2d) 145 QBD, which addresses implied licenses to use software sold without enforceable licenses.

56. See *British Leyland Motor Corp. v. Armstrong Patents Co. Ltd.*, [1986] FSR 221 (HL); *Saphena Computing Ltd. v. Allied Collection Agencies Ltd.*, [1995] FSR 616

57. Section 27(2).

58. *R. v. James Lorimer & Co. Ltd.*, (1984) 77 CPR (2d) 262 (Fed. CA); *Zamacois v. Douville*, [1943] 2 DLR 57 (Ex. Ct.); *Hubbard v. Vosper*, [1972] 2 QB 84 (CA).

59. Section 3(1)(f).

60. *Black v. Murray and Son*, (1870) 8 Sc. LR 261 (Ct. of Sess.); *Massie & Renwick Ltd. v. Underwriters Survey Bureau Ltd.*, *ibid.*

61. *Interlego A.G. v. Tyco Industries Inc.*, [1988] 3 WLR 678 (PC).

62. [1992] 19 FSR 320 (Ch.D.) at p. 325.

63. See, for instance, *International Scientific Communications Inc. v. Pattison*, [1979] 5 FSR 439 (Ch.D.); *Creditel of Can. Ltd. v. Faultless*, (1977) 36 CPR (2d) 88 (Ont. HC).

64. *R. v. Stewart*, [1988] 1 SCR 963 (SCC).

65. Section 63.

66. See Sookman, *Computer Law: Acquiring and Protection Information Technology* (Carswell 1989-1996) s. 4.2 in which examples of such actions are given.

67. Section 2.1(2).

Finland

R. OESCH

I. **Protection of databases themselves**

1. Does protection in any form turn on a distinction between electronic and non-electronic databases?

There is no distinction between electronic or non-electronic databases in the Finnish Copyright Act (law 34/91). Databases are protected without any distinction regarding the form of a collection of data.

2. (a) Are databases treated as copyright?

Databases are protected as works, provided they meet the required originality criteria.

(b) What type of work or other subject matter do they constitute?

Databases are treated either as (a) works (article 1 of the Finnish Copyright Act), (b) compiled works (article 5) or/and (c) catalogues (article 49 in the fifth chapter of the Act (Neighbouring Rights)).

(c) What test (of 'originality' or other characteristic) determines whether they qualify for copyright?

For 'work' protection, originality is required. The Finnish Copyright Act (article 1) presumes that the result is an intellectual creation, *i.e.* that any product that shows enough creativity in the form. The originality may be found in the selection or arrangement of the material recorded in the database. For compilations of works, *i.e.* products which consist of separate works or parts of works, the prerequisite is the original effort in the creation which often can be found in the selection or arrangement of works or parts of works. Catalogues (catalogue protection as a special neighbouring right in the fifth chapter; article 49 of the Act): a large number of information items has been compiled in one product (catalogue, table, a programme or similar kind of product, for example listings). The criteria thus is the 'largeness' of data included in the catalogue.

(d) Who is the initial owner of copyright? What is its duration? Is the database a collective work?

469

Right holder of a database protected as a work: as original right owner is to be regarded the natural person, who has made personal intellectual effort in the creation, *e.g.* in the choice or arrangement of information in a database. Also a group of natural persons can together make a database work. The cooperation can result in a joint work (article 6 of the Act). If a database work has been produced in the course of carrying out the duties of an employment contract, the employer can get the rights through contracts. Normally according to the contracts - explicit or implied - the employer gets the economic rights, although there are no specific provisions for the transfer to the employer except in case of computer programs and protected catalogues (articles 40b and 49 of the Act). The economic rights connected with computer programs and catalogues are thus transferred to the employer, if these are created (or 'produced' in case of catalogues) within the scope of duties in an employment situation. The same applies to civil servants (article 40b of the Finnish Copyright Act) (see also article 49 subsection 2, which refers to article 40b). Right holder of the *catalogue* is its maker: either the natural person or a group of natural persons or the legal person as the producer of the catalogue who have collected the several particulars on the same production from where the data can be accessed. It is exceptional in the Finnish copyright system that a judicial person can be an original right holder (also phonogram and film producers as neighbouring right holders).

The protection of database works starts at the moment of creation and lasts until 70 years of p.m.a., in cases of joint works 70 years after the year in which the last surviving author died. The protection period for catalogues is ten years counted from the year in which the catalogue was published. In any case, however, the term is restricted to expire at the latest when 15 years have elapsed from the year in which the catalogue was completed.

> *(e) What scope of protection attaches to this copyright? How far can it be used to protect a datum or data incorporated in the base?*

Scope of protection (as far as rights are concerned): basic economic rights connected with a database work are the right to make copies and the right to make it available to the public in any manner (for example by distributing, performing, exhibiting it publicly etc.) (article 2). Moral rights are mandatory by their nature: the creator of a database work can waive his moral rights with binding effect only in regard to clearly specified uses of the work (article 3). As far as the protected subject matter is concerned we can differ between following alternatives. When a group of data has been taken out of *a database consisting of mere data* infringement exists, if the part taken carries expression and demonstrates originality. The limits of protection in case of *database consisting of works* lie similarly as in the case of other works. The group works must carry original expression in order to belong to the scope of protection. For *catalogues* the part taken out from a catalogue must reach the required quantity for protection ('largeness').

As a conclusion I can say that copyright system may be endangered if the protection is extended too far, because the freedom of expression must be respected also from the copyright point of view.

(f) What limitations may apply particularly to this copyright? Can these limitations be overridden by a contractual term?

Limitations and their applicability in the database protection: all general limitations on copyright may apply, *e.g.* private copying, right to quote etc. Some of them may cause interpretation problems, for example the right to quote, when applied to database works. It is possible that the user and the right holder of a database agree that the user in his activities will not take advantage of relying on the limitations in the second chapter of the Finnish Copyright Act. There exists a full freedom of contract.

(g) What additions to the database will constitute a second work?

Databases are not often only updated but also provided with many additions for various purposes. Smaller alterations, additions and arrangements do not result in a totally new database. In case of stronger additions etc. the activity may change the identity of the database work either so that we can speak about an adaptation of a database work or a totally new work. In the first case the permission of the right holder is, of course, needed.

3. *(a) Are databases protected by trade secret, unfair competition or* sui generis *protection?*

The *sui generis* protection (catalogue protection) is explained above. Databases can also be protected by the Finnish Act on Unfair Competition (1978; Nr. 1061). It supplements the protection of intellectual property laws. The Act has both a general clause (article 1) and special articles concerning trade secrets. The importance of the general clause ('a procedure contrary to good business practice is not permissible and can be denied by the court') is diminished by the fact that the Act is applicable between entrepreneurs only, not for example between a private person and a company. The trade secret protection (with sanctions in the Penal Code) applies to the acts of natural persons. In practice the Act on Unfair Competition is less important than Copyright Act as a means against misuses of databases, although these laws protect different aspects.

(b) Is any such protection cumulative with copyright where the latter also applies?

The different forms of protection are cumulative although they protect different aspect and with varying sanctions.

(c) Who is entitled to the rights or rights ? How long do they endure? What further additions to the database would add to the period of protection?

See above 3(a). The questions concerning the right holder of copyright are dealt with after question 2(d).

(d) What is the scope of protection? How does it enable a datum or data be protected?

See above.

(e) What limitations may apply to these rights? May the limitations be overridden by contract?

See above.

II. Protection for copyright works included in databases

1. In what circumstances does a copyright work require to be authorised in order for it to be stored in a database? How far is the cataloguing of titles and other identifying data, abstracts and other summaries allowed without needing permission?

The storage of a work (input) into a database is of course regarded as reproduction. If only items and identifications are stored the permission is not needed. If abstracts or summaries are stored there are two possibilities: (1) if only unprotected items have been inputted (cataloguing), there is no reproduction of a work; (2) if abstracts and summaries (which already can be protected as such) are stored, permission is needed of the authors of abstracts and summaries. As a rule, a permission for the storage of a work into a database is thus required. Extraction of simple data does not normally constitute an infringement of copyright.

2. What extractions of copyright data constitute infringements of economic rights?

3. In what circumstances could extractions and manipulations of copyright data constitute a breach of moral rights? In practice, what contractual or other arrangements exist to allow material to be used without acknowledgement of authorship, or after alteration of content?

Finnish Copyright Act recognises especially the *droit au respect* and the *droit à la paternité*. The preconditions for infringement against *droit moral* are rather high: alterations must have been done in a manner that objectively (not only subjectively) are prejudicial to the original author's literary or artistic reputation or to his individuality (article 3). Regarding factual databases, infringements against moral rights of authors of databases are probably very uncommon. Material information, simple information items, may - of course - be used freely.

III. **Impact on database operations**

1. Are there considerable numbers of database operators in your country? How actively are they pressing the case for greater legal protection through copyright or other intellectual property protection? Will they be satisfied by legal reforms which may currently be under consideration?

There is a growing number of database operators. One may distinguish between different kinds of groups of interest. Except database operators, there are information providers, *i.e.* contents providers who produce the material that is included in a database (whether protected or not). Except content providers there are telecommunications service providers in a network environment. Producers of compilations of data and media houses as producers are more and more aware of the need for protection. Associations of the producing industries are in favour of the improved protection in the market. These associations are also claiming that the rights to the works made within an employment situation should be vested in the employer.

2. What other economic factors deserve to be given consideration in achieving adequate legal solutions to database problems?

How can the price of information be calculated? What are the grounds for its calculation and how can the collection of fees be technically administered? The price of use of a database is often calculated on time basis especially in a network environment.

France

A. KEREVER

I. **Protection des banques de données elles-mêmes**

1. Existe-t-il une distinction entre banques informatisées et banques analogiques?

Les banques informatisées ou non-informatisées font l'objet d'une définition juridique identique dans les textes suivants. *(a)* Article 2 § 5 de la CB: *"Recueils d'oeuvres littéraires ou artistiques ... qui, par le choix ou la disposition des matières, constituent des créations intellectuelles".* *(b)* Accord ADPIC, article 10: *"compilations de données ... qu'elles soient reproduites sur support exploitable par une machine ou sous toute autre forme, qui, par le choix ou la disposition des matières, constituent une création intellectuelle".* *(c)* Loi française, article L 112(3) CPI: protection des *"auteurs d'anthologies ou recueils d'oeuvres diverses qui, par le choix et la disposition des matières, constituent des créations intellectuelles".*

Mais il est évident que les banques informatisées présentent des caractères spécifiques: (a) l'importance des investissements financiers et intellectuels requis; (b) leur très grande capacité de stockage; (c) le fait que leur fonctionnement soit assuré par un ou plusieurs logiciels, qui, en eux-mêmes, sont des oeuvres progégées; et (d) l'obligation pour l'utilisateur, de reproduire la ou les données recherchées dans la mémoire de son propre ordinateur.

Le projet de Directive européenne (position commune du 10 juillet 1995) précise expressément que son champ d'application englobe aussi bien les banques analogiques que les banques numériques. Toutefois, ce projet contient au moins une disposition qui impose une distinction: l'article 6 institue une exception au droit de reproduction à des fins privées réservée aux seules banques analogiques. De plus, on peut penser que le "droit spécifique" ouvert par le chapitre III étant subordonné à l'importance des investissements, ce droit spécifique bénéficiera surtout, sinon exclusivement, aux banques informatisées.

2. (a) Les banques sont-elles traitées comme des oeuvres protégées par le droit d'auteur?

Oui, sous condition d'originalité. L'article 3 du projet de Directive définit la banque protégeable par le droit d'auteur comme *"des créations intellectuelles propres à leur auteur".* Cette définition est identique à celle exigée pour les logiciels par la Directive les concernant. On s'accorde, en France, pour estimer que l'originalité exigée pour les logiciels est moins forte que pour les autres oeuvres, pour lesquelles la protection n'est accordée que si l'oeuvre porte l'empreinte de la personnalité du créateur. On peut observer qu'en adoptant une condition d'originalité réduite, propre au numérique, l'effet de la Directive "banques de données" sera d'étendre cette exigence réduite d'originalité aux banques non-électroniques, anthologies ou compilations classiques. Bien que cet aspect soit évoqué sous la question 2(d) ci-après, il convient de mentionner dès maintenant que la condition d'originalité et l'octroi de la protection par le droit d'auteur ne concernent que la structure (composition) de la banque et non les données elles-mêmes.

(b) Quel type d'oeuvres ou d'autres objets de protection constituent-elles?

Il a déjà été répondu: cf. réponse à question 1. Les banques sont des oeuvres visées à l'article 25 de la CB ou à l'article 10 de l'accord ADPIC.

(c) A quel test d'originalité ou d'autres caractéristiques est subordonnée la protection des banques par le droit d'auteur?

Cf. réponse à la question 2(a) sur la notion d'originalité applicable aux banques.

(d) Quel est le titulaire initial du droit d'auteur? La banque est-elle une oeuvre collective? Durée du droit d'auteur?

A titre de remarque préliminaire, on mentionne que l'article 4 du projet de Directive renvoie la détermination de la titularité aux lois nationales des Etats membres. En droit français, la titularité se déterminera selon les règles de droit commun applicables aux "anthologies ou recueils d'oeuvres" mentionnées à l'article L 112(3) CPI. Il faut rappeler que l'oeuvre protégée constituée par la banque consiste à choisir et/ou organiser la composition et l'arrangement des données stockées, ainsi qu'à organiser son fonctionnement par des thésaurus ou des systèmes d'indexation. Cf. considérant n° 28.

Si la création de la banque, ainsi entendue est le fruit d'apports de plusieurs personnes physiques, il y a lieu d'appliquer, selon les modalités d'élaboration, le statut d'oeuvre de collaboration, d'oeuvre collective, ou d'oeuvre composite. (Cette dernière qualification pourrait être retenue si la banque incorpore un logiciel directement protégé sans la collaboration de l'auteur dudit logiciel.) La banque de données doit être distinguée de l'oeuvre multimédia. Elle est un "recueil" disposant systématiquement des données individuellement accessibles. On peut donc penser qu'une banque de données ne saurait être qualifiée d'oeuvre audiovisuelle, même si les données stockées sont elles-mêmes des oeuvres audiovisuelles.

La banque de données ne sera une oeuvre collective, au sens du droit français, que si les conditions juridiques pour une telle qualification sont réunies: il faut qu'il y ait plusieurs contributions dont la création a été suscitée par un "fédérateur" qui prend l'initiative de l'élaboration de la banque et qui l'édite sous son nom, qui rassemble et coordonne les diverses contributions de telle sorte que ces diverses contributions

475

se fondent dans un ensemble sans qu'aucun des contributeurs puisse revendiquer un droit indivis sur cet ensemble. En particulier, la qualification d'oeuvre collective devra s'effacer au profit de celle d'oeuvre de collaboration si la coordination des diverses contributions fusionnées dans l'ensemble est assurée par le concours des contributeurs eux-mêmes. Si la qualification d'oeuvre collective est retenue, le premier titulaire sera le "fédérateur" décrit ci-dessus, qui apparaîtra donc fréquemment comme la personne morale qui édite l'oeuvre sous son nom. En cas de qualification d'oeuvre de collaboration, les premiers titulaires sont les auteurs créateurs, collaborateurs et l'éditeur de la banque ne pourra intervenir que comme cessionnaire de leurs droits. La durée de protection par le droit d'auteur est celle du droit commun, compte tenu de la qualification retenue.

> *(e) Quelle est l'étendue de la protection attachée au droit d'auteur? Dans quelle mesure cette protection peut-elle être utilisée pour protéger une ou plusieurs données incorporées dans la banque?*

La protection par le droit d'auteur est limitée à la structure de la banque et ne s'étend pas aux données elles-mêmes. Cette distinction fondamentale est acquise en droit français pour les anthologies classiques non-informatisées. Cette distinction est consacrée par le projet de Directive du 10 juillet 1995, dans le Considérant n° 35 et l'article 3 § 2 qui précise que cette Directive ne s'applique qu'au choix ou a la disposition des matières, et non au contenu de la banque. La protection est étendue aux éléments nécessaires au fonctionnement ou à la consultation de certaines banques, tels que le thésaurus et les sytèmes d'indexation (considérant n° 20), et elle ne préjudicie pas aux droits subsistant sur ce contenu. L'article 5 du projet de Directive souligne encore cette distinction en précisant que les droits exclusifs d'auteur ne concernent que *"l'expression de cette banque pouvant faire l'objet d'une protection par le droit d'auteur"*.

Il résulte de ce qui précède que le droit d'auteur sur la banque elle-même ne peut être utilisé pour protéger une ou plusieurs des données stockées. Les droits d'auteur sur ces données ne sont ni réduits, ni amplifiés par le droit d'auteur sur la banque prise en elle-même. Mais il convient de rappeler que ce même projet de Directive investit l'auteur de la banque, originale ou non, d'un droit spécifique protégeant le producteur de la banque contre *"l'extraction ou la réutilisation de la totalité ou d'une partie substantielle du contenu"* de la banque. Ce droit, d'une durée de 15 ans à compter du 1er janvier de l'année de la fabrication de la banque, n'est pas un droit d'auteur et n'est, par suite, mentionné dans cette partie du questionnaire que pour mémoire. Il est cumulable avec le droit d'auteur lorsque ce dernier est reconnu.

> *(f) Quelles sont les limitations spécifiques au droit d'auteur applicables aux banques de données?*

A ma connaissance, il n'existe, en droit français, aucune limitation du droit d'auteur spécifique aux banques de données protégées en tant qu'anthologies ou recueils (article L 112(3) CPI). Le projet de Directive du 10 juillet 1995 traite de cette question. Des exceptions spécifiques aux banques informatisées sont définies par la combinaison des articles 5 et 6. Le droit d'extraction souffre des exceptions définies par les articles 8 et 9 (droit de l'utilisateur). Cette même Directive (article 15) confère un caractère d'ordre public à certaines exceptions (celles de l'article 6 § 1 pour le droit d'auteur; l'article 8 pour le droit spécifique).

(g) Quels ajouts à une banque peuvent aboutir à une seconde oeuvre?

Le droit français ne contient, sur ce point, aucune disposition spécifique ni pour les recueils/anthologies, ni a fortiori pour les banques de données protégeables par le droit d'auteur. Il convient donc d'appliquer le droit commun en cas d'arrangement, transformation ou adaptation d'oeuvres préexistantes (article L 112(3) 1er phrase CPI). Le projet de Directive du 10 juillet 1995 prévoit explicitement que s'agissant du droit spécifique et non du droit d'auteur, l'investissement nouveau et substantiel peut engendrer une nouvelle banque (article 10 § 3).

3. (a) (b) (c) Protection par d'autres législations que par le droit d'auteur. Y a-t-il cumul des protections? Qui en est le bénéficiaire? Quid en cas d'ajouts à une banque préexistante?

Jusqu'à transposition du projet de Directive du 10 juillet 1995 qui, on l'a déjà souligné, institue un droit spécifique d'extraction cumulable avec la protection du droit d'auteur, le droit français ne connaît aucun droit spécifique. La protection par les secrets commerciaux et celle par les règles relatives à la concurrence déloyale peuvent s'appliquer aux banques de données dans les conditions de droit commun et ces protections sont cumulables avec celles du droit d'auteur. La protection par le secret commercial s'obtient essentiellement par le droit contractuel et par les clauses pénales dont peuvent être assortis les contrats. L'action en concurrence déloyale suppose que celui qui l'intente est en mesure de prouver l'existence d'un préjudice subi dans son exploitation du fait d'agissements de concurrents qui désorganisent son marché en créant une confusion dans les produits, ou d'agissements dits "parasitaires" (utiliser à son profit les investissements réalisés par un concurrent). Ces agissements sont fautifs et leurs auteurs sont responsables envers les victimes.

(d) (e) Étendue de la protection par d'autres législations que celle du droit d'auteur.

Par sa nature même, la protection par la "concurrence déloyale" ne peut concerner que le "produit" constitué par une banque déterminée, et ne peut s'appliquer aux données incorporées dans la banque. Cette protection étant fondée sur le droit commun de la responsabilité, elle ne s'analyse pas en droit subjectif et ne comporte donc ni durée ni exceptions, sa mise en oeuvre supposant toujours l'obligation de prouver l'existence d'un préjudice résultant d'agissements fautifs de concurrents.

II. Protection des oeuvres incluses dans les banques de données

1. Le stockage d'une oeuvre protégée dans la banque doit-il être autorisé? Dans quelle mesure le cataloguage de titres, de données identifiantes, d'abstracts et autres résumés peut-il être incorporé sans autorisation?

(Première sous-question:) L'inclusion d'une oeuvre protégée dans une banque relève du droit de reproduction. En outre l'affichage de l'oeuvre sur l'écran terminal du récepteur engendre, en droit français, un droit de représentation (communication publique). (Seconde sous-question:) En principe, les titres sont protégeables, s'ils sont originaux, si - même non originaux - ils risquent de créer une confusion. Quant aux résumés, selon la doctrine classique, ils peuvent être élaborés sans le consentement de l'auteur de l'oeuvre préexistante dans la mesure ou ce résumé ne dispense pas le lecteur de se référer à l'oeuvre préexistante. Mais, par ses arrêts dits *Microfor* (9 novembre 1983 et 30 octobre 1987) la Cour de Cassation a établi une jurisprudence très libérale permettant aux banques de données de reproduire sans autorisation les titres et les résumés lorsque ces reproductions n'ont d'autres fonctions que d'identifier les oeuvres incorporées.

2. L'extraction de données protégeables constitue-t-elle une atteinte aux droits patrimoniaux?

La protection des données lorsqu'il s'agit d'oeuvres protégées par le droit d'auteur, est indépendante de la protection de droit d'auteur dont peut bénéficier la banque elle-même. Il en résulte que toute reproduction, représentation, traduction ou adaptation de la donnée individualisée n'est licite qu'avec l'autorisation de l'auteur. L'autorisation donnée par l'auteur d'incorporer son oeuvre dans une banque n'implique pas, par elle-même, qu'il ait accordé son autorisation pour d'autres utilisations, que ce soit par le producteur/éditeur de la banque ou par un tiers.

3. Dans quelles circonstances les "extractions" et manipulations d'oeuvres constituent-elles une atteinte au droit moral? En pratique, quelles sont les mesures contractuelles ou autres qui permettent d'utiliser du matériel sans reconnaissance du droit d'auteur, ou après modification de son contenu?

L'incorporation de données protégées dans une banque peut en effet, être une source d'atteinte aux droits moraux dont l'étendue et la portée sont importantes en droit français. L'omission du nom de l'auteur, des reprises partielles, voire des rapprochements insolites de deux oeuvres peuvent constituer des atteintes au droit au respect du nom et au droit au respect ou à l'intégrité de l'oeuvre. Comme l'indique la question, toute "manipulation" de l'oeuvre est susceptible de constituer une atteinte aux droits moraux. La pratique contractuelle peut, dans une certaine mesure, avec l'accord de l'auteur, ou pour les nécessités techniques dûment reconnues d'un mode d'exploitation déterminé, atténuer la rigueur de la protection des droits moraux. Mais les arrangements contractuels n'auront qu'une portée limitée; un contrat ne peut contraindre un auteur à renoncer définitivement et totalement à ses prérogatives d'ordre moral.

III. **Impact sur les opérations des banques de données**

1. Y a-t-il de nombreux opérateurs de banques de données dans votre pays? Tentent-ils activement de faire adopter une plus grande protection légale par le droit d'auteur ou un autre droit de propriété intellectuelle? Seront-ils satisfaits par des réformes légales qui sont actuellement prises en considération?

Il existe certainement un lobby ou groupe de pression formé par les opérateurs de banques de données en France. Nous n'avons que peu de renseignements sur leur attitude à l'égard de la propriété intellectuelle, en particulier. Leur attitude à l'égard du projet de Directive du 10 juillet 1995 n'est pas connue.

2. Quels sont les autres acteurs économiques à prendre en considération pour élaborer un cadre juridique adéquat aux activités de banques de données?

Il est évident que les éditeurs/producteurs de banques de données souhaitent obtenir le plus de liberté possible dans la collecte et l'incorporation des données, ainsi que la maîtrise de la stratégie de l'exploitation des banques. Cette double recherche peut créer des conflits d'intérêts avec les titulaires des droits sur les données, ainsi qu'avec les auteurs personnes physiques à l'origine de la création des banques. Cet effort a déjà été partiellement couronné de succès avec la jurisprudence *Microfor* déjà rappelée (interprétation libérale par la Cour de Cassation de l'exception au droit de reproduction pour les citations dans son application à l'incorporation des titres et résumés signalétiques des données individuelles). Il est certain que ces milieux jouent également de la fascination exercée par les nouvelles technologies pour justifier des "assouplissements" aux contraintes du droit d'auteur, présentés comme nécessaires à la diffusion du progrès technique.

A cet égard, l'octroi au profit des producteurs de banques, d'un droit spécifique dit "d'extraction" envisagé par le projet de Directive du 10 juillet 1995 devrait contribuer à persuader les producteurs d'accepter leurs obligations en matière de droit d'auteur. Il est également évident que les producteurs se préoccupent également d'aspects autres que le droit d'auteur, tels que la législation sur la protection des données nominatives, le régime fiscal ou les questions de nantissement qui s'étaient déjà posées pour les logiciels, l'édiction de dispositions pénales spécifiques etc.

Germany

S. von Lewinski

I. Protection of databases themselves

1. Does protection in any form turn on a distinction between electronic and non-electronic databases?

Databases as such are not even mentioned in the German Copyright Act (CA). They may be protected as 'collections' within the meaning of § 4 CA. The requirements for protection, set out in § 4 CA, must be fulfilled, irrespective of whether the collection/database is electronic or non-electronic. The same is true for databases protected as literary works under § 2 CA: the law does not provide any distinction based on the (electronic or non-electronic) form of the work.

2. (a) Are databases treated as copyright?

Databases themselves are protected as copyright works, if they fulfil the requirements set out in §§ 4 and 2 CA (cf. for the requirements the answer under *(c)* hereunder).

(b) What type of work or other subject matter do they constitute?

According to § 4 CA, they are protected as 'collections of works or of other contributions', similar to, but not identical to, collections within the meaning of article 2(5) of the Berne Convention. Databases which do not contain works or similar contributions may be protected as literary works under § 2(1)1 CA (see, for example, BGH *GRUR* 1987, 704 *et seq. - Warenzeichenlexika*, note Loewenheim). Such works, which contain collections of data rather than of works or similar contributions, have been called 'organized works' by a part of the academic literature (cf. Fromm/Nordemann, *Urheberrecht*, 8th edition, 1994, paragraph 2, no. 88). See however for the requirements for protection the remarks under *(c)* hereunder.

(c) What test (of 'originality' or other characteristic) determines whether they qualify for copyright?

The general criterium of 'personal intellectual creation' laid down in § 2(2) CA applies. With respect to collections of works or other contributions, § 4 CA states explicitly that this criterium of 'personal intellectual creation' refers to the selection or arrangement of the works or contributions. In other words, the selection or arrangement itself must fulfil the requirement of 'personal intellectual creation'. The criterium 'personal intellectual creation' covers, according to case law and academic literature, at least five main elements: a creation, an intellectual content, a certain form of expression, the so-called individuality, and a certain degree of individuality *('Gestaltungshöhe')* (see on these criteria in particular Loewenheim in: Schricker (ed.), *Urheberrecht*, München 1987, § 2, no. 4 *et seq.*).

'Creation', like 'personal', implies that only the activity of a human being (as opposed to machines etc.) is protected and that the activity must consist in shaping a work or providing a certain form of expression which will result in a work *('Gestaltung')*. In addition, the human intellect must be expressed in the work, be it thoughts or feelings. Thirdly, the work must be expressed in a form which is directly or indirectly perceptible to human beings. Fourthly, the work must be characterized by the individual intellect of the author, the 'individuality'. In general, the individuality may result from the particular form of expression or the concept of the work, as well as from all elements relating to the particular shaping or forming of the work.

With respect to collections, this individuality may result from the selection and arrangement of the material. Individuality presupposes a latitude or space for individual shaping. This excludes from copyright protection in particular such productions, which are shaped on the basis of pure rules of logic or appropriateness, technical necessities or other constraints which are in the nature of things. Individuality also excludes from copyright protection any common place, banal or ordinary productions as well as productions resulting from routine activities. The mere effort, investment of money or skill is not sufficient.

Finally, a certain degree of individuality *('Gestaltungshöhe')* must be achieved. It seems hardly possible to generally describe this degree of individuality. Regularly, the jurisdiction only requires a low degree of individuality; in particular, the so-called 'small change' *('kleine Münze')* is protected in principle. However, with respect to works of applied art, which are protected also by a separate design protection, the courts have required a higher degree of individuality than for other works. Also with respect to works in the scientific and technical field, the jurisdiction has required that the creative acitivity must be clearly above the general, average ability (cf. for example BGH *GRUR* 1986, 739, 741 - *Anwaltsschriftsatz*; BGH *GRUR* 1984, 659 *et seq.* - *Ausschreibungsunterlagen*). These high requirements were also applied to computer programs (BGH *GRUR* 1985, 1041, 1048 - *Inkasso-Programm*; BGH *GRUR* 1991, 449 - *Betriebssystem*). As a result of the EC Computer Directive, these demanding requirements will have to be lowered.

Although no decision on the very question of the requirements for protection has been rendered, two decisions of the Federal Court of Justice indicate that the Court is willing to lower the requirements in accordance with § 69a(3) CA (BGH *GRUR* 1994, 39 - *Buchhaltungsprogramm* and BGH *GRUR* 1994, 363 - *Holzhandelspro-gramm*). Given the fact that the European Database Directive, which is expected in 1996, will probably lay down similar requirements for protection as the EC Compu-ter Directive ('own intellectual creation'), one may expect that German courts will not apply the higher requirements to the protection of databases.

§ 4 CA covers only collections of works or 'other contributions'. Such contributions must be works in the public domain or contributions similar to works; however, mere data or facts do not constitute contributions within the meaning of § 4 CA. Collections of mere data or facts may be protected under § 2(1)1 CA (by some, they are called 'organized works', see above under *(b)*). As regards the protectability of these works, the courts apply the same criteria as under § 4 CA. Accordingly, the personal intellectual creation must be expressed in the selection or arrangement of the material (see, for example, BGH *GRUR* 1987, 704 *et seq. - Warenzeichenlexika*).

(d) *Who is the initial owner of this copyright? What is its duration? Is the database a collective work?*

According to the general rule, which applies also to authors of databases, the author is the creator of the work (§ 7 CA). Accordingly, the person who selects or arranges the works, contributions, data or facts and thereby creates the work, is its author. As regards traditional collections such as encyclopedias, this author is usually designed as 'editor' *('Herausgeber')*. If more than one person has selected and arranged material and thereby achieved a personal intellectual creation, these persons are joint authors of the database, if the conditions of § 8 CA are fulfilled (a joint creation by several persons and the fact that their respective contributions, which must be protectable themselves, cannot be exploited separately).

The concept of collective work *('Gruppenwerk')* was rejected by the legislator in 1965. Indeed, this concept would result in an author's right for an achievement which is of an organisational and economic nature rather than of a creative nature. Accordingly, such a right being granted to the editor or publisher would be in conflict with the general principle of § 7 CA, which recognizes only the creator of the work as its author. The introduction of a neighbouring right for the organisator or investor in such a 'collective work' would have been possible, but was not realized. (See Fromm/Nordemann, *loc. cit.*, § 8, no. 30, with further references).

The duration is determined by the general rules. Accordingly, if the database has been created by one author, it is protected during the life of the author and until 70 years p.m.a. In the case of joint authorship, the general rule applies, according to which the period of protection expires 70 years after the death of the last surviving co-author (§§ 64, 65(1) CA). The Copyright Act does not yet contain any specific rule which would take into account the problem of the ever changing contents of an electronic database, which has to be brought up to date and completed constantly. If a database is adapted (see for the conditions hereunder, *(g)*), the duration of the adaptation expires 70 years after the death of the adaptor (or the last surviving co-adaptor).

(e) *What scope of protection attaches to this copyright? How far can it be used to protect a datum or data incorporated in the base?*

Since the personal intellectual creation is expressed only in the selection or arrangement of the material contained in a database, the scope of protection only covers such selection or arrangement, as opposed to the material itself (see, for example, Loewenheim in: Schricker, *loc. cit.*, § 4, no. 12). A partial reproduction of a database may infringe the copyright therein. In each single case, an infringement of the protected elements (selection or arrangement) will have to be established. According to general rules, the higher the degree of individuality will be, the larger will be the scope of protection. Mere data themselves are not protected by copyright (see, for example, Katzenberger, *IIC* vol. 21, no. 3, 1990, p. 310, 323, referring to the protectability of certain data ('results of topographical surveys') under special statutes). However, they might be indirectly protected, as far as the database itself or parts thereof are protected. Such protection however does not result in a protection of the particular data, which may still be reproduced and otherwise exploited without any infringement of copyright.

As regards the rights granted to the author of a database, no special rules are provided. In particular, the exclusive rights of reproduction, distribution and rental apply. With respect to the exclusive right of communication to the public, which covers several forms of immaterial exploitation (§ 15(2) CA), the legal situation is not yet entirely clarified; in particular, it is unclear whether the on-line consultation of databases constitutes a communication 'to the public' within the meaning of § 15(3) CA, which so far has been interpreted as requiring the communication to different persons at the same time (see, for example, Von Ungern/Sternberg in: Schricker, *loc. cit.*, § 15, no. 30). Even if one agrees with this prevailing opinion, there is no unanimity regarding the particular form of communication to the public which should apply.

> *(f) What limitations may apply particularly to this copyright? Can these limitations be overridden by a contractual term?*

The general rules apply. There are no particular limitations for databases. The applicability of certain limitations will depend on the qualification of certain acts of exploitation. For example, if an on-demand use were regarded as broadcasting, the general limitations to the broadcasting right would apply. However, if such a use is not at all regarded as any form of communication to the public, but the rental or distribution right is applied by analogy, then the respective limitations apply (see however the critical analysis of Katzenberger, *GRUR Int.* 1983, p. 895, 908 *et seq.*). So far, the application of the existing rights and limitations to electronic databases creates a number of problems, which have not yet been clearly solved. This situation will of course change after the probable adoption of the Database Directive in 1996 and its implementation into German law. Under copyright in general, it is possible to 'license' certain uses which are not reserved to the copyright owner under copyright law. The user may decide not to envoke the limitations provided by the law. However, such contracts might rise problems under antitrust law.

> *(g) What additions to the database will constitute a second work?*

Additions to the database might amount to an adaptation, which is itself protected as a work under the conditions of § 3 CA. The adaptation itself must constitute a 'personal intellectual creation'. The same criteria as mentioned above (see answer to question *2(c)*) apply to the adaptation. Although the adaptation must allow the adapted work/database to be recognized, it must at the same time differ from the original work by an own, personal intellectual creation expressed in the adaptation. The degree of individuality of the adaptation depends on that of the original work. For example, the degree of individuality of an adaptation needs to be only low in the case of an original work with a low degree of individuality. According to these general rules, the mere addition of data to a database in order to bring it up to date, without changing the selection or arrangement of its contents, will not constitute an adaptation or any other form of 'second work'. If, however, the database is not only completed but also essentially changed in the protected elements, *i.e.* the selection and/or arrangement of the contents, such addition may be protected as an adaptation, if it constitutes itself a personal intellectual creation.

3. *(a) Are databases protected by trade secret, unfair competition or* sui generis *law?*

The protection of trade secrets is granted in §§ 17 *et seq.* Act against Unfair Competition *(UWG)*. A secret is known, by its nature, only to one person or a very limited number of persons, such as the employees of the database producer. Accordingly, as soon as the database is offered to the public for use, there is no trade secret anymore. Consequently, protection for trade secrets is conceivable only with respect to databases created within an enterprise or company and not yet made available to the public, or not even designed for the public but for internal use only.

A number of other conditions must be fulfilled, depending on the different situations covered by §§ 17 *et seq. UWG*: (1) an employee reveals a trade secret which has been confided to him on the grounds of the employment, at the time when the employment is still valid, without authorisation to another person, be it for the purpose of competition or for personal gain or in order to damage the owner of the business (§ 17(1) *UWG*); (2) a person secures himself illegally a trade secret by technical means, reproduction or taking away the object which incorporates the trade secret, for the purpose of competition, for personal gain or in order to damage the owner of the business (§ 17(2)1 *UWG*); (3) a person illegally exploits or communicates to another person a trade secret, which he has obtained through a communication as set out in § 17(1) *UWG* or through an own or a foreign act or the act of another person according to § 17(2)1 *UWG*, or otherwise secured illegally (§ 17(2)2 *UWG*); (4) a person exploits without authorisation the designs *('Vorlagen')* or instructions *('Vorschriften')* of a technical nature confided to him in the course of the business dealings, for the purposes of competition or for personal gain, or the person communicates such designs or instructions to another person (§ 18 *UWG*). § 18 *UWG* has already been interpreted as covering computer programs; as far as databases include any form of instructions, they will also be protected by § 18 *UWG*, which so far has been interpreted generously.

These acts are criminal acts; any person who fulfils these acts shall be liable to a term of imprisonment not exceeding three years (§ 17(1), (2) *UWG*) or two years (§ 18

UWG) or to a fine. At the same time, all these acts are giving rise to a claim for damages (§ 19 *UWG*) as well as civil law remedies, such as § 823(2) *BGB* (damages). Lists of clients and of agents have already been recognized as trade secrets (cf. RG MuW 33, 12 and RG HRR 27, 1367). Also, the courts have decided that computer programs may be protected as trade secrets, either because of their contents, or on the grounds of the programs themselves (cf. LG Mannheim, *BB* 1981, 1543/1556 *et seq.*; BayObLG, *GRUR* 1991, 694).

Protection by the law against unfair competition is possible also under § 1 *UWG*. Under the heading of 'direct copying of the performance of someone else' *('unmittelbare Übernahme fremder Leistung')*, a database may be protected against the entire or partial copying by a competitor. As a further condition, the so-called 'singularity in competition' *('wettbewerbliche Eigenart')* must have been taken over to the new database. In the case of a database, this element results from the effort of collection and organization and the thereby produced supply of information. This economic value, which is essential in the framework of competition, must have been taken over unfairly and for purposes of competition (see for a decision on the basis of § 1 *UWG*: BGH, *GRUR* 1988, p. 308 *et seq. - Informationsdienst*). So far, a *sui generis* protection for databases has not yet been provided. It is to be expected in the framework of the implementation of the future Database Directive.

> *(b) Is any such protection cumulative with copyright where the latter also applies?*

According to the prevailing opinion in academic literature, copyright protection is regarded as *lex specialis* in relation to unfair competition law. Accordingly, unfair competition law cannot be applied if copyright applies. (See Schricker, *loc. cit.*, introduction no. 39; see however also his criticism in nos. 39 and 38.)

> *(c) Who is entitled to the right or rights? How long do they endure? What further additions to the database would add to the period of protection?*

The protection under § 1 *UWG* may be asserted by any competitor, and, according to § 13(2) *UWG*, by any associations which are legal persons and which envisage the promotion of industrial interests as well as consumer associations and chambers of commerce, industry and handicraft. Since unfair competition law refers to acts of unfair competition, but does not provide for exclusive property rights in certain achievements, there is no precise duration of such protection. As far as the databases are not protected by copyright and if the complementary protection under § 1 *UWG* applies, the duration of protection under § 1 *UWG* should in any case not be longer than the duration under copyright, because the complementary protection under unfair competition law should not undermine copyright protection. The duration under § 1 *UWG* should rather be linked to the 'singularity in competition' *(`wettbewerbliche Eigenart')* of the database. With respect to computer programs, it has been proposed to acknowledge at least a duration which equals the period necessary for the amortisation of costs and, as a maximum, the whole period, in which the product is being marketed, to the corresponding copyright duration (see, with further details,

Lehmann (ed.), *Rechtsschutz und Verwertung von Computerprogrammen*, second edition, Köln 1993). Accordingly, further additions to the database might add to the period of protection.

(d) What is the scope of protection? How does it enable a datum or data to be protected?

The acts of reproduction and further exploitation of the database represent, under the above mentioned conditions (see *3(a)*), an infringement of § 1 *UWG*. The scope of protection extends to the 'singularity in competition'. The precise scope of protection has to be determined in every single case. However, as under copyright, data themselves are not protected (cf. in the context of computer programs Lehmann, *loc. cit.*, page 396, stating that all elements which are not protectable under copyright, such as the algorithm, ideas or a style, must remain free and may not be protected under unfair competition law).

(e) What limitations may apply to these rights? May the limitations be overridden by contract?

Since unfair competition law does not provide any property rights in a product but only protection against certain unfair acts, there are no 'limitations' of 'rights'. The protection is provided only if the above mentioned conditions are fulfilled.

II. Protection for copyright works included in databases

1. In what circumstances does a copyright work require to be authorised in order for it to be stored in a database? How far is the cataloguing of titles and other identifying data, abstracts and other summaries allowed without needing permission?

The storage of a protected work in a database is generally recognized to be a reproduction and therefore covered by the exclusive reproduction right. The limitations of § 53(2) CA, regarding certain forms of personal use, do not apply as regards the storage of works in databases, because the particular conditions of § 53(2) CA are not fulfilled. If an author has transferred *('eingeräumt')* his exclusive reproduction right without any specification, the contract will be interpreted as not covering the transfer of the exclusive right of reproduction in the form of electronic storage, since such storage represents a particular, separate type of use within the meaning of § 31(5) CA (see also, as far as this type of use is not yet known at the time of the transfer of the reproduction right, § 31(4) CA, according to which such transfer/*Einräumung* would not be valid). Thus, a new authorisation for the electronic storage would be necessary.

With respect to titles, other identifying data, abstracts and other summaries, the answer depends on their protectability under copyright. The general rules apply. The criteria mentioned above (see I.*2(c)*) have to be fulfilled. Data themselves are not protected by copyright, titles may be protected in principle, but rarely fulfil the requirements of a personal intellectual creation (see, for example, Loewenheim in:

Schricker, *loc. cit.*, § 2, nos. 35, 36). In fact, also abstracts and other summaries will rarely fulfil the conditions of a personal intellectual creation; if they reproduce important parts of the original text or constitute an adaptation thereof, they are protected, so that their cataloguing (understood as storage into the database) is subject to the exclusive reproduction right.

2. *What extractions of copyright data constitute infringements of economic rights?*

It is unclear what 'copyright data' means. Data themselves are not protected by copyright. In addition, it is not entirely clear what is meant by 'extraction'. The print-out or the copy on a disc or in the computer of copyright works constitutes a reproduction which is, in principle, subject to the exclusive right of the author. This exclusive right is, however, subject to a legal licence in favour of certain forms of private or personal use under § 53 CA. Accordingly, all acts of reproduction which do not fulfil the conditions of any exemption under § 53 CA constitutes infringements of the reproduction right, unless they are done with the authorization of the right owner.

3. *In what circumstances could extractions and manipulations of copyright data constitute a breach of moral rights? In practice, what contractual or other arrangements exist to allow material to be used without acknowledgement of authorship, or after alteration of content?*

The extraction of protected copyright works or parts thereof, understood as a reproduction, from a database does not infringe the moral rights of the author. The situation corresponds to the traditional situation of a person making a copy, for example from a book or a part of a book. Of course, the manipulation of protected works or parts thereof constitutes an infringement of the integrity right under § 14 CA if the manipulation amounts to a distortion or any other mutilation of the work which would jeopardize the author's legitimate intellectual or personal interests in the work. It depends on the single case, whether or not these requirements are fulfilled. No specific rules are provided for moral rights in the context of databases. This is also true for contractual or other arrangements as regards the use of works without acknowledgement of authorship, or after alteration of content. Under § 13 CA, regarding the acknowledgement of authorship, the author may decide whether the work is to bear his name or other designation. In other words, the right of authorship even includes the right to decide that the work is to be used without any name or author's designation.

According to the general rules, which apply also in the context of databases, the author may give his consent to alterations of the work. This follows from § 39(1) CA. However, if the author has generally agreed to any kind of alterations without any specification, he may still rely on his right of integrity under § 14 CA, which, as part of his moral rights, cannot be transferred. Accordingly, any contractual agreements concerning the permitted alterations should be sufficiently precise and concrete (see, for example, Dietz in: Schricker, *loc. cit.* § 39, nos. 8 *et seq.*).

III. Impact on database operations

1. Are there considerable numbers of database operators in Germany? How actively are they pressing the case for greater legal protection through copyright or other intellectual property protection? Will they be satisfied by legal reforms which may currently be under consideration?

In Germany there is a growing number of database operators, including for example *Juris* in the field of law and databases in the economic field, which is run by banks. However, they do not yet represent a strong block of lobbyists. Anyway, in view of the European Database Directive, which is expected in 1996, the need for further lobbying does not seem to be strong.

2. What other economic factors deserve to be given consideration in achieving adequate legal solutions to database problems?

Italy

A. Pojaghi

I. Protection of databases themselves

1. Does protection in any form turn on a distinction between electronic and non-electronic databases?

No, there is no distinction between electronic and non-electronic systems.

2. (a) Are databases treated as copyright? / (b) What type of work or other subject matter do they constitute? / (c) What test (of 'originality' or other characteristic) determines whether they qualify for copyright? / (d) Who is the initial owner of this copyright? What is its duration? Is the database a collective work? / (e) What scope of protection attaches to this copyright? How far can it be used to protect a datum or data incorporated in the base? / (f) What limitations may apply particularly to this copyright? Can these limitations be overridden by a contractual term? / (g) What additions to the database will constitute a second work?

At the present time, there is no specific protection for databases. Therefore, as long as they are not endowed with the indispensable requisite of creativity, it must be concluded that databases cannot be protected under copyright law, unless they can be included in the software protection. *De jure condendo*, and in accordance with the draft-Directive presently under study at the EU Commission, I believe that databases could, in the future, find protection in the framework of neighbouring rights (the so-called '*sui generis* right' of the mentioned draft-Directive).

3. (a) Are databases protected by trade secret, unfair competition and sui generis law? / (b) Is any such protection cumulative with copyright where the latter also applies? / (c) Who is entitled to the right of rights? How long do they endure? What further additions to the database would add to the period of protection? / (d) What is the scope of protection? How does it enable a datum or data to be protected? / (e) What limitations may apply to these rights? May the limitations be overridden by contract?

I believe that databases can be protected by unfair competition and unjust enrichment rules. Such protection is granted to the creator of the database from its realization. The right should be disposable or renouncable by contract.

II. **Protection for copyright works included in databases**

1. In what circumstances does a copyright work require to be authorised in order for it to be stored in a database? How far is the cataloguing of titles and other identifying data, abstracts and other summaries allowed without needing permission?

2. What extractions of copyright data constitute infringements of economic rights?

Under no circumstances may a copyright work be stored in a database without the authorization of the right owner, so that any unauthorized reproduction - even partial - of the work in the database constitutes a copyright violation.

3. In what circumstances could extractions and manipulations of copyright data constitute a breach of moral rights? In practice, what contractual or other arrangements exist to allow material to be used without acknowledgement of authorship, or after alteration of content?

A moral right violation, according to the general principles, takes place when the unauthorized utilization involves a prejudice to the honour or to the reputation of the author, such as in the case of unauthorized modification of the work.

III. **Impact on database operations**

1. Are there considerable numbers of database operators in your country? How actively are they pressing the case for greater legal protection through copyright or other intellectual property protection? Will they be satisfied by legal reforms which may currently be under consideration? / 2. What other economic factors deserve to be given consideration in achieving adequate legal solutions to database problems?

There are no precise elements to answer this question.

The Netherlands

P.B. HUGENHOLTZ

1. Introduction: the European Database Directive

The protection of databases figured prominently on the agenda of the 1989 ALAI Congress in Quebec, *'L'informatique et le droit d'auteur'*. An extensive Report on behalf of the Dutch Group was prepared for that occasion;[1] the present Report primarily serves as an update thereof.

The 1989 Dutch Report concluded with a brief reflection on the (then embryonic) proposal of the European Commission to extend protection to electronic databases containing material not protected by copyright. In 1996 the Commission's plan has finally materialized; on 11 March 1996 the European Database Directive was adopted by the Council and the European Parliament.[2]

The Directive provides for a two-tier protection scheme. In the first place, Member States are to grant copyright protection to *'databases which, by reason of the selection or arrangement of their contents, constitute the author's own intellectual creation...'*. In addition, the Directive provides for a *safety net* in the form of a *sui generis* right to prevent extraction or re-utilization.

Initially, the ideas of the Commission on database protection, which were presented in its *Green Paper on Copyright and the Challenge of Technology* of 1988,[3] did not receive the attention they deserved. At a hearing which took place in Brussels on 26-27 April 1990, interested parties were given the opportunity to express their views. During the hearing a general preference for a copyright approach was expressed. As the Commission reported in its *Follow-Up to the Green Paper*,[4] no support at all was given to a *sui generis* approach.

The opinions expressed at the hearing were, at that time, illustrative of legal thinking on the protection of databases in Europe. For many years, copyright protection was generally regarded as an appropriate instrument for protecting database producers. Perhaps, in retrospective, the European consensus was influenced by an amount of wishful thinking. As in the case of computer programs, copyright is *prima facie* a very attractive solution. Copyright offers worldwide protection on a non-discriminatory basis, for a relatively long period of time, on relatively 'soft' conditions.

Serious doubts about a copyright approach were first publicly expressed during the 1989 ALAI Congress in Quebec. As some commentators pointed out, database producers can derive only limited protection from copyright. From the database producer's perspective copyright protection is misdirected. Protection of an original *arrangement* of the data is weak, and, in practice, rather useless. Moreover, copyright protection based on original *selection* is at odds with the essential purpose of a database, which is to provide the user with a comprehensive set of data.[5] The Rapporteur-general to the Congress, Prof. Lucas, concluded: '*If copyright is to meet all the expectations of database producers, it must be capable of protecting the greatest possible number of producers and providing a decisive weapon by which to combat all parasitic behaviour. This dual result can not be guaranteed*'.[6]

In 1996 it has become quite clear that the critics were right and the consensus was ill-founded. As the *Van Dale v. Romme*[7] decision by the *Hoge Raad* (the Dutch Supreme Court), which will be discussed below, clearly illustrates, traditional copyright concepts can no longer be trusted as the appropriate instrument of database protection. The European Database Directive thus comes at a timely moment.

The Directive must be implemented into national law by the Member States of the European Union by 1 January 1998. Until that date, national disparity in the level of protection granted to database producers may persist. As will become clear from the present Report, copyright protection of databases in the Netherlands is quite different from the law in most other (European) countries. In fact, due to the ancient printer's right surviving in the present Act, database producers enjoy much better protection than elsewhere.

2. Copyright protection for non-original compilations

The Dutch Copyright Act (DCA)[8] is one of the oldest 'living' copyright laws in the world. It was adopted in 1912, the year the Netherlands adhered to the Berne Convention; hence the Act's official title *Auteurswet 1912*.[9] The Act has since been amended many times, but never thoroughly revised. Thus, the Act has retained its original structure, which has proven to be surprisingly flexible and modern. Even in the 'digital' 1990's, no need for thorough revision is currently felt.

The Act protects 'works of literature, science or art', as exemplified in the non-exhaustive list of work categories of article 10(1), which is reminiscent of article 2(1) BC. Article 10(2) clarifies that the Act protects '*every production in the domain of literature, science or art, whatever may be the mode or form of its expression*'. Of course, as in other Berne Convention countries, *originality* is a prerequisite to protection under Dutch copyright law. According to the *Hoge Raad*, a work must have an individual character and bear the personal imprint of its creator.[10]

Non-original writings

Departing from continental European *droit d'auteur* tradition, the Dutch Act also protects so called *non-original writings, i.e.* texts, compilations of data and other information products expressed in alphanumerical form, that do not meet the test of originality. This regime, the so-called *geschriftenbescherming* (protection of writings), is a remnant of an ancient 18th century printer's right, that still survives in the work catalogue of article 10(1): 'books, brochures, newspapers, magazines and *all other writings*'.

Over the years, the words 'all other writings' have caused lively debates in Dutch copyright circles. Eventually, in a series of three decisions concerning the protection of radio and television program listings, the *Hoge Raad* decided that these three words were to be taken literally. According to the Court, even the most banal or trivial writings are protected by copyright law, provided they have been published or are intended for publication.[11] Thus, in the Netherlands, producers of price lists,[12] telephone directories,[13] Top 40 lists,[14] address books,[15] arithmetic tables,[16] compendia,[17] cryptograms,[18] and all sorts of other compilations of facts[19] are safely protected by copyright. No copyright protection is awarded, however, to non-original compilations for strictly private or internal purposes.[20]

The copyright in non-original 'writings' is rather thin. Such writings are protected only against copying from the written document. Thus, the owner of the copyright in a protected writing does not acquire a monopoly in the information recorded therein.[21] Moreover, it remains unclear to what extent the copyright owner is protected against various forms of non-literal copying, *e.g.* re-arranging the data taken from a protected writing.[22]

Because of the absence of originality, proof of copying from non-original 'writings' is, sometimes, difficult to establish. In order to facilitate such a finding, database producers routinely include small errors or bogus data in their files. Due to the Dutch copyright in non-original 'writings' no need currently exists for additional protection under the general misappropriation doctrine, based on article 6:162 of the Dutch Civil Code. Even so, in a few cases lower courts have applied this doctrine to compilations of facts, such as a street guide and a television program guide.[23]

3. Original compilations: the *Van Dale v. Romme* case

The quasi-copyright in 'unpersonal writings' was not an issue in the case of *Van Dale v. Romme*, which was decided by the *Hoge Raad* applying traditional copyright principles.[24] The case involved massive copying from Van Dale's dictionary, *the* authoritative dictionary of the Dutch language. Copyright protection was sought for the approximately 230,000 alphabetically ordered headwords contained in the 1984 edition of the dictionary. A certain Rudolf Jan Romme, whose hobbies included the solving of crossword puzzles and the making of anagrams, had copied all of the Van Dale headwords on several computer disks, and rearranged the words into a database. In combination with a simple searching algorithm, Romme was now able to speed up, or practically automate, the process of solving these puzzles.

Van Dale was granted copyright protection in two instances (the District Court of Utrecht and the Amsterdam Court of Appeals). The *Hoge Raad*, however, reversed. According to the Court a collection of words will only be protected by copyright '*if it results from a selection process expressing the author's personal views*'. Since this rather severe test had not been applied by the Court of Appeal, the *Hoge Raad* granted the appeal and remanded the case to the The Hague Court of Appeal for further decision. Van Dale did eventually prevail; the Court of Appeal found sufficient personal expression in the selection process employed by the Van Dale lexicographers.[25]

Even so, the *Van Dale* decision clearly demonstrates that compilations of data or public domain materials will qualify as protected works of authorship only in special circumstances.[26] Databases are definitely not safely protected under traditional copyright doctrine. The test of originality, as applied by the *Hoge Raad*, will pose a major problem if the aim of the database producer is to gather or compile *all* data relevant to a certain subject.[27] Thus, in many cases a database will not qualify as an original work.

One of the many interesting aspects of the *Van Dale* decision is the standard of originality set by the *Hoge Raad*. In order for an object to qualify as a work of literature, science or art, *'it is necessary for it to have an original and individual character bearing the personal imprint of its maker'*, the Court declared. According to some commentators, this formula implies a higher standard of originality than previously applied by the Court. If this is true, Dutch law may be somewhat out of step with the emerging European norm of 'the author's own intellectual creation', as found in article 1(3) of the Software Directive and article 3(1) of the Database Directive.

4. Relevant exemptions

The Dutch Copyright Act provides for a number of exemptions (mostly in the form of legal licenses) which may be beneficial to database producers using pre-existing material.

Private use

The first provision that comes to mind is the private use exemption of article 16b DCA. In the case of 'writings' (*i.e.* works in alphanumerical form), the legal license is limited to the reproduction of *portions* of the work. Clearly, article 16b leaves ample room for the creation of all sorts of private databases.

Press reviews

Another exemption worth mentioning is article 15a DCA, allowing *(inter alia)* for the use of brief citations from daily or weekly newspapers and magazines in press reviews. Presumably, this provision will apply as well to a 'press review' communicated by an electronic database or an Internet Web Site.

News reports and clipping services

Electronic information providers will probably not be able to benefit from the 'news reports' exemption of article 15 DCA. The scope of this provision, which permits the free exchange of news items and articles, is expressly limited to the use in newspapers or in radio, television or cable transmissions.

The scope of the news reporting exemption (article 15) was discussed in the case of *Stichting Reprorecht v. NBLC*.[28] Defendant, the Dutch national organisation of public libraries, provided a clipping service for library users. Could the service qualify as an exempted 'newspaper' or 'magazine' within the meaning of article 15? Failing to find a guiding principle in article 10*bis*(1) of the Berne Convention, the Court turned to the legislative history of article 15. During the parliamentary debate the responsible ministers had stated repeatedly that clipping services would fall under the scope of this provision. This 'authentic' interpretation of the provision led the Court to hold that clipping services are, indeed, exempted under article 15. In a later decision by the District Court of The Hague,[29] the Court refused to treat a CD-ROM containing literary reviews 'clipped' from a large number of Dutch newspapers, as an exempted clipping service.

Government information

Government documents are important source materials for database producers. According to article 15b DCA, a work published by a government agency may be freely reproduced and republished, provided the copyright in the document is not expressly reserved. No copyright reservation is possible in respect of laws, ordinances, by-laws, governmental decrees, judicial and administrative decisions. According to article 11 DCA these documents are totally exempt from copyright.

Towards an open system of exemptions?

Of prime importance to the Dutch system of copyright exemptions is the *Hoge Raad*'s recent decision in *Dior v. Evora*.[30] Evora, a large retailer of perfumes and cosmetics, offered for sale parallel-imported Dior products. Because of the exhaustion rule the sale of these products could not be prevented. When Evora advertised its Dior products in an illustrated brochure, containing photographs of the products involved, Dior scented its chance. Dior claimed Evora's advertisements infringed the copyrights in the packing of the perfume bottles pictured in the brochure. Evora countered that the exhaustion rule must imply that the products may be displayed without authorization in advertisements. Moreover, Evora drew an analogy with the art catalogue exemption of article 23 DCA. Under this provision the owner of a work of art is free to reproduce it in a sales catalogue. The Dutch *Hoge Raad* observed that no existing copyright exemption could be applied to the facts of the case. The Court then held that there must be room to draw the borderlines of copyright *outside* the existing system of exemptions, on the basis of a balancing of interests similar to the rational underlying the existing exemption(s).

In an earlier decision by the District Court of Amsterdam[31] the Court ruled that, under certain circumstances, the copyright owner's exclusive rights might be set aside by the freedom of expressing and information guaranteed under article 10 of the European Convention on Human Rights, even if no statutory exemption were applicable.

5. Conclusion

As can be learned from the *Van Dale v. Romme* decision, producers of databases are by no means safely protected under traditional copyright concepts. Under the severe test of originality applied by the *Hoge Raad*, a database or other compilation will only rarely qualify as an original work of authorship. Fortunately, the existing Dutch Copyright Act provides for a 'safety net': the uniquely Dutch copyright in non-original writings, oft criticized in legal doctrine, but regularly applied in practice. Thus, a precursor of the 'extraction right' introduced by the Database Directive already exists in the Netherlands for more than a century. Will this ancient regime, a direct descendant from the printer's privileges of old, survive the new Directive? So far, the Directive has not yet generated any legislative activity in the Netherlands. If the implementation of the European Software Directive (Council Directive 91/52/ EEC)[32] is a valid precedent, the days of the *ancient regime* may be numbered. The amended Dutch law expressly excludes computer programs from the category of 'writings'.

According to the legislature, the Directive's originality requirement does not allow for copyright protection of non-original programs. Thus, producers of computer programs no longer may enjoy the 'quick and easy' (and, admittedly, somewhat dirty) protection provided by the quasi-copyright in non-original writings. It remains to be whether, in the near future, the same fate will await the producers of non-original compilations of data.

Footnotes

1. P.B. Hugenholtz, Report on the Netherlands, in: *L'informatique et le droit d'auteur*, Proceedings of the 1989 ALAI Congress in Quebec City, Cowansville (Que.), 1990, p. 390-397.
2. Directive 96/9/EC of the European Parliament and of the Council on the legal protection of databases, 11 March 1996, *OJ* No. L 77/20 of 27 March 1996.
3. Commission of the European Communities, *Green Paper on Copyright and the Challenge of Technology. Copyright Issues Requiring Immediate Action*, COM (88) 172 final, Brussels 7 June 1988.
4. Commission of the European Communities, *Follow-up to the Green Paper on Copyright and the Challenge of Technology*, COM (90) 584, Brussels 5 December 1990.
5. See *e.g.* Report on the Netherlands, *supra* note 1, at p. 396.
6. Proceedings ALAI Congress 1989, *supra* note 1, at p. 346. See also A. Lucas, *Le droit de l'Informatique*, Paris 1987, pp. 298-300.
7. Hoge Raad (Supreme Court of the Netherlands) 4 January 1991 *(Van Dale Lexicografie BV v. R.J. Romme)*, *Nederlandse Jurisprudentie (NJ)* 1991, 608; published in English in: E.J. Dommering & P.B. Hugenholtz (eds.), *Protecting Works of Fact*, Deventer/Boston 1991, pp. 93-96.
8. Act of 23 September 1912, *Staatsblad* 308; a full text of the Act (as amended to 1973) is published in *Copyright*, 1973, p. 181.
9. The Netherlands have ratified the Paris Act of the Berne Convention; Act of 30 May 1985, *Staatsblad* 1985, 306.
10. See generally F.W. Grosheide, Standards of qualification for the protection of literary and artistic property in Dutch copyright law, in: J.H.M. van Erp & E.H. Hondius (eds.), *Netherlands Reports for the Fourteenth International Congress of Comparative Law*, Athens 1994, The Hague 1995, p. 175.
11. Hoge Raad 17 April 1953 *(Radioprogramma)*, *NJ* 1954, 211; Hoge Raad 27 January 1961 *(Explicator)*, *NJ* 1962, 355; Hoge Raad 25 June 1965 *(Televizier)*, *NJ* 1966, 116.
12. District Court of Amsterdam 14 January 1934, *NJ* 1934, 254.
13. Hoge Raad 1 November 1937, *NJ* 1937, 1092.
14. President District Court of Amsterdam 10 February 1977, *Auteursrecht* 1977, p. 66.

15. President District Court of Arnhem 15 January 1947, *NJ* 1947, 474; President District Court of Arnhem 19 January 1990 *(Blauwe Kommunikatiegids)*, *Computerrecht* 1990/3, p. 136.
16. President District Court of Zwolle 15 March 1948, *NJ* 1949, 55.
17. District Court of Amsterdam 17 May 1989 *(De Toorts v. Oedip)*, *Computerrecht* 1990/3, p. 132.
18. President District Court of Zutphen 18 August 1992 *(Win v. De Denker)*, *NJ* 1994, 137.
19. President District Court of Amsterdam 16 April 1992, *Kort Geding* 1992, 176,
20. President District Court of Haarlem 5 December 1989 *(VNU v. Speets)*, *Computerrecht* 1990/3, p. 133.
21. Cf. President District Court of The Hague 5 November 1991 *(Subsidiedisk)*, *Computerrecht* 1992, p. 77.
22. See P.B. Hugenholtz, *Auteursrecht op informatie*, Deventer, 1989, at p. 117.
23. President Dictrict Court of Haarlem 23 December 1960, *Bijblad bij de Industriële Eigendom* 1962, p. 26; President Disrict Court of Amsterdam 25 June 1981 *(De Piraat)*, *Bijblad bij de Industriële Eigendom* 1983, p. 147.
24. *Supra* note 7.
25. Court of Appeals The Hague 1 April 1993, *NJ* 1994, 58.
26. Cf. President District Court of Breda 23 December 1992 *(Rode Scheen)*, *Informatierecht/AMI* 1993, p. 90.
27. President District Court of The Hague 5 November 1991 *(Subsidiedisk)*, *Computerrecht* 1992, p. 77. Cf. US decision *Feist Publications, Inc. v. Rural Telephone Service Co. Inc.*, 111 S.Ct. 1282 (1991).
28. Hoge Raad 10 November 1995, *Intellectuele Eigendom en Reclamerecht* 1995, 41.
29. District Court of The Hague 3 May 1995 *(LiteROM)*, *Informatierecht/AMI* 1995, p. 116.
30. Hoge Raad 20 October 1995, *Informatierecht/AMI* 1996, p. 51.
31. District Court of Amsterdam 19 January 1994 *(Boogschutter)*, *Informatierecht/AMI* 1994, 51.
32. Act of 7 July 1994, *Staatsblad* 1994, 521; entry into force on 1 September 1994.

Suisse

P. Brügger

I. Protection pour les banques de données

Dans l'énumération à l'article 2 de la Loi du 9 octobre 1992 sur le droit d'auteur et les droits voisins (LDA) des oeuvres protégées, nous ne trouvons pas les bases ou banques de données. Mais il n'est pas question que celles-ci - électroniques ou non-électroniques - soient attribuables aux créations littéraires ayant un caractère individuel et, plus précisément, à la définition à l'article 4 alinéa 1 LDA des recueils protégés. Le choix des données, la structuration, la disposition et/ou la réunion des informations singulières en paquets d'informations sont des éléments susceptibles de donner à un recueil une physionomie individuelle, ce qui permet de lui conférer dans l'ensemble la protection du droit d'auteur.

Si une base de données concrète peut être jugée comme objet protégé par le droit d'auteur, il s'en suit que l'entreprise privée ou l'entité publique qui l'a produite n'est pas originairement titulaire du droit d'auteur. Les droits appartiennent d'origine à l'individu ou au groupe d'individus qui a créé la banque de données. Le terme "oeuvre collective" n'existe pas dans la LDA de 1992, mais dans la plupart des cas, la banque de données sera créée par des coauteurs, qui ne peuvent - sauf convention contraire - utiliser la base de données que d'un commun accord.

La durée du droit d'auteur pour une banque de données est de 70 ans après le décès du dernier coauteur survivant.

Indépendamment du fait qu'une base de données peut être dans l'ensemble objet du droit d'auteur une donnée singulière, par exemple le résumé d'un roman peut être qualifié d'oeuvre par sa propre originalité.

Il semble que les conflits d'intérêts entre les producteurs de fonds documentaires informatisés et les concurrents et les utilisateurs concernent moins la question de la qualification (oeuvre: oui ou non) que celle de l'accès aux banques de données et du mode d'utilisation des bases, qui sont dirigés par les logiciels comme clés pour travailler sur ces fonds documentaires. A la condition qu'on accepte que des structures statiques d'information soient jugées comme parties de programmes protégés par le droit d'auteur, on atteint le but de la protection de ces trésors plus directement. Il fallait définir les structures d'une banque de données par recours à des langages spécialisés (langage objet) pour recevoir des composantes de programme protégé et - ce qui est essentiel - qui se laissent commercialiser en relation avec des banques de données ou des système de gestion intégrés des données.

Une banque de données peut constituer une oeuvre dérivée (article 3 LDA) si par exemple la structure ou le plan d'une banque de données préexistante reste reconnaissable dans son caractère individuel bien que la conception de la banque nouvelle manifeste une propre originalité.

En Suisse, nous ne connaissons pas (encore) de protection *sui generis* pour les banques de données. Le piratage d'une banque de données - peu importe qu'elle se présente comme un trésor électronique ou un recueil sur papier -, est en général l'acte d'un concurrent sur le marché. Ce vol pourrait être sanctionné par la Loi contre la concurrence déloyale (LCD) et être basé sur l'article 5 lettre c LCD qui dispose qu'agit *"de façon déloyale celui qui reprend grâce à des procédés techniques de reproduction et sans sacrifice correspondant le résultat de travail d'un tiers prêt à être mis sur le marché et l'exploite comme tel"*. En utilisant cet instrument de défense, le problème primordial peut être la charge de la preuve que la copie est réalisée "par moyens techniques de reproduction".

II. Protection pour des oeuvres intégrées dans des banques de données

L'intégration d'une oeuvre protégée par le droit d'auteur dans une banque de données - soit qu'elle est qualifiée comme recueils selon l'article 4 LDA ou comme oeuvre dérivée selon l'article 3 LDA - n'est licite qu'avec le consentement de l'auteur, parce que l'auteur a le droit exclusif de décider *"si, quand et de quelle manière l'oeuvre peut être utilisée pour la création d'une oeuvre dérivée ou être incorporée dans un recueil'* (article 11 alinéa 1 lettre b LDA). Il semble utile dans ce contexte de souligner que selon le droit suisse, le multimédia peut être compris comme création dérivée. Selon l'argumentation de Jaques de Werra qui se réfère à Lucas & Lucas (*Traité de la propriété littéraire et artistique*, Paris 1994, p. 200): *"Le multimédia offre des possibilités d'individualisation qu'une anthologie de poèmes sous la forme d'un simple livre n'est pas en mesure d'offrir. Il ne se limite donc pas à simplement juxtaposer des oeuvres préexistantes, mais leur donne un nouvel attrait par les moyens de l'informatique. Dès lors, il sera en principe susceptible d'acquérir le statut d'oeuvre dérivée"* (Le multimédia en droit d'auteur, *RSPI* 1995, p. 240).

Une simple composition alphabétisée de données "non-oeuvres" ne suffirait pas pour atteindre des critères exigés pour la protection par le droit d'auteur. Le seul critère du choix ou de la sélection de données conduit à écarter du bénéfice de la protection par exemple les terminologies exhaustives, conséquence paradoxale dont le but est de permettre la rémunération des investissements des producteurs. Mais on peut conclure que sur la base de l'article 5 lettre c LCD (précité), les banques de données se voient appliquer un droit d'empêcher l'"extraction" déloyale des citations de contenus à des fins commerciales.

L'article 11 alinéa 2 LDA est un instrument de protection du droit moral: *"Même si un tiers est autorisé par un contrat ou par la loi à modifier l'oeuvre où à l'utiliser pour créer une oeuvre dérivée, l'auteur peut s'opposer à toute altération de l'oeuvre portant atteinte à sa personnalité"*. Même si un auteur a cédé ses droits pour rassembler ses poèmes d'amour dans une banque de données, il peut s'opposer à leur intégration dans une banque de données pornographiques. Il se justifie que pour la banques de données ainsi que pour les multimédias, le droit à l'intégrité subisse quelques *"restrictions de manière à faciliter leurs modifications et leurs mises à jour ainsi que l'élimination d'éventuels bogues"* (voir J. de Werra, *op. cit.,* p. 245 avec références).

III. Impact sur la gérance des banques de données

Nous ne disposons pas de statistiques valables sur les gérants des banques de données. Leur nombre ne semble pas très considérable, mais il est certainement croissant. Un lobbying de ces cercles demandant une adaptation de la législation sur les bases de données n'est pas encore très actifs. Mais il est fort probable que la Suisse suive la ligne de la Directive de l'Union européenne concernant la protection juridique des bases de données. Les voix qui demandent une réglementation légale expresse pour les bases de données et le multimédia se font de plus en plus entendre. Si l'on se rend compte que bientôt tout le monde pourra se servir d'archives électroniques universelles, les demandes impératives concernant un barème de tarifs particuliers pour le multimédia, *"de manière à permettre aux producteurs de monter des projets financièrement équilibrés"* (J. de Werra, *op. cit.,* p. 246) semblent justifiées.

United States of America*

M.A. LEAFFER

I. Protection of databases themselves

1. *Does protection in any form turn on a distinction between electronic and non-electronic databases?*

No.

2. *(a) Are databases treated as copyright?*

Yes, if original. (See response in I.2(c) below.)

(b) What type of work or other subject matter do they constitute?

Literary work, compilation, collective work.

(c) What test (of 'originality' or other characteristic) determines whether they qualify for copyright?

A database must meet the standard of originality. The standard is: does the database as a whole manifest originality in the selection, ordering, or arrangement, of the data? (17 USC § 101.) Industrious labour, *i.e.* 'sweat of the brow' in collecting the data, does not constitute protectible authorship under copyright. See *Feist Publications Inc. v. Rural Telephone Service Company Inc.*, 499 US 340 (1991).

(d) Who is the initial owner of this copyright?

The author or the employer of a work made for hire are the initial owners of copyright. (17 USC § 201(a)(b).)

What is its duration?

Life plus 50 years. If the database is an anonymous, pseudonymous, or work made for hire the duration is 100 from creation or 75 years from publication whichever is less. (17 USC § 302(a)(b)(c).)

---

*) *Editorial note:* Prof. Leaffer's National Report consists of two parts; his answers to the questionnaire and a paper titled *'Database protection in the United States'*. These contributions are included in this order.

Is the database a collective work?

Yes, a database can be a collective work if separate and independent databases, each of which constitute independently copyrightable works in themselves, are assembled into a collective whole. In US law, the term compilation includes collective works. (17 USC § 101.)

[No (e) - ed.]

(f) What limitations may apply particularly to this copyright?

There are no limitations to copyrightability of databases except that they must meet the originality requirement stated above. Facts *per se* are not copyrightable. See response in I.*2(c)* above.

Can these limitations be overridden by a contractual term?

Contractual provisions can be enforced between the contracting parties as to the use of and access to the subject matter contained in a database. However, there exits a substantial degree of uncertainty as the state of the law. For example, in *ProCD Inc. v. Zeidenberg*, 908 F. Supp. 640 (W.D. Wis.), rev'd 86 F.3d 1447 (7th Cir. 1996), the District Court held that state contract claims for violation of a shrinkwrap license were unenforceable on two grounds: (1) the contract was invalid and (2) the contract was pre-empted by federal copyright law. The court reversed on both grounds holding that the shrinkwrap license constituted a valid contract and that the Copyright Act did not pre-empt the contractual terms.

(g) What additions to the database will constitute a second work?

A database can be considered a derivative work if new authorship is added to pre-existing database as to the selection, ordering, and arrangement of the material added.

***3.** (a) Are databases protected by trade secret, unfair competition or sui generis law?*

Databases can be protected by trade secret and unfair competition law. No *sui generis* law protects databases.

(b) Is any such protection cumulative with copyright where the latter also apply?

Protection under trade secret, unfair competition law or both can be cumulative with copyright protection.

(c) Who is entitled to the right or rights?

The owner of the database or his exclusive licensee can enforce these rights.

How long do they endure?

Rights under trade secret and unfair competition law have no fixed duration.

What further additions to the database would add to the period of protection?

If new authorship were added to the database and a derivative work were created, the term of protection for the new authorship would be based on the durational terms for copyright set forth above. See response to I.*2(d)* above.

(d) What is the scope of protection? How does it enable a datum or data to be protected?

In general, the data or datum *per se* cannot be protected under copyright law. See response to I.*2(c)* above. However, data may be protected under trade secret and unfair competition law.

(e) What limitations may apply to these rights? May the limitations be overridden by contract?

The scope of trade secret and unfair competition law may be overridden by contract but would only be effective as to the parties to the contract. But see response to I.*2(e)* above.

II. **Protection for copyrighted works included in databases**

1. In what circumstances does a copyrighted work require to be authorized in order for it to stored in a database?

To store a copyrighted work in a database, one must obtain permission form the copyright owner.

How far is the cataloguing of titles and other identifying data, abstracts and other summaries allowed without needing permission?

The cataloging of titles generally would not require permission because titles *per se* are not protected under US law. A person may abstract another's work if the abstract does not constitute an abridgement of the pre-existing work. An abridgement would be considered a derivative work, and as such, the author of the abridgement would need permission of the owner of the pre-existing work to avoid copyright infringement.

2. What extractions of copyright data constitute infringements of economic rights?

503

Copying individual data does not constitute copyright infringement. Infringement consists in copying the original authorship in the selection, ordering and arrangement of the data as a whole. See response in I.2*(c)* above.

> **3.** *In what circumstances could extractions and manipulations of copyright data constitute a breach of moral rights?*

Under US law, databases do not enjoy moral rights protection.

> *In practice, what contractual or other arrangements exist to allow material to be used without acknowledgment of authorship, or after alteration of content?*

Nothing prevents the parties from entering into contractual arrangements to allow the material to be used or altered.

III. Impact on database operations

> **1.** *Are there considerable numbers of database operators in your country?*

Yes.

> *How actively are they pressing the case for greater legal protection through copyright or other intellectual property protection?*

Some would like special recognition of protection of data in electronic form because of the ease of copying and disseminating works in electronic form. Others would like protection for the industrious labour involved in creating a database. One trade group is working on a proposal to modify US law by providing databases *sui generis* protection similar to the proposed database directive of the European Union. See legislation introduced before the US Congress proposing a 25-year term of *sui generis* protection unfair extraction: *Database Investment and Intellectual Property Antipiracy Act*, H.R. 3531 104th Cong. 2d Sess (30 May 1996). Also the US has proposed similar protection before WIPO in conjunction with the deliberations on the Berne Protocol: see *Proposal of the United States of America on* Sui Generis *Protection of Databases* of 20 May 1996 (Committee of Experts on a Possible Protocol to the Berne Convention, Sixth Session Geneva, 22-24 May 1996). The provisions have been incorporated in large part into the *Basic Proposal for the Substantive Provisions of the Treaty on Intellectual Property in Respect of Databases in Conjunction with the Diplomatic Conference on Certain Copyright and Neighboring Rights Questions* taking place in Geneva, 2-20 December 1996.

> *Will they be satisfied by legal reforms which may currently be under consideration?*

Certain legal reforms are not directed explicitly to databases but affect all copyright owners whose works are distributed on electronic networks. *Intellectual Property and the National Information Infrastructure: The Report of the Working Group on*

Intellectual Property Rights (1995) has recommended that the Copyright Act be amended to expressly recognize that copies or phonorecords can be distributed to the public by transmission and that such transmissions fall within the exclusive distribution right of the copyright owner. This proposed amendment would affect the scope of protection for all copyrighted works but would have particular importance to owners of databases who have a special interest in obtaining the strongest possible protection of their works in electronic networks.

> **2.** *What other economic factors deserve to be given consideration in achieving adequate legal solutions to database problems?*

Some owners of databases would like to see the following bases of protection: (a) whether databases should be given *sui generis* protection rather than under copyright law; (b) whether the industrious labour expended in amassing a database should be protected absent originality in the selection ordering and arrangement of the data; (c) whether databases in electronic form, or, for that matter, any public domain work placed into electronic form should be given protection under copyright law or *sui generis* protection.

Database protection in the United States

1. Introduction

Electronic databases and other compilations of factual material are indispensable to the American economy on the verge of the new century. These informational products are an essential tool for improving productivity, advancing education, and promoting science. They are the linchpin of a dynamic commercial information industry in the United States.

Creating commercially significant databases often requires a substantial financial investment. Until recently the database owner was able to protect his work more or less adequately under traditional copyright principles, but several legal and technological developments threaten the incentives for investment to create these valuable informational products.

From a technological standpoint, copying factual material from a database is cheaper than ever through digital technology in widespread use. In cyberspace, the database has less and less control over his work where copying occurs ever more cheaply and with low visibility. In addition, the legal developments in the United States have been less than hospitable in extending broad protection to the database owner. On the legal front, the Supreme Court decision in *Feist v. Rural Telephone* denied copyright protection to databases not manifesting originality in the traditional copyright terms. This landmark case required that a databases cannot be protected on amount of value of the investment expended in creating it. Rather, a claim for copyright in a database must be based on originality in the selection, arrangement or organization of the database. Database owners were hardly more successful in applying other legal theories, such as contract law, to protect their works. Recent cases have wavered on the ability of database owners to protect their works under contract principles.[1]

Against this background, the United States has taken initiatives both nationally and internationally to protect database owners against piracy and unfair competition. On the national scene, legislation has been proposed for a *sui generis* protection of databases similar to the provisions of the European Database Directive.[2] On the international level, the United States have proposed similar *sui generis* protection of databases before the Committee of Experts on a Possible Protocol to the Berne Convention.[3] This proposal in turn was incorporated in large part into the *Basic Proposal for the Substantive Provisions of the Treaty on Intellectual Property in Respect of Databases in conjunction with the Diplomatic Conference on Certain Copyright and Neighbouring Rights Questions* (taking place in Geneva, 2-20 December 1996).[4] This paper will focus on the United States initiatives to provide enhanced protection for databases both nationally and internationally. To properly understand the need for these initiatives, one must consider the current state of database protection in the United States.

2. The current status of database protection in the US

Under US law, databases, whether in electronic or other form, are protected under copyright law as a literary work.[5] In addition, the 1976 Act specifically protects compilations, as a category of copyrightable subject matter that includes databases. Compilations are defined under the Act as: *a work formed by the collection and assembling of pre-existing materials or of data that are selected, coordinated, or arranged in such a way that the resulting work as a whole constitutes an original work of authorship. The term 'compilation' includes collective works.*[6]

Their duration is life of the author plus fifty years.[7] Because of their nature, databases are often created by more than one author, raising problems of joint work authorship.[8] In addition, databases are created in a business setting by persons hired specifically to gather and organize information to create databases. Accordingly, work made for hire issues arise when databases are at issue. Most important, a database is protected as for any copyrighted work must meet the standard of originality.

Copyright in a compilation consists of the original elements an author has added to the assembled pre-existing materials or data. Compilations vary widely in original authorship. Some contain facts plus extensive authorial analysis and judgment in the selection and organization of the pre-existing data: other compilations contain nothing more than an arrangement of facts such as certain databases. For all varieties of compilations, however, copyright in the compilation extends not to the pre-existing materials or data themselves, but to the author's judgment in selecting and arranging the disparate materials or data and organizing them into a unified work. This fundamental principle about the requisite standard for copyright protection was raised to the level of a constitutional requirement in *Feist Publications Inc. v. Rural Telephone Service Co.*[9]

3. **The originality requirement under *Feist* and its aftermath**

Compilations, particularly those which assemble public domain materials, reflect basic tensions in copyright policy. Modern copyright law has had difficulty with that are low in personal authorship even though the works themselves may be high in commercial value.[10] Suppose A, without doing independent research, appropriates the factual information contained in a telephone book or a catalogue produced at great expense by B. Suppose also that A has not taken the original elements added to the public domain, such as A's subjective arrangement or organization of the compilation. Can B be protected under copyright law from A's total appropriation of A's hard work in gathering the facts? Under traditional copyright law principles, facts *per se* are not protectable. Nevertheless, some courts have stretched copyright law to protect a compilation from similar free riders like A who have appropriated the fruits of another's labour. To limit protection to the expressive elements in this instance would seem to confer inadequate protection a compilation containing little expression.[11]

The application of the standard of originality had been a question of controversy until the Supreme Court resolved a serious split in the Circuits in *Feist v. Rural Telephone Service.*[12] As indicated above, one line of cases protected a database if the creator manifested industrious labour in collecting and arranging the data. For these courts, substantial investment supplied the necessary degree of original authorship to meet the standard of protection. Under this 'sweat-of-the-brow' doctrine infringement took place when a third party appropriated a substantial amount of the data for incorporation into a competing work. Under this 'sweat-of-the-brow' theory, copyright law was transformed into a more generalized theory of unfair competition, sometimes called the 'misappropriation' doctrine.[13]

The other line of cases would only protect a database that manifested a degree of original authorship in the selecting or arranging the data. Because facts *per se* are not protected, no amount of industrious labour could suffice for copyright protection. And an action for infringement could not be sustained, even if a third party wholly appropriated the database. Under this infringement could only take place if a third party appropriated the originality in the selection, or arrangement of the data.[14]

The *Feist* case decided by the Supreme Court was a resounding decision in favour of the later view. The defendant in Feist specialized in publishing phone books for an entire geographic area. In developing the directory, Feist would license the listing from local phone companies. Plaintiff was one of those companies and refused to license the local listings in its book to Feist, who proceeded to use the listing without consent. The Supreme Court rejected plaintiff's claim of copyright infringement because the telephone listings at issue were not original. The Court stated that originality is a constitutional requirement that requires 'independent creation' plus a 'modicum of creativity'. Under this view, facts are uncopyrightable because they do not 'owe their origin to an act of authorship'. According to the Court, a compilation can be copyrightable if their is a minimum degree of originality in the selection arrangement or organization of the facts. Although originality is not a stringent requirement, plaintiff's alphabetically arranged telephone book was devoid of the slightest trace of originality as so defined.

Feist raises many questions even after it laid to rest copyright protection based on industrious authorship. First, what constitutes original authorship in the selection and arrangement of facts? Second, even if a compilation is original from that standpoint, at what point does infringement occur when another has made use of the facts in copyrightable compilation? A good example of these problems occurred in *Key v. Chinatown Today Publishing Enterprises,*[15] decided shortly after *Feist.* In *Key,* a lower court upheld copyright protection of plaintiff's business directory for the New York Chinese community, but found no infringement in defendant's copying which made up of 75 per cent of the listings. The court found it significant that defendant had only 28 categories in his book as compared with 260 categories in plaintiff's directory. Thus, it makes no difference what percentage or how many facts are taken from the plaintiff's work so long as the compiler does not appropriated the copyrightable selection and arrangement of the prior work. In *Bellsouth Advtg. & Pub. Corp. v. Donnelley Information Pub. Inc.,*[16] another Yellow Pages case, defendant copied into a computer both the directory's listings and the classification headings. The Court did not find sufficient originality in the structure of the compilation headings to be protectable. Although more intricate than Feist's alphabetical ordering of the White Pages, one could characterize plaintiff's Yellow Page classifications as obvious, typical, or commonplace. As the Court stated: *'Bellsouth can claim no copyright in the idea of dividing churches by denomination or attorneys by area of speciality'.*[17]

A compilation may display sufficient originality for copyright purposes if the work as a whole constitutes either original selection or original arrangement. Thus, a work may be arranged in a commonplace way (*e.g.* an alphabetical arrangement of a telephone book), but may nevertheless be copyrightable if the data are selected in an original way. For an example of what constitutes original selection, one might consider the pre-*Feist* case *Eckes v. Card Prices Update,*[18] in which a selection of 5,000 premium baseball cards from approximately 18,000 cards was held copyrightable. Here, the selection of data required creative rather than merely mechanical decisions of inclusion.[19]

Sometimes a court has found original selection and arrangement in the judgment used in the kinds of facts at issue. In *CCC Information Services Inc. v. MacLean Hunter Market Reports Inc.,*[20] the plaintiff published a used car valuation guide known as the *Red Book*. CCC copied a substantial portion of MacLean Hunter's guides into its database. The lower court held that the *Red Book* had no protectable selection, coordination and arrangement; that its values were unprotectable facts. The Court of Appeals reversed. It stressed that the requirement for originality was quite modest and that the district court was simply mistaken in analogizing the valuations in the *Red Book* to the phone numbers in *Feist*. The *Red Book* valuations were not facts but predictions by the *Red Book* editors of future prices, based on numerous data sources, as well as their professional judgment and expertise. *In sum*, the valuations were original creations. Moreover, the Court found that the selection and arrangement of data showed sufficient originality to be protectable. For example, the division of the market into geographic regions, the selection of optional features for inclusion, adjustment for mileage in 5,000 mile increments, and he selection of number of years models for inclusion.[21] *CCC* illustrates that the courts are willing to entertain originality when the selection, arrangement and organization of facts meets a minimum threshold of judgment and discretion.[22] Alternatively, where the selection, arrangement and organization of the facts is rote and mechanical, the work will not meet the standard of originality under *Feist*.[23]

Unfortunately, for enterprising compilers seeking copyright protection, the most useful ordering systems for compilations would not meet *Feist* criteria for originality. By contrast, highly original systems of arrangement often are of limited commercial value. For example, an alphabetical list of lawyers might be highly useful and valuable but uncopyrightable from the standpoint of arrangement. On the other hand, a list of local lawyers arranged and selected according to the size of their libraries or the square footage in their waiting rooms may contain sufficient originality in arrangement and selection for copyright protection. But who needs such a compilation? Accordingly, one might expect the issue of originality in compilations to arise with greater frequency over the selection rather than the arrangement of the facts or data.

4. Protection of databases under contract law

If certain non-original databases can no longer be protected under copyright, is there an alternative body of law under which they could be protected? In this regard, database owners have looked to contract law as a non-copyright means by which protection could be sought. The latest battleground has concerned the efficacy of the shrinkwrap license to circumvent the copyright problems.[24] The results have been less than satisfactory because of the legal uncertainty surrounding this mode of protection. The issues have concerned whether the shrinkwrap licence is inherently valid under contract principles[25] or whether it is invalidated by being pre-empted under the Copyright Act.[26]

ProCD v. Zeidenberg[27] involved both these issues, illustrating the uncertainty about protecting software products through contract law, specifically by the shrinkwrap licence. In *ProCD*, plaintiff produced a comprehensive national directory of residential and business listings on CD-ROM disks. Each disk contained both telephone listings and a software program used to access, retrieve, and download data. The sale of the product included a licence agreement contained in the user guide which limited data to personal use only. Defendant downloaded the data, added some of his own data, and eventually made his database available to users on the Internet. He had about 20,000 hits a day. Plaintiff sued for both copyright infringement and breach of contract. The District Court sided with the defendant on all grounds. As for the breach of contract issue, the court sided with the defendant based on the *Feist* case. It found that the telephone listings were not arranged in an original manner and were not copyrightable. As to the copyright claims, the court held that the shrinkwrap licence was not valid because its terms were not available for review, there was no assent to the terms of the contract.[28] Moreover, even if the contract was a good contract under traditional contract law, it was pre-empted under section 301(a) of the Copyright Act.[29] Section 301(a) of the Copyright Act pre-empts any legal or equitable rights under state law that are equivalent to any of the exclusive rights within the general scope of copyright. To allow a breach of contract claim under state law would allow parties to circumvent copyright law and its policies.

The Court of Appeals for the Seventh Circuit reversed the lower court on both the contract and pre-emption grounds. It accepted the District Court's ruling (based on *Feist*) that ProCD's telephone listing database could not be copyrighted, as the information contained within the database was not sufficiently 'original' but could nonetheless be protected by the shrinkwrap licence. Here, the Seventh Circuit focused on the more restrictive limitations imposed on the purchasers of the SelectPhone database through the shrinkwrap licence agreement. It held that shrinkwrap licences are enforceable unless, as with ordinary contracts, their terms violated a rule of positive law or were found to be unconscionable. The Court indicated that one cannot agree to hidden terms, but a term on the outside of the package which defendant agreed to with his purchase was that the transaction was subject to a licence.[30] The Seventh Circuit also reversed the District Court on the pre-emption issue. In so doing, it joined the Fourth, Fifth, and Eighth Circuits that have held that rights created by contract are not equivalent to any of the exclusive rights within the general scope of copyright.[31] The Court stated *'just as section 301(a) does not itself interfere with private transactions in intellectual property, so it does not prevent states from respecting those transactions'*. While some application of contract law could interfere with the goals of copyright law and therefore come within the domain of section 301(a) but the *'general enforcement of shrinkwrap licences of the kind before us does not create such interference'*.[32]

5. Toward a *sui generis* protection of databases

Despite the database owner's victory in *ProCD*, the scope of protection for non-original databases is fraught with uncertainty and the case law is hardly consistent on the questions of contract validity of shrinkwrap licences. Similarly, the courts are split on whether the Copyright Act pre-empts a contact that would protect a work that falls short of *Feist* orginality. The reaction to this legal uncertainty has taken place on two fronts: legislation to provide a *sui generis* protection of databases[33] and a proposal before WIPO in conjunction with Berne Protocol hearings for similar protection[34] later to be incorporated into a Draft Treaty on databases.[35]

a. *The WIPO Proposal and the Draft Treaty*

On 20 May 1996, the US delegation presented the Director General of WIPO a proposal for the *sui generis* protection of databases, most of which was later incorporated in a Draft Treaty on Databases for the Diplomatic Conference on Certain Copyright and Neighbouring Rights Questions in Geneva, 2-20 December 1996. The language of the Draft Treaty resembles the European Database Directive with certain variations. For example, the Treaty would confer a *sui generis* protection of databases, regardless of their form, representing qualitatively or quantitatively significant investment in their creation.[36] This *sui generis* protection shall exist without prejudice to copyright and other related rights.[37] Under the Treaty, two alternatives are provided as the term of protection: a 25 year alternative proposed by the United States, and 15 year alternative proposed by the European Union (identical to the Database Directive's term of protection). This is obviously a major difference, and it will be left to the Diplomatic Conference to resolve this issue.[38] The term of protection can be extended if significant changes are added to the database. If such changes occur, the database shall qualify the database for its own term of protection.[39] Certain works are specifically excluded from protection. The Treaty would not allow protection of computer programs, including those used in the manufacture and maintenance of a database.[40] The Treaty confers exclusive rights on the owner of the database. The maker of a database shall have the right to authorize or prohibit acts of extraction, or utilization of its contents.[41] In addition to these provisions, the Treaty contains a provision that shall make it unlawful to use or supply devices that would bypass mechanisms (such as encryption techniques) that inhibit the unauthorized exercise of rights.[42]

b. *Domestic legislation: Database Investment and Intellectual Property Anti-piracy Act*

In conjunction with the WIPO proposals, legislation has been drafted to confer a *sui generis* protection of databases under US law. The Database Investment and Intellectual Property Antipiracy Act[43] would prohibit the misappropriation of valuable commercial databases by free-riding competitors. The new federal law is not intended for incorporation into the Copyright Act but is based on the power of Congress under the Commerce Clause of the Constitution. It is modeled on the law of unfair competition and draws heavily on the language of the European Directive. The principal terms of protection are similar to the WIPO Proposal and the Draft Treaty, including the same definitions and the 25 year protection.

The motivation for this legislation is the recognition that databases are valuable to the US economy but are inadequately protected under US law and are progressively threatened by digital copying technology in cyberspace or elsewhere. As discussed above, not all commercially significant databases will meet the originality standard under *Feist*, while contract law provides an imperfect if not uncertain mode of protection. Other motivation for the legislation came from the European Union Directive on legal protection of databases. Among other things, the Directive, in creating a new non-copyright form of legal protection, would deny this protection to

511

US originated databases unless the United States is found to offer 'comparable' protection to European databases. Thus when fully implemented, in 1998, the European Directive could place US firms at an enormous competitive disadvantage throughout the entire European market.

The bill maintains existing protections for databases afforded by copyright and contract rights and is intended to supplement these rights, not replace them.[44] Taking its model from the European Union Directive, this legislation would protect databases manifesting a substantial investment from acts of unfair extraction by others.[45] Its provisions are aimed at actual or threatened competitive injury from the misappropriation of databases or their contents, not at non-competitive uses. The bill contains specific exemptions for use of insubstantial portions of databases.[46] Unlike the European Directive, the proposed legislation confers a twenty-five year term of protection measured from date when first made available to the public or the date when it was first placed into public use, whichever is the earliest. Changes of commercial significance to a database will make the resulting database subject to its own twenty-five year term as measured above.[47]

Much of the bill follows closely the non-copyright provisions of the NII Copyright Protection Act of 1995, introduced in the Fall of 1994.[48] In addition to the substantive provisions, the bill includes protection against technological means to circumvent database protection systems,[49] and would render illegal the knowing removal or alteration of database management information.[50]

6. Conclusion

Protection of databases under US law exists in an uncomfortable state of ambiguity. Under US law, the contours of copyright protection remain unclear and effective protection of databases under contract law finds the courts in disarray. This has led to initiatives for specialized legislation on the national scene and support of *sui generis* protection under treaty deliberations. Both these proposals incorporate stronger substantive protection of databases against unfair use, hitherto unknown in US law. In addition, these proposals both incorporate for the first time the unlawful importation, manufacture or distribution of protection-defeating devices. From a practical standpoint, it may turn out that this technologically oriented measure may be prove to be the most significant innovation for database owners in effectively protecting their works against acts of copying and unfair competition.

Footnotes

1. See *ProCd Inc. v. Zeidenberg*, 908 F. Supp. 640 (W.D. Wis), rev'd and remanded, 86 F. 3d 1447 (7th Cir. 1996).
2. See Database Investment and Intellectual Property Antipiracy Act, H.R 3531 104th Cong. 2d sess., 1280 (1996). *(Reproduced in Appendix I, hereunder.)*
3. *Proposal of the the United States of America on Sui Generis Protection of Databases*, Committee of Experts on a Possible Instrument for the Protection of the Rights of Performers and Producers of Phonograms, Sixth Session, Geneva, 22-24 May 1996 *(reproduced in Appendix II)*; Basic Proposal for

the Substantive Provisions of the Treaty on Intellectual Property in Respect of Databases in conjunction with the Diplomatic Conference on Certain Copyright and Neighbouring Rights Questions in Geneva, 2-20 December 1996. *(Reproduced in Appendix III.)*
4. See WIPO Document CRNR/DC/6, 30 August 1996.
5. In passing the 1976 Copyright Congress confirmed the application of the the law to compilations and databases. The House Report on the Act states: *'the term 'literary works' does not connote any criterion of literary merit or qualitative value: it includes catalogues, directories, and similar factual, reference, or instructional works and compilations of data. It also includes computer databases, and computer programs to the extent that they incorporate authorship in the programmer's expression of original ideas, as distinguished from the ideas themselves'*. H.R. Rep. No. 1476, 94th Cong., 2d sess. 54 (1976).
6. 17 USC § 101 (compilation). Compilations are similar to another category of copyrightable subject matter called the 'derivative work' which is a work based upon one or more pre-existing works, such as a translation, musical arrangement, etc.; see 17 USC § 101 (derivative work). Compilations and derivative works differ in one significant way. Unlike the derivative work author, the creator of a compilation does not recast, reform, or change the underlying materials but rather compiles (or assembles) them in his own manner.
7. Or the alternative duration for anonymous, pseudonymous or works made for hire of 75 years from publication or 100 years from creation, whichever is less.
8. 17 USC § 101 (joint work).
9. 499 US 340 (1991).
10. For a development of this idea see Jane C. Ginsburg, Creation and Commercial Value: Copyright Protection for Works of Information, 90 *Colum. L. Rev.* 1865 (1990).
11. The expansive view is represented by *Leon v. Pacific Telephone & Telegraph Co.*, 91 F2d 484 (9th 1937).
12. 111 S. Ct. 1282 (1991).
13. See *e.g. Schroeder v. William Morrow & Co.*, 566 F.2d 3 (7th Cir. 1977); *Hutchinson Telephone Co. v. Fronteer Dirctory Co.*, 770 F.2d 128 (8th Cir. 1985); *Leon v. Pacific Telephone and Telegraph Co.*, 91 F.2d 484 (9th Cir. 1937).
14. See *e.g. Financial Information, Inc. v. Moody's Investors Service*, 808 F. 2d 204 (2d Cir. 1986), cert. denied, 484 US 820 (1987); *Southern Bell Telephone & Telegraph Co. v. Associated Telephone Directory*, 756 F.2d 801 (11th Cir. 1985); *Eckes v. Card Prices Update*, 736 F.2d 859 (2d Cir. 1984).
15. 945 F2d 509 (2d Cir. 1991).
16. 999 F.2d 1436 (11th Cir. 1993).
17. *Id.* at 1444.
18. 736 F.2d 859 (2d Cir. 1984).
19. Compare *Financial Information v. Moody's Investors Service*, 751 F.2d 501 (2d Cir. 1984) (compilation of bond redemptions culled from bond tombstones in newspapers not copyrightable because no selection was involved in gathering the information).
20. 44 F.3d 61 (2d Cir. 1994).
21. *Id.* at 1188.
22. See *e.g. Mason v. Montgomery Data*, Inc. 967 F.2d 135 (5th Cir. 1992) (plaintiff's maps were original compilations because the mapmaker made selections as to which sources of information to use and how to depict that information), *Marshal & Swift v. BS&A Software*, 871 F. Supp. 952 (W.S. Mich. 1994) (plaintiff's estimates in evaluating property were copyrightable were the result of a creative process that entailed judgment and selection).
23. See *e.g. Mid America Title Co. v. Kirk*, F.3d (7th Cir. 1995) (the selection and arrangement process in the legal description fo certain property, information about mortgages, taxes, and other encumberances was too rote and mechanical to qualify as original).
24. Software companies have included such agreements, commonly known as 'shrinkwrap licences', with their products since the advent of the mass market software.The term 'shrinkwrap' refers to the transparent plastic in which mass market software is encased. (See Mark A. Lemley, Intellectual Property and Shrinkwrap Licenses, 68 *S.Cal. L. Rev.* 1239, 1241 (1995).)
25. Generally, the courts have invalidated shrinkwrap licences. See *Step-Saver Data Sys. Inc. v. Wyse Technology*, 939 F.2d 91 (3d Cir. 1991); *Arizona Retail Sys. Inc. v. Software Link Inc.*, 831 F.Supp. 759 (D. Ariz. 1993).
26. Section 301 governs pre-emption of state law claims that conflict with the federal copyright policies embedded in the Copyright Act (17 USC § 301).It comes into play only if both of two conditions are satisfied: (1) the work in which the state law right is asserted comes within the 'subject matter' of copyright as specified in 17 USC §§ 102, 103 and (2) the state law right asserted is equivalent to any of the rights specified in 17 USC § 106. See *e.g. Baltimore Orioles v. Major League Baseball Players*, 805 F.2d 663, 674 (7th Cir. 1986).
27. See *ProCD Inc. v. Zeidenberg*, 908 F. Supp. 640 (W.D. Wis), rev'd and remanded, 86 F.3d 1447 (7th Cir. 1996).
28. The court pointed out that despite the widespread use of shrinkwrap licenses and the intense academic interest in the subject, there has been little litigation on this subject and most commentators view shrinkwrap licenses as being of questionable validity. (908 F. Supp. at 650.)
29. 17 USC § 301(a) reads: *'On and after January 1, 1978, all legal or equitable rights that are equivalent to any of the exclusive rights within the general scope of copyright as specified by section 106 in works of authorship that are fixed in a tangible medium of expression and come within the subject matter of copyright as specified by sections 102 and 103, whether created before or after that date and whether*

published or unpublished, are governed exclusively by this title. Thereafter, no person is entitled to any such right or equivalent right in any such work under the common law or statutes of any State'.

30. The Seventh Circuit found further support in the Uniform Commercial Code for upholding the validity of ProCD's shrinkwrap licence. The UCC governs this transaction because the exchange was considered a sale of goods rather than a licence. The Court of Appeals applied UCC section 2-204 which allows a contract to be 'made in any manner sufficient to show agreement, including conduct'. (86 F.3d at 1452.)

31. See *National Car Rental System Inc. v. Computer Associates International Inc.*, 991 F.2d 426, 433 (8th Cir. 1993); *Taquino v. Teledyne Monarch Rubber*, 893 F.2d 1488, 1501 (5th Cir. 1990); *Acorn Structures Inc. v. Swantz*, 846 F.2d 923, 926 (4th Cir. 1988).

32. 86 F.3d 1454.

33. Database Investment and Intellectual Property Antipiracy Act (H.R. 3531, 104 Cong. 2d sess. (1996)).

34. Proposal of the United States of America on Sui Generis Protection of Databases, Committee of Experts on a Possible Protocol to the Berne Convention, Sixth Session, Geneva, 22-24 May 1996 *(reproduced in Appendix II, hereunder)*.

35. Basic Proposal for the Substantive Provisions of the Treaty on Intellectual Property in Respect of Databases to be Considered by the Diplomatic Conferce, Geneva, 2-20 December 1996, WIPO Document CRNR/DC/6, 30 August 1996 (herinafter Draft Treaty) *(reproduced in Appendix III, hereunder)*.

36. Draft Treaty, article 1.

37. Draft Treaty, article 12.

38. Draft Treaty, article 8.

39. Draft Treaty, article 8 par. 3.

40. Draft Treaty, article 1 par. 4.

41. Draft Treaty, article 3 par. 1.

42. Draft Treaty, article 10.

43. H.R. 3531 104th Cong. 2d sess, 1280 (1996) *(reproduced in Appendix I)*.

44. Section 9.

45. Section 3.

46. Section 5.

47. Section 6.

48. See the White Paper: Intellectual Property and the National Information Infrastructure, (September 1995); Information Infrastructure: A Preliminary Draft of the Report of the Working Group on Intellectual Property Rights (Green Paper) (July 1994).

49. Section 10.

50. Section 11.

Appendix I

Database Investment and Intellectual Property Antipiracy Act (HR 3531)

Mr Moorhead introduced the following bill on May 23, 1996, which was referred to the Committee on the Judiciary.

A bill

to amend title 15, United States Code, to promote investment and prevent intellectual property piracy with respect to databases.

Be it enacted by the Senate and House of Representatives of the United States of America in Congress assembled,

Section 1 *Short title*

This Act may be cited as the 'Database Investment and Intellectual Property Antipiracy Act of 1996'.

Section 2 *Definitions*

'Change of commercial significance' means a change that a reasonable user of a database would regard as affecting the quality, quantity or value of contents of that database as a whole.

'Commerce' means all commerce that may lawfully be regulated by Congress.

'Database' means a collection, assembly or compilation, in any form or medium now or later known or developed, of works, data or other materials, arranged in a systematic or methodical way.

'*Database maker*' means the natural or juristic person making a substantial investment, qualitatively or quantitatively, in the collection, assembly, verification, organization and/or presentation of the contents of the database. Unless provided otherwise by contract (1) where two or more persons qualify as the makers of a database, they are jointly the database maker; (2) where a database is made by employees within the scope of their employment, the employer is the database maker; and (3) where a database is made pursuant to special order or commission, the person who ordered or commissioned the database is the database maker.

'*Database management information*' means the name and other identifying information of the database maker, the name and other identifying information of the database owner, and terms and conditions for extraction and use or re-use of the contents of the database.

'*Database owner*' means the database maker or the natural or juristic person who is the database maker's successor in interest.

'*Extraction*' means the permanent or temporary transfer of all or a substantial part of the contents of a database or of a copy or copies thereof. Such transfer may be to an identical or different medium, and by any means or in any form, now or later known or developed.

'*Governmental entity*' means the United States Government, any State, any agency or instrumentality of either, and any officer or employee of any of the foregoing acting in his or her official capacity.

'*Insubstantial part*' of a database means any portion of the contents of a database whose extraction, use or re-use does not diminish the value of the database, conflict with a normal exploitation of the database or adversely affect the actual or potential market for the database.

'*Juristic person*' means any firm, corporation, union, association, non-profit institution, or other organization capable of suing and being sued in a court of law, but does not include a governmental entity.

'*Place in commercial use*' means to use or re-use, or to authorize use or re-use, for direct or indirect commercial advantage or for financial gain.

'*Person*' means any natural person, any juristic person, and any governmental entity.

'*Use*' and '*re-use*' means making available all or a substantial part, qualitatively or quantitatively, of the contents of a database, or access to all or such substantial part, whether or not for direct or indirect commercial advantage or financial gain, by any means now known or later developed, including any of the following: (i) marketing, selling, or renting; (ii) in the form of permanent or temporary copies; or (iii) by distribution, any on-line or other form of transmission.

Section 3 *Databases subject to the Act*

(a) A database is subject to the Act if it is the result of a qualitatively or quantitatively substantial investment of human, technical, financial or other resources in the collection, assembly, verification, organization or presentation of the database contents, and (i) the database is used or re-used in commerce; or (ii) the database owner intends to use or re-use the database in commerce.

(b) A database otherwise subject to this Act shall remain subject, regardless of whether it is made available to the public or in commercial use; the form or medium in which it is embodied; or whether the database or any contents of the database are intellectual creations.

(c) Except for a database made by a governmental entity, any database otherwise subject to this Act, is not excluded herefrom because its contents have been obtained from a governmental entity.

(d) Computer programs are not subject to this Act, including without limitation any computer programs used in the manufacture, production, operation or maintenance of a database. However, the contents of a database otherwise subject to this Act remain subject, notwithstanding their direct or indirect incorporation in a computer program or other work.

Section 4 *Prohibited acts*

(a) No person shall, without the authorization of the database owner

(1) extract, use or re-use all or a substantial part, qualitatively or quantitatively, of the contents of a database subject to this Act in a manner that conflicts with the database owner's normal exploitation of the database or adversely affects the actual or potential market for the database;

(2) engage, notwithstanding section 5(a), in the repeated or systematic extraction, use or re-use of insubstantial parts, qualitatively or quantitatively, of the contents of a database subject to this Act in a manner that cumulatively conflicts with the database owner's normal exploitation of the database or adversely affects the actual or potential market for the database; or

(3) procure, direct or commission any act prohibited by subsections (i) or (ii).

(b) Acts that conflict with a normal exploitation of the database or adversely affect the actual or potential market for the database include but are not limited to the extraction, use or re-use of all or a substantial part of the contents of a database

(1) in a product or service that directly or indirectly competes in any market with the database from which it was extracted; or

(2) in a product or service that directly or indirectly competes in any market in which the database owner has a demonstrable interest or expectation in licensing or otherwise using or re-using the database; or

(3) in a product or service for customers who might otherwise reasonably be expected to be customers for the database; or

(4) by or for multiple persons within an organization or entity *in lieu* of the authorized additional use or re-use (by license, purchase or otherwise) of copies of the database by or for such persons.

Section 5 *Exceptions to prohibited acts*

(a) Subject to section 4(a)(ii), a lawful user of a database made available to the public or placed in commercial use is not prohibited from extracting, using or re-using insubstantial parts of its contents, qualitatively or quantitatively, for any purposes whatsoever.
(b) Nothing in this Act shall in any way restrict any person from independently collecting, assembling or compiling works, data or materials from sources other than a database subject to this Act.

Section 6 *Duration of prohibitions*

(a) A database becomes subject to this Act when the necessary investment has been made to qualify its maker as such under section 2. The database shall remain subject to this Act for a period of twenty-five years from the first of January following the date when it was first made available to the public or the date when it was first placed in commercial use, whichever is earlier.
(b) Any change of commercial significance, qualitatively or quantitatively, to a database, including any such change through the accumulation of successive additions, deletions, reverifications, alterations, modifications in organization or presentation, or other modifications, shall make the resulting database subject to this Act for its own term, as calculated under subsection (a).

Section 7 *Civil remedies for violation of section 4*

(a) *Civil actions* - A database owner injured by a violation of section 4 may bring a civil action for such a violation in an appropriate United States district court without regard to the amount in controversy: provided however, that any action against a State governmental entity may be brought in any court that has jurisdiction over claims against such entity.
(b) *Temporary and permanent injunctions* - Any court having jurisdiction of a civil action arising hereunder shall have the power to grant temporary and permanent injunctions, according to the principles of equity and upon such terms as the court may deem reasonable, to prevent the violation of section 4. Any such injunction granted upon hearing, after notice to the party sought to be enjoined, by any district court of the United States, may be served on the party against whom such injunction is granted anywhere in the United States where such person may be found, and shall be operative and may be enforced by proceedings in contempt or otherwise by any United States district court having jurisdiction over such party.
(c) *Impoundment* - At any time while an action hereunder is pending, the court may order the impounding, on such terms as it deems reasonable, of all copies of contents of databases extracted and or used or re-used in violation of section 4, and of all masters, tapes, disks, diskettes, or other articles by means of which such copies may be reproduced. The court may, as part of a final judgment or decree finding a violation of section 4, order the remedial modification or destruction of all copies of contents of databases extracted, used or re-used in violation of section 4, and of all masters, tapes, disks, diskettes, or other articles by means of which such copies may be reproduced.
(d) *Monetary relief* - When a violation of section 4 has been established in any civil action arising hereunder, the plaintiff shall be entitled, subject to principles of equity, to recover (i) defendant's profit, (ii) any damages sustained by the plaintiff, and (iii) the costs of the action. The court shall assess such profits or damages or cause the same to be assessed under its direction. In assessing profits the plaintiff shall be required to prove defendant's sales only; defendant must prove all elements of cost or deduction claimed. In assessing damages the court may enter judgment, according to the circumstances of the case, for any sum above the amount found as actual damages, not exceeding three times such amount. If the court shall find that the amount of the recovery based on profits is either inadequate or excessive, the court may in its discretion enter judgment for such sum as it finds just. The court in its discretion may award reasonable attorney fees to the prevailing party.
(e) Subsections (b) and (c) shall not apply to any action against the United States Government.
(f) The relief provided under this section shall be available against a State governmental entity to the extent allowed by applicable law.

Section 8 *Criminal offenses and penalties for violation of section 4*

(a) Any person who violates section 4 willfully, and *(1)* does so for direct or indirect commercial advantage or financial gain; or *(2)* thereby causes loss or damage to a database owner aggregating $ 10,000 or more in any one-year calendar period, shall be punished as provided in subsection (b).
(b) An offense under subsection (a) shall be punishable by a fine of not more than $ 250,000 or imprisonment for not more than five years, or both. A second or subsequent offense under subsection (a) shall be punishable by a fine of not more than $ 500,000, imprisonment for not more than ten years, or both.

Section 9 *Relationship to other laws*

(a) The remedies against violations hereunder shall be without prejudice to any remedies under any copyright that may subsist in the database, any contents of the database, or the selection, coordination or arrangement of such contents. Such remedies shall not limit, impair, or otherwise affect the existence, scope or duration of protection under any such copyright.

(b) Nothing in this Act shall restrict the rights of parties freely to enter into licenses or any other contracts with respect to databases or their contents.

(c) Nothing in this Act shall prejudice provisions concerning copyright, rights related to copyright or any other rights or obligations in the database or its contents, including laws in respect of patent, trademark, design rights, antitrust or competition, trade secrets, data protection and privacy, access to public documents, and the law of contract.

Section 10 *Circumvention of database protection systems*

No person shall import, manufacture or distribute any device, product, or component incorporated into a device or product, or offer or perform any service, the primary purpose or effect of which is to avoid, bypass, remove, deactivate, or otherwise circumvent, without the authority of the database owner or the law, any process, treatment, mechanism or system which prevents or inhibits the extraction, use or re-use of the contents of the database in violation of section 4 hereof.

Section 11 *Integrity of database management information*

(a) *False database management information* - No person shall knowingly provide database management information that is false, or knowingly publicly distribute or import for public distribution database management information that is false.

(b) *Removal or alteration of database management information* - No person shall, without authority of the database owner or the law, *(i)* knowingly remove or alter any database management information, *(ii)* knowingly distribute or import for distribution database management information that has been altered without authority of the database owner or the law; or *(iii)* knowingly distribute or import for distribution copies of a database from which database management information has been removed without the authority of the database owner or the law.

Section 12 *Civil remedies for violation of sections 10 or 11*

(a) *Civil actions* - Any person injured by a violation of section 10 or section 11 may bring a civil action for such violation in an appropriate United States district court, without regard to the amount in controversy: provided, however, that any action against a State governmental entity may be brought in any court that has jurisdiction over claims against such entity.

(b) *Powers of the court* - In an action brought under subsection (a), the court

(1) may grant temporary and permanent injunctions on such terms as it deems reasonable to prevent or restrain a violation;

(2) at any time while an action is pending, may order the impounding, on such terms as it deems reasonable, of any device or product that is in the custody or the control of the alleged violator and that the court has reasonable cause to believe was involved in a violation;

(3) may award damages under subsection (c);

(4) in its discretion may allow the recovery of costs by or against any party other than the United States or an officer thereof;

(5) in its discretion may award reasonable attorney's fees to the prevailing party; and

(6) may, as part of a final judgment or decree finding a violation, order the remedial modification or the destruction of any device or product involved in the violation that is in the custody or control of the violator or has been impounded under subsection (ii).

(c) *Awards of damages*

(1) *In general* - Except as otherwise provided in this Act, a violator is liable for either (a) the actual damages and any additional profits of the violator, as provided by subsection (ii), or (b) statutory damages, as provided by subsection (iii).

(2) *Actual damages* - The court shall award to the complaining party the actual damages suffered by him or her as a result of the violation, and any profits of the violator that are attributable to the violation and are not taken into account incomputing the actual damages, if the complaining party elects such damages at any time before final judgment is entered.

(3) *Statutory damages* - (a) At any time before final judgment is entered, a complaining party may elect to recover an award of statutory damages for each violation of section 10 in the sum of not less than $ 200 or more than $ 2,500 per device, product, offer or performance of service, as the court considers just. (b) At any time before final judgment is entered, a complaining party may elect to recover an award of statutory damages for each violation of section 11 in the sum of not less than $ 2,500 or more than $ 25,000.

(4) *Repeated violations* - In any case in which the injured party sustains the burden of proving, and the court finds, that a person has violated section 10 or 11 within three years after a final judgment was entered against that person for another such violation, the court may increase the award of damages up to triple the amount that would otherwise be awarded, as the court considers just.

(5) *Innocent violations* - The court in its discretion may reduce or remit altogether the total award of damages in any case in which the violator sustains the burden of proving, and the court finds, that the violator was not aware and had no reason to believe that its acts constituted a violation.

(d) Subsections (b)(i) and (ii) shall not apply to any action against the United States Government.

(e) The relief provided under subsection (b) shall be available against a State governmental entity to the extent allowed by applicable law.

Section 13 *Criminal offenses and penalties for violation of section 11*

Any person who violates section 11 with intent to defraud shall be fined not more than $ 500,000 or imprisoned for not more than five years, or both.

Section 14 *Limitations on actions*

No action shall be maintained under this Act unless it is commenced within three years after the database owner knew or should have known of the claim.

Section 15 *Effective date*

(a) This Act shall take effect immediately upon enactment, and shall be applicable to acts committed on or after that date.
(b) No person shall be liable under this Act for use or re-use of database contents lawfully extracted from a database, prior to the effective date of this Act, by that person or by that person's predecessor in interest.

Appendix II

WIPO

Committee of Experts on a Possible Protocol to the Berne Convention - Seventh Session

Committee of Experts on a Possible Instrument for the protection of the rights of performers and producers of phonograms - Sixth Session

Geneva, 22-24 May 1996

Proposal of the United States of America on *sui generis* protection of databases

Text of the proposal

(Preamble)

Article 1 *Scope*

1.1. The legal protection under this [Instrument] extends to databases embodied in any form.
1.2. Contracting Parties shall protect substantial investments in databases in accordance with the provisions of this [Instrument].
1.3. Contracting Parties shall protect all databases that represent a substantial investment in the collection, assembly, verification, organization, or presentation of the database contents, whether or not such database is made commercially available or otherwise made available to the public, regardless of the form or medium in which the database is embodied, and regardless of whether the database or any of its contents are intellectual creations or are protected under other domestic legislation.
1.4. The protection under this [Instrument] shall not extend to any computer programs, including without limitation any computer program used in the manufacture, operation or maintenance of a database. However, a database incorporated into a computer program shall be protected under this [Instrument].

Article 2 *Definitions*

2.1. A 'database' is a collection, assembly or compilation of works, data, information or other materials arranged in a systematic or methodical way.
2.2. 'Extraction' means the permanent or temporary transfer to the same or another type of medium, by any means now known or later developed, of all or a substantial part of the database contents.
2.3. The 'maker of the database' is the natural or legal person or persons making a substantial investment in the collection, assembly, verification, organization or presentation of the contents of the database.
2.4. 'Substantial investment' means any qualitatively or quantitatively significant investment of human, financial, technical or other resources in the make of a database.
2.5. 'Substantial part' means any portion of the database that is of qualitative or quantitative significance when evaluated in relation to the entire database.
2.6. 'Use' and 're-use' mean the making available, by any means now known or later developed,

including by the distribution of copies, by renting, or by on-line or other forms of transmission, of all or a substantial part of the contents of a database, including making available of all or a substantial part of the database to members of the public at a place and at a time chosen by each member of the public, whether or not for direct or indirect commercial advantage or financial gain.

Article 3 *Rights in respect of database contents*

3.1. The maker of a database eligible for protection under this [Instrument] shall have the right to do, authorize or prohibit acts of extraction, use or re-use of all or a substantial part of the contents of the databases.
3.2. The protection provided under this [Instrument] shall not preclude any person from independently collecting, assembling or compiling works, data or materials from any source other than a protected database.

Article 4 *Right holders*

4.1. The rights provided under this [Instrument] shall be owned by the maker of the database or, where there is more than one maker, jointly by the makers.
4.2. The rights provided under this [Instrument] shall be freely transferable.

Article 5 *Exceptions to rights*

5.1. Subject to the limitations in paragraph 2 of this Article, a lawful user of a database made commercially available or generally made available to the public may extract, use or re-use insubstantial parts of its contents for any purpose whatsoever.
5.2. The repeated or systematic extraction, use or re-use of insubstantial parts of the contents of a database in a manner that cumulatively conflicts with the normal exploitation of the database or adversely affects the actual or potential market for the database shall not be permitted.
5.3. Contracting parties may, in their domestic legislation, provide for exceptions to or limitations on the rights provided in this [Instrument] so long as such limitations or exceptions do not unreasonably conflict with a normal exploitation of the database and do not unreasonably prejudice the legitimate interests of the right holder.
5.4. It shall be a matter of legislation in the Contracting Parties to determine the protection to be granted to databases made by a governmental entity or its agents or employees.

Article 6 *Term of protection*

6.1. The rights provided under this [Instrument] shall attach when the database meets the requirements of Article 1.3 and shall endure for at least 25 years.
6.2. For databases that have been made commercially available or generally made available to the public, the rights provided under this [Instrument] shall endure for at least 25 years from the first of January following, whichever of such acts has occurred earlier.
6.3. Any significant change, evaluated qualitatively or quantitatively, to the database, including any significant change resulting from the accumulation of successive additions, deletions, verifications or re-verifications, alterations, modifications in organization or presentation, or other modifications, shall qualify the resulting database for its own term of protection.

Article 7 *Relation to other laws*

7.1. The protection under this [Instrument] shall be without prejudice to provisions concerning copyright, rights related to copyright or any other rights or obligations in the database or its contents, including laws in respect of patent, trademark, design rights, antitrust or competition, trade secrets, data protection and privacy, access to public documents, and the law of contract.
7.2. No Contracting Party shall impair the ability to vary by contract the rights and exceptions to rights set forth herein.

Article 8 *Prohibition of protection-defeating devices*

Contracting Parties shall make it unlawful to import, manufacture or distribute any device, product, or component incorporated into a device or product, or offer or perform any service, the primary purpose or effect of which is to avoid, bypass, remove, deactivate, or otherwise circumvent, without authority, any process, treatment, mechanism or system which prevents or inhibits the authorized exercise of any of the rights under this [Instrument].

Article 9 *Application to existing databases*

9.1. Databases eligible for protection under this [Instrument] that are in existence at the time this [Instrument] comes into force in respect of a Contracting Party shall be protected. The duration of such protection shall be determined under Article 6.
9.2. The rights under this [Instrument] shall be without prejudice to any acts of exploitation performed

prior to its effective date. It shall be a matter for domestic legislation to provide for protection of any rights of third parties acquired before the effective date of this [Instrument].

Article 10 *Implementation*

10.1. Contracting Parties shall provide for the implementation of this [Instrument] in domestic legislation by its effective date in their territories.
10.2. The means by which this [Instrument] is implemented shall be a matter for national legislation, and may include protection under the laws related to intellectual property, unfair competition, misappropriation or other laws.

Article 11 *National treatment*

11.1. Databases whose makers are at the time of the making of the database either nationals of or habitual residents of a Contracting Party shall be protected under this [Instrument].
11.2. Right holders shall enjoy, in respect of databases that qualify for protection under this [Instrument], in Contracting Parties other than the country of the nationality or the habitual residence of the maker, the rights which their respective laws do now or may hereafter grant to their nationals, as well as the rights specially granted by this [Instrument].
11.3. Protection in the country of the nationality or habitual residence of the maker shall be governed by domestic law.
11.4. The enjoyment and the exercise of the rights hereunder shall not be subject to any formality; such enjoyment and exercise shall be independent of the existence of protection in the country of the database maker's nationality or habitual residence. Apart from the provisions of this [Instrument], the extent of protection, as well as the means and extent of redress, shall be governed exclusively by the laws of the Contracting Party where protection is claimed.

Appendix III

WIPO

Diplomatic Conference on Certain Copyright and Neighbouring Rights Questions

Geneva, 2-20 December 1996

Basic proposal for the substantive provisions of the Treaty on Intellectual Property in respect of databases to be considered by the Diplomatic Conference

prepared by the Chairman of the Committees of Experts on a Possible Protocol to the Berne Convention and on a Possible Instrument for the Protection of the Rights of Performers and producers of Phonograms.

Draft Treaty on Intellectual Property in respect of databases

Contents

Preamble (substantive provisions)
Article 1: Scope
Article 2: Definitions
Article 3: Rights
Article 4: Right holders
Article 5: Exceptions
Article 6: Beneficiaries of protection
Article 7: National treatment and independence of protection
Article 8: Term of protection
Article 9: Formalities
Article 10: Obligations concerning technological measures
Article 11: Application in time
Article 12: Relation to other legal provisions
Article 13: Special provisions on enforcement of rights (administrative and final clauses)
Annexe

Preamble

The Contracting Parties,

desiring to enhance and stimulate the production, distribution and international trade in databases,
recognizing that databases are a vital element in the development of a global information infrastructure and an essential tool for promoting economic, cultural and technological advancement,
recognizing that the making of databases requires the investment of uconsiderable human, technical and financial resources but that such databases can be copied or accessed at a fraction of the cost needed to design them independently,
desiring to establish a new form of protection for databases by granting rights adequate to enable the makers of databases to recover the investment they have made in their databases and by providing international protection in a manner as effective and uniform as possible,
emphasizing that nothing in this Treaty shall derogate from existing obligations that Contracting Parties may have to each other under treaties in the field of intellectual property, and in particular, that nothing in this Treaty shall in any way prejudice the rights granted to authors in the Berne Convention for the Protection of Literary and Artistic Works,
have agreed as follows:

Article 1 *Scope*

(1) Contracting Parties shall protect any database that represents a substantial investment in the collection, assembly, verification, organization or presentation of the contents of the database.
(2) The legal protection set forth in this Treaty extends to a database regardless of the form or medium in which the database is embodied, and regardless of whether or not the database is made available to the public.
(3) The protection granted under this Treaty shall be provided irrespective of any protection provided for a database or its contents by copyright or by other rights granted by Contracting Parties in their national legislation.
(4) The protection under this Treaty shall not extend to any computer program as such, including without limitation any computer program used in the manufacture, operation or maintenance of a database.

Article 2 *Definitions*

For the purposes of this Treaty:
(i) 'database' means a collection of independent works, data or other materials arranged in a systematic or methodical way and capable of being individually accessed by electronic or other means;
(ii) 'extraction' means the permanent or temporary transfer of all or a substantial part of the contents of a database to another medium by any means or in any form;
(iii) 'maker of the database' means the natural or legal person or persons with control and responsibility for the undertaking of a substantial investment in making a database;
(iv) 'substantial investment' means any qualitatively or quantitatively significant investment of human, financial, technical or other resources in the collection, assembly, verification, organization or presentation of the contents of the database;
(v) 'substantial part', in reference to the contents of a database, means any portion of the database, including an accumulation of small portions, that is of qualitative or quantitative significance to the value of the database;
(vi) 'utilization' means the making available to the public or all or a substantial part of the contents of a database by any means, including by the distribution of copies, by renting, or by on-line or other forms of transmission, including making the same available to the public at a place and at a time individually chosen by each member of the public.

Article 3 *Rights*

(1) The maker of a database eligible for protection under this Treaty shall have the right to authorize or prohibit the extraction or utilization of its contents.
(2) Contracting Parties may, in their national legislation, provide that the right of utilization provided for in paragraph (1) does not apply to distribution of the original or any copy of any database that has been sold or the ownership of which has been otherwise transferred in that Contracting Party's territory by or pursuant to authorization.

Article 4 *Right holders*

(1) The rights provided under this Treaty shall be owned by the maker of the database.
(2) The rights provided under this Treaty shall be freely transferable.

Article 5 *Exceptions*

(1) Contracting Parties may, in their national legislation, provide exceptions to or limitations of the

rights provided in this Treaty in certain special cases that do not conflict with the normal exploitation of the database and do not unreasonably prejudice the legitimate interests of the right holder.
(2) It shall be a matter for the national legislation of Contracting Parties to determine the protection that shall be granted to databases made by governmental entities or their agents or employees.

Article 6 *Beneficiaries of protection*

(1) Each Contracting Party shall protect according to the terms of this Treaty makers of databases who are nationals of a Contracting Party.
(2) The provisions of paragraph (1) shall also apply to companies, firms and other legal entities formed in accordance with the laws of a Contracting Party or having their registered office, central administration or principal place of business within a Contracting Party; however, where such a company, firm or other legal entity has only its registered office in the territory of a Contracting Party, its operations must be genuinely linked on an on-going basis with the economy of a Contracting Party.

Article 7 *National treatment and independence of protection*

(1) The maker of a database shall enjoy in respect of the protection provided for in this Treaty, in Contracting Parties other than the Contracting Party of which he is a national, the rights which their respective laws do now or may hereafter grant to their nationals as well as the rights specially granted by this Treaty.
(2) Protection of a database in the Contracting Party of which the maker of the database is a national shall be governed by nation legislation.
(3) The enjoyment and the exercise of rights under this Treaty shall be independent of the existence of protection in the Contracting Party of which the maker of a database is a national. Apart from the provisions of this Treaty, the extent of protection, as well as the means and extent of redress, shall be governed exclusively by the laws of the Contracting Party where protection is claimed.
(4) Makers of databases who are not nationals of a Contracting Party but who have their habitual residence in a Contracting Party shall, for the purposes of this Treaty, be assimilated to nationals of that Contracting Party.

Article 8 *Term of protection*

(1) The rights provided for in this Treaty shall attach when a database meets the requirements of Article 1(1) and shall endure for at least - *alternative A:* 25, *alternative B:* 15 - years from the first day of January in the year following the date when the database first met the requirements of Article 1(1).
(2) In the case of a database that is made available to the public, in whatever manner, before the expiry of the period provided for in paragraph (1), the term of protection shall endure for at least - *alternative A:* 25, *alternative B:* 15 - years from the first day of January in the year following the date when the database was first made available to the public.
(3) Any substantial change to the database, evaluated qualitatively or quantitatively, including any substantial change resulting from the accumulation of successive additions, deletions, verifications, modifications in organization or presentation, or other alterations, which constitute a new substantial investment, shall qualify the database resulting from such investment for its own term of protection.

Article 9 *Formalities*

The enjoyment and exercise of the rights provided for in this Treaty shall not be subject to any formality.

Article 10 *Obligations concerning technological measures*

(1) Contracting Parties shall make unlawful the importation, manufacture or distribution of protection-defeating devices, or the offer or performance of any service having the same effect, by any person knowing or having reasonable grounds to know that the device or service will be used for, or in the course of, the exercise of rights provided under this Treaty that is not authorized by the right holder or the law.
(2) Contracting Parties shall provide for appropriate and effective remedies against the unlawful acts referred to in paragraph (1).
(3) As used in this Article, 'protection-defeating device' means any device, product or component incorporated into a device or product, the primary purpose or primary effect of which is to circumvent any process, treatment, mechanism or system that prevents or inhibits any of the acts covered by the rights under this Treaty.

Article 11 *Application in time*

(1) Contracting Parties shall also grant protection pursuant to this Treaty in respect of databases that met the requirements of Article 1(1) at the date of the entry into force of this Treaty for each Contracting Party. The duration of such protection shall be determined by the provisions of Article 8.
(2) The protection provided for in paragraph (1) shall be without prejudice to any acts concluded or rights acquired before the entry into force of this Treaty in each Contracting Party.

(3) A contracting Party may provide for conditions under which copies of databases which were lawfully made before the date of the entry into force of this Treaty for that Contracting Party may be distributed to the public, provided that such provisions do not allow distribution for period longer than two years from that date.

Article 12 *Relation to other legal provisions*

The protection accord under this Treaty shall be without prejudice to any other rights in, or obligations with respect to, a database or its contents, including laws in respect of copyright, rights related to copyright, patent, trademark, design rights, antitrust or competition, trade secrets, data protection and privacy, access to public documents and the law of contract.

Article 13 *Special provisions on enforcement of rights*

Alternative A

(1) Special provisions regarding the enforcement of rights are included in the Annexe to the Treaty.
(2) The Annexe forms an integral part of this Treaty.

Alternative B

Contracting Parties shall ensure that the enforcement procedures specified in Part III, Articles 41-61, of the Agreement on Trade-Related Aspects of Intellectual Property Rights, Including Trade in Counterfeit Goods, Annex 1C, of the Marrakesh Agreement Establishing the World Trade Organization, concluded on April 15, 1994 (the 'TRIPs Agreement'), are available under their national law so as to permit effective action against any act of infringement of the rights provided under this Treaty, including expeditious remedies to prevent infringements, and remedies that constitute a deterrent to further infringements. To this end, Contracting Parties shall apply *mutatis mutandis* the provisions of Articles 41 to 61 of the TRIPs Agreement.

Interventions

F. POLLAUD-DULIAN:

Je voudrais dire d'abord quelques mots de la technique législative de la Commission, qui devrait être repensée à mon sens. D'abord, comme l'a souligné très justement M. Cornish, on ne peut qu'être troublé par la profusion des considérants par rapport aux articles, ce qui ne facilite pas la mise en oeuvre de telles directives. Par exemple, on confrontera avec curiosité le considérant et l'article pertinents sur les questions de droit international privé touchant au droit *"sui generis"*. Un autre aspect discutable de la méthode, c'est cette technique qui consiste à poser une règle, à la restreindre par une exception, puis à poser des exceptions à l'exception. La règle se dissout dans les cas particuliers. Je crois que cette directive, chacun en conviendra, est très compliquée et qu'elle sera à la fois difficile à intégrer dans les législations nationales d'une part et, d'autre part, qu'elle créera davantage d'insécurité juridique, ce qui n'était sans doute pas l'intention du législateur européen.

Ensuite, je voudrais dire quelques mots du droit *sui generis*, qui constitue, bien sûr, l'innovation la plus problématique et la plus contestée. Ce droit était-il nécessaire, est-il adéquat, est-il même légitime? Ce qui est immédiatement à souligner, à propos de la directive, c'est l'omniprésence de la notion d'investissement. On pourrait croire que cette référence fondatrice à l'investissement serait sans grande portée puisqu'il s'agit, non de droit d'auteur, mais d'un droit qualifié de *sui generis*. Mais la portée de cette référence ne doit pas être minorée. En effet, dans le Livre vert de la Commission, il est dit expressément (n. 87) que la directive "bases de données" revêt une grande importance car elle servira de pilote ou de base pour toute future initiative sur les aspects de droit d'auteur liés à la Société de l'information. Par ailleurs, ce droit *sui generis* est largement décalqué sur le droit d'auteur: on trouve même la reprise textuelle de passages de la Convention de Berne pour régir ce droit qui n'est pourtant pas un droit d'auteur. En outre, le droit *sui generis* est doté d'une durée potentiellement plus longue que celle du droit d'auteur, voire perpétuelle, par un système de renouvellement qui rappelle quelque-chose: ceci est d'autant plus curieux que ce droit ne porte pas sur une création ou sur une innovation, et qu'il ne se justifie que par le coût de l'investissement. Ces règles de durée, surprenantes, poseront sûrement des difficultés de mise en oeuvre importantes.

On doit se poser une question à propos de cette promotion de l'investissement comme fondement d'un droit exclusif ou d'un droit de propriété: est-ce que tout ce qui coûte de l'argent mérite d'être couvert par un droit de propriété intellectuelle? Celle-ci ne doit-elle pas être réservée aux créations et aux innovations? Est-ce que l'investissement, en soi, suffit à justifier la création de tels droits, je ne le crois pas, car ce que l'on veut faire ici, c'est permettre de sanctionner le parasitage de ces investissements. Il s'agit de sanctionner une faute de déloyauté dans la concurrence. C'est donc de responsabilité pour faute qu'il s'agit en réalité: il en résulte que c'est la concurrence déloyale qui était la solution adaptée au problème posé, et non ce droit *sui generis*. Le résultat est, au moins pour les juristes français, que la directive introduit une grave confusion parmi des catégories juridiques fondamentales (les droits de propriété intellectuelle, auxquels la directive accroche ce droit *sui generis* et l'action en concurrence déloyale, à laquelle ressortissait naturellement la question). L'intégration du texte dans les différentes législations promet de poser des questions très délicates.

Je voudrais attirer l'attention sur une autre source de difficultés potentielles très importantes: c'est l'interprétation de l'adjectif "substantiel", qui revient très souvent dans la directive et ce, dans différents contextes où il s'applique à des termes différents pour mettre en oeuvre des règles différentes (investissement, partie, modification). Le terme est trop souple pour ne pas poser des problèmes et notamment celui de savoir s'il doit recevoir une seule interprétation pour tout le texte ou pas. En ce qui concerne la prorogation de la durée de la protection, l'interprétation de cet adjectif est décisive.

Enfin, je signalerai un dernier point sensible: la définition du droit exclusif et celle des exceptions, qui me semblent excessivement compliquées. Je mets quiconque au défi de dire à l'utilisateur légitime ou non ce qu'il a le droit de faire ou pas, s'il est en état d'infraction ou non. Il en résultera, à mon avis, une grande insécurité juridique. D'ailleurs, même si la directive précise bien que le droit *sui generis* ne couvre ni les oeuvres, ni les données non couvertes par le droit d'auteur, on a quand même l'impression que ce droit *sui generis* tend à permettre une protectrion indirecte de faits ou d'idées. Par là même, si l'on tient compte de l'obscurité des limites du droit, il nous semble que la notion de domaine public est remise en cause. Le législateur européen a eu sans doute conscience de ceci et donc du caractère anticoncurrentiel de ce droit *sui generis*, puisqu'il évoque à plusieurs reprises le droit de la concurrence et envisage même la possibilité d'instaurer des licences obligatoires en cas d'atteinte à la libre concurrence.

W. ROTHNIE:

I should preface my remarks by acknowledging that I come from a country which applies the British 'sweat-of-the-brow' theory. But that said, my first question regards a difference in terminology between the US proposal and the European proposal/Directive. The European proposal/Directive requires a 'substantial' investment; the US a 'significant' investment. I wonder whether the US terminology therefore proposes a lower threshold perhaps flowing from *Feist*'s stress on the requirement for a modicum of creativity.

The second question I wonder about is the apparently universal agreement that we must have some sort of protection for the 'un-original' contents of databases. Surprisingly, there appears to be a general view that copyright cannot be the vehicle for this. This appears to contrast starkly with the approach taken over computer programs! I wonder why? I wonder also if we are re-embarking on a new phase. The debates over the protection of the contents of a database appear reminiscent of the great arguments over the protection of photographs. There was a serious view that there lacked sufficient originality for copyright protection. Are we now reviving this old, once thought extinct and intractable debates together with a new direction for intellectual property protection?

J.H. SPOOR:

Mr Chairman, Professor Cornish very rightly criticized the EC Database Directive's incredibly vast definition of what may constitute a database. Indeed, the situation may even be worse, for not only that definition is extremely broad, but one may also wonder what in fact constitutes 'a' database. Please let me explain. Professor Cornish also reminded us that databases must be substantially 'refreshed' from time to time in order to prevent the *sui generis* right from expiring. Now while some databases are being updated continuously, others just cannot be refreshed because they simply are complete. Take for example a database listing all books published in the Netherlands between 1900 and 1940. It may take some time to complete the work, but once that database is ready, no further work will be required. (Except perhaps for a thorough check-up, but one can hardly keep checking it over and over again.) After fifteen years, such a database will run out of protection.

Now suppose the same database producer also owns another database, listing all scholarly articles about books published in the Netherlands between 1900 and 1940. As long as new articles on this exciting subject keep being written and published, that database can be updated and expanded continuously, and thereby will keep being protected. Now why not simply *merge* both databases into one? The combined database as a whole will require regular updates and thus enjoy permanent protection. Of course, the database producer could still offer different access options to potential subscribers: access to all data at a certain price, or to part of the data (for example just those concerning the books, not the references to the scholarly articles) at a lower price.

In fact, whether we call a body of data 'a' database is largely a matter of labeling. With computerized databases, the location of the data has become irrelevant. Databases may merely consist of part of what is stocked on a server; they may also be distributed over different servers. In the end, the defining of 'a' certain database may simply depend on a piece of software: the search tool which permits users to access data of a certain nature, regardless of their precise location which may be anywhere in the world. To the outside world the database's limits may simply be defined by the label which the owner cares to give it. And since that label can be chosen at will, it may be carefully designed to make certain that 'the' database will need continuous updates so as not to run out of protection, or to make certain that it meets the originality requirement.

I mention this merely as another example of how vague the Database Directive's definition of what may constitute a database really is. In the end, the database concept may well turn out to have no 'natural' limits. I think that this aspect, as well as its potential consequences, should be studied more closely.

Allocution de clôture

V. Nabhan

Mesdames, Messieurs, Chers amis,

Mercredi matin, lors de mon allocution de bienvenue, je me faisais fort de prédire que nos journées d'études seraient intéressantes. C'est avec joie, et sans la moindre surprise d'ailleurs, que je constate m'être carrément trompé. Ces journées ne furent pas juste intéressantes ou instructives, elles furent plutôt éblouissantes. Pour utiliser une expression chère à M. André Françon, qui soit dit en passant, manie en cachette et avec dextérité la langue de Shakespeare: *"it was really marvelous"*.

Merveilleuses, ces journées le furent en raison de leur qualité scientifique remarquable. Exceptionnelles, aussi, elles le furent grâce à une organisation efficace, sans bavure.

L'aspect scientifique d'abord. Que puis-je ajouter que l'on ne sait déjà? Des rapports généraux de haut calibre, exhaustifs, éclairants. De nombreux rapports nationaux qui ont nourri de leur sève les rapporteurs généraux. Des présidents de séance bien préparés, qui ont su habilement doser souplesse et rigueur. Des panelistes qui sont intervenus avec brio et précision sur des sujets pointus. Et *last, but not least*, un public attentif, intéressé, et surtout fidèle, qui a su résister aux attraits extérieurs d'un soleil diaboliquement tentateur. Fidélité qui en l'occurrence, attestait, ô combien éloquemment, de la qualité des travaux.

Quelles conclusions tirer de ces journées? Je ne m'engagerai pas dans la voie périlleuse d'un rapport de synthèse, mais me contenterai de quelques remarques générales. Face à notre désarroi et inquiétude suscités par ces nouvelles techniques encore mal apprivoisées, la réponse presque unanime semble être la suivante: "tout baigne", "pas de panique", "il n'y a pas de révolution". *"Kein Problem". "Alles gut"*. Le droit d'auteur continuera à mener allègrement son petit bonhomme de chemin, sans accroc majeur, sur les autoroutes de l'information.

Les notions déjà connues, bien établies, vénérables, de droit de reproduction, et de droit de communication au public, suffiraient à la tâche. Ne les abandonnons pas. Courtisons-les encore. Poursuivons-les de nos assiduités. Elles ont encore bien des satisfactions à nous offrir.

Tout au plus pourrait-on leur donner çà et là un coup de pinceau législatif, éliminer une ride, ajouter une petite touche de maquillage. Mais point n'est besoin de s'en départir, car, au fond, rien n'a vraiment changé. Le droit d'auteur s'est de tout temps, et depuis sa naissance, heurté aux coups de boutoir de la technique et a toujours réussi à s'adapter grâce à la souplesse de ces concepts généraux. Donc, rien de nouveau sous le soleil. Et la première conclusion, je la formulerai en empruntant à mon ami Adolf Dietz une de ses expressions favorites: *"il faut rester calme"*.

Rien n'a changé, peut-être, mais en même temps, tout est différent. Il est dorénavant question de fournisseurs de contenus et de services d'accès, de diffusion planétaire non localisable, de nouveaux moyens techniques de protection et de gestion. Nouvelles réalités, nouvel environnement, nouvelles menaces, nouveaux problèmes. Mais là aussi, les discours sont plutôt rassurants. La machine n'est pas juste une menace, elle représente en même temps la solution. Elle permet d'assurer l'efficacité de l'exercice du droit exclusif, d'affiner l'exercice collectif du droit, par une gestion individuelle plus poussée. Mais aussi, ô paradoxe, elle renforce d'une certaine façon, nous dit le professeur Lucas, le droit moral. *What's wrong with that?* Donc deuxième conclusion: il y a lieu de rester modérément optimiste.

Mais, et c'est la troisième conclusion, il convient aussi d'être prudent, voire vigilant. S'il est vrai que le ciel demeure bleu, il risque d'être brouillé par des nuages qui auront vite fait d'en altérer la pureté. On ne peut souscrire à la fâcheuse tendance de ravaler l'oeuvre au rang d'information ou de simple produit. Il y a plus dans la Mona Lisa de Leonardo, ou la neuvième de Beethoven, qu'une simple addition de zéros et de uns. L'auteur, la personne, doit demeurer au centre de nos préoccupations. Ceci ne doit pas être perdu de vue, ni passer au second plan. Il faut savoir gré au président Koumantos de nous avoir rappelé cette vérité élémentaire, mais combien fondamentale.

Voilà pour l'aspect scientifique. L'organisation maintenant. Là dessus, il faut constater l'évidence. Organisation fluide, impeccable, qui frise la perfection. A l'instar de la panthère rose, le groupe néerlandais a frappé encore une fois, nous épatant par son savoir-faire. A cet égard, je dois d'abord rendre hommage au penseur, au concepteur, à l'architecte, celui dont la vision nous a guidés tout au long de ces journées. Tout le monde a compris que je vise le professeur Cohen Jehoram, un des piliers de notre association, à qui j'adresse nos remerciements et nos voeux de rétablissement et de bonne santé. Il fut physiquement absent, mais en réalité il était omniprésent durant ces trois jours. Avec votre permission, et sans doute votre accord unanime, je propose qu'il soit désigné président honoraire de ces journées.

Mais il faut aussi remercier non seulement le général, mais l'état-major. Je m'adresse ici à Nora, à Juliette, à Jaap. Ils ont été des hôtes exceptionnels. Leur disponibilité, leur discrétion, leur générosité, leur efficacité ont été constamment mises à rude épreuve sans jamais faire défaut. Le temps est venu de leur exprimer, ainsi qu'à l'ensemble du groupe néerlandais qui les a secondés dans leurs efforts, notre profonde appréciation, notre amitié, notre affection. Je m'adresserai à eux en néerlandais en ces termes: *"We houden van jullie"*. Ce qui veut dire: nous vous aimons. J'ai dû me fier à M. Hugenholtz pour la traduction. J'espère qu'il m'a donné la bonne version, et que ces mots ne cachent aucun message inavouable ou obscène. Enfin, il convient de ne pas oublier Madame Lidy Groot et son équipe, toujours serviables, efficaces, souriants. Et bien sûr, nous n'omettrons pas de mentionner, les traducteurs, ces héros discrets qui travaillent dans l'ombre, dans des conditions souvent éprouvantes, et qui ont accompli leurs tâches avec professionnalisme.

En 1982, c'était à Amsterdam: nous avons étudié la problématique de la transmission par câble touchant au droit d'auteur. En 1996: c'est encore à Amsterdam. Et cette fois-ci, nous avons réfléchi sur l'infrastructure globale d'information et le droit d'auteur. Je vous donne de nouveau rendez-vous, pour l'année 2010. Où? A Amsterdam, bien sûr. Pour aborder quel thème? Quel autre sinon les nouvelles techniques de communication et le droit d'auteur? Nous reviendrons alors dans cette ville au charme inouï, avec notre bagage d'interrogations et d'inquiétudes, suscitées par les nouvelles techniques du moment qui nous bouleverseront. Et nous en repartirons, vraisemblablement un peu moins inquiets, récitant les mêmes formules rassurantes: "pas de panique", "il n'y a pas de révolution", "rien n'a changé", "droit de reproduction", "droit de communication", *"kein Problem"*.

En attendant, chers amis, il faut s'armer de patience, et surtout ne pas oublier cette parole toute empreinte de sagesse: "IL FAUT RESTER CALME", et ce, jusqu'au Congrès suivant de l'ALAI qui se déroulera à Amsterdam en 2024. Je vous laisse le soin d'en deviner le thème. Ainsi que les conclusions.

D'ici deux jours, beaucoup d'entre nous seront partis. Et quelque part dans notre mémoire sera gravée de manière indélébile une trace de la magie d'Amsterdam. Et quelque part, en nos coeurs, nous emporterons avec nous le sourire et l'amitié de Nora, de Juliette et de Jaap.

List of participants

Abraham, Daniel - Graphic Artists Guild - New York, USA
Adamson, Birgitta - Swedish Television - Stockholm, Sweden
Åkerberg, Yngve - SAMI - Stockholm, Sweden
Anderzén, Matti - Sanoma Corporation - Helsinki, Finland
Arcomano, Nicholas - Broadcast Music Inc. - New York, USA
Arkenbout, Erwin - Ministry of Justice - The Hague, Netherlands
Aviles, Ricardo - Aviles & Roca - Barcelona, Spain

Badowski, Jerzy - Society of Authors ZAiKS - Warsaw, Poland
Beemsterboer, André - Buma/Stemra - Amstelveen, Netherlands
Bercovitz, Alberto - Estudio Juridico Bercovitz - Madrid, Spain
Bertrams, Heleen - Max-Planck-Institute - Munich, Germany
Best, Hubert - Biddle & Co. - London, United Kingdom
Bettinger, Torsten - Munich, Germany
Bigle, Gerald - Cabinet Bigle - Paris, France
Black, Jack - Radcliffes Crossman Block - London, United Kingdom
Blomme, Johan - IFPI Belgium - Ghent, Belgium
Bois, Rob du - Haarlem, Netherlands
Bouwes, M.Tj. - Ministry of Justice - The Hague, Netherlands
Brandsteder, Sylvia - Stichting Stemra - Amstelveen, Netherlands
Brett, Hugh - Dallas Brett - Oxford, United Kingdom
Brison, Fabienne - SABAM - Brussels, Belgium
Brown, Ralph - Yale Law School - New Haven, USA
Brügger, Paul - ALAI Suisse - Berne, Switzerland
Buch, Rikke - TV2 Denmark - Odense, Denmark

Calissendorff, Kerstin - Advokatfirman Cerderquist - Stockholm, Sweden
Capiau, Suzanne - Coppens Van Ommeslaghe Horsmans - Brussels, Belgium
Clark, Charles - Int. Publishers Copyright Council - London, United Kingdom
Cock Buning, Madeleine de - Amsterdam, Netherlands
Cohen Jehoram, Tobias - De Brauw Blackstone - The Hague, Netherlands
Corbet, Jan - Antwerp, Belgium
Cornish, William - Cambridge University - Cambridge, United Kingdom

Desurmont, Thierry - SACEM - Neuilly sur Seine, France
Diekman, W.J.M. - De Brauw Blackstone Westbroek - Amsterdam, Netherlands
Dietz, Adolf - Max-Planck-Institute - Munich, Germany
Dommering, Egbert - Institute for Information Law - Amsterdam, Netherlands
Dos Santos Gil, Alfredo - Centre for Intell. Prop. Law - Utrecht, Netherlands

Dreier, Thomas - Max-Planck-Institute - Munich, Germany
Dufrane, Sabine - SABAM - Brussels, Belgium
Dumont, Pierre-Henri - SSA - Lausanne, Switzerland

Empel, Geerten van - IKON Television - Groningen, Netherlands
Eskola, Jaakko - Finnish Copyright Society - Helsinki, Finland

Farrés, Juan - Barcelona, Spain
Flechsig, Norbert - Süddeutscher Rundfunk - Remshalden, Germany
Fornari, Domenico - Patentbyrå Zacco & Bruhn - Stockholm, Sweden
Franchi, Eric - Lapointe Rosenstein - Montreal, Canada
Françon, André - Secrétaire général du ALAI - Paris, France
Freegard, Michael - London, United Kingdom
Frequin, Michel - Nederlands Uitgeversverbond - Amsterdam, Netherlands

Galama, Maron - VECAI - Dordrecht, Netherlands
Gard, Lena-Liisa - Media Employers Ass. - Stockholm, Sweden
Gaubiac, Yves - Revue Int. du Droit d'Auteur - Neuilly sur Seine, France
Gautier, Pierre-Yves - Université Panthéon-Assas - Paris, France
Gendreau, Ysolde - Université de Montréal - Montreal, Canada
Gielen, Charles - Nauta Dutilh - Amsterdam, Netherlands
Gielen-Drion, Maria - Bussum, Netherlands
Gimeno, Luis - University of London - London, United Kingdom
Ginsburg, Jane - Columbia Law School - New York, USA
Goldsmith, Frédéric - SNEP - Paris, France
Gonzales, Agustin - SGAE - Madrid, Spain
Gotzen, Frank - Centre for Intellectual Property Rights - Louvain, Belgium
Goutal, Jean-Louis - CUERPI - Grenoble, France
Graninger, Gernot - AKM - Vienna, Austria
Grinbaum, Henrik - Swedish Television - Stockholm, Sweden
Grootenhuis, Inge - Schut & Grosheide - Amsterdam, Netherlands
Grosheide, Willem - Centre for Intellectual Property Law - Utrecht, Netherlands
Guibault, Lucie - McCarthy Tétrault - Montreal, Canada
Gutiérrez Vicen, Javier - VEGAO - Madrid, Spain
Gutton, Jean-Marc - ADAGP - Paris, France

Haberstumpf, Helmut - Nürnberg, Germany
Haeck, Jaap - Institute for Information Law - Amsterdam, Netherlands
Halén, Torsten - Taby, Sweden
Henning-Bodewig, Frauke - Max-Planck-Institute - Munich, Germany
Heremans, Tom - Loeff Claeys Verbeke - Brussels, Belgium
Hermans, Ruprecht - Nauta Dutilh - Amsterdam, Netherlands
Hétu, Michel - Commission du droit d'auteur - Ottawa, Canada
Hillerström, Helene - TV4 - Stockholm, Sweden
Hoffman, Barbara - Schwarz Weiss Steckler Hoffman - New York, USA
Hoogenraad, Ebba - Steinhauser Hoogenraad - Amsterdam, Netherlands
Hugenholtz, Bernt - Institute for Information Law - Amsterdam, Netherlands

Jaeger, Andrea - Wessing Berenberg-Gosslev - Düsseldorg, Germany
Janssens, Marie-Christine - Centre for Intell. Prop. Rights - Louvain, Belgium
Jehl, Joseph - Editions du Juris-Classeur - Paris, France
Jonkers, Juliette - Buma/Stemra - Amstelveen, Netherlands
Josselin, Muriel - Montrouge, France
Jutten, Ronald - VECAI - Dordrecht, Netherlands

Kabel, Jan - Institute for Information Law - Amsterdam, Netherlands
Kaplan, Adria - Columbia Law School - New York, USA
Karnell, Gunnar - Stockholm School of Economics - Stockholm, Sweden
Keuchenius, Pemea - Stichting Stemra - Amstelveen, Netherlands
Koivumaa, Ari - University of Lapland - Rovaniemi, Finland
Koriatopoulov, Pierrine-Angélique - Athens, Greece
Korman, Bernard - Dornbusch Mensch Mandelstam & Schaeffer - New York, USA
Koumantos, Georges - Athens, Greece
Kroeze, Anja - Goudsmit & Branbergen - Amsterdam, Netherlands
Kroft, Paul van der - Van der Kroft c.s. - Amsterdam, Netherlands
Krüger, Christof - Klaka & Partner - Munich, Germany
Kukuk, Christina - Hamburg, Germany

Latreille, Antoine - CERDI - Sceaux, France
Leaffer, Marshall - University of Toledo - Bloomington, USA
Ledger, Michèle - CRID - Namur, Belgium
Lehmann, Michael - Max-Planck-Institute - Munich, Germany
Lemyre, Patrice - Industry Canada - Ottawa, Canada
Lewinski, Silke von - Max-Planck-Institute - Munich, Germany
Liberg, Björn - Arbetsgivareföreningen SRAO - Stockholm, Sweden
Libert, Carine - SABAM - Brussels, Belgium
Lindström, Hans - SAMI - Stockholm, Sweden
Lingen, Niek van - Amsterdam, Netherlands
Linneman, Joost - Kennedy Van der Laan - Amsterdam, Netherlands
Loewenheim, Ulrich - J.W. Goethe-Universität - Frankfurt, Germany
Looye, Yvonne - Philips Media - Eindhoven, Netherlands
Lucas, André - Chéméré, France
Lund, Astri - Oslo, Norway

Majeau, Claude - Commission du droit d'auteur - Ottawa, Canada
Manz, Friederike - Max-Planck-Institute - Munich, Germany
Martin, Guy - Carter-Ruck & Partners - London, United Kingdom
Meeuwsen, B. - Ministry of Justice - The Hague, Netherlands
Messinger, Gloria - ALAI-USA - New York, USA
Michaux, Benoit - Loeff Claeys Verbeke - Brussels, Belgium
Miserachs, Paul - Miserachs Avocats - Barcelona, Spain
Mom, Gerard - University of Amsterdam - Amsterdam, Netherlands
Mout, Kees - Nauta Dutilh - Amsterdam, Netherlands
Mout-Bouwman, Nora - Nauta Dutilh - Amsterdam, Netherlands
Movsessian, Vera - Berlin, Germany

Nabhan, Victor - ALAI - Munich, Germany
Nefkens, Ruby - Van der Steenhoven Kolle Gilhuis - Amsterdam, Netherlands
Niesten, Raoul - Van der Kroft c.s. - Amsterdam, Netherlands
Niiranen, Valtteri - Finnish (...) Publisher's Associations - Helsinki, Finland
Nordell, Per Jonas - University of Stockholm - Stockholm, Sweden
Nordemann, Wilhelm - ALAI Germany - Potsdam, Germany

Oeconomidis, Dimitris - Oeconomidis & Partners - Athens, Greece
Oerle, Richard van - Nauta Dutilh - Rotterdam, Netherlands
Oesch, Rainer - University of Helsinki - Helsinki, Finland
Ojala, Jyrki - Finnish Copyright Institute - Helsinki, Finland
Oppenoorth, Frits - Vrije Universiteit - Amsterdam, Netherlands
Ova, Erik - Norwaco - Oslo, Norway

Pearson, Colin - Radcliffes Crossman Block - London, United Kingdom
Peeperkorn, D.H.M. - Hof Amsterdam - Amsterdam, Netherlands
Perot-Morel, Marie-Angèle - Faculté de Droite de Grenoble - Seyssins, France
Pina, David - APEPI - Lisbon, Portugal
Piriou, Florence - AFJPIDA - Paris, France
Pitta, Laura - Pacific Palisades, USA
Pojaghi, Alberto - Studio Legale Pojaghi - Milan, Italy
Pojaghi, Gianluca - Studio Legale Pojaghi - Milan, Italy
Pollaud-Dulian, Frédéric - Université de Bourgogne - Paris, France

Quaedvlieg, Antoon - Nijmegen University - Nijmegen, Netherlands

Racicot, Michel - McCarthy Tétrault - Montreal, Canada
Randes, Thomas - Swedish Copyright Society - Stockholm, Sweden
Reboul, Yves - Université Robert Schuman - Strasbourg, France
Rechardt, Lauri - Gramex Finland - Helsinki, Finland
Rengifo, Ernesto - Max-Planck-Institute - Munich, Germany
Ribbink, G.J. - Derks.Star Busmann.Hanotiau - Amsterdam, Netherlands
Richardson, Charlott - Swedish Media Employers Ass. - Stockholm, Sweden
Rijlaarsdam, Arie - Université Technique - Gouda, Netherlands
Rivers, Tom - Rivers Consultancy - London, United Kingdom
Rorbye Ronn, Maria - Danmarks Radio - Soborg, Denmark
Rosén, Jan - Stockholm University - Stockholm, Sweden
Rothnie, Warwick - Mallesons Stephen Jacques - Melbourne, Australia
Rouart, Nicolas - Soc. des Auteurs et Comp. Dramatique - Paris, France
Roussel, Ghislain - ALAI Canada - Montreal, Canada
Ruijsenaars, Heijo - Max-Planck-Institute - Munich, Germany
Rüter-Ehlermann, A.L. - Rasker Duvekot & Wibbens - Amsterdam, Netherlands

Salokannel, Marvot - University of Helsinki - Helsinki, Finland
Schlatter, Sibylle - Max-Planck-Institute - Munich, Germany
Schulze, Gernot - Schmidt Schulze Küster - Munich, Germany
Schwenzer, Oliver - Max-Planck-Institute - Munich, Germany

Scourtis, Dimitris - ALAI Hellenic Group - Athens, Greece
Seignette, Jacqueline - Goudsmit & Branbergen - Amsterdam, Netherlands
Shackleton, Eamon - Irish Music Rights Organisation - Dublin, Ireland
Sipilä, Katri - Finnish Composers Copyright Soc. - Helsinki, Finland
Sirinelli, Pierre - CERDI - Sceaux, France
Smith, Neil - Limbach & Limbach - San Francisco, USA
Solleveld, Paul - NVPI - Hilversum, Netherlands
Spoor, Jaap - Trenité Van Doorne - Amsterdam, Netherlands
Steinhauser, Paul - Steinhauser Hoogenraad - Amsterdam, Netherlands
Sterling, Adrian - London, United Kingdom
Strubel, Xavier - Institut National des Telecommunications - Evry, France
Struik, Hendrik - Derks.Star Busmann.Hanotiau - Utrecht, Netherlands
Stuyt, R. - VVA - Heemstede, Netherlands

Thum, Dorothee - Max-Planck-Institute - Munich, Germany
Timonen, Jukka-Pekka - Kopiosto - Helsinki, Finland

Vaillancourt, Benoit - Université du Quebec à Montréal - Montreal, Canada
Vallois, Thierry le - SCP Nataf & Fajgenbaum - Paris, France
Vallverdu, Mercedes - Soc. General de Autores & Editores - Madrid, Spain
Vecht, Ronald - Amsterdam, Netherlands
Vendrell, Eudald - Gay-Vendrell Advocats - Barcelona, Spain
Verhagen, Jan Hendrik - Manco Adviesbureau - Vijfhuizen, Netherlands
Verkade, D.W.F. - Stibbe Simont Monahan Duhot - Amsterdam, Netherlands
Vinje, Thomas - Morrison & Foerster - Brussels, Belgium
Visscher, Fernard de - Loeff Claeys Verbeke - Brussels, Belgium
Visser, Dirk - Leiden University - Leiden, Netherlands
Vogel, Martin - Bundestatengericht München - Munich, Germany

Walter, Michel - Vienna, Austria
Wand, Peter - Max-Planck-Institute - Munich, Germany
Werra, Jacques de - Mathias Neumann - Munich, Germany
Wieringa, Jelle - John de Mol Produkties - Hilversum, Netherlands
Wit, Paul de - Korte & De Wit - Bussum, Netherlands

Záborszky, Carien - Kennedy Van der Laan - Amsterdam, Netherlands
Zmirou, Nicole - SACD - Paris, France

ALAI Bureau and Executive Committee
Bureau et Comité Exécutif de l'ALAI

Members of the ALAI Bureau / *Membres du Bureau de l'ALAI*

Chairman / *Président*	M. V. Nabhan
Vice-Chairman / *Vice-Président*	M. H. Cohen Jehoram
	M. W. Cornish
	M. A. Dietz
	M. G.W.G. Karnell
Secretary General / *Secrétaire Général*	M. A. Françon
Treasurer / *Thésorier*	M. Y. Gaubiac

Members of the Executive Committee / *Membres du Comité Exécutif*

Mme L. Baulch, M. A. Bercovitz, M. J. Black, M. C.H.C. Bodenhausen, M. A. Bogsch, M. R. du Bois, Mme S. Bridge, M. P. Brügger, M. A. de Caluwé, Mme S. Capiau, M. H. Cohen Jehoram, M. J. Corbet, M. W. Cornish, M. Th. Desurmont, M. A. Dietz, Mlle M.C. Dock, M. Th. Dreier, M. P.H. Dumont, M. M. Fabiani, M. A. Françon, M. M. Freegard, Mme D. Gaudel, Mme J.C. Ginsburg, M. F. Gotzen, M. T. Halén, M. K. Hodik, M. F. van Isacker, Mme J. Jonkers, M. G.W.G. Karnell, M. A. Kerever, M. J. Kernochan, M. M. Koktvedgaard, M. G. Koumantos, Mme G. Krüger-Nieland, M. J. Lahore, M. N. Landry, M. M.A. Leaffer, M. J. Liedes, M. S. Ljungman, M. U. Loewenheim, M. A. Lucas, Mme A.M. Lund, M. P. Miserachs Sala, Mme N. Mout-Bouwman, M. V. Nabhan, M. W. Nordemann, Mlle S. Perlmutter, M. D. Pina, M. A.A. Quaedvlieg, M. J. Rosén, M. W.A. Rothnie, M. G. Roussel, M. P. Sirinelli, M. J.H. Spoor, M. R.A.E. Stuyt, M. M. Walter, M. J. Weisman, M. J.A. Ziegler

Acknowledgements
Remerciements

We gratefully acknowledge the support for the ALAI Study Days 1996 from:

Les Journées d'Étude de l'ALAI 1996 ont pu être organisées grâce au soutien des organismes suivants:

Boekel De Nerée
Buma/Stemra
Gemeente Amsterdam
Ministerie van Justitie
Nauta Dutilh
NOTU
NVPI
Reed Elsevier
Stichting LIRA
Stichting Reprorecht
VNU